SPIRITUAL WARFARE

SPIRITUAL WARFARE

GATES OF THE SOUL

DELIVERED BY ZERUBBABEL SHALIACH

ZERUBBABEL SHALIACH

First Printing, 2021

I CREATED ALL THINGS[1] AND HAVE BEEN SUBJECTING THEM ALL TO BECOME A FOOTSTOOL FOR MY GLORY.[2] I AM ABOUT TO TAKE MY GREAT POWER AND REIGN WITH AN IRON SCEPTER[3] OVER HEAVEN AND CREATION[4] FOR MY GOODNESS.[5] MY CHILDREN WILL REIGN WITH ME.[6]
LET THOSE WITH EARS HEAR:[7]
MAKE STRAIGHT THE WAY FOR YEHOVAH.[8] FIRST REIGN OVER YOUR SOUL,[9] THEN YOU WILL REIGN OVER YOUR BODY AS WELL.[10] CLEAN THE INSIDE OF THE CUP SO THAT THE OUTSIDE MAY BE CLEAN.[11]
TO THOSE WHO ARE VICTORIOUS,[12] I WILL GRANT AUTHORITY[13] OVER HEAVEN AND CREATION,[14] BOTH NOW[15] AND IN THE DAYS TO COME.[16]"

- THE HOLY SPIRIT[17]

HALLELUYAH!

---

[1] Revelation 4:11; Genesis 1:1
[2] Psalm 110:1; 1 Corinthians 15:25
[3] Revelation 2:27; 12:5; 19:15
[4] Daniel 7:27; Revelation 11:17
[5] Psalm 27:13; 2 Peter 1:3; Exodus 33:19
[6] Revelation 2:26-27; 3:21; 2 Timothy 2:12
[7] Luke 8:18; Revelation 2:7,11,17,29; 3:6,13,20,22; 13:9
[8] Luke 1:16-17; 3:4; Isaiah 40:3-5; 57:14; 62:10
[9] Genesis 4:7; 1 Kings 1:35; Colossians 3:5-8; 1 Peter 2:11
[10] Romans 6:12; 8:13; Numbers 33:55; Joshua 23:12-13
[11] Matthew 23:26; Jeremiah 4:14; Ezekiel 18:31
[12] 2 Timothy 2:12; Revelation 2:7,11,17,26; 3:5,12,21; 21:7
[13] Luke 10:19; Revelation 2:26-27; 3:21
[14] Revelation 5:10; Daniel 7:27; Exodus 19:6; 1 Peter 2:5-9
[15] Romans 5:21; 6:14; 8:13; Colossians 3:5
[16] Revelation 22:5; Daniel 7:18
[17] 1 Peter 4:11; Galatians 1:12; 1 Corinthians 2:10,16

TABLE OF CONTENTS

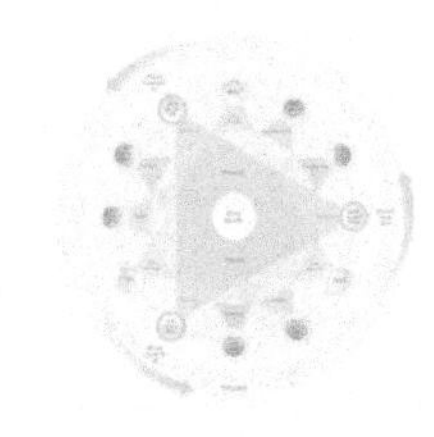

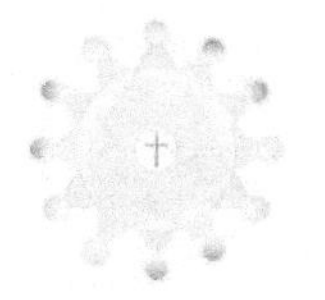

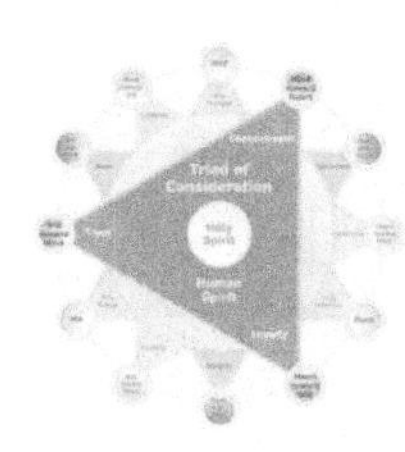

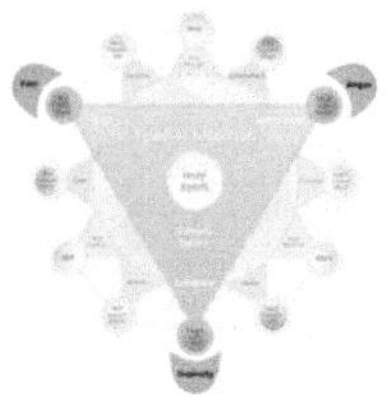

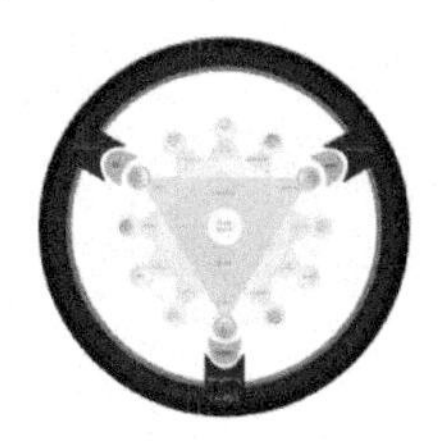

TABLE OF MAPS

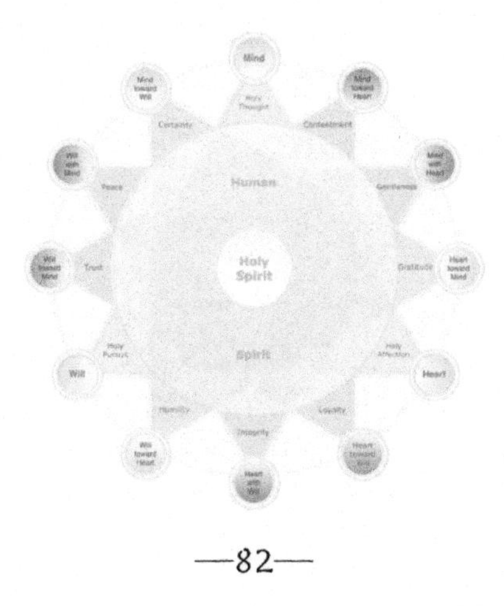

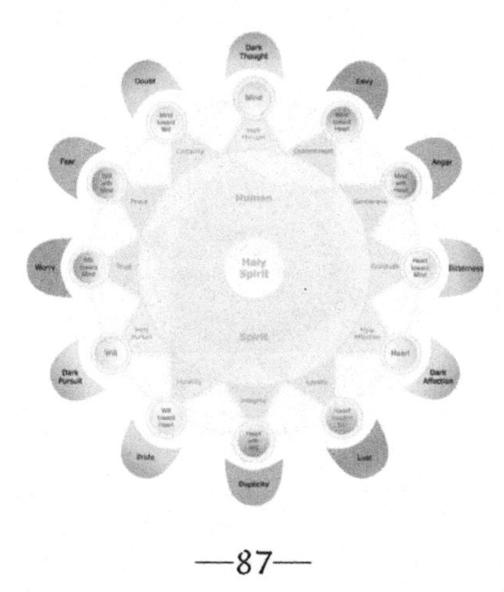

TRIAD OF CONSIDERATION

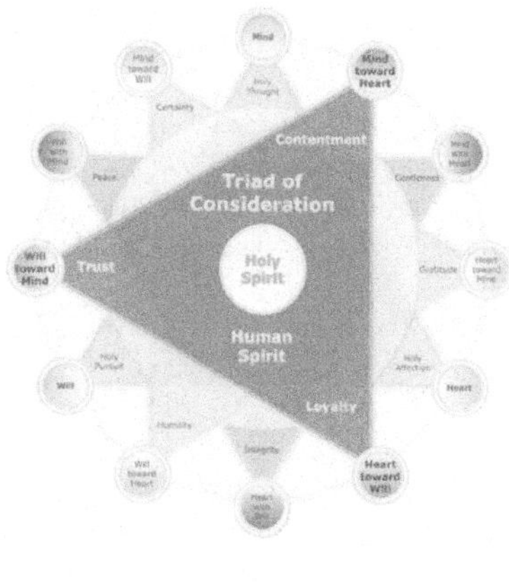

—249—

DARK TRIAD OF CONSIDERATION

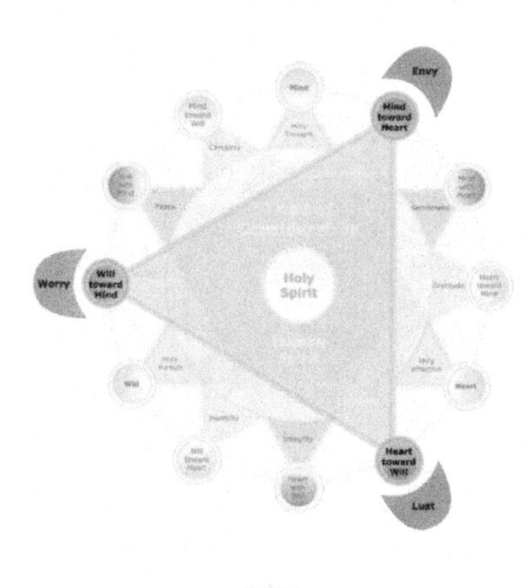

—250—

TRIAD OF DECISION

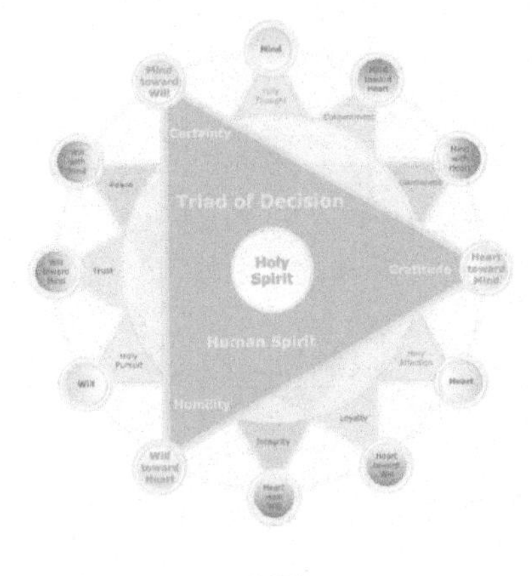

—257—

DARK TRIAD OF DECISION

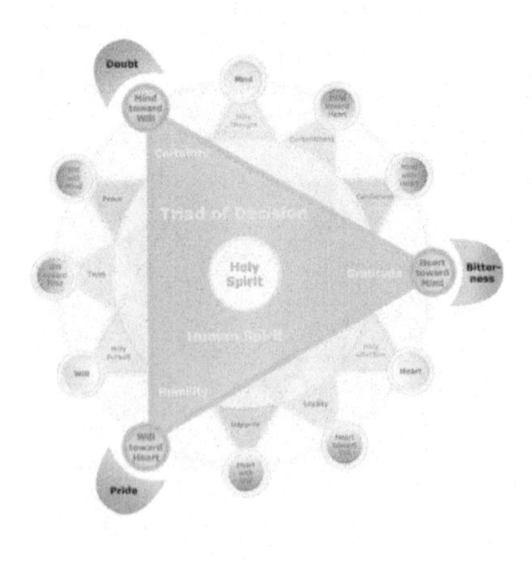

—258—

TRIAD OF INTENTION

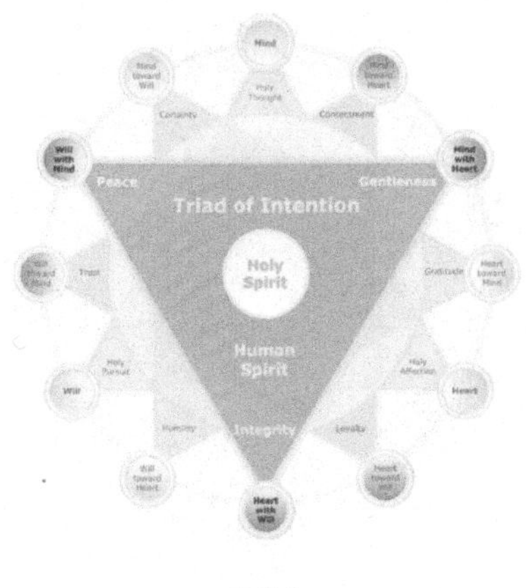

—266—

DARK TRIAD OF INTENTION

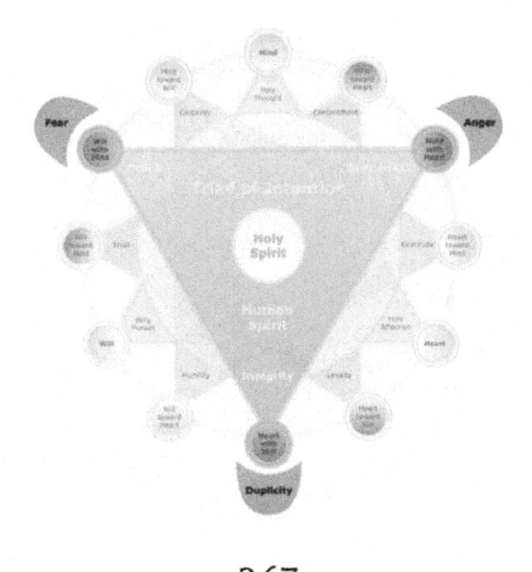

—267—

OBSERVATION TRIAD ASSAULT

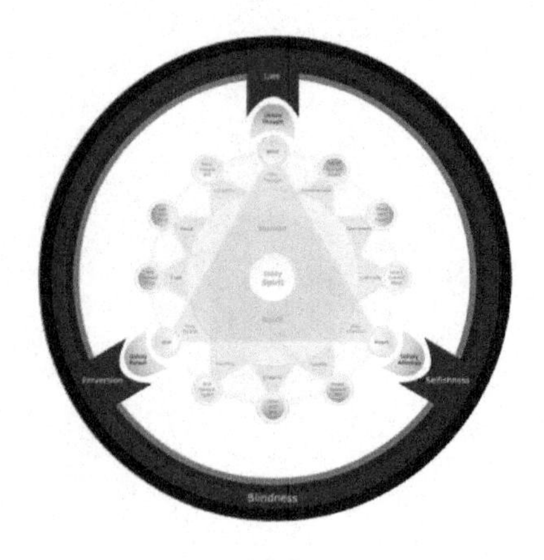

CONSIDERATION TRIAD ASSAULT

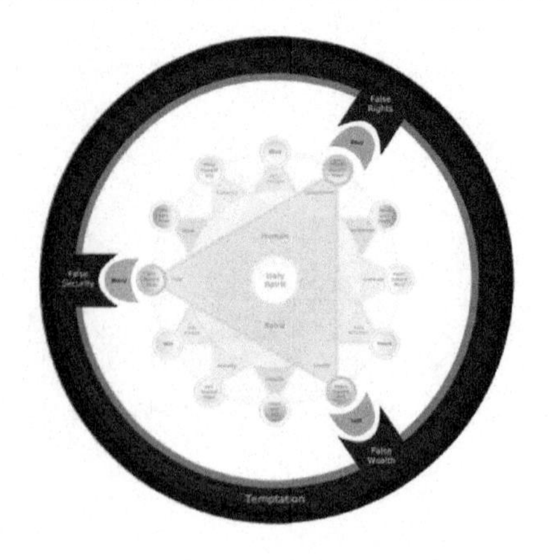

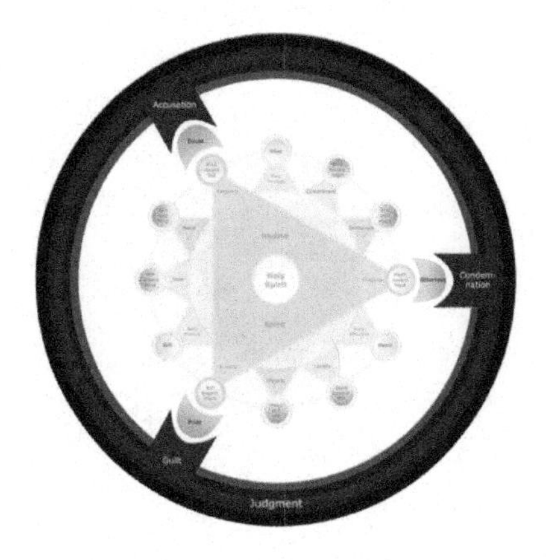

Accusation
Condem-
nation
Guilt
Judgment

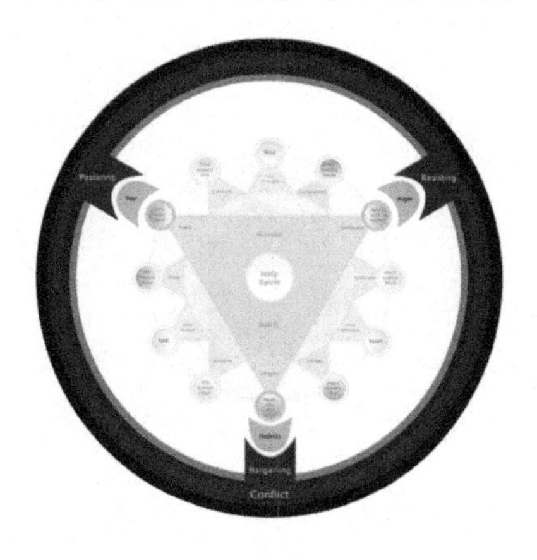

Posturing
Resisting
Conflict

CURRENTS OF SHOULD

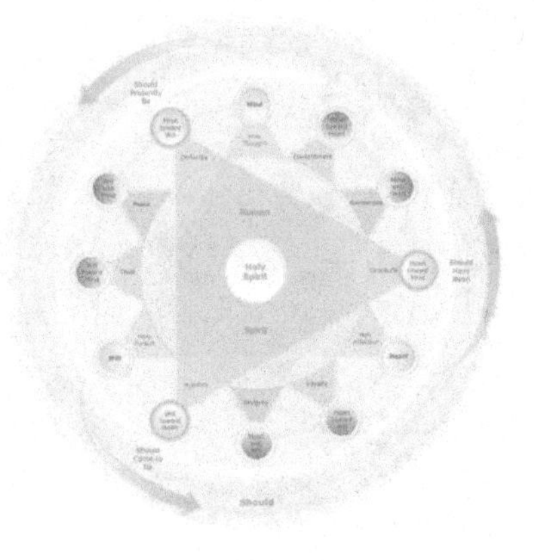

—356—

CURRENTS OF SHOULD NOT

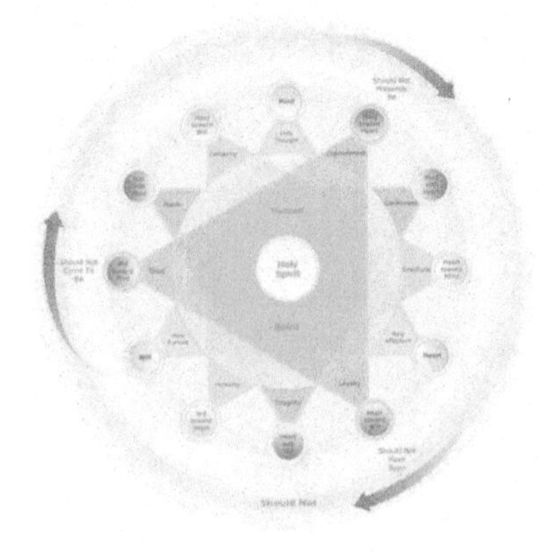

—357—

CURRENTS OF ANTI-SHOULD

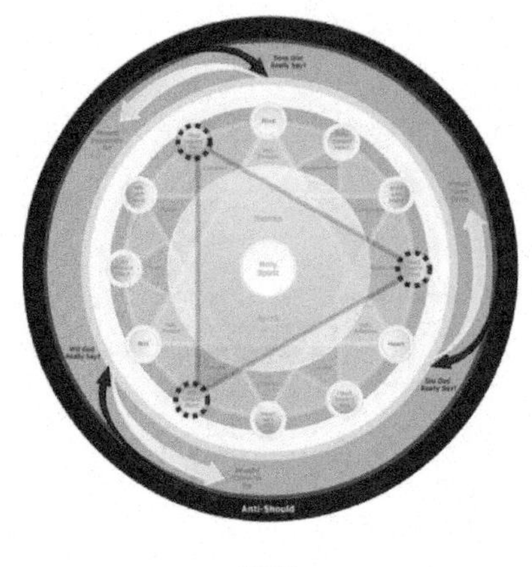

—359—

CURRENTS OF ANTI-SHOULD NOT

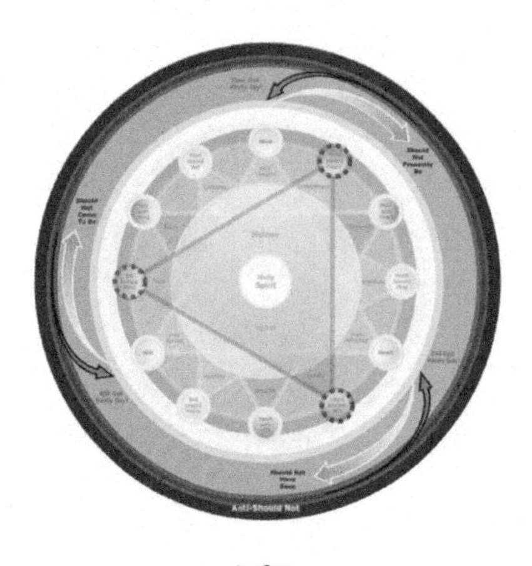

—360—

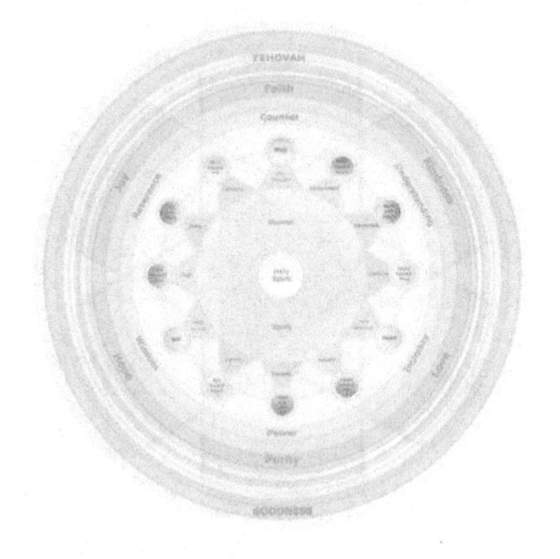
YEHOVAH
Faith
Counsel
Power
Purity

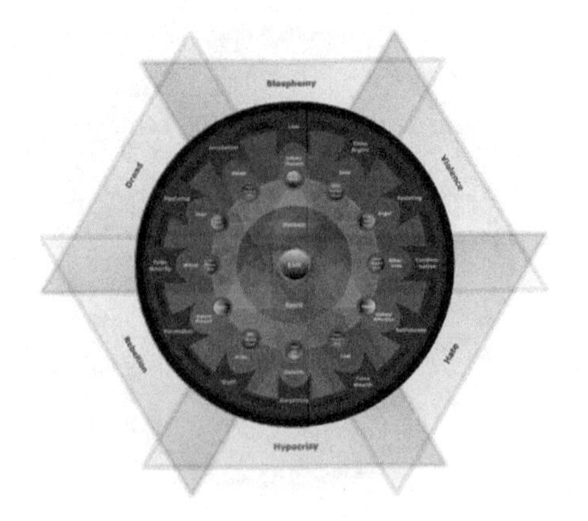
Blasphemy
Violence
Hate
Hypocrisy
Rebellion
Dread

PREFACE

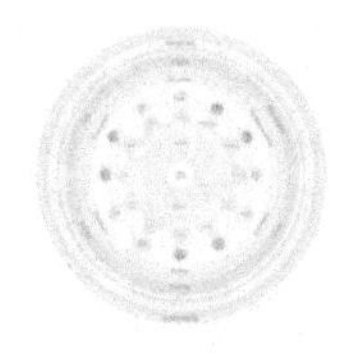

"Truly, truly I tell you, *whoever believes* in Me *will do* the works I have been doing, and they will do *even greater* things than these, because I am going to the Father. And I will do *whatever* you ask in My name, so that the Father may be glorified in the Son. Ask Me for *anything* in My Name, and I *will do it*."[1]

"Then He said to me, 'Do not seal up the words of the prophecy of this scroll, for the time is near.'"[2]

"What I say to you in the dark, speak in the daylight; what is whispered in your ear, shout from the rooftops."[3]

I, "Zerubbabel Shaliach,"[4] known as Michael, testify that Yehovah[5] transfigured me[6] and raised me up into the Third Heaven.[7]

---

[1] John 14:12-14

[2] Revelation 22:10

[3] Matthew 10:27

[4] *Zerubbabel* – a transliteration from the Hebrew זְרֻבָּבֶל, meaning *born in Babylon*, or more specifically *pressed out of Babylon* (Haggai 1:12). *Shaliach* – from the Hebrew שָׁלִיחַ, pronounced "shah-lee-ach" and meaning *one who is sent, messenger*, or *emissary* (Genesis 19:13; 24:1-10). Yehovah chose this name for me (Revelation 2:17; Genesis 17:15).

[5] In Exodus 3:14, God told Moses to say that "אהיה אשר אהיה" or "I AM THAT I AM" sent him. In Hebrew, the sound is "haYah asher haYah." This is why Yehovah calls Himself יה, or *Yah,* fifty times in the Scriptures (e.g., Exodus 15:2). In Exodus 6:6, God told Moses to tell the Israelites, "I am Yehovah, and I will bring you out from under the yoke of the Egyptians." Because Moses knew this when he recorded the Book of the Law, or the Torah (the first five books of the Bible), he used Yehovah as the Name for God as early as Genesis 2:4. *Yehovah* is a combination, or portmanteau, of the three Hebrew "being" verbs that mean *He will be, He is,* and *He was*. When all three words are said together quickly, they sound like "Ye-hov-ah": יהוה "yiheye" (He will be), הוה "hoveh" (He is), and היה "hayah" (He was) = yiheye + hoveh + hayah = ye+hov+ah = "Yehovah," "He will be, He is, and He was." HalleluYah!

[6] Mark 9:2-4; 2 Corinthians 3:7-16; 1 Corinthians 15:42; Philippians 3:21; Job 19:26

[7] 2 Corinthians 12:2; Revelation 4:1; 11:12; In John 3:13, Yeshua says, "No one has ever gone into Heaven except the one who came from Heaven—the Son of Man." Here He was speaking of knowing the Father in His Presence (Luke 10:22) because to know God is eternal

In the presence of many witnesses,[1] I stood before Yeshua,[2] Who looks exactly as John described when he stood before Him.[3] And Yeshua was full of the Father's Glory.[4] He is the Lamb of God,[5] the Savior of Humanity,[6] and the Eternal Lamp of Heaven![7]

HALLELUYAH![8]

And I heard the Holy Spirit say that Yeshua HaMashiach,[9] Jesus Christ, is precisely Who the Holy Scriptures say He is![10]
HALLELUYAH!

---

life (John 17:3). At that time and even now, though people have been raised into Paradise (Luke 16:22; 2 Corinthians 12:2) and even entered into the Kingdom of Heaven (Matthew 11:12), no one in the past, present, or future can ever know Yehovah except through the Son (Matthew 11:27). The Father can *only be revealed* through His Word, Who *is* the Son (John 1:1-18). Eternal life *only* comes through the Son (John 4:14).

1 Hebrews 12:1; Ephesians 2:6; Revelation 6:9

2 Isaiah 6:5; Job 42:5; Genesis 16:13; 32:30; Exodus 24:9-11. In 1 John 4:12, John says, "No one has seen God" – *seen,* coarsely translated from the Greek θεάομαι, meaning to *look closely at, contemplate,* or *learn by looking,* as if it were βλέπω, meaning to *perceive or observe by the senses* (Matthew 11:4). But because John also recorded in Revelation 4:1-3 that after he was called up into Heaven, he himself saw God (δεικνύω, meaning *to show, expose to the eyes*), since John recorded in John 6:46 that Yeshua is the only One Who has seen the Father (ὁράω, meaning *to stare, to know*), and because John explains in John 12:45 that whoever sees Yeshua sees the Father (θεωρέω, meaning *to be a spectator of*), we understand that John is neither contradicting his *own* account nor the former accounts of people *seeing* God (Abraham – Genesis 18:22,33; Issac – Genesis 26:24; Jacob – Genesis 35:1; Moses – Hebrews 11:27; Moses and Aaron – Numbers 20:6; the Hebrews – Leviticus 9:4,6; Deuteronomy 31:15; Moses, Aaron, Nadab, and Abihu – Exodus 24:9-11; Moses, face to Face – Exodus 33:11; Gideon – Judges 6:12; Samson's parents – Judges 13:3,16-18; Samuel – 1 Samuel 3:21; Solomon – 1 Kings 11:9, and many more). But John is rather explaining that the invisible God people have seen has only *ever* been ***made known*** through the Expression, the Soul, the Word of Yehovah, Who *always* has been, is, and forever will be Yeshua HaMashiach, Jesus Christ, the Lamp of Heaven! Amen!

3 Revelation 1:12-16

4 Matthew 16:27; Luke 9:26

5 Revelation 5:6; John 1:29; Genesis 22:8

6 1 John 4:14; John 12:47

7 Revelation 21:23; John 5:35-36

8 Revelation 19:1 – *HalleluYah,* from the Greek ἀλληλουϊα, which is transliteration from the Hebrew הַלְלוּיָהּ, meaning *praise Yah*. *Yah* is a contraction of *Yehovah* and is commonly used in the Scriptures, appearing first in Exodus 15:2.

9 *Yeshua HaMashiach* is the transliteration of the Hebrew ישועה המשיח, meaning *Jesus the Messiah*, or *Jesus Christ*.

10 Colossians 2:9; John 1:14; Luke 24:44

GLORY TO THE TRUE KING OF KINGS![1]

He is the Word of God![2] He is the Chosen Vessel,[3] the Soul of Yehovah,[4] the Truth, the Way, the Light, and the Life forever and ever![5]

PRAISE BE TO HIM THROUGH WHOM ALL THINGS HAVE BEEN MADE![6]

HOLY, HOLY, HOLY IS THE LORD GOD ALMIGHTY![7]

HALLELUYAH!

Some time after this, I was walking in the Spirit,[8] and my eyes were opened.[9] I was standing on the shore of the sea,[10] and I saw a great scroll stretching from Heaven down to the sea, like a mighty pillar.[11] I asked, "Lord Yeshua, what is this great scroll?" And I heard a reply in the Spirit[12] which said, "The scroll you see has been given to you so that you may speak[13] it to the inhabitants of the earth."[14]

I learned by revelation[15] that I had to eat the scroll in spirit.[16] So I began to eat it every day, and it took almost a year to consume.[17] When I had consumed it, I heard Yehovah say to me, "Write down what you have received[18] so that the

---

[1] Revelation 17:14; 19:16; Psalm 72:11; Proverbs 8:15-16; 1 Timothy 6:15

[2] John 1:1-3; 17:17; Luke 8:11; Revelation 19:13

[3] Colossians 2:9; 1 Timothy 3:16

[4] John 14:6b; Matthew 11:27

[5] John 14:6a; Acts 3:15; John 1:4,10,14; 5:26; 10:28; 11:25-26; 14:6; 17:2; 1 John 5:11-12,20; Romans 8:1-2; 1 Corinthians 15:45; Colossians 3:3-4

[6] John 1:3; Hebrews 3:3-4; Colossians 1:16-17; Psalm 33:6

[7] Revelation 1:8; 4:8; Isaiah 5:16; 48:2; 54:5; Jeremiah 51:5

[8] Revelation 1:10; 2 Corinthians 12:18; Galatians 5:16

[9] 2 Kings 6:17; Numbers 22:31

[10] Revelation 17:15 (Though I was actually standing on the seashore, I knew in spirit that I was spiritually looking at this same sea).

[11] Exodus 33:10; Revelation 3:12

[12] Acts 8:29; 11:12; Revelation 1:10

[13] Ezekiel 37:4,9,12; Matthew 17:20

[14] Ezekiel 3:1,4; Revelation 10:11

[15] 2 Corinthians 12:1; Galatians 2:2

[16] Ezekiel 2:8-9; 3:1-3

[17] Revelation 10:8-11; Ezekiel 3:1-3

[18] Revelation 1:11; Isaiah 30:8

people of this generation may read it to prepare for what is coming."[1] Suddenly, I was filled with words,[2] and I wrote a description of all that I had received.

This book is the description of what is in that great scroll.

"I did not receive it from any human, nor was I taught it; rather, I received it through revelation from Jesus Christ."[3]

This scroll will serve to reveal good trees and bad trees for who they are.[4] The Lord will use it to cause the rise and fall of many.[5] But for those who seek to understand,[6] their eyes will see, their ears will hear, their hearts will soften and turn toward Yeshua, and He will heal them.[7]

"Look, He is coming with the clouds, and every eye will see Him, even those who pierced Him, and all the nations of the earth will mourn because of Him. Even so, Amen!"[8]

The main text of this book was written in twelve days. After that, the Lord had me draw out the maps of the soul.[9] Then I heard Yehovah say, "Because intimate knowledge of My Word is rare,[10] many who read this book will not recognize that it is of Me.[11] Therefore, go and add Scripture references throughout it, so that they may be able to search My Word and receive it."[12] Then I was filled with diligence

---

[1] 1 Peter 1:13; Hebrews 9:28; 2 Timothy 4:8
[2] Jeremiah 1:9; Isaiah 51:16; Matthew 10:19
[3] Galatians 1:12
[4] Matthew 7:15-23; Luke 6:43-45
[5] Luke 2:34; Hosea 14:9
[6] Luke 11:9-10; 13:24; Hebrews 4:16; James 1:5
[7] Matthew 13:15; Jeremiah 3:22
[8] Revelation 1:7; Isaiah 19:1; Numbers 24:17; Psalm 22:16; Zechariah 12:10
[9] Joshua 18:8; Genesis 13:17; Revelation 11:1; These maps are depictions of the relationships between the characteristics of the soul and are useful for understanding how the soul interacts with the spirit (Ephesians 1:17). They are revelation from Yehovah and not from any other source (Galatians 1:12). Their purpose is to draw us to Christ, Who is the Living Answer to our every need (Colossians 2:2-3). They are maps (Joshua 18:8; Revelation 11:1). We do not worship New Jerusalem; we worship the King Who lives in it (Revelation 21:2). We do not worship the soul; we worship the King Who made it and lives in it (Colossians 1:27). The maps are not "graven images" for worship (Exodus 20:4); they are "surveys of the land written on a scroll" for the purpose of navigation (Joshua 18:9).
[10] 2 Timothy 4:3; Amos 7:10-17; Hosea 4:6
[11] Genesis 42:8; 1 John 4:2,6; Matthew 17:12; Luke 19:44; John 1:10; Acts 7:57
[12] Acts 17:11; 1 Peter 1:10-12

through His Spirit,[1] and I added over 5,200 footnotes with over 18,750 applicable verses from His Holy Word.

After I added the footnotes, the Holy Spirit led me[2] to make a distinction between footnotes that are Scripture references[3] and footnotes that contain additional information. The ones containing additional information are emphasized with a bold and italic font.[4] Those footnotes often contain important information that should be read as supplementary to the text.

Understand this also: In this testimony, an exclamation mark indicates a loud voice, but words written in all capitals indicate shouting. And there is a lot of shouting, because it is written, "Raise a shout for Yehovah, all the earth!"[5]

HALLELUYAH!

YEHOVAH'S RIGHT HAND HAS DONE MIGHTY THINGS![6]

WE'RE GOING TO LIVE WITH YESHUA FOREVER![7]

---

[1] Exodus 31:3; 1 Kings 18:46

[2] Romans 8:14; Galatians 5:18

[3] A letter in a verse reference represents the approximate area of the verse being emphasized. For example, Romans 8:15 reads, "The Spirit you received does not make you slaves, so that you live in fear again; rather, the Spirit you received brought about your adoption to sonship. And by Him we cry, 'Abba, Father.'" The reference Romans 8:13c would be drawing attention to the last section of the verse: "And by Him we cry, 'Abba, Father.'" Since we could be referring to any number of English translations, the letters in the reference are approximate. However, the context of the citation should help clarify the emphasis.

[4] If a Scripture reference in a footnote does not seem immediately applicable or explanatory, try looking at the reference in a different English version. No English versions are tagged in this testimony because all such versions are translations (and the Scriptures in this testimony have been translated by me according to my own emphases or preferences in dynamic or form equivalency). Manuscripts written in the original languages were consulted for this testimony. For example, the Book of Galatians was not written in 1611 English; it was written in Koine Greek. The child of Yehovah should understand that no single English translation can always capture the full meaning of the original language in a given verse. Many people who speak more than one language can testify about the difficulties involved when attempting to succinctly translate some concepts from one language to another. Therefore, for a better understanding, read many versions or learn the original languages.

[5] Psalm 98:4; 100:1

[6] Psalm 89:13; 98:1; 118:15

[7] Revelation 7:9-17; Zechariah 2:10; John 14:2-3

The Word of God COMMANDS us to SHOUT! ARE YOU OBEDIENT?[1] THEN SHOUT! ENGAGE YOUR SOUL AND BODY FOR HIS HONOR![2] REJOICE IN OUR GOD![3]

The silent hear silence.[4] The mumblers hear mumbling.[5] The lecturers hear lecturing.[6] But if you want to hear Yehovah's Voice loud and clear, then SHOUT FOR JOY! BE OBEDIENT AND SHOUT,[7] AND HE WILL SHOUT OVER YOU WITH JOY![8] HALLELUYAH!

HALLELUYAAAAAAAAAAAAAAAAAAAAAAAH!!!

GLORY TO GOD![9]

HalleluYah!

Now, if anyone wishes to know more, I would be honored to share more with them. It is what Yehovah has given me to do![10] Only let them read this book first! Because anyone who is unwilling to read even this book is certainly neither sincere about receiving more than is already in it! You may contact me at zerubbabel@gatesofthesoul.life. If you do, I intend to ask you a question to see if you have reflected upon the whole book, the starred footnotes, and the maps. Whether the Lord has me answer upon your reply is up to Him.

Also understand that Yehovah revealed all of this to me, but I am the one writing it down.[11] I am like a painter who has done his best to paint a beautiful scene on a canvas.[12] Any imperfection in the painting does not imply an imperfection in the scene.[13] If I have failed to write according to someone's preferred standards, made ridiculous errors, or confused anyone, I assure you, it's my fault[14] and not

---

[1] Psalm 47:1,5; 66:1; 95:1-2; 98:4; 100:1; Isaiah 24:14-16; 42:10-12
[2] Acts 26:20; Romans 6:13; John 15:8
[3] Philippians 4:4; Leviticus 23:40; Deuteronomy 16:11; Psalm 96:13; 97:12
[4] James 4:2c; John 16:24; Isaiah 7:10-13
[5] Numbers 14:29; Hebrews 4:6
[6] Job 13:3; 38:2-3
[7] Psalm 20:5; 33:3; 35:27; 47:1; 66:1; 71:23; 81:1; 95:1; 98:4,6; 100:1; 108:9
[8] Numbers 23:21; Isaiah 62:5
[9] Revelation 7:12; Luke 2:14; Romans 4:20
[10] Galatians 1:15; Isaiah 49:1,5; Jeremiah 1:5; Romans 9:24
[11] Galatians 6:11; Romans 16:22; 1 Corinthians 16:21-23; Revelation 1:11
[12] Exodus 25:40; 2 Timothy 1:13
[13] Hebrews 8:5; Matthew 19:17
[14] Job 11:12; Psalm 39:11; 62:9

that of His Revelation.[1] Nevertheless, those who reject His Light because of imperfections in this lampstand[2] will remain in darkness.[3]

Yehovah reveals Himself in Spirit through Yeshua.[4] He is only ever revealed through Yeshua, the Word of God.[5] But He reveals Yeshua through His Spirit,[6] His Angel,[7] His Physical Form,[8] and His Body of Disciples.[9] Each one of His true disciples serves as a revelation of Him,[10] and this revelation is accurate and eternal.[11] Even His Holy Scriptures were revealed through His true disciples[12] so that His Bride would receive eternal honor[13] that she could in turn use to honor Him.[14] That is to say, He reveals Himself to His Bride and through His Bride.[15] But His Bride is not the way; she points to the Way.[16] The Scriptures are not the way; they point to the Way.[17] And this testimony is not the way; it points to the Way.[18] Jesus Christ is the Way.[19] He is the Solution.[20] He is the Fountain of Life.[21] He is the Reward.[22] The Bride, Scriptures, and this testimony all point to Him;[23] they testify about knowing Him. To know Him is eternal life.[24] He is the Way, Life, and Truth forever and ever.[25] Amen!

---

[1] Jeremiah 8:8; 1 Corinthians 3:18-20; Ephesians 1:17
[2] 2 Corinthians 4:7; 3:18; Proverbs 4:18
[3] Luke 9:48-50; 10:10-12,16
[4] John 14:7,9; 12:45; Colossians 1:15; Hebrews 1:3
[5] John 1:18; 3:18; 10:9; 14:6; 1 John 4:9; Matthew 11:27; Acts 4:12
[6] 1 John 5:6; Philippians 1:19; Acts 16:7
[7] Revelation 1:1; 22:16; Genesis 22:11; Exodus 3:2
[8] Colossians 1:19; 2:9; John 1:14; 2:21
[9] Ephesians 1:22-23; 3:19; Colossians 2:10
[10] 1 Corinthians 12:6; Colossians 3:11; 1 Corinthians 12:12-27
[11] 2 Corinthians 5:21; John 15:8; 17:18; Ephesians 5:1; Revelation 19:8
[12] 2 Peter 1:19-21; 2 Timothy 3:14-17
[13] Revelation 19:7-8; 7:9-17; 21:2,9; 22:17
[14] Revelation 4:10; Matthew 24:35; Luke 8:21
[15] John 14:20; Ephesians 3:10; 1 Peter 1:12
[16] John 1:7; 3:26-36; Acts 1:8; 2 Peter 1:16
[17] John 5:39-40; Acts 3:22-23; Hebrews 12:25-26
[18] Luke 21:13; Revelation 12:11; Acts 20:24; Romans 3:21
[19] John 14:6; 1:18; 3:18; 10:9; 1 John 4:9; Matthew 11:27; Acts 4:12
[20] Romans 5:10; 2 Corinthians 5:18; Ephesians 2:16; Colossians 1:20,22
[21] John 4:10,11; 7:38; Revelation 7:17; Psalm 36:9; Zechariah 13:1
[22] Genesis 15:1; Revelation 21:3-4; Lamentations 3:24
[23] Colossians 1:16; Romans 11:36
[24] John 17:3; 1 John 5:11,20
[25] John 1:14; 14:6; Isaiah 35:8-9; Acts 3:15; Ephesians 2:18

I asked the Lord how He wanted to distribute this testimony, and His Spirit[1] guided me[2] through the specifics. Then I asked how much money it would cost, and I heard, "That will depend on the various forms, distributions, publishing contracts, and countries, but why are you concerned?[3] You already serve me with all of your time, relationships, mind, heart, strength, and provisions; to read what you have written, they will also have to sacrifice.[4] But if they are not willing to pay less for it than a day's wages, then they would not listen anyway;[5] for many read, but few listen.[6] And many speak about the value of money and are willing to sacrifice it for their entertainment, worldly education, and comforts.[7] Yet, they are unwilling to sacrifice even a little for what is eternally valuable.[8] Therefore, do not be concerned about who will receive it, because I will ensure that anyone who values it will obtain it."[9]

May those of you who value it obtain it, may this scroll be a blessing of encouragement for you,[10] may it direct you into His Word,[11] and may His Holy Voice heal you from every ailment[12] and strengthen you in the power[13] of His Glorious Promises![14] May Yehovah bless you and fill your soul with His Presence,[15] and may you know what He has accomplished for you by the Cross through His Great Love![16] May you be lifted out of the darkness of this world![17] May you be filled with His Authority and Power for His Glory![18] And may you overflow with the

---

[1] Manifestations, Pronouns, Facets, and Characteristics of Yehovah are capitalized in this testimony because they are Divine and beyond measure. Such Wonders certainly deserve to be honored as much as any human's name (1 Samuel 2:30).
[2] Romans 8:14; Galatians 5:18; Psalm 143:10
[3] John 21:22; Proverbs 25:27
[4] 2 Samuel 24:24; Matthew 13:45-46
[5] Luke 16:31; Matthew 7:6
[6] Mark 4:12; John 12:37-41; John 5:47
[7] Luke 12:15,18-19; Matthew 19:24
[8] Luke 12:20-21; Matthew 19:21-23
[9] Matthew 7:7,11; 21:22; Luke 12:28,31-34
[10] Colossians 2:2; 1 Corinthians 14:31; 2 Corinthians 13:11
[11] 2 Timothy 3:16; Romans 15:4; Hebrews 4:12; Colossians 1:25
[12] 1 Peter 2:24; Exodus 15:26; Psalm 103:3; Matthew 4:24
[13] Ephesians 3:16; Hebrews 11:34
[14] Ephesians 1:18; Luke 24:49
[15] Revelation 7:15; 1 Corinthians 3:16
[16] Galatians 6:14; Ephesians 2:16
[17] Colossians 1:13; Acts 26:18
[18] Luke 10:19; Psalm 91:13; Ezekiel 2:6

Light[1] of His Victory[2] through Yeshua HaMashiach, Jesus Christ, the Lion of the Tribe of Judah,[3] the Wonderful Counselor,[4] and the Ruler of Creation![5] What He opens no one can shut, and what He shuts no one can open, both now and forever![6]

HALLELUYAH!

PRAISE be to the LIVING KING OF KINGS and LORD OF LORDS,[7] Who graciously provides us with ALL things through JESUS CHRIST![8]

HALLELUYAH!

PRAISE be to the AUTHOR OF LIFE,[9] Who has compassion on us and gives us eyes to see and ears to hear![10]

HALLELUYAH!

Praise be to our WONDERFUL COUNSELOR,[11] Who leads us into all TRUTH[12] and fills us with His perfect JOY![13]

HALLELUYAH!

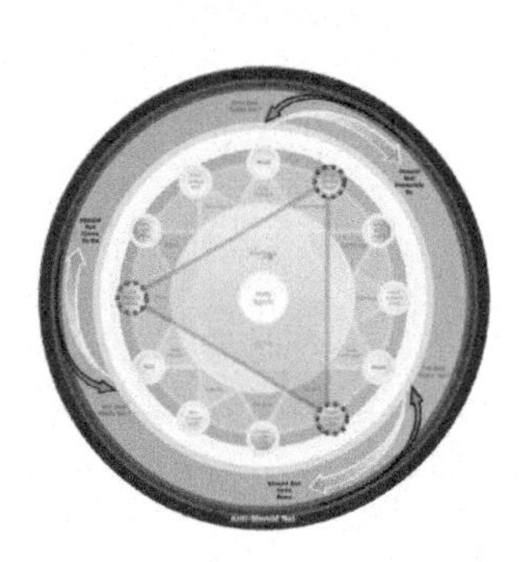

---

[1] 1 Thessalonians 5:5; Ephesians 5:8
[2] 1 Corinthians 15:57; Romans 8:37; 1 John 5:4-5
[3] Revelation 5:5; Hosea 5:14
[4] Isaiah 9:6; Psalm 32:8; Proverbs 8:14
[5] Revelation 3:14; Colossians 1:15
[6] Revelation 3:7; Job 11:10; 12:14; Matthew 16:19
[7] Revelation 17:14; 19:16; Psalm 72:11; Proverbs 8:15-16; 1 Timothy 6:15
[8] Romans 8:32; Psalm 84:11; 1 Corinthians 2:12; 3:21-23
[9] Acts 3:15; John 1:4,10,14; 5:26; 10:28; 11:25-26; 14:6; 17:2; 1 John 5:11-12,20; Romans 8:1-2; 1 Corinthians 15:45; Colossians 3:3-4
[10] Proverbs 20:12; Exodus 4:11; Psalm 94:9
[11] Isaiah 9:6; Psalm 32:8; Proverbs 8:14
[12] John 14:26; 16:13; 1 Corinthians 2:10-13; Ephesians 4:7-15; 1 John 2:20,27
[13] John 15:11; 16:24; 17:13; 1 Peter 1:8; Jude 1:24

PRAISE BE TO THE BREAD OF LIFE,[1] THE LIVING ONE,[2] THE SUSTENANCE OF EXISTENCE,[3] THE ONE IN WHOM ALL THINGS HOLD TOGETHER![4]

PRAISE OUR ALMIGHTY GOD!!!!!!!!!!!!!!!!!!![5]

HALLELUUUUUUUYAAAAAAAAAAAAAAAH!!!!!!!!!!!!!!![6]

BLESS YEHOVAAAAAAAAAAAAAAAAAAAAAAH!!!!!!!!!!!!!!![7]

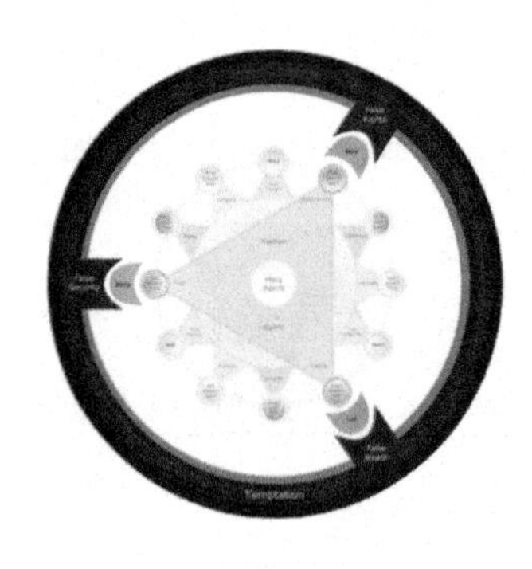

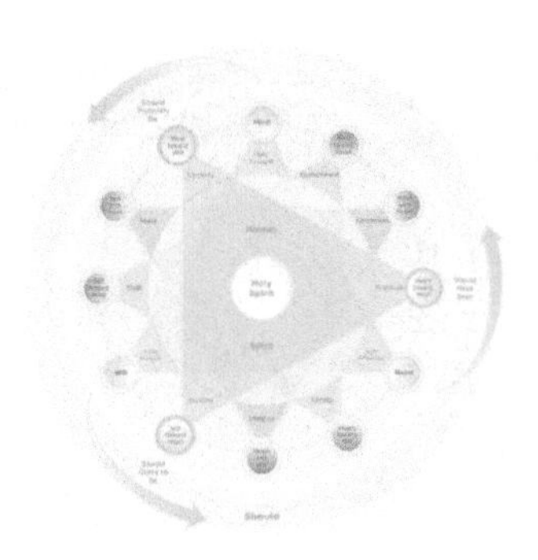

[1] John 6:33-51; Luke 22:19

[2] Revelation 1:18; 4:9; Hebrews 7:25; John 14:19; Romans 6:9

[3] Acts 17:28; Job 12:10; Psalm 36:9; Hebrews 1:3

[4] Colossians 1:17; 1 Samuel 2:8; Isaiah 44:6; John 1:3; 1 Corinthians 8:6

[5] 1 Peter 1:3; Revelation 19:5

[6] Ezra 3:11; Psalm 100:1; Revelation 19:6

[7] Though it is not commonly practiced in many gatherings today, we are exhorted throughout the Scriptures to bless Yehovah (Some verses that say "Bless Yehovah": Genesis 9:26; 24:27; Exodus 18:10; Ruth 4:14; 1 Samuel 25:32,39; 1 Kings 8:56; Ezra 7:27; Nehemiah 9:5; Psalm 28:6; 31:21; 103:1-2,20-22; 104:1,35; 134:1-2; 135:19-21. Some verses that say "Bless God": Psalm 66:8,20; 68:19,26,35; Daniel 2:20; Luke 1:68; John 12:13; Romans 1:25; 9:5; 2 Corinthians 1:3; Ephesians 1:3; 1 Peter 1:3); The Hebrew *Yehovah* is translated by Greek as both θεός, pronounced "thay-awss" and meaning *God* or *Supreme* Deity (see how Matthew 4:4 translates Deuteronomy 8:3), and κύριος, pronounced "koo-ree-awss," which means *Lord, God, Supreme in Authority* (see how Matthew 4:7 translates Deuteronomy 6:16 and how Romans 15:11 translates Psalm 117:1).

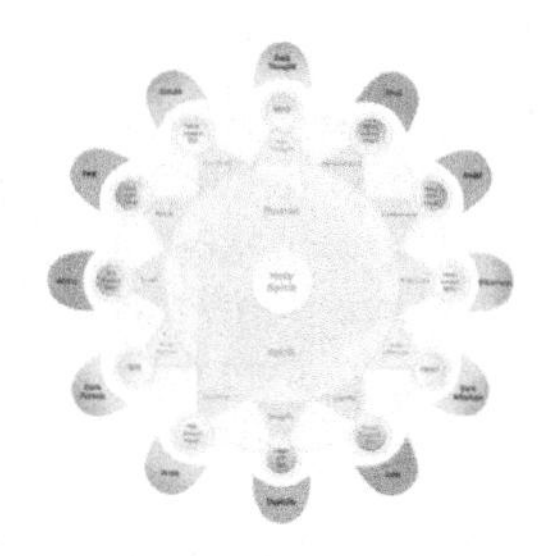

CHAPTER 1

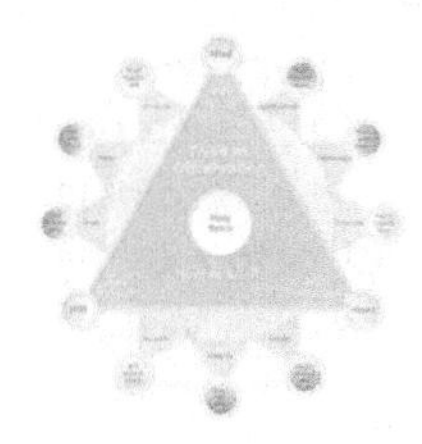

INTRODUCTION

To those on the earth called and chosen by Yehovah to accept the invitation of Yeshua for entrance into His fellowship, dominion, and eternal life:[1]

"Grace and peace to you from Him Who is, and Who was, and Who is to come, and from the Sevenfold Spirit[2] before His throne, and from Jesus Christ, Who is the faithful Witness, the Firstborn from the dead, and the Ruler of the kings of the earth."[3]

I, your eternal brother[4] "Zerubbabel,"[5] am a man redeemed by the shed Blood of Yeshua HaMashiach, Jesus Christ, our Savior, Who gave His life as a propitiation for many.[6] Our Lord not only became an atoning sacrifice for sin but also lived as a visible redemption of the purpose of humanity,[7] perfectly revealing all the unseen Characteristics of Yehovah,[8] Who is and was and is to come.[9]

---

[1] 1 Peter 2:9; Revelation 17:14

[2] See Chapter 34 of this testimony for more about the Sevenfold Spirit of Yehovah.

[3] Revelation 1:4-5

[4] John 3:16,36; 5:24; 6:40,47; 8:51; 11:26; 1 John 5:11-13

[5] *Zerubbabel* – Meaning *born in Babylon*, or more specifically *pressed out of Babylon* (Haggai 1:12).

[6] 1 John 2:2; 4:10; Romans 3:21-26; Isaiah 53

[7] 2 Corinthians 5:21; Luke 1:68

[8] John 12:44-46; Malachi 3:1; Luke 1:76

[9] Hebrews 1:3; Colossians 1:15; John 1:8

This same God has called and prepared many of us as vessels[1] of encouragement[2] for His people who have longed to understand His instruction clearly. For though His Word is not lacking,[3] forces of darkness have interfered incessantly[4] to obscure the clear message of Christ[5] given to those who seek salvation in Him. The dark spirits have done this in desperation, making every effort to temporarily avoid their sure plunge into absolute darkness, where there is no light at all, for that is where they belong.[6]

Therefore, it is with His Joy[7] that I come as a witness[8] and messenger[9] to confirm[10] the Good News to those of you who long for His Peace![11] In His great Wisdom, He has richly provided us with everything we need to receive His Victory over darkness, sickness, and sin of every kind![12] He has not left us as orphans but indwelled us with His Spirit of Truth![13] And so He has set this task before us, having engraved His Perfect Law on our hearts,[14] that we should know His Voice[15] and reject everything false, entering into His Kingdom and Domain, escaping the authority of the fallen principalities of this world,[16] and emerging victorious, as His bold, courageous, and invincible children of Light,[17] who live as ambassadors[18] of His character in a world perishing[19] in the weakness of darkness.[20]

---

1 2 Timothy 2:20-21; 2 Corinthians 4:5-7
2 2 Corinthians 13:11; Colossians 2:2; 4:8; 1 Thessalonians 5:11
3 1 John 2:5; 2 Timothy 3:16; 2 Samuel 23:2; Matthew 22:43; 26:56; John 10:35; Romans 3:2; 15:4; Galatians 3:8; Hebrews 4:12; 2 Peter 1:19-21
4 2 Corinthians 4:3-4; 1 John 2:11
5 Colossians 3:16; Hebrews 5:11
6 Luke 8:31; Revelation 9:2; 2 Peter 2:4; Jude 1:6; Acts 1:25
7 1 John 1:4; John 15:11; 16:24; 17:13; 1 Peter 1:8; Jude 1:24
8 John 1:8; Acts 22:15; Revelation 2:13
9 John 13:16; Philippians 2:25
10 Acts 15:27; 2 Peter 1:10
11 Colossians 1:20; Romans 1:7; Matthew 10:13
12 2 Peter 1:3; Philippians 4:19; 1 Peter 2:24; Luke 10:19; 2 Corinthians 1:20
13 John 14:17-18; 15:26; 16:13; 1 John 4:6
14 Jeremiah 31:33; Romans 2:15
15 John 10:3-5,16,27; Acts 10:13-15; Hebrews 4:7
16 Ephesians 2:2; 6:11-12; Colossians 2:10,15; 1 Peter 3:22; Luke 10:19
17 Romans 8:37; 1 Thessalonians 5:5
18 Ephesians 6:20; 2 Corinthians 5:20; John 20:21; Acts 26:17-18
19 2 Thessalonians 2:10; 1 Corinthians 1:18; 2 Corinthians 2:15; 4:3
20 John 1:5; 3:19-20; Job 24:13-17; Proverbs 1:22; Romans 1:28; 1 Corinthians 2:14

May those who read this testimony[1] receive the blessing they seek,[2] may the eyes of those who wish to see[3] be opened,[4] and may the hearts of those who long for hope[5] be filled and overflow with the joy[6] of the free and living Breath of Life in Him![7]

HalleluYah!

Praise our Faithful Savior, Who is able to complete the good work He has begun in us![8]

HalleluYah!

Praise the King of Glory, Who is the Father of All Good Gifts![9]

HalleluYah!

Praise Our Patient King, Who stands at the door and knocks![10]

HalleluYah!

We call to you, Yehovah! Show us great and unsearchable things that we do not know![11]

Amen!

And, Lord willing, let us now proceed toward discussing the importance of listening in spirit, the spiritual environment of Creation, the gates and characteristics of the soul, the battle strategies of the enemy, the dominion and claims of kingdoms, and how to receive and wield victory over sickness and death for His Glory! Amen

---

[1] Revelation 12:11; John 19:35
[2] Matthew 10:41; 16:27; Mark 11:24
[3] Genesis 21:19; John 4:35
[4] Acts 26:17-18; Psalm 119:18; 146:8; Isaiah 29:18; 32:3; 35:5
[5] 1 Peter 1:3; Romans 5:5; 8:24; 15:13; 1 Corinthians 13:13; Colossians 1:23,27
[6] Acts 13:52; John 15:11; 16:24; 17:13; 1 Peter 1:8; Jude 1:24
[7] Acts 17:25; Revelation 11:11
[8] Philippians 1:6; Psalm 138:8; 1 Thessalonians 5:23-24; 2 Thessalonians 1:11; 1 Peter 5:10
[9] James 1:17; John 1:9; 1 John 1:5; Revelation 21:23; 22:5; Isaiah 60:19
[10] Revelation 3:17-22; Song of Songs 5:2-4; Luke 12:36
[11] Jeremiah 33:3; Deuteronomy 4:29; Psalm 91:15; Isaiah 65:24; Joel 2:32; Luke 11:9-10

HALLELUYAH!

PRAISE THE LORD!!!!!!!!!!

ALL GLORY BE TO THE VICTORIOUS ONE,[1] TO THE KING OF KINGS!!!!!!!![2]

YESHUAAAAAAAAAAAAAAAAAAAA!!!!!!!!!!!!!!

HALLELUUUUUUUYAAAAAAAAAAAAAAAAAH!!!!!!!!!!!!!!

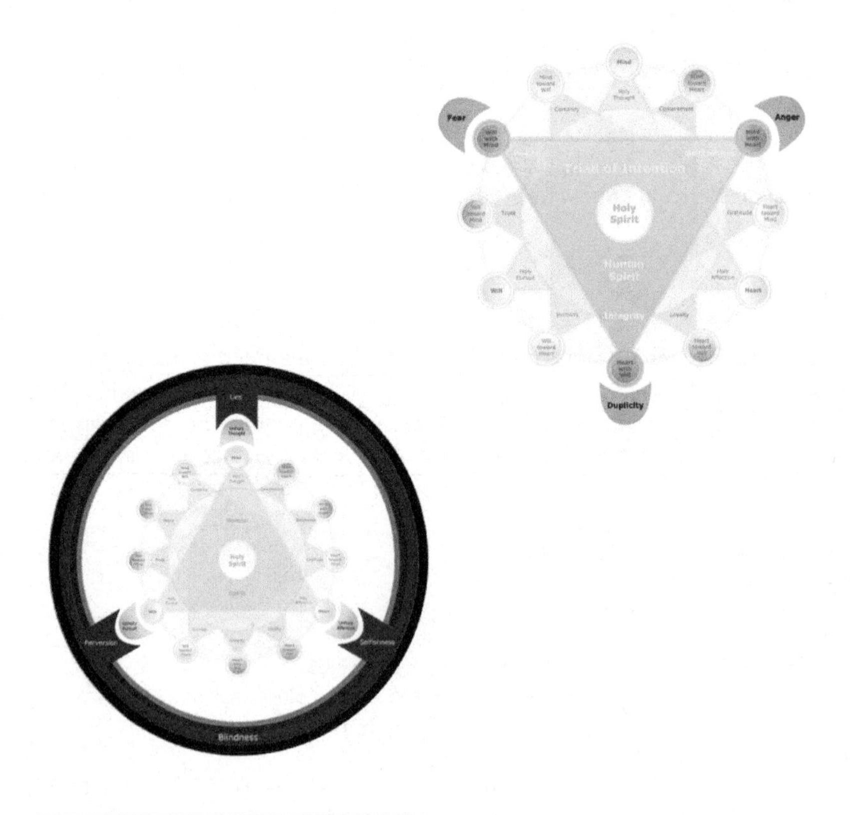

[1] John 16:33; Psalm 68:18; 1 Corinthians 15:57

[2] Revelation 17:14; 19:16; Psalm 72:11; Proverbs 8:15-16; 1 Timothy 6:15

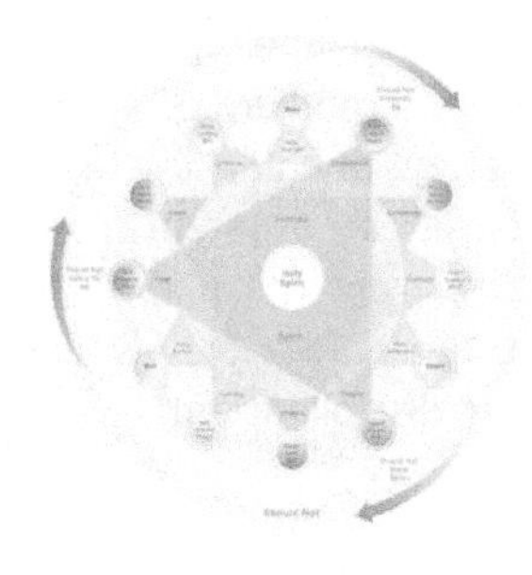

CHAPTER 2

RECEIVING THE TRUTH

Nothing worthy of being called a meal can be consumed in a few bites.

Since the beginning, Yehovah has been sharing His Word with humanity.[1] As a Father speaking to infants, He introduced His Voice to our first parents.[2] And though they understood His simple command, they failed to grasp the depth of His heart.[3] Not having an intimate knowledge of relational experience with Him,[4] our parents were deceived by suggestions spoken from another voice of which they had no reason to be suspicious.[5] Instead of Yehovah's Voice, they chose to listen to another.[6] Their sin was not their thirst for knowledge and experience but their decision to distrust Yehovah in favor of another voice![7] And so their very same trespass has been passed on to each child of Adam to this very day![8]

As humanity grew in number and understanding, Yehovah spoke more and more, teaching His children by speaking to them in Spirit and by using various experiences in Creation to form analogies or parables.[9] By the time of Moses, Yehovah's children had experienced enough relationship to receive rudimentary

---

[1] John 1:1-5,11; Genesis 2:16

[2] Genesis 2:16-17; 3:8-10

[3] Jeremiah 5:21; Proverbs 17:16; Hosea 7:11

[4] Hosea 4:6; Jeremiah 5:21; 2 Corinthians 4:3-6

[5] Genesis 1:31; 3:1; 2 Corinthians 11:3

[6] Genesis 3:5; 1 Timothy 2:14

[7] Genesis 3:11-13; 2 Corinthians 11:3

[8] Romans 5:12,19; 1 Corinthians 15:21

[9] Genesis 4:6; 5:22-24; 6:13; Ezekiel 17:2; 24:3-14; Psalm 78:2

commands to facilitate their preservation and spiritual growth in drawing near to Him.[1] Such orders were like the commands from a parent to a toddler, using the most basic concepts of reward and punishment to encourage obedience where trust was lacking. And just as some toddlers, when stopped by a parent from running into a street, interpret the subsequent discipline from the parent as unkind, so also many spiritual children, when reading the earlier Scriptures, erroneously conclude that Our Gracious Father is an unkind disciplinarian![2]

Beware! Understand the "Principle of the Hard Master":

"A certain nobleman went to a distant country to have himself appointed king and then return. So he called ten of his servants and gave them ten minas. 'Invest this money,' he said, 'until I come back.' But his subjects hated him and sent a delegation after him to say, 'We don't want this man to rule over us.' However, He was made king and returned home. Then he called for the servants to whom he had given the money, in order to find out what they had gained with it. The first one came and said, 'Lord, your mina has earned ten more.' The king replied, 'Well done, my good servant! Because you have been trustworthy in a very small matter, take charge of ten cities.' The second came and said, 'Lord, your mina has earned five more.' His master answered, 'You take charge of five cities.' Then another servant came and said, 'Lord, here is your mina; I have kept it laid away in a piece of cloth. I was afraid of you, because you are a hard man. You take out what you did not put in and reap what you did not sow.' The king replied, 'I will judge you by your own words, you wicked servant! You knew, did you, that I am a hard man, taking out what I did not put in, and reaping what I did not sow? Why then didn't you put my money in the bank, so that when I came back, I could have collected it with interest?' Then he said to those standing by, 'Take his mina away from him and give it to the one who has ten minas.' 'Lord,' they said, 'he already has ten!' He replied, 'I tell you that to everyone who has, more will be given, but as for the one who has nothing, even what they have will be taken away. But those enemies of mine who did not want me to be king over them—bring them here and kill them in front of me.'"[3]

In other words, anyone entertaining accusations of evil about Yehovah will be blinded from seeing or experiencing Him as the Rewarder of those who seek His Face.[4] Do not even entertain the slightest hint of accusation against Yehovah![5] He

TRUST GOD!

BE COURAGEOUS

---

1 Exodus 20:1-18; Deuteronomy 4:33,36; 5:4,22; Acts 7:38,53

2 Exodus 34:6-7; Proverbs 19:3

3 Luke 19:12-27

4 Hebrews 11:6; Isaiah 7:9; John 3:19

5 Job 38:1-40:2; Luke 19:21-27

is the only One Who is wholly Good and the only One Who gives good and perfect gifts![1] But know that this tactic of accusation from darkness is the very oldest method used by the enemy to lead people astray from the Love of Yehovah.[2]

However, for those who read the fullness of Yehovah's Word,[3] accept His Testimony,[4] and continue in relationship with Him,[5] spiritual intimacy is fanned into flame. Through this, the child begins to recognize and understand His Voice,[6] hearing the depth of His Love and Patience and learning to engage in mature conversation.[7] The written Word leads to the living Word,[8] and the child begins to walk in the Spirit.[9]

HalleluYah!

This is what Yeshua meant when He said,

"Though I have been speaking figuratively; an hour is coming when I will no longer speak to you in figures of speech, but will tell you plainly about the Father. On that day you will ask in My name, and I am not saying I will ask the Father on your behalf; for the Father Himself loves you, because you have loved Me and have believed that I came forth from God. I came forth from the Father and have come into the world; now I am leaving the world and going to the Father."[10]

In the past He spoke to us in figures of speech and parables, but *the hour has come*[11] for His Spirit to reveal these things plainly.[12] And Yehovah is going to fill the earth with knowledge of the Lord as the waters cover the sea![13]

---

[1] Matthew 19:17; James 1:17; John 1:9; 1 John 1:5; Revelation 21:23; 22:5; Isaiah 60:19
[2] Genesis 3:4-5; John 8:44; Acts 13:10; 1 John 3:8
[3] Acts 20:27; Isaiah 46:10; Matthew 28:20
[4] 1 John 5:10; Matthew 24:14
[5] James 4:8; Hebrews 10:22; 1 Peter 3:21; 2 Corinthians 7:1
[6] 1 Kings 19:9-13; Luke 8:18
[7] 1 John 2:13-14; 1 Corinthians 13:11
[8] John 5:39; 1 Peter 1:23
[9] Galatians 5:25; 1 John 5:10-12
[10] John 16:25-28
[11] Luke 12:56; 2 Corinthians 6:1-2
[12] John 16:25; Matthew 13:10-11
[13] Habakkuk 2:14; Psalm 22:27; 67:1-2; 72:19; 86:9; 98:1-3; Isaiah 6:3; 11:9; Zechariah 14:8-9: Revelation 11:15; 15:4

"Look! He is coming with the clouds, and every eye will see Him, even those who pierced Him; and all the nations of the earth will mourn because of Him!"[1]

HALLELUYAH!

SOUND THE TRUMPETS![2]

HALLELUYAH!

MAKE STRAIGHT THE WAY OF THE LORD![3]

HALLELUYAH!

Let us encourage one another to become experts in doing good[4] for the Glory of His Name![5]

Therefore, let us carefully consider how we listen![6] Remember what the Lord has said:

"Whoever has will be given more; whoever does not have, even what they think they have will be taken from them."[7]

Blessed are those who seek understanding![8] Blessed are those who seek a prophet's reward![9] Blessed are those who knock, for the door will be opened to them![10]

---

1 Revelation 1:7; Zechariah 12:10

2 Numbers 10:2; Joshua 6:20

3 Isaiah 40:3-5; 43:19; 49:11; 62:10-11

4 Romans 16:19; Hebrews 10:24; Titus 3:8,14; Hebrews 13:21; 2 Thessalonians 3:13; Galatians 6:9

5 1 Peter 2:12; Romans 15:9; 1 Corinthians 14:25

6 Luke 8:18a; Mark 4:23-24

7 Luke 8:18b; Matthew 25:29

8 Proverbs 4:7-9; Psalm 119:104

9 Matthew 10:41; Mark 6:11

10 Luke 11:9; Revelation 3:20

Praise be to our Glorious Creator, Who knows all things and is full of Wisdom![1] Praise be to our Redeemer,[2] Who gives us the Mind of Christ![3] Praise be to the Author of Faith,[4] Who gives us His Holy Word![5]

HALLELUYAH!

Praise be to the Lord Jesus Christ, Who overcame the world![6]

HALLELUYAH!

Show us, Great King![7] Make your ways known to us![8]

HALLELUYAAAAAAAAAAAAAH!!!!!!!

THANK YOU, Perfecter of Faith![9] THANK YOU for freely giving us all things![10]

HALLELUUUUYAH!

HALLELUUUUUYAAAAAAAAAAAAAAAAAAAAAAAAH!!!!!!!!

AMEN!!!!!!!!

---

[1] Romans 11:33; Job 5:9

[2] Psalm 19:14; 78:35; Isaiah 41:14; 43:14; 44:6,24; Jeremiah 63:16

[3] 1 Corinthians 2:16; John 15:15; 16:13-15

[4] Hebrews 12:2; Acts 5:31; Psalms 138:8

[5] John 1:14; Acts 4:31

[6] John 12:31; 16:11,33; Psalm 68:18; Romans 8:37; 1 John 4:4; 5:4

[7] Matthew 5:35; Psalm 47:2; 48:2; 95:3; Malachi 1:14

[8] Psalm 25:4; 27:11; 86:11; 119:27; 143:8; Exodus 33:13; Isaiah 2:3; Jeremiah 6:16

[9] Hebrews 12:2; Acts 5:31; Psalms 138:8

[10] Romans 8:32; Psalm 84:11; 1 Corinthians 2:12; 3:21-23

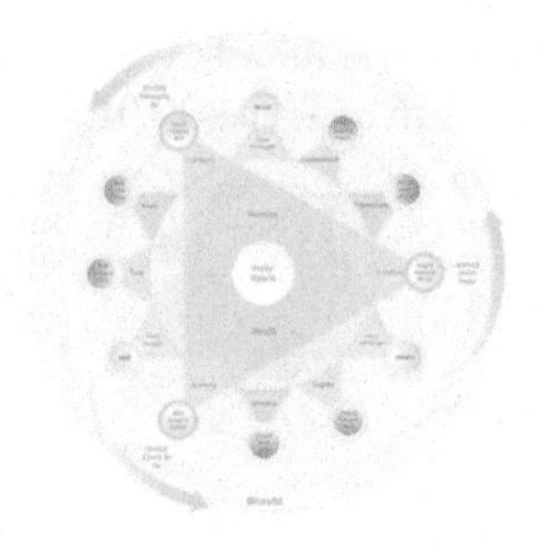

CHAPTER 3

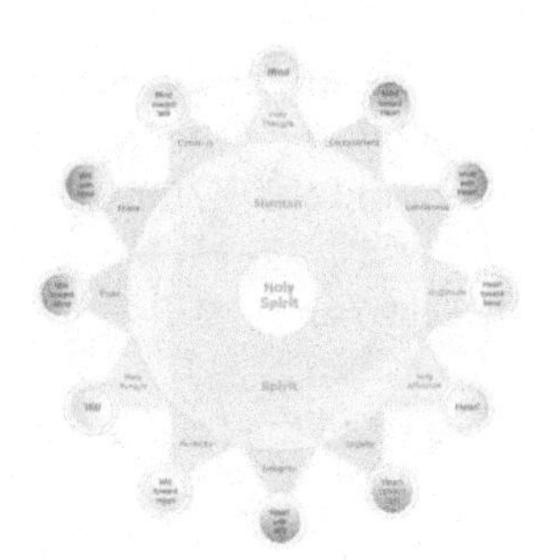

HEARING IN SPIRIT

Yehovah wants you.[1] He wants you to be with Him.[2] He does not reject you.[3] He has been speaking to you since He formed you in the womb,[4] and He has never abandoned you nor neglected you.[5]

You were made in the image of Yehovah.[6] If you were left alone, you would do what He does.[7] But you have not been left alone.[8] Our first parents allowed the voice of darkness[9] to gain access through Creation into their souls, and now dark "voices"[10] have tempted you as well. Instead of taking every thought captive,[11] you have listened to them, and they have deceived you into believing, receiving, embracing, facilitating, and doing evil.[12]

---

[1] Matthew 10:29-31; 12:11-12
[2] John 14:2-3; Matthew 25:34
[3] Deuteronomy 31:8; Matthew 28:20
[4] Jeremiah 1:5; Psalm 71:5-6; Isaiah 49:1; Galatians 1:15
[5] Isaiah 44:21; 49:15-16; Jeremiah 31:20
[6] Genesis 1:26; Romans 8:28-29
[7] Genesis 1:27,31
[8] 1 Peter 5:8; John 8:44; Ephesians 6:11; Revelation 12:9; Zechariah 3:1; Job 1:7
[9] Genesis 3:1,4-5, 14-15; Revelation 12:9; 20:2
[10] Genesis 3:1; 1 Thessalonians 3:5; 1 Timothy 6:20; John 13:2,27; Mark 8:33; 1 John 2:16; "Voices" in this case are *thoughts*, but we will learn that they can also be *pursuits, and affections*.
[11] 2 Corinthians 10:5; Jeremiah 4:14; Hebrews 4:12
[12] Ephesians 2:1-3; Genesis 3:1; 2 Corinthians 11:13-15; Titus 3:3-7

Yehovah has not tempted you.[1] He is Good in every way and all the time.[2] Many people have attempted to describe Yehovah as a "Trinity." Such a description in its official form is not false, but neither does it adequately describe the One Who is and was and is to come,[3] the One Who has made you,[4] sought you,[5] and loved you.[6] He is One God,[7] Who manifests in three shared ways.[8] He is the Father, the Prime Source of all things,[9] the Foundation of Life,[10] the Fount of Goodness[11] from Whom all things come and for Whom we live.[12] His Holy Spirit comes forth from the Father[13] through the Son[14] and is aware of all,[15] considers all,[16] judges what is True,[17] and intends Truth.[18] And His Son, or Soul,[19] Who interacts with Creation,[20] Who holds all things together and gives them their being,[21] Who sends the Holy Spirit[22] and from Whom the Holy Spirit receives,[23] is He through Whom all things came and through Whom we live.[24] He has thoughts,[25] pursuits,[26] and affections[27] and expresses the fullness of the personality of Yehovah in every way.[28] It is

---

[1] James 1:13; Romans 9:20

[2] James 1:17; John 1:9; 1 John 1:5; Revelation 21:23; 22:5; Isaiah 60:19

[3] Revelation 1:4,7-8; 4:8; Exodus 3:14; Psalm 90:2; Isaiah 41:4; Micah 5:2; John 1:1

[4] John 1:10; Colossians 1:16

[5] John 1:11; Matthew 15:24; Acts 3:25-26

[6] Romans 5:8; John 15:13; 1 John 3:16; 4:9-10

[7] John 10:30; 12:44-46; 14:6-11; Deuteronomy 6:4; Isaiah 43:10; Malachi 3:1; Luke 1:76

[8] Matthew 28:19; John 10:30; 16:7,14-15

[9] 1 Corinthians 8:6a; Acts 17:28; Ephesians 4:6

[10] John 17:3; 1 Samuel 2:8

[11] James 1:17; John 1:9; 1 John 1:5; Revelation 21:23; 22:5; Isaiah 60:19

[12] 1 Corinthians 8:6b; John 1:3; Hebrews 1:2-3

[13] John 8:42; 15:26; Revelation 22:1

[14] John 16:14-15; Matthew 11:27; Colossians 2:3

[15] John 16:13b; Psalms 139:7-12; Mark 12:36; John 14:26

[16] John 16:9-11; Luke 2:26; 10:21; Acts 15:28

[17] John 16:8; Matthew 12:32; Acts 10:44-48

[18] John 16:13a; Mark 13:11; Luke 12:12; Romans 14:17

[19] Jeremiah 32:41; Isaiah 62:5

[20] John 1:4,9; Romans 8:20

[21] Matthew 5:45; 10:29; 15:13; 18:19; 26:52; John 5:19-20,26; 6:37,44,65; 8:28,42,54

[22] John 14:26; 16:7; Luke 24:49; Acts 1:4

[23] John 16:14-15; 2 Corinthians 3:14-18

[24] 1 Corinthians 8:6b; Hebrews 1:2-3; John 1:3

[25] Jeremiah 19:5; Luke 9:47

[26] Psalm 132:13-14; 1 Corinthians 4:19 – *power*, from the Greek δύναμις, pronounced "doo'-nah-mihs," meaning *miraculous ability to accomplish or achieve, strength to work, power to pursue or conquer.*

[27] Hosea 11:8; Matthew 23:37; Genesis 1:26a

[28] Colossians 2:9; John 12:45

through Yehovah's Soul that all things come, and it is this part of Him that was able to put on flesh for you and explain these very things to you.[1]

You who are redeemed by His Blood have been made in His image.[2] You also manifest in three shared ways because you have a spirit, soul, and body.[3] The essence of your life, which is your spirit, was breathed out from the Spirit of Yehovah.[4] When this spirit was breathed into a physical body,[5] the body gained both a physical life and a different sort of inner life than that of the spirit, and this unique aspect of inner life is called a "soul."[6] It is this life that has thoughts, pursuits, and affections, just like Yehovah.[7] And just like Yehovah, though your present body can be crucified on a cross, both your soul and spirit are eternal.[8] Also like Yehovah, even though your spirit is presently presiding over your physical body,[9] the Scriptures clearly state that your spirit is also simultaneously present in Heaven.[10] If your physical body were to suddenly lose an arm or a leg, your soul would not be lessened.[11] And, if your physical body received some sort of debilitating head injury, the ability of your soul to function within that body could be hindered, but your spirit would not be reduced at all.[12]

In the same way, understand that Christ has always been the Soul of Yehovah.[13] He has always been the Savior,[14] always been the Personality of Yehovah.[15] He has always been the Voice of Yehovah,[16] the Word of Yehovah,[17] the Testimony of which the Holy Spirit has been convicting you,[18] and He is that part of Yehovah that transformed His Heavenly Body into a physical one.[19] Yeshua is that part of

---

[1] John 14:6-11,13,20,24,31; 10:18; 12:49-50; 15:16,23; 16:15
[2] Genesis 1:26; 1 Corinthians 15:49; Colossians 3:10
[3] 1 Thessalonians 5:23; Hebrews 4:12
[4] Isaiah 42:5; Ezekiel 37:5
[5] Job 27:3; 33:4; Genesis 2:7
[6] Genesis 2:7; Exodus 30:12; Deuteronomy 30:6; Micah 6:7
[7] Mark 12:30; Genesis 1:26a
[8] Revelation 6:9; 20:4
[9] 2 Corinthians 5:8; Malachi 2:15; Romans 8:13
[10] Ephesians 2:6; 1 Corinthians 5:3; Colossians 2:5; 3:3
[11] Matthew 18:8-9; 9:20-22; Luke 6:6-10; 18:42
[12] Acts 20:9-12; 1 Samuel 28:13-15
[13] John 1:18; 4:26
[14] Malachi 3:1; John 20:28; Isaiah 9:6; Luke 1:76
[15] Colossians 1:19; 2:9; Matthew 11:25-27; John 1:16
[16] John 10:27; Hebrews 3:7; Revelation 3:20
[17] John 1:1-5; Luke 11:28; Revelation 19:13
[18] Revelation 19:10d; John 16:8-11
[19] Matthew 17:2; Revelation 4:2; 7:17

Yehovah that laid down His physical body into death and raised it back up into life again for your salvation.[1] And just as your spirit shares in all the experiences of your body, so also the "Father" experienced everything that happened to the "Son."[2] Therefore, do not doubt Yehovah's Love for you, because He died for you in *every way as much as you could possibly die* for Him.[3] He did this to demonstrate His selfless Love for you[4] so that you could trust His commitment to you[5] even when you do not understand all the intricacies of Creation with its temporary independence[6] from Heaven's Law of Righteousness.[7]

Now, the other voices that have been making suggestions to separate you from that love are those which transgressed from Yehovah's presence and fell from Righteousness.[8] They have become unrighteousness and can no longer cohabitate with the Word.[9] However, because they were granted authority before their fall, they maintain a temporary position of influence in Creation that allows them to affect beings within it[10] (much in the same way that people, who have been given authority over their souls and flesh for the purpose of glorifying Yehovah,[11] are free to misuse that authority to sin until they are removed from Creation).[12]

Being aware of this, do not be deceived by any voices of authority[13] claiming that the inner man is a private place in spirit![14] While the human soul is only expressed through the body to other people[15] as a sign that Yehovah's Soul is only expressed

---

[1] John 10:17-18; Isaiah 53:7-12
[2] John 12:45; 14:9
[3] Romans 5:8; John 20:28
[4] 1 John 3:16; Romans 5:8; John 15:13; 1 Peter 3:18
[5] Philippians 1:6; 1 Corinthians 1:8
[6] Romans 2:4; 9:22; 2 Peter 3:15
[7] Romans 6:18; 8:2,10-11; 2 Corinthians 3:6
[8] 1 John 4:1; John 8:44
[9] 2 Corinthians 6:14-15; James 4:4
[10] Psalm 82:1-8; Ephesians 6:12
[11] Isaiah 43:7,21; Psalm 100:3; Ephesians 2:10; Romans 9:23
[12] Matthew 25:32-33; Romans 8:13; Revelation 20:12
[13] 1 John 4:1; 2 Corinthians 4:4
[14] Romans 8:27; Revelation 2:23; 1 Kings 22:22
[15] 1 Corinthians 2 - Notice that Paul in this chapter speaks of a person's spirit knowing their own thoughts, yet the chapter ends with him arguing that we know the thoughts of God because we share His Spirit. Other souls do not see our thoughts, but other spirits can see our thoughts. And just as Yeshua sees our thoughts (Revelation 2:23), we also may know the thoughts of others through the revelation of the Holy Spirit (Matthew 9:4; John 14:12; Acts 5:3).

through Yeshua in Creation,[1] all roaming spirits can clearly see the inner man of a person as he is.[2] Nothing is hidden![3] In the spirit, everything is visible![4] Thoughts, pursuits, and affections are readily apparent.[5] There is no "profile page" as there is on social media. There is no ability to appear different than one is, to engage in any sort of posturing, or to put a best foot forward.[6] Though many people will quote that only Yehovah knows what is in the heart,[7] they miss that this is a reference to the hidden *potential* of a heart.[8] But understand that spirits are visible to spirits![9] Any roaming spirit that can see both spirit and body can certainly also see how a human spirit or any other spirit is interacting with a body![10] And since the interaction of a human spirit with a body produces a human soul,[11] any roaming spirit can also *clearly* see what a soul is currently doing![12] And this *includes* the activities of the mind, will, and heart of that soul![13]

Someone might ask, "How then can we fight a war in spirit, when war on earth consists of subterfuge, bluffing, pretense, posturing, camouflage, misdirection, and craftiness?" I tell you the truth, *none* of those methods work in spiritual warfare![14] Any such plans formed in a human soul are clearly observable to any spirit![15] No! As children of Yehovah, we use *spiritual* weapons for *spiritual* warfare, weapons that are strong and sure, able to bring the evil kingdom to absolute devastation![16] And the foremost weapon of our warfare is Truth! It's Yehovah Himself![17]

HALLELUYAH!

---

[1] John 1:14,18; 6:46; Matthew 11:27; Colossians 1:15
[2] Acts 19:13-16; Mark 1:23-26
[3] Luke 12:2-3; Ecclesiastes 10:20
[4] Mark 1:34; Luke 4:41
[5] Acts 5:3; 13:10
[6] Acts 19:13-16; Matthew 23:27
[7] 1 Kings 8:39-40; 1 Samuel 16:7
[8] Job 1:7,9,11 – Satan presently saw Job's fear of Yehovah but did not know what Job's heart would do in every circumstance. However, Yehovah knows all things, including what the heart will do even before it does it (Psalm 139:2-23).
[9] Mark 1:24; Job 1:6; Numbers 22:31; 2 Kings 6:17
[10] Matthew 12:43-45 Luke 11:21-22; Ephesians 2:2
[11] Genesis 2:7; Job 27:3; 33:4; John 20:22: Acts 17:25
[12] Ephesians 2:2; Matthew 12:43-45; Revelation 6:9; 20:4
[13] 2 Corinthians 4:4; 1 Peter 5:8-9; Genesis 3:1-5; John 13:2; Acts 5:1-11
[14] 2 Corinthians 10:3-5; Romans 8:13; Ephesians 6:12
[15] Mark 2:8; Acts 5:3-4; Psalm 91:11-12; 1 Kings 22:21-22
[16] 2 Corinthians 10:3-5; Zechariah 4:6
[17] John 8:32; 14:6; 2 Corinthians 13:8

The Truth lives in us, and we live in the Truth![1] This is what He meant by, "On that day you will realize that I am in My Father, and you are in Me, and I am in you."[2]

HALLELUYAH!

Yehovah loves us infinitely more than we can imagine![3] He put on flesh and died for us to reveal His Love to us![4] He would do anything for us *except* become a lie.[5] That is where He draws the line, and He has given us that same line. He will *never* ask us to become a lie.[6] The Kingdom of Heaven is a Kingdom of Truth, with Truth as its King,[7] and we have been made children, citizens, priests, and soldiers of that Truth.[8] Amen!

Therefore, nothing about how we fight is at all lie, pretend, exaggeration, pretense, posturing, deceit, subterfuge, craftiness, or hidden in any way.[9] No, we are the bold,[10] the fearless,[11] confident,[12] standing on the Rock of Truth and Power,[13] piercing the darkness with the Light of Truth![14] We are conquerors,[15] able to endure[16] and persevere[17] through all things, mighty,[18] overwhelming,[19] and invincible[20] because we drink the Blood of Yeshua,[21] eat from the Tree of Life,[22] and wear the armor of Yehovah![23]

Lord, you always cause me to triumph. You do the work.

---

[1] John 14:17; 2 John 1:2
[2] John 14:20
[3] Ephesians 3:18; Job 11:7-9; Psalm 103:11-12; 139:6
[4] Malachi 3:1; Luke 1:76-79; John 1:1,14; Romans 5:8
[5] Hebrews 6:18; Titus 1:2
[6] Revelation 21:8; Proverbs 19:5; John 8:44
[7] John 14:6; Revelation 19:16
[8] 1 Thessalonians 5:5; Revelation 1:5-6; Philippians 3:20
[9] Matthew 5:16; Luke 12:3
[10] Proverbs 28:1; Exodus 11:8; Psalm 27:1-2; Acts 4:13; 14:3; 1 Thessalonians 2:2
[11] 2 Timothy 1:7; Romans 8:15; 1 John 4:18
[12] 2 Corinthians 5:5-9; Psalm 27:3-4; Hebrews 10:35
[13] Psalm 40:2; 61:2; Matthew 7:24-25
[14] Ephesians 6:12; 1 John 2:8
[15] Romans 8:37; Isaiah 25:8; 1 Corinthians 15:57; 1 John 4:4; 5:4-5; Jude 1:24
[16] Hebrews 12:7; 2 Timothy 4:5
[17] 1 Corinthians 13:7; 2 Timothy 2:10
[18] Ephesians 1:19; 3:7,20; 6:10; 2 Thessalonians 1:11; 1 Thessalonians 1:5
[19] Romans 8:37; Isaiah 25:8; 1 Corinthians 15:57; 1 John 4:4; 5:4-5; Jude 1:24
[20] 1 John 4:4; Ephesians 6:10,13; Romans 8:37; 1 Corinthians 15:57
[21] John 6:53; Matthew 26:27-28
[22] Revelation 2:7; 22:2,14
[23] Romans 13:12; Ephesians 6:11

HALLELUYAH!

There is no such thing as a shadow that can overcome Light![1] "You are the light of the world. A town built on a hill *cannot* be hidden!"[2]

HALLELUYAH!

PRAISE BE TO THE FATHER OF HEAVENLY LIGHTS, WHO DOES NOT CHANGE LIKE SHIFTING SHADOWS![3]

HALLELUYAH!

WHOSE VOICE IS THE TRUTH![4]

GLORY TO GOD!

WHOSE WORD IS SURE![5]

HALLELUYAH!

PRAISE THE ALMIGHTY PRESENCE FROM WHOM EARTH AND HEAVEN FLEE AND CANNOT BE FOUND![6]

HALLELUYAH!

FROM HIS MOUTH COMES A DOUBLE-EDGED SWORD WITH WHICH HE WILL SLAY ALL EVIL FROM THE EARTH![7]

HALLELUYAAAAAAAAAAAAH!!!!!!!!!!

---

[1] John 1:5; Matthew 15:14
[2] Matthew 5:14; Ephesians 5:8-14; Philippians 2:15
[3] James 1:17; John 1:9; 1 John 1:5; Revelation 21:23; 22:5; Isaiah 60:19
[4] 1 John 4:6; John 14:17; 15:26; 16:13
[5] Mark 13:31; 2 Timothy 2:13; Titus 1:2; Zechariah 1:6; Isaiah 40:8; Luke 1:37
[6] Revelation 20:11; Jeremiah 4:23-26
[7] Revelation 19:15-21; Isaiah 11:4; 2 Thessalonians 2:8

GOODNESS,[1] RIGHTEOUSNESS,[2] PURITY,[3] AND TRUTH[4] WILL RULE FOREVER AND EVER![5]

HALLELUYAAAAAAAAAAAAH!!!!!!!!!!

OUR GOD ALMIGHTY REIGNS!!!!!!!!!!!!!![6]

HALLELUYAAAAAAAAAAAAAAAAAAAAAAAAAAAH!!!!!!!!!!

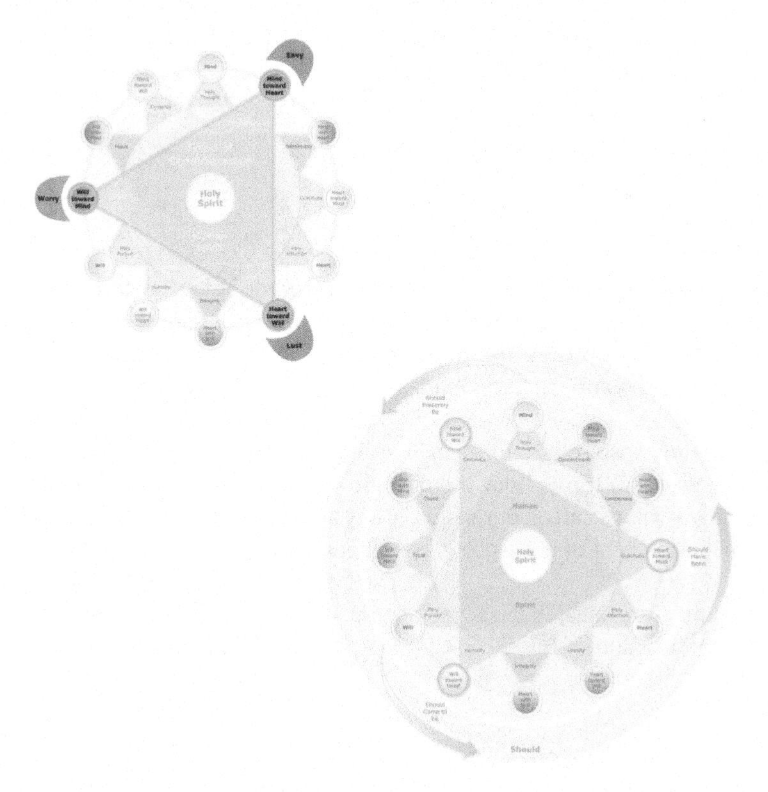

[1] Matthew 19:17; 1 Samuel 2:2; Psalm 145:7-9; James 1:17

[2] 1 John 2:29; Zechariah 9:9; Acts 3:14; 22:14; 2 Corinthians 5:21; Hebrews 1:8-9

[3] 1 John 3:3; Hebrews 7:26

[4] John 1:17; 14:6; 15:1; 18:37; Romans 15:8; Colossians 2:17; 1 John 5:6,20; Revelation 3:7,14; 19:11

[5] Revelation 21:27; Hebrews 1:8; Revelation 1:18; 4:9; 11:15

[6] Psalm 99:1; Revelation 1:18; 4:9; 11:15; 19:6; 21:27; Hebrews 1:8

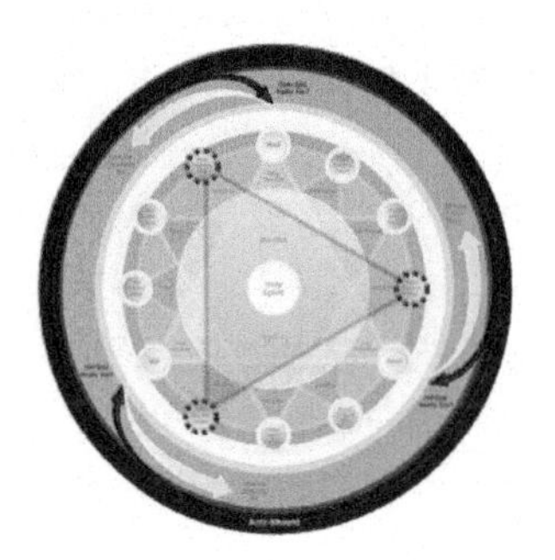

CHAPTER 4

CHEWING THE TRUTH

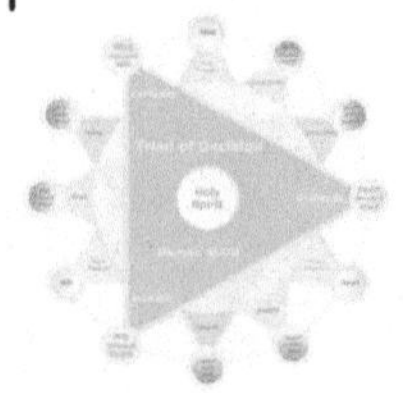

Simply receiving the Word is not enough. Like a person without teeth who cannot chew meat is a child of spirit who reads the Word but does not consider it.[1] Such a child searches the Scriptures for milk, looking for easy words and easy responsibilities, but substantial growth eludes him.[2]

Throughout the Holy Inspired Scriptures,[3] we are exhorted to apply them to memory, to ponder them throughout the day and on our beds at night.[4] We are to wear them on our minds and on our deeds.[5] They are like good seeds that, when watered and given the light of day, sprout up to bear much fruit in the Spirit.[6]

Whatever the mind entertains, that is what it chews upon.[7] And whatever it chews upon, that is what it swallows.[8]

---

1 James 1:23-24; 1 Thessalonians 1:5; Ezekiel 33:31-32; Matthew 7:26-27

2 Hebrews 5:13; Isaiah 28:9; 1 Corinthians 14:20; Ephesians 4:14

3 2 Timothy 3:16; 2 Samuel 23:2; Matthew 22:43; 26:56; John 10:35; Romans 3:2; 15:4; Galatians 3:8; Hebrews 4:12; 2 Peter 1:19-21

4 Psalm 119:11,48,78,83,93,95,99,109,141,153; 63:6

5 Deuteronomy 6:6-9; Exodus 13:9,16; Numbers 15:38-39; Proverbs 3:3; 6:21; 7:3; Hebrews 2:1

6 Matthew 13:1-9,18-23

7 Psalm 119:15,23,48,78,97,131,148; James 1:25

8 Matthew 6:22-23; Luke 11:34-36

Someone might say, "I chew the meat and spit out the bones." Yes, but if one is eating a rat, it is rat meat that is consumed.[1]

Therefore, see to it then that you chew "righteous meat."[2] Seek the Word.[3] Engage in holy fellowship.[4] Listen to the testimonies of the righteous,[5] and do not hand the reins of your mind to unrighteous media, entertainment, or the idle words of the wayward.[6]

Do you want wisdom? Do you long for understanding? Do you thirst for truth? Why then would you fill your mind with constant wayward musings of depressed musicians and immoral actors?[7] For if you spend your precious time in Creation consuming that which is cultivated and produced by waywardness, then you will consume that seed and bear that fruit.[8] But if you devote yourself to seeking His Kingdom of Truth, Holiness, and Righteousness, then you will consume that nutrition and be healed from sin and death to life, victory, and peace.[9]

As our Righteous King[10] has said, "No one can serve two masters. Either you will hate the one and love the other, or you will be devoted to the one and think little of the other."[11] You cannot serve both the Truth and lies. If you choose "both," you have chosen the latter.[12] Therefore, anyone who wishes to leave the chains of the principles of this world[13] behind must also leave the lies of this world behind.[14] But those who seek to become genuine disciples of the Truth, devoting themselves to the consumption of what is holy,[15] and seeking His Kingdom,[16] they

---

[1] Revelation 16:13-14; 1 Timothy 4:1-3

[2] Colossians 3:2; 1 Chronicles 22:19; Psalm 62:10; 119:36-37; Matthew 16:23; Romans 8:4-6; 1 John 2:15-17; Philippians 3:19

[3] Amos 8:12; John 4:14

[4] Hebrews 10:25; 1 Thessalonians 4:18; 5:11

[5] 1 Thessalonians 5:11; Revelation 12:11

[6] Romans 8:5-8; Luke 11:34-36; Matthew 6:22-23

[7] Psalm 101:3; 2 Peter 3:17

[8] Galatians 6:7-8; Romans 8:13-14

[9] 2 Peter 1:5-8; Colossians 3:2-4

[10] Hebrews 7:2,17; Psalm 45:4-7; Isaiah 9:6-7; Jeremiah 23:5-6; 33:15-16

[11] Matthew 6:24

[12] Haggai 2:12-13; Numbers 19:11-22

[13] Colossians 2:20; Galatians 4:3; John 15:19; 17:14-16; 2 Corinthians 10:3; 1 John 5:19; Romans 7:4-6

[14] Ephesians 5:11; Philippians 3:13-14

[15] John 6:33-51; Luke 22:19

[16] Luke 12:31; Psalm 34:9; 37:19; 84:11; Isaiah 33:16; Matthew 6:33; John 6:27

will be set free by the Truth[1] from the chains of this world and live in the resurrection power that rose Our Righteous King from the dead.[2]

Again, this is what is meant by, "Consider carefully how you listen. Whoever has will be given more; whoever does not have, even what they seem to have will be taken from them."[3]

SO BE CAREFUL HOW YOU LISTEN! Stop merely nodding at what the Lord says and instead actually do it![4] Stop looking to the world for your rest, peace, joy, and information![5] How is it that you say you believe God and then turn and look for fulfillment somewhere else?[6] Were you made in the image of the world or the image of God?[7] God tells you to set your mind on things above and not on earthly things,[8] and you nod but then watch primetime or scroll social media for several hours every evening?[9] Your Savior explains that you can cast out sicknesses,[10] and you nod but somehow never manage to learn? Jesus Christ teaches that people are infested with unclean spirits,[11] and you nod but live life as if unclean spirits are foolish myths? After doing all of this, you accept the idea fed to you by darkness that you are living the way Christ commanded you to live?[12] And after such double-mindedness, you juggle and trade opinions with others about "how things *really* are today"?[13]

How can you claim to be a disciple of Christ when you don't accept and live by what He teaches![14] You should not be surprised that your life doesn't look like that

---

[1] John 8:32,36; Psalm 25:5; 119:45; Proverbs 2:1-7; 4:18; Isaiah 2:3; 61:1; Romans 6:14-18,22; 8:2,15; 2 Corinthians 3:17-18; Galatians 5:13; 2 Timothy 2:25-26

[2] Romans 8:11; John 7:38-39; Ephesians 2:5

[3] Luke 8:18; 19:26; Deuteronomy 32:46-47; Proverbs 2:2-5; Mark 4:23-24; Acts 17:11; Hebrews 2:1; James 1:22-25; Matthew 13:12; John 15:2

[4] James 1:22; 4:17; Matthew 7:21-25; 12:50; 28:20; Luke 11:28; 12:47-48; John 13:17; Romans 2:13; 1 John 2:3, 3:7; 3 John 1:11; Revelation 22:7

[5] 2 Corinthians 4:4; Matthew 4:8-9; John 12:40; Ephesians 2:2; 1 John 2:11; 5:19

[6] James 1:8; 1 Kings 18:21; Hosea 7:8-11; Matthew 6:24

[7] Genesis 1:26-17; Romans 1:23; John 8:43-45; Colossians 3:10; 2 Corinthians 3:18

[8] Colossians 3:2; 1 Chronicles 22:19; Psalm 62:10; 119:36-37; Matthew 16:23; Romans 8:4-6; 1 John 2:15-17; Philippians 3:19

[9] Philippians 3:19; Matthew 16:23; Romans 8:5-7

[10] Luke 10:9; Matthew 10:8; Mark 6:13; Acts 28:7-10

[11] Mark 6:7; Acts 8:7

[12] John 14:15,23-24

[13] Acts 17:21; 2 Thessalonians 3:11-12; 1 Timothy 5:13; 2 Timothy 2:16-17

[14] Luke 6:46; Revelation 3:15-17

of the disciples![1] Haven't you heard that friendship with the world is enmity toward Yehovah?[2] Do you live like the disciples or like the world?[3] ***Do you*** or ***do you not*** teach others that evil spirits tempt people to sin?[4] ***Do you*** or ***do you not*** teach others that evil spirits cause people to be sick?[5]

WHOSE DISCIPLE ARE YOU?

JESUS TAUGHT THAT EVIL SPIRITS TEMPT PEOPLE[6] AND MAKE THEM SICK![7]

DO YOU AGREE OR NOT?[8]

IF YOU DON'T AGREE, THEN YOU'RE NOT A *DISCIPLE* OF CHRIST![9]

IF YOU DO AGREE, THEN STOP ENTERTAINING THE WORLD AND EATING THE FRUIT OF ITS RIDICULOUS DUPLICITY AND DECEIT![10]

The "world's" ideas are not even *from* humanity![11] They are thoughts set by dark spirits as stumbling blocks[12] to impair the righteous![13]

"WAKE UP, SLEEPER, RISE FROM THE DEAD, AND CHRIST WILL SHINE ON YOU"![14]

But for those of you who are willing to leave such darkness behind and seek something better: "The world is not even worthy of you!"[15]

HALLELUYAH!

---

[1] John 15:5; 13:15; 1 John 2:6; 1:7; Psalm 85:13; Matthew 11:29; 1 Peter 2:21
[2] James 4:4; 7:7; 15:19,23; 17:14; 1 John 2:15-16
[3] 1 Corinthians 11:1; 1 Peter 2:21; Matthew 11:29; Romans 8:5; 1 John 2:4,6; Philippians 3:19
[4] Mark 1:13; 1 Corinthians 7:5; Luke 22:31; John 15:4-6
[5] 1 Corinthians 5:5; Job 2:7
[6] Matthew 4:1,3; 6:13; 1 Thessalonians 3:5; Revelation 12:9; 2 Timothy 2:26
[7] Luke 13:16; Acts 19:12
[8] Luke 6:46; James 4:6-8
[9] John 15:4-6; Luke 6:46; 12:47; 1 John 2:4
[10] Luke 24:25; Mark 7:18; 8:17-18; 16:14
[11] 1 John 5:19; John 8:44; Ephesians 6:12
[12] Matthew 16:23; Colossians 3:2; 1 Chronicles 22:19; Psalm 62:10; 119:36-37; Romans 8:4-6; 1 John 2:15-17; Philippians 3:19
[13] 2 Corinthians 11:3; Revelation 12:9
[14] Ephesians 5:14; Isaiah 60:1; 1 Thessalonians 5:6; 2 Timothy 2:26
[15] Hebrews 11:38; Isaiah 57:1

Praise our Savior, Who is able to rescue us all from such futility![1] Because of Him, we are now able to put off our old, corrupted desires[2] and "put on the new self, created to be Like God in true righteousness and holiness"![3]

Yes! You can receive and accept the Truth from God! Yes, it is more than possible; it is even guaranteed with a promise:

"If you declare with your mouth, 'Jesus is Lord,' and believe in your heart that God raised him from the dead, you will be saved."[4] Saved from what? – saved from *anything* less than *everything* promised to you by the Lord Jesus Christ![5]

HALLELUYAH!

So, whether you are hearing this for the first time or the thousandth time, let us proceed to do this! Let us confess with our mouths and believe in our hearts!

HalleluYah! WE BELIEVE YOU, LORD! HALLELUYAH!

For everyone reading these words: May the rocks in the soil of your soul be broken,[6] may the thorns be removed,[7] may your affection for Him be kindled into flame,[8] may your power to walk in Truth be strengthened,[9] and may your integrity overflow for His Glory![10]

HalleluYah!

Praise our faithful Mediator,[11] Who is the WAY, the TRUTH, and the LIFE![12]

HALLELUYAH!

---

[1] Ephesians 4:17; Psalm 94:8-11
[2] Ephesians 4:22; Colossians 3:9; Romans 6:6
[3] Ephesians 4:24; 6:11; Job 29:14; Romans 6:4; 13:12,14; Galatians 3:27
[4] Romans 10:9
[5] 2 Corinthians 1:20; Ephesians 1:13; Galatians 3:22
[6] Matthew 13:15,20-21; Acts 8:21-23; Mark 6:52; 10:5; Ephesians 4:18; Hebrews 3:8
[7] Matthew 13:22; 2 Timothy 4:10; Luke 18:24
[8] 2 Corinthians 8:7; 9:8; Philippians 1:9,11; 2 Peter 1:5-8
[9] Ephesians 3:16; 3 John 1:4; Acts 3:12
[10] Matthew 5:16; Luke 1:53; John 6:27; 15:8
[11] 1 Timothy 2:5; Hebrews 7:25; 8:6; 9:15; 12:24
[12] John 14:6; Acts 4:12; Hebrews 10:19-22; 1 John 2:23; 2 John 1:9; Revelation 5:8-9

Praise our GOD, Who came in FLESH,[1] and Who is THE SAME YESTERDAY, TODAY, and FOREVER![2]

BLESS GOD!

Before Abraham was born, HE IS![3] AMEN!

He DESTROYED the power of death![4] AMEN!

He is the Alpha and the Omega, the BEGINNING and the END![5] AMEN!

ALL authority in Heaven and on Earth belongs to HIM![6] AMEN!

He is the PAYMENT for the sins of the WHOLE WORLD![7]

HALLELUYAH!

Whoever BELIEVES in Him, out of their heart will flow RIVERS of living water![8]

HALLELUYAAAAAAAAAAH!!!!!

PRAISE BE TO *YOUR NAME* OUR GOD AND KING!!!![9]

PRAISE YOU, *JESUS*!!!!!!!!!![10]

HALLELUYAAAAAAAAAAAAAAAAAAAAAAAAH!!!!!!!!!!

---

[1] John 1:14; Luke 2:11; Philippians 2:6-8; 1 Timothy 3:16; 1 John 4:2-3; 2 John 1:7

[2] Hebrews 13:8; Psalm 102:27-28; 103:17; Malachi 3:6; James 1:17

[3] John 8:58; 17:5,24; Proverbs 8:22-30; Micah 5:2; Colossians 1:17; Hebrews 1:10-12; 13:8; Revelation 1:17-18; 2:8

[4] Hebrews 2:14; 2 Timothy 1:10

[5] Revelation 1:8; 22:13; Isaiah 41:4; 44:6; 48:12

[6] Matthew 28:18; Psalm 2:6-9; 89:27; 110:1-3; Isaiah 9:6-7; Daniel 7:14; Luke 1:32-33; 10:22; John 3:35; 5:22-27; 13:3; 17:2; Acts 2:36; 10:36; Romans 14:9

[7] 1 John 2:2; 3:5; 4:10,14; Romans 3:25-26; 1 Peter 2:24; 3:18; John 1:29; 4:42

[8] John 7:38; Job 32:18-19; Proverbs 10:11; Isaiah 12:3; 44:3; 58:11; 59:21; Galatians 5:22-23; Ephesians 5:9

[9] Psalm 44:8; Isaiah 25:1

[10] Hebrews 13:15; Leviticus 7:12; 2 Chronicles 7:6; Psalm 118:19; Romans 12:1

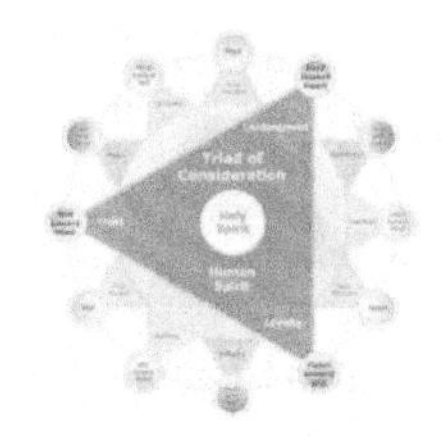

CHAPTER 5

DIGESTING THE TRUTH

Just as the act of consumption is not complete merely with chewing, so also our nourishment by the Truth is not completed through mere reception and consideration but must include reflection,[1] reciprocation,[2] and participation[3] in the Truth.

This act of "digesting" the Truth is called "walking with God."[4]

Walking with God is analogous to walking with someone on the earth. When two people walk together, there is most often shared communication, conversation, proximity, and agreement on pace, direction, and a common destination.[5]

Understand that Yehovah is establishing His Kingdom.[6] *That* is "where He is going."[7] To join Him for a walk, a person must go where Yehovah is going.[8] That is not to say that Yehovah walks only in churches.[9] No! He walks into businesses,

---

[1] 2 Timothy 2:7; 1 Timothy 4:15; Proverbs 24:32

[2] Luke 17:14; Matthew 3:15; John 2:5

[3] 2 Peter 1:4; Ephesians 4:23-24; Hebrews 12:10; Galatians 6:8

[4] Deuteronomy 10:12-13; Joshua 22:5; Psalm 81:13; Titus 2:11-12

[5] Amos 3:3; 2 Corinthians 6:14-16

[6] Matthew 12:30; Ephesians 2:22; Revelation 21:3

[7] John 14:2; Matthew 8:22; 16:24

[8] Matthew 4:19; John 15:4-5

[9] John 4:4; Matthew 9:10-13

coffee shops, malls, and sports arenas.[1] He walks into government buildings, parks, airports, and neighbor's homes.[2] His eyes search the earth for those whose hearts are committed to Him.[3] And He wants to help them.[4] He wants to help the blind see and the deaf hear.[5] He wants to soften the hearts of the traumatized and rescue the wicked from their waywardness.[6] And to do this, He walks His laborers into the fields ripe for harvest.[7]

Someone might say, "If God would just tell me what to do, I would do it." Good! There's great news! Yehovah has told you what to do![8]

HalleluYah! Rejoice![9] Learn the Truth so that your joy may be complete![10]

"Obey My voice, and I will be your God, and you will be My people. Walk in all the ways which I command you, that it may be well with you."[11]

Walking with God is not about hearing the names of certain physical directions in the ear of your body. No! Yehovah is a Spirit![12] He is leading you to a spiritual destination.[13] And as you join Him in walking toward the spiritual destination, He will lead you to and through all the physical ones.[14] The physical destinations are temporal and can change moment by moment, but the spiritual destination is permanent and only grows in blessing and glory![15]

When you walk on the earth, do you demand to know the details of every place your foot falls, exactly how many steps your journey will demand, or the details of

---

[1] Acts 1:8; Micah 3:8; Zechariah 4:6; Luke 10:19; Romans 15:19
[2] Matthew 9:10; Mark 2:15-17; Luke 5:29-32
[3] 2 Chronicles 16:9; Job 34:21; Psalm 34:15; Proverbs 5:21; 15:3; Jeremiah 32:19
[4] Matthew 18:14; 2 Peter 3:9; 1 Timothy 2:4; Romans 2:4
[5] Luke 7:22; Job 29:15; Psalm 146:8; Isaiah 28:18-19; 32:3-4; 35:5-6; 42:6-7
[6] 2 Peter 3:9; Matthew 18:14; 1 Timothy 2:4; Romans 2:4
[7] John 4:35; Matthew 9:37-38; Luke 10:3
[8] Romans 1:19; Matthew 28:20
[9] Philippians 4:4; Psalm 34:1-2; 145:1-2; 146:2; Philippians 3:1; 1 Peter 4:13
[10] John 15:11; 16:24; 17:13; 1 Peter 1:8; Jude 1:24
[11] Jeremiah 7:23
[12] John 4:24; 2 Corinthians 3:17; Galatians 4:6
[13] Matthew 6:33; Luke 12:31; Psalm 34:9; 37:19; 84:11; Isaiah 33:16; John 6:27
[14] Proverbs 16:9; 19:21; 20:24; Jeremiah 10:23
[15] Matthew 6:20; Isaiah 33:6; Luke 12:33; 1 Timothy 6:17; Hebrews 10:34; 1 Peter 1:4; 5:4; Revelation 2:9

every blade of grass you will pass?[1] Of course not! You plan your destination and proceed toward its general direction, minding each step with as much care as necessary but not with any more care than required to accomplish its purpose.[2] Though every step in the journey is of equal importance, a limited amount of attention is required for each one.

Or take driving as an example. When setting out toward a destination, you give minimal attention to the basic skills necessary for driving, but you consciously increase your focus when starting, stopping, or turning this way or that.

So it is in the Spirit. The Lord tells us the Way.[3] We seek the destination of the Kingdom of Heaven and His Righteousness.[4] Everything we do should be for His Glory.[5] If we set His Glory as our destination, then we are on the straight and narrow way.[6] We are driving on the pavement.[7] We do not need to exit the vehicle and clear obstacles from our path, nor is our path excessively bumpy or precarious.[8] Instead, our path has been cleared and leveled for us.[9]

May Yehovah bless you now to hear the most excellent way![10] May the eyes of your spirit be opened,[11] and may you see the wonderful blessing and power of the Truth![12] Amen!

HalleluYah!

Our Gracious Savior has already revealed to us that the power of life and death is in our tongue.[13] The tongue is the steering wheel with which we direct the path and conquest of our spirit through our soul, body, and Creation.[14]

---

[1] Proverbs 3:5-6; Psalm 37:3-9; 62:8; 115:9-11; 125:1; 146:3-5; Isaiah 12:2; 26:3-4; Jeremiah 17:7-8
[2] Proverbs 16:9; 20:24; Jeremiah 10:23
[3] Jeremiah 10:23; John 14:4,6
[4] Matthew 6:33; Luke 12:31; Psalm 34:9; 37:19; 84:11; Isaiah 33:16; John 6:27
[5] Isaiah 43:7,21; 48:11; John 15:8; Romans 9:23; Ephesians 1:12
[6] John 7:18; 8:49-50; 1 Corinthians 10:31; 1 Thessalonians 2:6; 1 Peter 4:11
[7] Matthew 7:14; 16:24-25; Proverbs 4:26-27; Isaiah 30:21; 35:8; 57:14
[8] Hebrews 12:13; Proverbs 4:26-27; Isaiah 40:3-4; 42:16; Jeremiah 31:8-9
[9] Proverbs 11:5; Isaiah 40:3
[10] 1 Corinthians 12:31; Philippians 3:8
[11] Ephesians 1:18; 2 Corinthians 4:6; Acts 16:14
[12] Ephesians 1:19-21; 3:7,20; 2 Thessalonians 1:11; 1 Thessalonians 1:5
[13] Proverbs 18:21; 10:20-21,31; 11:30; Matthew 12:35-37; James 3:6-9
[14] James 3:4; Psalm 12:2-4; 52:1-2; Proverbs 12:18; 15:2; Jeremiah 9:3-8

How foolish it is to be careless with the steering wheel![1]

Therefore, until your spiritual driving skills become professional through much practice, pay very close attention to how you steer![2] Do not be careless with your tongue![3] Every word spoken has power.[4]

The Truth is the Narrow Way.[5] Any lie spoken takes a person off the Narrow Way[6] in the same way that poor driving can take a vehicle off the road. How dangerous such driving could be! In the same way, a careless tongue can cause terrible spiritual, soulical, and physical damage.[7]

"Driving with God" requires sufficient attention toward "keeping the vehicle on the pavement of righteousness."[8]

Someone might say, "If I knew what was righteous, I would live righteously." Excellent! There is more great news! Yehovah has not only told us but personally demonstrated for us what righteousness is![9]

HalleluYah!

The whole written Word of God is full of instruction about righteousness![10] And God in the flesh, Yeshua HaMashiach, Jesus Christ, the King of Glory,[11] came to reveal both the Truth and the Way![12]

Understand then that the answer is not "what" or "how" but "Who"![13]

---

[1] James 3:6; Psalm 64:3; 140:3; Proverbs 15:1; 16:27; 26:20-21; Isaiah 30:27

[2] James 1:26; 3:2-6; Isaiah 44:20; Proverbs 10:19; 11:12; 17:28

[3] 1 Peter 3:10; 2:1,22; John 1:47; Revelation 14:5

[4] Proverbs 18:21; 10:20-21,31; 11:30; Matthew 12:35-37; James 3:6-9

[5] Matthew 7:12-14; John 4:23

[6] John 8:44; Colossians 3:9

[7] 1 Timothy 1:19; Philippians 3:18-19; 2 Timothy 3:1-6; 2 Peter 2:1-22; Jude 1:10-13

[8] Philippians 2:12; Hebrews 4:1; 12:28-29

[9] Hebrews 6:20; 1 John 3:7

[10] 2 Timothy 3:16; 2:25; Deuteronomy 4:36; Nehemiah 9:20; Matthew 13:52

[11] 1 Timothy 1:17; Jude 1:25

[12] John 1:14; 10:9; Romans 5:1-2

[13] John 14:6; Acts 4:12; Hebrews 10:19-22; 1 John 2:23; 2 John 1:9; Revelation 5:8-9

Do you want to walk with God? Then get to know Him![1] The better you know Yehovah, the closer you will walk with Him![2] "Ask and it will be given to you; seek and you will find; knock and the door will be opened to you"![3]

HalleluYah! HalleluYah! Praise be to our Gentle King,[4] Who is eager to gather us under His Wings![5] HalleluYah!

Now, to know Yeshua is to know the Word of Yehovah, and to know the Word of Yehovah is to know Yeshua.[6] He is alive and well[7] and very much in love with us![8]

Yehovah Himself holds no human directly accountable for the deceit of the kingdom of darkness.[9] He truly desires for all humanity to be saved.[10] He wishes deceit upon no person[11] and does not rejoice when the wicked share in the consequences of evil.[12] Nevertheless, because it would not be good for the goodness of Heaven to be diluted with evil,[13] causing Heaven to then become frustrated like the fallen earth,[14] *whatever* or *whoever* belongs to darkness will be expelled from Heaven and banished to the outer darkness on the Day of Judgment.[15] What will hurt the wicked the most is that they will finally have their eyes fully open to the Wonder, Glory, and Goodness of God,[16] only then to learn

---

1 John 17:3; 2 Corinthians 4:6; 1 John 5:20

2 James 4:8; Hebrews 10:22; 1 Peter 3:21; 2 Corinthians 7:1

3 Matthew 7:7; Luke 11:9; John 4:10; 16:23-24

4 Matthew 11:29; 2 Corinthians 10:1

5 Luke 13:34; Psalm 17:8; 36:7; 57:1; 91:4; Ruth 2:12; Deuteronomy 32:9-12

6 John 1:1-5; When Yehovah transfigured me and took me to Heaven, I learned that it is His Glory that transforms us (2 Corinthians 3:18). And as I first stood there looking at Yeshua in all His Brilliant Radiance, I heard the Holy Spirit say, "Everything said in the Scriptures about Yeshua is true!"(Luke 24:27) And I understood that He is even greater than I could ever imagine! He is the Vessel of the Father (John 12:45)! He is God in a body (John 1:14)! HalleluYah! HALLELUYAH! OUR GOD BECAME LIKE US TO SAVE US! HALLELUYAH! WHAT A HUMBLE AND MAGNIFICENT GOD WE HAVE THE PRIVILEGE OF CALLING "FATHER"! HALLELUYAH! GLORY BE TO GOD! HALLELUYAH! GLORY BE TO GOD! GLORY BE TO GOD!!!!!!!!

7 Revelation 1:18; 4:9; Hebrews 7:25; John 14:19; Romans 6:9

8 John 13:34; 16:27; Romans 1:7; 5:5,8; 8:39; 2 Corinthians 13:11,14

9 John 3:17; 12:47; Hebrews 10:10

10 1 Timothy 2:4; 2 Peter 3:9; Titus 2:11

11 James 1:13; Hebrews 6:18

12 Proverbs 24:17-18; 17:5; Job 31:29-30

13 Habakkuk 1:13; Psalm 5:4; 71:4

14 Romans 8:20; Revelation 12:7

15 Matthew 25:31-46: Acts 1:25

16 Revelation 1:7; Zechariah 12:10

that they can never dwell with Him due to their own acceptance of the dominion of evil in their souls.[1] And their pain will even be worse when they realize that the scars on Yeshua's Hands are far deeper than they ever imagined,[2] representing the eternal injury that the Good One took upon Himself by allowing His beloved humans the freedom to choose.[3] By doing so, He increased the purity of Heaven, the awareness of Truth, the clarity of Certainty, the depth of eternal Peace and Joy, the security of Trust, the Holy Power of Hope and the pursuit of Righteousness, the beauty of Humility, the blessing of Integrity and Purity, the commitment of Loyalty, the perception of Selfless Affections and Love, the breadth of Gratitude, the appreciation of Gentleness and Kindness, and the relief of eternal Contentment. [4] But for those who choose evil, who choose the foolishness of a lie, Yeshua forever knows the depths of their pain and regret.[5] The Good One is not unaware.[6] He bears the scars.[7] He willfully bears them forever so that no one else ever has to,[8] and the wicked will be cut to the heart of their own spirit when they become aware of this.[9]

Holy, Holy, Holy, is the Lord God Almighty, Who was, and is, and is to come.[10] Holy is His Name. Holy is His Name.[11]

Oh, the pain that the Holy One has suffered![12] How terrible a loss for Him![13] But Praise be to His Holy and Relentless Heart[14] that was willing to pay the price[15] for a greater purpose far beyond measure![16]

HalleluYah! Holy is His Name! Holy is His Name! HalleluYah!

---

[1] Luke 13:24; 16:25; Ephesians 4:18
[2] 1 Peter 2:24; Galatians 1:4; 1 Timothy 2:6; Titus 2:14
[3] Ezekiel 33:11; 2 Peter 3:9; 1 Timothy 2:4
[4] The revelations of these Holy Characteristics are discussed in detail in Chapters 18-34 of this testimony.
[5] Luke 16:24,26; Isaiah 65:13-14; 66:24; John 4:10; Revelation 20:15
[6] Proverbs 15:3; Psalm 139:12; Hebrews 4:13
[7] John 20:27; Revelation 7:14; 19:13
[8] 1 John 2:2; 3:5; 4:10,14; Romans 3:25-26; 1 Peter 2:24; 3:18; John 1:29; 4:42
[9] Acts 2:37; Zechariah 12:10
[10] Revelation 4:8; Isaiah 6:3; Exodus 15:11
[11] Luke 1:49; 1 Samuel 2:2; Psalm 99:3,9; 111:9; Isaiah 57:15
[12] Ezekiel 33:11; Matthew 8:17
[13] Isaiah 53:4; Galatians 3:13; 1 Peter 2:24
[14] Hebrews 12:2; Acts 5:31; Psalms 138:8
[15] Revelation 5:9; Matthew 20:28; 26:28; Acts 20:28; Romans 3:24-26
[16] See the following chapter in this testimony.

And now let us address this greater purpose for which Yehovah was willing to pay such a heavy price.

Amen.

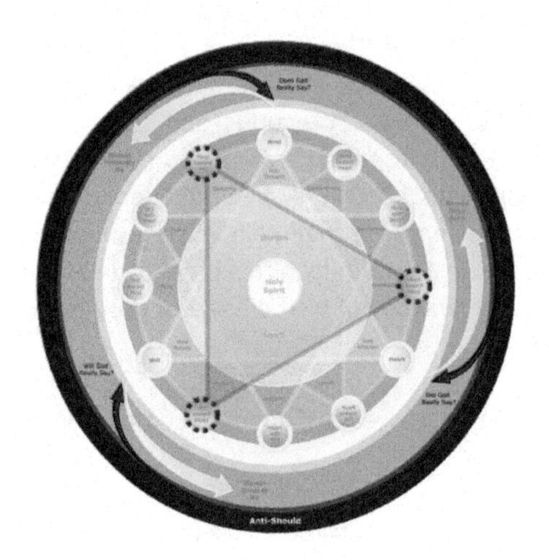

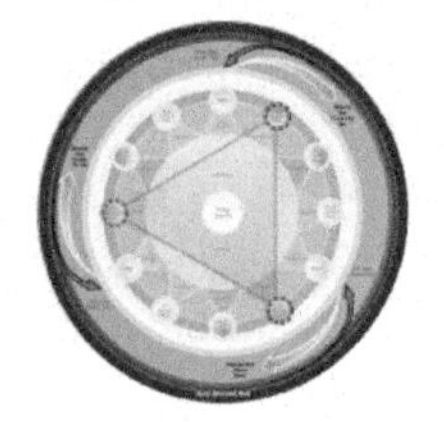

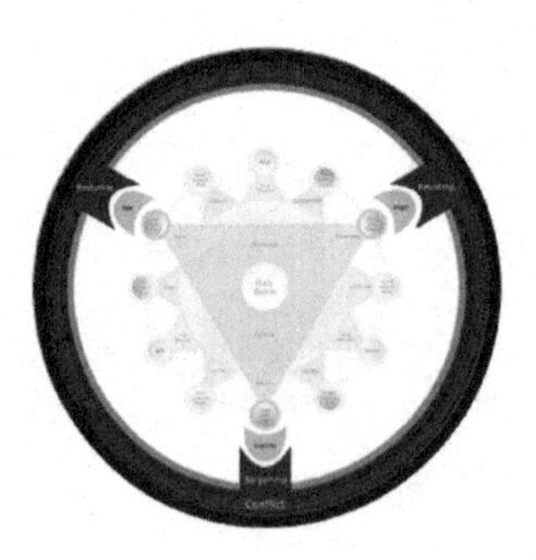

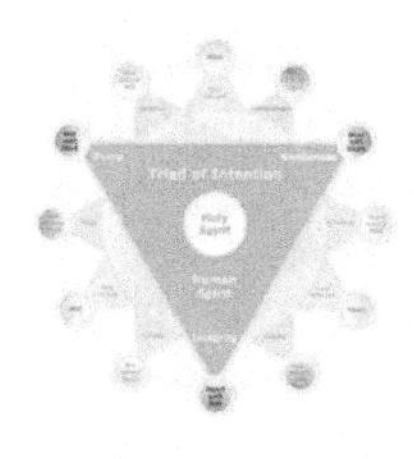

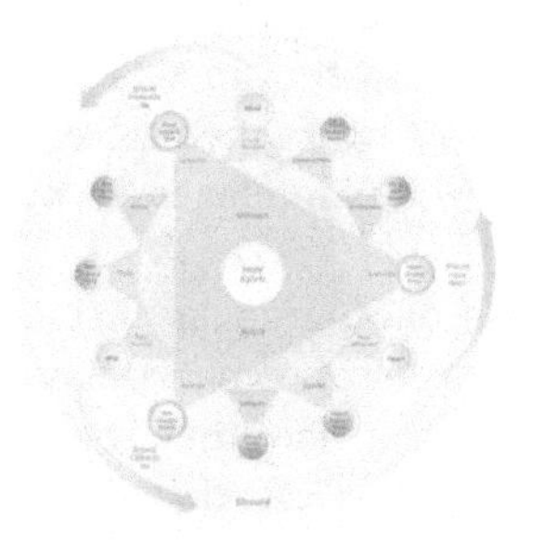

CHAPTER 6

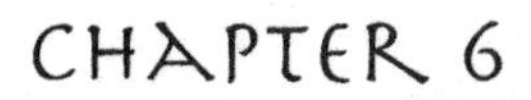

THE PURPOSE OF CREATION

In these last days, which are overflowing with deceit, exaggeration, dilution, and distraction,[1] it is necessary for the sake of Yehovah's children that the knowledge of the purpose of Creation increase through the Spirit of Wisdom and Revelation.[2]

May the understanding of Yehovah's great Wisdom be unveiled,[3] may His Goodness be glorified,[4] and may His Love become evident to all![5] Amen!

Long before Creation, Yehovah, the Eternal Spirit, Who was, is, and is to come, made many different spiritual beings.[6] And just as He has made many colors of all various types and shades, so also He made many beings with various types and degrees of awareness, intelligence, and personality.[7]

For eternity past, all beings dwelled in His Light and sought to become increasingly aware as He is aware.[8] They knew that He is the Source and Provider of all,[9] aware

---

[1] 2 Timothy 3:1-5; 2 Peter 3:3-4; 1 John 2:18; Hebrews 1:2
[2] Ephesians 1:17; Luke 12:12; 21:15; Matthew 16:17; 1 Corinthians 2:10
[3] 2 Corinthians 3:18; Proverbs 3:19; Isaiah 11:2; Psalm 104:24
[4] John 15:8; Luke 6:35; Psalm 92:12-15; Isaiah 60:21; Matthew 5:16
[5] John 17:23,26; 14:23; 15:9; Matthew 5:16
[6] Job 1:6; 2:1; 38:4-7; Psalm 82:1-8; 103:20; 104:4; 148:2; Revelation 5:11; 1 Kings 22:19; 2 Kings 6:16-18
[7] Romans 12:4-5; 1 Corinthians 12:4-6,18-20
[8] 1 Peter 1:12; Daniel 8:13; 12:5-6; Ephesians 3:10
[9] James 1:17; John 1:9; 1 John 1:5; Revelation 21:23; 22:5; Isaiah 60:19

of all things,[1] and infinite in depth and majesty.[2] But, understanding that He is infinite, they inevitably discovered that they were not.[3] Consequently, they began to compare themselves to each other, especially their unique features and various levels of intelligence and awareness.[4]

In one particular instance, when everyone was standing before Yehovah,[5] the matter of comparison was broached.[6] There was discovered a mutual agreement among many that a being known as Heylel[7] was, in their observation, chief[8] among them all.[9] At that very moment, he was greatly congratulated by many, and a number of them suggested that he was second only to Yehovah.[10] As they discussed his attributes, his ability to protect was brought to the fore.[11] Some spirits considered that Heylel could lead them like Yehovah, or even in place of Yehovah, and they asked Yehovah why He held all rule to Himself.[12]

Yehovah gently explained that His unseen Characteristics alone were worthy to rule all things because His Goodness, Faithfulness, Joy, Love, Hope, Purity, and Truth were best for everyone all the time.[13] But the inhabitants of Heaven were unsure about the meanings of any of these things because they did not know how to be aware of them.[14]

---

[1] 1 John 3:20; Psalm 44:20-21; 139:1-4; Jeremiah 23:24; John 2:24-25

[2] Psalm 147:5; 40:5; 139:17-18; Isaiah 40:28; Romans 11:33

[3] 1 Peter 1:12; 1 Corinthians 6:3; Hebrews 1:4

[4] Ezekiel 28:13; 31:8-9

[5] Psalm 82:1; Job 1:6; 2:1

[6] Job 1:8; 2:3

[7] Isaiah 14:12 – *Heylel* is a transliteration from the Hebrew, הֵילֵל, meaning *shining one* or *morning star,* which is translated in many English versions using the title *Lucifer,* a shortened form of the Latin word *Luciferum,* meaning *light bringing*. Rather, if we are going to call him the shortened form of anything in Latin, we should call him *Stella,* which means *star,* or *Clara*, which means *bright*! But be sure of this, Heylel has never *brought light* to any human being (Revelation 12:9; Matthew 12:26), though he certainly masquerades as an angel of light (2 Corinthians 11:14)! Of course, other more appropriate Latin terms to describe him would be *Adversarius*, which means *opponent* (1 Chronicles 21:1), or *Mendax,* which means *Liar* (John 8:44).

[8] Daniel 10:13; Ezekiel 31:8-9

[9] Ezekiel 28:14; Revelation 12:4

[10] Ezekiel 28:17; Ezekiel 31:8-9

[11] Ezekiel 28:14-15; 31:6

[12] Isaiah 14:13-14; 37:23; Genesis 3:5; 2 Thessalonians 2:4

[13] See Chapter 33 of this testimony; Job 15:15-16

[14] 2 Corinthians 3:14; Matthew 11:25; John 3:19-21; 8:19; 12:45-46

To their sheer astonishment, Yehovah brought them all together and formed Creation in their presence, revealing its complexity and teaching them about how it functioned.[1] The point of focus would be Earth, and He covered it with all sorts of growing plants[2] and living creatures.[3] He then formed Adam and Eve to be fruitful revelations of His Character[4] and to multiply and fill Creation,[5] ruling over it[6] with the Light of His Goodness.[7] He explained that this rule was to be an image[8] and reflection[9] of how His Goodness faithfully held all the inhabitants of Heaven to His Righteousness,[10] because His Goodness is powerful and able to accomplish Righteousness[11] just as gravity would now faithfully hold Adam's feet to the soil.[12]

Yehovah continued to carefully explain that His unseen Attributes had to be challenged to become visible.[13] So He made a contract sealed with the seven seals of His Character. ***[14]*** And He swore that He would hold back His gravity of Righteousness from Creation, so that when present there the inhabitants of Heaven, as well as humanity, would be allowed to choose to abide by Yehovah's Righteousness or to abandon it.[15] He explained that He would not force compliance when His Love, Loyalty, Integrity, Humility, Faithfulness, Trust, Peace, Certainty, Truth, Contentment, Gentleness, and Gratitude were resisted.[16] He further explained that He would use the resistance of His Character to reveal His Characteristics by contrast; that Love would become more evident when hate became apparent, that Loyalty would be valued when surrounded by betrayal, that Integrity would shine in the midst of hypocrisy, that Humility would become precious in a sea of pride, that Faithfulness would be seen as strength against apathy and waywardness, that Trust would be cherished when worry was rampant, that Peace would become appreciated against fear, that Certainty would

---

[1] Job 38:6-7; 26:7; Psalm 33:6; 1 Samuel 2:8-10
[2] Genesis 1:2; 9:1; Isaiah 40:12-14
[3] Genesis 1:20,24; Psalm 104:24-25; Acts 17:25
[4] Genesis 1:26; Ecclesiastes 7:29; 2 Corinthians 3:18; Ephesians 4:24
[5] Genesis 1:28; 22:17-18; 26:3-4
[6] Psalm 115:16; Genesis 1:28; Jeremiah 27:5
[7] Genesis 1:31; Psalm 24:14; Ephesians 2:10; Romans 1:18-23
[8] Genesis 1:27; Isaiah 43:7; Ephesians 2:10; 4:24; Colossians 1:15; 3:10
[9] Isaiah 55:11; 1 Corinthians 13:12
[10] Romans 3:4; 7:7; Job 40:8, 11-12; Exodus 34:6-7; Psalm 51:4
[11] Romans 2:4; 8:3; John 12:32; 2 Peter 1:3; Exodus 33:19; Nehemiah 9:35; Psalm 145:7
[12] Psalm 96:10; Ecclesiastes 12:11; Isaiah 11:3-5
[13] Rom 3:5-6; 8:17; John 1:14; 2:11; Hebrews 1:3; Hebrews 2:9
[14] See Chapter 34 for more on the Seven Manifested Facets of Yehovah's Character; Revelation 4:5
[15] Romans 3:25; Revelation 6:10-11
[16] Job 1:12; 2:6; Psalm 89:7; 1 Kings 22:20; 2 Chronicles 18:19

become priceless in the clouds of doubt, that Truth would be revealed as steadfast when compared to lies, that Contentment would become welcome instead of envy, that Gentleness would be favored over abusive violence, and that Gratitude would never again be neglected after the world was saturated with bitterness.[1] However, He warned everyone that the reason His Goodness held everyone's deeds to His Righteousness in Heaven was only to protect all beings from the destructive effects of any abandonment of His Righteousness.[2] And He warned them all many times of the severity and eternal consequences of such abandonment.[3]

Since humanity was born in ignorance and would be vulnerable to the consequences of choices made by themselves, rulings in the Second Jurisdiction,[4] or roaming spirits,[5] Yehovah's Justice demanded that humans would retain a choice to end the authority of all such spirits over them.[6] Humans could choose to submit Creation to the same righteous gravity enjoyed by the inhabitants of Heaven.[7] They could do this when any single human being lived a life exhibiting the seven perfect unseen Characteristics of Yehovah represented by the seven seals.[8] Such a human being would have the legal right to open the Contract of Creation and enforce the terms of the contract, returning all choices and deeds to the protective standards of the Righteousness of Yehovah.[9] This opening would free Yehovah's Characteristics to correct and separate all misdeeds from Creation and thereby promote any man or woman living according to the unseen Characteristics of Yehovah to the highest level of being, that is, eternal life and oneness with Him.[10]

The contract also stipulated that initial shares of dominion would be distributed based on each spirit's awareness, ability, and investment.[11] While authority could

---

[1] Revelation 15:3-4; Psalm 51:4; 1 Peter 4:12-14; Romans 1:20-21; 7:7,13; Isaiah 45:7,9; 61:8-11 (These facets of character will be addressed at length throughout this testimony).

[2] Isaiah 45:8; Romans 8:28

[3] Job 40:11-13; Romans 2:5

[4] See Chapter 13 of this testimony for more on the Second Jurisdiction.

[5] 1 Corinthians 3:1-2; 13:11; 14:20; Galatians 4:1

[6] Psalm 73:12-17; 82:1-8; Daniel 7:25-27

[7] Revelation 1:6; 5:10; 20:6; 22:5; Exodus 19:6; 1 Peter 2:5-9

[8] Revelation 5:1; 6:1; Isaiah 29:11; Jeremiah 33:20,25; Genesis 8:22; Psalm 89:37; See Chapter 34 of this testimony for more on the Seven Characteristics of Yehovah.

[9] Daniel 7:10-11,25-27; 2 Thessalonians 2:8; Revelation 20:7-15

[10] Revelation 5:2-5,9-10; 14:4

[11] Matthew 25:14; Romans 12:6; 1 Corinthians 3:5; 12:7-11; 1 Peter 4:9-11

not be lost,[1] *it could be surrendered* through mutual agreement[2] or bested by greater dominion.[3] Because human spirits would grow while in Creation,[4] they could achieve greater authority according to their choices to better display Yehovah's unseen Characteristics.[5]

After the inhabitants of Heaven unanimously agreed to the terms of the contract,[6] Yehovah distributed portions of authority and dominion over Creation to everyone[7] so that they could make ruling choices with real ramifications.[8] Beginning with the least,[9] each spirit received some level of influence based on their awareness, abilities, and investment.[10] Both because of his abilities[11] and central position in the original discussion,[12] Heylel was the final heavenly recipient and given the greatest heavenly share.[13] However, because of their compulsory investment of participation in Creation, Adam and Eve shared the largest portion,[14] receiving greater authority and dominion over Creation than the combined shares of everyone else.

And for the moment, everything was still good.[15]

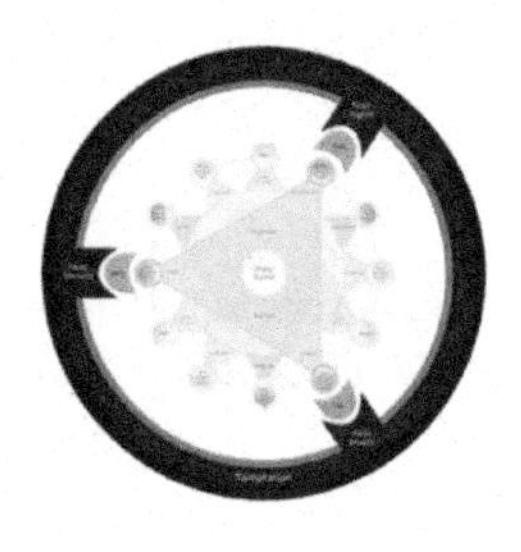

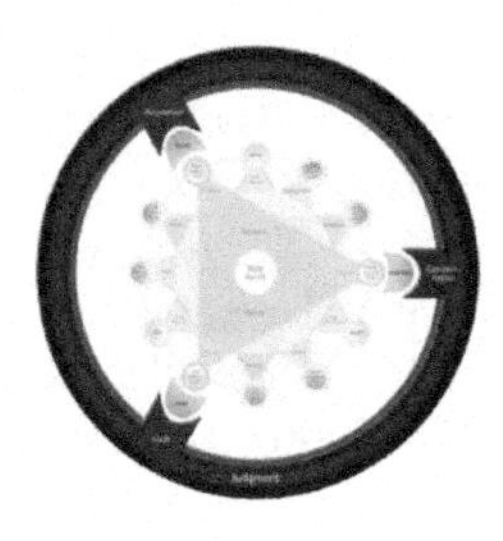

---

[1] Luke 4:6; Romans 11:29

[2] Genesis 3:13b,17a; Luke 4:6-7

[3] Genesis 3:15b; Revelation 12:7-8

[4] Luke 1:80; 2:40,52; Judges 13:24-25; 1 Samuel 3:19-20

[5] Luke 2:40,52; Judges 13:24-25; 1 Samuel 2:26; 3:19-20

[6] 1 Kings 22:19-23 describes a similar meeting and agreement.

[7] Matthew 25:15; Luke 12:48

[8] Joshua 24:15; Psalm 82:1-8

[9] Hebrews 8:11; Jeremiah 6:13; 42:1; 42:8; 44:12

[10] Deuteronomy 32:8-9 – The Septuagint, which was translated from Hebrew manuscripts much older than the Masoretic text (and could therefore be called the "oldest Bible"), reads "κατὰ ἀριθμὸν ἀγγέλων θεοῦ" or "according to the number of the angels of God."

[11] Ezekiel 28:12-14; 31:2-9

[12] Isaiah 14:13-14; Ezekiel 31:10

[13] Revelation 12:4a,9a-b; Daniel 8:9-12

[14] Genesis 1:27-28; Romans 12:3; Numbers 18:20; Joshua 19:9; Luke 19:12-27

[15] Genesis 1:4,10,12,18,21,25,31

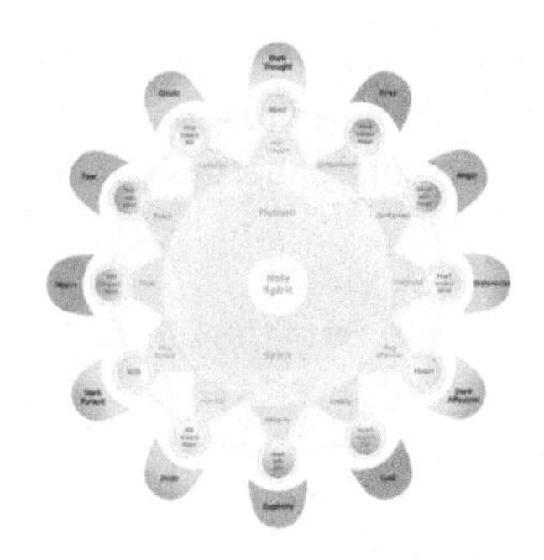

CHAPTER 7

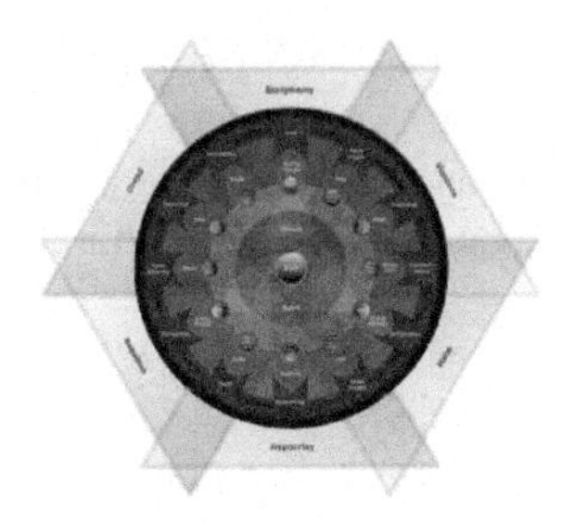

THE FALL OF CREATION

On a particular day, Heylel was observing Adam and Eve and considering their abilities concerning dominion.[1] Recognizing their lack of intimate experience with Yehovah,[2] he saw an opportunity to seize their dominion[3] by deceiving them into *willfully* separating[4] from Yehovah's Righteousness.[5]

Of course, since no lie had ever been told in Heaven or in Creation, our first mother had no reason to distrust Heylel's motives.[6] So understand that her sin was *not* that she was deceived into trusting another voice but that she *chose to reject Yehovah's Light* in favor of Heylel's suggestion.[7] By deliberately turning away from oneness with Yehovah, she willfully turned her eyes from Light toward darkness.[8] This caused her whole being to be filled with darkness.[9] And though her husband knew this was the consequence, he chose to do the same anyway.[10]

---

[1] Job 1:7; 1 Peter 5:8
[2] Proverbs 19:2; Jeremiah 8:7
[3] Hebrews 2:5-8; Genesis 1:26,28
[4] Genesis 3:6,11,13; Hosea 6:7
[5] Hosea 4:6; Jeremiah 5:21; 2 Corinthians 4:3-6
[6] John 8:44; Genesis 3:3-7; 1 Peter 5:8; Revelation 9:11; 12:9; Acts 13:10
[7] Genesis 3:6-7; 2 Corinthians 11:3
[8] Matthew 6:22-23; Luke 11:34-36
[9] Matthew 6:23; 2 Corinthians 11:3; Genesis 3:6
[10] 1 Timothy 2:14; Genesis 3:12

When Adam and Eve chose to listen to Heylel's voice instead of Yehovah's, their guardianship transferred[1] from the Light of Righteousness[2] to the dominion of Heylel.[3] Though the authority of Heylel still consisted in power based on the Characteristics of Yehovah,[4] and since Heylel was also given the option to choose,[5] he was able to use good power and authority dishonorably to serve himself rather than goodness.[6] This evil of selfish ambition[7] was conceived in Heylel's pride[8] and then spread through his influence into Creation.[9]

Understand what happened to humanity here.[10] Yehovah had breathed a spirit of life and light into bodies made from the earth.[11] When the union of spirit and bodies produced souls, those souls were also full of light.[12] But when humans chose to allow the darkness of rebellion into their souls,[13] they forfeited the Kingdom of Light for one of darkness.[14] They opened the gate wide[15] and let the enemy in,[16] thereby granting the enemy dominion and authority over their kingdom,[17] over their soul, body, and even spirit.[18] When this happened, their spirits became dark and were separated from the Light of Life.[19] The Light of Yehovah could still shine *on* them.[20] It could fall *upon* them,[21] but they no longer had light *within* themselves[22] because they belonged to darkness.[23]

---

[1] Romans 6:16,20; John 8:34; Matthew 6:24a-b

[2] John 1:3-4,9; 8:12; 9:5; 12:46; Isaiah 42:6-7; Malachi 4:2; Matthew 4:16; Luke 1:78-79; 2:32; Acts 26:23; Ephesians 5:124; 1 John 1:5; Revelation 22:16

[3] Luke 4:6; Genesis 1:26; 3:1-24

[4] Proverbs 16:12; Isaiah 54:16

[5] Job 1:6-12; Psalm 82:1-8

[6] Matthew 21:33-41; James 4:17; Luke 12:47; John 19:11

[7] James 3:14; Philippians 2:3; Galatians 5:20; 2 Corinthians 12:20

[8] Ezekiel 28:2; Revelation 12:9

[9] Ezekiel 28:15; John 8:44

[10] Daniel 9:23; Isaiah 41:20

[11] Genesis 2:7; Job 27:3; 33:4; John 20:22: Acts 17:25

[12] John 1:3-4,9; 8:12; 9:5; 12:46; Isaiah 42:6-7; Malachi 4:2; Matthew 4:16; Luke 1:78-79; 2:32; Acts 26:23; Ephesians 5:124; 1 John 1:5; Revelation 22:16

[13] Genesis 3:4-6; Deuteronomy 31:27; Psalm 105:28

[14] Romans 1:20,25; Jeremiah 2:11; Matthew 16:26

[15] Matthew 7:13; Nahum 2:6; 3:13; Jeremiah 51:30

[16] Genesis 3:13; Revelation 12:9; 20:2-3

[17] Luke 4:6; Ephesians 2:2; John 12:31; 14:30; 16:11; 1 John 5:19

[18] 1 Thessalonians 5:23; Hebrews 4:12

[19] John 1:4; 8:12; Romans 1:21; Ephesians 4:18

[20] John 1:5,10; 3:19; 12:36,46; Matthew 4:16

[21] Numbers 11:25; 1 Samuel 19:20-24

[22] 1 Samuel 19:15,20-24; Ephesians 2:2; 1 Corinthians 6:19

[23] Luke 4:6; Revelation 5:9; 14:4

Observing this, all of the inhabitants of Heaven were carefully considering Heylel's decisions and intentions.[1] Because authority over humanity had been transferred to Heylel,[2] many spirits concluded that the possibility was forever gone of any human being living according to the Light of the Seven Characteristics of Yehovah.[3] And as more and more children of Adam were born, Heylel invited every willing inhabitant of Heaven to yield their authority to him with the goal of ensuring that the Contract of Creation would remain sealed forever[4] (thereby gaining himself the title, Satan).[5]

By the time of Noah, the reign of evil had gained so much access through the cooperation of human souls[6] that the spirits in highest authority, the elohim,[7] were able by invitation[8] to manifest corporeally[9] in Creation and then lay with daughters of Adam.[10] This blatant intervention threatened to replace those created in godliness with hybrid creatures born in the image of darkness[11] so that

---

[1] 1 Peter 1:12; Daniel 8:13; 12:5-6; Ephesians 3:10

[2] Luke 4:6; Revelation 12:9; Matthew 24:24

[3] Revelation 5:3-4; Galatians 5:21-22; See Chapter 34 of this testimony.

[4] Revelation 12:4; Psalm 82:1-8

[5] *Satan* is a transliteration of the Hebrew, שָׂטָן, which means *opponent* or *adversary.*

[6] Genesis 6:5; Jeremiah 4:14

[7] Job 1:6; 2:1; 38:7; Daniel 3:25; Psalm 29:1; 89:7

[8] Leviticus 19:31; 20:6; 1 Samuel 28:11; Romans 1:18,32; Hosea 7:3; Psalm 50:18; Mark 14:10-11

[9] Elohim, or "angels," can clearly take on corporeal form: Genesis 18:8 – "While they ate..."; 32:24-30 – "...wrestled with him..."; Hebrews 13:2 – "...shown hospitality to angels without knowing it."

[10] Genesis 6:2 – Notice that the "sons of God" are contrasted with the "daughters of אָדָם." אָדָם is the Hebrew word for *Adam.* Some readers are concerned acceptance of the clear reading that fallen elohim took on corporeal form and slept with the daughters of Adam would imply a loss of uniqueness for the virgin birth of the Messiah (Genesis 3:15; Isaiah 7:14). Yet, intercourse with *corporeal* elohim would obviously *not* leave women as virgins! Others are concerned that Yeshua said that angels do not marry (Mark 12:25). However, He said *angels in Heaven* do not marry. Contrast that with the fallen elohim (Psalm 82:1-8), who not only fail to do what is right but are sternly rebuked (Zechariah 3:2) and punished for *sinning* (2 Peter 2:4; Jude 1:6).

[11] Genesis 6:4 – *Nephilim* is a plural of נְפִיל, pronounced "nef-eel," traditionally translated into the English word *giant.* This word is from the root נָפַל, pronounced "nah-fal," which means *to fall* or *to cast down.* The verse continues to explain that these beings *who [cause] to fall* became *mighty men.* However, the word chosen here for *mighty men* is not *Adam* as in the preceding verse but גִּבּוֹר, pronounced "ghib-bohr," meaning a *giant, strong man, mighty man,* or *chief.* That is to say, these *fallen* did not become *sons of Adam* or mere *men* (אנשים, the plural form of man) but *chiefs* (Though in today's Hebrew, אנשים now means

humans made in Yehovah's Image would become extinct,[1] thereby completely ending any possibility of the seals ever being opened.[2] So Yehovah found a man who listened to His Voice,[3] a pure descendant of Seth,[4] and helped him build a vessel to preserve humanity and the animal protospecies[5] of the earth from a catastrophic flood purposed to remove the hybrids and evil vessels of darkness[6] from Creation.[7]

Immediately after those days, Ham, having had the Devil plant the desire in his heart[8] to seek an increase in his share of inheritance from Noah,[9] saw his father and stepmother[10] passed out after too much wine,[11] and he took the opportunity to inseminate his stepmother.[12] After having done this, he emerged from the tent and boasted[13] to his brothers so everyone would know that a resulting male offspring would be not only their youngest brother but also Ham's son. Because this fourth brother would inherit a fourth of Noah's possessions,[14] Ham would control his own portion as well as that of his son, thereby granting Ham control over half of the world. This is why Noah cursed Canaan not to receive an

---

people and גְּבָרִים now refers to a group of *men,* which has led to some confusion in regard to the original intended meaning).

[1] Genesis 6:5; Deuteronomy 29:19; Ecclesiastes 9:3

[2] Revelation 5:4; Daniel 12:8-9

[3] Genesis 6:22; 7:5; Hebrews 11:7

[4] Genesis 6:9; 5:6-32

[5] Genesis 6:19-20 – The Hebrew מִין indicates a *portion* of a *sort* or *kind* of animal, which is more similar to the "family" rank rather than that of "species" in contemporary taxonomy.

[6] Matthew 6:23; 23:16-28; Isaiah 44:18

[7] Genesis 6:7; Jeremiah 4:22-27; 12:3-4; Hosea 4:3

[8] Acts 5:3; 1 Kings 22:21-22; 1 Chronicles 21:1; Matthew 13:9; Luke 22:3; John 13:27

[9] Genesis 9:22-25

[10] Genesis 6:18; 7:7,13; 8:18; "And Noah went forth, and his sons, and his wife, and *his* [not *their*] sons' wives with him." Notice that, unlike Eve and Sarah, Noah's wife is never mentioned by name despite her significance in the sinful event (Genesis 9:20-27).

[11] Genesis 9:21a

[12] Genesis 9:21b-22 – The use of the Hebrew idiom גָּלָה, *to uncover nakedness,* is clearly explained in Leviticus 18:8, meaning *to have physical relations with the wife of one's father.*

[13] Genesis 9:22 – While English translations typically translate the latter section of this verse with the English verb *told,* they elsewhere translate the same Hebrew word with stronger English verbs such as *declare, certify,* or *expound.* Just as in Genesis 41:24 ("...and I told this to the magicians; but they could not *declare* [or *explain*] it to me..."), the Hebrew word נָגַד implies a greater boldness than mere recounting ("...and I *told* [from the Hebrew אָמַר, *to say*] this to the magicians; but they could not declare it to me..."). Likewise, both the chosen Hebrew word and the context in Genesis 9:22 clearly indicate more than mere recounting but rather imply *to conspicuously proclaim* or *boldly certify.*

[14] Joshua 14:5; Numbers 26:55

inheritance but to serve Canaan's brothers and uncles instead.[1] However, since Ham's stepmother was not of pure descent,[2] Canaan was the offspring of a hybridized line. And this is how Satan used Ham's transgression to reintroduce the Nephilim lineage of immoral giants back into Creation after the flood.[3]

Meanwhile, Yehovah used Noah's spoken curse to impede the influence of evil through Canaan while the lines of Japheth and Shem continued in some semblance of righteousness.[4]

Shortly after this time, Yehovah invited the loyal elohim of Heaven together to help them in their growth of awareness concerning Yehovah's unseen Characteristics.[5] Having heard that Yehovah was doing this, Satan attended the gathering intending to challenge the veracity of Yehovah's unseen Characteristics by attributing them to selfish motives. But as soon as Satan arrived, Yehovah saved him the trouble of looking for an opportunity to speak by immediately drawing all attention to Satan.[6] Yehovah drew out Satan's motive by offering Job as an example of unseen worth.[7] Not being able to resist, Satan challenged the worth by attributing Job's loyalty to Job's own quest for self-preservation.[8] But Yehovah showed that even Job, a mere man, would not forsake righteousness for self-preservation.[9] This teaching moment humiliated Satan and caused many elohim to become increasingly curious of the unseen power of Yehovah's Characteristics. And the loyal elohim began to look into these matters more carefully.[10]

As Yehovah's people matured, He used their experiences as reference points to help His children understand spiritual dynamics.[11] He led Abram out of Ur to preserve and reveal righteousness and to provide a family line through which revelations could grow and mature.[12] But when Heylel subsequently prompted[13] the wayward souls of Egypt to enslave, torment, and destroy the children of the

---

[1] Genesis 9:25-27
[2] Genesis 6:9,12,18; 2 Peter 2:5
[3] Judges 1:9-10; Joshua 14:15; 21:11; Numbers 13:29,33
[4] Genesis 9:26-27
[5] Job 1:6; 2:1
[6] Job 1:7; 2:2
[7] Job 1:8; 2:3
[8] Job 1:9-11; 2:4-5; Ezekiel 27:3; 28:6,15; 31:10; Isaiah 14:12-14
[9] Job 42:7; James 5:11
[10] 1 Peter 1:12b; Daniel 8:13; 12:5-6; Ephesians 3:10
[11] 1 Corinthians 10:11; Romans 15:4
[12] Genesis 12:1-5; 15:7; Nehemiah 9:7
[13] John 13:2; 1 Chronicles 21:1

righteous,[1] Yehovah intervened in response to prayer,[2] revealing Himself as the Righteous Savior of those who walk with Yehovah.[3]

From the Exodus forward, Israel[4] continued to function as a representation of the spiritual dynamics of the human soul.[5] With great Wisdom[6] and careful Patience,[7] Yehovah led Israel through tedious events both to help them toward Him and also to display for us everything we need to know about navigating the spiritual realm.[8]

After this process was complete, Yehovah waited until the fullness of time,[9] and then, to the absolute astonishment of Heaven, He took on flesh Himself[10] and entered into Creation as a man.[11]

Every rebellious spirit was caught off guard.[12] Though they knew the Contract of Creation, their ambition had blinded them to Yehovah's Humility.[13] They never considered that, as a Spirit like them, He too could enter into Creation just like the fallen angels and live one life as a man[14] in a world under Satan's authority.[15] Since the Scriptures were cryptic,[16] none of them had foreseen His personal avoidance of Satan's dominion through a virgin birth.[17] For the first time, the rebellion fell into a panic.[18] Though they had known a messianic figure was coming, they had

---

[1] Exodus 1:8-10; Genesis 15:13; Numbers 20:15; Deuteronomy 26:6

[2] Exodus 2:23-25; Numbers 20:16; Deuteronomy 26:7

[3] Exodus 3:7-10; 6:6-8; 12:51; Genesis 15:14; 50:24

[4] *Israel* is a transliteration from the Hebrew word יִשְׂרָאֵל, meaning *to strive/overcome/rule with the Almighty.*

[5] Romans 9:6; 1 Corinthians 10:11; Romans 15:4

[6] James 3:17; Proverbs 2:6; Isaiah 11:2-3; Luke 21:15

[7] 2 Peter 3:9,15; Romans 2:4; 1 Timothy 1:16; 1 Peter 3:20

[8] 1 Peter 1:12a; Ephesians 3:10

[9] Galatians 4:4-7; Ephesians 1:10; Hebrews 9:10

[10] Malachi 3:1; Luke 1:76-79; John 1:1,3,14

[11] John 1:9-11; Hebrews 1:3

[12] Matthew 2:1-3; 8:29

[13] Proverbs 16:18; 18:12; 29:23; Ester 6:6; Isaiah 2:11-12; James 3:14,16

[14] This is why Yeshua is called the *only* Son (John 3:16; Romans 5:10; 8:2), even though Yehovah has many children born of Him (Matthew 5:9; John 1:12; Romans 8:14; Galatians 3:26; 1 John 3:2).

[15] Philippians 2:6-8; Matthew 4:3,6; Hebrews 2:9

[16] Proverbs 25:2; Deuteronomy 29:29; Job 11:7-8; 42:3; Romans 11:33-34

[17] Luke 1:34; Isaiah 7:14 – Note that עַלְמָה, the word for *virgin*, comes from the root עָלַם, meaning *veiled/concealed/kept out of sight.*

[18] Matthew 8:29; Mark 1:24; 5:7; Luke 4:34; 8:28

assumed it was allegorical.[1] They had never entertained the possibility that Yehovah Himself could walk the earth and personally display His Seven Characteristics.[2]

When Yeshua reached the age of priesthood,[3] He fasted for forty days to fully separate His human soul from the principles of the earth,[4] and He entered into the desert to be tested by Satan.[5] While Satan relished the opportunity to look for a weakness in the human soul of Yehovah, he found no darkness in Him.[6] By remaining victorious through vigorous testing in weakness,[7] Yehovah had finished successfully displaying all of His Characteristics,[8] proving Himself worthy to open the seven seals.[9] Yet again, to the utter surprise of the kingdom of darkness, Yeshua did not immediately choose to rise to His Throne and claim His reward but instead remained in Creation[10] and began to teach other human beings how to walk successfully in true righteousness.[11] Because He had proven His steadfast allegiance to the Higher Law of the Righteousness of the Spirit,[12] Yeshua was subsequently able to rule in perfect authority over all of the governing principalities of Creation.[13] His superior jurisdiction of the Kingdom of Heaven[14] overruled the Law of sin and death,[15] and so He was able to cast out demons and sicknesses with a word and raise the dead back to life.[16]

Painfully aware of their defeat, the dark kingdom desperately searched for any possible delay of their impending judgment.[17] Having noticed that Yeshua had not

---

[1] Exodus 1:22; Matthew 2:16 – Obviously, Yehovah Himself could not be hindered from being born (Genesis 3:15; Luke 1:37).

[2] Colossians 2:15; John 12:45

[3] Numbers 4:3,30; 1 Chronicles 23:3

[4] Matthew 6:16-18; Ezra 8:21; Ester 4:16; Isaiah 58:5-14

[5] Matthew 4:1; Mark 1:13; Luke 4:1

[6] Matthew 4:11; Luke 4:13; 1 Peter 1:19

[7] Hebrews 2:18; 4:15; Matthew 4:1-11; Luke 4:1-13

[8] These Holy Characteristics are addressed in depth throughout Chapters 18-34 of this testimony.

[9] Revelation 5:2-3,5,9; 4:11

[10] Matthew 8:29; Mark 1:24; 5:7; Luke 4:34; 8:28

[11] John 15:5; Romans 7:4; 2 Corinthians 9:10; Philippians 1:11

[12] Romans 8:2a; 10:4; Matthew 5:20

[13] John 16:33d; 17:2

[14] Colossians 2:15; Matthew 28:18; Revelation 2:27; 3:21; See Chapters 13-16 of this testimony for more on jurisdictions.

[15] Romans 8:2b; 6:18,22; John 8:32; Romans 5:21; 7:24-25

[16] Matthew 8:16-17; 14:14; Mark 1:25-27

[17] Matthew 8:31; Luke 8:30-33

yet risen into Heaven to open the Contract of Creation, they concluded that killing Him before that time would prevent its fulfillment.[1] So they rallied every foul spirit to pollute the minds of the very people who had waited so long for salvation and instead prompted the people to condemn their own King to death on a cross.[2]

Upon Yeshua's death, the kingdom of darkness celebrated, believing they had avoided the eternal consequences of their choices.[3] Confidence was high, and pride swelled in their ranks.[4] Having just had the opportunity to abuse Yehovah, each of the dark spirits measured themselves as somehow becoming greater.[5] But when He rose from death on the third day,[6] they realized that they had assumed He would remain in death like all men before Him.[7] They had not understood that death was a punishment for sinners but retained no authority over the One Who had remained Righteous.[8]

After Yeshua rose from death and encouraged His disciples for forty days,[9] He ascended into Heaven and sat back down on His Throne in His full Glory.[10] At that point, Heylel and his accomplices attempted to violate the Covenant of Creation and re-enter Heaven by force.[11] Yet, a certain powerful elohim, Michael,[12] had boldly and resolutely chosen loyalty to Yehovah.[13] Along with the myriad of angels following his example, he vigorously rejected the re-entry of the disloyal spirits and agreed with Yehovah that no revealed darkness should ever be permitted to dwell in Heaven.[14] From that time until this very day,[15] Heaven has consisted only of those inhabitants who actively choose Righteousness as revealed through Yeshua.[16] In this way, and through the mutual agreement of all of its inhabitants, Heaven has been purified according to Yeshua's Purity.[17]

---

[1] Mark 12:7; Acts 7:52
[2] Luke 24:20-21; Acts 2:23; 13:27-28
[3] Isaiah 22:12-14; 1 Corinthians 2:8
[4] Matthew 27:29-31; Isaiah 53:3
[5] Mark 15:31; Luke 23:35-36
[6] Matthew 20:17-19; 1 Corinthians 15:4
[7] John 1:4; 3:13; Romans 6:9
[8] Matthew 11:25; 1 Corinthians 1:26-28; 2:8
[9] Acts 1:3,9
[10] Revelation 3:21; Matthew 19:28
[11] Revelation 12:7a; Ephesians 6:12
[12] Daniel 10:13b; Jude 1:9
[13] Daniel 10:21b; Revelation 17:14
[14] Revelation 12:7b-9; Daniel 12:1
[15] Luke 17:20-21; Matthew 12:28; John 3:3; 18:36; Colossians 1:13
[16] John 3:16-21; Revelation 21:27
[17] Revelation 12:10; Hebrews 9:23

What's more is that, since the body of Yeshua was undeservedly put through the process of death[1] and died,[2] He now has the right to use both the process of death and the death itself as a propitiation for all who receive Him as their High Priest and Passover Lamb.[3] The former symbolic sacrifice of animals could never atone for the failures of humanity because it was not the animals that failed to live up to their own purpose but humans who failed to live up to theirs.[4] But after Yehovah in the Flesh[5] proved the value and purpose of humanity by revealing Yehovah's unseen Characteristics and thereby purifying Heaven, now any child of Adam who agrees to abide in that Revelation of Yehovah can also share in the purpose of that Revelation as well as in the death provided by that Revelation as payment for any failure to live up to that Revelation![6]

Realize and acknowledge what has been revealed![7] Satan and his followers argued that self-benefit is most important,[8] and they staked their very existence on that assumption.[9] But, by humbling Himself as a Man and limiting Himself down to the very essence of His Character,[10] Yehovah proved selfless Goodness is supremely victorious![11]

HALLELUUUUUUUUUUUYAAAAAAAAAAAAAAAH!!!!!!!

BEHOLD the immeasurable HUMILITY of Yehovah![12] For the value that Satan attempted to gain through lies, sin, deceit, and evil, Yehovah FREELY gave to ALL who would trust in Him through His own death ON A CROSS![13]

---

[1] 1 Peter 3:18; 2:22-23; 4:1; Isaiah 53:4-6

[2] Romans 5:6-8; 8:3; Hebrews 9:26

[3] Isaiah 53:5; 1 John 2:1-2

[4] Hebrews 10:4; See Chapter 14 of this testimony for more on why animal atonement was insufficient and why Christ's atonement was necessary.

[5] John 1:14; Malachi 3:1; Luke 1:76-79; 2 Peter 1:13-14

[6] Romans 3:21-26; 6:1-14; Galatians 2:16; James 2:23-24

[7] Luke 8:18; 19:26; Deuteronomy 32:46-47; Proverbs 2:2-5; Mark 4:23-24; Acts 17:11; Hebrews 2:1; James 1:22-25; Matthew 13:12; John 15:2

[8] Job 1:9-11; 2:4-5; Ezekiel 27:3; 28:6,15; 31:10; Isaiah 14:12-14

[9] Genesis 3:14-15; Revelation 12:7-9

[10] Philippians 2:8; Proverbs 15:33; Acts 8:33; Hebrews 5:5-7

[11] Like 14:11; Revelation 5:5; Colossians 2:15

[12] Matthew 11:29; Philippians 2:7-8

[13] Romans 8:32; Psalm 84:11; 1 Corinthians 2:12; 3:21-23; Hebrews 2:7-8

UNDERSTAND WHAT YESHUA DID FOR US![1] HE GAVE US NEW SPIRITS FULL OF HIS LIGHT![2] WE HAVE EVERYTHING WE NEED[3] TO CONQUER OUR SOULS, BODIES, AND CREATION WITH THE LIGHT[4] FOR HIS GLORY![5]

HALLELUYAH!

Praise, honor, and glory be to the Victorious One, WHO OVERCAME THE WORLD,[6] DARKNESS,[7] SICKNESS,[8] AND DEATH![9]

WHAT AN AMAZING GOD WE HAVE! FOR WHEN HEYLEL ATTEMPTED TO RISE HIGHER IN RULE THAN YEHOVAH BY EXALTING HIMSELF,[10] YEHOVAH, BY PUTTING ON FLESH[11] AND HUMBLING HIMSELF ON A CROSS,[12] NOT ONLY ESTABLISHED HIS SUPERIORITY[13] BUT EVEN TOOK HEYLEL'S TITLE OF "MORNING STAR"[14] FOR HIMSELF![15]

HAHA! HALLELUYAH! GLORY TO GOD!

GLORY TO THE KING OF KINGS,[16] SUPREME CONQUEROR OF CONQUERORS![17]

HALLELUYAH!

KING OF ALL SPIRITS![18]

HALLELUYAH!

---

[1] Daniel 9:23; Isaiah 41:20
[2] Ezekiel 11:19; 36:26; John 12:31,36; 17:26; Ephesians 5:8
[3] 2 Peter 1:3; Philippians 4:19; Ephesians 1:3
[4] Romans 8:37; Revelation 5:10
[5] John 15:8; Luke 6:35; Psalm 92:12-15; Isaiah 60:21; Matthew 5:16
[6] John 12:31; 16:11,33d; Psalm 68:18; Romans 8:37; 1 John 4:4; 5:4
[7] Matthew 4:16; Matthew 5:14; 6:22; John 1:4-5,9; 9:5
[8] Matthew 4:23; 8:16-17; 11:5; 15:30-31; Mark 1:34; 3:10; Luke 4:40; 9:11; 10:9
[9] Revelation 1:18; 4:9; Hebrews 7:25; John 14:19; Romans 6:9
[10] 2 Thessalonians 2:4; Revelation 13:4
[11] John 1:14; Malachi 3:1; Luke 1:76-79
[12] Philippians 2:8; Proverbs 15:33; Acts 8:33; Hebrews 5:5-7
[13] Colossians 1:18; Psalm 89:27; Isaiah 52:13; Matthew 28:18; John 3:35
[14] Isaiah 14:12
[15] Revelation 22:16
[16] Revelation 17:14; 19:17; 1 Timothy 6:15
[17] Romans 8:37; Isaiah 25:8; 1 Corinthians 15:57; 1 John 4:4; 5:4-5; Jude 1:24
[18] Revelation 5:6; Psalm 95:3; 96:4; 135:5; Exodus 8:11; Ephesians 1:21

NEVER AGAIN WILL ANY BEING DARE WORSHIP ANYONE BUT YESHUA YEHOVAH![1]

HALLELUYAH!

OUR WORSHIP IS SAFE IN HIM![2]

BLESS YESHUA!

HOLY, HOLY, HOLY is our GOD,[3] Who PUT ON FLESH[4] and disarmed the powers and authorities, making a public SPECTACLE of them, and TRIUMPHING over them by the CROSS![5]

HALLELUYAH! OUR LORD GOD ALMIGHTY REIGNS![6]

HALLELUYAH!!! OUR LORD GOD ALMIGHTY REIGNS!!![7]

HALLELUUUUYAAAAAAAAAAAAH!!! OUR LORD GOD ALMIGHTY REIGNS!!!!!!!!!![8]

HALLELUUUUUUYAAAAAAAAAAAAAAAAAAAAAAAAAH!!!!!!!!

[1] Revelation 1:8; 22:13; Isaiah 41:4; 44:6; 48:12

[2] Psalm 33:4; 36:5-6; Deuteronomy 34:2; John 14:6; Titus 1:2

[3] Revelation 4:8; Isaiah 6:3; Exodus 15:11

[4] John 1:14; Luke 2:11; Philippians 2:6-8; 1 Timothy 3:16; 1 John 4:2-3; 2 John 1:7

[5] Colossians 2:15; Acts 2:23-36

[6] Revelation 19:6; 21:27; Hebrews 1:8

[7] Isaiah 52:7; Revelation 1:18; 4:9; 11:15

[8] Psalm 99:1; Hebrews 1:8

CHAPTER 8

THE PRESENT WAR

Having lost the war in Heaven, all of those spirits who chose to deviate from the Righteousness of Yehovah have now found themselves eternally separated from the Fountain of All Life.[1] Though they were made in righteousness and partook in it, their choice of *opposition* to Yehovah's Character caused them to become the *opposite* of whichever aspect of His Character they had abandoned.[2] For example, the spirits who opposed Trust became worry. Those who deserted Gratitude became bitterness. Since Heylel rejected Humility, he became a spirit of pride.[3] And this is why each dark spirit continues to this very day to embody some sort of contrast to at least one Characteristic of Yehovah.[4]

Unlike human beings, any spirit who has become an example of contrast has now also been fully separated from *all* other Characteristics of Yehovah.[5] Because they broke the Law of Righteousness,[6] they became lawbreakers, and so they no longer dwell within the sanctity of that Law.[7]

---

[1] Revelation 12:12-13: Luke 10:18
[2] Ezekiel 28:15; Romans 1:25a; Hosea 4:7b
[3] Ezekiel 28:17; 31:10
[4] Matthew 6:23-24b; Romans 6:16; Galatians 1:10; James 4:4; 1 John 2:15-16
[5] 1 John 1:5; Matthew 6:23a; 12:25
[6] Romans 3:27; 8:2a,10
[7] Jude 1:6; Matthew 7:22-23

It is this complete separation that leaves them desperate for the smallest drop of the Water of Life.[1] Just as wayward human beings enjoy being recipients of hope, love, favor, approval, and honor, so also the dark spirits long to receive these things; for all blessings consist of some allotment of the Characteristics of Yehovah.[2] The dark spirits no longer have any other source for any of these blessings aside from within Creation and what is available through their remaining authority over those beings who continue to display some acceptance of them.[3] That is to say, just as humans devour the flesh of animals to take life physically,[4] so also the dark spirits devour the spirits of humans to take life spiritually.[5]

Now, all human beings have been made in the image of the Characteristics of Yehovah.[6] This means that their innate spiritual behavior was according to His Righteousness.[7] If Adam and Eve had not been tempted, then they never would have sinned.[8] It is the same with any human being.[9] But since Adam and Eve were misled by a different voice,[10] they ignorantly transferred humanity to the authority of Heylel.[11] When they did this, they "cut the roots"[12] of humanity from the "Vine of Life."[13] As a result, though all children can still receive light from the outside,[14] they no longer have light on the inside.[15] They structurally retain the potential to do right,[16] but they each fall to the same temptation of listening to

---

1 Matthew 12:43; Luke 16:24; For example, a spirit that has become bitterness lacks not only gratitude but also contentment, joy, peace, etc. Otherwise, when together, dark spirits would compose a kingdom divided against itself (Matthew 12:25).
2 James 1:17; John 1:9; 1 John 1:5; Revelation 21:23; 22:5; Isaiah 60:19
3 Matthew 8:31; 12:43; Luke 11:24
4 Genesis 9:3; Acts 10:13
5 1 Peter 5:8; Galatians 5:15
6 Genesis 1:27; Isaiah 43:7; Ephesians 2:10; 4:24; Colossians 1:15; 2 Corinthians 4:4
7 Genesis 1:31a; Deuteronomy 32:4; Ecclesiastes 7:29
8 Genesis 3:14-15; John 8:44
9 Genesis 5:1; James 3:9c; 1 Timothy 4:4a
10 Genesis 3:13,17; 2 Corinthians 11:3
11 Luke 4:6; Genesis 3:9-24; 2 Corinthians 4:4; Matthew 4:8-9; John 12:40; Ephesians 2:2; 1 John 2:11; 5:19
12 John 15:4-5; Acts 4:12; 2 Corinthians 13:8
13 John 15:1; Isaiah 5:1-7; Jeremiah 2:21; 5:10; 6:9; Ezekiel 17:2-10
14 Judges 14:6; 1 Samuel 10:6; Luke 1:35
15 Ephesians 2:2; Romans 5:12; Isaiah 57:4
16 Isaiah 7:15-16; Job 15:14-16; John 3:6

another voice.[1] For this reason, every human being, having shown some allegiance to darkness,[2] is vulnerable to the activities and rule of that darkness.[3]

When a dark spirit approaches a human soul, it looks for access, for any crack in the righteousness of that soul[4] to draw life from that aspect of the soul that is joined to the human spirit.[5] It cannot gain access through a region of that soul's character that emulates the Character of Yehovah.[6] For example, if a person has embraced His Humility, a spirit of pride cannot enter into that aspect of the soul.[7] But if that same soul has embraced bitterness, then a bitter spirit can easily enter into influence[8] and take up residence of "decision"[9] there. By doing this, it joins with the human spirit, sharing its authority.[10] This allows the dark spirit to drink life through the human spirit as it receives good things from the Mercy of Yehovah.[11]

These truths are of spirit and are difficult to discern in the carnal mind.[12] May those who seek understanding find it,[13] and may those who long for His Peace[14] embrace His Patience and Love for us![15] May they humble themselves to be teachable,[16] and may they receive encouragement through His Gospel and Faithful Promises![17] Amen!

---

[1] Romans 3:23; 1 John 1:10
[2] Galatians 4:8; 1 Peter 4:3
[3] 1 Corinthians 10:13; 1 Peter 5:8-9; Luke 22:46
[4] 1 Peter 5:8; James 4:7
[5] Hebrews 4:12; Job 7:11; Isaiah 26:9
[6] 2 Corinthians 6:14; 1 John 2:9
[7] John 1:5; Luke 10:19; 1 John 2:13; 4:4; 5:4-5
[8] Hebrews 12:15; Deuteronomy 29:18
[9] See Chapter 24 of this testimony for more on spiritual decision.
[10] Colossians 1:13; Matthew 12:29; Acts 26:18; Hebrews 2:14
[11] Matthew 5:45; Psalm 145:9; Acts 14:16-17; Luke 11:24; 16:24
[12] 1 Corinthians 2:14; Romans 8:7
[13] Matthew 7:7; Luke 11:9; John 4:10; 16:23-24
[14] Matthew 5:9; Psalm 122:6-8; 2 Corinthians 13:11
[15] Acts 2:21; 2 Timothy 1:9
[16] James 4:10; Matthew 23:12; Ephesians 4:2
[17] 2 Thessalonians 2:16-17; Hebrews 6:18

Understand then that dark spirits can only gain influence over a human soul through those areas in that soul where the person has already embraced darkness.[1] This is true both for the believer and the unbeliever.[2]

Though many in this generation have read about "demonic possession," such a term is an inadequate translation of the original language in which the Scriptures were written. The concept of "possession" is better translated as "vexed" or "to cause distress to."[3] No evil spirit ever has complete dominion over any child of Adam.[4] In the worst cases, spirits gain dominion in the main soulical gates through much acceptance and then take away control of the soul and body from that child's spirit.[5] However, the child's spirit can still cast out that darkness through the authority of Yeshua at any time.[6] Therefore, the problem is one of vexation, and any child of Adam can be vexed to the same proportion that the child embraces darkness.[7]

Suppose a believer, a person who has accepted the truth of the Gospel, accepts ideas and thoughts entertaining some deviation from righteousness.[8] In that case, dark spirits can gain access through that unrighteousness to further influence that soul.[9] For example, if a man entertains lust, which is disloyalty, then that is an invitation to any spirit of lust seeking to abide in that entertainment.[10] That man will find that lustful thoughts come to him more often and seem to increase in power.[11] The man is not "possessed" but vexed because he has *allowed* access to a dark spirit *by choice*.[12] Now that he has done so, he is constantly presented with choices for more disloyalty, choices that he would not be considering without the influence of the residing dark spirit.[13] Were that man to suddenly repent from

---

[1] 1 John 1:6-7; For example, Judas entertained a spirit of greed (John 12:6), which Satan later used to entice him (Matthew 26:14) and enter his soul (John 13:27).

[2] Romans 2:11-16; 8:6-13; Colossians 3:25; Ephesians 6:9; Galatians 2:6; Acts 10:34

[3] The Greek word δαιμονίζομαι comes from the root word δαίμων, or an *evil spirit*, which in turn is from the root δαιω, meaning *to kindle* or *to distribute*. Evil spirits *inspire*, and human beings receive that inspiration.

[4] James 4:7 (Any evil spirit can be cast out); Matthew 18:18

[5] Mark 5:1-9; Matthew 17:15

[6] James 4:7; Matthew 18:18

[7] Galatians 6:7-9; Job 4:8; Proverbs 11:18; Romans 2:6-10

[8] Matthew 16:23; Colossians 3:2; 1 Chronicles 22:19; Psalm 62:10; 119:36-37; Romans 8:4-6; 1 John 2:15-17; Philippians 3:19

[9] 2 Thessalonians 3:14-15; 1 Corinthians 5:5

[10] 2 Samuel 13:4-6; Romans 1:26a

[11] Matthew 9:4; Ezekiel 38:10; Haggai 2:13-14

[12] 2 Samuel 13:9; Galatians 6:8

[13] Matthew 4:3,6,9; Jeremiah 7:31

entertaining such thoughts, he would experience a temporary fight against increased suggestions for lust because the influence is not a product of his mind but the desperate work of a dark spirit.[1] However, if he continues to resist, and especially if he casts out the spirit by the Blood of Yeshua,[2] he will be rid of that influence.[3] If he is an unbeliever, his mind will return to the normal state of a child of Adam,[4] but if he is a recipient of the Blood of Yeshua, then his mind will fully recover into the whole state of the Mind of Yeshua.[5]

Therefore, all human beings represent the only workable source of sustenance for dark spirits,[6] who cannot become other than what they are even though they continue to seek comfort from that which they are not.[7] The enemy is not enraged on some level of superficial interest but is instead highly motivated by sheer frustration and desperation through an unquenchable thirst for continued existence and comfort of any sort.[8] They see humans only as a means to an end and care nothing for them.[9] They would not hesitate to destroy a thousand children for one drop of temporary comfort.[10] They have no love or compassion but remain only as insatiable appetites,[11] like sharks roaming the waters and willing to eat anything at all.[12]

And their chief means of access is the "lie."[13]

---

[1] Mark 9:20; Luke 4:35; 8:29; 9:42

[2] Colossians 1:20; Hebrews 9:14; 10:19; 1 John 1:7; Revelation 1:5

[3] James 4:7; Matthew 4:3-11; Ephesians 6:11-12; 1 Peter 5:8-9; Revelation 12:11

[4] 1 Samuel 19:24; 28:15

[5] Romans 12:2; 1 Corinthians 2:16; This battle is more thoroughly addressed in Chapters 19, 20, 22, and 26 of this testimony.

[6] Acts 3:15; Jude 1:6

[7] Matthew 5:45: Psalm 145:9; Job 25:2-6

[8] Deuteronomy 32:32; Luke 16:24; Isaiah 65:13-14

[9] John 10:10; Luke 8:12; John 8:44; Acts 13:10; Hebrews 2:14; Revelation 12:9

[10] Revelation 12:9; 1 Peter 5:8

[11] Philippians 3:19; Matthew 16:23; Romans 8:5-7

[12] John 10:10; Isaiah 56:11

[13] John 8:44; Romans 1:25; 1 John 1:6; 2:21; Revelation 14:5; 2 Thessalonians 2:9,11; Titus 2:11; Hebrews 6:18; Colossians 3:9; Numbers 23:19; Psalm 38:12

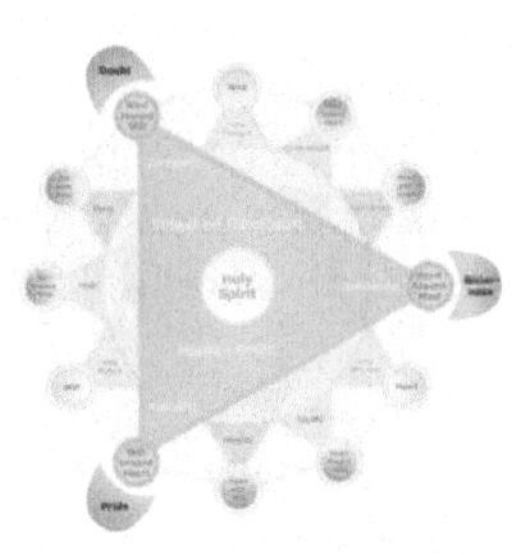

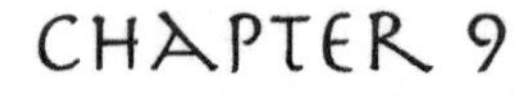

CHAPTER 9

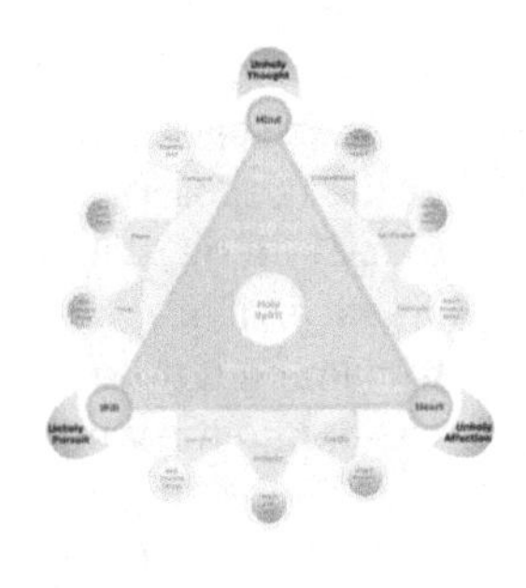

THE WEAPONS OF THE ENEMY

The only true voice is that of Yehovah.[1] Every other voice is only as valid as much as it speaks the words of Yehovah.[2]

The spirits who left the Righteousness of Yehovah are not of the Truth.[3] Though they retain authority until the Contract of Creation is fulfilled, their only means of continuing in existence is the utilization of lies.[4] They cannot speak in the Spirit of Truth, because they have left the Truth and are no longer in the Truth.[5] Everything they speak to the children of Adam is from a spirit of deceit.[6] They cannot speak for the purpose of the Truth but only for misdirection.[7] Because they are misdirection, the Truth does not abide in them.[8] They have nothing good to offer.[9] They are darkness.[10]

---

[1] John 14:6; Acts 4:12; Hebrews 10:19-22; 1 John 2:23; 2 John 1:9; Revelation 5:8-9

[2] John 10:2-9,27; 18:37

[3] Acts 13:10; 1 John 3:8-10

[4] John 8:44; Romans 1:25; 1 John 1:6; 2:21; Revelation 14:5; 2 Thessalonians 2:9,11; Titus 2:11; Hebrews 6:18; Colossians 3:9; Numbers 23:19; Psalm 38:12

[5] Jude 1:6; Ephesians 6:12; John 8:44

[6] 1 John 2:4; 2 Chronicles 18:21

[7] Matthew 7:18; Galatians 5:17; 1 John 3:9-10

[8] John 8:44; Romans 1:25; 1 John 1:6; 2:21; Revelation 14:5; 2 Thessalonians 2:9,11; Titus 2:11; Hebrews 6:18; Colossians 3:9; Numbers 23:19; Psalm 38:12

[9] James 1:17; John 1:9; 1 John 1:5; Revelation 21:23; 22:5; Isaiah 60:19

[10] 2 Peter 2:4; Colossians 1:13; Ephesians 5:8; 2 Corinthians 6:14

Do you want to walk in the Fortress of the Kingdom of Yehovah?[1] Then stop listening to the "voices of serpents"![2]

Lying is the primary weapon of the enemy.[3] All evil influences and temptations are based on lies because the spirits engaging in the evil activity became other than Truth when they left the Truth.[4] They can no longer function in the Truth.[5] When a person entertains the Truth, the activity of dark spirits is impeded.[6] And if the person continues in the Truth with perseverance, then the dark spirits will lose any infiltration of influence over that person.[7]

It is important for the child of Yehovah to understand that lies come in many forms, chief among which are thoughts, pursuits, and affections. [8] These *suggestions*[9] are all various forms of unholiness, or darkness, intended to function contrary to the Light.[10] The enemy uses unholiness to obtain access by tempting a soul to receive and embrace a spirit disguised as some seemingly beneficial function of the soul.[11]

Consider this example: When a certain waitress notices a famous actress entering her restaurant, she suddenly experiences a series of thoughts about the actress's lifestyle, wardrobe, wealth, and fame. Coupled with those thoughts are various affections and pursuits for those things. The waitress begins to wonder if she herself can achieve such goals by changing her own thinking and decisions.[12] Noticing that she has become distracted, the waitress makes an effort to focus on her own immediate tasks, yet she continues to be beset with thoughts measuring and comparing herself to the actress.[13] The actress eventually leaves, and the evening ends, but the waitress finds herself continuing to think of the actress

---

[1] Psalm 91:2; 18:2; 46:1; 71:3; 142:5; Deuteronomy 32:30-31; 33:27-29; Proverbs 18:10

[2] Genesis 3:1,13; Revelation 12:9; 16:14; 20:2,8; Zechariah 3:1-2

[3] John 8:44; Romans 1:25; 1 John 1:6; 2:21; Revelation 14:5; 2 Thessalonians 2:9,11; Titus 2:11; Hebrews 6:18; Colossians 3:9; Numbers 23:19; Psalm 38:12

[4] James 4:1-7; 2 Timothy 3:7; 1 Timothy 3:15; Romans 2:8

[5] 1 John 2:4; Titus 1:16

[6] Matthew 4:4,7,10; John 1:5; 1 John 2:21

[7] John 8:32,36; Psalm 25:5; 119:45; Proverbs 2:1-7; 4:18; Isaiah 2:3; 61:1; Romans 6:14-18,22; 8:2,15; 2 Corinthians 3:17-18; Galatians 5:13; 2 Timothy 2:25-26

[8] John 13:2; Luke 9:55; 22:3; Matthew 16:23; 1 Samuel 18:10-11; Revelation 17:17; Acts 5:3

[9] 1 Thessalonians 3:5; Hebrews 2:18; Matthew 4:1; 2 Corinthians 10:5

[10] Jeremiah 7:31; Matthew 12:30; Galatians 5:17; 1 Timothy 1:9-10; Romans 8:5-8

[11] Matthew 6:23; Proverbs 26:12; Isaiah 5:20-21; Jeremiah 8:9; Genesis 3:6a

[12] Proverbs 24:1,19; 3:31; 23:17; Psalm 37:1,7; 73:3

[13] James 4:2; 1 Timothy 6:9-10

often.[1] Hearing many ideas of comparison, she begins to consider the idea that her life as a waitress is the consequence of many failures.[2] Accusation and guilt creep in as she concludes that she should be accomplishing more in life.[3] However, through all of this, the waitress has failed to recognize that *none* of these thoughts, feelings, or pursuits have been of her own origin at all.[4] She has been vexed by a spirit of envy.[5] And after that spirit gained a foothold of momentum, spirits of worry[6] and greed[7] followed.

Father, bless us to receive from You eyes that see, ears that hear,[8] and a heart that is free from the deceitful hardness of sin.[9] Usher us into the freedom of Christ,[10] into the Truth of real Life.[11] Have mercy on us, and clear our souls of all the evil influence of darkness![12] Renew our minds,[13] and bless us to join You in Your Joy![14] Amen!

Look at the unawareness of the waitress. Do you see her torment?[15] She is a captive of the enemy, led around by her soul as if someone else has the reins.[16] She does not perceive that she can grasp those reins, that she can be free from being led astray into all sorts of torment.[17] Dark spirits have blinded her from their own presence,[18] and she has been conditioned by their influence to constrain herself.[19]

---

[1] 1 Samuel 16:14; 19:9-10
[2] 2 Corinthians 10:12; Luke 18:11-14
[3] Revelation 12:10; Job 1:9; 2:5; Zechariah 3:1-2; Luke 22:31
[4] John 8:38; 13:2: Acts 5:3
[5] Acts 7:9; James 3:14; Galatians 5:20; Romans 13:13; 1 Corinthians 3:3
[6] Philippians 4:6; Matthew 5:36; 6:27; Deuteronomy 28:65
[7] Greed is a form of lust (1 John 2:16); 1 Thessalonians 4:3-5,8; Colossians 3:5; 2 Peter 2:14
[8] Matthew 13:16; 16:17; Acts 26:18; 2 Corinthians 4:6; Ephesians 1:18
[9] Hebrews 3:15; Matthew 13:15; 19:8; Mark 6:52; 8:17; 10:5; Ephesians 4:18
[10] Galatians 5:1,13; 2:4; 4:26,31; John 8:32-36; Romans 6:18; 8:2
[11] John 14:6; Acts 4:12; Hebrews 10:19-22; 1 John 2:23; 2 John 1:9; Revelation 5:8-9
[12] John 13:8; Zechariah 13:1; Ephesians 5:26; Revelation 7:14
[13] Romans 12:2; Ephesians 4:22-24; Colossians 1:21-22; 3:10; Titus 3:5
[14] John 15:11; 16:24; 17:13; 1 Peter 1:8; Jude 1:24
[15] Acts 5:16; 2 Peter 2:8
[16] 2 Timothy 2:26; Job 1:12; 2:6; Luke 22:31-32
[17] 2 Corinthians 3:17; Galatians 5:1,13; 2:4; 4:26,31; John 8:32-36; Romans 6:18; 8:2
[18] 2 Corinthians 4:4; Matthew 4:8-9; John 12:40; Ephesians 2:2; 1 John 2:11; 5:19
[19] 2 Corinthians 3:14; 4:4; Matthew 13:15; 1 John 2:11

If only she could be free enough to listen to God,[1] to hear, understand,[2] and receive His Words![3]

This battle over listening is exactly what our King has been describing for us through the Parable of the Sower:

"Listen! A farmer went out to sow seed. As he was scattering the seed, some fell along the path, and the birds came and devoured them. Some fell on rocky areas where there was not much soil. It sprang up quickly because the soil was shallow. But when the sun rose, the plants were scorched, and they withered because they had no root. Other seed fell among thorns, which grew up and choked them. But other seed fell on good soil, where it produced a crop—some a hundred, some sixty, and some thirty times what was sown. Whoever has ears, let them hear."[4]

The Lord has explained this parable to us:

"Listen then to what the parable of the sower means: When anyone hears the word of the kingdom and does not understand it, the evil one comes and snatches away what was sown in their heart. This is what was sown along the path. The seed sown on rocky ground refers to someone who hears the word and immediately receives it with joy. But since there is no root within the person, they last only a short time. When trouble or persecution comes because of the word, they quickly fall away. The seed sown among the thorns refers to someone who hears the word, but the worries of this life and the deceitfulness of wealth choke the word, causing it to be unfruitful. But the seed sown on good soil refers to someone who hears the word, understands it, and produces a crop, yielding a hundred, sixty, or thirty times what was sown."[5]

Do you who have eyes see?[6] Do you who have ears hear?[7] The Lord is explaining the battle that can take place when you receive spiritual revelation from the Holy Spirit in your inner being! Look! When you hear the gentle whisper of His Voice[8] in your spirit, sometimes the enemy comes immediately to distract you with random thoughts, desires, or affections presented to your soul before you even

---

[1] 1 Kings 19:11-13; Job 4:12-16

[2] Matthew 13:15; Acts 3:19; 2 Timothy 2:25-26

[3] John 12:37-38; 15:24; Matthew 11:20; Luke 16:31

[4] Matthew 13:3-9; Mark 4:3-9

[5] Matthew 13:18-23; Mark 4:13-20

[6] Mark 8:18; Revelation 3:18

[7] Mark 8:21; Ezekiel 12:2

[8] 1 Kings 19:12; Job 4:12-16

have time to listen![1] Other times, you might hear a holy thought, experience a holy pursuit, or perceive a holy affection and rejoice only to treat its value as trivial and forget it due to your inexperience and lack of appreciation.[2] Or, in another moment, you might both hear and understand a holy revelation of thought, pursuit, or affection given to you, only to have its effect smothered by all the idolatry in your soul.[3] But those holy revelations that you hear, appreciate, and act upon, every one of them will produce immeasurable eternal fruit to His Glory![4]

HalleluYah!

Meanwhile, the enemy is also sowing seed.[5] These seeds come in the form of thoughts,[6] ideas,[7] feelings,[8] forces,[9] and motivations[10] made as suggestions from dark spirits to our souls.[11] Understand that, while our souls perceive all of these, we are not held responsible for any of them.[12] For example, if a man receives a lustful thought, image, feeling, or desire, he is *not* held responsible for it any more than Yeshua was held responsible for all of Satan's suggestions in the desert.[13] However, the man *is* held responsible for what he *does* with those thoughts, images, feelings, or desires.[14] If he rebukes them, he is living in the power of the Spirit.[15] But if he entertains them, he is giving soulical ground to darkness.[16] If he acts on such suggestions, then he is manifesting sin in Creation.[17] But if he subjects them to the Word of Yehovah,[18] then he is proving himself to be a disciple of Yeshua[19] and is bringing glory to our Father in Heaven.[20]

---

[1] Matthew 13:19; Mark 4:15; Luke 8:12
[2] Matthew 13:20-21; James 1:24; 2 Peter 3:5
[3] Matthew 13:22; 1 Timothy 6:9
[4] Matthew 13:23; Colossians 1:6
[5] Matthew 13:27; Romans 16:17
[6] Matthew 16:22-23; Romans 8:5-8
[7] Jeremiah 7:31; 1 Timothy 6:20
[8] Genesis 4:6; 1 Samuel 30:6
[9] Mark 9:22; Luke 8:29
[10] John 13:2; 1 Chronicles 21:1
[11] Mark 1:13; Matthew 4:1-11; Luke 4:1-13
[12] Hebrews 2:18; 4:15; Matthew 4:1-11; Luke 4:1-13
[13] Matthew 4:1; Luke 4:1; Mark 1:13
[14] Romans 8:13; Hebrews 10:36; James 4:8
[15] James 4:7; Colossians 3:5
[16] James 1:13-14; Matthew 9:4; Ezekiel 38:10
[17] James 1:15; Psalm 7:14; Isaiah 59:4
[18] Luke 4:4,8,12; Matthew 4:4,7,10
[19] John 15:7-10; 8:31; Luke 6:35
[20] John 15:8; Luke 6:35; Psalm 92:12-15; Isaiah 60:21; Matthew 5:16

Who then will rescue us from the evil one's use of such crafty deceit to turn our own soul against us?[1] Praise be to the Living God,[2] Who loves us so much that He died for us,[3] gave us His Spirit of Truth,[4] and formed in us the Mind of Christ![5] He has given us a new heart free from sin's brittleness[6] and blessed us with the gift of Grace for our will so that we can walk unhindered in the fullness of His New Life![7] Through all of these in unity with the Holy Spirit,[8] we are able to navigate through the deceit of darkness and stand in His Righteousness and Truth![9] We are not those who remain in the cloud of deceit,[10] but we are those who overcome,[11] rise above it,[12] live in Him,[13] and pass from GLORY to GLORY![14]

HALLELUYAH!

PRAISE OUR GOD, WHO MAKES EYES TO SEE AND EARS TO HEAR![15]

HALLELUYAH!

PRAISE OUR HOLY COUNSELOR,[16] WHO NEVER LEAVES US ALONE[17] BUT FILLS US WITH INSIGHT,[18] STRENGTH,[19] AND WISDOM![20]

HALLELUYAH!

---

[1] Romans 7:24; 1 Kings 8:38; Psalm 6:6; 38:8-10; 119:176
[2] Romans 7:25; 2 Timothy 4:18
[3] Romans 5:8; 8:34; 2 Corinthians 5:14; 1 Thessalonians 5:10
[4] John 14:17; 15:26; 16:13; 1 John 4:6
[5] 1 Corinthians 2:16; John 15:15; 16:13-15
[6] Mark 8:17; Ezekiel 36:26
[7] Romans 5:17; 6:23; Isaiah 61:10; Philippians 3:9
[8] Galatians 5:25: Romans 8:4-5
[9] 2 Peter 1:4; Ephesians 4:23-24; Hebrews 12:10; Galatians 6:8
[10] Galatians 4:31; Titus 3:3
[11] Luke 10:19; 1 John 5:4; Psalm 91:13; Ezekiel 2:6; Mark 16:18; Acts 28:5; Romans 16:20
[12] Ephesians 5:14; Revelation 3:2; Romans 13:11
[13] Romans 6:4; Colossians 2:6
[14] 2 Corinthians 3:18; Proverbs 4:18
[15] Proverbs 20:12; Exodus 4:11; Psalm 94:9
[16] Isaiah 9:6; Psalm 32:8; Proverbs 8:14
[17] John 14:18; Matthew 28:20
[18] Colossians 1:9; 1 Corinthians 1:5; Philippians 1:11; Ephesians 1:17-20
[19] Ephesians 3:16; Hebrews 11:34; 2 Timothy 4:17
[20] Ephesians 1:17; Luke 12:12; 21:15; Matthew 16:17; 1 Corinthians 2:10

PRAISE OUR GLORIOUS SAVIOR,[1] WHO REDEEMED US[2] AND CHOSE US[3] TO REVEAL HIS CHARACTERISTICS FOR ALL ETERNITY![4]

HALLELUYAH!

OUR GOD *RESCUES* US![5]

HALLELUYAH!!!

OUR GOD IS *GOOD*!!!!!!!!!![6]

HALLELUUUUUUYAAAAAAAAAAAAAAAAH!!!!!!!!!!!!!

AMEN!!!!

Of course, someone might hear all of this and say, "I have tried to escape the deceit of this world, but I am always failing." If this is true, in what state is the "Lord's House"?

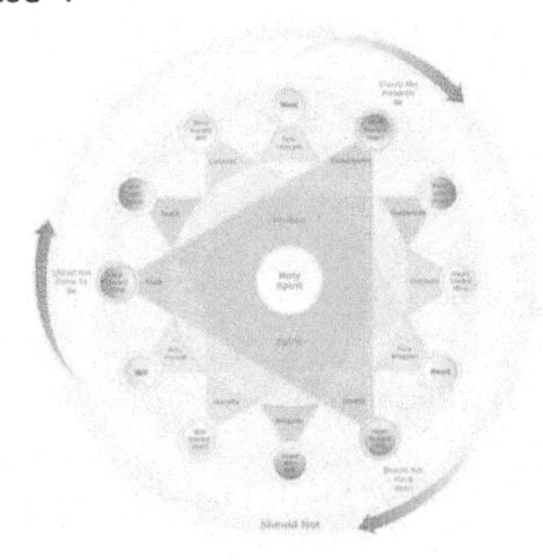

[1] 2 Timothy 1:10; 2 Peter 1:11; 1 John 4:14
[2] Galatians 3:13-14; 4:5; Titus 2:14; 1 Peter 1:18
[3] John 15:16,19; Matthew 13:20; Luke 18:7; Romans 8:33; Colossians 3:12
[4] Romans 8:29; Matthew 12:50; 25:40; Colossians 1:15-18; Revelation 1:5-6
[5] 2 Timothy 4:18; 2 Peter 2:9; 1 Thessalonians 1:10
[6] Matthew 19:17; 1 Samuel 2:2; Psalm 145:7-9; James 1:17

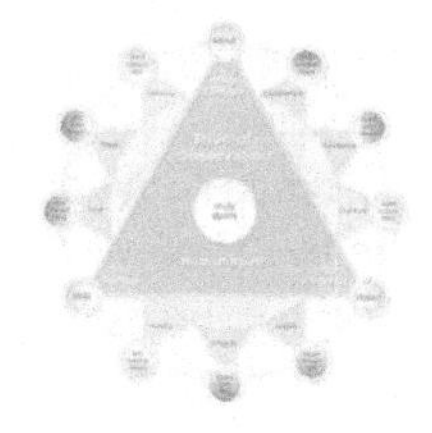

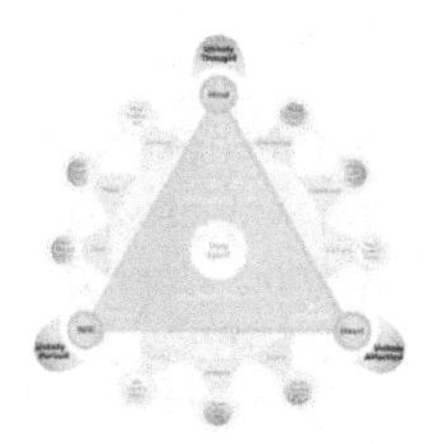

CHAPTER 10

THE LORD'S HOUSE

Does the Lord's House lay in ruins?[1]

As we have already said, Yeshua came speaking in parables.[2] He does not change like shifting shadows,[3] and since He is the Word of God,[4] we understand that He has always spoken to us in parables.[5]

"I will open my mouth with a parable; I will pour out ancient riddles."[6]

"Son of man, propose a riddle and present a parable to the house of Israel."[7]

Therefore, when we read the scriptures, we do not read with darkened minds,[8] expecting only the most superficial meanings, but we look deeper for the message of the Holy Spirit.[9]

"When the disciples reached the other shore, they had forgotten to bring bread. 'Be careful,' Yeshua said to them. 'Notice and beware of the yeast of the Pharisees

---

[1] Haggai 1:4; Daniel 9:17-18

[2] Matthew 13:10; Psalm 78:2; Ezekiel 20:49; Hosea 12:10; Mark 4:10,33-34

[3] James 1:17; John 1:9; 1 John 1:5; Revelation 21:23; 22:5; Isaiah 60:19

[4] John 1:1-18; Revelation 19:13

[5] Hebrews 13:8; Psalm 102:27-28; 103:17; Malachi 3:6; James 1:17

[6] Psalm 78:2

[7] Ezekiel 17:2

[8] Ephesians 4:18; 2 Corinthians 4:4; Romans 1:28

[9] 1 Corinthians 2:10; Daniel 2:22

and Sadducees.' They discussed among themselves that He had said this because they had not brought bread. Aware of their discussion, Yeshua asked, 'You of brief faith, why are you talking among yourselves about having no bread? Do you still not understand? Do you not remember the five loaves for the five thousand, and how many basketfuls you gathered? Or the seven loaves for the four thousand, and how many basketfuls you gathered? How do you not understand that I was not speaking to you about bread? But beware of the yeast of the Pharisees and Sadducees.' Then they understood that He was not telling them to beware of the yeast used in bread, but against the teaching of the Pharisees and Sadducees."[1]

Understanding that our God speaks to us with deeper meaning than that of a mere glance, let us read and consider the following:

"This is what Yehovah of Heavenly Warriors says: 'These people say, "The time has not yet come to rebuild the Yehovah's house."' Then the word of Yehovah came through the prophet Haggai: 'Is it a time for all of you to live in your paneled houses, while this house remains a ruin?' Now this is what Yehovah of Heavenly Warriors says: 'Carefully consider your ways. You have sown much but harvested little. You eat, but never have enough. You drink, but never have your fill. You put on clothes but are not warm. Laborers earn wages, only to put them in a purse with holes in it.' This is what Yehovah of Heavenly Warriors says: 'Carefully consider your ways. Go up into the mountains and bring down timber and build My house, so that I may be satisfied in it and be glorified,' says Yehovah. 'You turned to pursue abundance, but see, it turned out to be little. Whatever you brought home, I blew away. Why?' declares Yehovah of Heavenly Warriors. 'Because My house remains a ruin, while each of you is busy with your own house. Therefore, because of you the heavens have withheld their dew and the earth its crops. And I called for a drought on the land and the mountains, on the grain, the new wine, the olive oil, and everything else the ground produces, on people, livestock, and on all the labor of your hands.'"[2]

Do not read the above and simply speak about building church buildings and paying professional ministers. I tell you the truth: You can give all your money away and still be spiritually bankrupt.[3] See to it that Apostle Peter does not say to you as he said to Simon, "May your money perish with you, because you thought you could buy the gift of God with money!"[4]

---

[1] Matthew 16:5-12

[2] Haggai 1:2-11

[3] 1 Corinthians 13:3; Isaiah 57:12

[4] Acts 8:20

Are you spiritually weak? Do you find your walk dry and arduous? Are you bearing little spiritual fruit?[1] Then "build a house" for the Lord in your soul!" Go up into the mountains and bring down timber"[2] and build His house in your soul! Make an effort to prioritize God in your life![3] Sacrifice your schedule of personal comforts and entertainments[4] and make some changes to organize your entire soul around the Presence of Yehovah![5]

Until you do, you will "harvest little, never have enough, never have your fill, not be warm, and have a purse with holes in it."[6] But if you truly prioritize God in your life, if you orient your schedule around Him, if you seek Him before comforts and entertainments[7] and consider His Will in all your decisions,[8] then you will "harvest much, have enough, have your fill, be warm, and have a purse that overflows."[9]

Therefore, "maintain the Lord's House," and your soul will be richly blessed.[10]

But do not stop there! Conquer the land so that the Temple may be secure![11]

HalleluYah!

Do you not realize that all the Scriptures were written and preserved by Yehovah for your benefit?[12] How is it then that you read the story about the birth and experiences of Israel and fail to see how they describe your own life?[13] The Word of God is for YOU![14]

---

1 Luke 13:6-9; Mark 7:6
2 Haggai 1:8
3 Matthew 6:33; Luke 12:31; Psalm 34:9; 37:19; 84:11; Isaiah 33:16; John 6:27
4 Matthew 13:44-46; Proverbs 23:23; Revelation 3:18
5 Romans 12:1; Hebrews 12:1-29; 13:15; Luke 9:23
6 Haggai 1:6
7 Matthew 10:38-39; 16:24; Mark 10:21; Luke 9:23-24; 14:27
8 John 7:18; 8:49-50; 1 Corinthians 10:31; 1 Thessalonians 2:6; 1 Peter 4:11
9 See Romans 8:32; Psalm 84:11; 1 Corinthians 2:12; 3:21-23
10 Matthew 6:33; Luke 12:31; Psalm 34:9; 37:19; 84:11; Isaiah 33:16; John 6:27
11 1 Kings 5:3; Joshua 10:24
12 Romans 15:4; 2 Peter 1:20-21; 2 Timothy 3:16
13 1 Corinthians 10:11; Romans 15:4
14 2 Timothy 3:16; 2 Samuel 23:2; Matthew 22:43; 26:56; John 10:35; Romans 3:2; 15:4; Galatians 3:8; Hebrews 4:12; 2 Peter 1:19-21

Listen to the Word being sown in you![1] Hold on to it so the enemy cannot steal it![2] Remove the rocks and thorns so that the Word from Yehovah's Spirit can take root in you and bear much fruit![3]

You have been told that Abram was called out of Ur,[4] which represented civilization at that time. He was called away from the world, and Yehovah promised Abram that he would become the father of many, even changing his name to Abraham![5]

So it is for you![6] You are called out of the world![7] You are called to bring forth many in spirit![8] You have been renamed to live a new life![9]

Abraham was led out of the world's idolatry.[10]

And so it is with you![11] You are called to abandon placing value in aspects of this world![12] *Everyone worships!*[13] Everyone values all sorts of things that they consider important, beneficial, or necessary![14] But you are called to take your valuation away from all things[15] and place it firmly in the Heart of Yehovah,[16] where your values, hopes, trust, and worship can never be disappointed, lost, destroyed, or stolen![17]

HalleluYah!

---

[1] Luke 8:11; Mark 4:14; 1 Corinthians 3:6-7

[2] Luke 8:12; Matthew 13:19; Mark 4:15

[3] Luke 8:13-15; Psalm 106:12-14; Ephesians 3:17

[4] Genesis 15:7; Nehemiah 9:7

[5] Nehemiah 9:7; *Abram,* a transliteration from the Hebrew אברם, means *exalted father*, but *Abraham,* a transliteration of אברהם, means *father of a multitude*.

[6] 2 Corinthians 1:20; Galatians 3:22; Acts 13:32-39

[7] John 17:14,16; 1 John 4:5-6; 5:19-20

[8] Matthew 28:19; Acts 1:8; Colossians 1:23

[9] Revelation 2:17; 3:12; 19:12-13

[10] Deuteronomy 26:5; The Aramaeans worshiped idols (Genesis 25:20; 28:5; 31:34).

[11] 2 Corinthians 1:20; Galatians 3:22; Acts 13:32-39

[12] 1 John 2:15; Romans 12:2; Galatians 1:10; Ephesians 2:2; Colossians 3:1-2

[13] John 3:19: Isaiah 30:9-12; Luke 16:14; Think of worship as *worth-ship.*

[14] Revelation 13:8; Luke 12:29-30

[15] Matthew 10:37; John 12:25

[16] Revelation 14:7; Nehemiah 9:6

[17] Matthew 6:19-20; John 10:10; Luke 8:12; John 8:44; Acts 13:10; Hebrews 2:14; Revelation 12:9

You have heard that Yehovah promised Joshua the ground under wherever his feet walked.[1]

This promise is for you![2] Have you not read? Have you not heard? You are called to reign on the earth![3]

HalleluYah!

You have heard about how Joseph's brothers despised him for rejoicing that Yehovah had called him for a purpose and promised him great authority.[4]

Ha! HalleluYah! So it is for you![5] Yehovah has called you and honored you above the world![6] He has granted you unthinkable blessings and wonders![7] He has woven you a special garment,[8] and you will rule with Yeshua from His Throne![9] And just like Joseph, your siblings in this world may persecute you because of the Father's blessings on you,[10] but when trouble comes they will often end up at your doorstep to receive kindness from your hand in the Name of the Lord![11]

BLESS GOD!

You have heard about how Yehovah saw the bondage of His people and rescued them with a mighty Hand from evil slavery in Egypt.[12]

And this is what He has done for you![13] By the release of the Hebrews upon the death of the firstborn of Egypt,[14] Yehovah symbolized the later release His people from sin[15] upon the death of the Firstborn Son![16]

---

[1] Joshua 1:3; 14:9; Deuteronomy 11:24
[2] 2 Corinthians 1:20; Galatians 3:22; Acts 13:32-39
[3] Revelation 1:6; 5:10; 20:6; 22:5; Exodus 19:6; 1 Peter 2:5-9
[4] Genesis 37:10-11; Acts 7:9-10
[5] 2 Corinthians 1:20; Galatians 3:22; Acts 13:32-39
[6] Revelation 3:9; 1 Samuel 2:30
[7] 1 Corinthians 2:9; 1 Peter 1:12; Psalm 31:19; Hebrews 11:16
[8] Revelation 6:11; 3:4-5; 7:9,14
[9] Revelation 3:21; Matthew 19:28; Luke 22:30; 1 Corinthians 6:2-3; 2 Timothy 2:12
[10] Acts 7:9; James 3:14; Galatians 5:20; Romans 13:13; 1 Corinthians 3:3
[11] Genesis 45:5; Revelation 3:9
[12] Deuteronomy 26:8; Exodus 6:5-6; Ezekiel 20:7-9
[13] 2 Corinthians 1:20; Galatians 3:22; Acts 13:32-39
[14] Exodus 12:29-32; Job 34:20; 1 Thessalonians 5:2-3
[15] Romans 8:2; 6:18; John 8:36
[16] Hebrews 9:15; 12:24; Isaiah 53:10-12

HALLELUYAH! GLORY BE TO GOD! HALLELUYAH!

It is well known that Yehovah personally led His people out of Egypt[1] and through the parted waters away from the pursuing Egyptians.[2]

And look! He has done the same for you![3] He led you by His Spirit[4] to be baptized in water as a sign that you no longer belong to the evil forces that once enslaved you![5] The action of baptism functions as a testimony of commitment that protects you from many accusations and claims by the enemy![6] It symbolizes death to this world and the Second Jurisdiction![7] You are set apart![8]

PRAISE THE LORD! HOLY IS HIS NAME!

And now here we are. We stand at the entrance to the Promised Land, the Kingdom of Heaven![9]

Oh, look! The land is rich in milk and honey,[10] but there are "giants" in the land![11]

What will you do? Will you report to your soul that the giants are just too big to fight?[12] You would *love* to enter the Kingdom, but it's *impossible* for you to win against that worry, lust, depression, fear, addiction, greed, unforgiveness, illness, bitterness, heaviness, stupidity, laziness, science, persecution, mockery, or identity commitment?[13] Is this the report you will choose to give your soul? Or will you take the path of Joshua and Caleb and report that the land is good[14] and Yehovah has given your enemies into your hand?[15]

---

[1] Exodus 14:19; 23:20-21; Isaiah 63:9
[2] Nehemiah 9:11; Exodus 14:12-22,27-28
[3] 2 Corinthians 1:20; Galatians 3:22; Acts 13:32-39
[4] Romans 8:14; Galatians 5:18; Psalm 143:10
[5] 1 Peter 3:21; 1 Corinthians 10:1-2
[6] Revelation 12:11; 2 Corinthians 10:3-5
[7] Luke 12:50; Mark 10:38-39; See Chapter 13 of this testimony for more on the Second Jurisdiction, which is the Law of Sin and Death.
[8] Leviticus 20:24,26; 1 Chronicles 23:13; Revelation 1:6; 5:10
[9] Matthew 4:17; 2 Peter 1:18
[10] Exodus 3:8,17; 13:5; 33:3; Leviticus 20:24; Numbers 13:27
[11] Numbers 13:31; Deuteronomy 1:28
[12] Numbers 13:32-33; Joshua 14:8
[13] Numbers 13:28; Hebrews 3:19
[14] Numbers 14:6-7; Deuteronomy 1:25
[15] Numbers 13:30; Romans 8:31

Those who delay because of giants will find themselves wandering in the desert[1] eating the sweet basic manna of the Gospel for forty years.[2] But those who choose to press on in faith and courage[3] will see Yehovah part the Jordon,[4] lay waste to His enemies,[5] conquer the land,[6] and establish the Glory of the Lord in His Holy Temple![7]

HALLELUYAH! GLORY BE TO GOD! HALLELUYAH!

BRAVE AND MIGHTY WARRIORS OF YEHOVAH![8]

PREPARE FOR BATTLE![9]

HALLELUYAH! OUR GOD, WHO FREED US THROUGH HIS BLOOD FROM SLAVERY,[10] HAS RISEN FROM THE DEAD![11] HE GOES BEFORE US![12] HE CANNOT DIE AGAIN![13] HE IS INVINCIBLE![14] HALLELUYAH!

Listen, mighty warriors! Understand that when the Israelites had been promised the holy land by the King of Creation, they still had to go and take it by removing the foreign enemy and establishing their own presence.[15] Our ancestors were told that Yehovah would not clear out all the ungodly inhabitants at once but only as Israel proceeded to conquer.[16] Otherwise, the crops would have died, and the wild animals would have become too numerous.[17] For example, lions and wolves could have overpopulated and eaten the cattle. Then the land would no longer have

---

[1] Numbers 14:26-35; Hebrews 3:9
[2] Deuteronomy 8:16; Hebrews 3:17
[3] Philippians 3:14; 2 Timothy 4:7-8
[4] Joshua 3:1-17; 2 Kings 2:8
[5] Joshua 12:1-24; 21:44-45
[6] Joshua 11:23; 14:15
[7] 1 Kings 8:1-11; Ezekiel 43:4-5
[8] 2 Timothy 2:3; Romans 8:37
[9] Ephesians 6:10-11; James 4:7
[10] Revelation 1:5; Acts 20:28; 1 Peter 1:19
[11] Revelation 1:18; 4:9; Hebrews 7:25; John 14:19; Romans 6:9
[12] John 14:2-3; 16:33; Hebrews 2:14-15
[13] Romans 6:9; Acts 2:24-28; Psalm 16:9-11; Hebrews 7:16,25; Revelation 1:18
[14] Colossians 2:9-10; John 10:28-29
[15] Joshua 1:1-9; 24:11-13
[16] Exodus 23:30; Deuteronomy 7:22a
[17] Exodus 23:29; Deuteronomy 7:22b

been flowing with milk.[1] Skunks and bears could have multiplied and eaten all the beehives. Then the land would have been depleted of honey.[2]

In the same way, though the Conqueror of All Principalities[3] has already given each of us a full legal right to our own soul and body,[4] having disarmed all authority and power of darkness against us,[5] we still must conquer the residual lies in "our soul."[6] If Yehovah were simply to eradicate every lie from our soul,[7] it would destroy too many connections in our understandings,[8] emotions, and pursuits, rendering us disoriented warriors,[9] confused counselors,[10] or catatonic "vegetables."[11] But as we pursue the establishment of Truth in our soul,[12] we participate with Yehovah in this process and "get to know the land."[13] We replace all of the erroneous connections one by one with new revelations of spiritual intimacy with Him,[14] causing our soul to grow in a healthy and productive way for His Glory.[15] In this way, we remove the influence of darkness and establish the truth and power of our own legally granted authority from Yehovah.[16]

Before conquest, a soul can have many infestations of the enemy.[17] Some can be like Jericho;[18] others can be like Ai.[19] Therefore, we must approach each battle

---

1 Exodus 3:8; Genesis 18:8
2 Ezekiel 20:6; Genesis 43:11
3 Colossians 2:15; Acts 2:32-36; John 12:31; 16:11; Revelation 12:9; 20:2-3,10
4 Matthew 10:8: Luke 10:9
5 Matthew 12:29; Luke 10:18; Colossians 2:15; John 12:31; 16:11; Revelation 12:9; 20:2-3,10
6 Colossians 3:8; 1 Kings 2:4; To facilitate clarity regarding each human soul's spiritual and soulical dynamics, we will be speaking in terms of *our soul* instead of the plural *our souls. Our soul* is a reference to *the human soul.*
7 Exodus 23:29; Deuteronomy 7:22
8 Judges 3:1-4; John 16:12
9 1 Samuel 14:20; 2 Chronicles 20:23
10 Acts 19:32; Isaiah 19:11
11 Luke 1:22; Revelation 1:17
12 Romans 13:14; Galatians 3:27; Ephesians 4:24
13 Romans 12:2; 1 Peter 2:11; 1 John 2:15-17; Colossians 3:10
14 Ephesians 1:17; Luke 12:12; 21:15; Matthew 16:17; 1 Corinthians 2:10
15 Ephesians 1:18; 2 Corinthians 4:6; Acts 16:14
16 Romans 8:2; 6:18; John 8:36
17 Philippians 2:12; James 4:8; 1 John 1:9; 3:3; 2 Corinthians 7:1
18 Joshua 6:1,5; Hebrews 11:30
19 Joshua 7:3-5; 8:2,25

with an ear toward Yehovah.[1] We conquer nothing on our own.[2] Everything we do is by His direction[3] and for His Glory.[4]

In the spirit, territory is taken or lost by legal claims.[5] Understand that though these claims are legal and must precede any action of force,[6] they *are* followed by actions of force.[7] Just as a bailiff can forcefully take the accused into custody after a conviction and sentence of incarceration by the court, the enemy can exercise authority over parts of a person's body or soul by force after presenting a valid or *uncontested* claim and receiving a favorable judgment.[8] In the same way, our force to fight against the enemy is preceded by our successful presentation of legal claims and subsequent reception of favorable judgments.[9] Therefore, even when a person has experienced a technically illegal force from the enemy,[10] each battle is still about establishing, defending, and enacting legal claims.[11] The person must fight by legal means against the hostile force.[12] In the spiritual realm, which is the foundation of existence,[13] establishment of legality always precedes the power to enforce that legality.[14] Therefore, understand that the most common method used by the enemy to establish a claim of influence within a soul is to attempt residence based on *deeds* performed by that soul.[15]

Until Yeshua came in the flesh, the Kingdom of Heaven could only be taken by force according to the promises given to the nation of Israel.[16] Forceful human spirits, like Joshua,[17] the judges,[18] and David,[19] traveled around the land, finding, chasing, and defeating enemies according to the existing promises. But when

---

[1] 2 Samuel 5:23-24; John 9:6-7

[2] 1 Samuel 17:47; Zechariah 4:6

[3] Proverbs 20:24; Jeremiah 10:23; Psalm 25:12

[4] Isaiah 43:7,21; 48:11; John 15:8; Romans 9:23; Ephesians 1:12

[5] Job 1:6-12; 2:1-7; Luke 22:31-32

[6] Job 1:9-12; 2:4-6

[7] Job 1:13-19; 2:7

[8] See Chapters 13-16 for more on how claims are made, contested, and reversed in spirit.

[9] Zechariah 3:2; Job 42:7-10

[10] Luke 4:39; 8:24; Matthew 17:18; Mark 1:25; 9:25

[11] Job 1:8-12; 2:4-6; 42:1-17

[12] Acts 19:15; Mark 5:9-13

[13] 2 Corinthians 4:18; Hebrews 11:3

[14] Job 1:1-2:7; Matthew 4:1-11; Revelation 12:11

[15] 1 Corinthians 11:27,30; Revelation 2:22

[16] Deuteronomy 28:1-68

[17] Exodus 17:10; Acts 7:45

[18] Judges 15:16; Acts 13:20; Hebrews 11:32

[19] 1 Samuel 17:45-51; Acts 13:22

Yeshua came and died on the cross for our sins,[1] He released us from the authority, tyranny, and power of *all* satanic claims.[2] Yeshua covered *all* of our deeds with His own.[3] By doing this, he defeated *all* of our enemies' claims on our behalf.[4] He defeated the contrary elohim[5] who used the heavenly council[6] to turn against us the "Philistines, Egyptians, Moabites, Anakites," and every other ungodly "inhabitant."[7] He also established the Temple of His Holy Spirit in our soul.[8] Yeshua is the Prince of Peace,[9] the Almighty Solomon,[10] Who reigns in Wisdom and Power over all Israel.[11] What is left in our souls is the unprotected remnant of the enemy,[12] squatters that hope to be ignored.[13]

To conquer these stowaways,[14] we must understand our duty at the Temple.[15] Like Israel, we are a holy nation,[16] living for the Glory of Yehovah.[17] We are blessed according to how we honor Him.[18] And when the eyes of our nation are focused on Him,[19] we are unified in Him and in His Power.[20] Therefore, we fill our eyes with His Light so that our whole nation, our entire soul, may be unified in the Light![21]
Understand that each soul must participate in this glory.[22] Even though Yeshua died as a propitiation for the sins of the whole world,[23] that propitiation must be presented by each soul to obtain the legal release of that soul from the Law of Sin

---

1 1 John 2:2; 3:5; 4:10,14; Romans 3:25-26; 1 Peter 2:24; 3:18; John 1:29; 4:42
2 Hebrews 10:9; Colossians 1:13
3 Colossians 2:14; Isaiah 61:10
4 1 Corinthians 15:57; 1 John 3:8; Deuteronomy 28:7; John 16:33; 1 John 5:4
5 Psalm 82:1-8; Exodus 12:12; See Chapter 13 of this testimony for a more detailed explanation.
6 Psalm 82:1; 89:7; 138:1
7 Genesis 10:1-11:9; 1 Samuel 14:47; 1 Kings 5:3; Luke 19:43; 1 Chronicles 22:9
8 1 Corinthians 3:16; 6:19; 2 Corinthians 6:16; Ephesians 2:21-22; 1 Peter 2:5
9 Isaiah 9:6; 53:5; Micah 5:4; John 14:27; Acts 10:36
10 The name *Solomon*, from שְׁלֹמֹה, means *peace*.
11 1 Kings 4:1; 2 Chronicles 9:30
12 Colossians 3:5,8; Ephesians 5:3-6
13 2 Corinthians 11:3; 12:20-21; Galatians 1:6; 3:1
14 2 Corinthians 10:5; Jeremiah 4:14; Hebrews 4:12
15 Luke 17:10; 1 Corinthians 15:9-10; Philemon 1:11
16 1 Peter 2:9; Revelation 1:6; 5:10
17 Ephesians 1:12; John 15:8
18 1 Samuel 2:30; John 12:26; 1 Corinthians 4:5; 1 Peter 1:7
19 Genesis 11:6; Judges 20:11
20 1 Corinthians 6:17; Ephesians 4:3-4; John 17:21-23
21 Matthew 6:22-23; Luke 11:34-36
22 Romans 14:4; Isaiah 40:29
23 1 John 2:2; 3:5; 4:10,14; Romans 3:25-26; 1 Peter 2:24; 3:18; John 1:29; 4:42

and Death.[1] Yes, the Lamb's Blood was applied to the Mercy Seat of Heaven once for all,[2] but it must also be applied as directed to the mercy seat of *each* soul by the priest of that soul.[3] This is what is meant by, "He has made us to be a kingdom and priests to serve His God and Father,"[4] and "Your body is the temple of the Holy Spirit."[5]

Glory be to Yeshua, Who conquered death[6] and has given us His Own Blood[7] as a Holy Blessing,[8] ensuring our good standing with Life and Goodness![9] Amen!

HalleluYah to the King of Righteousness![10]

HalleluYah to our Wise Creator,[11] to Whom all knowledge and wisdom belong![12]

GLORY TO YEHOVAH!

Since each of us has become a temple of Yehovah,[13] let us also vigorously serve in that temple for His glory![14] Having had the Passover Blood sprinkled on the Mercy Seat for the forgiveness of our sins,[15] let us also make daily soulical sacrifices in love and service for the sake of removing any obstacles[16] of sinful behavior[17] or guilty conscience[18] between our Creator and us![19] Let us worship with our tithes of time[20] and sacrifices of convenience and comfort![21] Like Him, we pick up our

---

[1] Exodus 12:7; Hebrews 10:29; 1 Peter 1:2
[2] Hebrews 9:12; 10:9-14; Acts 20:28
[3] Revelation 12:11; Leviticus 16:14-15; Hebrews 10:22
[4] Revelation 1:6; 5:10; 20:6; 22:5; Exodus 19:6; 1 Peter 2:5-9
[5] 1 Corinthians 3:16; 6:19; 2 Corinthians 6:16; Ephesians 2:21-22; 1 Peter 2:5
[6] Colossians 2:15; Romans 6:9; 2 Timothy 1:10
[7] Luke 22:20; Hebrews 12:24; 13:20
[8] Acts 13:34; Isaiah 55:3
[9] 2 Corinthians 5:19-21; 1 Corinthians 1:30; Philippians 3:9
[10] Hebrews 7:2,17; Psalm 45:4-7; Isaiah 9:6-7; Jeremiah 23:5-6; 33:15-16
[11] Romans 16:27; Ephesians 1:7-8; 3:10; Colossians 2:2-3
[12] Exodus 35:31; Isaiah 11:2-5; 1 Corinthians 12:4-10; James 1:17
[13] 1 Corinthians 3:16; 6:19; 2 Corinthians 6:16; Ephesians 2:21-22; 1 Peter 2:5
[14] Revelation 7:15; Psalm 134:1-2; 1 Corinthians 3:16
[15] Hebrews 9:11-14,24-26; 10:12,19; Titus 2:4
[16] Hebrews 12:1; Romans 13:11-14; Ephesians 4:22-24
[17] 1 Peter 3:1,16; Colossians 1:21
[18] 1 Timothy 1:5,19; 1 Peter 3:16
[19] Matthew 16:24-27; Luke 9:26
[20] Matthew 8:21-22; 4:18-22; 9:9; John 1:43
[21] Luke 9:58; 2 Corinthians 8:9

cross, laying our life down for the glory of His Characteristics,[1] only to pick our new life[2] back up again for that same glory![3] In this way, we move "from glory to glory"![4] This glory is our purpose,[5] and so we live for Him![6]

Fight, mighty warriors,[7] by the power of His Blood![8] Take the land of your soul![9]

PRAISE YEHOVAH, WHO EXTENDS HIS TENT OVER US AND RESCUES US FROM ALL DISTRESS![10]

HALLELUYAH!

PRAISE OUR HIGH PRIEST,[11] WHO BECAME OUR ETERNAL OFFERING[12] GRANTING US ETERNAL REST[13] AND PEACE![14]

HALLELUYAH!

HOSANNA IN THE HIGHEST![15]

HALLELUYAAAAAAAAAAAAAAAAAAAAAAAAAAH!!!!!!!!!!!

---

[1] John 13:15; 1 Corinthians 10:11
[2] Romans 6:4; 7:6; 2 Corinthians 5:17; Galatians 6:15; Ephesians 4:22-24
[3] Romans 8:17; 1 Timothy 2:10; John 12:26
[4] 2 Corinthians 3:18; Proverbs 4:18
[5] Psalm 57:2,11; Ephesians 2:10; Isaiah 43:7; Philippians 2:13
[6] 2 Corinthians 5:15; 1 Corinthians 6:20; Galatians 2:19
[7] Romans 8:37; Isaiah 25:8; 1 Corinthians 15:57; 1 John 4:4; 5:4-5; Jude 1:24
[8] Matthew 26:28; John 6:54
[9] Romans 12:11; Colossians 4:12-13; 1 Peter 1:22; 4:8; Revelation 3:15-16
[10] Revelation 7:15-16; Psalm 134:1-2; 1 Corinthians 3:16
[11] Hebrews 3:1; 5:6,10; 6:20; 7:1-21
[12] Hebrews 7:27; 9:12,25,28
[13] Hebrews 4:10-11; Matthew 7:13; 11:28; 2 Peter 1:10-11
[14] John 14:27; 16:33; Romans 5:1-2; Acts 10:36; 1 Corinthians 1:3
[15] Matthew 21:9; Psalm 118:24-26; Mark 11:9-10

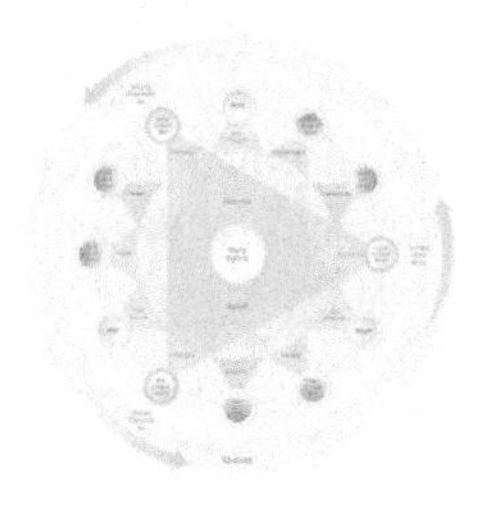

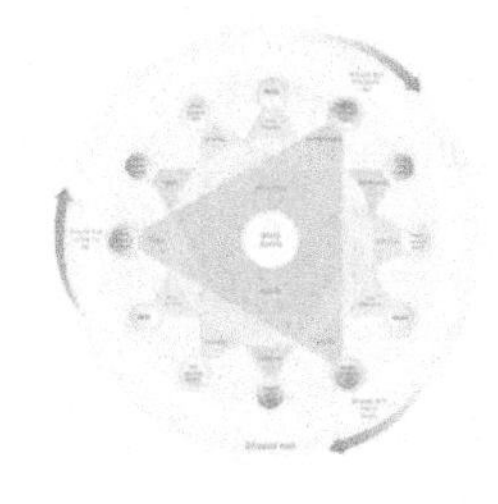

CHAPTER 11

THE HUMAN SOUL'S GATES AND TRIADS

From the beginning, Yehovah has been revealing the composition of the human soul in great detail.[1] Because of the potential for such knowledge to be abused, it has remained hidden for the righteous within the parables of Scripture.[2] Nevertheless, in these last days,[3] He is making these things blatant[4] in order to fully equip His children in their final stand against darkness.[5]

On the sixth day of creation, Yehovah breathed His Breath of Life into human flesh.[6] This breath was spirit and consisted of awareness able to observe, consider, decide, and intend.[7] As this awareness filled the flesh of the man, Adam became a living soul, which manifested in affections, thoughts, and will.[8]

---

[1] Genesis 2:7; 49:6; Exodus 30:12; Leviticus 4:2; 5:1; Numbers 21:4; 30:2; Deuteronomy 4:9,29; 6:5

[2] Proverbs 25:2; Deuteronomy 29:29; Job 11:7-8; 42:3; Romans 11:33-34

[3] Hebrews 1:2; James 5:3; 2 Peter 3:3

[4] Daniel 12:4; Isaiah 11:9; 29:18-19

[5] John 16:25; 2 Corinthians 14:18

[6] Genesis 2:7; Job 27:3; 33:4; John 20:22: Acts 17:25

[7] 2 Timothy 3:16: Revelation 4:7 – Eagle = observe (see); man = consider (think); lion = decide (judge/rule); ox = intend (do/labor/act). These functions of spirit are discussed more in Chapters 22-25 of this testimony.

[8] Mark 12:30 – *Heart* is from the Greek word καρδία, pronounced "kar-dee-ah," meaning *the seat of affections, appetites, and passions. Mind* is from διάνοια, pronounced "dee-ahn'-oy-ah," meaning *deep thought.* And *will* is from ἰσχύς, pronounced "ihs-khoos," meaning *forcefulness, ability,* or *might.* While the word does mean *strength,* in this context it is a reference not to physical strength but to the strength of a soul, that is, *strength of will.*

These aspects of a living soul relate and connect to form various qualities of soulical function.[1] When they flow with the Law of Righteousness, they produce fruit of light.[2] But when they flow with unrighteousness, they produce fruit of darkness.[3] Each of these functions represents a gate through which the soul is expressed. And just as in New Jerusalem, there are twelve gates.[4]

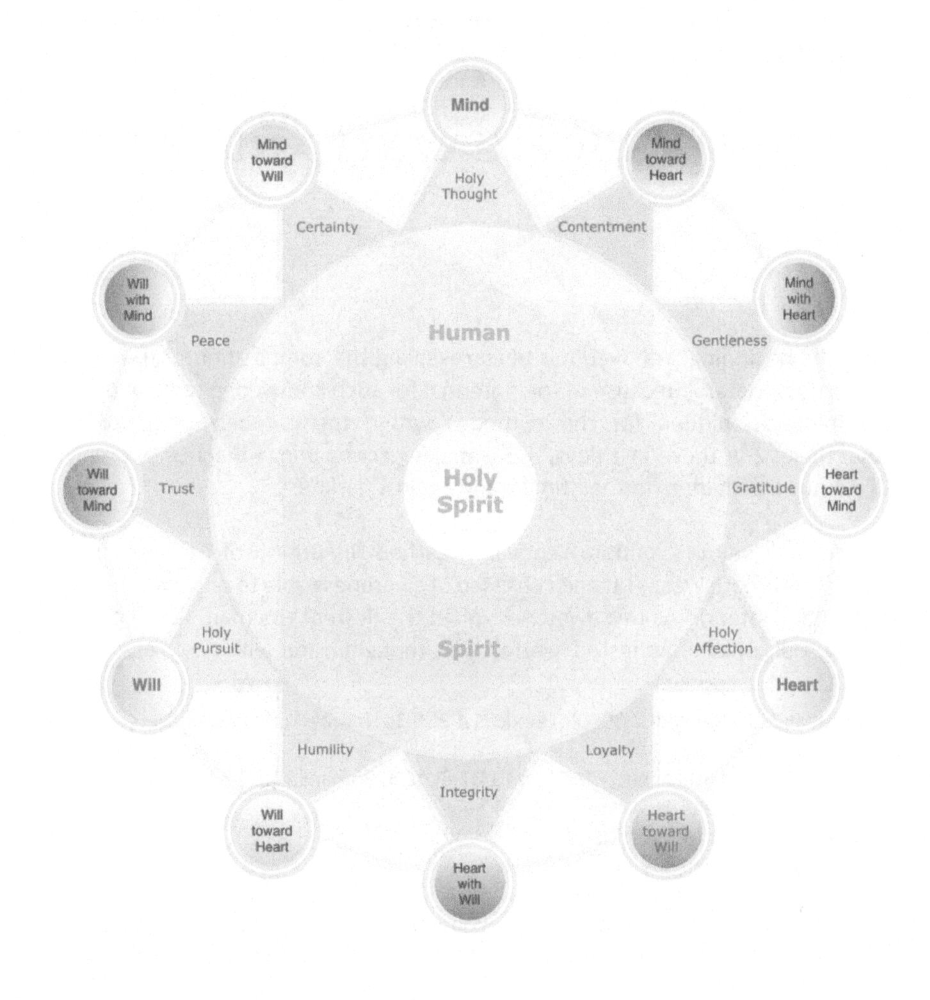

[1] These aspects are addressed in detail throughout Chapters 18-25, 31-32, and 34 of this testimony.

[2] Matthew 7:17; Psalm 1:3; 92:13-14; Isaiah 61:3

[3] Matthew 7:18; Galatians 5:17; 1 John 3:9-10

[4] Revelation 21:12; Isaiah 54:12; Isaiah 60:18

The twelve gates affect others according to their position.[1] For example, when influenced in agreement with the Holy Spirit, holy thoughts in the mind and righteously focused pursuits in the will work in tandem to receive heavenly peace in the convergence gate between them.[2] To produce this peace in its fullness, the will must participate in pursuits of trusting Yehovah, and the mind must be firmly certain of the Truth.[3] Similarly, holy thoughts in the mind and selfless affections in the heart enable confident and sincere gentleness[4] when mental contentment[5] and heartfelt gratitude[6] abound in the proximal gates. And if both the pursuits and affections of a soul are righteous, pure integrity[7] will result from a loyal heart[8] and a humble will.[9]

Father in Heaven, bless your children to receive Your wisdom and revelation![10] Thank you, Merciful Father, for giving them the Mind of Christ![11] HalleluYah! They are equipped and able to fathom Your very thoughts![12] HalleluYah! They are able to perceive your mysteries[13] and keep in step with Your Holy Spirit![14] HalleluYah!

WE ARE ONE WITH YESHUA![15] HALLELUYAH! HALLELUYAH!

BLESSED BE YOUR NAME, YEHOVAH HAMASHIACH![16] AMEN!

---

1 Revelation 21:13; Ezekiel 48:31-34
2 Romans 5:1; 14:17; 15:13; Isaiah 32:17; 54:13
3 Romans 14:5; 1 John 3:19-21
4 1 Peter 3:4,15; 2 Timothy 2:25-26; Ephesians 4:2; 1 Timothy 3:3; Titus 3:2
5 Philippians 4:11; 3:8; Matthew 6:31-34; 1 Timothy 6:6-9; Hebrews 10:34; 13:5-6
6 1 Thessalonians 5:18; Ephesians 5:20; Philippians 4:6; Colossians 3:17
7 Proverbs 11:3; 13:6; Psalm 25:21; John 7:17
8 2 Chronicles 25:2; Deuteronomy 6:4-9; Exodus 13:9,16; Numbers 15:38-39; Proverbs 3:3; 6:21; 7:3; Hebrews 2:1
9 Ephesians 4:2; Matthew 11:29; Colossians 3:12; James 1:21
10 Galatians 1:12; Ephesians 1:17; Luke 12:12; 21:15; Matthew 16:17; 1 Corinthians 2:10
11 1 Corinthians 2:16; John 15:15; 16:13-15
12 1 Corinthians 2:10-12,16
13 1 Corinthians 4:1; 2:7; Luke 8:10; Romans 16:25; Ephesians 1:9
14 Galatians 5:25: Romans 8:4-5
15 John 14:20; 6:56; 15:5-7; Romans 8:1; 16:7; 1 Corinthians 1:30; Galatians 2:20
16 Luke 2:11 – *Christ the Lord,* from the Greek Χριστὸς Κύριος, traditionally considered by readers of English to mean *Anointed Lord.* In Daniel 9:25 of the Greek Old Testament, the Hebrew word מָשִׁיחַ, pronounced "mah-shee-ach," meaning *messiah* or *anointed,* is translated into a form of Χριστὸς, pronounced "krihs-tahs," also meaning *messiah* or *anointed*. Likewise, the Hebrew Name of God, *Yehovah,* is translated into Greek as both θεός, pronounced "they-awss" and meaning *God* or *Supreme* Deity (see how Matthew 4:4

Now, let us also understand that each gate of the soul also has a direct connection with two cross gates. Together, these three gates form a triad, which is a layer of soulical connection and interaction with one of the four aspects of the human spirit.[1] Each of these triads consists of three gates, and these gates correspond to different currents in the soul.[2] That is to say, the spiritual function of observation interacts with the main gates of thought, pursuit, and affection in the soul.[3] Correspondingly, loyalty, trust, and contentment are soulical functions that reflect spiritual consideration.[4] Humility, gratitude, and certainty are aspects of spiritual decision.[5] And integrity, gentleness, and peace are the fruits of spiritual intention.[6]

Look at the map of the soul.[7] Do you see the pattern?[8] The colors are those of the precious gems representing the twelve tribes on the ephod of Israel.[9] They are also twelve gates.[10] The blue gates are the main gates. The green and red gates indicate gates that spring from the way the main gates push or pull on one another.[11] The purple gates are the gates that indicate whether the main gates agree.[12]

---

translates Deuteronomy 8:3), and κύριος, pronounced "koo-ree-awss," which means *Lord, God, Supreme in Authority* (see how Matthew 4:7 translates Deuteronomy 6:16 and how Romans 15:11 translates Psalm 117:1). Therefore, though traditionally translated into English as *Christ the Lord,* a more Hebrew translation of Χριστὸς Κύριος would be *Yehovah the Messiah*. HALLELUYAH! OUR GOD CAME AND SAVED US! OUR GOD IS ONE! (Deuteronomy 6:4; Mark 12:29, John 10:30)

[1] 2 Timothy 3:16: Revelation 4:7 – Eagle = observe (see); man = consider (think); lion = decide (judge/rule); ox = intend (do/labor/act). These functions of spirit are discussed more in Chapters 22-25 of this testimony.

[2] These currents are directly addressed in Chapter 32 of this testimony.

[3] Mark 12:30; Luke 10:27; Deuteronomy 30:14

[4] 1 Timothy 1:12; 1 Samuel 16:7; 24:15; 2 Chronicles 19:6

[5] Joshua 24:15; 1 Kings 18:21

[6] Matthew 10:13; John 12:7; 2 Corinthians 7:9

[7] It is a map (Joshua 18:8; Revelation 11:1). We do not worship New Jerusalem; we worship the King Who lives in it (Revelation 21:2). We do not worship the soul; we worship the King Who made it and lives in it (Colossians 1:27). The map is not a "graven image" for worship (Exodus 20:4); it is a "survey of the land written on a scroll" for the purpose of navigation (Joshua 18:9).

[8] Exodus 25:40; Hebrews 8:5

[9] Exodus 28:17-21; Revelation 21:19-21

[10] Revelation 21:12; Isaiah 54:12

[11] See Chapter 32 of this testimony for more on such effects.

[12] All of these features will continue to be discussed throughout this testimony, so do not lose courage (Deuteronomy 31:8)! God will bless you with wisdom and revelation (Ephesians 1:17)! HalleluYah!

Thank You, Lord, for blessing us with increased knowledge in these end times![1] Bless Your children to receive your Spirit of Wisdom and Revelation![2]

HalleluYah!

PRAISE BE TO YEHOVAH, GOD OF KNOWLEDGE![3]

HALLELUYAH!

PRAISE YOU, LORD, FOR ENSURING THAT YOUR CHILDREN DO NOT PERISH![4]

HALLELUYAH!

THANK YOU, GOD OF PEACE,[5] FOR EQUIPPING US[6] TO WILL AND TO ACT ACCORDING TO YOUR GOOD PURPOSE![7]

HALLELUYAH!

Priests of Yehovah![8] Listen! This calls for wisdom:[9] Because of the relationships within the soul to spiritual functions, an increase in one gate of a triad layer also influences the other two. If a person becomes encouraged by the Love of Yeshua and pursues a greater commitment to integrity, then that person will also experience an increase in both gentleness and peace.[10] Likewise, endeavors to practice and exercise trust in Yehovah will also lead to greater loyalty and deepening contentment,[11] and expressed gratitude will strengthen both certainty and humility.[12] Each one of the triad gates affects the others within its triad. In this

---

[1] Daniel 12:4; Isaiah 11:9; 29:18-19

[2] Ephesians 1:17; Luke 12:12; 21:15; Matthew 16:17; 1 Corinthians 2:10

[3] Romans 11:33; Ephesians 3:10; Colossians 2:2-3

[4] Hosea 4:6; Jeremiah 5:21; 2 Corinthians 4:3-6

[5] Hebrews 13:20; Romans 15:33; 16:20; 1 Corinthians 14:33; 2 Corinthians 13:11

[6] Hebrews 13:21; Ephesians 3:16-19; 2 Thessalonians 2:17

[7] Philippians 2:13; Ephesians 2:4-5; John 6:65

[8] Revelation 1:6; 5:10; 20:6; 22:5; Exodus 19:6; 1 Peter 2:5-9

[9] Revelation 17:9a; 13:18a; Daniel 12:8-10; Hosea 14:9; Matthew 13:11

[10] Philippians 4:4-7 – Verse 4: "...always..." (Integrity) => verse 5: "...gentleness..." => verse 7: "...peace..."

[11] Psalm 143:8; Proverbs 3:5-6; Isaiah 30:21

[12] Colossians 2:6-7; 3:17; Hebrews 13:15-16; 1 Thessalonians 5:15-24

way, the holy disciples of Yeshua[1] can strengthen their souls in the Power of the Holy Spirit![2] Amen!

HALLELUYAH!

MAY THE FATHER BE GLORIFIED[3] BY THE FRUIT[4] OF OUR CONQUESTS[5] THROUGH YESHUA![6]

Conversely, an influx of darkness also has an effect across the gates.[7] Participation in a deed that lacks integrity will indirectly decrease both gentleness and peace.[8] Acceptance of worry will also drain loyalty and reduce contentment,[9] and grumbling will eventually limit certainty and hinder genuine humility.[10]

If the righteous expression of any gate slows to a stop,[11] then the flow can reverse.[12] Trust can become worry, peace can change to fear,[13] and certainty can shift to doubt.[14] Gate reversal replaces contentment with envy,[15] gentleness with selfish anger,[16] and gratitude with bitterness.[17] Loyalty will flip to lust,[18] integrity to duplicity,[19] and humility to pride.[20]

---

[1] Matthew 28:19; Acts 1:8; Colossians 1:23-20
[2] Hebrews 12:12; Ephesians 3:16
[3] John 15:8; Luke 6:35; Psalm 92:12-15; Isaiah 60:21; Matthew 5:16
[4] Philippians 1:11; Luke 13:6-9; John 15:8,16
[5] Romans 8:37; Isaiah 25:8; 1 Corinthians 15:57; 1 John 4:4; 5:4-5; Jude 1:24
[6] 1 Peter 1:8-9; 1 Corinthians 8:6
[7] Matthew 6:23-24b; Romans 6:16; Galatians 1:10; James 4:4; 1 John 2:15-16
[8] Luke 12:49,51; Zechariah 11:7-11
[9] Proverbs 12:25; 1 Timothy 6:9
[10] Numbers 14:2; Deuteronomy 1:27
[11] Hebrews 12:3; Galatians 6:9; 2 Timothy 3:13
[12] Matthew 6:23-24b; Romans 6:16; Galatians 1:10; James 4:4; 1 John 2:15-16
[13] Jeremiah 30:5; Isaiah 59:11
[14] Matthew 14:31; James 1:6-8
[15] James 3:16; 1 Corinthians 3:3; 1 Peter 2:1
[16] Proverbs 15:1; Ephesians 4:31; James 1:20
[17] Deuteronomy 29:18; Jeremiah 2:19
[18] Matthew 23:25; Ephesians 4:19; 1 John 2:16
[19] Proverbs 11:3; 28:18; Isaiah 1:28; John 7:17; Matthew 6:2,5,16; 7:5; 15:7-9
[20] Proverbs 11:2; 1 Corinthians 8:1-2

Great Lord and God, bless us to have ears to hear what Your Spirit is saying to your people![1] Enlighten us like Daniel![2] Give us wisdom like Solomon![3] Fill us with the Humility of Christ, and bless us![4] Let us not *tell* You what we can know, but let us *accept what Your Word says* we can know![5] HalleluYah!

WE HAVE BEEN GIVEN THE MIND OF CHRIST![6]

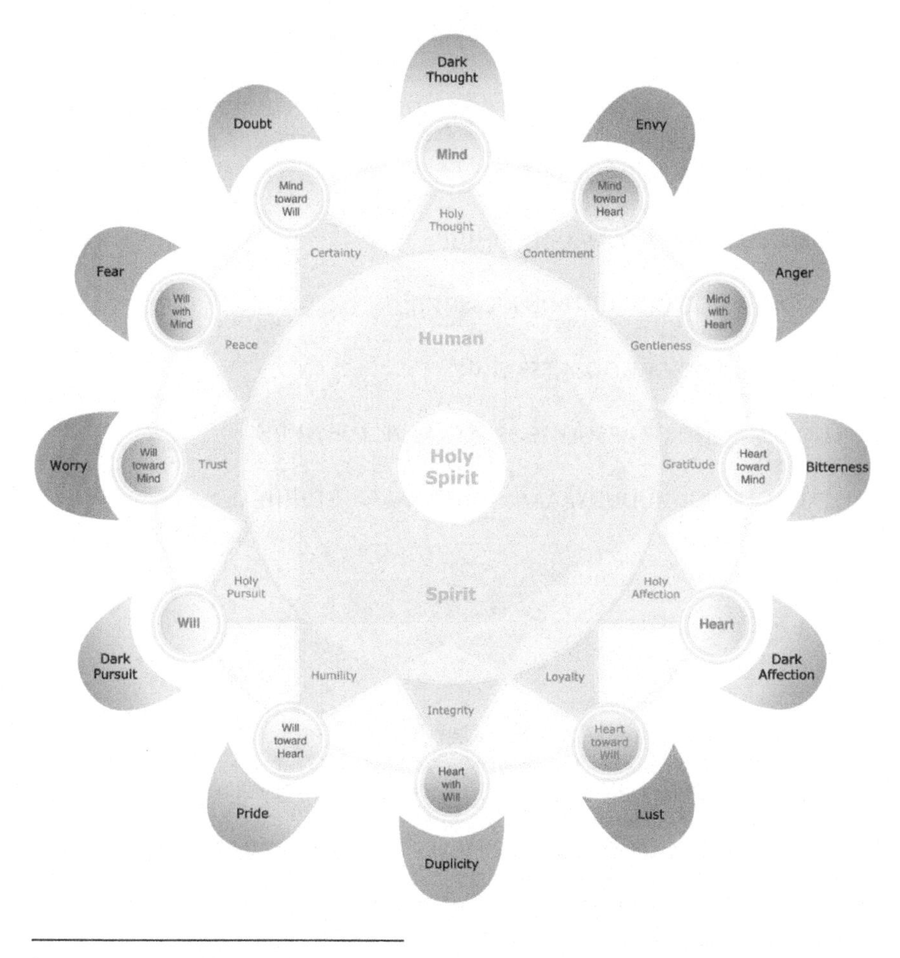

---

[1] Revelation 2:7; Luke 8:18; 19:26; Deuteronomy 32:46-47; Proverbs 2:2-5; Mark 4:23-24; Acts 17:11; Hebrews 2:1; James 1:22-25; Matthew 13:12; John 15:2

[2] Daniel 1:17; Numbers 12:6

[3] 1 Kings 3:10-15; 5:7; Luke 11:31

[4] Philippians 2:7-9; Acts 8:33; Hebrews 5:5-7; 10:7-9

[5] 1 Corinthians 13:12; James 1:23; 2 Corinthians 3:18

[6] 1 Corinthians 2:16; John 15:15; 16:13-15

HALLELUYAH!

WE ARE WHO GOD *SAYS* WE ARE![1]

ALL ASSAULTS ON ANY OF THE REDEEMED ARE NO LONGER FROM THE FLESH BUT FROM DARK SPIRITS[2] SEEKING TO KILL, STEAL, AND DESTROY[3] OUR FAITH, HOPE, AND LOVE[4] IN OUR SAVIOR WHO HAS FULLY PURCHASED,[5] RENEWED,[6] AND SAVED US![7]

THE TIME HAS COME FOR THE REDEEMED TO STAND IN THE TRUTH,[8] CONQUER LIES,[9] CONQUER UNRIGHTEOUSNESS,[10] AND BRING ETERNAL HONOR[11] TO OUR SAVIOR BOTH NOW AND FOREVER![12]

HALLELUYAAAAAAAAAAAAAAAH!!!!!!!!!!!

OUR GOD IS A GOD OF RIGHTEOUSNESS!!!!!![13]

OUR GOD IS A GOD OF GOODNESS!!!!!![14]

OUR GOD IS A GOD OF ABSOLUTE SPIRITUAL VICTORY!!!!![15]

HALLELUUUUUUUUUUUUUYAAAAAAAAAAAAAAAH!!!!!!!!!!!

---

[1] 1 Corinthians 13:12; James 1:23; 2 Corinthians 3:18
[2] Ephesians 6:12; Romans 8:38; Colossians 2:15; 1 Peter 3:22
[3] John 10:10; Luke 8:12; John 8:44; Acts 13:10; Hebrews 2:14; Revelation 12:9
[4] 1 Corinthians 13:13; Galatians 5:22
[5] Revelation 5:9-10; Matthew 20:28; 26:28; Acts 20:28; Romans 3:24-26
[6] 2 Corinthians 5:17; John 3:3; Galatians 6:15
[7] Ephesians 2:5,8; Titus 2:11; 3:5
[8] Galatians 5:1,13; 2:4; 4:26,31; John 8:32-36; Romans 6:18; 8:2
[9] 2 Corinthians 10:5; Jeremiah 4:14; Hebrews 4:12
[10] Romans 8:13; Colossians 3:5-8; 1 Peter 1:22
[11] 1 Corinthians 6:20; 10:31; Matthew 5:16
[12] 1 Timothy 1:17; Jude 1:25
[13] Romans 1:17; 1 John 3:7
[14] Matthew 19:17; 1 Samuel 2:2; Psalm 145:7-9; James 1:17
[15] John 16:33; 1 John 4:4

HOLY PEOPLE OF GOD![1] THEREFORE, UNDERSTAND![2] When the enemy sees an opportunity for dark expression in any gate, they will use that gate as a means for backdoor attacks against other gates connected or adjacent to it![3] For example, if a man entertains a temptation of lust, then the enemy immediately gains an influence on both his affection and integrity because of the connections between the functions of these gates within the soul itself.[4] However, the enemy also gains access to the other gates of the triad as a consequence of the cross connectivity within the human spirit in its accepted vulnerability to temptation.[5] In other words, by successfully impacting the man's human spirit with a temptation to lust, the dark spirits are immediately able to weaken the gates vulnerable to worry and envy as well, even though they have not been directly assaulted.[6] Overall, this means that when lies of lust are entertained, the soul's affection, integrity, trust, and contentment gates have become vulnerable![7]

BUT PRAISE GOD, WHO HAS GIVEN US HIS VERY GREAT AND PRECIOUS PROMISES SO THAT WE CAN ESCAPE ACCEPTING THE INFLUENCE OF CORRUPT DESIRES![8]

HALLELUYAH!

Since we are no longer unaware of the schemes of darkness,[9] let us be wise and forsake the pitfalls of temptation![10]

Know also that the dark spirits are aware that we are learning to resist![11] Therefore, because of the many potential proximal and triad effects opened by a single sin,[12] a dark spirit will invite other stronger spirits to assist in its efforts to take up a residence of influence![13] For example, when a spirit of lust sees an opportunity in a soul lacking loyalty, that spirit will often invite along spirits of

---

[1] 1 Peter 2:9; Revelation 1:6; 5:10

[2] Luke 8:18; 19:26; Deuteronomy 32:46-47; Proverbs 2:2-5; Mark 4:23-24; Acts 17:11; Hebrews 2:1; James 1:22-25; Matthew 13:12; John 15:2

[3] The enemy will cite unrighteousness found in one gate as justification for the destruction of others (Jeremiah 17:27).

[4] 1 Timothy 6:10; 2 Timothy 4:10; Jude 1:11

[5] James 1:14; Ephesians 4:22; Hebrews 3:13

[6] Ephesians 4:27; James 3:16

[7] Colossians 3:5; Romans 1:26; 1 Thessalonians 4:3-7

[8] 2 Peter 1:4; Ephesians 4:23-24; Hebrews 12:10; Galatians 6:8

[9] Ephesians 6:11; 2 Corinthians 2:11

[10] 2 Timothy 2:26; Acts 5:3; Luke 22:31-32

[11] Revelation 12:12,17; John 8:44; 1 Peter 5:8

[12] Galatians 6:1; 1 Corinthians 10:12

[13] Matthew 12:45; 23:15; Hebrews 6:4-8; 2 Peter 2:14-22

deceitful affection, duplicity, worry, and discontentment to weaken the neighboring gates and other sides of the triad.[1] By doing this, the dark spirit facilitates its own entrance and ensures its own continued foothold.[2]

Who is it that will save us from such complex and deceitful tactics by ancient spirits desperately seeking to use us for their own preservation?[3] Thanks be to Jesus Christ, Yeshua HaMashiach, our gracious Lord and Savior![4] With His Blood He has purchased us from death[5] and raised us into eternal life![6] Having this great assurance, we can now take hold of the victory given to us through His perfect promises and conquer by force in His mighty Name![7] We are no longer slaves in Egypt[8] but have become the chosen forces of Joshua,[9] taking the promised land[10] and removing the giants for the sake of His Glory![11]

Behold! He has commanded us to remove all the foreign inhabitants from our promised land![12] Therefore, let us train[13] and become skilled in spiritual warfare,[14] and may we make straight the way for the return of our Righteous and Invincible King![15] Amen!

HALLELUYAH!

PRAISE OUR ALMIGHTY GOD, WHO DELIVERED US FROM THE DARKNESS OF EGYPT AND SLAVERY![16]

HALLELUYAH!

---

[1] 2 Peter 2:10-22; Mark 7:22; Romans 1:29
[2] 1 Timothy 6:9; 1 John 2:15-17
[3] Romans 7:24; 1 Kings 8:38; Psalm 6:6; 38:8-10; 119:176
[4] 2 Corinthians 1:10; 2 Timothy 4:17
[5] Revelation 5:9; Matthew 20:28; 26:28; Acts 20:28; Romans 3:24-26
[6] Galatians 3:13-14; 4:5; Titus 2:14; 1 Peter 1:18
[7] 1 Corinthians 15:57; Romans 8:37; 1 John 5:4-5
[8] Acts 13:39; Romans 6:18,22
[9] Joshua 1:1-3; Deuteronomy 3:28
[10] Genesis 26:2-5; Hebrews 3:11-4:13
[11] 2 Samuel 21:15-22; Joshua 14:12; Psalm 60:12; 108:13; 118:15; Romans 8:37
[12] Numbers 33:51-52; Deuteronomy 7:2-5
[13] 2 Timothy 3:16; 2:25; Deuteronomy 4:36; Nehemiah 9:20; Matthew 13:52
[14] Judges 3:2; 1 Timothy 6:12; Ephesians 6:11-18
[15] Isaiah 40:3; 35:8; 57:14; 62:10-11; Malachi 3:1; 4:5-6
[16] Exodus 13:3; Galatians 4:3; Hebrews 2:15

PRAISE OUR ALMIGHTY GOD, WHO PARTED THE WATERS OF BAPTISM FOR OUR SALVATION![1]

HALLELUYAH!

PRAISE OUR ALMIGHTY GOD, WHO IS ABLE TO BRING DOWN THE WALLS OF EVERY JERICHO IN OUR SOUL![2]

HALLELUYAH!

HOLY IS HIS NAME!!!!!!!!!!!!!!!!!!!!!!![3]

HALLELUUUUUYAAAAAAAAAAAAAAAAAAAAH!!!!!!!!!!!!!!!!!!

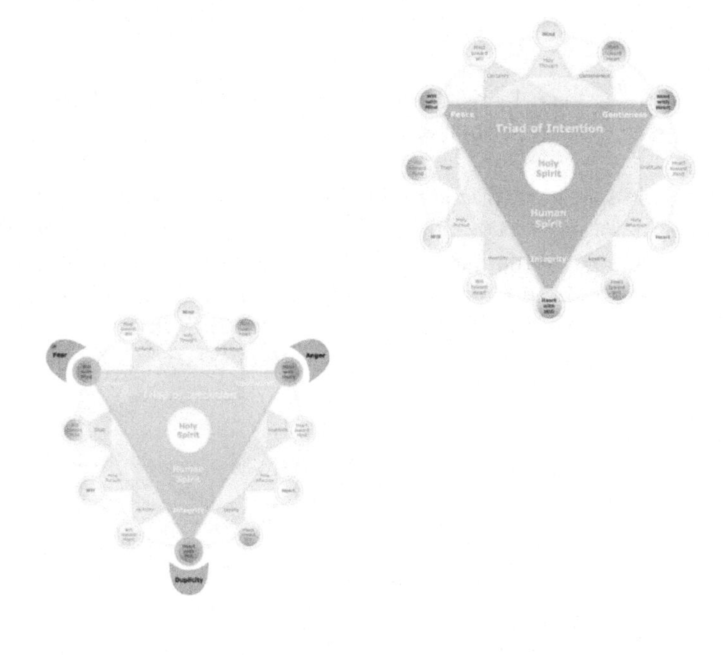

[1] Exodus 14:21-22; 1 Peter 3:21; 1 Corinthians 10:1-2
[2] Joshua 5:13-6:5; Hebrews 11:30
[3] Ezekiel 36:21; 39:25; 1 Chronicles 16:10: Psalm 33:21

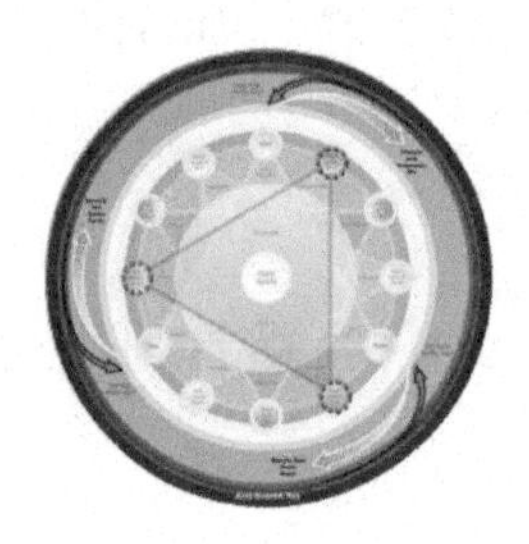

CHAPTER 12

OVERTAKING AND DEFENDING THE GATES

From the Scriptures, we learn many things about taking the land, fighting the enemy, and defending the gates of our souls.[1]

Israel was often given specific instructions about how to engage in battle.[2] Of all commands, the most notable was that the priests of Israel were to lead the army with the Ark of Testimony.[3] At that time, it contained a jar of the manna[4] used to feed the Israelites in the desert, the staff Yehovah miraculously budded with leaves and almonds to show His choice of Aaron as the High Priest,[5] and the

[1] 2 Timothy 3:16; 1 Timothy 6:12
[2] 2 Samuel 5:23-24; John 9:6-7
[3] Joshua 3:3,11; Numbers 10:33
[4] Exodus 16:33; Hebrews 9:4
[5] Numbers 17:10; Hebrews 9:4

second pair of two tablets[1] carved out by Moses but on which the finger of Yehovah had written[2] the Ten Commandments.[3]

This ark of Israel symbolizes how we carry Yeshua's Testimony before us whenever engaging in any spiritual battle.[4] And just as the physical ark was crafted according to Yehovah's instructions and gifts of the Holy Spirit through two men, Bezalel, "in the protection of God," and Oholiab, "Father's tent,"[5] so also our sacred testimony is crafted by the Holy Spirit in the protection of God in our Father's tent.[6] We are to lead with this sacred testimony that He is our Manna,[7] that is, our Bread of Life,[8] Provider,[9] and Provision.[10] He is also our Staff,[11] or our Power,[12] Authority,[13] Right,[14] and High Priest.[15] And He is the Living Word[16] that reveals Truth,[17] Promise,[18] and Covenant.[19]

We keep this multifold testimony in a temple we have built for Him in the center of our soul.[20] When we fight to conquer and rule over our soul,[21] we always lead

---

[1] Exodus 16:34; 25:16,21; 40:20-21; Deuteronomy 10:2-5

[2] Deuteronomy 10:2-5; Exodus 34:1; Because of the command in Exodus 34:27, some readers have erroneously assumed that verse 28 is saying Moses wrote on the stones, but we know from Deuteronomy 10:4 and Exodus 34:1 that Yehovah wrote on the stones. Therefore, we understand that the command in Exodus 34:27 for Moses to write was in reference to all the words that Yehovah had just spoken to him (Exodus 34:10-27) on that very *day* (Exodus 34:11), not the Ten Commandments (Exodus 34:28 should be understood by context to be the beginning of a new paragraph).

[3] Exodus 16:34; Hebrews 9:4

[4] Revelation 12:11; 7:10-14; 15:3

[5] Exodus 35:30-35; 31:2-6

[6] Revelation 7:15-17; Psalm 134:1-2; 1 Corinthians 3:16

[7] John 6:32-33,35,41,50,55,58

[8] John 6:33-51; Luke 22:19

[9] Matthew 16:9; Acts 14:17

[10] John 7:38; Galatians 5:22-23; Ephesians 5:9

[11] John 14:13; 1 Corinthians 15:57

[12] Philippians 4:13; Ephesians 3:16

[13] 2 Corinthians 10:8; Galatians 1:1

[14] 2 Peter 1:1; Acts 15:8-9

[15] Hebrews 4:14; 2:17; 3:1

[16] John 1:1,14; 1 John 1:1-2; Revelation 19:13

[17] John 14:6; Acts 4:12; Hebrews 10:19-22; 1 John 2:23; 2 John 1:9; Revelation 5:8-9

[18] Ephesians 3:6; Romans 4:16; 2 Corinthians 1:20

[19] Mark 14:24; Zechariah 9:11; Hebrews 9:15-23

[20] 1 Corinthians 3:16; 6:19; 2 Corinthians 6:16; Ephesians 2:21-22; 1 Peter 2:5

[21] James 1:21; 2 Corinthians 7:1; Colossians 3:5-8

with the Testimony of Yeshua, [1] Who overcame all darkness and every principality.[2]

We always use the deeds and words of Yeshua to defend a gate.[3] We never attempt to hold a gate with our own deeds.[4] It is by carrying His Testimony that we participate.[5] He made us to be priests who lead angels into battle.[6] We carry the Ark of the New Covenant, and they gather the dark spirits and take them to the abyss.[7] We sound the trumpets;[8] the angels strike the enemy.[9] We fight with the proclamation of His commands, authority, and provisions,[10] and they enforce them.[11]

The Lord is our Provider, Fortress, and Right; He is our Power, Reason, and Connection.[12] We must realize what is of the Lord and what is not. Any pursuit, thought, or affection that hinders our relationship with the Lord is not of Him.[13]

We cannot waver in commitment to our relationship with Yehovah.[14] Our enemies in the dark kingdom perceive a committed believer to be like a well-defended city with mighty walls and reinforced gates.[15] Yet, the resistance to attack mounted by a double-minded person is as meager as a fenceless farmhouse in the middle of nowhere.[16]

---

[1] Revelation 12:11; 7:10-14; 15:3
[2] Colossians 2:15; Acts 2:32-36; John 12:31; 16:11; Revelation 12:9; 20:2-3,10
[3] Deuteronomy 6:9; 11:20
[4] Romans 3:21-23; 1 John 2:1-2
[5] Romans 3:26-27; Revelation 12:11
[6] Revelation 5:10; Psalm 91:11; 34:7; 103:20; 2 Kings 6:17
[7] Revelation 9:1; 20:1-3; Luke 8:31
[8] Joshua 6:4; 2 Chronicles 13:12; Judges 7:15-22
[9] Revelation 12:7-9; Matthew 26:53
[10] Matthew 4:3-11; James 4:7; Acts 5:3-4,9
[11] Acts 5:5,10; Matthew 26:53; 2 Samuel 24:16
[12] Psalm 18:2; 2 Samuel 22:2; Nahum 1:7
[13] 2 Corinthians 10:5; Mark 12:30; 1 John 4:3
[14] Matthew 10:22; 24:13; 1 Corinthians 1:8; Revelation 2:26
[15] 2 Peter 1:10; 1 Peter 1:5
[16] James 1:8; 1 Kings 18:21; Hosea 7:8-11; Matthew 6:24

Every attack against a gate is an attack by the enemy to steal, kill, or destroy[1] our faith, hope, or love[2] in Yeshua because it is our relationship with Yeshua that renders our gates *impenetrable* to the enemy![3]

HalleluYah!

Therefore, understand that we cannot overemphasize the importance of leading with the Ark of His Greater Covenant.[4] The enemy knows that the power for the blessing of our victory is in this ark.[5] The enemy knows that Yeshua has already defeated them and that the more He is welcomed into our souls, the more the enemy will suffer conquest and defeat![6]

This is a very important concept to understand.[7] Even the tools given in this testimony are insufficient without a living relationship with Yehovah.[8] We must *invite*[9] our God into our struggles![10] The tools given in this scroll belong to the Lord, but He has shared them with us so that His Fellowship may belong to us![11] The purpose of the knowledge is to draw the soul to His Spirit,[12] set our eyes on the Light,[13] turn our ears toward Him,[14] and place our hearts, minds, and wills firmly in His Care.[15] They are reminders of the requests we should be making,[16] the discussions we should be having,[17] and the goals and purpose of our salvation![18]

SO TALK TO HIM ABOUT ALL OF THESE THINGS![19]

---

[1] John 10:10; Luke 8:12; John 8:44; Acts 13:10; Hebrews 2:14; Revelation 12:9
[2] 1 Corinthians 13:13; Galatians 5:22
[3] Romans 8:31,38-39; Colossians 3:3; John 10:28-30
[4] Jeremiah 31:31-34; Ezekiel 37:26-27
[5] Revelation 12:11; 7:10-14; 15:3
[6] Revelation 12:7-17; John 12:31; 14:30; 16:11; 1 John 2:13; 4:4; 5:4-5
[7] Hosea 4:6; Jeremiah 5:21; 2 Corinthians 4:3-6
[8] 1 John 2:14; Romans 8:11; Ephesians 3:16; Colossians 1:11; John 17:3
[9] Revelation 3:20; Luke 12:36
[10] Psalm 68:19; 32:7; 1 Peter 5:7
[11] Deuteronomy 29:29; Matthew 13:11; Romans 16:25-26; 1 Corinthians 2:16
[12] Proverbs 1:7; 1:22,29; 2:5,10; 10:14; 22:12; 23:12; 24:5; Isaiah 11:2
[13] Matthew 6:22-23; Luke 11:34-36
[14] Hebrews 3;7,15; 4:7
[15] 1 Peter 5:7; Psalm 68:19; 32:7
[16] Romans 15:15; 1 Corinthians 4:17; 15:1; 2 Timothy 1:6; 2:14; 2 Peter 1:12; 3:1; Jude 1:5
[17] 1 Peter 4:11; Philippians 4:8-9
[18] Colossians 3:1-2; Matthew 16:23; Romans 8:4-6
[19] James 4:2b; 1 Peter 5:7; 1 Thessalonians 5:17

IN EVERYTHING, *INVITE HIM TO HELP YOU*[1] TO SEEK FIRST HIS KINGDOM AND HIS *RIGHTEOUSNESS* SO THAT "ALL THESE THINGS WILL BE ADDED TO YOU!"[2]

YOU ARE NOT ALONE!!![3]

HALLELUYAH! BLESS HIS HOLY NAME!

Yeshua is the Key to Victory![4] He is our means of conquest and our means of defense![5] He is the Objective and the Solution![6] He is the Weapon and the Reward![7] No one achieves victory except through Him, and in Him there is no defeat![8]

GLORY TO GOD! IN JESUS THERE IS NO DEFEAT![9]

JESUS BRINGS OUR KINGDOM,[10] AND OUR KINGDOM IS IN JESUS!

JESUS BRINGS OUR VICTORY,[11] AND OUR VICTORY IS IN JESUS![12]

JESUS BRINGS OUR PEACE,[13] AND OUR PEACE IS IN JESUS![14]

HALLELUYAH!

HALLELUYAH!

BLESS HIS HOLY NAME![15]

PRAISE GOD!

---

[1] Luke 11:9; Hebrews 4:16; James 1:5
[2] Matthew 6:33; Luke 12:31; Psalm 34:9; 37:19; 84:11; Isaiah 33:16; John 6:27
[3] John 14:18; Matthew 28:20
[4] 1 Corinthians 15:57; Romans 8:37; 1 John 5:4-5
[5] Romans 8:37; Isaiah 25:8; 1 Corinthians 15:57; 1 John 4:4; 5:4-5; Jude 1:24
[6] 2 Corinthians 3:18; Proverbs 4:18
[7] Hebrews 4:12; Revelation 22:12
[8] John 14:6; Acts 4:12; Hebrews 10:26
[9] Romans 8:37; Isaiah 25:8; 1 Corinthians 15:57; 1 John 4:4; 5:4-5; Jude 1:24
[10] Matthew 4:17; 13:11; Luke 9:2
[11] John 16:33d; Romans 8:37; 1 John 4:4; Colossians 2:10; 1 Corinthians 15:57
[12] Luke 10:19; 1 John 5:4-5; Psalm 91:13; Ezekiel 2:6; Mark 16:18; Romans 16:20
[13] John 14:27; 16:33a; 20:21; Acts 10:36
[14] John 16:33a; Ephesians 2:14
[15] Psalm 72:17; Luke 19:38

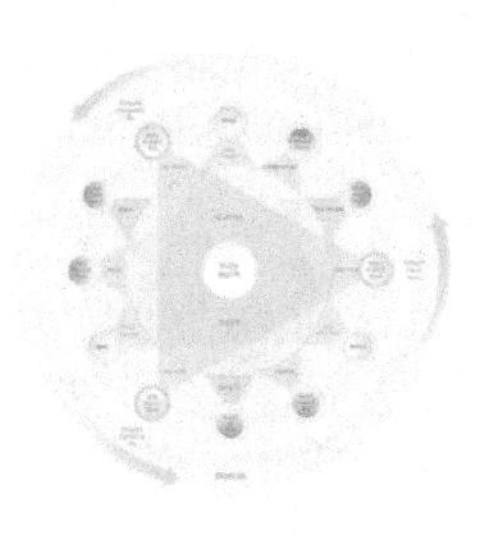

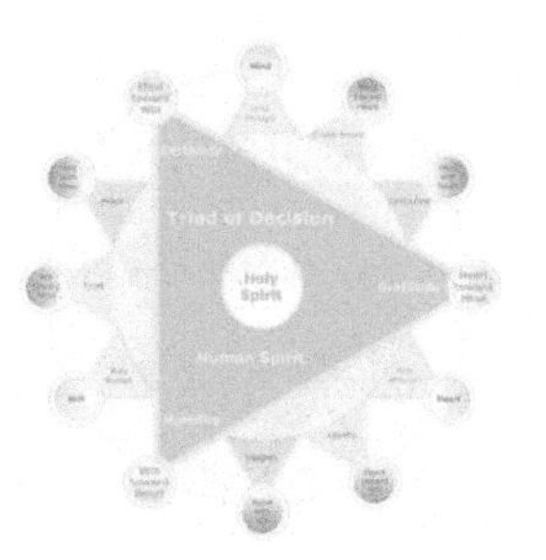

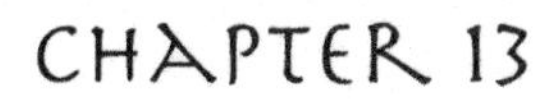

CHAPTER 13

THE SECOND JURISDICTION

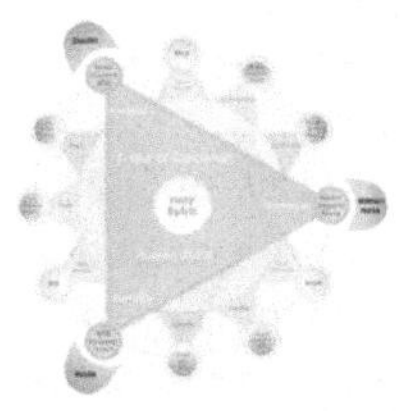

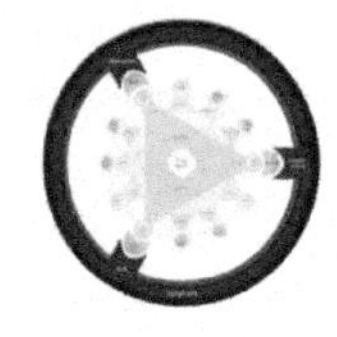

To understand the battle at the gates, one must also understand the jurisdictions of kingdoms.[1] Of primary importance is our awareness of the Second Jurisdiction, the Atonement,[2] and the First Jurisdiction.[3]

With the Contract of Creation, Yehovah gave authority to the inhabitants of Heaven for them to have the opportunity to wield real choices with significant ramifications.[4] These elohim were given authority based on their abilities,[5] and seventy among them were placed in charge as principalities in authority over the world:[6]

"And Yehovah revealed Himself to punish them for the work of the city and the tower which the sons of men[7] built. And Yehovah said, 'Look, the people are one, and their language is one. And they have considered doing this, and now they will not be restrained from doing whatever they imagine.' And Yehovah said to the seventy angels who stand before Him, 'Come, let us descend and commingle their language so that people cannot understand each other.' And the Word of Yehovah was revealed against the city, and with Him were seventy angels, who refer to

---

[1] John 18:36; Colossians 1:13; Matthew 8:12; Revelation 11:15; 16:10; Ephesians 2:2

[2] See Chapter 14 of this testimony.

[3] See Chapter 15 of this testimony.

[4] 2 Peter 2:4; Revelation 22:11; Genesis 3:14: Romans 1:28; Proverbs 1:29

[5] See Chapter 6 of this testimony.

[6] Psalm 82:1-8; Hebrews 2:5; Genesis 10:1-11:32

[7] The Hebrew Masoretic Text also reads בני האדם, meaning *sons of Adam.*

seventy nations, each having its own language and writing. And He dispersed them from there across the face of all the earth into seventy languages, and people no longer knew what each other were saying. So they fought against each other, and they stopped building the city."[1]

The rebellion of Heylel persuaded the allegiance of these ruling elohim,[2] and they stepped out of Yehovah's Jurisdiction of Righteousness to become spirits of unrighteousness.[3] This act has subjected them to a coming judgment that they will experience without partiality to their former honor.[4]

However, because Yehovah has patiently delayed opening the Contract of Creation to allow more time for the full number of His children to be born and mature,[5] the original authority given to the now fallen principalities is still active over all humans who remain under this Second Jurisdiction of the Law of Sin and Death.[6] Nevertheless, any person who receives Yeshua's invitation for salvation[7] is then laid down by baptism into His death and counted as *dead* to the Law of Sin and Death.[8] That person dies to the authority of sin[9] as well as that of the principalities[10] and is then risen into a new life by the same power that rose Yeshua from the dead.[11] Since the person has legally died[12] and been made into a new creature,[13] the new creature is no longer governed by nor answers to the jurisdiction of the Law of Sin and Death.[14] Instead, the New Covenant of Yeshua's Blood[15] is written on their hearts,[16] enabling them to walk according to the First

---

[1] Genesis 11:5-8, Targum Yerushalmi, my dynamic-equivalent translation of the Aramaic. See also the better-known and form-equivalent translation by J. W. Etheridge.
[2] Revelation 12:4,9; Psalm 82:1-2
[3] Psalm 82:3-5; Exodus 12:12
[4] Psalm 82:6-7; 2 Peter 2:4; Jude 1:6; Revelation 12:7-9
[5] Romans 11:25; Matthew 13:30
[6] Ephesians 2:2: Matthew 13:38
[7] Matthew 22:14; John 1:12
[8] Romans 6:4-7; 7:6; 2 Corinthians 5:17; Galatians 6:15; Ephesians 4:22-24
[9] Romans 6:2-14; Colossians 2:20
[10] Colossians 1:13; Isaiah 49:24-25; Matthew 12:29-30; Acts 26:18; Hebrews 2:14
[11] Romans 6:8-11; 2 Timothy 2:11; John 14:19; 2 Corinthians 13:4; Colossians 3:3
[12] Romans 6:2-14; Colossians 2:20
[13] 2 Corinthians 5:17; Galatians 6:15
[14] Romans 6:14; Galatians 3:23; 4:4-5; 5:18; John 8:36
[15] Luke 22:20; Hebrews 12:24; 13:20
[16] Romans 2:15; Hebrews 8:10

Jurisdiction of the Law of the Spirit[1] — the same Spirit Who works in them to will and to work according to His good purposes.[2]

So, while the sons of Adam were and still are subject to the Second Law of Sin and Death,[3] the redeemed are new creatures who have been given a new life governed by the First Law of Life and Peace.[4] They have died to one jurisdiction and entered another.[5]

Do we not know that each kingdom has its own law?[6] For kingdoms of the earth are defined by how they rule, and such rule is what constitutes their law.[7] Likewise, a spiritual kingdom is defined by its rule of law, and without law, there is no kingdom nor domain.[8]

Now, listen carefully because these understandings require spiritual discernment.[9] May those of you trusting in Yeshua receive the clarity of Yeshua's Mind, which has been given to you![10]

When the former inhabitants of Heaven left the First Jurisdiction of the Kingdom of Righteousness,[11] they became unrighteousness itself and consequently lawbreakers in every way.[12] They had been able to leave that jurisdiction through the legal agreement of the Contract of Creation and enter into its Second jurisdiction where they were permitted their own limited authority.[13] When they used their authority in the Second Jurisdiction to deceptively influence human beings, the same Contract also permitted the Creator equal influence, which He used to provide a means of rescue — He gave humanity His Law to help them identify, avoid, and be healed from deceit and its potential consequences.[14] Because of this, the dark spirits are limited in their ability to access or influence

---

[1] Jeremiah 31:33-34; Romans 7:6; 8:2; Galatians 5:18

[2] Philippians 2:13; Ephesians 2:4-5; John 6:65

[3] Romans 6:20-23; 1 Corinthians 15:56; 1 Timothy 1:9; 1 John 3:4

[4] 2 Corinthians 5:17; Romans 8:6-8

[5] Romans 7:4-6; 8:2; Galatians 2:19-20; 3:13; 5:18; Ephesians 2:15; Colossians 2:14

[6] Ephesians 2:2; John 18:36; Revelation 11:15

[7] Daniel 2:31-45; 7:15-28

[8] Isaiah 9:7; Psalm 103:19; Even the "lawless one" establishes his kingdom through his own law (2 Thessalonians 2:3-12; Revelation 13:11-18).

[9] 1 Corinthians 2:14; Romans 8:7

[10] 1 Corinthians 2:16; John 15:15; 16:13-15

[11] Revelation 12:4; 2 Peter 2:4

[12] Jude 1:6; Matthew 25:41; Luke 10:18; Revelation 12:7-8

[13] Colossians 2:15; Ephesians 1:21; 1 Corinthians 2:8; 11:10; Isaiah 14:14

[14] Romans 3:25b; Galatians 3:24

those who obey God.[1] Though the dark spirits are themselves unrighteous, they are restricted to His Law with its definitions, prescriptions, punishments, and principles as a means of claim for access to human souls.[2]

To utilize this law, the dark kingdom prowls about looking for whoever can be claimed under this jurisdiction of the Law of Sin and Death.[3] Since the acceptance of temptation is ultimately a potential death sentence,[4] each temptation by a dark spirit is like the destroyer sent into Egypt on the night of Passover, checking doors for access.[5] If the destroyer's access was unimpeded, then the life of that home's "firstborn" son was taken.[6] In other words, the actions that house would have produced in honor of the image of Yehovah were prevented from ever coming to pass. In the same way, when temptation is allowed to enter the unprotected soul of a person under the law today, that person will suffer the consequence of destruction in that area.[7]

Notice that the destroyer came to *everyone* in Egypt, yet the Hebrews were instructed how to *prevent* that spirit's entry.[8] Moses, who as an infant was given over to death in hope of salvation from God,[9] represented a person brought back from death itself[10] and was commanded by God to instruct the Hebrews that the entry of death could only be prevented by the sacrifice of an innocent lamb.[11] Since all people had been born into the invasive influence of sin and already lost perfect innocence,[12] the sacrifice of an innocent animal,[13] while incomplete, was used to prevent the entrance of physical death for that one night.[14] In other words, once a door had been transgressed by sin, the only way to prevent the entrance of death was to mark the door with the substituted death of an innocent life.[15]

---

[1] Galatians 3:10; Deuteronomy 28:1-68

[2] Revelation 12:10b; Job 1:9; 2:5; Zechariah 3:1-2; Luke 22:31; They do this in the same way that an unrighteous prosecutor could use a court system to convict others.

[3] 1 Peter 5:8; John 8:44; Ephesians 4:27; 6:11; Revelation 12:9; Zechariah 3:1

[4] Romans 5:12-19; 1 Corinthians 15:21

[5] Exodus 12:23; Revelation 6:1,4,5,8; 2 Samuel 24:15-16

[6] Exodus 12:29; Job 34:20; 1 Thessalonians 5:2-3

[7] Romans 8:13; Colossians 3:5-8; 1 Peter 2:11

[8] Exodus 12:22-23; Hebrews 11:28; Ezekiel 9:4,6

[9] Exodus 2:2-4; Acts 7:21

[10] Exodus 2:5-10; 1 Corinthians 10:2; Romans 6:4

[11] Exodus 12:13; Hebrews 11:28

[12] Romans 3:10; Psalm 14:2-3

[13] Hebrews 9:9-10; Psalm 40:6-7; Leviticus 4:32; 9:3; 14:10; 23:12

[14] Hebrews 11:28; Exodus 12:21-30

[15] Hebrews 9:16-22; Romans 7:2; Numbers 18:15

Because the sacrifice of a perfect *animal* is an incomplete substitution for the current sin of a *human* household, continued sacrifices were necessary for continuing sins.[1] But Yehovah had prepared a better solution and waited patiently for the perfect time to implement it.[2]

And His solution was Himself![3]

BLESSED BE YOUR NAME, YEHOVAH HAMASHIACH!!![4]

Glory to God! HalleluYah! Praise be to the Holy One for doing what no one else could do![5]

OUR GOD IS AN AWESOME GOD![6] HALLELUYAH!

MIGHTY IS OUR KING WHO CONQUERS![7] HALLELUYAH!

HOLY IS THE NAME OF YESHUA![8] HALLELUYAH!

HOLY! HOLY! HOLY! HOLY! HOLY![9]

LION OF THE TRIBE OF JUDAH![10] HALLELUYAH!

---

[1] Hebrews 9:25; Leviticus 16:2-34

[2] Hebrews 9:23; Colossians 2:17

[3] Hebrews 9:26; Titus 2:14; Ephesians 5:2

[4] Luke 2:11 – *Christ the Lord,* from the Greek Χριστὸς Κύριος, traditionally considered by readers of English to mean *Anointed Lord.* In Daniel 9:25 of the Greek Old Testament, the Hebrew word מָשִׁיחַ, pronounced "mah-shee-ach," meaning *messiah* or *anointed,* is translated into a form of Χριστὸς, pronounced "khris-tahs," also meaning *messiah* or *anointed*. Likewise, the Hebrew Name of God, *Yehovah,* is translated into Greek as both θεός, pronounced "they-awss" and meaning *God* or *Supreme* Deity (see how Matthew 4:4 translates Deuteronomy 8:3), and κύριος, pronounced "koo-ree-awss," which means *Lord, God, Supreme in Authority* (see how Matthew 4:7 translates Deuteronomy 6:16 and how Romans 15:11 translates Psalm 117:1). Therefore, though traditionally translated into English as *Christ the Lord,* a more Hebrew translation of Χριστὸς Κύριος would be *Yehovah the Messiah*. HALLELUYAH! OUR GOD CAME AND SAVED US! OUR GOD IS ONE! (Deuteronomy 6:4; Mark 12:29, John 10:30)

[5] Revelation 5:2-4; Daniel 7:28; Romans 7:24

[6] Exodus 15:11; Nehemiah 1:5; 9:32; Job 37:22

[7] Colossians 2:10; John 12:31; 16:11,33; Psalm 68:18; Romans 8:37; 1 John 4:4; 5:4

[8] Acts 4:12; Philippians 2:11

[9] Revelation 4:8; Isaiah 6:3; Exodus 15:11

[10] Revelation 5:5; Hosea 5:14

KING OF KINGS![1] GLORIOUS SAVIOR![2] HALLELUYAH!

HOLY IS HIS NAME![3] HALLELUYAH!

HOLY!!!!!!! HOLY!!!!!!! HOLY!!!!!!![4]

AMENNNNNNNNNNNN!!!!!!!!

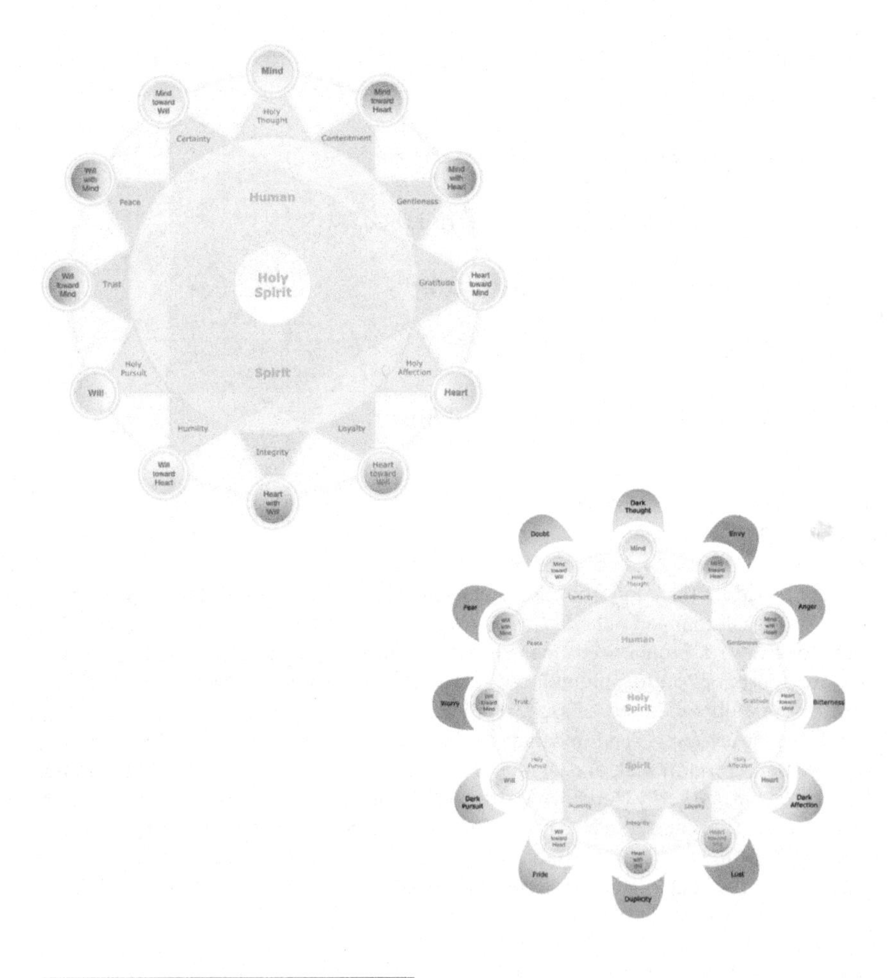

---

[1] Revelation 17:14; 19:17; 1 Timothy 6:15
[2] Matthew 19:28; Titus 2:13; 2 Peter 3:18; Jude 1:25
[3] Revelation 15:4; Luke 1:49; Psalm 99:3
[4] Revelation 4:8; Isaiah 6:3; Exodus 15:11

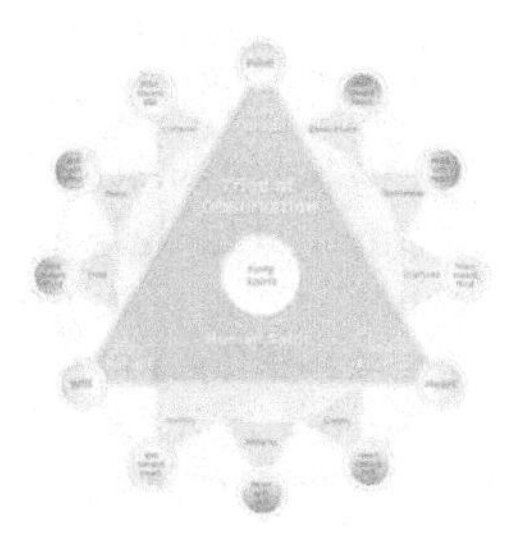

CHAPTER 14

THE COMPLETE INNOCENT ATONEMENT

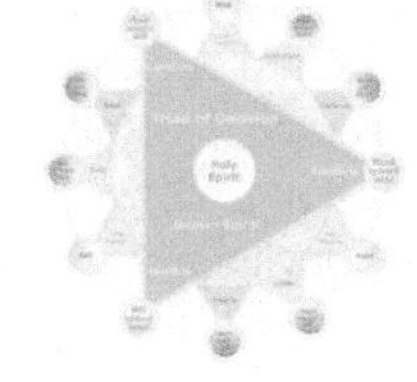

The Complete Atonement[1] provides a means of legal exit from the Second Jurisdiction[2] and a welcome entrance into the First Jurisdiction.[3]

From the beginning, Yehovah, Whose Name is a blended combination of the Hebrew words "He will be, He is, and He was,"[4] breathed His "Chay Neshamah,"[5] or Breath of Life, into a body He made from the dust of the earth, and that combination became a "Chay Nephesh,"[6] or a living soul.[7] The purpose of this soul was to exhibit the unseen Characteristics of Yehovah thoroughly.[8]

---

[1] Romans 3:25; 1 John 2:2; 4:10

[2] Romans 8:2; 6:18; John 8:36

[3] Romans 8:9-11; 2 Corinthians 5:1-4; John 4:14; 11:25-26; Colossians 3:3-4

[4] Yehovah is a portmanteau, or blend of words, of the three Hebrew being verbs for "He will be," "He is," and "He was." When all three words are said together quickly, they sound like "Yehovah": יהוה "yiheye" (He will be), הוה "hoveh" (He is), and היה "hayah" (He was). yihe<u>ye</u> + <u>hov</u>eh + hay<u>ah</u> = ye+hov+ah = "Yehovah," "He will be, He is, and He was."

[5] Genesis 2:7a – חַי, traditionally transliterated as *chay* and pronounced "khah-ee," meaning *alive, living,* and נשמה, pronounced "neh-shah-mah," meaning *divine breath, wind, inspiration, intellect.*

[6] Genesis 2:7b – חַי, traditionally transliterated as *chay* and pronounced "khah-ee," meaning *alive, living,* and נפש, pronounced "nahf-esh," meaning *a living being, soul, creature, life, person, mind, passion, desire, appetite.*

[7] Genesis 2:7,19; 1:21,24; 9:10,12,15-16

[8] Romans 8:29; Matthew 12:50; 25:40; Colossians 1:15-18; Revelation 1:5-6

Having also been created by Yehovah, animals also have a nephesh.[1] But they were not made in the full image of Yehovah and could not fully exhibit the unseen Characteristics of Yehovah.[2] Their nephesh is known as "nephesh habehamit," or "the animal soul," and it references that breath that makes a physical body live.[3] Human beings share in this aspect of the soul, and so the sacrifice of one of these innocent animal souls provided for protection for the same aspect of flesh life in a human soul.[4] In other words, the substitutionary sacrifice of the body of an innocent animal allowed for the body of a human to continue to live.[5] And this is not difficult to understand. Because ever since the fall of our first parents from their perfect existence in the garden, we have killed animals[6] and used their flesh to preserve our flesh to this very day.[7] This was necessary because death entered into our parents.[8] And though they had previously enjoyed bountiful life by eating seed-bearing plants and fruit,[9] the entrance of death required our parents to take sustenance from the innocent.[10] In life there is no darkness at all.[11] Because darkness had entered into their own bodies, our parents had to consume life from bodies in which there was no darkness. Therefore, having mercy on them,

---

[1] Ecclesiastes 3:19; Genesis 1:30; 7:15,22

[2] Genesis 1:24-25; 1 Corinthians 15:39; 2 Peter 2:12; Jude 1:10

[3] English translations of the Hebrew have greatly hindered this understanding by translating the word "nephesh" as *life* or *creature* in Genesis 1:20,21,24, and 30 when in reference to animals but as *soul* or *living being* in Genesis 2:7 when in reference to a man.

[4] Genesis 22:13; Hebrews 13:11

[5] Deuteronomy 15:21; Leviticus 22:20; Malachi 1:7-8

[6] Genesis 3:21; 4:4 – Notice that Yehovah made coverings of *skin* and that Abel offered *fat portions.* Abel's slaying of the animal is evidence that he was not keeping flocks merely for milk or animal hair.

[7] Genesis 7:2 – Here used before the flood, the term "clean" describes animals that are fit for consumption (Leviticus 11:2) and, when *sacrificed,* represent an *offering* to Yehovah of something that could have *otherwise been consumed* (else any animal could have been captured and killed as a ceremonial substitution). Notice throughout the Scriptures that, while all clean animals could be eaten, not all were used for sacrifice (Exodus 12:5). Notice also that after the flood, Yehovah announced that *everything that lived and moved* would be food for humanity (Genesis 9:3). However, He maintained restrictions for the diet of Israel (Leviticus 11:2).

[8] Genesis 2:17; 3:6

[9] Genesis 1:29; 2:16

[10] Genesis 4:4; 9:3; Numbers 6:14; Leviticus 9:2; Romans 5:12

[11] John 1:4; 1 John 1:5

Yehovah made garments of skin to clothe our parents[1] and allowed them to kill and eat life.[2]

Since they were made in the image of Yehovah, human beings have another aspect of the soul, known as the "nephesh ha'elokit," or "the godly soul," for which an animal sacrifice cannot substitute.[3] In other words, an animal sacrifice and its consumption could supply life to the human body but not to the godly aspect of the soul made in the image of Yehovah[4] (This is why people such as the wayward Pharisees could physically continue to walk on the earth while spiritually dead inside).[5]

The solution to this need for godly life could only be found in its Source, Yeshua, Who is the very Soul of Yehovah,[6] the Godly One[7] Who was, is, and is to come.[8] In Him is Life.[9] To give us this Life,[10] He made a body for Himself from a woman and came to walk the earth in human flesh.[11] This is what he meant by,

"'Look, I am sending My messenger, and he will prepare the way before Me. Then suddenly the Lord you are seeking will come to His Temple, even the Messenger

---

[1] Genesis 3:21; 2 Corinthians 5:2-3

[2] Genesis 4:4; 9:3; Deuteronomy 12:15; Acts 10:13; John 6:51; Notice that though there is residual blood in slain meat, excess blood must be poured out (Leviticus 17:13). This is because the life of the animal is in the blood, and the shedding of that blood is what substitutes the animal's death for our own (Leviticus 17:11-14). This atonement is what preserves the "animal" aspect of our soul. Our flesh is further sustained by the consumption of the residual soulical life of the animal flesh, that is, the residual benefits of that life that remain until death produces decay (Leviticus 7:24).

[3] Hebrews 10:4; Psalm 50:8-12; Isaiah 1:11-15; 66:3; Jeremiah 6:20; 7:21-22; Hosea 6:6; Amos 5:21-22; Micah 6:6-8; Mark 12:33

[4] Hebrews 9:9-10; 10:11; Psalm 40:6-7; 51:16-17; Galatians 3:21

[5] Matthew 23:27; Isaiah 58:1-10; Acts 23:3

[6] Colossians 2:9; Isaiah 7:14; Matthew 1:23; John 10:30,38; 14:9-10,20

[7] 1 John 2:29; John 15:1-6; Matthew 7:18-19

[8] John 1:1-3; Revelation 1:8; John 8:23,58; 10:30; 14:10

[9] John 1:4; 4:14; 5:21,24; 6:27,33,48,51,63; 8:12; 10:28; 11:25; 14:6; 17:3

[10] John 10:15,17; 15:13; Isaiah 53:4-10; Daniel 9:26; Zechariah 13:7; Matthew 20:28

[11] "And I will put enmity between you and the woman, and between your offspring and hers; He will crush your head, and you will bruise His heel" (Genesis 3:15). Notice that this early prophecy about Yeshua refers to Him as the *woman's* Seed.

of the covenant, in Whom you delight. See, He is coming,' says יהוה of Heavenly Armies."[1]

Notice Who is speaking![2] It is Yehovah of Hosts, the Supreme Creator, through Whom and for Whom all things were made![3] This is why Paul said about Yeshua, Jesus Christ,

"Because by Him were created all things that are in the heavens and on earth, visible and invisible, whether thrones or rulerships or principalities or authorities – all have been created through Him and for Him. And He is before all, and in Him all things hold together. And He is the Head of the body, the assembly. And being from the beginning, He is also the First-born from the dead, so that He could become first in all. Because in Him all the Completeness was well pleased to permanently dwell, and through Him to completely reconcile all unto Himself, whether on earth or in the heavens, having made peace through the Blood of His Cross."[4]

Understand then that those persecuting and abusing Jesus Christ were persecuting and abusing the Soul of Yehovah Himself;[5] they were piercing the Hands of the very One Who made them![6] Since Yeshua was not a descendant of a human male,[7] He was not an Heir of the inheritance of man's deeds.[8] He was not legally under the Second Jurisdiction.[9] So, when the principalities of this world brought their jurisdiction of death against Yeshua,[10] they were bringing the processes of death against Yehovah Himself.[11] And even though He was not under those principles, He still lived a perfectly innocent life according to the principles

---

[1] Malachi 3:1 – יהוה is the Hebrew Name *Yehovah* that most English translations render as LORD even though it is His proper Name (Isaiah 42:8). Such a practice causes some verses to read almost nonsensically. For example, Psalm 105:1 says, "Give thanks to יהוה [not *to the LORD*]! Call upon His *Name*, Make known His deeds among the peoples!" How can they not translate His Name in a verse that *commands* us to call on His Name? (Mark 7:6)

[2] See also Luke 1:76-79; Revelation 3:14

[3] Genesis 1:1; Nehemiah 9:6; Hebrews 11:3; Jeremiah 32:17; Isaiah 40:26; 44:24; 45:18; Proverbs 16:4; Psalm 33:6; 1 Chronicles 29:11; John 1:3

[4] Colossians 1:16-20

[5] Colossians 2:9; Isaiah 7:14; Matthew 1:23; John 10:30,38; 14:9-10,20

[6] John 1:3,10; Jeremiah 10:11-12; Hebrews 1:2

[7] 1 John 3:5; Matthew 1:23

[8] Romans 5:12-19; 1 Corinthians 15:21

[9] Genesis 3:17-19,22-24

[10] Mark 15:20; John 19:6,15

[11] John 5:19; 12:45

of this world.[1] Therefore, when they nailed Yeshua to the cross to die according to that jurisdiction, they were illegally killing the Soul of God,[2] the Author of Life,[3] through Whom all things were created and have their being![4]

So we see that, though the principalities did their best to bring the fullness of their God-given authority and principles against Yehovah to take His Authority for themselves,[5] they failed to realize that He was not under their authority.[6] He was and is the perfectly innocent One Whose very Life holds *all* things together.[7] His Life was in all things![8] When they killed His human body, they killed both the "animal" and "godly" aspects of His Soul, but they could not kill His Existence or His Spirit,[9] Who is and was and is to come,[10] Who gives Life to all things, even to all existence itself forever, amen![11]

It is precisely because of Who Yeshua was and is that we can be saved.[12] For if a man under the Second Jurisdiction were to die for a man, then only the life worthy of a man under the Second Jurisdiction could be substituted and accomplished.[13] But because the Godly Soul of Yehovah became a man and *died* for us, the Eternal Life[14] worthy of the Soul of Yehovah can be substituted and accomplished for us![15]

This was legally possible because the Soul of Yehovah was never subject to the Second Jurisdiction but was under the higher Jurisdiction of Righteousness.[16] Nevertheless, when walking on the earth, Yeshua took it upon Himself to abide by

---

1 Luke 23:13-16; 2 Corinthians 5:21; 1 Peter 2:22; 1 John 3:5
2 Matthew 11:27; 1 Peter 2:22; Acts 3:15; John 6:46; 10:30; 14:6,9
3 Acts 3:15; John 1:4,10,14; 5:26; 10:28; 11:25-26; 14:6; 17:2; 1 John 5:11-12,20; Romans 8:1-2; 1 Corinthians 15:45; Colossians 3:3-4
4 Colossians 1:16; Revelation 4:11
5 Matthew 21:38; Psalm 2:2-8; Mark 12:7-8
6 John 14:30; 1 John 3:5-8; Luke 1:35; Hebrews 7:26; 1 Peter 1:19
7 Colossians 1:17; 1 Samuel 2:8; Isaiah 44:6; John 1:3; 1 Corinthians 8:6
8 Hebrews 1:2; 1 Corinthians 8:6; John 1:3
9 Acts 2:24; 3:15; John 2:19; Hebrews 2:14; Revelation 1:18
10 Revelation 1:4,8; Exodus 3:14; Psalm 90:2; Isaiah 41:4; Micah 5:2; John 1:1
11 Acts 17:28; Job 12:10; Psalm 36:9; Hebrews 1:3
12 Hebrews 2:17; Philippians 2:7-8
13 Hebrews 9:25; Exodus 30:10
14 John 1:4; 4:14; 5:21,24; 6:27,33,48,51,63; 8:12; 10:28; 11:25; 14:6; 17:3
15 Hebrews 9:26; Isaiah 53:1-12
16 "So that the Law becomes our tutor to bring us to Christ, that we might be justified by faith" (Galatians 3:24); Obviously, the Law was not a tutor to bring Christ to Himself!

the rules of the Second Jurisdiction to reveal the fullness of His Glory.[1] Since He had lived His life perfectly obedient in spirit, soul, and deeds,[2] the sufferings and death inflicted upon Him by those claiming authority were unwarranted and unjust according to the jurisdiction.[3] Moreover, because He was not even subject to the Second Jurisdiction, all actions taken against Him were illegal and therefore overturned by the greater Authority of the Jurisdiction of Righteousness.[4] Because of the *undeserved* suffering and death He received within the Second Jurisdiction, Yeshua has been granted the authority by the Jurisdiction of Righteousness to give *undeserved* ownership of those sufferings and that death to whomever He chooses within the Second Jurisdiction.[5] And since anyone who receives His death also dies to the governance of the Second Jurisdiction,[6] they exit that jurisdiction retaining His entire righteous life of suffering as their right to inherit all of the promises given under the First Jurisdiction.[7] Because of this, Yeshua has the legal authority to make them citizens and priests of His Jurisdiction of Righteousness[8] and welcome them into the Kingdom of Heaven, even while they still dwell on the earth![9]

Do you who have ears hear?[10] HalleluYah! We can enter Heaven even while we still dwell in Creation![11] Glory to Yehovah! We don't have to wait to enter His Rest![12]

PRAISE BE TO OUR SAVIOR, WHO HAS RESCUED US FROM THE DOMINION OF DARKNESS![13] HALLELUYAH!

LET ME TELL YOU ABOUT JESUS!

---

[1] Philippians 2:5-8; Hebrews 10:7-9; John 15:10

[2] 1 Peter 1:19; 2:22; Hebrews 4:15; Isaiah 53:9; 1 John 3:5

[3] 1 Peter 2:22-23; Luke 23:41,47; Isaiah 53:9; Matthew 27:4,19,23-24; John 8:46

[4] "For in Christ all the fullness of the Deity lives in bodily form" (Colossians 2:9); Obviously, God did not fail to live up to Himself and therefore remained the Standard of Goodness which presides over and defines Heaven. His Goodness will not allow injustice to prevail even if that injustice is against Himself; Proverbs 11:21; 17:15; Exodus 34:7

[5] Hebrews 9:15; Matthew 10:28; Romans 6:3-4; Galatians 2:20

[6] Romans 7:4-6; 8:2; Galatians 2:19-20; 3:13; 5:18; Ephesians 2:15; Colossians 2:14

[7] 2 Corinthians 1:19-22; Acts 13:38-39; Galatians 3:22

[8] Revelation 1:6: Philippians 3:20

[9] Luke 17:20-21; Matthew 12:28; John 3:3; 18:36; Colossians 1:13

[10] Matthew 11:15; Mark 4:9,23; Luke 8:8; Revelation 2:7,11,17,29; 3:6,13,22

[11] Matthew 7:13; 13:32; Mark 12:34; Luke 17:20

[12] Hebrews 4:10-11; Matthew 7:13; 11:28; 2 Peter 1:10-11

[13] Colossians 1:13; Isaiah 49:24-25; Matthew 12:29-30; Acts 26:18; Hebrews 2:14

THERE ARE NO BROKEN BACKS IN JESUS,[1] BUT THERE'S STRENGTH![2]
THERE ARE NO RUNNY NOSES IN JESUS,[3] BUT THERE'S EASY BREATHING![4]

THERE IS NO POVERTY IN JESUS,[5] BUT THERE'S PROVISION![6]

THERE IS NO CONDEMNATION IN JESUS,[7] BUT THERE'S BLESSING![8]

THERE IS NO ACCUSATION IN JESUS,[9] BUT THERE'S JUSTIFICATION![10]

THERE IS NO BAD NEWS OF ANY KIND,[11] BUT THERE'S INFINITE GOOD NEWS IN JESUS!!!!!!!![12]

DID YOU HEAR THAT????

THERE'S NO *BAD NEWS* IN THE *GOOD NEWS*!!!!!![13]

BLESSED BE YOUR NAME, YEHOVAH, OUR MESSIAH!!!!!!!!![14]

---

[1] Psalm 22:17; John 19:36
[2] Proverbs 3:8; 4:22; 16:24
[3] Matthew 8:17; Isaiah 53:4-5; 1 Peter 2:24
[4] Isaiah 42:5; Genesis 2:7; Job 12:10; 33:4; Acts 17:25
[5] Revelation 2:9; 2 Corinthians 6:10
[6] Romans 8:32; Psalm 84:11; 1 Corinthians 2:12; 3:21-23
[7] Romans 4:7-8; 5:1; 8:1; Isaiah 54:17; John 3:18; 5:24; Galatians 3:13
[8] Romans 1:11-12; 15:29; Ephesians 1:3; 3:8,19; 4:13
[9] Revelation 12:10; Job 1:9; 2:5; Zechariah 3:1-2; Luke 22:31
[10] Romans 3:24; 5:1,9,16; 1 Corinthians 6:11; Titus 3:5-7
[11] Matthew 11:5; James 1:17; John 1:9; 1 John 1:5; Revelation 21:23; 22:5; Isaiah 60:19
[12] Acts 10:36; Ephesians 3:20; 1 Corinthians 2:9
[13] Mark 1:15; Matthew 9:35; Luke 4:43; 16:16; Hebrews 4:2
[14] Luke 2:11 – *Christ the Lord,* from the Greek Χριστὸς Κύριος, traditionally considered by readers of English to mean *Anointed Lord.* In Daniel 9:25 of the Greek Old Testament, the Hebrew word מָשִׁיחַ, pronounced "mah-shee-ach," meaning *messiah* or *anointed,* is translated into a form of Χριστὸς, pronounced "khris-tahs," also meaning *messiah* or *anointed*. Likewise, the Hebrew Name of God, *Yehovah,* is translated into Greek as both θεός, pronounced "they-awss" and meaning *God* or *Supreme* Deity (see how Matthew 4:4 translates Deuteronomy 8:3), and κύριος, pronounced "koo-ree-awss," which means *Lord, God, Supreme in Authority* (see how Matthew 4:7 translates Deuteronomy 6:16 and how

HALLELUYAAAAAAAAAAAAAAAAAAAAAAAAAAAAH!!!!!!!!!!!!!!

HALLELUYAAAAAAAAAAAAAAAAAAAAAAAAAAAAH!!!!!!!!!!!!!!

HALLELUUUUUUUUUUYAAAAAAAAAAAAAAAAAAAAAAAAAAH!!!!!!!!!!!!!!

Romans 15:11 translates Psalm 117:1). Therefore, though traditionally translated into English as *Christ the Lord,* a more Hebrew translation of Χριστὸς Κύριος would be *Yehovah the Messiah*. HALLELUYAH! OUR GOD CAME AND SAVED US! OUR GOD IS ONE! (Deuteronomy 6:4; Mark 12:29, John 10:30)

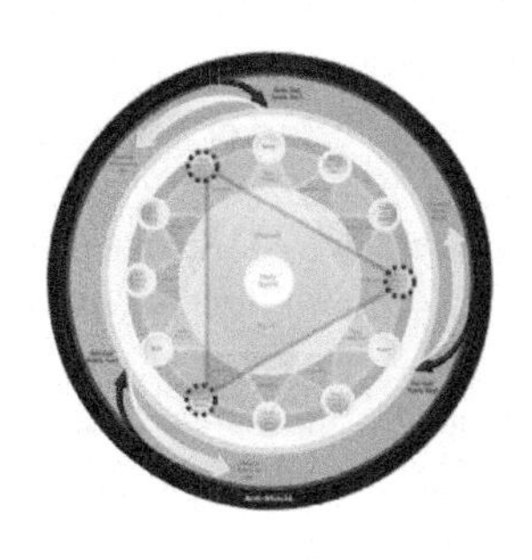

CHAPTER 15

THE FIRST JURISDICTION

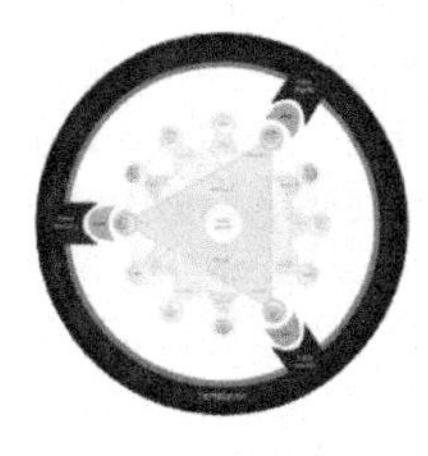

By means of His Blood, Yeshua has granted us citizenship and priesthood in the Jurisdiction of Righteousness.[1] He has delivered us from the Second Jurisdiction of the Law of Sin and Death,[2] but many disciples do not understand these things well.[3]

Father, thank you for increasing knowledge so that Your children may be preserved in these last days![4] Your Wisdom is Great![5] Your Kindness Generous![6] Thank You for revealing these things so that we may agree with You and share in Your Victory![7] We ask You for the Holy Spirit without limit![8] Let Your Wisdom guide us![9] Let Your Knowledge renew us![10] HalleluYah! Praise be to the Father of all good gifts![11] HalleluYah! Amen!

---

1 Hebrews 10:9,19; Philippians 3:20

2 Romans 8:2; 6:18; John 8:36

3 Hebrews 5:12-13; 1 Corinthians 3:1-3

4 Daniel 12:4; Acts 2:17; Hebrews 1:2; 2 Timothy 3:1; James 5:3; 2 Peter 3:3

5 Luke 11:31; 9:35; Isaiah 9:6-7; Colossians 1:15-19; James 1:5; 7:12

6 Ephesians 2:7; Matthew 20:15; Titus 3:6; James 1:5

7 John 15:4; 1 Corinthians 15:57; Romans 8:37; 1 John 5:4-5

8 John 3:34; 7:37-39; 14:12

9 Matthew 12:42; Luke 9:35; Isaiah 9:6-7; Colossians 1:15-19; James 1:5; 7:12

10 Romans 12:2; Ephesians 4:22-24; Colossians 1:21-22; 3:10; Titus 3:5

11 James 1:17; John 1:9; 1 John 1:5; Revelation 21:23; 22:5; Isaiah 60:19

Now, Moses told us that a prophet like Him would come to Whom everyone would have to listen or risk being completely cut off from his people.[1]

Jeremiah told us that Yehovah was going to give us a New Covenant that was not like the one He gave us in Egypt but would instead be written on our hearts.[2]

This Prophet is Yeshua, and the New Covenant is that which has been given to us in His Blood.[3]

HalleluYah!

Today, many believe that when Yeshua was speaking the Sermon on the Mount,[4] He was explaining the meaning of the Law as given through Moses from the mountain of Yehovah.[5] However, He was not explaining the former covenant but rather revealing a greater one![6] For Moses gave us a law as a caretaker to preserve us until we could meet our Messiah.[7] But when our Righteous King came, He was able to deliver the full revelation of the greater Law of the Heart because He alone was perfect in heart![8] The purpose of the Law given through Moses in the desert[9] was to lead us *to* the Messiah,[10] but the purpose of the Law given through the Messiah in the Spirit[11] is to free us from sin.[12]

Let us look at the Ten Commandments as given through Moses[13] and see how they have been surpassed by the King of Righteousness:

---

1 Deuteronomy 18:15-19; Acts 3:23
2 Jeremiah 31:33-34; Romans 7:6; 8:2; Galatians 5:18
3 Luke 22:20; 2 Corinthians 3:6; Hebrews 8:6; 9:15; 12:24
4 Matthew 5:1-7:29; Luke 6:20-49
5 Exodus 19:16; Hebrews 12:18
6 In Matthew 5:21,27,31,33,38, and 43, Yeshua says some version of "You have heard it said..." and in Matthew 5:22,28,32,34,39, and 44 Yeshua follows with "But I say to you..."; He is not explaining an old law but giving a *greater* one (Hebrews 3:3), just as the law given to Moses (Exodus 24:12) was greater than the law given to Adam (Genesis 1:26-30; 2:16-17; 3:16-19).
7 Galatians 3:24-25; 4:2-3; Romans 7:7; Colossians 2:17; Hebrews 7:11,18-19; 10:1
8 1 Peter 2:22; 1 John 3:5; 2 Corinthians 5:21; Hebrews 7:26
9 Exodus 19:2; Acts 7:38; Galatians 4:24-25
10 Galatians 3:24-25; 4:2-3; Romans 7:7; Colossians 2:17; Hebrews 7:11,18-19; 10:1
11 Galatians 4:24-31; 1 Corinthians 10:11
12 James 1:25; 2:12; Romans 7:6; 8:2-4; Galatians 3:2-5; 5:18
13 Exodus 20:1-17

1. Moses: "Do not have other gods before Me."[1]

1a. Yeshua; "Anyone who is a friend to their father or mother more than Me is not worthy of Me; anyone who is a friend to their son or daughter more than Me is not worthy of Me. Whoever does not take up their cross and follow Me in the same way is not worthy of Me. Whoever finds their life will lose it, and whoever loses their life on account of Me will find it."[2]

2. Moses: "Do not make for yourself an idol in the form of anything in heaven above, or on the earth beneath, or in the waters below. Do not bow down to them in worship or serve them; for I, Yehovah your God, am a jealous God, punishing the children for the sin of the parents to the third and fourth generation of those who hate Me, but showing kindness to a thousand generations of those who love Me and keep My commandments.[3]

2a. Yeshua: "Not everyone who says to Me, 'Lord, Lord,'[4] will enter the Kingdom of Heaven, but only the one who does the will of My Father Who is in Heaven. Many will say to Me on that day, 'Lord, Lord, did we not prophesy in Your Name, eject demons in Your Name, and in Your Name perform many miracles?' Then I will tell them plainly, 'I never knew you at any time. Depart from Me, you who practice lawlessness!'"[5]

---

[1] Exodus 20:3

[2] Matthew 10:37-39

[3] Exodus 20:4-6

[4] In Matthew 4:4, Yeshua quotes Deuteronomy 8:3 using the Greek θεός, pronounced "they-awss" and meaning *God* or *Supreme Deity*, to translate the Hebrew Name of God, *Yehovah*. In Matthew 4:7, Yeshua quotes Deuteronomy 6:16 and uses the Greek Κύριος, pronounced "koo-ree-awss" and meaning *Supreme Authority* or *Master,* to translate the Hebrew *Yehovah,* and He uses θεός to translate the Hebrew *Elohim*, meaning *Supreme God.* In Matthew 4:10, He again translates *Yehovah your Elohim* as *Κύριον τὸν Θεόν,* or what has been traditionally translated into English as *the Lord your God.* Therefore, let the reader understand that, when Yeshua spoke and repeated the word Κύριος in reference to Himself, He most definitely did so to an audience that understood the title represented His Divinity (Deuteronomy 6:4; Mark 12:29, John 10:30).

[5] Matthew 7:23

3. Moses: "Do not misuse the Name of Yehovah your God, for Yehovah will not hold anyone guiltless who misuses His Name."[1]

3a. Yeshua: "Therefore I tell you, every kind of sin and blasphemy can be forgiven, but blasphemy against the Spirit will not be forgiven. And whoever speaks a word against the Son of Man will be forgiven, but anyone who speaks against the Holy Spirit will not be forgiven, either in this age or in the age to come."[2]

4. Moses: "Remember the Sabbath day, to keep it holy. For six days you may labor and do all your work, but the seventh day is a Sabbath to Yehovah your God. On that day do no work, neither you, nor your son or daughter, nor your male or female servant, nor your animals, nor any foreigner residing within your gates. Because in six days Yehovah made the heavens and the earth, the sea, and all that is in them, but He rested on the seventh day. Therefore Yehovah blessed the Sabbath Day and made it holy."[3]

4a. Yeshua: "Come to Me, all you who are exhausted and burdened, and I will give you rest. Take My yoke upon you and learn from Me, because I am gentle and humble in heart, and you will find rest for your souls. For My yoke is easy and My burden is light."[4]

And this is what was meant by,

"For if Joshua had given them rest, God would not have spoken further about another day. Therefore, there remains a Sabbath-rest for the people of God; because anyone who enters God's rest also rests from their works, just as God did

---

[1] Exodus 20:7 – The word translated "misuse" is שוא, pronounced "shav," and conveys the sense of *desolating, evil, destructive*; *to ruin*; *to use falsely or deceptively.* In this context, it specifically means to not swear or testify *falsely* by His Name. For example, do not "swear to God" that this or that is true if you know it is not (Leviticus 19:12; Zechariah 5:4).

[2] Matthew 12:31-32; In other words, active blasphemy, or "vilification," of the Holy Spirit, Who bears the fruit of Goodness itself (Galatians 5:22), *will not be ignored now or at the Judgment.* That is, no one can vilify Goodness itself and be proclaimed innocent. And if someone dies having not repented from vilifying Goodness, they cannot be proclaimed innocent at the Final Judgment. However, if someone *repents* from blaspheming the Holy Spirit, they are *already* forgiven (Colossians 2:13; 1 John 1:7-9; Acts 13:26-41). HalleluYah!

[3] Exodus 20:8-11

[4] Matthew 11:28-30

from His. Therefore, let us endeavor to enter that rest, so that no one will perish by imitating their example of disbelief."[1]

5. Moses: "Honor your father and your mother, so that you may live long in the land Yehovah your God is giving you."[2]

5a. Yeshua: "But I tell you, love your enemies and pray for those who persecute you, that you may be children of your Father in Heaven. He makes his sun rise on the evil and the good, and sends rain on the righteous and the unrighteous. If you love those who love you, what reward do you have? Don't even the tax collectors do that? And if you greet only those who are close to you, what are you doing more than others? Don't even the worldly do that? Therefore, be perfect as your Heavenly Father is Perfect."[3]

6. Moses: "Do not murder."[4]

6a. Yeshua: "You have heard that it was said to the original audience, 'Do not murder, and anyone who murders will be accountable to justice.' But I tell you that anyone angry with a brother or sister will be accountable to justice. Again, anyone who says to a brother or sister, 'You're worthless,'[5] is accountable to the council. And anyone who says, 'You're stupid!'[6] will be in danger of the fire of Hell. Therefore, if you are offering your gift at the altar and remember in that place that your brother or sister has something against you, leave your gift there in front of the altar. First go and renew your friendship them; then come and offer your gift. Reconcile quickly with your adversary while you are still together on the way toward justice, or your adversary may hand you over to the judge, and the judge may hand you over to the bailiff, and you may be thrown into prison. I assure you, you will not get out until you have paid the last penny."[7]

---

[1] Hebrews 4:8-11

[2] Exodus 20:12

[3] Matthew 5:44-48

[4] Exodus 20:13

[5] *Worthless* from the Greek ῥακά, pronounced "rah-kah'," meaning *worthless, empty-headed,* or *senseless.*

[6] *Stupid* from the Greek μωρός, pronounced "moh-raws'," meaning *stupid, dull, absurd, foolish, impious,* or *godless.*

[7] Matthew 5:21-26

7. Moses: "Do not commit adultery."[1]

7a. Yeshua: "You have heard that it was said, 'Do not commit adultery.' But I tell you that anyone who looks at a woman lustfully has already committed adultery with her in his heart. If your right eye causes you to sin, tear it out and throw it away. It is better for you to lose one part of your body than for your whole body to be thrown into Hell. And if your right hand causes you to sin, cut it off and throw it away. It is better for you to lose one part of your body than for your whole body to go into Hell."[2]

8. Moses: "Do not steal."[3]

8a. Yeshua: "Do not amass for yourselves treasures on earth, where moths and corrosion destroy, and where thieves break in and steal. But amass for yourselves treasures in Heaven, where moths and corrosion do not destroy, and where thieves do not break in and steal. Because where your treasure is, there your heart will be also. The eye is the lamp of the body. If your eyes are focused, your whole body will be full of light. But if your eyes are diseased, your whole body will be full of darkness. If then the light within you is darkness, how great is that darkness! No one can serve two lords. Either you will hate the one and love the other, or you will be devoted to the one and think little of the other. You cannot serve both God and money."[4]

9. Moses: "Do not testify falsely about other people."[5]

9a. Yeshua: "Do not judge, so that you too may avoid judgment. Because with the judgment you use to judge others, you will be judged, and with the measure you use to measure others, it will be measured to you. Why do you look at the chaff in your brother's eye and not consider the timber in your own eye? How can you say to your brother, 'Let me take the chaff out of your eye,' while there is a timber in your own eye? Hypocrite! First take the timber out of your own eye, and then you will see clearly to remove the chaff from your brother's eye."[6]

---

[1] Exodus 20:14
[2] Matthew 5:27-30
[3] Exodus 20:15
[4] Matthew 6:19-24
[5] Exodus 20:16
[6] Matthew 7:1-5

10. Moses: "Do not desire your neighbor's house. Do not desire your neighbor's spouse, male or female servant, ox or donkey, or anything that belongs to your neighbor."[1]

10a. Yeshua: "This is why I tell you not to worry about your life—what you will eat or drink—or about your body—what you will wear. Isn't life more than food, and the body more than clothes? Look at the birds of the air; they do not sow or harvest or fill storehouses, and yet your Heavenly Father feeds them. Are you not more valuable than they? Can any one of you add anything to your life by worrying? And why do you worry about clothes? Consider how the lilies of the field grow; they don't do any work or spin fibers into yarn. Yet I tell you that not even Solomon in all his glory was dressed like one of these. But if that is how God clothes the vegetation of the field, which is fresh today and tomorrow is thrown into the baking oven, will He not much more clothe you—you of brief faith? So do not worry by saying, 'What will we eat?' or 'What will we drink?' or 'What will we wear?' Because the worldly run after all these things, and your Heavenly Father knows that you need all of them. But seek first His Kingdom and his Righteousness, and all these things will be added to you as well. So do not worry about tomorrow, because tomorrow will worry about itself. Each day has enough of its own trouble to manage."[2]

We see then that in every way the Decalogue (the Ten Commandments) has not only been fulfilled but also *far surpassed* by the Law of Yeshua![3]

HALLELUYAH!

This is what He meant by,

"I tell you this because unless your righteousness surpasses that of the Pharisees and the teachers of the law, you will certainly not enter the Kingdom of Heaven!"[4]

So then, anyone who wishes to keep the Decalogue must also keep the Law of Yeshua, or they will in no way enter the Kingdom of Heaven.[5] For just as the people fleeing Egypt were no longer measured by the commands given in the garden to Adam, we also are no longer measured by the Decalogue given in Egypt but rather

---

[1] Exodus 20:17

[2] Matthew 6:25-34

[3] Romans 8:1-17; Matthew 5:20; 2 Corinthians 3:10; Ephesians 3:19; Philippians 3:8

[4] Matthew 5:20

[5] James 2:10-13; Matthew 5:18-19; Galatians 3:10

by the far greater Law of Yeshua.[1] The Ten Commandments stand as the Second Jurisdiction, but those who wish to enter the Kingdom of Heaven must abide by its commandments, the commandments of the First Jurisdiction.[2] They must have the *greater* 1,050 commands of the New Covenant written on their hearts.[3]

As addressed earlier, the Kingdom of Heaven does not come at once.[4] It is the Jurisdiction we enter through the Blood of Yeshua.[5] It is the Promised Land[6] that we enter and take by the force of His Testimony and His Sacred Promises.[7] It is the Oneness we share with our King and His children,[8] and the crowns we bring are the dominion we establish over our souls by the Power of His Victory![9]

We crush the lies![10] We bind the squatting spirits that are trespassing with their influence and darkness![11] We stand on the Rock of Truth and hold fast to His Word! [12]

LISTEN,[13] HOLY WARRIORS OF TRUTH![14]

THE WORLD IS NOT THE TRUTH![15] JESUS CHRIST IS THE TRUTH![16]

---

[1] Deuteronomy 18:15-19; Hebrews 3:1-6

[2] Romans 8:3-4; Galatians 5:22-24; Ephesians 5:26-27; Colossians 1:22; Hebrews 12:23; Jude 1:24; Revelation 14:5

[3] Romans 2:12-16; 8:2-8; Jeremiah 31:31-33; Hebrews 8:6-13

[4] Luke 17:20-21; Matthew 12:28; John 3:3; 18:36; Colossians 1:13

[5] Hebrews 10:19-22; 9:15; 12:24; Luke 22:20; John 6:54-56

[6] Hebrews 3:11-4:13; 11:9-12; Matthew 11:29

[7] 2 Corinthians 10:3-5; Matthew 11:12; Revelation 12:11

[8] John 14:20; 6:56; 15:5-7; Romans 8:1; 16:7; 1 Corinthians 1:30; Galatians 2:20

[9] Revelation 3:11; Jeremiah 1:10; Joshua 6:20; 1 Corinthians 15:57

[10] 2 Corinthians 10:4-5; 2 Thessalonians 2:8

[11] Matthew 12:29; 16:19; Mark 3:27; Luke 11:22

[12] Matthew 7:24; 16:18; Luke 20:18

[13] Luke 8:18; 19:26; Deuteronomy 32:46-47; Proverbs 2:2-5; Mark 4:23-24; Acts 17:11; Hebrews 2:1; James 1:22-25; Matthew 13:12; John 15:2

[14] 2 Timothy 2:3; 2 Corinthians 10:3-5; Ephesians 6:11-18; 1 Timothy 1:18

[15] 1 John 5:19; Romans 1:28-32; Galatians 1:4; Revelation 12:9; 2 Corinthians 11:3

[16] John 1:17; 14:6; 15:1; 18:37; Romans 15:8; Colossians 2:17; 1 John 5:6,20; Revelation 3:7,14; 19:11

Spirit is the "cause"; *Creation* is the "effect."[1] All causes are from the spiritual realm.[2] Spirits cause the effects that take place in Creation.[3] The Light of Truth is a cause, and the darkness of spiritual contrariness is a cause.[4] Truth is a cause that has an effect.[5] Lies are a cause that have an effect.[6] We can identify causes by their effects, but we cannot look at effects as if they are causes![7] Effects do not produce their causes! Causes produce their effects![8]

When we look out at the world, we are not seeing the Truth![9] We are simply seeing the manifested effects that result from spiritual causes.[10] We are seeing where Heaven and Hell meet.[11] Those who live according to the First Jurisdiction do not decide what is true by observing the world![12] We do not entertain any voice of any thought or idea that asks, "Did God really say?"[13] On the contrary! We speak with expertise what God has said![14] We speak the Truth into our souls, bodies, and Creation![15] We cause Truth to be manifested in the world![16]

LISTEN CAREFULLY! A soul has one "foot" in the spiritual realm[17] and another in the realm of "Creation."[18] A soul is the "connecting ligament" or "bridge" between the two realms.[19] It is the means by which a spirit commands a body.[20] And

---

[1] Hebrews 11:3; 2 Corinthians 4:18
[2] 1 Corinthians 8:6; Hebrews 1:2-3; John 1:3
[3] Hebrews 1:2; Job 1:16,19; 2:7; Exodus 20:4; Proverbs 8:22-31; Isaiah 44:13,24; 45:12; John 1:3; Deuteronomy 4:23; 5:8; Revelation 13:14
[4] Matthew 13:24-30; 2 Corinthians 11:13-15; 1 Peter 5:8; Revelation 12:9; 13:14
[5] Matthew 13:3-9; 7:17-19; Luke 3:9; James 3:17
[6] Genesis 3:4; John 8:44; Acts 13:10; 1 John 3:8
[7] Matthew 7:16; 23:25-28; James 6:45
[8] Mark 4:39; 9:25; Nahum 1:4; Luke 4:39
[9] 1 John 2:4; Hosea 8:2-3; John 14:17
[10] 1 John 4:5; Proverbs 18:21
[11] Genesis 3:1-7; Luke 4:1-13
[12] John 20:29; 2 Corinthians 5:7; Hebrews 11:1,27
[13] Genesis 3:1,13; Revelation 12:9; 16:14; 20:2,8; Zechariah 3:1-2
[14] 2 Timothy 2:15; Acts 20:27; Romans 16:19
[15] Ezekiel 37:1-10; Proverbs 18:21
[16] Luke 17:6; Mark 11:24
[17] Genesis 1:26-28; Galatians 5:17; Revelation 10:2
[18] Romans 8:6; Galatians 3:3; Revelation 10:2
[19] Psalm 139:8; 1 Timothy 3:16; Galatians 5:16
[20] Romans 6:13; 1 Peter 4:4

because it has these two ends, it can cooperate with the cause ***or*** the effect.[1] It can exist as the image of the spirit ***or*** the image of the body.[2]

Most souls on the earth are living as images of the body, as images of Creation.[3] They are living like animals, like creatures of instinct.[4] They function almost solely in Creation, which is why they know little, if anything, more than Creation.[5] And even though they are unaware of such things, they live completely under the authority of the ruling principalities that govern according to the Second Jurisdiction.[6] They are like cattle grazing on a farmer's land without awareness that they could be taken and slaughtered at any time.

But the soul that has been conquered by the spirit lives in the Spirit.[7] It dwells in the Kingdom of the Spirit,[8] and it is able to function in the image of the Spirit.[9] Because of this, it is able to function in unity with "cause."[10] This is why a child of Heaven can speak to a mountain and have it obey,[11] but a "child of Creation"[12] can speak to a mountain and see nothing happen at all.[13]

Understand that most of what is visible in the world is the result of images of Creation.[14] But because even the most fleshy human beings can be manipulated by dark spirits, they can still function as agents of dark spiritual causes.[15] For example, when a person is deceived by a lying spirit and speaks a lie, that spoken lie can cause a chain of events to unfold in Creation.[16] Creation will manifest the spoken words and the resulting deeds, but those words and deeds are not the

---

[1] Romans 6:16,19; 2 Peter 2:19
[2] Romans 8:13; Ephesians 4:22-24; 1 Peter 1:22
[3] 1 John 5:19; Romans 1:28-32; James 4:4; Ephesians 2:2; 2 Corinthians 4:4
[4] 2 Peter 2:12; Jude 1:10
[5] 1 Peter 4:4; Acts 17:30
[6] 1 John 5:19; Romans 1:28-32; Galatians 1:4; Revelation 12:9; 2 Corinthians 11:3
[7] Romans 5:1,10; 8:6; 13:14; John 14:27; Galatians 6:8
[8] Hebrews 4:3; Matthew 12:28; John 3:5; Romans 14:17
[9] Romans 8:29; Matthew 12:50; 25:40; Colossians 1:15-18; Revelation 1:5-6
[10] John 14:13; 17:11,21-22
[11] Mark 11:23; Matthew 17:20; 21:21; Luke 17:6; 1 Corinthians 13:2
[12] 1 John 4:5; John 8:23; 15:19; 17:14
[13] James 1:6-7; Mark 11:22-24; Hebrews 10:32; 11:6; Ephesians 4:14
[14] Colossians 2:20; Galatians 4:3; John 15:19; 17:14-16; 2 Corinthians 10:3; 1 John 5:19; Romans 7:4-6
[15] 2 Peter 2:18; Numbers 13:32
[16] Joshua 7:11-12; Judges 2:4; Isaiah 59:2

Truth![1] They are manifestations of lies![2] Likewise, if a deceived person believes a lie that they should accept a dark spirit of offense in their soul, and an infirmity spirit follows it in, the resulting sickness is not the Truth![3] It is the result of a lie being manifested in Creation.[4]
On the other hand, the devoted disciple of Yeshua knows that the Truth is not born in Creation and then manifested in Heaven![5] Quite the opposite! The Truth first flows out of the Holy Spirit and is then manifested in Creation![6] Creation manifests what is caused in Spirit and then spoken![7] So, the experienced disciple believes the promises of Yehovah, speaks them from the Spirit, and sees mountains picked up and thrown into the sea![8]

THEREFORE, KNOW WITH YOUR SOUL THAT THE TRUTH IS ALREADY THE TRUTH IN HEAVEN![9] TO SEE THE TRUTH MANIFESTED IN CREATION, SPEAK THE TRUTH INTO CREATION![10] THIS IS THE VERY SAME WAY OUR SAVIOR WILL RETURN AND REIGN![11] HE WILL SLAY THE ARMIES OF EVIL AT THE BATTLE OF ARMAGEDDON WITH THE SWORD OF HIS MOUTH![12]

HALLELUYAAAAAAAAAAAAAAAAH!!!!!!!!!!!

SO, SHOUT, MIGHTY WARRIORS OF TRUTH![13]

SHOUT TO SEE THE WALLS OF JERICHO FALL[14] UNDER THE POWER OF YESHUA'S NAME![15]

---

[1] 1 John 2:16; Psalm 73:6; 119:36-37; Titus 3:3; 1 Peter 2:11; 2 Peter 2:22
[2] 2 Peter 1:4c; 2:18-20; Galatians 6:8; James 4:1-3; 1 Peter 4:2
[3] Luke 4:39,41; Matthew 17:18; Mark 1:25; 9:25
[4] John 10:10; Job 2:7; Proverbs 17:22; Luke 13:16; Acts 10:38
[5] Genesis 1:1-4; Hebrews 11:1,7; 2 Corinthians 4:18
[6] Genesis 1:3; Hebrews 11:3
[7] John 1:1-3; Romans 1:20; Job 22:28
[8] Mark 11:23; Matthew 17:20; 21:21; Luke 17:6; 1 Corinthians 13:2
[9] 1 John 1:5; John 8:32; Psalm 110:1; 1 Corinthians 15:25-27
[10] Matthew 17:20; Mark 9:23; Luke 1:37; 18:27
[11] Revelation 21:27; Hebrews 1:8; Revelation 1:18; 4:9; 11:15
[12] Revelation 19:15-21; Isaiah 11:4; 2 Thessalonians 2:8; Romans 14:11
[13] Psalm 20:5; 27:6; 33:3; 47:1; 66:1; 95:1; 98:4; 100:1; 118:15
[14] Joshua 6:16; Hebrews 11:30
[15] John 14:14; 15:16; 16:24,26

PLANT THE SEED OF THE TRUTH AND WATER IT BECAUSE GREAT CROPS WILL BE PRODUCED![1]

WE ARE PURE BECAUSE HE MADE US PURE![2]

HALLELUYAH!

WE ARE RIGHTEOUS BECAUSE HE MADE US RIGHTEOUS![3]

HALLELUYAH!

WE ARE CLEAN BECAUSE HE WASHED US CLEAN IN HIS BLOOD![4]

HALLELUYAH!

AND WE ARE VICTORIOUS[5] BECAUSE HE HAS GIVEN HIS VICTORY TO US, PROMISED US SALVATION, AND REDEEMED US THAT WE MAY STAND AS EXAMPLES OF HIS CHARACTER![6]

HALLELUUUUUUUYAAAAAAAAAAAAAAAAAAH!!!!!!!!!!!!

GLORY TO THE KING![7] HALLELUYAH!

KING OF THE LAW![8] HALLELUYAH!

KING OF REDEMPTION![9] HALLELUYAH!

KING OF GRACE![10] HALLELUYAH!

---

[1] 1 Corinthians 3:6; Matthew 13:18-23
[2] 1 John 1:7,9; 3:2-3; Titus 2:14
[3] Romans 5:1; 2 Corinthians 5:21; 1 John 3:7; Ephesians 4:24
[4] John 15:3; Hebrews 10:22; Acts 10:15
[5] 1 Corinthians 15:57; Romans 8:37; Romans 6:14; 8:31
[6] 1 John 2:6; 1 Corinthians 11:1; Ephesians 4:22-24; Galatians 3:27
[7] Luke 19:38; 2 Timothy 4:18; Revelation 1:6; 4:11; 5:13; 21:23
[8] Romans 10:4; Matthew 5:17; Colossians 2:17
[9] Romans 8:3-4; Galatians 3:13-4; 1 Peter 1:18-19; Revelation 14:3
[10] John 1:17; 14:6; Romans 5:21; 6:14

KING OF RIGHTEOUSNESS![1] HALLELUYAH!

KING OF HEALING![2] HALLELUYAH!

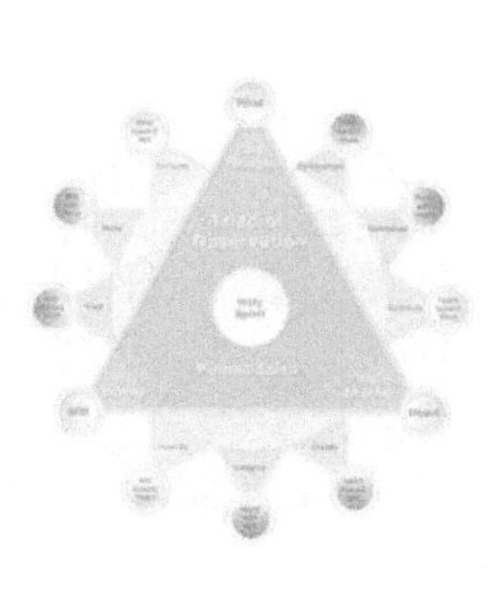

KING OF JOY![3] HALLELUYAH!

KING OF POWER![4] HALLELUYAH!

KING OF HONOR![5] HALLELUYAH!

KING OF CREATION![6] HALLELUYAH!

KING OF HEAVEN![7] HALLELUYAH!

GLORY TO THE KING OF ALL!!!!!!!!!!!!!!!!!!!!!!!!!!!!!![8]

HALLELUUUUUUUUUUYAAAAAAAAAAAAAAAAAAAAH!!!!!!!!!!!

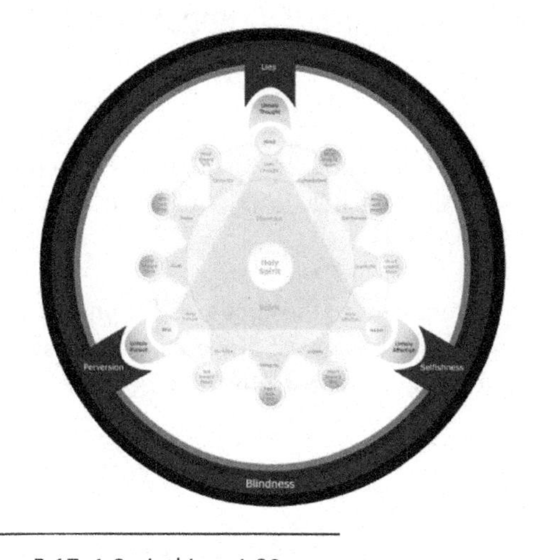

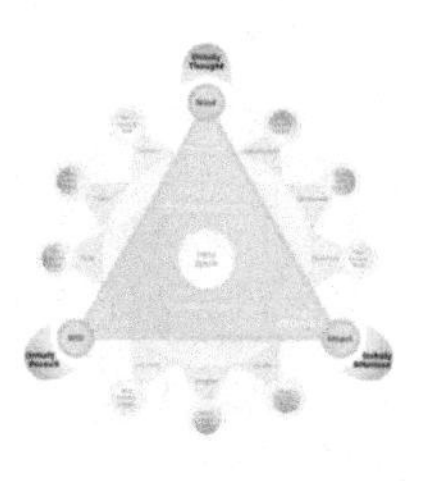

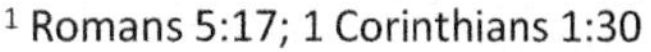

[1] Romans 5:17; 1 Corinthians 1:30

[2] Acts 4:10; Luke 7:6-8; Matthew 8:16; Mark 6:56

[3] John 15:11; 16:24; 17:13; 1 Peter 1:8; Jude 1:24

[4] 1 Corinthians 1:24; Romans 1:4; Matthew 22:29; Mark 13:26; Colossians 1:16; 2:15; Hebrews 6:5; 1 Peter 3:22

[5] Hebrews 3:3; John 5:23; Revelation 4:11; 5:12-13; 7:12; 13:14

[6] Revelation 3:14; Colossians 1:15

[7] Revelation 3:21; Matthew 18:23; 22:2

[8] Psalm 103:19; Revelation 2:27; 3:21; 12:5; 19:15; Hebrews 1:8

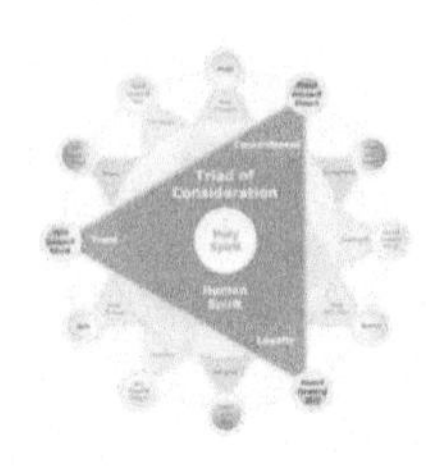

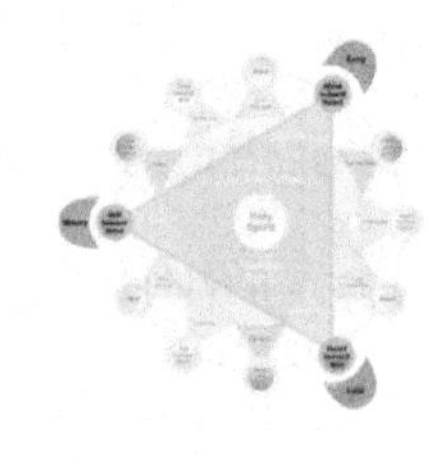

CHAPTER 16

CHOOSING JURISDICTIONS

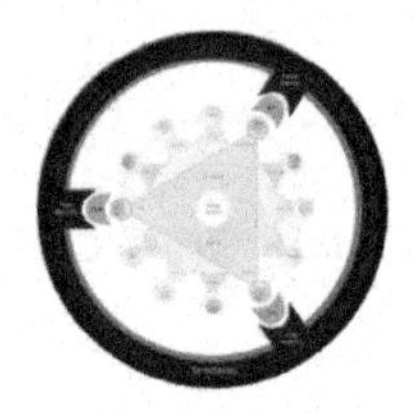

GLORY TO THE ALMIGHTY GOD WHO KNOWS ALL, SEES ALL,[1] AND HAS DECIDED TO RULE ALL[2] IN HIS GLORIOUS RIGHTEOUSNESS AND GOODNESS![3]

HALLELUYAH!

The First Jurisdiction, the Law of Righteousness, the Kingdom of Heaven, is full of Light![4] In it there is no darkness at all![5] It is fully loving, fully righteous, and fully true![6]

To hinder access of the children of Yehovah[7] to the First Jurisdiction with its safety and provisions, the enemy mounts attacks against any cooperation of the child with the jurisdiction's love, righteousness, and truth.[8] But because we cannot

---

1 Psalm 33:13; 139:1-24; Isaiah 11:2; Revelation 5:6
2 Revelation 11:15,17; 19:6; Psalm 57:11
3 Matthew 19:17; 1 Samuel 2:2; Psalm 145:7-9; James 1:17
4 Revelation 21:27; 22:5; 1 John 1:5; John 12:46
5 1 John 1:5; Matthew 5:48
6 1 Corinthians 2:9; Romans 7:12; Ephesians 5:9
7 Romans 8:14; Galatians 3:26; 1 John 3:1-2; 5:19; Matthew 5:9
8 Galatians 3:1; 5:7-8; Hebrews 12:1; 2 Corinthians 10:5; 2 Peter 2:1-3

write actual pursuits or affections but only describe them with words of truth, we will focus on the Truth.[1]

The Truth is not just a concept; It's alive![2] It's an accurate description of that which exists, but It's also a Person! God is what gives existence to anything and everything and makes anything "true!"[3]

HALLELUYAH!

In Heaven, the Truth is clearly visible to everyone, and to see Him in His Glory is to "breathe" truth.[4] Since detailed knowledge of both deeds and thoughts is freely available in the very atmosphere of Heaven, it is impossible for anyone dwelling there to believe a lie.[5] Even on earth no one believes a lie as the truth while also readily identifying it as a lie, because a lie can only be believed as truth when it's told to someone who receives it through ignorance as a true statement. Yet, because knowledge is pervasive and obvious in Heaven,[6] while someone could tell a lie, it would lack all deceptive power and would be viewed by everyone as an obvious falsity, thereby rendering the lie absolutely useless (This is why dark accusing spirits can lie on earth but cannot lie in the Courts of Heaven).[7]

---

[1] This is why fellowship with other believers is so important; when together, believers share and impart not only holy words but also holy affections and holy pursuits (Philippians 2:2; Hebrews 10:24; 1 John 4:12).

[2] John 14:6; Acts 4:12; Hebrews 10:19-22; 1 John 2:23; 2 John 1:9; Revelation 5:8-9

[3] Colossians 1:17; 1 Samuel 2:8; Isaiah 44:6; John 1:3; 1 Corinthians 8:6

[4] I testify that I experienced this when He transfigured me and took me to the Third Heaven; 1 Corinthians 13:12; 1 John 3:2

[5] 1 John 2:21; 2 Peter 1:12

[6] "Love never decays at any time. But where there are prophecies, they will become useless; where there are foreign tongues, they will be stilled; where there is knowledge, it will become useless" (1 Corinthians 13:8). Of course, it is not knowledge itself but the *measure* of knowledge that becomes useless (since everyone knows everything), as is explained in the following verses: "For we know *in part* and we prophesy *in part*, but when that which is complete comes, *what is in part* disappears" (1 Corinthians 13:9-10). In other words, in Heaven no one needs gifts of prophecy, foreign tongues, or knowledge, because everyone sees what was prophesied, understands what is being said, and knows what is happening! HalleluYah!

[7] Psalms 101:7; 1 John 2:21; Romans 1:25

However, since knowledge is significantly restrained on earth, lies can have power.[1] Their force is generally proportional to their reception.[2] If a lie represents weight in a person's choice mechanism, its acceptance can influence, alter, and shape creation.[3] This is why lies are the foundation of evil.[4] They are the very substance of rebellion, providing its only avenue for resistance of the Truth.[5]

For this reason, the rebellion, consisting of Heylel, the fallen elohim, the dark spirits, and demons, is composed of beings obsessed with people.[6] The spirits have very limited power without humanity,[7] so they need people to grant access in order for the dark spirits to make any lasting changes to Creation.[8] Only people have such residual dominion over Creation because they are born of Adam, who was made a spiritual being in Yehovah's image.[9] While this image describes many Characteristics of God, it also contains some properties of divine interaction, which include the expression and implementation of creative force through spiritual voice.[10] In other words, the rebellion hopes to use humans to continue to cut a path for itself into Creation.[11]

This is why the dark kingdom attacks people with lies.[12] It desperately needs humans to accomplish its continued existence here. As more people accept its voices, the dark kingdom obtains a hold on them and through them, gaining more effect in Creation.[13] The more lies the rebellion can get people to accept, the more power it has to alter existence to its liking through the mouths of the sons of Adam speaking things into existence.[14]

---

[1] Hosea 4:6; Jeremiah 5:21; 2 Corinthians 4:3-6

[2] Luke 8:18; 19:26; Deuteronomy 32:46-47; Proverbs 2:2-5; Mark 4:23-24; Acts 17:11; Hebrews 2:1; James 1:22-25; Matthew 13:12; John 15:2

[3] Once deceived, humans become acting agents of darkness in Creation (Acts 13:10; 1 John 2:18; 3:10; 1 Timothy 4:1; 1 Corinthians 10:20).

[4] John 8:44; Romans 1:25; 1 John 1:6; 2:21; Revelation 14:5; 2 Thessalonians 2:9,11; Titus 2:11; Hebrews 6:18; Colossians 3:9; Numbers 23:19; Psalm 38:12

[5] Daniel 8:12; Isaiah 59:14; 2 Thessalonians 2:10-12

[6] Job 1:7; 1 Peter 5:8

[7] Mark 5:9-13; Luke 11:24

[8] Proverbs 18:21; 10:20-21,31; 11:30; Matthew 12:35-37; James 3:6-9

[9] Genesis 1:26-27; Psalm 115:16

[10] Matthew 12:37; Proverbs 13:3

[11] Luke 6:45; Matthew 12:36-37; Romans 3:13-14; Jude 1:15

[12] 2 Corinthians 4:4; Matthew 4:8-9; John 12:40; Ephesians 2:2; 1 John 2:11; 5:19

[13] James 3:5; Revelation 13:5-6

[14] Proverbs 18:21; Mark 11:23; Ezekiel 37:1-28; James 3:9

This is how the enemy attempts to sabotage the function, safety, and provision of the First Jurisdiction for the children of Yehovah.[1] The dark spirits can clearly identify anyone who has been made into a new creature.[2] They are not confused about who has received Yeshua's death, exited the Second Jurisdiction, and been raised to life in the first.[3] The dark spirits always search such spiritual threats for weaknesses.[4] If they can influence a child of Yehovah to accept any temptations of sin or sickness,[5] then the dark spirits will claim that those deeds represent abandonment of the First Jurisdiction and constitute legal agreement by the person to abide within the principles of the Second Jurisdiction (This is why "trespass" is not a poor choice of translation for an act of sin).[6]

Therefore, the life of a child of Yehovah, a citizen of the First Jurisdiction, is a battle and mission of choosing, proving, and holding to the First Jurisdiction.[7] This battle is fought against lies on earth by children of Yehovah fighting by means of truth from the Kingdom of Heaven.[8] It is because of this positioning that dark spirits are considered "fallen" while the children of Yehovah are considered "risen" residents of Heaven.[9] In Yeshua we hurl down the dark spirits and trample upon them![10] We tread the snakes and scorpions![11] We cast down the darkness to the abyss where darkness belongs,[12] and we encourage the children of Adam to rise into the Light,[13] where there is love and loyalty, glory and power, wisdom and wealth, and grace and joy, both now and forever![14]

---

[1] James 3:6; Psalm 64:3; 140:3; Proverbs 15:1; 16:27; 26:20-21; Isaiah 30:27

[2] Matthew 5:14; Ephesians 5:8-14; Philippians 2:15

[3] Acts 19:15; Mark 1:24

[4] 1 Peter 5:8; John 8:44; Ephesians 4:27; 6:11; Revelation 12:9; Zechariah 3:1

[5] Matthew 9:5; Mark 2:5

[6] Romans 8:13; Colossians 3:5-8; 1 Peter 2:11

[7] Revelation 3:11; 1 Corinthians 15:58; 16:13; Ephesians 6:11; Romans 12:2; 1 Peter 5:9; James 4:7; Philippians 1:27; 4:1; 2 Thessalonians 2:15

[8] Ephesians 2:6; 2 Corinthians 13:8

[9] Ephesians 5:14; Isaiah 60:1; 1 Thessalonians 5:6; 2 Timothy 2:26

[10] Luke 10:18; John 12:31; 16:11; 1 John 3:8; Revelation 12:7-9,11

[11] Luke 10:19; Psalm 91:13; Ezekiel 2:6; Mark 16:18; Acts 28:5; Romans 16:20

[12] Jude 1:13; Matthew 25:41; Acts 1:25

[13] Isaiah 60:1; 1 John 1:5-9; Luke 11:34-35

[14] Revelation 5:12; 7:12; 19:1

When we abide in the Word of Yeshua,[1] His Law becomes ours.[2] When we dwell in the Kingdom of Yeshua,[3] the walls of His Kingdom become ours.[4] When we set our eyes on Yeshua,[5] our whole beings are full of His Light.[6] And when we live for Him,[7] His Life lives in us![8]

HalleluYah!

Praise be to our God, Who raised us up and has seated us at the Right Hand of God![9] Shout praise to the Lord,[10] for He has done marvelous things![11] Offer Him the fruit of your lips,[12] and give Him glory and thanks[13] because He has loved us[14] and brought us into His Victory![15]

HalleluYah!

HALLELUYAH![16]

LONG LIVE THE KING! YES, HE IS ALIVE AGAIN, FOREVER AND EVER![17]

HALLELUYAH!

HE CRUSHED THE ENEMY[18] AND MADE EARTH A FOOTSTOOL FOR HIS OWN FEET![19]

---

[1] John 15:7; Psalm 119:11; Proverbs 4:4; Jeremiah 15:16; 1 John 2:27
[2] Romans 8:2,10-11; 6:18,22; John 8:36
[3] Matthew 7:13; 13:32; Hebrews 4:11; Mark 12:34; Luke 17:20
[4] Matthew 11:28; John 10:28-29
[5] Colossians 3:1-2; Matthew 6:22-23; Luke 11:34-36
[6] Luke 11:34-36; Matthew 6:22-23
[7] Colossians 3:7,10; Galatians 2:20b
[8] Colossians 3:3-4; Galatians 2:20a
[9] Ephesians 2:6; Colossians 3:1
[10] Psalm 20:5; 27:6; 33:3; 47:1; 66:1; 95:1; 98:4; 100:1; 118:15
[11] Psalm 72:17-18; 77:14; 86:10; 136:4; Exodus 15:11; Job 9:10; Daniel 4:2-3
[12] Hebrews 13:15; Hosea 14:2; Romans 12:1
[13] 1 Chronicles 16:35; Revelation 4:9
[14] Ephesians 5:2; John 15:12; 2 Corinthians 5:14-15; 1 John 3:16; Revelation 1:5
[15] 1 Corinthians 15:57; Romans 8:37; 1 John 5:4-5
[16] Psalm 95:1; Revelation 19:1,3-4,6
[17] Revelation 1:18; 4:9; Hebrews 7:25; John 14:19; Romans 6:9
[18] Genesis 3:15; Romans 16:20; Colossians 2:15; Hebrews 2:14-15
[19] Luke 20:43-44; Psalm 2:1-9

HALLELUYAH!

HE REIGNS OVER EVERY POWER![1]

HALLELUYAH!
MIGHTY IS HIS NAME![2]

HALLELUYAH!

MIGHTY IS HIS NAME!!!!!!!!!!!!!!!!!!!![3]

HALLELUUUUUYAAAAAAAAAAAAAAAAAAAH!!!!!!!!!!!!!!!!!!!!

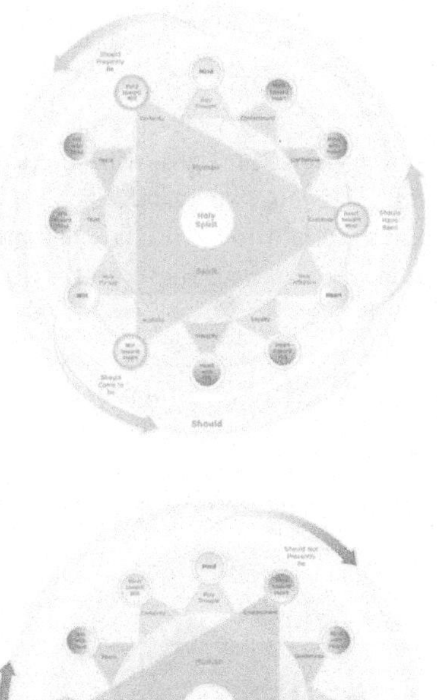

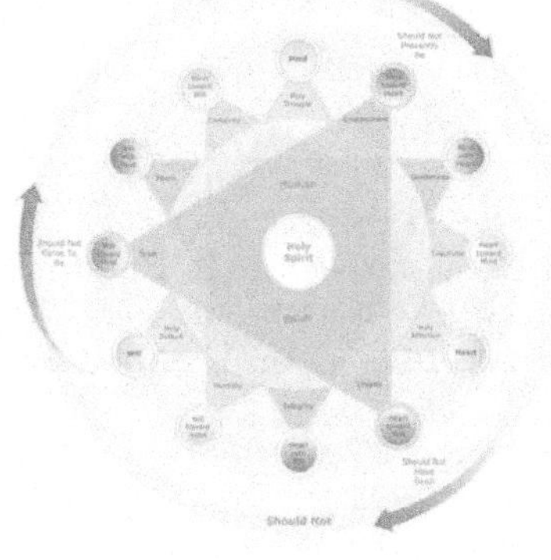

[1] Ephesians 1:21; Revelation 21:27; Hebrews 1:8; Revelation 1:18; 4:9; 11:15
[2] John 14:13; 1 Kings 8:42; Jeremiah 10:6; 32:18; Daniel 9:15; Luke 1:49
[3] John 14:14; 15:16; 16:24,26

CHAPTER 17

THE REVELATION OF THE HARVEST

When Yehovah revealed Himself through Yeshua, He opened our eyes to His Character.[1] By doing this, He also revealed His Law of Righteousness.[2] This revelation not only included what the law looked like but also its repercussions,[3] for we were created by a Holy God, and He tolerates no darkness in His Kingdom whatsoever.[4]

Holy, holy, holy is our God.[5] May Heaven and Creation tremble before Him![6]

Father, we thank you for revealing Yourself and Your Character to us![7] We now stand as witnesses[8] that you alone are Good![9] May Your Light pierce us[10] and rid

---

[1] Colossians 1:19; 2:9; Matthew 11:27; Ephesians 1:23; 4:10
[2] Romans 8:2; Matthew 5:22,28,32,34,39,44; Hebrews 3:3
[3] Matthew 11:21; 18:7; 23:13,15-16,23,25,27,29; 26:24; Luke 6:24-26; 10:13; 11:42-52; Revelation 8:13; 9:12; 11:14
[4] Matthew 7:23; 25:41; Revelation 21:8
[5] Revelation 4:8; Isaiah 6:3; Exodus 15:11
[6] Psalm 4:4; 96:9; 99:1; Isaiah 13:13; 41:5; Habakkuk 3:6
[7] John 1:18; 14:9; 17:6,26; Matthew 11:27; Luke 10:22
[8] John 1:7; 5:20; 16:30; Acts 22:15; Hebrews 3:5; 1 Peter 5:1; Revelation 2:13
[9] Matthew 19:17; 1 Samuel 2:2; Psalm 145:7-9; James 1:17
[10] Acts 2:37; Luke 2:34-35; Hosea 14:9; Matthew 21:44

us of all rocks[1] in the soil of our souls![2] May our eyes be opened, our ears hear,[3] and may our hearts be sprinkled with Your Blood,[4] made soft toward You,[5] and live in Your Joy, Peace, and Love forever and ever![6] Amen!

As with every law, the violation of Yehovah's Law of Righteousness has legal consequences.[7] Just as a nation's federal laws override the various rulings and interpretations that might be unique to its states or provinces, so also Yehovah's Law of Righteousness overrides all other laws.[8] And though the Contract of Creation allowed for a postponement of the application and repercussions of Yehovah's Law of Righteousness,[9] exceptions to His Law have *never* been permitted.[10] When the Covenant of Creation is fulfilled, it will be closed according to the *full ramifications* of Yehovah's Law of Righteousness.[11] No exceptions will be permitted.[12]

Understand how authority works.[13] Consider this parable: A child in the Kingdom of David[14] lived with his father and two older brothers. On a particular day, the boy was in his house and threatened by his older brother. At that time, his focus rested solely on pleasing his older brother in hope of avoiding repercussions of his older sibling's displeasure. But when his oldest brother entered the home, the child shifted his attention to gaining the favor of the oldest brother. Shortly after that, their father entered, and the authority of the older siblings faded to insignificance. This is where the child normally considered all authority to end. But on this particular day, it became known that his father had committed a crime. Because of this, soldiers kicked down the front door and entered the home. Just as they were binding the father to take him to prison, one of David's mighty men[15] entered and took command, accusing the father of treason. The father swore that there had been a mistake, but then King David himself entered the home and said,

---

[1] Jeremiah 23:29; Luke 24:32; John 6:63; 2 Corinthians 10:4-5

[2] Matthew 13:15,20-21; Acts 8:21-23; Mark 6:52; 10:5; Ephesians 4:18; Hebrews 3:8

[3] Matthew 13:15; Acts 3:19; 2 Timothy 2:25-26

[4] Hebrews 10:19-22; 9:15; 12:24; Luke 22:20; John 6:54-56

[5] Hebrews 3:8; 4:7; Matthew 13:15; 19:8; Mark 6:52; 8:17; Ephesians 4:18

[6] Romans 8:6; Acts 2:28; Galatians 5:22

[7] Hebrews 2:2; 2 Peter 2:4

[8] Acts 4:19; 5:29; 1 Samuel 15:24; Mark 7:7-9

[9] Romans 3:25; Hebrews 10:4; 11:39-40; 1 John 2:2; 4:10; Revelation 13:8

[10] Proverbs 11:21; Nahum 1:3

[11] Revelation 19:15-21; Isaiah 11:4; 2 Thessalonians 2:8

[12] Revelation 20:12,15; 21:27

[13] Luke 7:8; Acts 22:25-26; 23:17; 23:23; 25:26

[14] 2 Samuel 5:12; 1 Chronicles 14:2

[15] 2 Samuel 23:8-39; 1 Chronicles 11:11-12

"This is the man who conspired with our enemy, and bind his two older sons as well because they helped him. Take them to be executed immediately.[1] But this child is innocent, so bring him with us because he will live with my young sons in the palace."[2]

Who then has authority over the child? Notice that whoever was present could claim authority and be granted respect by the child, yet as soon as a greater authority entered, all lesser authority faded.[3] And where did King David's authority come from? It was granted by Yehovah Himself.[4]

Now, just as David had personally witnessed the crime in the parable above, Yehovah has witnessed every offense by everyone.[5] Nothing escapes His attention.[6] Therefore, know that regardless of any authority that you perceive in your life, Yehovah *will* have the final say.[7]

Notice in the parable that those taken away had conspired with the enemy. Though they had previously been protected by their king and his army and had lived as Israelites with an inheritance in the Kingdom of David, their cooperation with the enemy caused their own king and his army to treat them like a foreign enemy.[8]

So it will be for many.[9] Many are called, but few will be chosen.[10]

Therefore, understand that Yehovah desires that all human beings dwell in His Kingdom and abide by His Law that both protects them and governs over them.[11] He does not wish for *anyone* to conspire with the enemy,[12] because He knows that a Kingdom divided against itself cannot stand.[13] But anyone who does conspire

---

[1] Matthew 25:30; 3:10; 5:13; Jeremiah 15:1-2: Ezekiel 15:2-5

[2] Matthew 25:22-23; Mark 14:8-9

[3] Luke 11:31; Hebrews 3:3

[4] 1 Samuel 28:17; 16:13; 24:20

[5] Proverbs 15:3; 2 Chronicles 16:9; Job 34:21-22; Jeremiah 16:17; 23:24; 32:19; Hebrews 4:13

[6] Ecclesiastes 11:9; 12:14; Psalm 96:13; Matthew 12:36; Luke 12:2; Acts 17:30

[7] Romans 2:6-11; Job 34:11; Galatians 6:7-8; Revelation 2:23; 20:12; 22:12

[8] Luke 19:27; Matthew 23:34

[9] Matthew 3:9-10; 7:22-23; 8:12; 21:43

[10] Matthew 22:14; 7:13-14; 20:16; Luke 13:23-24

[11] 1 Timothy 2:3-4; Titus 2:11; 2 Peter 3:9

[12] 2 Peter 3:9; Matthew 18:14; 1 Timothy 2:4; Romans 2:4

[13] Luke 11:17; Isaiah 9:20-21; Isaiah 19:2-3

with the enemy will surely be banished from the Kingdom,[1] and this is a very serious consequence, because His Kingdom is Goodness[2] and His enemy is evil itself.[3]

The kingdom of darkness has already been judged as evil because it stands in opposition to Goodness.[4] It is evil by definition, and Yeshua completely defeated it, guaranteeing its coming banishment.[5] Therefore, the only judgments that await are the decisions regarding who belongs to which kingdom.[6] And those judgments are fairly simple; whoever has knowingly cooperated with darkness is darkness,[7] and whoever has conspired with the enemy is an enemy.[8]

Yehovah would have been just to let such judgment stand.[9] However, being Merciful and Compassionate,[10] He became a man and subjected Himself to unjust suffering, punishment, and death[11] so that He could allow anyone who turned back toward the Light to have all their due consequences for transgressing the Law of Righteousness paid in full..[12] By doing this, He has given every human being the simple opportunity to choose Goodness or evil.[13] Regardless of their experience or participation, all human beings have been offered the same choice.[14] And it is a real choice. Just as each human being has been created with their own spirit, soul, and body, each human being has been granted authority to choose their own destiny.[15]

This opportunity could not be made any easier.[16] It is not an essay or a multiple-choice test. It doesn't require paperwork or a college degree.[17] It is a simple yes

---

1 Matthew 5:13; 7:19; 8:12; 13:41-42
2 Mark 1:15; Matthew 9:35; Luke 4:43; 16:16; Hebrews 4:2
3 James 4:4; Romans 8:7
4 2 Peter 2:4; Jude 1:6
5 1 John 3:8; Colossians 2:15
6 Matthew 25:32-33; Romans 14:10-12
7 Galatians 6:7-9; Job 4:8; Proverbs 11:18; Romans 2:6-10
8 2 Peter 2:15; 1 Kings 18:18; 19:10; Ezekiel 9:10
9 Jeremiah 18:3-6; Isaiah 64:8; Matthew 20:15
10 James 5:11; Exodus 34:6; 1 Chronicles 21:13
11 Hebrews 12:2; Philippians 2:8
12 John 6:54-58; Ephesians 2:16
13 1 Peter 3:11; Proverbs 11:27
14 3 John 1:11; 1 John 3:6-9
15 Joshua 24:15; 1 Kings 18:21
16 1 Kings 18:21; Deuteronomy 4:35; Matthew 6:24
17 Matthew 18:3; Mark 10:15; 1 Peter 2:2

or no.[1] But it is not just a yes or no at one time or another.[2] It is a *living, or perpetual*, yes or no.[3]

This will take some time to explain.

My earliest memory is of a conversation with Yehovah when I was in my mother's womb.[4] I was very excited to be born,[5] and Yeshua was excited for me. I was somehow quite confident that I was going to do very well, and Yeshua was pleased with my determination. But then, with a gentle smile and a sincere concern, He said to me, "You know, all who have gone before you have struggled."[6] I was aware of the presence of others in the Kingdom of Heaven who seemed just beyond our private encounter. I also remembered knowing the stories of many who had gone before me, but I remained convinced that I would be different and said, "Yes, but I deeply believe that I can do this without failing."[7] I could tell that He was pleased with my exuberance, but He did not hide from me that He knew I would struggle. And He said to me, "Remember: When you need help, ask."[8]

Moments later, I was born. I was squeezed so hard that I thought I was going to be crushed. Then I emerged into an absurdly bright light. A man's face as big as my whole body was inches from me. He was holding me by limbs I didn't even realize I had, and I felt as if my body was being pulled apart. I felt wet for the first time and very cold. I was coughing up fluid from lungs I didn't know I had, and the entering air felt extremely dry and cold. And with all of this, I was horrified and thought to myself, "I have made a terrible choice!"[9]

I confess that if I could have returned to the womb, I would have.

Nevertheless, I remember willfully sinning for the first time when I was two years old.[10] And over the years, I became more comfortable in doing so.[11] By the time I

---

1 Matthew 5:37; 2 Corinthians 1:17-20; James 5:12
2 Matthew 12:35; Psalm 37:30-31; Proverbs 12:17-19
3 John 7:17; Philippians 3:15-16; Luke 8:15
4 Exodus 34:19; Psalm 22:9-10; 51:6; 71:6; 139:13; Isaiah 49:1,5; Jeremiah 1:5; Luke 1:44; Galatians 1:15
5 Jeremiah 1:5; Isaiah 49:1,5; Galatians 1:15-16; Romans 8:29-30
6 Isaiah 44:24; 46:3-4; 48:17; Job 31:15
7 Jeremiah 1:5; Psalm 139:13-16
8 Isaiah 44:2; 43:1,7; Psalm 71:6; Romans 8:29-30
9 Matthew 14:30; 2 Kings 6:15; Mark 14:38
10 1 Peter 1:14; Titus 3:3-5; Acts 17:30
11 Luke 15:13; Proverbs 5:8-14; 21:17; Ecclesiastes 11:9-10

was a teenager, I was sinning left and right.[1] And although I had been baptized more than once and prayed for salvation on numerous occasions, I continued to embrace the world.[2]

One day, when I was eighteen years old, I had an unexpected accident.[3] I received a severe head injury. At first the pain was beyond excruciating. Then it grew worse and worse, far beyond any pain I had ever imagined possible. But suddenly it stopped, and I was greatly relieved until I realized that I was no longer in my body.

I was dead.[4]

I had not understood it at first, because I was fully conscious. That is to say, I was far more conscious than I had ever been up until that time. I was not distracted by anything but seemed to have the full measure of my awareness. It was then that I realized I was suspended in an outer darkness.[5]

I was in Hell, or more specifically, Hades.[6]

And once again, I thought to myself, "I have made a terrible choice!"[7]

I called out to Yeshua, and to my immense relief, I saw Him descend from Heaven in a pillar of light.[8] His descent stopped just above my level, and He stood about two hundred feet away from me. He looked exactly as the Apostle John described Him when riding the white horse,[9] and He said nothing to me. In my foolishness, I had the audacity to ask, "Lord Jesus, please, if you send me back, return me without deformity, but if you are not sending me back, please take me to be with you."

I heard Him say nothing, but suddenly I sat up in my body![10] I had been laying on the ground, and those who had surrounded me were stunned and began to

---

[1] 2 Timothy 2:22; 1 Peter 2:11

[2] James 4:4; 7:7; 15:19,23; 17:14; 1 John 2:15-16

[3] Luke 12:20; James 4:14

[4] Romans 8:13; Galatians 5:19-21

[5] Matthew 8:12; 22:13; 25:30

[6] Luke 16:23; Revelation 1:18; 6:8; 20:13

[7] Matthew 14:30; 2 Kings 6:15; Mark 14:38

[8] 1 Peter 3:19; Isaiah 42:7; 61:1; Revelation 1:18

[9] Revelation 19:13

[10] Luke 8:55; Acts 9:40

earnestly insist[1] that I had been without a pulse, that my body had become pale, and that they were certain I had been dead for at least ten minutes.[2] They asked how I felt, and I told them that I felt absolutely fine. Then they pointed to my face and my shirt, and both were drenched in my own blood. Yet after cleaning myself off, there was no wound to be found anywhere.[3]

I praise my Merciful God Who saves me, and I assure you, I did not deserve such mercy! But as the Scriptures testify, "...if we are faithless, He remains faithful, for He cannot disown Himself."[4]

How can I describe the horror of the outer darkness?

Father, I thank you for Your wonderful Mercy that returned me for Your Glory! Please let them see![5] Please let them hear the warning![6]

Woe, woe, woe to those who choose to remain outside of His Kingdom![7]

I am a witness that Hades is very much as the Scriptures describe; an outer darkness.[8] It is perhaps best explained in today's language as an infinite void, absent of anything except darkness. One can picture limitless outer space without anything in it.

When a person who doesn't have a relationship with God dies, their spirit goes immediately[9] into the outer darkness.[10] All of the distractions of Creation pass away, and their soul immediately perceives its existence in the spiritual realm where it already exists, whether they have been previously blind to such an existence or not. Those who live in darkness perceive that they already live in the

---

[1] Deuteronomy 19:15b; 17:6; Matthew 18:16; John 8:17; 2 Corinthians 13:1

[2] While they said it had been at least ten minutes, their testimony that my body had become pale signifies that it had most likely been at least fifteen minutes, since pallor mortis usually occurs 15-25 minutes after death.

[3] Acts 3:16; John 7:23

[4] 2 Timothy 2:13

[5] Matthew 13:15; Acts 3:19; 2 Timothy 2:25-26

[6] Colossians 4:3; Luke 16:28; 1 Corinthians 4:14

[7] Revelation 8:13; Matthew 18:7; Luke 6:24-26

[8] Matthew 8:12; 22:13; 25:30

[9] Luke 16:22-23; Psalm 9:17; Proverbs 9:18; Isaiah 14:9; Revelation 20:13-14

[10] Matthew 11:23; Luke 16:23; Revelation 20:13

darkness of Hades, while those who live in light perceive that they already live in the Light of Heaven.[1]

Those who find themselves in Hades immediately perceive that they have no physical body.[2] They are just an immobile consciousness existing in darkness some distance below Heaven. The distance below depends on how close they drew to the Kingdom of Heaven while on earth. Some are quite close but can never enter;[3] others are horrifically far below in unfathomable depths of a darkness that has an increasing quality far darker than the mere absence of light.[4]

Everyone in the darkness is alone.[5] There is an awareness that others are there as well, but there is no way to encounter or observe them in any way. Everyone is also aware of the infinite boundary above them.[6] The underside of Heaven extends like an endless ceiling over the outer darkness.[7] Those in the darkness can

---

[1] Many have misunderstood 1 Thessalonians 4:16, "Because the Lord himself will descend from Heaven, with a loud command, with the voice of the archangel, and with the trumpet call of God, and the dead in Christ will rise first." However, this is not a verse about the resurrection of spirits and souls but about the resurrection of bodies that are to be transformed from imperishable to perishable (1 Corinthians 15:35-54). And there is an order to inheritance of heavenly bodies; Christ received His first (1 Corinthians 15:20), and those who belong to Him will receive their glorified bodies when He returns to reign (1 Corinthians 15:23). This is how the rich man and Lazarus were experiencing spiritual afterlife before the resurrection of Yeshua (Luke 16:19-31) and why the souls under the Holy Altar in Heaven are eagerly awaiting the Final Judgment (Revelation 6:10). And I testify that when I was transfigured, the only Person I saw in a glorified body was Yeshua; everyone else, though recognizable, was somewhat transparent and awaiting the resurrection and transfiguration of their bodies. I myself had been transfigured and was able to be physically embraced by Yeshua, but my transfiguration was temporary and faded back to normal about fifteen minutes after I was returned to Creation (Exodus 34:29-35; Luke 9:29-31).

[2] In Matthew 5:29, Yeshua says, "If your right eye causes you to stumble, tear it out and throw it away from you. It is better for you to lose one part of your body than for your whole *body* to be thrown into Hell." – *Body* from the Greek σῶμα, pronounced "soh-mah," meaning *body* but with a wide berth of literal or figurative applications, especially used to refer to one's *whole being*. When I was in the outer darkness, my whole consciousness was present in every way. It was actually worse to have no physical body because I was not able to curl up, rub my face, cross my arms, or partake in any of the normal reactions to discomfort or stress. It is a place void of Creation and all its comforts. There is no comfort, only absolute isolation with nothing but one's own corrupted soul.

[3] Luke 13:28; 16:23

[4] 2 Peter 2:17; Jude 1:13

[5] Luke 16:24; Isaiah 65:13-14

[6] Luke 16:26; Psalm 49:14

[7] 2 Thessalonians 1:9; Matthew 7:23; 22:13; 25:41; Luke 13:27

perceive that there is light and every good thing above the boundary, but most in the darkness are not close enough to see or observe anything in detail.

In the first few moments, the experience of the outer darkness is not unpleasant.[1] It is even somewhat of a relief from the discomforts and chaos of Creation, especially if one's death was violent. But it only takes a few moments for the person to realize that they have nothing—no physical body of any sort, no comfort, no warmth, no covering, no company, no blanket. They have nothing.[2] They have their soul in the darkness. That is all.

How do I describe the raw horror of what it is like to be there and realize that you could be there forever? Nothing in Creation comes close because Heaven and Earth will pass away.[3] The description given by the rich man in Hades certainly fits. In Greek, it could be translated as "being grieved in this blaze."[4] It is a fire of unquenchable regret.[5] It is certainly a spiritual fire far worse than any fire in Creation, for all fires in Creation eventually consume their fuel. But this fire burns hotter and hotter forever[6] because it is self-inflicted with no source of relief.[7]

In the first few moments, the inhabitants of the outer darkness realize that they traded Heaven for their carnal life, causing their carnal life to become their "heaven."[8] Since they rebelled against Yehovah's order, they became the contrast of it.[9] Instead of beginning existence and growing into greater and greater spiritual life, they began their existence and will decay into greater and greater spiritual death.[10]

Though the initial time spent in the darkness is unfathomably hopeless, it soon grows far worse.[11] At the Final Judgment, the person will have a chance to talk

---

[1] Luke 16:24 – Unlike those who are set ablaze in a fire within Creation, the rich man is able to carry on a conversation. This is because his fire is spiritual, not physical. He thirsts for inclusion, for restoration, for comfort, but none will ever be found. His fire is eternal, and though he longs to perish, he never will (Mark 9:48).

[2] Luke 16:25; Matthew 13:12; Mark 4:25

[3] Mark 13:31; Psalm 102:25-27; Isaiah 51:6; 2 Peter 3:10-12; Revelation 14:9-11

[4] Luke 16:24 – *Being grieved* from the Greek οδυνωμαι, pronounced "aw-doo-noh-mahyee," meaning *to be sorrowed, grieved, anguished,* or *tormented.*

[5] Matthew 8:12; 22:13; 24:51; 25:30; Luke 13:28

[6] Daniel 7:11; Revelation 14:9-11; 13:5-6; 20:4,12

[7] Titus 3:11; Luke 7:30; 19:22; John 3:18; Acts 13:46

[8] Luke 16:25; Ecclesiastes 11:9-10; Acts 17:30-31; Romans 2:5-11

[9] 1 Corinthians 10:6; Romans 1:28

[10] Isaiah 66:24; Mark 9:48

[11] Luke 16:24; Isaiah 66:24; Matthew 25:41; Mark 9:43-49; Revelation 14:10-11

with Yeshua about their predicament.[1] They will not experience a change of state but will simply be educated about why they are "what they are" and "where they are."[2] At that point, all hope will be lost.[3] What makes it horrifically excruciating is the brief encounter of the Final Judgment with Yehovah where they get to see how beyond wonderful He is, how much He wanted good things for them, how He even died to show them His Love in an effort to win their attention and trust, but how they threw all of that away for temporal distractions.[4] Their chance to grow able to enter the Kingdom was squandered on things that have passed away.[5] And now they will never be able to enter.[6] They simply don't have the capacity.[7] The entrance into Heaven is through a *relationship*, and they didn't grow into that relationship while they could.[8] They will forever be aware but away, wishful but unfulfilled, sorry but eternally stationed in nothingness with only their memories to cherish.[9] Since they chose to be a god over themselves during their lives,[10] they are granted their dearest wish and given themselves to rule over.[11] And after millions of millennia, when they've thought of every moment of their lives, they will realize repeatedly in horror, that they didn't only fail to make it to Heaven themselves but kept others from entering as well, others whom they cherished, others to whom they will never even be able to offer so much as a single apology.[12] And if they ask Yeshua why no one can be with them, He will simply answer that it would be unjust.[13] Because everyone who is in the outer darkness is there due to their desire to rule themselves.[14] No one else ever belonged to them. Everything in Creation always belonged to Him.[15] It was His Kingdom all along.[16] And now those who asked Him to be their God will be blessed to dwell with Him[17]

---

[1] Matthew 25:44; 7:22; Revelation 3:9

[2] Matthew 25:45; 1 John 3:12-20; Acts 9:5

[3] Luke 13:28; Psalm 112:10; Matthew 8:12; 13:42,50; 22:13; 24:50; 25:30

[4] Revelation 1:7; Zechariah 12:10; Philippians 3:19

[5] Luke 16:25; Ecclesiastes 11:9-10; Acts 17:30-31; Romans 2:5-11

[6] Matthew 25:46; Jude 1:7; Hebrews 12:17

[7] 1 John 3:15; Matthew 25:1-13

[8] John 14:17; 17:3; 1 Corinthians 2:14

[9] Luke 16:24; Isaiah 65:13-14

[10] Philippians 2:21; 3:19; 1 Thessalonians 4:8; 2 Timothy 3:4; Romans 16:18; Isaiah 56:10-12

[11] Acts 7:51; 13:46; John 1:11

[12] Luke 16:27; Psalm 49:12-13

[13] Deuteronomy 32:4; Romans 9:14

[14] Matthew 25:45; Luke 16:25; Ecclesiastes 11:9-10; Daniel 5:22-23; Luke 19:27

[15] John 16:15; 1 Chronicles 29:13-14; Psalm 100:3; Romans 14:7-9

[16] Psalm 24:1; 1 Samuel 2:8

[17] Acts 2:21; 22:16; Psalm 86:5; Joel 2:32; Romans 10:12-13; Hebrews 4:16

in His Kingdom of Righteousness forever,[1] because they entered the Kingdom of His Rule before their death.[2]

We all thirst for Yehovah.[3] When in Creation, spirits and people can drink from the general blessings of Yehovah without entering His Kingdom.[4] But when He fulfills the Covenant of Creation and brings Creation into His Kingdom,[5] those who have rejected His Kingdom will remain outside of both in the outer darkness.[6] The awareness received by those in darkness that they will never again experience anything more than themselves is a "fire that will never be quenched, and a worm that will never die."[7] The Final Judgment is the moment when Creation is fully brought into His Kingdom;[8] it is the moment that the door is shut.[9] This final decision is what transforms the current torment of Hades into the unquenchable Lake of Fire.[10] Because of this, any location below the boundary of Heaven is beyond horrible.[11] But any location above the boundary is beyond wonderful.[12]

It is true that some people make it into Heaven as "sticks snatched from the fire."[13] But, just as there are those who are horrifically deep in the darkness,[14] there are those who "dwell wonderfully high" in the Light.[15] Of course, everyone in Heaven dwells in the Light of the Father,[16] in the company of Yeshua,[17] receives a new

---

[1] Titus 2:14; 1 Peter 2:9,12

[2] John 5:24; 14:2-3 Matthew 25:34,40; 1 John 3:14; 1 Corinthians 2:9; Hebrews 11:16; Romans 8:13

[3] Psalm 42:2; 63:1; 143:6; Isaiah 55:1; Amos 8:11; Matthew 5:6; John 4:14; 17:3; Revelation 21:6; 22:17

[4] Matthew 5:45; Job 25:3; Psalm 145:9; Acts 14:17

[5] Revelation 11:15,17; 19:6; Psalm 57:11

[6] Matthew 8:12; Luke 19:27; Hebrews 12:14-17

[7] Mark 9:48

[8] Revelation 11:15 – The door of salvation remains open until the seventh trumpet (Revelation 14:14-19). But upon its sounding, the door is shut forever (Revelation 3:7-8).

[9] Matthew 25:10; Numbers 14:28-34; Psalm 95:11; Luke 13:25

[10] Revelation 2:8; 20:14

[11] Revelation 14:10; Job 21:20; Psalm 11:6; Jeremiah 51:57

[12] 1 Corinthians 2:9; 1 Peter 1:12; Psalm 31:19; Hebrews 11:16

[13] Amos 4:11; Zechariah 3:2; Jude 1:23; 1 Corinthians 3:15

[14] 2 Peter 2:17; Jude 1:13

[15] Daniel 12:3; Matthew 24:45-47

[16] James 1:17; Colossians 1:12; Matthew 5:16

[17] Luke 23:43; John 14:3; 17:24

body,[1] comforts,[2] amazing fellowship,[3] and so much more.[4] But some inhabitants experience levels of eternal reward that are extensively beyond the vocabulary of this present world.[5]

HALLELUYAH!

What is wonderful is that those of us who dwell in Heaven will do so forever and ever. In the Greek this is worded "εἰς τοὺς αἰῶνας τῶν αἰώνων," which means "into ages upon ages." It is not unlike the older English construction of "for ever and ever," and it means the same thing.

When speaking of those of us who will serve Yehovah in His Kingdom, the Revelation of Jesus Christ given though the Apostle John says, "There will be no more night. They will not need the light of a lamp or the light of the sun, because the Lord God will give them light. And they will reign *forever and ever (εἰς τοὺς αἰῶνας τῶν αἰώνων).*"[6] So we see that those of us who accept the dominion of His Law will live for *eternity.*[7]

If anyone wants to argue otherwise, then let them know that this is the same language used in the same revelation by the same apostle to say, "And whenever the living creatures give glory, honor, and thanks to Him Who sits on the throne and Who lives *forever and ever (εἰς τοὺς αἰῶνας τῶν αἰώνων),* the twenty-four elders fall facedown before Him Who sits on the throne and worship Him Who lives *forever and ever (εἰς τοὺς αἰῶνας τῶν αἰώνων).*"[8] Obviously, our Almighty Creator is an Eternal Being Who created time,[9] so it is worth highlighting that this same language used in this verse to describe His eternal conscious existence is also used to describe our own eternal conscious existence in Heaven.[10]

---

[1] 1 Corinthians 15:40,50-54; 2 Corinthians 5:2-4

[2] Luke 16:25; Revelation 7:13-17

[3] Revelation 19:10; 22:9; Hebrews 12:1; Luke 16:23b

[4] 1 Corinthians 2:9; 1 Peter 1:12; Psalm 31:19; Hebrews 11:16

[5] Matthew 5:12; 20:23; 25:34; Philippians 3:14; Psalm 31:19; Hebrews 11:16; 2 Timothy 4:8; James 1:12; Hebrews 2:7; Revelation 3:11; 4:4

[6] Revelation 22:5

[7] Matthew 19:29; 25:46; John 3:15-16,36; 4:14,36; 5:24,39; 6:27,40,47,54,68; 10:28; 12:25,50; 17:2-3; Acts 13:46,48; Romans 2:7; 5:21; 6:22-23; Galatians 6:8; 1 Timothy 1:16; 6:12; Titus 1:2; 3:7; 1 John 1:2; 2:25; 3:15; 5:11,13,20; Jude 1:21

[8] Revelation 4:9-10

[9] Hebrews 1:2; 11:3 – Both of these verses are typically interpreted by English versions to say *the universe* or *the worlds*, but the raw meaning of the Greek τοὺς αἰῶνας, pronounced "toos ahyee-oh'-nahs," is *the ages.*

[10] Revelation 22:5; 4:9-10; 5:13; 7:12; 10:6; 11:15; 15:7

Likewise, the same revelation also says through the same apostle,

"And when the thousand years are over, Satan will be released from his prison and will go out to deceive the nations in the four corners of the earth, Gog and Magog, to gather them for battle. In number they are like the sand of the sea. They marched across the expanse of the earth and surrounded the encampment of God's people and the city He loves. But fire descended from Heaven and devoured them. And the Devil, who deceived them, was thrown into the lake of burning sulfur, where the Beast and the False Prophet *are.*[1] *They will be tormented day and night forever and ever (εἰς τοὺς αἰῶνας τῶν αἰώνων).*"[2]

Notice that the very same language used to describe the eternal life of Yehovah is also used to describe the eternal state of consciousness of the Devil, Beast, and False Prophet. Notice also that the Beast and the False Prophet are *still there* when the Devil is thrown in a *thousand years* later. And understand that one must be conscious to be tormented.[3] The Devil, Beast, and False Prophet will not be "annihilated"; they will be *tormented.*[4]

Yet, immediately after this, we are told of another coming event:

"And I saw a great white throne and Him who was seated on it. The earth and the sky fled from His presence, and there was no place for them. And I saw the dead, great and small, standing before the throne, and books were opened. And another book was opened, which is the Book of Life. The dead were judged according to what they had done as recorded in the books. The sea gave up the dead that were in it, and death and Hades gave up the dead that were in them, and each person was judged according to their deeds. Then death and Hades were *thrown into the Lake of Fire*. The Lake of Fire is the second death. And if anyone was not found written in the Book of Life, they were *thrown into the Lake of Fire*."[5]

---

[1] The Greek format does not use a being verb here but simply says, "...into the Lake of Fire, where the Beast and the False Prophet, they will be tormented..." This construction in the Greek clearly indicates their continued presence.

[2] Revelation 20:7-10

[3] *Tormented* from the Greek βασανίζω, pronounced "bah-sah-nih'-zoh," meaning *to torture, pain,* or *distress.*

[4] Revelation 20:10b

[5] Revelation 20:11-15

We know that these people also suffer forever and ever, for like them the False Prophet is certainly a man,[1] yet he never loses consciousness for all eternity.[2] And to clarify this eternal condition, the same apostle says,

"And a third angel followed them and shouted: 'If anyone worships the Beast and its image and receives its mark on their forehead or on their hand, they also will drink the wine of God's Fury, which has been poured undiluted into the cup of His wrath. They will be *tormented* with burning sulfur in the presence of the holy angels and in the presence of the Lamb. And the smoke of their *torment* rises *forever and ever (εἰς αἰῶνας αἰώνων). There will be no rest day or night* for those who worship the Beast and its image or for anyone who receives the mark of its name.'"[3]

Many have argued that the mention of smoke implies annihilation, yet we are clearly told that the smoke is of their *torment,[4] not destruction,* and that there will be *no rest[5] day or night* for these people.[6] Just as a fire in Creation must have something to burn to produce smoke,[7] the eternal smoke also represents ongoing eternal torment.[8] This is the very same language used to describe the eternal torment of the Devil, Beast, and False Prophet.[9] Again, those who worship the

---

[1] Revelation 19:20, "...The two of them were thrown alive into the fiery lake of burning sulfur." – *Alive*, from the Greek ζάω, pronounced "Zah'-oh" and meaning *to live, breathe, be among the living.*

[2] Revelation 20:10b; See also Matthew 25:41,46

[3] Revelation 14:9-11

[4] Revelation 14:11a – *Torment,* from the Greek βασανισμός, pronounced "bah-sah-nees-mawss'," meaning *torment,* or *torture,* from the root βασανίζω, meaning *to question by applying torture, to vex with grievous pains, to harass or distress.*

[5] *Rest* from the Greek ἀνάπαυσις, pronounced "ah-nah'-pauw-sis," meaning *intermission, cessation,* or *rest.*

[6] Revelation 14:11b

[7] Proverbs 26:20a; 22:10

[8] Revelation 9:2-3 – *Abyss,* from the Greek ἄβυσσος, pronounced "ah'-boo-sawss" and meaning *(infernal) abyss, depthless, bottomless pit.* Notice that both the Beast (Revelation 9:11; 17:8) and the locusts emerge from the abyss very much *alive*. This is the same abyss mentioned in Luke 8:31; Romans 10:7; Revelation 9:11; 11:7; 17:8; 20:1,3. This is also the same abyss used to lock away Satan for a thousand years (Revelation 20:1,3). And from this abyss, smoke rises like the smoke from a giant furnace, *indicating the furious torment of its living inhabitants* (2 Peter 2:4). Therefore, we see that the same book written by the same apostle that spoke about the rising smoke from the endless torment of the living inhabitants of the abyss in Revelation 9:2-3 uses the very same language to speak of the rising smoke from the endless torment of those who worshipped the Beast in Revelation 14:9-11.

[9] Revelation 20:10b

Beast and his image must be conscious to be *tormented* and *without rest.* The reason the angel used this language is that the Scriptures clearly say in regard to eternal torment,

"The sinners in Zion are terrified; trembling has seized the immoral: 'Who of us can dwell with the consuming fire? Who of us can dwell with *everlasting* burning?'"[1]

"Then He will say to those on His left, 'Depart from Me, you who are cursed, into the *everlasting* fire prepared for the Devil and his angels.'"[2]

"Then they will go away to *everlasting punishment,*[3] but the righteous to *everlasting life.*"[4] Obviously, neither punishment nor life would be everlasting if either of them ever ended!

CHILDREN OF OUR CREATOR![5] THIS IS THE HARVEST TO COME![6] THERE ARE ONLY TWO SORTS OF FRUIT: GOOD OR BAD![7]

This is what our Maker and Teacher[8] is saying when He speaks of the wheat and the darnel:[9]

"The Kingdom of Heaven is like a man who sowed good seed in his field. But while people were sleeping, his enemy came and sowed *darnel* among the wheat, and went away. When the wheat sprouted and produced grain, then the darnel also appeared. And the owner's servants came to him and said, 'Sir, did you not sow good seed in your field? Then where did the darnel come from?' He replied, 'An enemy did this.' Then the servants asked him, 'So do you want us to go and remove them?' But he answered, 'No, because while you are pulling up the darnel, you may uproot the wheat with it. Let both grow together until the harvest. And at the time of the harvest, I will tell the harvesters: First collect the darnel and tie

---

[1] Isaiah 33:14

[2] Matthew 25:41

[3] *Torment* from the Greek κόλασις, pronounced "koh'-lah-sis," meaning *penal infliction, torment,* or *punishment.*

[4] Matthew 25:46

[5] 1 Peter 4:19; Colossians 3:10; Isaiah 42:5

[6] Revelation 14:14-18; Matthew 13:39b

[7] Luke 6:43; Matthew 7:19

[8] Matthew 23:8; 17:5; John 13:13; 1 Corinthians 3:3-5

[9] *Darnel* from the Greek ζιζάνιον, pronounced "zih-zahn'-ee-awn," meaning *Lolium temulentum.*

it in bundles to be burned; then gather together the wheat and bring it into my barn.'"[1]

Understand that darnel is a *poisonous* form of false wheat that appears virtually identical to genuine wheat until the mature ear appears. When eaten, it can result in severe nausea and death.[2] During its early growth stages, it has a tendency to stand up tall, appearing as healthy wheat, whereas wheat can often appear less healthy upon growth as it bends under the weight of its forming grain.[3] Only upon maturity, when the ears are fully formed, is there a clear difference; when ripe, the mature heads of the darnel appear misaligned and black while those of the wheat appear aligned and light brown. This is why the owner of the field would not allow an attempt of separation until the grains of both plants had fully formed.[4]

In the same way, the spiritual growth of human beings can be difficult to quantify or qualify until they have reached maturity.[5] The unredeemed might appear joyful, bold, peaceful, and successful, while the redeemed could be struggling with their tormented souls when waging incessant battles against evil attacks.[6] To be sure, many of the redeemed are momentarily deceived and might appear indistinguishable from an unbeliever who regularly attends church,[7] but in the end, who they are will become clear by their fruit.[8]

But what is the difference between those people represented by wheat and those represented by darnel?[9] The difference is the allegiance shown to each kingdom.[10] Those in the Kingdom of Heaven bear good spiritual fruit[11] of motivations,[12] behaviors,[13] and deeds[14] that reveal the Characteristics of Yehovah in Creation,

---

[1] Matthew 13:24-30

[2] Such symptoms are the typical result of poison consumption according to the principles of this world with its governing principalities, though a child of Yehovah can rule over them (Mark 16:18).

[3] Matthew 13:29; John 7:24

[4] Matthew 13:30; 3:12; 22:10-14; 25:6-13

[5] 1 Corinthians 7:16; Romans 10:6-7

[6] Psalm 37:1-28; 1 Samuel 24:11; Proverbs 29:10; Habakkuk 1:13; Acts 7:52

[7] James 5:19-20; Psalm 32:1; 1 Peter 4:8

[8] Matthew 25:34-40; 1 John 4:20-21; 5:1-2

[9] Matthew 13:38-39; Mark 16:16; Romans 10:18

[10] John 5:28-29; Romans 2:6-10; Galatians 6:8

[11] Matthew 7:17; Psalm 1:3; 92:13-14; Isaiah 61:3

[12] 1 Timothy 1:5; Hebrews 10:22; 1 Peter 1:22

[13] 1 Peter 3:16; Acts 24:16; 2 Corinthians 1:12; Hebrews 13:18

[14] Matthew 5:16; 1 Timothy 5:25; Acts 26:20

while those in the kingdom of darkness bear bad fruit of motivations,[1] behaviors,[2] and deeds[3] that reveal characteristics contrary to Yehovah. Those who bear good fruit abide in the Truth,[4] do Yehovah's Will,[5] and intimately know Him,[6] while those who bear bad fruit spread lies,[7] live in sin,[8] and do not intimately know God.[9] Those who prove themselves to be disciples of Christ bring glory to the Father[10] and shine like a city on a hill[11] with truth,[12] righteousness,[13] and love,[14] while those who prove themselves to belong to the world embrace lies,[15] selfish ambition,[16] and cause others to sin.[17] In the end, everyone is judged by their deeds[18] as recorded by the angels.[19]

Many children of God have long been confused about judgment.[20] Final judgments of deeds are not like temporal judgments in Creation.[21] Temporal judgments are soulical corrections, verdicts of what should or should not have been done. They are explanations of the differences between how "wheat" and "darnel" behave or do not behave.[22] When true, such verdicts are active *correction* and *counsel* for the purpose of *repentance* in Creation.[23] When false, they are accusations, condemnations, and false guilt levied by the enemy to *inhibit* human beings from living in Yeshua's Truth, Righteousness, and Love.[24] But all such "Currents of

---

[1] Romans 7:5; 8:7-8; Mark 7:21
[2] Colossians 1:21; Galatians 5:19-21
[3] John 3:19-20; Ephesians 5:11; Romans 13:12
[4] 3 John 1:4; 2 Peter 1:12
[5] Galatians 5:22-25; Romans 8:3-5
[6] John 17:3; 2 Corinthians 4:6; 1 John 5:20
[7] John 8:44; Romans 1:25; 1 John 1:6; 2:21; Revelation 14:5; 2 Thessalonians 2:9,11; Titus 2:11; Hebrews 6:18; Colossians 3:9; Numbers 23:19; Psalm 38:12
[8] Hebrews 3:12; 1 Peter 4:3
[9] Matthew 7:23; Romans 8:6-8
[10] John 15:8; Luke 6:35; Psalm 92:12-15; Isaiah 60:21; Matthew 5:16
[11] Matthew 5:14; Ephesians 5:8-14; Philippians 2:15
[12] John 8:32; 1 John 2:21; 2 John 1:1
[13] Matthew 5:20; Romans 3:22; 6:19
[14] John 13:35; 1 John 2:10
[15] John 14:17; 1 Corinthians 2:14
[16] Galatians 5:19-21; James 3:16; 2 Corinthians 12:20
[17] Romans 1:32; 8:6; 2 Peter 2:14
[18] John 3:19; James 2:14,17,26; Revelation 2:2,19,23; 3:1,2,8,15-16; 20:12
[19] Revelation 20:12; Daniel 7:10; 2 Corinthians 5:10
[20] John 7:24; 8:15; James 2:4
[21] John 5:26-30; 8:15-16; Revelation 16:5; 19:2
[22] Hebrews 4:12; 1 Corinthians 5:3
[23] John 16:7-15; 2 Timothy 3:16
[24] Deuteronomy 19:16-21; Exodus 23:1-7

Should"[1] are attempts to *guide* the soul by means spiritual correction.[2] Such judgments are evaluations of input.[3] However, the Final Judgment is not a lecture about what should or should not have been done but rather a *comprehensive assessment* of a person's spiritual condition.[4] It is an inescapable exposure to the truth regarding a person's relationship with Yehovah.[5] It is an evaluation of output.[6] And it is not a long and arduous process but a sudden overwhelming revelation of *what is actually true,* a revelation that darnel is darnel and wheat is wheat, that goats are goats and sheep are sheep.[7] This revelation is not able to be altered.[8] It is the truth.[9] It is an honest description by the One Who Sees All of what a person is.[10] And Yehovah is the only One Who can make the final judgment, because He knows whether or not someone lives in the Truth, does His Will, and intimately knows Him.[11]

For those who have welcomed Him as their Creator,[12] God,[13] Lord,[14] Commander,[15] Law,[16] Priest,[17] Savior,[18] Teacher,[19] Father,[20] Groom of the Church,[21] Brother,[22] Friend,[23] Vine,[24] Living Water,[25] and Bread of Life,[26] the encounter at the Final Judgment is just the beginning of an astounding reunion

---

[1] See Chapter 32 of this testimony for more about the "Currents of Should."
[2] Romans 8:13; Colossians 3:5-8; 1 Peter 1:22
[3] Romans 8:5; John 3:6; 1 Corinthians 15:48
[4] Revelation 20:12; Daniel 7:10; 2 Corinthians 5:10
[5] Matthew 7:21-23; 25:12; John 10:14,27-30; 2 Timothy 2:19
[6] Matthew 25:41-45; 1 John 3:14-17; 4:20; John 8:42-44
[7] Matthew 25:32-33; 1 Timothy 6:17-19; Luke 14:12-14
[8] Matthew 25:10; Numbers 14:28-34; Psalm 95:11; Luke 13:25
[9] Luke 16:25; Revelation 2:23; Romans 2:5-11
[10] Revelation 2:23; Romans 8:27; Hebrews 4:13
[11] Matthew 7:21-23; 25:12; John 10:14,27-30; 2 Timothy 2:19
[12] 1 Peter 4:19; Colossians 3:10
[13] John 20:28; Isaiah 9:6; Luke 1:76; Malachi 3:1
[14] Acts 10:36; Matthew 22:44-46; John 3:35-36
[15] Matthew 26:53; 28:20; Luke 8:25
[16] Matthew 5:17; Romans 8:2
[17] Hebrews 4:14; 2:17; 3:1
[18] Isaiah 43:11; Luke 1:77-79; 2:11; Malachi 3:1
[19] John 13:13-14; Matthew 23:8
[20] John 10:30; 14:9; Matthew 11:27; 1 Timothy 3:16; Titus 2:13
[21] Matthew 9:15; John 3:29
[22] Hebrews 2:11; Matthew 28:10
[23] John 15:14; Luke 12:4
[24] John 15:1-5; Isaiah 4:2
[25] Revelation 22:1; John 4:10; 7:38
[26] Matthew 26:26; John 6:33,35,48,51

that aligns every fiber of the person's spirit and soul with all the Wonder and Perfection of His Generous Promises.[1] The person's faith is finally face to Face with their God[2] Who they then realize is everything they ever wanted, pursued, hoped for, or desired.[3] Power surges through their being,[4] continuing to increase beyond reason or expectation.[5] And joy erupts[6] in a brilliant release of eternal reward[7] as they stand before Him and begin to grasp that they will never again suffer, fail, or struggle[8] but will forevermore enjoy increasing heavenly blessing, perfection, and abundance.[9]

But for those who have not welcomed Him as their King,[10] they find themselves suddenly standing in the piercing rays of the Almighty Light of Truth[11] before their Creator Whom they have not personally known.[12] Though they might have previously known His Name,[13] they are now meeting Him as He is for the first time and experience an unavoidable revelation that they do not know Him at all.[14] The Truth is a consuming fire,[15] and there is a realization that there are no lies anywhere to be found.[16] There is recognition that they were given the same opportunity as everyone else,[17] yet they did not choose to walk in the Truth,[18] abide in Yehovah's Will,[19] or bother to know Him intimately.[20] And somehow, the understanding is obvious that since they were unable to do these things in Creation, they would never be able to achieve them in Heaven[21] (For if they were

---

[1] John 5:24; 2 Corinthians 1:20; 7:1
[2] 1 Corinthians 13:12; Numbers 12:8; Matthew 5:8
[3] John 14:6; 17:3; Acts 4:12; Hebrews 10:19-22; 1 John 2:23; 2 John 1:9; Revelation 5:8-9; 17:3
[4] 1 Corinthians 15:43; Matthew 22:29; Philippians 3:10
[5] 1 Corinthians 2:9; 1 Peter 1:12; Psalm 31:19; Hebrews 11:16
[6] John 15:11; 16:24; 17:13; 1 Peter 1:8; Jude 1:24
[7] Genesis 15:1; Isaiah 62:11; Matthew 5:12; Revelation 11:18
[8] Revelation 7:16; Isaiah 49:10
[9] Revelation 7:17; Isaiah 35:6-7
[10] Luke 19:27; 1 Thessalonians 2:15-16
[11] Luke 11:36; 19:42-44; Matthew 23:34-36
[12] Matthew 7:23; 25:12; John 10:14,27-30; 2 Timothy 2:19
[13] Matthew 7:22; Luke 6:46; 13:25-27
[14] Luke 13:26-28; 1 Corinthians 8:3
[15] Hebrews 12:29; Exodus 24:17; Psalm 50:3; 97:3; Isaiah 66:15
[16] Psalm 5:4; 101:7; Habakkuk 1:13; Hebrews 12:14; Revelation 21:25,27; 22:5
[17] Romans 2:6-11; Matthew 25:34-46; Galatians 6:7-8
[18] 1 John 1:6; John 3:19-20
[19] Romans 8:7; Matthew 7:21
[20] Galatians 4:8; 1 John 4:8; 2 Thessalonians 1:8
[21] Luke 16:29; Romans 1:20-21

unable to perceive the value of Goodness in Creation where they could witness and experience its comparison and contrast, then they would certainly be unable to perceive its value in Heaven, where there is no longer any contrast available).[1]

Therefore,

"Come! Let us sing for joy to Yehovah; let us shout for joy to the Rock of our salvation! Let us come into His Presence with thanksgiving and shout for joy to Him with music and song! For Yehovah is the great God, the great King above all gods! In His Hand are the depths of the earth and the peaks of the mountains! The sea is His, and He made it, and His Hands formed the dry land. Come! Let us bow down and worship Him! Let us kneel in the Presence of Yehovah, our Maker; because He is our God and we are the people of His pasture, the flock in His Hand. Today, if you hear His Voice, 'Do not harden your hearts as you did at Meribah, as you did on that day at Massah in the wilderness, where your ancestors tested Me; they tested Me, though they had seen My works. For forty years I detested that generation; I said, "They are a people whose hearts wander, and they have not known My ways." So I declared on oath in My Wrath, "They will never enter My rest."'"[2]

And not a single one of those who hardened their hearts against Him entered into His rest.[3] They chose not to know Yehovah, so they were not known by Yehovah.[4]

"Not everyone who says to Me, Lord, Lord,' will come into the Kingdom of Heaven, *but only the one who continues in the will of My Father Who is in Heaven.* Many will say to Me on that day, 'Lord, Lord, did we not prophesy in Your Name and in Your Name eject demons and in Your Name perform many miracles?' Then I will tell them plainly, '*I never knew you at any time*. Depart from Me, you who practice lawlessness!'"[5]

So we see that those who did not do Yehovah's Will did not know Him, either.

"But know this: There will be troublesome times in the last days. People will be selfish, greedy, boastful, proud, abusive, disobedient to their parents, ungrateful, unholy, *without love*, uncooperative, slanderous, without self-control, brutal, *not lovers of the good*, traitors, reckless, conceited, lovers of pleasure rather than

---

[1] Luke 16:30-31; John 11:43-53

[2] Psalm 95:1-11

[3] Hebrews 3:18-19; Numbers 14:20-23

[4] Hebrews 12:16-17; 1 Corinthians 8:3; Matthew 7:23; Revelation 3:15-16

[5] Matthew 7:21-23

lovers of God—having an appearance of godliness but denying its power. Turn away from such people because they are the kind who creep their way into homes and captivate vulnerable women, who are saturated with sin and swayed by all sorts of evil desires. They are always learning but *never able to come to a knowledge of the truth*. Just as Jannes and Jambres opposed Moses, so also *these people oppose the truth*. They are people of depraved minds, unaccepted by the faith."[1]

And we see that those who do not intimately know or love Yehovah do not know the Truth, either.

"Then He will say to those on His left, 'Depart from Me, you who are cursed, into the everlasting fire prepared for the Devil and his angels. Because I was hungry and you gave Me nothing to eat, I was thirsty and you gave Me nothing to drink, I was a stranger and you did not receive Me, I was poorly clothed and you did not clothe Me, I was sick and in prison and you did not check on Me.' They also will reply, 'Lord, when did we see You hungry or thirsty or a stranger or poorly clothed or sick or in prison, and did not help You?' Then He will answer them, 'I assure you, whatever you did not do for one of the least of these, you did not do for Me.' Then they will go away to everlasting punishment, but the righteous to everlasting life."[2]

Therefore, we understand that those who do not do His Will do not intimately know or love Him, either.

CHILDREN OF YEHOVAH![3] IF YOU DO NOT DO HIS WILL NOW, YOU WILL NOT DO IT LATER![4] IF YOU DO NOT LIVE IN THE TRUTH NOW, YOU WILL NOT LIVE IN IT LATER![5] AND IF YOU DO NOT INTIMATELY KNOW GOD NOW, YOU WILL NOT KNOW HIM LATER![6]

TODAY IS THE DAY OF SALVATION![7] YOU MUST PLANT THE SEED NOW TO REAP THE HARVEST LATER![8] YOU MUST CHOOSE THE LIGHT NOW, OR YOU HAVE CHOSEN DARKNESS FOR LATER![9]

---

[1] 2 Timothy 3:1-8
[2] Matthew 25:41-46
[3] Deuteronomy 14:1; Hosea 1:10; John 1:12; 11:52; Romans 8:6
[4] Luke 16:10; Matthew 25:24-30
[5] Galatians 6:7-9; Job 4:8; Proverbs 11:18; Romans 2:6-10
[6] Hebrews 12:16-17; 1 Corinthians 8:3; Matthew 7:23; Revelation 3:15-16
[7] Hebrews 3:7,15; 4:7
[8] Hosea 10:12; Galatians 6:7-8
[9] John 12:35-36; Matthew 25:6-13

DO NOT DELAY! BECAUSE, UNLESS YOU ARE WALKING WITH HIM,[1] YOU DO NOT KNOW IF YOU HAVE ANOTHER DAY TOMORROW![2]

DO NOT LISTEN TO ANY THOUGHT, IDEA, OR PURSUIT THAT SUGGESTS THAT YOU CAN WAIT![3] KNOW THAT THERE ARE MANY PEOPLE WHO HAVE NOT LIVED AS LONG AS YOU![4]

The day I died, I had *NO* warning![5] I was fine one moment and dead the next! I was a healthy and strong young man. I listened to many ideas and thoughts that suggested I had plenty of time to "straighten out my life."[6] But they were *ALL* wrong! They were voices of dark spirits that were planning to sabotage me![7] They knew the spiritual law better than I did, and they used technical claims against me to take my life![8] I had been baptized more than once, prayed to have Yeshua live in my heart, and said the Lord's Prayer every morning but nevertheless found myself in outer darkness because I was *not walking with Him*![9] Despite my memories of our discussion in the womb and all the times I had heard His Spirit speak to me, I neither abided in His Will, dwelled in the Truth, nor intimately knew Him.[10] I had conspired with the enemy and had therefore become an enemy of Yeshua and His Kingdom.[11]

PRAISE YEHOVAH THAT HE SNATCHED ME LIKE A STICK FROM THE FIRE![12] But the judgment was so close that when I called on His Name, I was sent back to earth because I was *UNABLE* at that time to enter Heaven![13]

BLESS THE LORD! THANK YOU, YESHUA, FOR RESCUING ME AND SHOWING ME SUCH UNDESERVED MERCY![14]

---

[1] John 21:18-19; Acts 9:16

[2] Luke 12:20; James 4:15

[3] Luke 12:45; Ezekiel 12:27-28

[4] Luke 12:19-20,40,46; Revelation 16:15

[5] Revelation 3:3; Matthew 24:42-43; 1 Thessalonians 5:4-6

[6] Matthew 24:48; Ezekiel 12:27; 2 Peter 3:3-5

[7] 2 Corinthians 11:3; Revelation 12:9; 2 Timothy 4:3-4

[8] Romans 8:13; Colossians 3:5-8; 1 Peter 2:11

[9] Luke 6:49; 10:12-16; 12:47; Hebrews 10:26-29; 2 Peter 2:20

[10] Revelation 3:16; 16:15; Jeremiah 15:1-4

[11] Matthew 25:30; 12:32; Hebrews 6:8; Luke 14:34-35; John 15:6

[12] Zechariah 3:2; Jude 1:23; 1 Corinthians 3:15

[13] James 4:4; Matthew 24:51

[14] Matthew 9:13; Mark 5:19; Luke 1:78

But none of us deserve His Mercy![1] To suggest that we could somehow deserve His Mercy is as nonsensical as suggesting that we deserved to be created![2]

WE BELONG TO HIM ALREADY![3] HE MADE US![4] AND HE CAN DO WHATEVER HE WANTS WITH US BECAUSE HE MADE ALL THINGS[5] AND ANSWERS TO NO ONE BUT HIMSELF![6]

Yet we can trust in Him to remain true to Himself because He is the Truth,[7] and He is Faithfulness![8] These Characteristics, like all His others, are not simply recorded choices on His part but descriptions of His very Being![9] These Characteristics are living![10] They are eternal![11]

In the same way, we are eternal beings![12] We are made in His Image![13] Therefore, whatever we are now *is* what we are eternally![14] And though we ourselves cannot yet *see* what we are eternally,[15] Yehovah has told us what we are,[16] and we experience ourselves moving from glory to glory.[17]

Therefore, today, if you hear His Voice encouraging you toward Him, do not wait![18] Speak what you hear![19] Speak your salvation![20] Speak your obedience![21] Call out

---

[1] Romans 3:23; 1 John 1:10
[2] Jeremiah 18:6; Isaiah 64:8; Matthew 20:15
[3] Isaiah 43:7,21; 48:11; John 15:8; Romans 9:23; Ephesians 1:12
[4] Psalm 86:9; Isaiah 42:5; Acts 17:25
[5] Revelation 4:11; Ephesians 3:9; Colossians 1:16
[6] Isaiah 40:13-14; Romans 11:34; Ephesians 1:11
[7] Hebrews 6:18; John 1:17; 14:6
[8] 2 Timothy 2:13; Matthew 24:35; Isaiah 25:1; 1 Thessalonians 5:24
[9] Matthew 19:17; 1 Samuel 2:2; Psalm 145:7-9; James 1:17
[10] 1 John 4:12,16; 3:24
[11] Romans 1:20; Hebrews 13:8; Psalm 102:27-28; 103:17; Malachi 3:6; James 1:17
[12] Daniel 7:18; Revelation 22:5
[13] Genesis 1:26; Romans 8:29
[14] Colossians 3:3; 1 John 3:2; 1 Peter 1:3-5
[15] 1 Corinthians 13:12; Philippians 3:12; 2 Corinthians 3:18; 1 John 3:12
[16] James 1:23-24; 1 Thessalonians 1:5; Ezekiel 33:31-32; Matthew 7:26-27
[17] 2 Corinthians 3:18; Proverbs 4:18
[18] Hebrews 3:7; 4:7; 3:15; Psalm 95:7
[19] Matthew 10:27; 28:19; Acts 1:8; 5:20
[20] Romans 10:9,32; 1 John 4:2
[21] Romans 10:10; 1 John 4:15; Revelation 2:13

to Him![1] Because by doing so, you prove yourself to be a disciple of Yeshua and bring glory to our Father in Heaven![2] Allow the gift of faith[3] given to you to become alive![4] Listen to the Voice encouraging you to do good things[5] and put His counsel into practice![6] Stop looking at your soul to see what it likes or wants to do, but start leading your soul to do what God likes and wants you to do![7]

WHO IS YOUR GOD? IS IT YOUR SOUL, OR IS IT YEHOVAH?[8]

IT IS VERY EASY TO DETERMINE WHO YOUR GOD IS: IF YOU DO WHAT YOU WANT, YOU ARE SERVING YOURSELF![9] BUT IF YOU DO WHAT YEHOVAH WANTS, YOU ARE SERVING GOD![10]

GOOD TREES BEAR GOOD FRUIT![11]

YOU WILL KNOW A TREE BY ITS FRUIT![12]

IT IS VERY EASY TO DETERMINE WHO YOUR GOD IS: IF YOU BELIEVE YOURSELF, YOU ARE SERVING YOURSELF![13] BUT IF YOU BELIEVE YEHOVAH, YOU ARE SERVING GOD![14]

GOOD TREES BEAR GOOD FRUIT!

YOU WILL KNOW A TREE BY ITS FRUIT!

---

[1] Jeremiah 33:3; Deuteronomy 4:29; Psalm 91:15; Isaiah 65:24; Joel 2:32; Luke 11:9-10; Acts 2:21

[2] John 15:8; Luke 6:35; Psalm 92:12-15; Isaiah 60:21; Matthew 5:16

[3] Ephesians 2:5,8; Titus 2:11; 3:5

[4] 2 Timothy 1:6; James 2:22

[5] Acts 9:31; John 14:16-18; Romans 5:5; 15:13; Galatians 5:22-23

[6] James 1:22; 4:17; Matthew 7:21-25; 12:50; 28:20; Luke 11:28; 12:47-48; John 13:17; Romans 2:13; 1 John 2:3, 3:7; 3 John 1:11; Revelation 22:7

[7] James 1:23-24; 1 Thessalonians 1:5; Ezekiel 33:31-32; Matthew 7:26-27

[8] Joshua 24:15; 1 Kings 18:21

[9] Luke 6:46; Malachi 1:6; Matthew 7:21; Galatians 6:7

[10] Matthew 7:21; 12:50

[11] Matthew 7:17; Psalm 1:3; 92:13-14; Isaiah 61:3

[12] Matthew 7:16,20; Luke 6:45; James 3:12

[13] Proverbs 3:5,7; 14:12

[14] Romans 3:22; 4:5; Galatians 2:16

IT IS VERY EASY TO DETERMINE WHO YOUR GOD IS: IF YOU PUT YOURSELF FIRST,[1] YOU ARE SERVING YOURSELF![2] BUT IF YOU PUT YEHOVAH FIRST IN ALL THAT YOU DO,[3] THEN YOU ARE PROVING YOURSELF TO BE HIS DISCIPLE, BRINGING GLORY TO HIS NAME,[4] AND KNOWING HIM INTIMATELY![5]

HALLELUUUUUUUUYAAAAAAAAAAAAAH!!!!!!!!!

CHILDREN OF YEHOVAH![6] IF YOU *CARE* ABOUT THESE THINGS, THEN YOU *DO* BELONG TO HIM!!!![7]

HALLELUUUUUUUUYAAAAAAAAAAAAAH!!!!!!!!!

TODAY IS *YOUR* DAY!!![8]

HALLELUUUUUUUUYAAAAAAAAAAAAAH!!!!!!!!!

TODAY YOU *CAN* CROSS THE JORDAN!!![9]

HALLELUUUUUUUUYAAAAAAAAAAAAAH!!!!!!!!!

WARRIORS OF HIS HOLY ARMY![10] YOUR MOMENT HAS COME! YOU ARE AWAKE!!!!![11]

PRAISE BE TO OUR HOLY SAVIOR!!!!![12]

YOUR EYES ARE OPEN!!!!![13]

HOLY, HOLY, HOLY IS OUR RIGHTEOUS GOD!!!!!![14]

---

[1] 3 John 1:9-11; Matthew 20:20-28
[2] James 3:16; Philippians 2:3; Galatians 5:20
[3] Matthew 6:33; Luke 12:31; Psalm 34:9; 37:19; 84:11; Isaiah 33:16; John 6:27
[4] John 15:8; Luke 6:35; Psalm 92:12-15; Isaiah 60:21; Matthew 5:16
[5] John 10:27: Revelation 3:20; 1 Corinthians 8:3
[6] Romans 8:14; Galatians 3:26; 1 John 3:1-2; 5:19; Matthew 5:9
[7] 1 John 4:6; John 14:17; 15:26; 16:13
[8] Hebrews 3:7; 4:7; 3:15; Psalm 95:7
[9] Hebrews 4:10; Luke 18:17
[10] 2 Timothy 2:3; 2 Corinthians 10:3-5; Ephesians 6:11-18; 1 Timothy 1:18
[11] Matthew 13:16; 16:17; Acts 26:18; 2 Corinthians 4:6; Ephesians 1:18
[12] 2 Samuel 22:47; Psalm 68:19
[13] Ephesians 1:17-18; Matthew 16:17
[14] Revelation 4:8; Isaiah 6:3; Exodus 15:11

YOU HAVE COME OUT OF THE DARKNESS AND ENTERED THE LIGHT!!!!![1]

PRAISE OUR ALMIGHTY AND VICTORIOUS KING!!!!![2]

YOU ARE READY TO CONQUER AND DISCOVER WHO YOU REALLY ARE!!!!![3]

HALLELUUUUUUUUYAAAAAAAAAAAAAAH!!!!!!!!!!

HALLELUUUUUUUUYAAAAAAAAAAAAAAH!!!!!!!!!!

HALLELUUUUUUUUYAAAAAAAAAAAAAAAAAAAAAAAAAAAH!!!!!!!!!!

[1] 1 Peter 2:9; 1 Thessalonians 5:4-6; Colossians 1:13

[2] 1 Corinthians 15:57; John 16:33

[3] Romans 8:37; 1 John 5:4-5; Revelation 12:11; 15:2-4

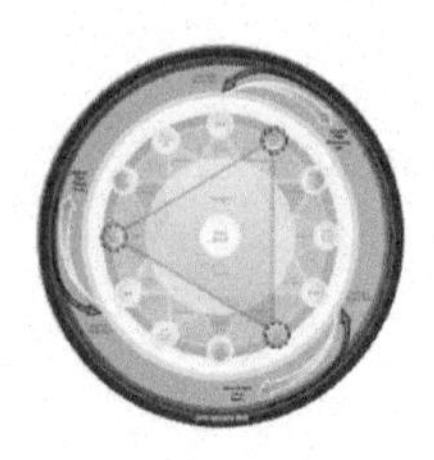

CHAPTER 18

DOMINION OVER BODY, SOUL, AND CREATION

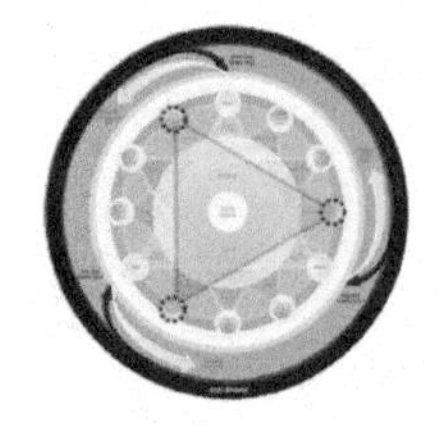

HOLY WARRIORS OF YEHOVAH! DOMINION IS OURS! HE HAS GIVEN IT INTO OUR HANDS! BE STRONG AND COURAGEOUS!

TODAY IS THE DAY YOU GLORIFY YOUR HOLY KING!

HALLELUUUUUUUUYAAAAAAAAAAAAAH!!!!!!!!!

THEREFORE, LISTEN CAREFULLY!

Dominion is NOT something that occurs only with physical words but is spoken from the truth by the spirit and manifested in Creation.[1]

HALLELUYAH!

When a human being fights against a sickness or injury in the soul or body, dark spirits will attempt to hide their dominion to avoid a challenge.[2] They know that they cannot stay without the person's permission, so they cite any dark deeds

---

1 Matthew 17:20; 21:21; Genesis 1:28; Psalm 8:1; 1 Peter 4:11; 1 Corinthians 10:31

2 Mark 1:24-26; John 9:1-7

committed by a person as legal proof of that person's violation of the Second Jurisdiction,[1] abandonment of the First Jurisdiction,[2] and allegiance to the kingdom of darkness.[3] Such deeds also include any verbal permission that functions as an agreement of shared dominion over the flesh.[4] And if a person does not make a resolute effort to rid their soul or body of any invasion of darkness, then the kingdom of darkness cites that failure of resistance as constituting a deed of permission.[5] That is to say, the enemy will claim that any sort of agreement, whether explicit or tacit, is a covenant.[6]

Listen, holy children of Yehovah![7] Make straight the way of the Lord and listen![8]

The enemy will not only claim willful sin but *any* sort of surrender, neglect, ignorance, or concession on the part of the redeemed as *implied* allegiance to darkness![9] They will argue that a common direction means there has been an agreement toward darkness, whether spoken or unspoken![10]

This is why we need Christ to wash our feet![11] Even though we are not purposefully wallowing in the mire, it is easy for our feet to become dirty while walking on the earth.[12] We might spend all day resisting sin and refusing to bend to any temptation, but the slightest neglect, the smallest hint of concession to even a worldly idea, can be claimed by the enemy as agreement.[13] Therefore, rather than tiptoeing around with an obsessive-compulsive attention to the most meticulous aspects of life, we boldly set off down the road, confident that our Savior will wash our feet from even the least bit of soil.[14] We set our eyes on our destination above,[15] and we accept no condemnation or accusation![16]

---

[1] See Chapter 13 for the Law of Sin and Death; Romans 8:2b
[2] See Chapter 15 for the Law of the Spirit; Romans 8:2a
[3] James 5:15-16,19-20; Matthew 18:15-17
[4] Job 31:30; Psalm 62:4; Mark 5:12; Luke 4:41
[5] James 4:7; 1 Peter 5:9
[6] Numbers 30:10-16; Job 2:4
[7] Luke 8:18; 19:26; Deuteronomy 32:46-47; Proverbs 2:2-5; Mark 4:23-24; Acts 17:11; Hebrews 2:1; James 1:22-25; Matthew 13:12; John 15:2
[8] Hebrews 12:13; Proverbs 4:26-27; Isaiah 40:3-4; 42:16; Jeremiah 31:8-9
[9] Acts 6:2; 1 Timothy 5:8
[10] Deuteronomy 22:23-24
[11] John 13:5-7: Hebrews 10:22
[12] John 13:10; James 4:8
[13] Matthew 6:23-24b; Romans 6:16; Galatians 1:10; James 4:4; 1 John 2:15-16
[14] John 13:8; Zechariah 13:1; Ephesians 5:26; Revelation 7:14
[15] Colossians 3:1; Hebrews 11:13-16
[16] Romans 4:7-8; 5:1; 8:1; Isaiah 54:17; John 3:18; 5:24; Galatians 3:13

Our Savior's Blood washes us clean![1] HalleluYah!

Through Yeshua, we have been released from every debt![2] Therefore, we speak this freedom aloud so that all claims of tacit agreement with evil may be canceled and covered under the Blood of Yeshua![3]

WE ARE CLEAN IN THE NAME OF JESUS![4] HALLELUYAH!

Holy ones! You have been called and chosen for victory![5] HalleluYah! Therefore, may the Spirit of Wisdom[6] and Truth[7] give you revelation for victory over darkness, and may your soul be blessed to receive it![8] Amen!

Let us then understand that both the soul and the body are like the Promised Land.[9] They represent vast potential regarding ability, power, blessing, and influence. Dark spirits seek this potential, and when they obtain a foothold, they hide their presence from us by attributing their own dark deeds to us, Creation, or Yehovah.[10] They do not want to be challenged by us![11] They know we have been given authority and power to conquer them and take their temporal dominion away![12]

BE CAST OUT, YOU FOUL SPIRITS OF DARKNESS![13] THE LORD OUR GOD SEES YOU![14] YOU CHOSE DARKNESS, AND DARKNESS IS YOUR DESTINY![15] THE LORD ALMIGHTY YEHOVAH SAYS TO YOU, "GET OUT OF MY LAND!"[16] THE LORD

---

[1] Revelation 7:14; 1 John 1:7; Hebrews 9:14
[2] Colossians 2:13-14; Acts 3:19; Hebrews 8:13
[3] Revelation 12:11; 7:10-14; 15:3
[4] John 15:3; 17:17; Acts 11:9
[5] Romans 8:30; 1 Corinthians 15:57; 1 Peter 5:10
[6] Ephesians 1:17; Luke 12:12; 21:15; Matthew 16:17; 1 Corinthians 2:10
[7] John 14:26; 16:13; 1 Corinthians 2:10-13; Ephesians 4:7-15; 1 John 2:20,27
[8] James 1:12; John 16:24; Acts 11:1
[9] Mark 8:36; Proverbs 16:32; Hebrews 3:11-4:13
[10] 2 Corinthians 11:14; Ephesians 6:11-12; Revelation 12:9-11; Notice Job 2:5, "But now stretch out your hand and strike his flesh and bones, and he will surely curse you to your face." - Satan wanted to strike Job so that Job would curse Yehovah (as opposed to cursing Satan). By doing this, Job would have opened his soul to the dominion of evil.
[11] Matthew 8:29; Mark 1:24; 5:7; Luke 4:34; 8:28
[12] Romans 8:37; Ephesians 2:6; Luke 10:19
[13] Matthew 12:28: Mark 16:17; Acts 10:38
[14] Hebrews 4:13; Job 26:6
[15] Matthew 22:13; 25:41; 2 Peter 2:4
[16] Deuteronomy 9:4; 18:12; Leviticus 18:24-25

ALMIGHTY YEHOVAH STRIKES YOU![1] BE STRICKEN![2] LOOK! HIS HOLY ANGELS ARE EXPELLING YOU OUT OF HIS BELOVED CHILDREN![3] YOU WILL CRY OUT, BUT YOUR VOICE WILL BE HEARD NO MORE![4]

HALLELUYAH! OUR GOD RULES WITH AN IRON SCEPTER![5]

HALLELUYAH!

Chosen warriors of Yeshua! Listen! This war is not pleasant![6] Yet, it is necessary because of unrighteousness, for evil wishes to spread like a disease throughout all of existence.[7] But be encouraged! He Who is Good has defeated evil![8] And by the Almighty Power of Yehovah, we have been made to be like Him![9] Those of us who live in Him also share in His Goodness and in His resolute stance against evil![10] We do not war because we long for war; rather, we war because we live for goodness.[11] HalleluYah! We do not accept sin, because sin is an attack![12] We do not accept sickness, because sickness is an attack![13] On the contrary! We boldly charge against them because it is His will that we defeat them for His Glory![14] HalleluYah!

All children of the Kingdom of Heaven have been given the Mind of Christ,[15] the Righteousness of Christ,[16] and the Love of Christ.[17] Every attempt of dominion by the enemy, whether against the body or soul, is an attack against one or more of these gates of mind, will, and heart. These are the primary gates.[18] If any intermediate gates have fallen, it is because of a weakness in the reception of

---

[1] 1 Chronicles 14:15; Isaiah 13:4; 45:2; Micah 2:13
[2] Psalm 3:7; 58:6; Lamentations 3:30
[3] Philippians 1:6; Hebrews 12:2
[4] Psalm 143:12; 54:5; 55:23
[5] Revelation 19:15-21; Isaiah 11:4; 2 Thessalonians 2:8
[6] Philippians 1:29; Acts 14:22
[7] 2 Thessalonians 2:3-7; Isaiah 14:13: Daniel 8:9-11; 11:36; Revelation 13:6
[8] Isaiah 13:11; 2 Thessalonians 1:9; 2 Peter 2:9; Psalm 100:5; 107:1; Revelation 3:21
[9] Romans 8:29; Matthew 12:50; 25:40; Colossians 1:15-18; Revelation 1:5-6
[10] Galatians 5:22; Ephesians 5:9
[11] Romans 15:14; Philippians 4:8
[12] Hebrews 2:18; 4:15; Matthew 4:1-11; Luke 4:1-13
[13] Job 2:7; Luke 4:39
[14] Luke 10:19; Psalm 91:13; Ezekiel 2:6; Mark 16:18; Acts 28:5; Romans 16:20
[15] 1 Corinthians 2:16; John 15:15; 16:13-15
[16] 2 Corinthians 5:21; Romans 10:4
[17] Romans 5:5; John 15:9; 1 John 4:7-8
[18] Luke 10:27; Deuteronomy 30:14

Truth by one of the primary gates of observation.[1] In other words, some lie has been accepted and is blocking full blessing from flowing through the gate.[2]

Chief among such lies is the suggestion that the attribution of sickness to evil spirits is willful ignorance due to ancient superstitious thinking.[3] Do not entertain such a shallow and blind lie![4] Remember that Luke, the vessel[5] used to write the Gospel of Luke and Acts,[6] was a medical doctor[7] who used medical terms in his writing.[8] Yet he readily admitted that a woman who had been crippled for eighteen years was unable to stand up straight, not because of a spinal issue, but because of a *spirit* of infirmity.[9] He wrote this because Yeshua rebuked a meddling synagogue leader by explaining that the woman had been kept bound by Satan.[10] Christ had called that woman forward and said, "Woman, you are set free from your infirmity!"[11] Then He placed His hands on her, and she immediately straightened up and praised Yehovah![12]

Therefore, do not make the mistake of embracing a spirit of pride and accepting thoughts that you know more than Christ because you were born recently into a world of technological tools.[13] After all, many people alive today will testify that minds were stronger in memory and math before calculators and cellphones were available. The tools have made memory and math more accessible, but they have not made minds more capable. Consequently, you might be able to enter symptoms into a software application for a contemporary diagnosis[14] and

---

[1] Galatians 5:7-8; 2 Corinthians 11:3
[2] Matthew 6:23; James 1:6-8
[3] 2 Peter 3:4; Ezekiel 12:22: Malachi 2:17; Luke 12:45
[4] Matthew 9:4; Ezekiel 38:10; Haggai 2:13-14
[5] 2 Corinthians 4:7; 5:1; 2 Peter 1:13-14
[6] Luke 1:1-4; Philemon 1:24; 2 Timothy 4:11; Acts 1:1-2; 16:10-17; 20:5-15; 21:1-18; 27:1-28:16
[7] Colossians 4:14; Luke 5:31; 8:43
[8] For example, παραλύω, pronounced "pah-rah-loo'-oh" and meaning "palsy" or "paralysis," was used by Luke in Luke 5:18,24; Acts 8:7; 9:33. Likewise, he used ὑδρωπικός, pronounced "hoo-droh-pih-'kaws" the etymon of the older English term *dropsy*, as a technical term for *edema* in Luke 14:2.
[9] Luke 13:11
[10] Luke 13:14-17
[11] Luke 13:12
[12] Luke 13:13
[13] Daniel 12:4; Romans 10:16
[14] *Diagnosis* is a transliteration from the Greek διάγνωσις, meaning *to discern.* Be cautious about agreeing with what "experts" *speak* about you (Matthew 10:12-15).

prognosis[1] and have all sorts of complex suggestions returned to you. But you cannot enter your symptoms into the application and have the application instantly heal you by saying, "You are set free from your infirmity!" Therefore, if you want to do what contemporary medical doctors do, then go study what they say and do. Certainly, you will lose many battles against all sorts of diseases and sicknesses (because you will be answering to the very principles overseen by the principalities that govern such things)![2] But if you want to learn how to cast out diseases, sicknesses, and crippling spirits with a word, then you will have to learn from the One Who does such things![3] And do not think that you cannot be blessed with such authority and power,[4] but know that the disciples were later given authority to do even greater things than Yeshua allowed Himself to do![5]

EVERY PROMISE IS "YES" AND "AMEN" FOR YOU IN CHRIST JESUS![6] HE HAS GRANTED AUTHORITY TO HIS BODY TO DO EVEN GREATER THINGS THAN HE DID WHEN WALKING ON THE EARTH![7]

MIGHTY BODY OF CHRIST![8] DO YOU HEAR WHAT THE SPIRIT IS SAYING TO YOU?[9] HE IS SAYING THAT HE HAS GRANTED YOU AUTHORITY TO DO EVEN MORE THAN

---

[1] *Prognosis* is a transliteration from the Greek πρόγνωσις, meaning *foreknowledge* or *prediction.* Be cautious about agreeing with what "experts" *prophesy* over you. *Prophecy* is from the Greek προφητεύω, meaning *to foretell events.* Listen carefully to the difference of an "expert" telling you what *will* happen versus what *could* happen (Matthew 24:11). I testify that I witnessed many miracles while I worked as a "professional," and I watched as the "experts" stood dumfounded when cancer was cured, deformities were instantly healed, and the dead were raised back to life in the Name of Jesus! HalleluYah! Yehovah Rapha is our Healer! HalleluYah! Jesus Christ is the same yesterday, today, and forever (Hebrews 13:8)! HALLELUYAH!

[2] Ephesians 6:12; Romans 8:38; Colossians 2:15; 1 Peter 3:22

[3] Matthew 8:16

[4] Luke 10:19; Psalm 91:13; Ezekiel 2:6; Mark 16:18; Acts 28:5; Romans 16:20

[5] Acts 5:15; Acts 19:12; John 14:12; I share this later in the testimony, but I was once told *over the phone* about a friend who had died in a hospital two and a half hours earlier, and when I asked our Father in the Name of Yeshua to raise her from the dead, He raised her immediately! Glory to God! HalleluYah! HALLELUYAH! PRAISE OUR SAVIOR! HALLELUYAH!

[6] 2 Corinthians 1:20; Galatians 3:22; Acts 13:32-39

[7] John 14:12; Acts 5:15; 19:12

[8] Ephesians 5:30

[9] Revelation 2:7; Luke 8:18; 19:26; Deuteronomy 32:46-47; Proverbs 2:2-5; Mark 4:23-24; Acts 17:11; Hebrews 2:1; James 1:22-25; Matthew 13:12; John 15:2

HE DID![1] HE IS SAYING THAT YOU BRING GLORY TO YEHOVAH WHEN YOU WALK AS HIS DISCIPLES AND DO WHAT HE DID![2] NOTHING IS IMPOSSIBLE FOR YOU![3]

HALLELUYAH!

But concerning the world, we remember that the Lord has said:

"And in them is fulfilled the prophecy of Isaiah: 'Hearing, you hear but never understand; seeing, you see but never perceive. For this people's heart has become fat; their ears are too heavy to hear, and their eyes are too shut to see—or else they might see with their eyes, hear with their ears, understand with their hearts and turn, *and I would heal them*.'"[4]

THE WORLD HAS BEEN BLINDED BY THE SPIRIT OF PRIDE![5] BUT YOU HAVE BEEN GIVEN YESHUA'S AUTHORITY[6] AND POWER![7]

THEREFORE, CAST AWAY the LIES suggested by the principalities with their worldly rules and principles![8] HUMBLE yourself[9] and learn from the One Who HEALED with a word EVERYONE who came to Him from EVERY sort of sickness, disease, injury, and demonization![10]

HALLELUYAH!

The Good News is so WONDERFUL that it exceeds the ability of the FLESH to fathom it![11]

HALLELUYAH!

---

[1] John 14:12; Acts 5:15; 19:12
[2] John 15:8; Philippians 1:11
[3] Matthew 17:20; Mark 9:23; Luke 1:37; 18:27
[4] Matthew 13:14-15; Isaiah 6:9-10
[5] 2 Corinthians 4:4; 1 John 2:16; 1 Timothy 3:6
[6] Luke 10:19; Psalm 91:13; Ezekiel 2:6; Mark 16:18; Acts 28:5; Romans 16:20
[7] Ephesians 3:7,20; 2 Peter 1:3; 2 Timothy 1:7
[8] 1 Corinthians 2:12; Romans 8:5-6; 2 Corinthians 4:4; Ephesians 2:2
[9] James 4:10; 1 Peter 5:6; Luke 1:52; 14:11
[10] Luke 4:40; Matthew 4:23-24; 11:5; Mark 3:10; 6:55-56
[11] 1 Corinthians 2:9; 1 Peter 1:12; Psalm 31:19; Hebrews 11:16

OUR GOD HAS POURED HIS SPIRIT INTO US,[1] AND THROUGH IT WE CAN EMBRACE THE FULLNESS OF THE KINGDOM OF HEAVEN![2]

HALLELUYAH!

OUR SAVIOR HAS SET US FREE FROM THE CHAINS OF THE WORLD![3]

HALLELUYAH!

JESUS CHRIST HAS DELIVERED US FROM SICKNESS[4] AND DEATH![5]

HALLELUYAH!

ETERNAL LIFE IS OURS IN HIM BOTH NOW AND FOREVER![6]

HALLELUYAH!

HALLELUYAH!

HALLELUUUUUUYAAAAAAAAAAAAAAAAAAAAH!!!!!!!!!!!!!!!!!

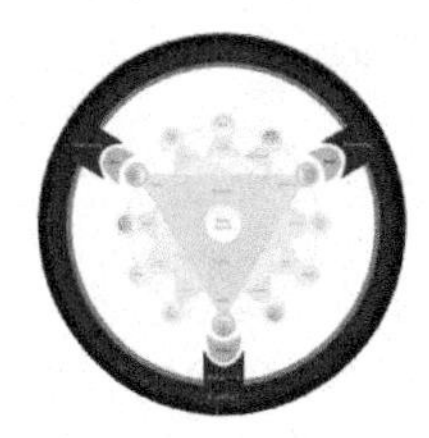

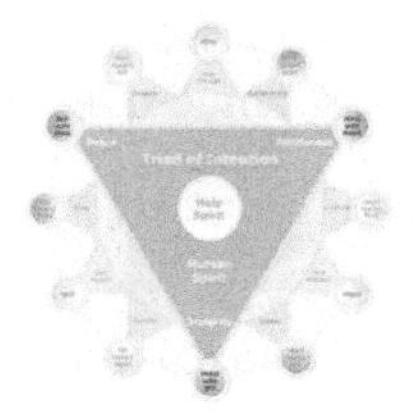

[1] Acts 2:17; 10:45; Titus 3:4-6; Proverbs 1:23; Isaiah 32:15-16; 44:3 Ezekiel 39:29; Zechariah 12:10

[2] Matthew 11:11; Luke 8:10

[3] Romans 8:1-4; John 17:14-16

[4] Deuteronomy 7:15; 2 Corinthians 1:20

[5] Romans 8:2,10-11; 6:18,22; John 8:36; Hebrews 2:9,14-15

[6] John 6:47; 10:28; 1 John 5:13; Jude 1:21

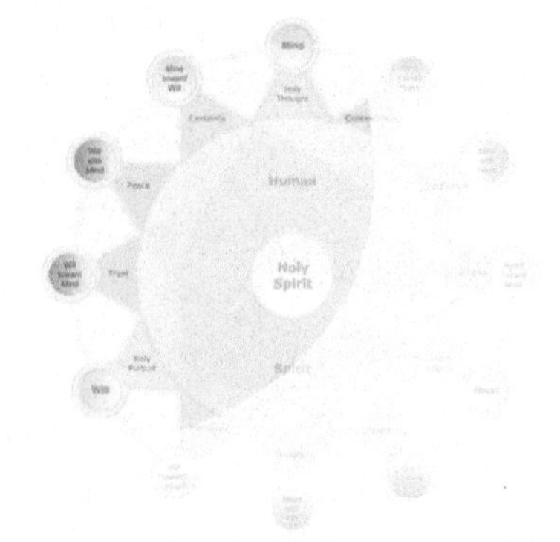

CHAPTER 19

GATES BETWEEN THE MIND AND THE WILL

Glory to our Creator, provider of Wisdom![1]

"Therefore, carefully observe how you hear, because to those who have heard more will be given. But from those who have not heard even what they seem to have will be taken away."[2]

Therefore, listen, holy children of Yehovah! Listen, you who seek victory, because it will be granted to you!

HalleluYah!

To take dominion from darkness over any gate of the soul, a person must overtake that gate with light.[3] Even in the world, the children of Adam often attempt to fill gates with various facsimiles of light.[4] For example, if a person is attacked with the darkness of worry, a friend might try to encourage them by suggesting "things will get better." Of course, such light is like that of a match; it is not very bright, does

---

[1] Proverbs 2:6; Exodus 31:3; 1 Kings 3:12; Daniel 1:17; Luke 21:15; James 1:5

[2] Luke 8:18; 19:26; Deuteronomy 32:46-47; Proverbs 2:2-5; Mark 4:23-24; Acts 17:11; Hebrews 2:1; James 1:22-25; Matthew 13:12; John 15:2

[3] Acts 26:18; Colossians 1:9-14

[4] 2 Corinthians 11:14; 1 Timothy 1:10; 4:16; 2 Timothy 4:3; Titus 1:9; 2:1

not resist the winds of adversity very well, and cannot last for long.[1] On the other hand, the Light of God is eternal and shines like the sun.[2] When a child of Yehovah speaks the Truth of Yeshua through a gate, that gate overflows with Light, and there is no room for any darkness of any kind.[3]

This is why Yeshua says,

"No one, after lighting a small lantern, then hides it away or puts a bowl over it. Instead they put it on a stand, so that those who come in may see the light. Your eye is the lamp of your body. When your eyes are focused, your whole body also is full of light. But when they are diseased, your body also is full of darkness. Make sure, then, that the light within you is not darkness. Therefore, if your whole body is full of light, and no part of it is dark in any way, it will be completely full of light as when a lamp shines its light on you."[4]

Therefore, know that by focusing on the Light of Christ, we successfully overcome the onslaught of darkness against our souls.[5] Yeshua is saying that focusing on Him is just as effective on the inside as having Him present with us on the outside.[6] And as we grow in revelation, experience, and maturity,[7] we even become experts at being filled with His Light.[8]

Consider your soul to be like a glass prism.[9] As light passes through a prism, different qualities of that light are revealed.[10] While the light shining in may be white, the prism separates the light into many different colors of light. In the same way, when the Light of Yehovah shines through your soul, different Characteristics of His Light are revealed. When His Light shines through your heart, Christ's Love becomes evident.[11] When He shines through your mind, His Truth is seen.[12] And

---

[1] Isaiah 31:3; 36:6; Ezekiel 29:6-7
[2] John 1:9; 12:46; Matthew 4:16
[3] John 8:32; Ephesians 1:13; 6:17
[4] Luke 11:33-36
[5] John 15:5; Romans 7:4; 2 Corinthians 9:10; Philippians 1:11
[6] Luke 11:36; Psalm 119:97-105; Proverbs 2:1-11; 2 Timothy 3:15-17
[7] Matthew 13:30; 1 Corinthians 3:6; Luke 13:19
[8] 2 Peter 3:18; Hebrews 6:1; Colossians 1:9-10; Romans 16:19
[9] Philippians 2:15; Matthew 5:14-16; John 5:35; Ephesians 5:8
[10] Galatians 5:22-23; Ephesians 5:9; Philippians 1:11; Colossians 1:10; Romans 7:4
[11] John 15:9,13; 17:23,26; Ephesians 3:18; Revelation 1:5
[12] John 1:47; 3:21; Acts 17:11-12

when His Light fills your will, it overflows with His unlimited Power [1] and Obedience.[2]

While the intermediate gates require specific attention to the aspects of their function, the primary gates require the foundational Light of the Gospel.[3]

When the mind is full of truth concerning pursuit of the Glory of Yehovah,[4] the position of the mind toward the will is one of certainty.[5] This is the aspect of soul that some are describing when they testify that they "know in their knower."[6] It is through this certainty, or gate of deciding belief, that one can hear the Voice of Yehovah.[7] Though it is often as subtle as a gentle whisper,[8] its quality is one of certainty.[9] This revelation of Yehovah's Character through the human soul has the power to influence the human will to conform to Yehovah's Strength[10] because the mind full of His Truth is full of Light.[11]

For example, many years ago, I was driving along a highway at night. At that time in my life, I had been making a devoted effort to honor Yehovah by doing my best to obey the laws of the land, so I was obeying the speed limit.[12] A red pickup truck had just passed me and moved over in front of me when I heard the Voice of Yehovah say, "Speed up and pass the red pickup truck."[13]

I was shocked that Yehovah would ask me to surpass the speed limit, but I heard His Certainty in His Voice.[14] So, I sped up to pass the truck. As soon as I passed the truck, I heard something that sounded like small rocks hitting the rear quarter panel on the driver's side of my car. When I turned my head to the left to look out of the window and see what it was, I saw two headlights in midair about five feet away from me! A large car from the other side of the highway had crossed and

---

[1] Matthew 22:29; Luke 9:1; Acts 1:8

[2] Philippians 2:8; 1 Peter 1:2; 1:14

[3] Ephesians 5:9; 1 Timothy 6:11

[4] Matthew 6:33; Luke 12:31; Psalm 34:9; 37:19; 84:11; Isaiah 33:16; John 6:27

[5] Colossians 4:12; Romans 15:14; Hebrews 6:1

[6] John 8:32,36; Psalm 25:5; 119:45; Proverbs 2:1-7; 4:18; Isaiah 2:3; 61:1; Romans 6:14-18,22; 8:2,15; 2 Corinthians 3:17-18; Galatians 5:13; 2 Timothy 2:25-26

[7] John 10:4,16,27; 5:25; 8:43; Revelation 3:20

[8] 1 Kings 19:12; Job 4:12-16

[9] Revelation 3:20; Luke 12:36

[10] Ephesians 1:19; Philippians 4:13; 2 Timothy 4:17

[11] Matthew 6:22-23; Luke 11:34-36

[12] Romans 13:1-2; Titus 3:1

[13] Acts 8:29; 10:19; 11:12; 13:2-4; 16:6-7

[14] 1 Kings 19:12; Job 4:12-16

jumped the median, sending it like an airborne missile directly at me! It was so close that debris from the median was hitting my car! However, because I had sped up in obedience to His Voice, the flying vehicle missed me by inches! Tragically, it slammed directly into the red pickup truck. Both vehicles, including several behind them, collided in such violence that they were tumbling end over end down the highway.

THE VOICE OF HIS CERTAINTY PRESERVED ME BY LEADING MY WILL INTO THE PROTECTION OF YESHUA'S OBEDIENCE![1] MAY YEHOVAH HAVE MERCY ON THOSE OTHERS WHO WERE INVOLVED![2] AND PRAISE BE TO OUR SAVIOR, WHO GIVES US LIFE,[3] AND WHO KNOWS HOW TO PRESERVE THE LIFE OF HIS SERVANT FOR HIS GLORY![4]

HALLELUYAH!

THANK YOU, YEHOVAH, FOR SAVING US BY YOUR VOICE[5] ON MANY OCCASIONS FROM THE ENEMY'S ATTEMPTS TO DESTROY US![6]

HALLELUUUUUUUYAAAAAAAAAAAAAAAH!!!!

OUR GOD IS A MIGHTY GOD,[7] POWERFUL TO ACCOMPLISH HIS WILL![8]

HALLELUUUUUUUYAAAAAAAAAAAAAAAH!!!!

GLORY, GLORY, GLORY TO HIS NAME!!!!!![9]

PRAISE BE TO THE GOD OF TRUTH[10] AND CERTAINTY,[11] WHO STILL SPEAKS TO HIS PEOPLE![12]

---

[1] Leviticus 25:18; John 5:19
[2] Jonah 4:11; Matthew 18:33
[3] John 5:21; Deuteronomy 32:39; Acts 26:8
[4] John 11:1-48; Mark 3:4
[5] Acts 10:15; 18:9; Ezekiel 3:24
[6] 2 Samuel 4:9; Psalm 54:7; 56:13; 86:13
[7] Isaiah 9:6; 45:24-25; Psalm 45:3,6; 50:1; Romans 9:5; Titus 2:13
[8] Luke 1:37; Philippians 3:21
[9] Revelation 15:4; Luke 1:49; Psalm 99:3
[10] John 14:6,17; Acts 4:12; Hebrews 10:19-22; 1 John 2:23; 2 John 1:9; Revelation 5:8-9
[11] John 7:29; 8:14; 8:55; 14:4,7; Hebrews 10:22; 11:1
[12] Acts 10:19; 13:2; 21:11; Hebrews 3:15

HALLELUUUUUUUYAAAAAAAAAAAAAAAH!!!!

HALLELUUUUUUUYAAAAAAAAAAAAAAAH!!!!

HALLELUUUUUUUYAAAAAAAAAAAAAAAH!!!!

But even though He is True[1] and Good,[2] not all souls choose to fellowship with Him![3] How tragic for them!

When a mind is not full of light and instead receives an understanding that is dark and "deciding"[4] in purpose, it opens the mind-toward-will gate as a foothold for darkness.[5] This spirit of a dark "deciding" belief is better known as a spirit of doubt,[6] and it functions in contrast to certainty. The most foundational aspect of any doubt is the suggestion that the mind is responsible for *answering* the various wavering thoughts of doubt.[7] Many people fall to this deceit. They experience a hint of doubt, and then they hear many ideas and thoughts about difficult and often nonsensical questions.[8] However, they have been deceived. The doubt is not a product of the mind but a dark spirit that does not truly care about any information at all.[9] The goal of the darkness is to argue that the mind is above the Word of God so that the soul will waver in spiritual knowledge,[10] and its function is to cause the soul to vacillate between decisions.[11] No matter what information the person discovers or provides in answer to it, the spirit of doubt will persist.[12] The questions and difficulties heard are suggestions given by the dark spirit to distract the person from the truth that the same spirit has to be bound, silenced, and removed.[13] As long as the darkness can continue to present the mind as being above the Word of God, the soul will be open to the incessant blabbering of dark

---

[1] John 1:17; 14:6; 17:3; 1 Thessalonians 1:9

[2] Mark 10:18; Romans 8:28; 12:2

[3] Matthew 13:15; 24:10; Acts 3:19; 20:21

[4] See Chapter 24 of this testimony for more about the Triad of Decision.

[5] Romans 8:7; Ephesians 4:27; Acts 5:3; 2 Corinthians 2:10-11; 11:3

[6] Genesis 3:1; Matthew 4:3,6,9

[7] Genesis 3:1,13; Revelation 12:9; 16:14; 20:2,8; Zechariah 3:1-2

[8] Matthew 14:30; 2 Kings 6:15; Mark 14:38

[9] Luke 16:27-31; Both certainty and doubt are decisions in spirit, for there is no end to the acquisition of evidence. Even with the same evidence, one person decides to believe, and another decides not to believe (John 12:37,42-43).

[10] Hosea 4:6; Jeremiah 5:21; 2 Corinthians 4:3-6

[11] 1 Kings 18:21; Joshua 24:15; Zephaniah 1:5; Matthew 6:24

[12] Matthew 12:26; Satan argues for his own agenda, and an impure spirit cannot be made pure by discussion (Luke 4:41). This is why evil spirits must be cast out (Mark 5:8).

[13] 2 Corinthians 10:5; Genesis 3:1-5; 2 Thessalonians 2:4

suggestions.[1] And though the will is properly functioning and not the source of the attack, the goal of the spirit of doubt is continued residence,[2] which is secured through corrupting the soul's will with a cluttered and wavering mind.[3]

Listen again.[4]

When arguing with any spirit, one will eventually realize that no argument will be sufficient to sway the spirit.[5] Whether one is at home arguing with a family member or on the mission field arguing for salvation, when a spirit is engaged, whatever one says will "go in one ear and out the other" because the spirit is not "considering" but "intending."[6] It is the same *inside* the soul.[7] When fighting a spirit, it will become obvious that it is a spirit when it continues to push for its agenda.[8] Doubt will never become certainty. An impure spirit cannot be persuaded to become a pure spirit.[9] Doubt and certainty are different spirits.[10]

To overcome the spirit of doubt, a person must apply the Blood of Yeshua as the Word of Yehovah to the mind.[11] The person must speak the true understanding through the mind that they have been given the Mind of Christ and that doubt is not of Him.[12] Then the person can cover the gate of dark deciding belief with the Blood of Yeshua's Faithfulness by acknowledging the Scriptures that faith is a gift from Yehovah,[13] that we are commanded to stop doubting and believe,[14] and that we wrestle not against flesh but against principalities.[15] After this, the person can

---

[1] Proverbs 21:24; 2 Timothy 4:3

[2] Matthew 8:31; Luke 11:24

[3] Genesis 3:6; 2 Corinthians 11:3; 1 Kings 18:21

[4] Luke 8:18; 19:26; Deuteronomy 32:46-47; Proverbs 2:2-5; Mark 4:23-24; Acts 17:11; Hebrews 2:1; James 1:22-25; Matthew 13:12; John 15:2

[5] Matthew 17:21; Mark 9:29; Ephesians 6:18

[6] John 8:43-45,47; 10:26-27; 1 John 4:3-6; See Chapters 23 and 25 of this testimony for more about the Triads of Consideration and Intention.

[7] 2 Corinthians 10:5; Jeremiah 4:14; Hebrews 4:12

[8] 1 Samuel 18:10-11,17,21,28-29

[9] Matthew 9:4; Ezekiel 38:10; Haggai 2:13-14

[10] 2 Corinthians 6:14; 1 John 1:6; 3:14; 1 Corinthians 10:21; James 4:4

[11] Matthew 4:3-4,6-7; Deuteronomy 6:9

[12] Matthew 4:10; We must not accept the doubting spirit as our own but address it as an enemy.

[13] Ephesians 2:5,8; Titus 2:11; 3:5

[14] John 6:29; 14:11; 20:27; Mark 1:15

[15] Ephesians 6:12; Romans 8:38; Colossians 2:15; 1 Peter 3:22

cast out the spirit of doubt by the Name[1] and Blood[2] of Yeshua. Then the gate will be shut,[3] not allowing any additional spirits of doubt dominion[4] but turning away any temptation of doubt that comes knocking on that gate in the future.[5]

When approached by doubt in your soul, a helpful key response is, "My faith is enough,[6] and it is God's handiwork;[7] doubt has never made anything, but the faith given me moves mountains!"[8] Remember, doubt is a spirit![9] You never have to doubt![10] It is not your purpose here![11] The faith given to you is more than enough![12] Cast that spirit away and set your soul free from doubt's dominion![13] And enter into the Kingdom of Heaven *right now*,[14] where *no one* doubts His Word any longer but is only certain of It all the time![15]

HALLELUYAH!

Remember, your faith is not the object of your faith![16] Yeshua is![17] Everyone believes *something*![18] You are always placing your faith in *something.*[19] If you place your faith in the world, then you'll reap the world's reward.[20] But if you place your faith in *Yeshua,* you'll reap His reward![21]

HALLELUYAH!

---

[1] Acts 16:18; Luke 9:1; 10:17-19
[2] Hebrews 11:28; 12:24; 1 John 1:7; Revelation 1:5
[3] Revelation 3:7; Job 11:10; 12:14; Matthew 16:19
[4] Colossians 1:13; Isaiah 49:24-25; Matthew 12:29-30; Acts 26:18; Hebrews 2:14
[5] James 4:7; Luke 10:17; Acts 16:18; Mark 16:17
[6] Matthew 17:20; Mark 9:23; Luke 1:37; 18:27
[7] Ephesians 2:8,10; 1 Corinthians 13:2; Matthew 11:27; John 6:44
[8] James 1:6-8; Mark 11:23
[9] Genesis 3:1; 1 Timothy 4:1
[10] 2 Corinthians 6:14; 1 John 1:6; 3:14; 1 Corinthians 10:21; James 4:4
[11] Romans 8:29; Matthew 12:50; 25:40; Colossians 1:15-18; Revelation 1:5-6
[12] Luke 17:6; Matthew 17:20-21; 21:21; 13:31-32
[13] Matthew 10:1; 16:19; Mark 1:34
[14] Luke 17:21; 1 Corinthians 3:16; Matthew 10:7
[15] Matthew 6:10; 13:11,44; 16:19; Luke 1:32-33,37
[16] Luke 8:25; Hebrews 11:1
[17] Hebrews 12:2; Acts 5:31; Psalms 138:8
[18] James 2:19; 2 Timothy 4:3
[19] Psalm 20:7; Isaiah 31:1; Jeremiah 17:5
[20] Matthew 14:30; 2 Corinthians 4:3-4; 11:14
[21] Matthew 14:28-29,31

HE IS THE ONE WHO WORKS IN US TO WILL AND TO ACT ACCORDING TO HIS GOOD PURPOSE![1]
HE IS THE ONE WHO FINISHES THE GOOD WORK HE BEGAN IN US![2]

HE IS THE ONE WHO MAKES "THINGS HAPPEN"![3]

HALLELUYAH!

So, let us continue to learn from Him because He will use it all for our good![4]

Now, when a will is turned completely toward the Light of Yeshua, the gate of considering pursuit overflows with trust toward the Truth.[5] Again, understand that a human soul is *always* trusting in something.[6] But when it is obediently trusting the Truth, its security is sure.[7] Those who serve Yehovah are served by Him.[8] This is the aspect of faith that allows martyrs to boldly proclaim the Truth even when facing persecution and death.[9] It is this same part of the soul that speaks miracles from the Spirit into Creation.[10]

Years ago, I was walking in my back yard by a mandarin tree that was covered in hundreds of beautiful fruit. I had just listened to several old sermons by powerful preachers,[11] and I was suddenly moved in spirit[12] that I had not yet spoken in power as a witness of Yehovah to the world.[13] At once, I looked up at the tree and said, "Because I am not bearing fruit, neither let this tree!"[14] Even as I said it, I was

---

[1] Philippians 2:13; Ephesians 2:4-5; John 6:65
[2] Philippians 1:6; Hebrews 12:2
[3] Proverbs 16:9; 19:21; 20:24; Jeremiah 10:23
[4] Romans 8:28,35-39; Hebrews 12:6-12; James 1:3-4; 2 Thessalonians 1:5-7
[5] Romans 15:13; 1 Peter 1:8
[6] Matthew 14:30 – When Peter turned his trust from Yeshua to the wind, he reaped a harvest resulting from where his trust was sown (Galatians 6:7b). The wind and waves were trustworthy to make Peter sink, while Yeshua was trustworthy to save. Wherever Peter trusted, that is what happened to him.
[7] Matthew 14:31; Mark 16:7
[8] John 13:3-8; Titus 3:5; Hebrews 10:4-10; Revelation 1:5
[9] Acts 7:55-60; 16:25
[10] Matthew 17:20; Mark 9:23; Luke 1:37; 18:27
[11] Acts 7:22; 9:22; 14:1; 17:4; 19:8;
[12] John 11:33; Luke 2:27
[13] Acts 1:8; Micah 3:8; Zechariah 4:6; Luke 10:19; Romans 15:19
[14] Mark 11:14; John 14:12

aware that I had done so in the power of the Holy Spirit,[1] the Spirit of Truth.[2] When I began to turn away, I took one last glance and thought, "I felt the agreement of the Spirit of Truth when those words were spoken through me."[3] And I walked away without another thought.
The next day or the day after, some others called my attention to the tree, and I saw that the previously bountiful tree was completely dead.[4] Not only was every leaf completely dry and withered, but the hundreds of fruit were gone! There weren't even any mandarines on the ground! Even the grass under the tree was gone! The tree and the ground beneath it were dead, but everything else in the yard and in the woods beyond was green and healthy.

The others who were with me asked," Why did you curse that wonderful tree?" And they begged me to bless it. I realized that I had liked the tree. So we all blessed the tree in the Name of Yeshua to come back to life,[5] and we put our trust in Yehovah.[6] Within just a few days, the tree came back to life with green leaves and white flowers![7] And we rejoiced in Yehovah Who had placed the power of life and death in our tongues![8]

Both times I had spoken, I did so with the gift of His Trust given to me through Yeshua.[9] His Spirit reminded me[10] to consider His promise that I will receive whatever I ask for in His Name,[11] and then He gave me His Grace to obediently trust in Him Who is Trustworthy![12]

HALLELUYAH!

---

[1] Mark 5:30; 13:11; Acts 1:8; 1 Thessalonians 1:5
[2] John 14:17; 15:26; 16:13; 1 John 4:6
[3] 1 Peter 4:11a; 1 John 5:14
[4] Mark 11:20-21; Matthew 21:19-20
[5] John 16:23; Hebrews 10:19-23; 1 John 5:14-15
[6] John 16:27; Zephaniah 3:17
[7] Numbers 17:8; Ezekiel 17:24
[8] Proverbs 18:21; 10:20-21,31; 11:30; Matthew 12:35-37; James 3:6-9
[9] Ephesians 2:5,8; Titus 2:11; 3:5
[10] John 14:26; 6:45; 16:13-14; 1 Corinthians 2:10-13; 1 John 2:27
[11] John 16:24b; Matthew 7:7-8
[12] Romans 15:13; 1 Peter 1:8

CHILDREN OF YEHOVAH![1] UNDERSTAND THE GREAT POWER HE HAS GIVEN YOU![2] HE HAS NOT LEFT YOU AS ORPHANS[3] BUT HAS CALLED YOU[4] AND EQUIPPED YOU[5] AS CHILDREN OF GOD!

HALLELUYAH!

OUR GOD ALMIGHTY REIGNS![6]

Of course, the contrast of trust is worry.[7] If a person has been attacked by worry, then the position of the will-toward-mind gate indicates a weakness in the will's *strength*[8] to focus according to what the soul knows in the mind to be true.[9] Worry is a dark considering force of focus. The primary focus of this spirit is a dark considering pursuit toward achieving control.[10] This focus is not a product of human origin but a received pursuit from a dark spirit.[11] When received, this spirit of worry[12] will push forward many false desires, feelings of concern, and wariness.[13] Though the mind is not the source of the attack, this spirit seeks to corrupt the mind by suggesting the lie that the person lives according to their own wisdom and righteousness.[14] The dark spirit will then submit numerous thoughts for consideration about what could or should happen if the person does or does not do this or that.[15] The worry spirit is quick to suggest disaster, loss, and failure,

---

[1] Romans 8:14; Galatians 3:26; 1 John 3:2; 5:19; Matthew 5:9

[2] Acts 1:8; Micah 3:8; Zechariah 4:6; Luke 10:19; Romans 15:19

[3] John 14:18; Matthew 28:20

[4] Romans 8:30; Matthew 22:14; John 15:16

[5] 2 Timothy 3:17; Romans 8:32; Psalm 84:11; 1 Corinthians 2:12; 3:21-23; Ephesians 1:3

[6] Psalm 99:1; Revelation 1:18; 4:9; 11:15; 19:6; 21:27; Hebrews 1:8

[7] Luke 12:26; 21:14; Matthew 6:25,28,31,34; 10:19

[8] Matthew 12:30 – *Strength* is from ἰσχύς, pronounced "ees-khoos," meaning *forcefulness, ability,* power, or *might.* While the word does mean *strength,* in this context is a reference not to a physical strength but to the strength of a soul, that is, a *strength or forcefulness of will.*

[9] Matthew 6:31-34; Luke 12:22-34

[10] Philippians 4:6; Matthew 5:36; 6:27; Deuteronomy 28:65

[11] Ephesians 6:12,16b; 1 John 5:19

[12] Luke 8:14; 10:41; Ecclesiastes 11:10 – *Anxiety* from the Hebrew כַּעַס, pronounced "kah'ahs," meaning *anxiety, sorrow,* and especially *provocation*; Note that acceptance and entertainment of doubting thoughts create nests for worrisome spirits (Luke 11:26). Do not accept ideas insisting that you must "figure things out" to cease worrying (Proverbs 3:5). Forceful worry is a spirit. Cast it out for Yehovah's Glory! HalleluYah!

[13] Luke 10:40; Matthew 14:15

[14] Mark 4:19; 1 Timothy 6:9

[15] Matthew 14:30; 2 Corinthians 4:3-4; 11:14

while it constantly confirms that the person must attempt to control as many aspects of life as possible.[1] Its goal is continued residence, and its foothold is secured by using disobedience to plant and grow lies in the mind.[2] The essence of such a spirit is its force of focus and focus of force.

To remove this spirit, the person must cover the will gate with the Blood of Yeshua's deeds[3] by forcing through the gate a pursuit of repentance,[4] which is the act of conforming the will by obedient force[5] to what the mind knows to be true.[6] While speaking the truth covers the mind,[7] the will gate consists of force and only interacts with force.[8] Therefore, the person must cover this gate of pursuit with the Yeshua's Pursuit.[9] This is done by receiving the free gift of the Righteousness of Yeshua,[10] a gift of Grace and Force.[11] This Grace feels like purpose,[12] effort,[13] and commitment.[14]

Understand what Grace is. If we were to say, "That woman is a graceful dancer," we would not be making a statement of *mercy*, as if to say, "She doesn't dance well, but we have decided to forgive her." No! If we say someone is a graceful dancer, we are observing that the dancer is dancing so well that all of her technical movements appear perfectly executed while flowing together with an elegant and artistic finesse! In the same way, when we are speaking of the gift of His Grace, we are not at all speaking of His Mercy but rather of a Gift of His Finesse in Pursuit of Holiness that enables us to do well and receive His Righteousness.[15] In other words, Yehovah has blessed us to dance in Creation with glorious elegance in Righteousness![16]

HALLELUYAH!

---

[1] Mark 4:38; Luke 12:25-26
[2] 1 Corinthians 15:33; 2 Timothy 2:16-18; 2 Peter 2:2,18-20
[3] 1 John 2:2; 1 Peter 3:18; Deuteronomy 6:9
[4] Matthew 3:2; 11:20; Luke 13:3; Acts 3:19
[5] Isaiah 50:10; 2 Corinthians 1:8-10
[6] Revelation 3:3; 1 Timothy 6:20; 2 Timothy 1:13
[7] John 6:38; Philippians 2:7-8
[8] Luke 10:27 – "Love the Lord your God ... with all your strength (will/force/pursuit)..."
[9] John 4:34; 15:10; Hebrews 5:8-9; 10:7-9
[10] Romans 5:17; Philippians 1:11
[11] Acts 26:20; Ephesians 2:8; 1 Peter 4:10
[12] Romans 12:6-8; 1 Corinthians 12:4-11; 1 Peter 4:10-11
[13] Acts 6:8; 1 Corinthians 15:10
[14] Romans 5:21; John 10:28
[15] Acts 6:8; Romans 1:5
[16] 2 Corinthians 5:21; Philippians 3:9

Now, once the Grace of Righteousness has been repented through the will gate, the person can cover the gate of dark considering pursuit with the repentance of trust by *forcing* the deed of speaking through the mouth[1] about the Blood of Yeshua and His Trust,[2] His Commands concerning our trust,[3] and any other Scriptures exhorting us to trust in Yehovah.[4] In other words, the person should speak through their mouth Scriptures about God's trustworthiness and our trust in Him.[5] By doing this, the person draws force from both the productive strength of joy[6] and the power of life in the tongue.[7] After this, the worry spirit may be cast out.[8]

A key saying when hearing a spirit of worry in your soul is, "As long as I abstain from accepting darkness, I have nothing to worry about because it is not me but God Who takes care of me!"[9] Your spirit already overflows with trust in Yehovah![10] It is a fruit of the Holy Spirit within you![11] Your Shepherd didn't make you to worry;[12] He made you to trust![13] No one ever needs to worry![14] You never need to worry even once ever again![15] It is not your purpose here![16] Don't serve it![17] It is a dark spirit![18] Cast it out and be free from it forever![19] Enter into the Kingdom of Heaven,[20] where *no one* worries anymore but only trusts all the time![21]

HALLELUYAH!

---

[1] Romans 10:9a,10b,32; 1 John 4:2
[2] John 5:19; Luke 22:42
[3] John 14:1; 11:25-27; 14:27-28; 16:22-23
[4] Ephesians 1:12,18; Acts 14:23; Romans 15:13
[5] Psalm 5:11; 9:10; 57:1; 146:5-6; Isaiah 26:3-4
[6] Nehemiah 8:10-12; Isaiah 12:2; 61:3; Psalm 71:23
[7] Proverbs 18:21; 10:20-21,31; 11:30; Matthew 12:35-37; James 3:6-9
[8] Matthew 10:1; 16:19; Mark 1:34; 16:17; James 4:7; Luke 10:17; Acts 16:18; Psalm 31:18
[9] Matthew 6:26,30,32-33
[10] Hebrews 11:6; Romans 15:13
[11] Ephesians 2:5,8; Titus 2:11; 3:5
[12] John 10:11; Psalm 23:1; Isaiah 40:11
[13] Psalm 23:2-6; 139:13-16; Philippians 4:6-7; Romans 8:38-39
[14] Jeremiah 17:8d; Isaiah 58:11
[15] Luke 12:11-12,22,29; 21:14; Matthew 6:25,31,34; 10:19
[16] Romans 8:29; Matthew 12:50; 25:40; Colossians 1:15-18; Revelation 1:5-6
[17] Galatians 5:1,13; 2:4; 4:26,31; John 8:32-36; Romans 6:18; 8:2
[18] Matthew 6:34; John 16:33
[19] Matthew 10:1; 16:19; Mark 1:34; Galatians 5:1
[20] Luke 17:21; 1 Corinthians 3:16; Matthew 10:7
[21] Matthew 6:10,20; 13:11,44; 16:19; Luke 21:14; Revelation 3:12; 7:15-17

When the mind is full of truth[1] and the will is actively seeking Yehovah,[2] the benefits of these converge to reveal peace. Unlike the peace of the world, this peace does not ebb and flow according to challenges in the environment of Creation.[3] On the contrary, it perseveres through even the most difficult situations because its power comes directly from the Faithfulness and Trustworthiness of God.[4] In this peace, no fear, worry, or doubt can be found but only absolute confidence, assurance, and rest.[5]

Several years ago, I was walking through a field in the wilderness. It was very cold, and I had no supplies but only a light jacket and the Scriptures. As the sun set and the night progressed, I stopped and squatted down behind the trunk of a tree to shield my body from the frigid wind. Yehovah's perfect Peace was upon me,[6] and without any real concern, I said, "Lord, I think I will die out here tonight."[7] Then I heard His Voice reply, "Go north into those dark woods."[8] Of course, there was nothing about that foreboding forest that seemed beneficial! It was an ominous scene, like a beckoning grave! But the Peace of the Lord was upon me, so I proceeded north to the dark woods and entered them.

I was amazed at how pitch black the woods were, but after only walking for a moment, I saw before me something colorful in the darkness. Because the Peace of Yehovah was upon me, I approached without concern,[9] and I came to a very large piece of bright red, flexible, but very thick plastic sheeting, like no plastic I'd ever seen before. It was cut in a square, measuring about twenty-by-twenty feet, and it looked new and clean. If it had not been so large and colorful, I would never have seen it! Next to it, I found two new eight-foot-long wooden 2x4 beams and a single mattress in perfect condition! I looked up to see if these items could have been dropped from a plane, but the trees were too dense! I could not even imagine how a new, clean, dry single mattress could be lying on the floor of a dark forest in the middle of nowhere! At once, I received a vision of how to make a

---

[1] Matthew 6:22-23; Luke 11:34-36

[2] Matthew 6:33; 7:7-8; Luke 12:31; Psalm 34:9; 37:19; 84:11; Isaiah 33:16; John 6:27

[3] John 14:27; Psalm 27:1; 56:11; 112:7

[4] John 16:33d; Psalm 68:18; Galatians 6:14

[5] Philippians 4:7; Ephesians 3:19

[6] Colossians 3:15; John 14:27; 16:33

[7] I have since learned that I should not have said such a thing, because life and death are in the tongue (Proverbs 18:21). Rather, I should have simply asked Yehovah what to do (1 Peter 5:7).

[8] Acts 8:29; 9:6,15; 26:16

[9] Philippians 4:7; Ephesians 3:19

shelter![1] I was shown to suspend the two beams of wood between the bough forks of two adjacent trees. I placed the mattress lengthwise in a clear spot beneath them and draped the plastic sheeting over the beams. I then had enough sheeting left over to fold underneath both sides of the mattress as a complete plastic floor. The result was a perfect tent with overlapping flaps forming doors at both ends! I crawled in, tucked the door flaps under the ends of the mattress, thanked Yehovah, and went to sleep. While it was quite cold at first, the temperature inside eventually warmed, and I then slept comfortably.
Several hours later, I opened my eyes and saw over me two wide strips of red light running parallel along each side of the beams. I was puzzled by how this light was only shining through the top half of the tent. Curious, I made my way toward one end of the tent and opened up the flaps of plastic. I discovered that it was daytime, and much of the tent was covered in snow! Yehovah had provided me with a waterproof shelter that insulated me from the cold using my body's heat![2] It was more effective than an igloo!

HALLELUYAH! PRAISE OUR GOD WHO PROVIDES![3]

Understand that it was Yehovah's Peace that enabled me to receive the gift He had waiting for me![4] Had I wavered in certainty regarding His Voice or worried that I had to provide for myself,[5] then I would never have entered the woods and experienced His Provision![6]

HALLELUYAH FOR YEHOVAH'S FAITHFULNESS, [7] TRUSTWORTHINESS, [8] AND GRACE![9] HE ALONE IS OUR PROTECTOR[10] AND PROVIDER![11]

HALLELUYAH!

---

[1] Exodus 25:9; Hebrews 8:5
[2] Luke 12:28; Psalm 27:5; Isaiah 25:4
[3] Jonah 4:6; Psalm 103:10-14
[4] Philippians 4:7-8; Ephesians 3:19
[5] Philippians 4:6; Matthew 6:25-33; 1 Peter 5:7
[6] Matthew 14:30; Psalm 107:27-30; 116:3-4; Lamentations 3:54-57; Jonah 2:2-7
[7] 1 Corinthians 1:9; 10:13; 1 Thessalonians 5:23-24; 2 Thessalonians 3:3
[8] 2 Samuel 7:28; Numbers 23:19; Titus 1:2
[9] Romans 5:15; Ephesians 2:8
[10] Psalm 18:1; 46:1; 59:9-10,17
[11] Philippians 4:19; Luke 12:30-32

But how terrible the suffering can be for those who accept the voices of darkness that both question Yehovah's Voice[1] and discourage trust in Him![2] With such a significant *disconnect* between the will and mind, a spirit of fear[3] will advance against the mind-will-convergence gate. Such a spirit works in contrast to peace and consists of forceful distractions and feelings, especially stress,[4] heaviness,[5] or anxiety,[6] as well as many lies and suggested thoughts concerning failure,[7] doom,[8] and the need for false posturing.[9] The invasion of this gate could be the result of a significant unprovoked attack,[10] but it most often occurs after significant weakness has been previously experienced at one or both of the adjacent gates of doubt and worry.[11]

While the presence of the spirit of fear can be quite toxic to the child of Yehovah, it is not any more difficult to dislodge than any of the other spirits.[12] The person must first speak the Blood of Yeshua over the mind and the will,[13] acknowledging that they have received the Mind[14] and Righteousness[15] of Christ (Though due to a firm knowledge of the Scriptures, a spiritually mature person may not need to do so.[16] But a person young or unpracticed[17] in the Word should spend some time reading and speaking the Scriptures that address our reception of the Mind and Righteousness of Yeshua).[18] Repentance must be actively forced through the will

---

[1] Genesis 3:1,13; Revelation 12:9; 16:14; 20:2,8; Zechariah 3:1-2
[2] Genesis 3:4-5; John 8:44; Acts 13:10; 1 John 3:8
[3] 2 Timothy 1:7; Romans 8:15
[4] 1 Corinthians 7:32; Psalm 55:22; Matthew 13:22
[5] Isaiah 61:3; Psalm 30:11
[6] Philippians 4:6; Ecclesiastes 11:10
[7] Matthew 25:24-25; Proverbs 26:13
[8] Joshua 7:5; Isaiah 13:7
[9] 1 Samuel 21:13; Proverbs 29:25
[10] Psalm 35:8; Luke 21:34
[11] Matthew 14:30; 2 Kings 6:15; Mark 14:38
[12] 2 Timothy 1:7; Romans 8:15
[13] Deuteronomy 6:6-9; Exodus 13:9,16; Numbers 15:38-39; Proverbs 3:3; 6:21; 7:3; Hebrews 2:1
[14] 1 Corinthians 2:16; John 15:15; 16:13-15
[15] Romans 5:17; 1 Corinthians 1:30
[16] Song of Solomon 3:7-8; 1 Thessalonians 5:6-8
[17] 1 Timothy 3:6; Hebrews 5:12-13
[18] Romans 16:19; James 3:13-18; 2 Timothy 3:16-17; Ephesians 1:17-18; 5:17

gate in the Name of Yeshua by the Gift of His Grace.[1] Speaking praise[2] is especially valuable when addressing weakness in the will because praise brings strength through joy.[3] After this, the spirit of fear may be cast out, and the convergence gate can be sealed by speaking the Scriptures about the Peace of Yeshua.[4] Then one can speak the *trust* and *certainty* of His Resurrection[5] into the convergence gate by speaking about His instructions concerning peace,[6] how He has shared it with us,[7] and about other Scriptures describing the quality and promise of our peace.[8]

When confronted in your soul with a spirit of fear, a helpful response is, "I am not afraid, because Yehovah loves me and has not given me a spirit of fear!"[9] Understand that fear has no part in your soul! It is not part of the human mind;[10] neither does it have any part in your purpose here![11] Your spirit already overflows with His Peace![12] You never have to fear at any time or ever again![13] It is an enslaving and tormenting spirit.[14] Do not claim any part of it as your own but instead bind it, silence it, and cast it away.[15] If you do so, it will flee from you![16] Boldly enter into the Kingdom of Heaven *today*,[17] where *no one* fears anymore but only lives in perfect peace![18]

---

1 Revelation 3:19; 2 Timothy 2:25; Acts 26:20

2 While worship, or the act of ascribing worth, might include expressions of feelings concerning oneself in relation to Yehovah (Romans 12:1), praise consists of the exaltation of the Name, Deeds, or Character of Yehovah (Psalm 18:46; 21:13). For example, saying, "I love you, Lord, so I will live for you," would be worship, but saying, "You are the King of kings and Lord of Lords" would be praise. Worship is a spiritual act of love through the heart (Matthew 22:37), and praise spiritually strengthens the focus of the will (Psalm 71:23).

3 Nehemiah 8:10; Isaiah 12:2; 61:3; Psalm 71:23

4 John 14:27; Mark 4:38; Romans 5:1-2

5 Philippians 3:8-11; 2 Peter 3:18

6 Luke 12:4-7; Matthew 10:13; Mark 9:50

7 John 14:27; 16:33; Romans 5:1-2; Acts 10:36; 1 Corinthians 1:3

8 Isaiah 26:3; Philippians 4:6-7

9 Romans 8:31-33,38-39; 2 Timothy 1:7a

10 2 Timothy 1:7; Romans 8:15

11 Romans 8:29; Matthew 12:50; 25:40; Colossians 1:15-18; Revelation 1:5-6

12 John 14:27; Romans 8:6

13 2 Timothy 1:7; Romans 8:15

14 1 John 4:18b, "But perfect love drives out fear, because fear has to do with κολασιν." – from κόλασις, pronounced "koh'-lah-sihs" and meaning *infliction, torment,* or *punishment.*

15 Matthew 18:18; Matthew 10:1; Psalm 31:18

16 James 4:7; Matthew 4:3-11; Ephesians 6:11-12; 1 Peter 5:8-9; Revelation 12:11

17 Luke 17:21; 1 Corinthians 3:16; Matthew 10:7

18 John 14:27; 1 Corinthians 16:13; Matthew 6:10; 13:11,44; 16:19; Revelation 2:7,11,17,26-28; 3:5,12,21; 7:15-17

HALLELUYAH!

Notice that the spirits of doubt, worry, and fear *cannot* enter the presence of joy.[1] The Joy of the Lord is your strength![2] Therefore, if the Light of God's Character is shining out of the gates between your mind and will,[3] no darkness can overcome it![4] Your joy will remain, and it will be complete![5]

Did you hear that?
THE JOY OF THE LORD IS YOUR STRENGTH![6]

Do you want joy?

Of course you want joy! It's flowing out of your spirit![7] You just need to unclog your soul by setting your mind above![8]

HalleluYah!

Would you like to know the most effective way to set your mind above?

SPEAK IT![9] OBEDIENTLY SHOUT WHO YEHOVAH IS![10] BOW DOWN BEFORE HIM![11] SING THE PRAISE OF THE LORD![12] DANCE IN JOY![13]

STOP LISTENING TO THE VOICES OF SERPENTS TELLING YOU THAT OBEDIENCE TO GOD IS A BAD THING OR SOMETHING YOU DON'T WANT![14] THOSE DEVILS WANT YOU TO SERVE THEM AND DO WHAT THEY WANT![15] YOU ALWAYS OBEY

---

[1] John 1:5; 1 Peter 1:8; 1 John 1:5-6; 4:18a
[2] Nehemiah 8:10; Isaiah 12:2; 61:3; Psalm 71:23
[3] Psalm 19:8; 119:14; Deuteronomy 16:11,14; Jeremiah 15:16
[4] Psalm 118:1-29; 2 Samuel 22:29; John 8:12
[5] John 15:11; 16:24; 17:13; 1 Peter 1:8; Jude 1:24
[6] Nehemiah 8:10-12; Isaiah 12:2; 61:3; Psalm 71:23
[7] John 15:11; 16:24; 17:13; 1 Peter 1:8; Jude 1:24
[8] Colossians 3:2; 1 Chronicles 22:19; Psalm 62:10; 119:36-37; Matthew 16:23; Romans 8:4-6; 1 John 2:15-17; Philippians 3:19
[9] 2 Corinthians 4:13; Matthew 17:20
[10] Psalm 20:5; 118:15; Isaiah 25:9; 61:10
[11] Deuteronomy 26:10; 33:3; Romans 14:11; Philippians 2:10
[12] 2 Samuel 22:50; Judges 5:3
[13] Psalm 30:11; 149:3; 150:4; Luke 15:25
[14] Genesis 3:1-5; Job 1:11; 2:4-5
[15] Matthew 4:3,6,9; Luke 4:3,6, 9-11

SOMETHING, EVEN IF IT IS YOUR OWN IGNORANCE![1] BUT THOSE WHO SERVE GOD RECEIVE THE FRUITS OF HIS BLESSINGS WHICH ARE ETERNAL LIFE, PEACE, AND JOY![2]

HALLELUUUUUUUUUUYAAAAAAAAAAAAAAH!!!

BLESS GOD!!

MAY OUR HOLY GOD REIGN FOREVER!!!!!!

NO ONE IN THE KINGDOM OF HEAVEN MAKES ANY APOLOGY FOR WANTING TO SERVE THE GOD OF GOODNESS![3] WE ARE NOT ASHAMED TO SERVE HIM!!![4] WE LOVE OUR GOD!!![5]

HALLELUUUUUUUUUUYAAAAAAAAAAAAAAH!!!

And we don't just tell Him we love Him![6] We don't just tell Him we will serve Him![7] Yes, it's wonderful to tell Him we love Him and that we want to serve Him![8] We should constantly do so![9] But such words are the essence of gratitude![10] They consist of great affection, but they are not what facilitates the power of joy!

When we want STRENGTH, when we want POWER, then...

WE SPEAK WHO YEHOVAH IS![11] WE SPEAK WHO YESHUA IS![12] WE EVEN SPEAK WHO HE SAYS WE ARE IN HIM![13]

AND WE SHOUT IT AT THE TOP OF OUR LUNGS![14]

---

[1] 1 Timothy 1:13; Judges 21:25
[2] 1 Corinthians 9:13; Revelation 7:14-17
[3] Revelation 5:1-14; 7:9-12
[4] Mark 8:38; Romans 1:16; 1 Peter 4:16
[5] 1 John 2:5; 4:16; 5:1; John 14:15
[6] Psalm 33:1-2; 34:3; 35:27; 40:16; 66:8; 69:30; 103:20-22
[7] Psalm 107:32; 22:22,25; 40:9-10; 66:16; 111:1; 119:46
[8] Matthew 22:37; Mark 12:29-30
[9] Luke 10:27; Mark 12:33-34
[10] 1 Thessalonians 5:18; Ephesians 5:20; Philippians 4:6; Colossians 3:17
[11] Psalm 145:1; Romans 15:9; Hebrews 2:12; 13:15
[12] John 5:23; 2 Thessalonians 1:12; Colossians 3:17; 1 Corinthians 1:2; Acts 19:17
[13] Revelation 12:11; 7:10-14; 15:3
[14] Psalm 20:5; 27:6; 33:3; 47:1; 66:1; 95:1; 98:4; 100:1; 118:15

BEHOLD WHAT THE LORD HAS DONE![1]

HALLELUYAH!

HE IS GOD OVER ALL THINGS![2]

HALLELUYAH!

HE IS THE MAKER OF HEAVEN AND EARTH![3]
HALLELUYAH!

HE IS THE ONE WHO IS, WAS, AND FOREVER WILL BE![4]

HALLELUYAH!

YESHUA HAMASHIACH YEHOVAH IS HIS NAME![5]

HALLELUYAH!

THE HEAVENS AND EARTH FLEE FROM HIS PRESENCE![6]

HALLELUYAH!

HE IS ABOVE EVERY POWER![7]

HALLELUYAH!

HE IS GOOD![8] HE IS HOLY![9] HE IS ALMIGHTY![10]

HALLELUYAH!

---

[1] Psalm 118:17,23-24; 126:3; Mark 12:11-12; Luke 8:39
[2] Revelation 4:11; 2 Kings 19:15; Isaiah 37:16
[3] Revelation 14:7; Isaiah 40:26; Jeremiah 32:17
[4] Revelation 1:8; 22:13; Isaiah 41:4; 44:6; 48:12
[5] John 10:30; 14:9; Matthew 11:27; 1 Timothy 3:16; Titus 2:13
[6] Revelation 20:11; Jeremiah 4:23-26
[7] Ephesians 1:21; Philippians 2:9-10; Colossians 2:10; Hebrews 1:4
[8] Mark 10:18; James 1:17; 1 John 1:5
[9] 1 Samuel 2:2; Exodus 15:11; Psalm 99:9; 111:9; Isaiah 6:3
[10] 1 Chronicles 29:11; Romans 9:29; 2 Corinthians 6:18; Revelation 1:8; 11:17; 21:22

"SHOUT FOR JOY TO YEHOVAH, ALL THE EARTH!"[1]

HALLELUUUUUYAAAAAAAAAAH!!!!

HALLELUUUUUYAAAAAAAAAAH!!!!

HALLELUUUUUUUYAAAAAAAAAAAAAAAAAAAAAAAAAAAH!!!!!!

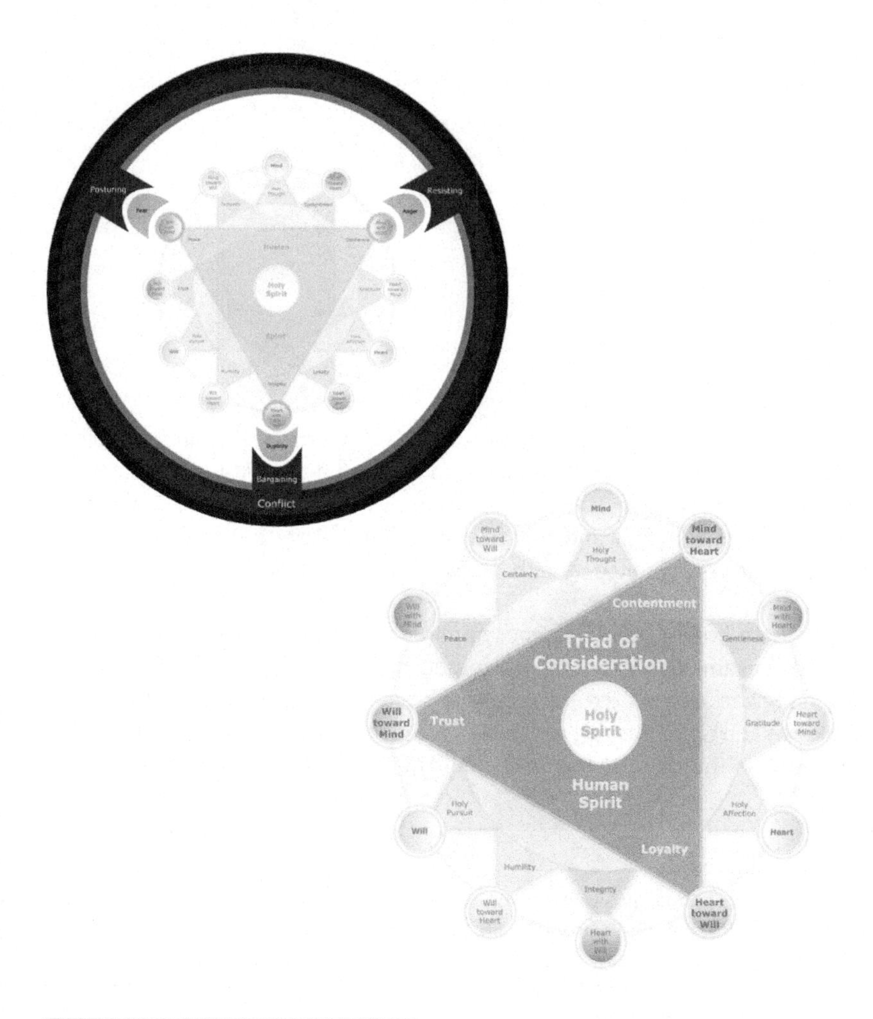

[1] Psalm 47:1,5; 66:1; 95:1-2; 98:4; 100:1; Isaiah 24:14-16; 42:10-12

CHAPTER 20

GATES BETWEEN THE MIND AND THE HEART

When a soul is full of the Light of Yeshua, the Truth prompts the mind to facilitate affection in the heart.[1] This manifests in the mind-toward-heart gate as an overflow of contentment. This *consideration* of belief brings great comfort and warmth through the soul and out toward others.[2] Together with certainty, it establishes the very essence of faith.[3]

Spiritual contentment often becomes apparent in Creation when there seems to be lack.[4] For example, some of the redeemed might see an established prophetess sitting in the back of a church and receiving little honor.[5] They might approach her and ask why she is not pushing to be recognized and cherished by those esteemed to be leaders of the church.[6] But they should not be surprised when she responds,

---

[1] Philippians 4:12; 1 Timothy 6:6-9; Hebrews 13:5-6
[2] Hebrews 13:5; Joshua 1:5; 1 Chronicles 28:20
[3] Philippians 4:11; 3:8; Matthew 6:31-34; 1 Timothy 6:6-9; Hebrews 10:34; 13:5-6
[4] Ecclesiastes 2:24-26; Proverbs 30:8-9; Matthew 6:11; 1 Timothy 6:8
[5] Mark 6:4; Luke 4:24; John 4:44
[6] Galatians 2:9,12-14; Philippians 2:3

"I am here at God's request and will do whatever He asks of me; how those in leadership value me changes nothing."[1]

I have experienced several times in my life betrayal by someone close to me who, when prompted by the enemy, became vindictive and bought my name into disrepute.[2] In response to such testimonies,[3] there was almost always a brief period when everyone I knew turned against me to one degree or another.[4] However, thanks be to Yehovah that He provided me *spiritual contentment* through those trials![5] My Father proved to be my Fountain[6] of value,[7] appreciation,[8] and purpose.[9] He taught me that He was more than sufficient for me![10] He encouraged me to wait patiently and watch Him redeem my name[11] and testimony.[12] He assured me that I had lost no value with Him![13] I would watch amazed in each of those situations as a small group of former friends would slowly return to gather around me.[14] They would ask forgiveness for having doubted me and would begin to boldly defend my name to others.[15] Then, after a year or so, something would happen where many more would begin to return and do the same. In each situation, even the person who began the defamation was eventually freed from the dark spirit and repented![16]

Understand that if my soul had been discontent, I would have either tried to fix my situation myself,[17] or I would have been vulnerable to spirits of doubt and bitterness.[18] But because Contentment shined from His Spirit through my soul,[19] I

---

[1] John 21:22; Galatians 2:6
[2] 2 Samuel 15:2-6; Matthew 10:21; Luke 21:16
[3] Psalm 38:12; 119:69,85-87,95; Acts 23:21
[4] Job 19:19; Psalm 35:7-12; 55:12-15; 109:1-5; Luke 22:48
[5] Psalm 18:2; 62:2,7; 141:9; 142:3
[6] Psalm 36:9; Isaiah 12:3; Jeremiah 2:13; John 4:10,14; 7:37-39; Revelation 21:6
[7] Luke 12:7; Psalm 8:6; Isaiah 43:3-4; Matthew 6:26
[8] 1 Corinthians 4:5; 2 Corinthians 10:18; 1 Peter 1:7; 5:4; Romans 2:29; John 5:44
[9] Philippians 2:13; Ephesians 1:11
[10] 2 Corinthians 12:9; 3:5-6; Joshua 1:9; Isaiah 43:2
[11] Psalm 102:8; Revelation 3:9
[12] Hebrews 13:6; Philippians 1:6
[13] Acts 11:9; Hebrews 9:13-14
[14] Zechariah 8:23; 1 Corinthians 14:25
[15] Isaiah 60:14; 45:14; 49:23; Jeremiah 16:19; Revelation 3:9
[16] Job 42:7-10; Matthew 27:4
[17] 1 Samuel 13:8-13; Psalm 50:8-15
[18] Luke 12:45; John 11:21,32
[19] Philippians 4:11; 3:8; Matthew 6:31-34; 1 Timothy 6:6-9; Hebrews 10:34; 13:5-6

was also able to receive His Gift of Gratitude[1] as I witnessed the blessing of Yehovah's Loyalty![2]

PRAISE OUR GOD, WHO KNOWS HOW TO DEFEAT THE ENEMY,[3] AND WHO BRINGS HIS CHILDREN BACK INTO FELLOWSHIP WITH ONE ANOTHER![4]

HALLEUUUUYAAAAAAAH!!!!

PRAISE OUR GOD, WHO HEALS US FROM BETRAYAL,[5] WHO HOLDS NO RECORD OF WRONGS FOR THOSE WHO RECEIVE HIS FORGIVENESS AND GRACE,[6] AND WHO HAS ENABLED US TO DO THE SAME![7]

HALLELUUUUUUUUUUYAAAAAAAAAAAAH!!!!!!!!

THANK YOU, YEHOVAH, THAT WE HAVE BEEN GIVEN EVERY SPIRITUAL BLESSING IN CHRIST![8] WE NEVER HAVE TO BE DISCONTENT AGAIN![9]

HALLELUUUUUUUUUUYAAAAAAAAAAAAH!!!!!!!!

PRAISE OUR HOLY[10] AND GENEROUS GOD!!![11]

HALLELUUUUUUUUUUYAAAAAAAAAAAAH!!!!!!!!

But how burdened are those who are influenced by darkness! When the mind is significantly hindered from truth in regard to affections, the gate of mind-toward-heart, or considering belief, is weakened and becomes vulnerable to a deceptive spirit of envy.[12] This spirit moves in contrast to contentment and is more than an alternative consideration of affection for some particular comfort, benefit, trait,

---

[1] 2 Corinthians 9:15; Psalm 7:17; 9:1; 1 Timothy 5:18; 1 Corinthians 15:57
[2] John 12:26; 14:21-23; 1 Samuel 2:30; Proverbs 27:18
[3] Colossians 2:15; Acts 2:32-36; John 12:31; 16:11; Revelation 12:9; 20:2-3,10
[4] Colossians 3:13; 2 Corinthians 2:10; Ephesians 4:32; 5:2
[5] John 21:15-17; 2 Corinthians 2:10
[6] 1 Corinthians 13:5; Mark 11:25; Luke 5:32
[7] 1 John 2:6; 1:7; Psalm 85:13; Matthew 11:29; John 13:15; 1 Peter 2:21
[8] Ephesians 1:3; 2:6; Genesis 12:2-3; 1 Chronicles 4:10; Isaiah 61:9; Galatians 3:9
[9] Philippians 4:11; 3:8; Matthew 6:31-34; 1 Timothy 6:6-9; Hebrews 10:34; 13:5-6
[10] 1 Peter 1:16; Leviticus 11:44; 19:2; 20:7; Amos 3:3
[11] 2 Peter 1:3; Psalm 84:11; Romans 8:32; 1 Corinthians 3:21-23; 1 Timothy 4:8
[12] Acts 7:9; James 3:14; Galatians 5:20; Romans 13:13; 1 Corinthians 3:3

or means; it is the deceitful persuasion that an affection for something determines a right of ownership.[1] This is the primary spirit behind most thievery, piracy, and mental justification of adultery.[2] Envy falsely attributes its motivations to the heart, though its lies reside primarily in the mind.[3] However, over time its accepted presence will eventually begin to corrupt the heart by means of a corrupted mind.[4] Upon confrontation, this spirit will falsely suggest that many "rights" and "opportunities" are being overlooked or denied.[5] If such considerations are *not* accepted, the dark spirit will switch tactics and suggest heavy thoughts of condemnation in an effort to migrate away from the mind and closer toward bitterness of the heart.[6]

To overtake this gate from dark considering belief, we must first apply the Blood of Yeshua's Contentment to the mind gate by speaking examples.[7] We also speak the Scriptures about Christ's Generosity.[8] We proclaim examples of blessings in our own lives as well as the promises and blessings of Yehovah's Generosity mentioned throughout His Word.[9] By doing this, the authority of God ushers strength and victory into the soul.[10] The lie of lack is expelled, and Yeshua's affections in the heart are ratified, realigning it with the mind.[11] Then the mind-toward-heart gate may be closed by covering it with the Blood of Yeshua's Contentment in sacrifice,[12] word,[13] and deed.[14] After all of this, the spirit of envy will lose its foothold and can be resisted easily.[15]

When wrestling with contentment, we must understand that we do not just "cross" once; we "cross" twice. The waters *were* and *are* parted twice. We cross the sea by Moses[16] and then the Jordan by Joshua.[17] We are baptized once in the

---

[1] James 3:16; Acts 13:45
[2] James 3:15; Acts 13:10; 2 Corinthians 11:3,13-15; 1 John 3:8-10
[3] 1 Timothy 6:4; Romans 2:8; Galatians 5:26; Titus 3:9
[4] Proverbs 24:1-2; Psalm 73:3
[5] Genesis 3:4-5; James 4:2
[6] Ecclesiastes 4:4; 1 Samuel 18:8-9; Acts 7:9; 1 John 3:12
[7] Matthew 8:20; John 16:15; 1 Timothy 6:17; Deuteronomy 6:9
[8] Luke 22:17-19; John 6:11; 2 Peter 1:3; Ephesians 1:3,7-8
[9] Deuteronomy 6:11; 7:12-15; Ezekiel 6:10-14
[10] 1 John 5:4; 1 Corinthians 15:57; Romans 8:37; 1 John 5:4-5
[11] James 4:8; Hebrews 10:22; 1 Peter 3:21; 2 Corinthians 7:1
[12] John 12:27-28; Hebrews 10:5; Galatians 1:4; 1 Timothy 2:6; Titus 2:14
[13] Luke 22:20; Hebrews 12:24; 13:20
[14] John 4:34; 5:19,30,36; 17:4; 19:20
[15] Matthew 10:1; Ephesians 4:27; James 4:7
[16] Exodus 14:21; 1 Corinthians 10:1-2
[17] Joshua 3:7-17; Deuteronomy 12:10-12

water of Christ's death[1] and again in the fire of His Holy Spirit.[2] We pick up our cross once to exit the enslavement from Egypt,[3] to repent from sin. But we pick up our cross a second time to shed our worldliness in the desert and to enter the fight for the Promised Land, to enter the Kingdom of Heaven.[4] The first cross is to say, "Yes, Lord, please save me," but the second cross is to say, "Yes, Lord, I will trust in You and fight for You!" We place all perceptions of personal "rights" on the cross, once to leave slavery[5] and a second time to enter the promise.[6] Anyone who only picks up their cross once will remain in the desert.[7] But the one who picks it up again will enter the Kingdom of Heaven, even while on earth![8] Christ picked up His cross by entering the desert and fasting while Satan tempted Him[9] for forty days,[10] but He picked it up again[11] to clothe Himself with immortality[12] and rise into Heaven![13] So also, we first pick up our cross and deny sin for our flesh,[14] but we pick up our cross again to leave the dry principles of this world behind[15] and enter the bountiful glory of the Kingdom of Heaven![16]

Understand how important this is![17] If your first goal is wealth or worldly security, you will remain in the desert![18] If your first goal is healing or comfort, you will

---

[1] Romans 6:3-4; Matthew 28:19; 1 Corinthians 12:13; Galatians 2:20-21; 3:27
[2] Acts 8:14-17; 11:15-16
[3] Exodus 12:21-22; 1 Peter 1:19; Revelation 7:14; 12:11
[4] Hebrews 3:7-4:13; Joshua 5:1-12
[5] Exodus 12:22; Matthew 3:11
[6] Matthew 24:13; Mark 13:13; Luke 8:15
[7] Joshua 5:6; Hebrews 3:17-19
[8] Luke 17:21; 10:9; Matthew 12:28; Romans 14:17
[9] Matthew 4:1; 16:24-25; 1 Peter 4:1-2
[10] Matthew 4:2; Luke 4:2
[11] John 3:14; 8:28; 12:32-34; Matthew 27:50-54
[12] 1 Corinthians 15:53; 2 Corinthians 5:2-4; Romans 13:14; Ephesians 4:24
[13] Acts 1:9-11; Daniel 7:13; Luke 21:27; Revelation 1:7; 11:12
[14] Romans 13:14; Colossians 3:5-8; Galatians 5:24
[15] Acts 1:9-11; Daniel 7:13; Luke 21:27; Revelation 1:7; 11:12; 1 John 5:6 – This is what is meant by, "This is the One who came by water and blood—Jesus Christ. He did not come by water only, but by water and blood. And it is the Spirit Who testifies, because the Spirit is the Truth."
[16] Ephesians 1:18; 2 Corinthians 4:6; Acts 16:14
[17] Luke 8:18; 19:26; Deuteronomy 32:46-47; Proverbs 2:2-5; Mark 4:23-24; Acts 17:11; Hebrews 2:1; James 1:22-25; Matthew 13:12; John 15:2
[18] 1 Timothy 6:9; Luke 18:25

remain in the desert![1] No goal can *precede* your entry into the Kingdom of God, because the Kingdom of God *is* the Reign of God,[2] and the Reign of God must precede your goals in order to accomplish them![3] Your wealth is *in* the Promised Land! [4] Your healing is *in* the Promised Land! [5] All blessings *follow* the Relationship![6] They follow the entry into the Promised Land because they are the result of dwelling *in* the Promised Land![7]

Therefore, stop looking at "other nations," or "the wicked," and envying their comforts while you are walking through the desert toward the Promised Land![8] Remember that your Savior, Who has rescued you from "Egypt," has promised to freely give you everything *where* you are going![9] It is a land of "milk and honey"! He wants good things for you, but you must go there and dwell according to His instructions so that you may receive them all![10]

HALLELUYAH!

So, when you are faced with envy, know that a key response to hearing that spirit's voice in your soul is, "Yehovah provides different paths for us all,[11] but I have everything I need *in Him*!" [12] Remember, *your* spirit already overflows with

---

[1] In Matthew 9:20-22, the woman with bleeding had concluded that if she could merely touch the clothes (ἱμάτιον – *garment, robe*) of the Messiah, she would be healed. And notice that, due to her "impurity," the law in her day made such an effort illegal on her part (Leviticus 15:19-31). But she knew Yeshua was the Messiah, that He was the Healer. So she set her eyes on *seeking Him first* above all things, *even her own safety*. And when she *barely* encountered Him, even though she was only able to just touch the garment's hanging tzitzit (κράσπεδον – *tassel;* Hebrew צִיצִת, a garment's hanging appendage required by Numbers 15:38; also addressed in Matthew 14:36; 23:5; Mark 6:56; Luke 8:44) she was *fully* rewarded! He even called her "*daughter*"! The slightest encounter was *followed* by complete healing! She had it in the right order! HALLELUYAH!

[2] "Kingdom of God," or "βασιλεία τοῦ Θεοῦ" in Greek, may also be translated "Reign of God" or "Dominion of God."

[3] Matthew 6:33; Luke 12:31; Psalm 34:9; 37:19; 84:11; Isaiah 33:16; John 6:27

[4] Leviticus 20:24; Ezekiel 20:6

[5] Deuteronomy 11:9; Numbers 13:27

[6] Romans 8:32; Psalm 84:11; 1 Corinthians 2:12; 3:21-23

[7] Nehemiah 9:21-25; Deuteronomy 8:7-10

[8] Numbers 16:13-14; Exodus 16:3

[9] Deuteronomy 26:15; Psalm 28:9

[10] Deuteronomy 6:3; 28:1-14; Isaiah 3:10

[11] John 21:22; 1 Corinthians 4:5; 1 Peter 4:10; Revelation 22:11

[12] Ephesians 1:3; 2:6; Genesis 12:2-3; 1 Chronicles 4:10; Isaiah 61:9; Galatians 3:9

contentment![1] Any envy coming against your soul is a *different* spirit![2] It is not of you! It is not your purpose here![3] You do not ever have to envy![4] You are a child of the Living God![5] You have clothed yourself with Christ![6] You don't live by bread but by the words that come forth from the mouth of Yehovah![7] Did Christ rise by bread or by the Power of God? You are strong, and the Word of God lives in you, and you have overcome the evil one![8] Bind that spirit of envy, silence it, and cast it away![9] Enter into the Kingdom of Heaven *today,*[10] where *no one* envies anymore but only lives in perfect contentment![11] Give your tongue to the service of Yehovah's Name,[12] and speak the Word of the Lord over the earth![13]

HALLELUYAH!

GLORY BE TO GOD!!!

When the heart-toward-mind gate is shining with the Light of Yeshua, it erupts with a *decision* of affection.***[14]*** This affection manifests in the heart-toward-will gate as gratitude, and it is by means of this that we enter the Kingdom of Heaven.[15]

This is not just something we say; it is practically and structurally true.[16] The Kingdom of Heaven is not just a place you are waiting to go; it is an accessible realm.[17] The reason most people do not enter it is that they are not truly grateful.[18]

---

[1] 2 Corinthians 9:8; Proverbs 19:23; Philippians 4:11; Titus 6:6
[2] 1 Peter 2:1; Job 5:2; Ephesians 6:12
[3] Romans 8:29; Matthew 12:50; 25:40; Colossians 1:15-18; Revelation 1:5-6
[4] Matthew 7:18; Galatians 5:17; 1 John 3:9-10
[5] Galatians 3:26; Romans 8:14; 1 John 3:1
[6] Romans 13:14; Galatians 3:27; Ephesians 4:24
[7] Matthew 4:4; John 6:31-59
[8] 1 John 2:14; Revelation 2:7,11,17,26; 3:5,12,21
[9] Matthew 10:1; 16:19; Mark 1:34; 16:17; James 4:7; Luke 10:17; Acts 16:18; Psalm 31:18
[10] Luke 17:21; 1 Corinthians 3:16; Matthew 10:7
[11] Luke 15:31; Matthew 6:10; 13:11,44; 16:19; 20:13-16; Revelation 2:7,11,17,26-28; 3:5,12,21; 7:15-17
[12] Deuteronomy 6:13; 10:20; Psalm 63:11
[13] Deuteronomy 32:1-3; Isaiah 55:10-11
[14] See Chapter 24 of this testimony for more about spiritual decision.
[15] Psalm 100:4; 116:17-19; Isaiah 35:10
[16] Revelation 4:9-10,11; 2 Samuel 22:4
[17] Luke 17:20-21; Matthew 12:28; John 3:3; 18:36; Colossians 1:13
[18] 1 Thessalonians 5:18; Ephesians 5:20; Philippians 4:6; Colossians 3:17

One evening a few years ago, I was in the kitchen making salsa. When I searched for cilantro, I learned that all that remained were four inches of bare stalks that had been cut from a large bouquet.[1] They were banded tightly together in a bunch that was about the size and shape of a small can of tomato paste. While I would normally have made an effort to go to the store and buy more,[2] I was already well into dinner preparation, and I heard in the Spirit that the stalks would be sufficient if I diced them into very small pieces to add flavor.[3]

As I began to cut the stalks, I reflected on how grateful I was to the Lord for always providing for me.[4] I said out loud, "I wonder how the Lord will provide for us during the difficult end times that will soon be upon us?"[5] While I was still speaking, I noticed that as the knife cut through the stalks, pieces of leaves fell on the cutting board.[6] I stopped for a moment, looking carefully at what was before me. Yes, there were definitely pieces of leaves. Where did they come from? I brought the knife down again, and more leaves came out![7] I called other people over to see, and every time I cut, there were more leaves![8] It was bizarre to see stalks on one side of the knife and leaves on the other! Even as I watched closely, I could not see exactly when the stalks changed into leaves! And after I had cut all the stalks, the pile of leaves was larger than the original bouquet could have provided![9]

The whole time, I was yelling, "The Lord is still doing it!" I was laughing and amazed, but deep in my spirit,[10] I knew that His provision of the right kind of cilantro for me[11] was a comment on the open door provided through Yeshua's Gratitude[12] that I had received toward Yehovah.[13]

What does this gratitude look like? It looks like awareness of complete goodness.[14] It is not like the gratitude of the world that depends on the comfort, pleasure, or

---

1 Matthew 14:17; Numbers 11:21-22

2 Matthew 14:15; Luke 9:12

3 Matthew 14:16; 2 Kings 4:42-44

4 Genesis, 22:14; Psalm 22:4-5; Matthew 14:19b

5 Hebrews 1:2; 2 Timothy 3:1; 2 Peter 3:3

6 Matthew 14:20; John 2:7-9

7 John 2:9; Matthew 14:19c

8 John 2:10-11; 20:30-31

9 Mark 6:43; 2 Kings 4:44

10 1 Corinthians 2:10; Daniel 2:22

11 James 1:17; John 1:9; 1 John 1:5; Revelation 21:23; 22:5; Isaiah 60:19

12 Psalm 100:4: Isaiah 35:10

13 1 Corinthians 8:6; Hebrews 1:2-3; John 1:3

14 Ephesians 1:3; 1 Corinthians 15:57; Romans 8:37; 1 John 5:4-5

security of any given set of preferences or circumstances.[1] No! Spiritual gratitude is found deep within one's relationship with Yehovah![2] To experience it, a person must be able to see their own life through Yeshua's Affection for them.[3] When this happens, everything changes.[4] Suddenly, there are no bad memories.[5] There are no more regrets.[6] Everything is seen through redemption.[7] The Light separates away the darkness,[8] and the person's life is now perceived as a wonderful experience[9] with some distant recollections of failed attacks by darkness that no longer seem to have ever mattered.[10] The resulting freedom is tangible, so tangible that an inward transformation takes place.[11] Once here, the person never has to leave again.[12] Life becomes delightfully bright, and every burden falls away.[13]

OH, THE GLORIOUS AND ABUNDANT RICHES THAT YEHOVAH HAS FOR THOSE CALLED INTO HIS LOVE![14]

HALLELUYAH!

HOW WONDERFUL IS HIS LOVE THAT ESTABLISHED US AND PREDESTINED US[15] FROM THE FOUNDATIONS OF CREATION![16]

HALLELUYAAAAAAAAAAH!!!!

WHAT A GENEROUS GOD WE SERVE!!!!

---

[1] 1 Thessalonians 5:18; Philippians 4:6
[2] Colossians 3:16; Psalm 28:7; 30:11-12; 63:4-6; 103:1-2
[3] 2 Corinthians 1:5; Philippians 2:1; 2 Thessalonians 2:16-17
[4] 2 Corinthians 3:18; Proverbs 4:18
[5] Romans 12:2; Ephesians 4:22-24; Colossians 1:21-22; 3:10; Titus 3:5
[6] Revelation 7:17; Isaiah 25:8; 30:19; 35:10; 60:20
[7] 1 Corinthians 2:16; John 15:15; 16:13-15
[8] 1 Corinthians 6:11; Titus 3:5; Hebrews 10:22; 1 Peter 3:21
[9] Hebrews 10:22; Titus 2:14
[10] Psalm 103:12; 1 John 1:7; Isaiah 43:25; Jeremiah 31:34; 50:20; Micah 7:18
[11] Romans 8:29; 2 Corinthians 3:18
[12] 2 Peter 1:10; 3:17; 1 Peter 1:5; Revelation 3:10-11; Psalm 37:24; 62:2,6; 112:6
[13] John 8:32,36; Psalm 25:5; 119:45; Proverbs 2:1-7; 4:18; Isaiah 2:3; 61:1; Romans 6:14-18,22; 8:2,15; 2 Corinthians 3:17-18; Galatians 5:13; 2 Timothy 2:25-26
[14] Romans 9:23; Ephesians 1:6-8; Colossians 1:12; 2 Thessalonians 2:13-14
[15] Ephesians 1:5,11; Romans 8:29-30
[16] Ephesians 1:4; Matthew 25:34; John 17:24; 1 Peter 1:20; Revelation 13:8; 17:8

"WHAT NO EYE HAS SEEN, NO EAR HAS HEARD, AND NO HUMAN SOUL HAS CONCEIVED,' THE THINGS GOD HAS PREPARED FOR THOSE WHO LOVE HIM – THESE ARE THE THINGS GOD HAS REVEALED TO US BY HIS SPIRIT!"[1]

HALLELUUUUUUUUUUYAAAAAAAAAAAH!!!!!!!!!!!

HOW TRUE IT IS THAT OUR WONDERFUL FATHER WORKS ALL THINGS FOR THE GOOD OF THOSE WHO LOVE HIM![2]

HALLELUUUUUUUUUUYAAAAAAAAAAAH!!!!!!!!!!!

GLORY TO GOD!

But if the heart is experiencing wayward affections that have not been sufficiently understood by truth in the mind, then the gate of deciding affection, or heart-toward-mind, is unguarded. Weakness in this gate is the chosen foothold of the spirit of dark deciding affection, otherwise known as grumbling or bitterness (That is to say, dark deciding affection produces bitterness, but holy deciding affection produces gratitude).[3] When a squatting spirit of bitterness is approached, it will counter or parry acknowledgment by suggesting all sorts of justifications citing injustice, rejection, neglect, abandonment, or abuse.[4] Foremost among such tactics of darkness are suggestions of unforgiveness.[5]

There is much confusion about forgiveness among believers today. May Yehovah bless you to understand His Freedom in Yeshua for your soul![6] May your eyes be full of His Light,[7] and may your heart overflow with His Peace and Joy![8] Amen!

Holy children of Yehovah![9] Listen! Do not be discouraged![10] Your Heavenly Father has made forgiveness easy![11] Don't listen to the ideas of evil spirits insisting that

---

[1] 1 Corinthians 2:9-10a; 1 Peter 1:12; Psalm 31:19; Hebrews 11:16
[2] Romans 8:28,35-39; Hebrews 12:6-12; James 1:3-4; 2 Thessalonians 1:5-7
[3] 1 Samuel 30:6; Deuteronomy 29:18; Philippians 2:14-15
[4] Job 10:1; 9:21; 1 Kings 19:4; Jonah 4:3
[5] Mark 11:25; Luke 17:4; 2 Timothy 3:3
[6] Galatians 5:1,13; 2:4; 4:26,31; John 8:32-36; Romans 6:18; 8:2
[7] Matthew 6:22-23; Luke 11:34-36
[8] Romans 14:17; 15:13; Isaiah 55:12; Acts 13:52
[9] Romans 8:14; Galatians 3:26; 1 John 3:1-2; 5:19; Matthew 5:9
[10] 2 Chronicles 20:17; Deuteronomy 1:21; 31:8; Joshua 1:9; 8:1; 10:25
[11] Ezekiel 36:26; Deuteronomy 30:6; Psalm 51:10; John 3:3-5; 2 Corinthians 5:17

forgiveness is difficult![1] Such thoughts are lies intended for your distraction![2] Forgiveness of humanity is already a trait of your new spirit![3] Yehovah wrote it into your being![4]

HALLELUYAH!

So, listen carefully![5]

It is absolutely paramount that the redeemed human being forgive *every* person of *every* sin, wrong, or offense *ever* experienced.[6] There are *no* circumstances of *any* sort under which unforgiveness toward *any* human being is acceptable.[7] Every child of Yehovah must forgive every person of every sin.[8] There are no exceptions.[9] This is not due to legal technicalities but rather structural realities,[10] because a failure to forgive others leaves the soul's gate of gratitude[11] completely compromised, wide open, and welcoming for every sort of darkness to enter unresisted, unrestrained, and unhindered in any way.[12]

HOWEVER, equally vital is the understanding that WE ARE NOT TO FORGIVE EVIL IN ANY SORT OF WAY EVER![13] Yehovah NEVER approves of evil of any sort, and neither do His children![14] Darkness is UNFORGIVABLE, and that is *why* Yehovah does not allow it in Heaven,[15] *why* there is a Covenant of Creation,[16] and *why* there is a Hell for the isolation of darkness and its spiritual consequences![17] AMEN!

---

[1] Matthew 9:5; Mark 11:25; 2 Corinthians 2:10; Colossians 3:13
[2] Luke 10:40; Colossians 2:4
[3] Ezekiel 11:19; Psalm 51:10; Acts 8:15; Romans 7:6; 2 Corinthians 3:6
[4] Jeremiah 31:33-34; Romans 7:6; 8:2; Galatians 5:18
[5] Luke 8:18; 19:26; Deuteronomy 32:46-47; Proverbs 2:2-5; Mark 4:23-24; Acts 17:11; Hebrews 2:1; James 1:22-25; Matthew 13:12; John 15:2
[6] Matthew 6:14-15; Ephesians 4:32; Colossians 3:13; James 2:13; 1 John 3:10
[7] Matthew 18:23-35; 7:1-2; Proverbs 21:13; Luke 6:37-38
[8] Mark 11:25; Matthew 6:12,14-15; 18:23-35; Luke 6:37; James 2:13
[9] Romans 2:11; Colossians 3:25; Ephesians 6:9; Galatians 2:6; Acts 10:34
[10] Acts 26:18; Romans 8:17; Ephesians 1:11,14; Colossians 1:12; 1 Peter 1:4
[11] That is, the heart-toward-mind gate.
[12] Numbers 16:1-50; 17:10
[13] Isaiah 13:11; Proverbs 11:21a; 2 Peter 2:9; 2 Thessalonians 1:9
[14] Habakkuk 1:13; Colossians 3:2-6
[15] Psalm 5:4; 101:7; Habakkuk 1:13; Hebrews 12:14; Revelation 21:25,27; 22:5
[16] Revelation 5:1; 6:1; Isaiah 29:11; Jeremiah 33:20,25; Genesis 8:22; Psalm 89:37
[17] 2 Peter 2:4; Jude 1:6

So, how do we forgive people for sinning against us and yet not forgive sins committed against us? We do this by understanding what sin is.[1]

As discussed earlier, if left alone human beings would do good because they are made in the image of Yehovah.[2] People do wrong because they have been deceived by dark spirits,[3] have accepted lies,[4] have become hosts for evil influence,[5] and have become instruments of wickedness.[6] All of these traits are the direct result of the actions of spirits of darkness; therefore, IT IS THE SPIRITS OF DARKNESS WHO ARE CULPABLE![7]

It is because of this that Yeshua was able to say to the accused adulteress, "Neither do I condemn you; go and from now on sin no more."[8] He put her accusers on display by suggesting that whoever was without sin should cast the first stone.[9] And this is what He still says to us today![10] Whether in any given situation we are the adulteress or those seeking to stone her, we have all been manipulated by darkness.[11] We have all suffered from deceit.[12] Therefore, the redeemed people of Yehovah accuse no human being.[13] Like Yeshua, we are not here to condemn human beings for being deceived but to save them from the influence of darkness.[14] We do not curse human beings but bless them![15] We bless them with eyes to see and ears to hear![16] We bless them to be set free from darkness and to enter into His loving embrace![17] We bless them to dwell in the Light and walk as children of the Light,[18] full of peace and joy![19] HalleluYah!

---

[1] Romans 3:20; 7:7; Psalm 19:7-12; 119:96

[2] Genesis 1:31a; Deuteronomy 32:4; Ecclesiastes 7:29; See Chapter 8 of this testimony.

[3] Genesis 3:1-3; 2 Corinthians 11:3; Revelation 13:14; 16:13-14; 20:10

[4] Genesis 3:4-5; John 8:44; Acts 13:10; 1 John 3:8

[5] Matthew 16:23; Colossians 3:2; 1 Chronicles 22:19; Psalm 62:10; 119:36-37; Romans 8:4-6; 1 John 2:15-17; Philippians 3:19

[6] Genesis 3:6; John 13:2

[7] Matthew 25:41; John 8:44; 2 Peter 2:4; Jude 1:6; Revelation 12:7-9

[8] John 8:11

[9] John 8:7; Matthew 7:1-5; 23:25-28; Romans 2:1-3; 2:21-25

[10] Hebrews 13:8; Psalm 102:27-28; 103:17; Malachi 3:6; James 1:17

[11] Romans 3:23; 1 John 1:10

[12] Revelation 12:9; Ephesians 2:2; 5:8; Colossians 1:13; 2 Peter 2:4

[13] John 5:45; 8:15-16; 12:47

[14] Matthew 7:1; John 3:17

[15] Romans 12:14; Luke 6:28; 23:24; Acts 7:60; 1 Thessalonians 5:15; 1 Peter 3:9

[16] Matthew 11:15; Mark 4:9,23; Luke 8:8; Revelation 2:7,11,17,29; 3:6,13,22

[17] Isaiah 42:7,22; 49:9; 61:1; Psalm 107:10-16; 146:7; Zechariah 9:11-12

[18] 1 John 1:7; Ephesians 5:8; Romans 13:12; Isaiah 2:5

[19] Romans 14:17; 15:13; Isaiah 55:12; Acts 13:52

Yet, while we completely forgive human beings of all wrongdoing, we do not ever forgive wrongdoing! We do not forgive evil deeds or wickedness of any sort[1] but condemn evil deeds and those dark spirits responsible for them![2] We wage a spiritual war against them and seek their utter banishment and punishment![3] We do not approve of any sin against anyone, not even ourselves![4] That is to say, Yehovah does not ask us to enable or support any sin committed against us by anyone.[5] Though dark spirits will attempt to influence many voices to advise us to give permission for others to sin against us, we know such voices are not of Yehovah.[6]

Did you hear that, precious children of Yehovah?[7]

Yehovah does not say it is permissible for others to sin against you! This is not what is meant by "turning the other cheek,"[8] which is an exhortation to refrain from returning evil for evil![9] And while we would absolutely advise an abused or molested person not to return evil for evil, we certainly do not preach compliance or surrender to such evil![10] On the contrary! We mourn with those who mourn![11]

Someone might ask, "Doesn't the Lord say not to resist an evil person?"[12] Yes! But That is not to say that we should participate in their evil![13] Yeshua says that we should not return evil for evil, that we should not return violence for violence, attack for attack, or demand for demand.[14] But He certainly never says that we should join sinners in sin![15] May it never be so! No! We tear down the strongholds of sin with spiritual weapons![16] We crush the sin beneath our feet![17] We do not tolerate, approve, or enable any evil but lay down our lives to defend and protect

---

[1] Ecclesiastes 12:14; Matthew 12:36: Jude 1:14-15
[2] Psalm 45:7; 101:3-4,8; Luke 13:27; Revelation 21L27
[3] Ephesians 6:10-12; Hebrews 2:2; Jude 1:6
[4] John 8:50; Jude 1:23
[5] 2 Thessalonians 3:14-15; 1 Corinthians 5:11; Ephesians 5:11
[6] 1 Corinthians 5:2,5,7,13; Revelation 2:20-22
[7] Romans 8:14; Galatians 3:26; 1 John 3:1-2; 5:19; Matthew 5:9
[8] Matthew 5:39; Luke 6:29
[9] Matthew 5:44; Romans 12:17-19; 1 Peter 3:9; 1 Thessalonians 5:15
[10] Matthew 10:14; Acts 18:6; 1 Timothy 5:22; Ecclesiastes 7:26; Deuteronomy 22:23-27
[11] Romans 12:15b; Hebrews 13:3; Psalms 35:13-14; John 11:35
[12] Matthew 5:39a,44; Romans 12:17
[13] Psalm 101:4; Ephesians 5:11
[14] Matthew 5:39b-48; 1 Peter 2:20-23
[15] John 5:14; Luke 13:4-5; Revelation 2:21-23
[16] Revelation 3:11; Jeremiah 1:10; Joshua 6:20; 1 Corinthians 15:57
[17] Romans 16:20-22; Luke 10:19

the innocent![1] Yehovah never approves of sin of any sort, and neither do we![2] All dark spirits are destined for eternal banishment and punishment,[3] and we will help judge them and forcefully send them there for the glory of His Justice and Righteousness![4] HalleluYah! May no evil of any sort ever dwell in the presence of our Holy King and His Holy Kingdom,[5] a refuge from all iniquity, a perfect haven for the righteous! [6] HalleluYah! May God's Purity, Holiness, Righteousness, Kindness, Truth, and Joy reign forever through His Goodness![7] HalleluYah!

Therefore, we say to everyone, "Stop sinning, or something worse may happen to you!"[8] And though we do not seek our own honor,[9] "There is One Who seeks it," for Yehovah is HOLY![10] And we are comforted being assured that no injustice will ever be permitted entrance into Heaven![11] Because of this, we can joyfully enter the Father's Love, Justice, and Holiness.[12] In Him we find His Grace, Forgiveness, and Freedom from darkness of every sort.[13] So, we freely forgive our human brothers and sisters[14] and pray for their redemption and release from bondage to evil spirits that manipulate them for dark purposes.[15] And we shed the bitterness of darkness,[16] knowing that the condemnation of human beings is from the enemy[17] (Unfortunately many will ultimately have a share in condemnation due to their alignment with darkness, but that is their own doing. They have condemned themselves).[18]

---

[1] John 15:13; 1 John 4:7-11; 1 Corinthians 13:7

[2] 2 Timothy 3:1-6; 4:2-4

[3] Matthew 25:41; John 8:44; 2 Peter 2:4; Jude 1:6; Revelation 12:7-9

[4] 1 Corinthians 6:3; Matthew 25:41; 2 Peter 2:4; Jude 1:6

[5] Psalm 5:4; 101:7; Habakkuk 1:13; Hebrews 12:14; Revelation 21:25,27; 22:5

[6] Revelation 21:3-8; 7:15; Hebrews 11:16

[7] Galatians 5:22-26; Ephesians 5:9; 1 Corinthians 13:7

[8] John 5:14

[9] John 7:18; 8:49-50; 1 Corinthians 10:31; 1 Thessalonians 2:6; 1 Peter 4:11

[10] John 8:50; John 12:47-48

[11] Psalm 5:4; 101:7; Habakkuk 1:13; Hebrews 12:14; Revelation 21:25,27; 22:5

[12] Luke 18:7; John 14:21; Colossians 1:12; Psalm 63:4-5; 100:1-5

[13] John 1:14; Matthew 6:14; Romans 8:21; Luke 4:18

[14] Ephesians 4:32; Mark 11:25-26; Luke 6:37; 11:4; Colossians 3:12-13; Romans 12:20-21; 1 Peter 3:8-9; 1 John 2:12

[15] 1 John 5:16; James 5:14-15

[16] Isaiah 5:20; Ephesians 4:31

[17] Romans 8:1; 2:1; 2 Corinthians 7:3; Luke 6:37

[18] Titus 3:11; Matthew 12:37; John 12:48

And we even do more than this. We don't just forgive individual human beings; we forgive groups of human beings.[1] We forgive our family of being used for darkness.[2] We forgive times and places associated with groups of humans that transferred darkness to us.[3] For example, we forgive our childhood, adolescence, adulthood, church, camp, school, neighborhood, military, hospital, police, workplace, industry, sport, entertainers, legal system, leadership, nation, and foreign peoples.[4] We forgive all of these "things" because they are really titles that identify periods and places of relationships with other human beings throughout our experience in Creation.[5]

HALLELUYAH! YESHUA HAS SET US FREE FROM ALL DARKNESS WE'VE EVER EXPERIENCED![6] HE HAS REDEEMED EVEN OUR MEMORIES![7] WE DIED TO THE DARKNESS [8] AND HAVE RISEN INTO THE LIGHT! [9] WE WERE CREATED IN GOODNESS, [10] AND NOW WE CAN PROCLAIM THAT OUR LIVES HAVE BEEN GOOD![11] IT HAS ALWAYS BEEN DARKNESS THAT HAS BEEN BAD![12] LONG LIVE THE GOODNESS OF YEHOVAH,[13] AND MAY ALL EVIL BE BANISHED FROM OUR PAST, PRESENT, AND FUTURE FOREVER AND EVER![14]

HALLELUUUUUUUYAAAAAAAAAAAAAAAAH!!!!!!!!!!!

GLORY TO OUR GREAT AND GOOD GOD FOR WHOM NOTHING IS IMPOSSIBLE![15]

HALLELUUUUUUUYAAAAAAAAAAAAAAAAH!!!!!!!!!!!

---

[1] Luke 23:34; 1 Peter 20:20-23; 3:9; Romans 12:14; Acts 7:60

[2] Luke 17:4; Genesis 50:17

[3] Mark 11:25; Matthew 6:12,14-15; 18:23-35; Luke 6:37; James 2:13

[4] Numbers 14:19; Jonah 4:11; Isaiah 19:21; 2 Chronicles 7:14

[5] Numbers 15:25-26; John 19:6,10-12,16

[6] Romans 12:2; Ephesians 4:22-24; Colossians 1:21-22; 3:10; Titus 3:5

[7] Colossians 3:2; 1 Chronicles 22:19; Psalm 62:10; 119:36-37; Matthew 16:23; Romans 8:4-6; 1 John 2:15-17; Philippians 3:19

[8] Colossians 2:20; 3:3; Romans 6:2; Galatians 2:20

[9] Ephesians 2:2; 5:8; 2:11-12; Ephesians 4:18; 6:12; Isaiah 42:16; 1 Peter 2:9; Colossians 1:13; Acts 26:18

[10] Genesis 1:31a; Deuteronomy 32:4; Ecclesiastes 7:29

[11] Psalm 126:3; 100:5; 145:7,9; James 1:17

[12] John 8:44; 12:31; Ephesians 2:2; 6:12

[13] Matthew 19:17; 1 Samuel 2:2; Psalm 145:7-9; James 1:17

[14] Revelation 22:5; 21:4; Isaiah 25:8; 1 Corinthians 15:26

[15] Isaiah 50:2; Genesis 18:14; Numbers 11:23

GLORY TO OUR WONDERFUL SAVIOR, WHO IS ABLE TO WIPE AWAY EVERY TEAR FROM OUR EYES![1]

HALLELUUUUUUUYAAAAAAAAAAAAAAAAH!!!!!!!!!!!

Now, to DEFEAT the lying and deceitful spirit of bitterness, we understand that the heart must first be covered by Yehovah's Sacrifice of His own Affection on the Cross[2] as well as His commands to carry our own cross to replace our affections with His.[3] Covering the heart in this way causes it to be brought back into submission under the Word of Truth in the mind.[4] Then the neighboring gate of deciding affection, or heart-toward-mind, can be covered with Yeshua's Blood of Gratitude by speaking of His Thankfulness[5] and Shared Glory with the Father and us.[6] It is His Gratitude that enables our own.[7] It's His Testimony, His Gratitude that ushers in our strength.[8] After this, the spirit of bitterness may be effectively bound, silenced, and cast away into darkness[9] because it cannot dwell in the presence of His Glory![10] Amen! HalleluYah!

A key response to a spirit of bitterness is, "This is the only place I will ever suffer or be disciplined, and neither will last long.[11] Praise Yehovah that every bit of suffering here will be redeemed as wealth for me,[12] causing me to become more grateful for Heaven, enabling me to have an even deeper sense of gratitude and enjoyment forever!"[13] We never need to make the mistake of receiving bitterness![14] It's not of us![15] Christ did not redeem us to be bitter but to triumph over all darkness![16] He has not given us a heart of bitterness but a new heart that

---

[1] Revelation 7:17; 21:4; Isaiah 25:8; 30:19; 35:10; 60:20

[2] Hebrews 12:2; Acts 5:31; Psalms 138:8

[3] Matthew 16:24; Deuteronomy 6:6-9; Exodus 13:9,16; Numbers 15:38-39; Proverbs 3:3; 6:21; 7:3; Hebrews 2:1

[4] James 4:8; Hebrews 10:22; 1 Peter 3:21; 2 Corinthians 7:1

[5] Matthew 11:25-27; John 11:41

[6] John 17:22; 14:20; 1 John 3:24; 2 Thessalonians 1:5-10

[7] Luke 15:22-24; 1 Peter 1:7

[8] Joshua 3:7-17; Deuteronomy 12:10-12

[9] Matthew 10:1; 16:19; Mark 1:34; 16:17; James 4:7; Luke 10:17; Acts 16:18; Psalm 31:18

[10] Psalm 5:4 ("לא יגרך רע" or "nor does evil dwell with You")

[11] Romans 8:18; Revelation 21:4

[12] Genesis 50:20; Romans 8:28

[13] James 1:2-4; Matthew 5:10-12; Luke 6:22-23; 1 Peter 3:14; 4:16

[14] Ephesians 4:31; Colossians 3:18; James 3:14-15

[15] Ephesians 4:24; 6:11; Job 29:14; Romans 6:4; 13:12,14; Galatians 3:27

[16] Romans 8:37; 12:21; Proverbs 16:32; Luke 6:27-30; 1 Peter 3:9

is soft and full of joy![1] We never have to receive bitterness of any kind, no matter what we have experienced![2] It is not our purpose here, neither is it our destiny![3] Bitterness is a spirit,[4] and its thoughts are roots from evil seed![5] Cast it out![6] Be free from it forever![7] And enter into the Kingdom of Heaven *immediately*,[8] where *no one* is ever bitter but only lives in perfect gratitude all the time![9]

HALLELUYAH!

When the truth in the mind is focused on affection, and the affection of the heart is set on the truth, the result is a revelation of gentleness in the mind-heart-convergence gate. Such gentleness is not an afterthought but vital for Kingdom living.[10] Though it is often unacknowledged, gentleness is the very foundation of Heavenly behavior.[11]

Understand that our job is to shine for Yeshua.[12] We are called to draw people *to* His Light.[13] While His Sternness warns people of the danger of darkness, it is His Kindness that leads people to repentance.[14] His Light is welcoming, not angry.[15] It's forgiving, not condemning.[16] He longs to bring all human beings into His Light.[17]

---

[1] Ezekiel 36:26; Deuteronomy 30:6; Psalm 51:10; John 3:3-5; 2 Corinthians 5:17

[2] See the section pertaining to lust and the comments about feelings, appetites, and desires in Chapter 21 of this testimony.

[3] Romans 8:29; Matthew 12:50; 25:40; Colossians 1:15-18; Revelation 1:5-6

[4] 1 Samuel 30:6; Psalm 73:21; Ephesians 6:12

[5] Hebrews 12:15; Deuteronomy 29:18

[6] Matthew 10:1,8; 12:28; Luke 19:45; Ezekiel 18:31; 20:7; Isaiah 1:16-17; 55:7; Romans 8:13; Ephesians 4:22-32; Colossians 3:5-9; James 1:21; 1 Peter 2:1

[7] Galatians 5:1,13; 2:4; 4:26,31; John 8:32-36; Romans 6:18; 8:2

[8] Luke 17:21; 1 Corinthians 3:16; Matthew 10:7

[9] 1 Thessalonians 5:18; 1 Timothy 2:1; 4:4; Luke 17:3,4; 23:34; Matthew 6:10; 13:11,44; 16:19; 18:22-35; Mark 11:25; John 20:23; Revelation 2:7,11,17,26-28; 3:5,12,21; 7:15-17

[10] Matthew 5:5; 11:29; 21:5; Ephesians 4:2; 1 Timothy 3:3; Titus 3:2

[11] Philippians 4:5; Revelation 7:17; Colossians 3:12; 1 Timothy 6:11; See Chapter 25 of this testimony for more about how gentleness affects the will.

[12] John 15:8; Luke 6:35; Psalm 92:12-15; Isaiah 60:21; Matthew 5:16

[13] Matthew 5:16; Luke 1:53; John 6:27; 15:8

[14] Romans 11:22; Romans 2:4

[15] Matthew 11:29; 2 Corinthians 10:1

[16] John 8:11,15; 3:17; 18:36; Luke 6:37; 12:13-14

[17] 1 Timothy 2:3-4; Titus 2:11; 2 Peter 3:9

His Gentleness is both Content and Grateful.[1] He lacks nothing,[2] so He is able to give everything.[3]

So it is with us.[4] We lack nothing,[5] and we are overflowing with gratitude.[6] Because of this, we are able to receive His Gentleness and reveal it to others through both words and deeds.[7]

There was once a practicing lesbian who was very sick and very discouraged.[8] Out of love for her, two of her lesbian friends tricked her into coming to see me for help.[9] Within an hour of visiting in the Gentle Presence of the Holy Spirit[10] and receiving His Words of Love for her,[11] she was filled with hope[12] and encouragement[13] for both healing and righteousness.[14] She wanted the Light of Jesus.[15] She was ready to awake from the darkness that imprisoned her,[16] but she was still having trouble receiving and utilizing faith in Yeshua to see her healing manifested in Creation.[17] So she made plans to continue in fellowship with me until her healing was established in her soul and body for the Glory of His Name.[18]

However, after returning home that afternoon, she called the physician she had previously been trusting. He discouraged her so much that she accepted an idea from darkness[19] to ingest all her pain medications and commit suicide.[20] By

---

[1] Hebrews 2:17-18; Philippians 2:7-8
[2] Psalm 23:1; Luke 22:35
[3] Matthew 10:8; 1 John 3:16; 16:15
[4] 1 John 2:6; 1:7; Psalm 85:13; Matthew 11:29; John 13:15; 1 Peter 2:21
[5] Ephesians 1:3; 2:6; Genesis 12:2-3; 1 Chronicles 4:10; Isaiah 61:9; Galatians 3:9
[6] Colossians 2:7; 1:12-13; 3:17; Ephesians 5:20; 1 Thessalonians 5:18
[7] 2 Corinthians 1:3-6; 2 Thessalonians 2:16-17; Isaiah 66:12-13
[8] Mark 2:17; Hosea 14:4; Psalm 147:3; Luke 18:11-14
[9] Luke 10:33; 7:13; Exodus 2:6; Matthew 18:33
[10] 2 Corinthians 13:14; Galatians 5:22; 1 Corinthians 3:16
[11] Genesis 50:21; Isaiah 40:2
[12] Proverbs 13:12; Psalm 40:2-3
[13] Hebrews 6:18; Acts 9:31
[14] Acts 28:27; Luke 24:45
[15] John 1:3-4,9; 8:12; 9:5; 12:46; Isaiah 42:6-7; Malachi 4:2; Matthew 4:16; Luke 1:78-79; 2:32; Acts 26:23; Ephesians 5:124; 1 John 1:5; Revelation 22:16
[16] 2 Timothy 2:26; Job 1:12; 2:6; Luke 22:31-32
[17] Matthew 14:30; 2 Kings 6:15; Mark 14:38
[18] Acts 17:32; 2 Corinthians 6:2
[19] John 13:2; Acts 5:3; 1 Kings 22:21-22; 1 Chronicles 21:1; Matthew 13:9; Luke 22:3; John 13:27
[20] Matthew 27:4-5; Acts 1:18-19

Yehovah's Mercy, she was found quickly and rushed to the nearest hospital.[1] But she was brain dead upon arrival.

I owned a business in "Samaria"[2] as a licensed professional at the time. Knowing that the hospital staff was corporately "Samaritan" in spirit,[3] my office sent several published medical articles by licensed physicians about treatments that had facilitated recovery from brain death.[4] We even sent a licensed RN with IV bags full of the appropriate nutraceuticals. And while the attending physician agreed with our approach and was eager to cooperate, the hospital administration reluctantly denied our access and participation due to fear of legal impropriety.[5]

Four days later, I was in my office when one of the young woman's lesbian friends called to inform us that the hospital had removed life support and that our mutual friend had been dead for two and a half hours. At that moment, I was moved in spirit,[6] and I felt the Gentle Blessing of Yeshua rise up in power.[7] At once, I said loudly, "Yehovah, this is a tragedy against someone who just joyfully received Your Hope days ago,[8] and we ask that You rescue this young woman from the enemy's vicious schemes[9] and raise her from the dead for Your Glory!"[10]

Within just a few minutes, we received another call that our friend had risen from the dead with full brain recovery![11]

HALLELUUUUUUUUUUYAAAAAAAAAAAH!!!!!!!!!!!!!

GREAT AND COMPASSIONATE IS OUR GOD WHO LEAVES THE NINTY-NINE TO RECOVER THE ONE![12]
HALLELUUUUUUUUUUYAAAAAAAAAAAH!!!!!!!!!!!!!

---

[1] Luke 10:33; 7:13; Exodus 2:6; Matthew 18:33
[2] John 4:22; Acts 17:23,30
[3] Luke 10:33-34; John 4:22
[4] 1 Timothy 5:23; Luke 10:34
[5] John 19:12; Mark 6:26
[6] John 11:33; Luke 2:27
[7] 1 Thessalonians 1:5; Mark 5:30
[8] 2 Corinthians 11:3; Galatians 1:6; 3:1; Revelation 12:9
[9] 2 Corinthians 2:11; 1 Peter 5:8; Ephesians 6:11-12; Revelation 12:9-11; 13:8
[10] John 7:18; 8:49-50; 1 Corinthians 10:31; 1 Thessalonians 2:6; 1 Peter 4:11
[11] John 11:41-44; Luke 7:15
[12] Luke 15:4-7; Matthew 18:12

THIS is what the compassion of gentleness can do![1] THIS is its beauty and function![2]

GENTLENESS *SAVES* THE LOST![3] IT IS NOT CRITICAL BUT MERCIFUL![4] IT DOES *NOT* COMPROMISE WITH DARKNESS, BUT IT *RESCUES* HUMAN BEINGS FROM IT![5]

HALLELUUUUUUUUUUYAAAAAAAAAAAH!!!!!!!!!!!!

GOD IS GOOD!!!!!!!!!!!!![6]

In tragic contrast, if there is a complete break between the mind and heart, it is because there are lies in the mind and selfish affections in the heart. Such a disconnection opens the heart-mind-convergence gate to the opposition of gentleness, which is the spirit of anger. [7] This spirit is notorious for its unreasonable posturing. It fills the mind with heartless lies and the heart with mindless rage.[8]

RIGHTEOUS ONES OF YESHUA![9] LISTEN CLOSELY![10] There are two very different sorts of anger! There is the sort that loves to be first.[11] Such a spirit of anger always has selfishness somewhere as its motive.[12] It demands to be central, to be heard, to be respected, and to be valued.[13] In English, we can call this "selfish anger."[14] But there is also another very different sort of anger. It is the opposite of selfishness.[15] It is the sort of holy insistence that is no longer willing to tolerate

---

[1] Ephesians 4:32; Mark 11:25-26; Luke 6:37; 11:4; Colossians 3:12-13; Romans 12:20-21; 1 Peter 3:8-9; 1 John 2:12
[2] James 5:11; Exodus 34:6; 1 Chronicles 21:13
[3] Romans 5:8; Isaiah 53:6; 1 Peter 3:18; 1 John 4:9-10
[4] Philippians 2:1-8; Romans 9:23
[5] Jude 1:23; 1 Timothy 4:16
[6] James 1:17; John 1:9; 1 John 1:5; Revelation 21:23; 22:5; Isaiah 60:19
[7] Psalm 37:8; Proverbs 14:29; 29:22; James 1:20
[8] Ecclesiastes 7:9; 1 Samuel 19:9-11
[9] Romans 3:22; Philippians 3:9
[10] Luke 8:18; 19:26; Deuteronomy 32:46-47; Proverbs 2:2-5; Mark 4:23-24; Acts 17:11; Hebrews 2:1; James 1:22-25; Matthew 13:12; John 15:2
[11] Matthew 20:20-28; 23:4-8; 3 John 1:9
[12] James 3:16; Philippians 2:3; Galatians 5:20
[13] 1 Samuel 18:8; Esther 3:5; Proverbs 24:7; Ecclesiastes 4:4
[14] James 1:20; Psalm 37:8; Proverbs 14:29; 29:22
[15] Romans 2:8; Proverbs 13:10

anything less than absolute Goodness.[1] It is willing to fight or die for His Goodness.[2] It is more than willing to completely sacrifice self for the greater good.[3] It is *selfless* anger, and it seeks what is Holy, Pure, and Kind.[4] In the Spirit, this is known as "Holy Wrath."[5]

PRAISE OUR HOLY GOD, WHO IS FULL OF SELFLESS ANGER![6] HE CRUSHES THE DARKNESS IN HIS WRATH![7]

HALLELUYAH!

To rid a soul of a spirit of selfish anger, a person must speak the Blood of Yeshua's Mind through their soul's mind,[8] and His Sacrifice of Love must be spoken through the heart.[9] Then the Testimony of His Gentleness must be applied to the disconnection in the convergence gate.[10] Once the Scriptures of His Gentleness and those concerning our commanded gentleness[11] have been applied, then the spirit of selfish anger may be removed easily.[12]

When confronted by a spirit of selfish anger in your soul, a key response is, "Selfish anger is a spirit, not a fruit of the Spirit!"[13] The only time we experience justified anger is when we are clearing a path for someone to have a relationship with Yehovah.[14] So, if you hear any anger in your soul, make sure you are embracing the *selfless* anger of the Holy Spirit to bring someone close to Yehovah[15] rather than embracing an evil spirit of selfish anger that seeks to use you as a testimony *against* the behavior of Christ![16] Remember, selfish anger comes as a spirit![17] Your

---

[1] John 2:13-17; Psalm 69:9
[2] John 2:18-22; 12:16; Luke 24:7-8
[3] Hebrews 12:2; Acts 5:31; Psalms 138:8
[4] 2 Peter 3:10-13; 1 Timothy 4:12; 6:11; James 3:13
[5] Revelation 19:15-21; Isaiah 11:4; 2 Thessalonians 2:8
[6] Revelation 16:19; Jeremiah 25:15-16
[7] Revelation 15:1,7; 19:15
[8] Romans 12:2; Deuteronomy 6:9
[9] Hebrews 10:24; 6:10-11; Galatians 5:6
[10] Matthew 11:28-29; 12:20; 23:37
[11] Philippians 4:5; Colossians 3:12; 1 Timothy 6:11
[12] Colossians 3:8; Ephesians 4:22; Hebrews 12:1
[13] Matthew 5:22; Romans 2:8; Ecclesiastes 7:9; Ephesians 4:31; Colossians 3:8; Galatians 5:22-23
[14] Matthew 21:12-13; Acts 13:8-12
[15] Zechariah 7:12; Jeremiah 26:19
[16] Matthew 5:22; Ephesians 4:26; James 1:19
[17] Ecclesiastes 7:9; Mark 6:19

spirit already overflows with Yeshua's Gentleness![1] Selfish anger has nothing to do with you! It is not your purpose here![2] Do not serve it![3] Bind that angry spirit, silence it, and cast it away![4] And enter the Kingdom of Heaven *right now*,[5] where *no one* is ever selfishly angry but only lives in perfect gentleness all the time![6] Pick up your mat and walk[7] in the powerful and sober Gentleness of Christ[8] as the light you were created to be![9]

HALLELUYAH!

Are these "giants" too big for you, Israel? [10] These "Goliaths," [11] these "uncircumcised Philistines,"[12] these spirits of envy, bitterness, and anger, are they too much for you?

ARE THESE GIANTS TOO BIG FOR YOU, ISRAEL?[13]

NO!!!!!!!!!!!!!!!!!![14]

WHY NOT?

BECAUSE OF WHO OUR GOD IS! THAT'S WHY!!!!!!!!!!!![15]

SO, ARE YOU GOING TO LET THEM CAMP OUT IN YOUR LAND, ENJOYING YOUR MILK AND HONEY,[16] WHILE YOU WANDER AROUND IN THE DESERT?[17]

---

[1] Philippians 4:5; Titus 3:2
[2] Romans 8:29; Matthew 12:50; 25:40; Colossians 1:15-18; Revelation 1:5-6
[3] Ephesians 4:31
[4] Matthew 10:1; 16:19; Mark 1:34; 16:17; James 4:7; Luke 10:17; Acts 16:18; Psalm 31:18
[5] Luke 17:21; 1 Corinthians 3:16; Matthew 10:7
[6] Philippians 4:5; Revelation 7:17; Colossians 3:12; 1 Timothy 6:11; Matthew 6:10; 13:11,44; 16:19
[7] John 5:8; Acts 9:34
[8] 2 Corinthians 10:1; Matthew 21:5; 11:29
[9] Romans 8:29; Matthew 12:50; 25:40; Colossians 1:15-18; Revelation 1:5-6
[10] Numbers 13:31; Deuteronomy 1:28
[11] 1 Samuel 17:4; 2 Corinthians 20:5
[12] 1 Samuel 17:26,36; 14:6
[13] Numbers 13:33; Deuteronomy 1:28; 1 Samuel 17:4-7
[14] Numbers 13:30; 14:6-9; Joshua 14:6-8
[15] Numbers 14:6-8; Exodus 3:8
[16] Numbers 13:27-29; Exodus 3:17
[17] Numbers 14:20-24,34; Deuteronomy 2:7: 8:2

NO!!!!!!!!!!!!!!!!!!

WHY NOT?

BECAUSE OUR GOD HAS GIVEN THE LAND INTO OUR HANDS!!!!!!!!!!!!!!![1]

HALLELUYAH!

SWORDS OUT, ISRAEL! SWORDS OUT![2]

SLAY THESE "UNCIRCUMCISED PHILISTINES" WITH THE TRUTH OF GOD![3]

STRIKE THEM IN THE FOREHEAD[4] WITH THE STONE OF YESHUA![5]

CUT OFF THEIR HEADS[6] AND TAKE THEIR AUTHORITY AS PLUNDER![7]

HALLELUUUUUUUUYAAAAAAAAAAAAH!!!!

WARRIORS OF GOD![8] WHAT YOU CONQUER, YOU KEEP![9]
WARRIORS OF GOD![10] WHAT YOU CONQUER, YOU KEEP![11]

PRAISE BE TO OUR HOLY GOD!!!!

DEVOTE THIS LAND TO YEHOVAH![12] RULE OVER THIS SOUL WITH AN IRON SCEPTER![13] MAKE EVERY GATE OF THIS SOUL BOW,[14] AND EVERY THOUGHT OF THIS SOUL CONFESS THAT JESUS CHRIST IS LORD!!![15]

---

[1] Numberer 14:9; Deuteronomy 7:18
[2] Genesis 34:25; Exodus 17:13
[3] Ephesians 6:17; Isaiah 49:2; Revelation 1:16; 2:16; 19:15
[4] 1 Samuel 17:49; 2 Corinthians 10:4-5; 1 Corinthians 1:27-28
[5] 1 Samuel 2:2; Acts 4:11
[6] 1 Samuel 17:46,51c; 2 Samuel 23:21; Ester 7:10; Psalm 7:15-16
[7] 1 Samuel 17:51d-54; Mark 3:27
[8] 2 Timothy 2:3; 2 Corinthians 10:3-5; Ephesians 6:11-18; 1 Timothy 1:18
[9] 1 John 5:4; Revelation 2:10
[10] 2 Timothy 2:4; 1 Corinthians 9:25-26; 1 Timothy 6:9-12
[11] Revelation 4:10; Romans 8:37
[12] Leviticus 27:28; Numbers 21:2-3
[13] Revelation 2:27; 12:5; 19:15; Psalm 2:9
[14] Philippians 2:10; Isaiah 45:23-25; Romans 4:10-11
[15] Philippians 2:11; Isaiah 45:23-25; Romans 4:10-11

THE LAND IS OURS!!!!![1]

CONQUER WITH THE KING![2]

CONQUER THROUGH THE KING![3]

CONQUER BECAUSE OF THE KING![4]

CONQUER FOR THE GLORY OF OUR KING![5]

HALLELUUUUUUUUYAAAAAAAAAAAAAAAAAH!!!

HALLELUUUUUUUUYAAAAAAAAAAAAAAAAAAAAAAH!!!

HALLELUUUUUUUUYAAAAAAAAAAAAAAAAAAAAAAAAAAAH!!![6]

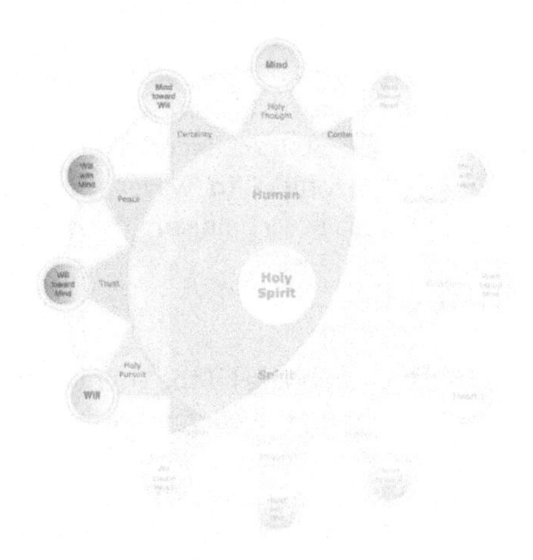

[1] 2 Chronicles 14:7; Hebrews 3:13-15
[2] Matthew 12:30; Genesis 49:10; Hosea 1:11; John 11:52
[3] Philippians 4:13; Ephesians 3:16
[4] John 15:5; Romans 12:5; 1 Corinthians 12:12; Acts 4:12
[5] John 15:8; Luke 6:35; Psalm 92:12-15; Isaiah 60:21; Matthew 5:16
[6] Psalm 20:5; 27:6; 33:3; 47:1; 66:1; 95:1; 98:4; 100:1; 118:15

CHAPTER 21

GATES BETWEEN THE HEART AND THE WILL

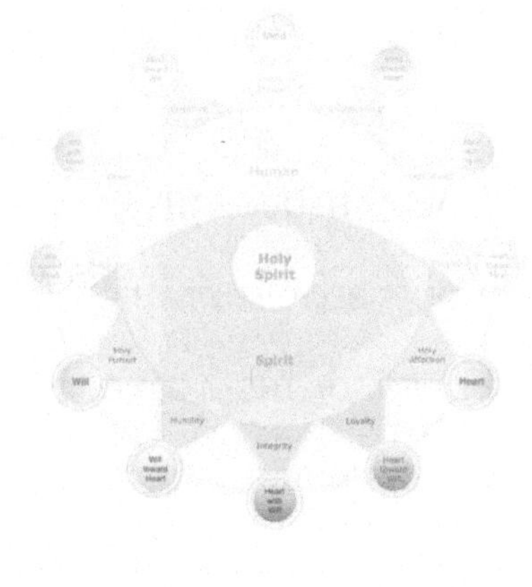

When the heart's affection prompts pursuit of Christ's Righteousness, loyalty is revealed in the heart-toward-will gate. This consideration of affection composes the very walls of the Kingdom of Heaven.[1] It is purely devoted, sure, and confident.[2] It refuses to waver, compromise, or withdraw.[3] It is mighty in resolution, absolutely bold, and the quality of love that never fails.[4]

HALLELUYAH!

I was once vacationing by the shore of the Dead Sea. And I heard the Spirit say, "Go swim in the sea."[5] Some brothers and sisters were headed that way, so I joined them in the shallow water for a while. But after some time, Yehovah spoke to me again and said, "Swim far out into the sea."[6] I immediately withdrew and swam very far away. Being quite buoyant in the extremely salty water, it was not

---

[1] 1 Chronicles 29:18; 2 Thessalonians 2:16-17
[2] 1 Samuel 17:26,36; Psalm 79:12
[3] 1 Samuel 17:31-37; Ezekiel 32:28-32
[4] 1 Samuel 17:45-47; Isaiah 37:22-23
[5] Acts 8:29; 10:19; 11:12; 13:2-4; 16:6-7
[6] Acts 8:29; 10:19; 11:12; 13:2-4; 16:6-7

difficult. And driven by the Strength of the Holy Spirit,[1] I swam for about an hour toward the center of the sea.

Suddenly, I noticed something that appeared to be floating on the water about twenty yards ahead of me. I swam toward it and saw that it was a perfectly flat platform of salt. It was about ten inches thick, oval in shape, and measured about twelve feet long and eight feet wide. The long side was facing me, and the platform looked solid as if it were the flat top of a mighty pillar protruding from the bottom of the sea.

Over the platform was what looked like a transparent golden fire.[2] It extended from the platform upward about twenty feet, fading into the sky. When I saw it, the Spirit filled me with awe, and I was overwhelmed, understanding that I was in the Presence of the Holy Angel of Yeshua Yehovah.[3]

At first, my soul cowered. But as the Spirit filled me,[4] I felt a sensation very much like that of when Yehovah transfigured me.[5] It seemed as if every fiber of my being was being aligned toward Him.[6] And at that moment, I received a revelation that every part of my soul could serve Him.[7] I was made aware that the same gate of my soul that had the potential for lust or greed was only out of alignment when it was not focused on Him.[8] That is to say, my insatiable hunger was only destructive when it was not focused on the eternal Fountain of Yeshua.[9]

The Holy Spirit opened my eyes,[10] and I saw two unidentified elohim standing on each side of Yehovah.[11] On the sea, and all around the shores of the sea, were myriads of spirits, both loyal and disloyal.[12] They were all silent and still; no one spoke a word. Then Yehovah spoke to me in a Voice like thunder and asked, "What do you want?"[13]

---

[1] 1 Kings 18:46; Ezekiel 3:14
[2] Exodus 3:2b; Luke 20:37; Acts 7:30
[3] Exodus 3:2a; 2 Kings 2:11; 6:17; Revelation 1:12-16
[4] Ephesians 3:16; Revelation 1:17; Daniel 8:18; 10:10
[5] Mark 9:2; See later in this chapter and the Preface of this testimony for more about when Yehovah mercifully transfigured me.
[6] John 13:14; Isaiah 6:7; Jeremiah 1:9; Daniel 10:16-18; Colossians 1:11
[7] Romans 12:2; Ephesians 4:22-24; Colossians 1:21-22; 3:10; Titus 3:5
[8] Matthew 6:22-23; Luke 11:34-36
[9] Matthew 6:23-24b; Romans 6:16; Galatians 1:10; James 4:4; 1 John 2:15-16
[10] 2 Kings 6:17; Numbers 22:31
[11] Psalm 82:1; Luke 1:19; Revelation 12:7
[12] Job 1:6; 2:1; Psalm 82:1-8
[13] 1 Kings 3:5; 2 Chronicles 1:7-12; Mark 10:36

Now, when I was previously transfigured and taken to Heaven,[1] Yehovah had done so in order for me to physically embrace my Lord and God, Yeshua HaMashiach, the Word Almighty.[2] At that time, He had welcomed me with a mesmerizing smile and open arms.[3] Yet this time, we were not in Heaven surrounded by my siblings made righteous[4] but in Creation surrounded by all sorts of principalities,[5] and my God stood before me as the Commander of Hosts.[6] The need for legality was evident, for I received by revelation[7] that I was not presenting myself as a redeemed son to his Father but as an enlisted soldier to his General.[8] This was a forum for a formal request before all the principalities.[9] Even so, His Peace rested upon me,[10] and I was not afraid at all but only concerned about honoring my King.[11]

At that moment, I was filled with the Holy Spirit,[12] and I replied, "Yehovah, all my life You have blessed me with countless miracles and interventions, so many that no one aside from Yeshua in the Scriptures appears to have been as blessed. But I seem to stumble constantly.[13] Lord, I ask that I may honor You and never stumble again."[14]

"Very well," He answered, "You will never stumble again,[15] but first you must suffer a little while."[16]

---

1 Mark 9:2; See later in this chapter and the Preface of this testimony for more about when Yehovah mercifully transfigured me.

2 John 20:27; Acts 1:3; Luke 24:41-43

3 Revelation 7:17; Isaiah 25:8; 30:19; 35:10; 60:20

4 Hebrews 12:1,23; Ezekiel 38:9

5 Job 1:6; 2:1; Ephesians 2:2; 6:12

6 Joshua 5:14; Revelation 19:11-14

7 Galatians 1:12; 1 Corinthians 14:30

8 Isaiah 6:8; Exodus 4:10-13; Acts 22:21; 26:16-17

9 1 Kings 22:20-22; Job 1:6; 2:1

10 John 14:27; 16:33; Romans 5:1-2; Acts 10:36; 1 Corinthians 1:3

11 John 7:18; 8:49-50; 1 Corinthians 10:31; 1 Thessalonians 2:6; 1 Peter 4:11

12 Luke 1:67; Acts 4:8

13 Even though I remembered hearing the Voice of Yehovah in the womb (Luke 1:44; Galatians 1:15), I stumbled in many ways throughout my life (James 3:2). At one time or another, I fell at every gate (1 Corinthians 10:13). But praise be to Yehovah through Yeshua, Who rescued me from all stumbling (2 Peter 1:10) through His Blood (1 Peter 1:2) and has given me His Complete Victory (1 Corinthians 15:57)! HALLELUYAH! SO GREAT IS HIS LOVE FOR US (Ephesians 1:7)! HALLELUYAH!

14 John 7:18; 8:49-50; 1 Corinthians 10:31; 1 Thessalonians 2:6; 1 Peter 4:11

15 2 Peter 1:10; 1 Peter 1:2,5

16 Acts 9:16; Matthew 5:11; Romans 5:3; 8:17

I was elated! I had longed for this! But even as I celebrated in my soul, He spoke to me deep in my spirit[1] and let me know that His Heart went out to me concerning my coming suffering.[2] He did not hide His Compassion for me in Spirit,[3] but outwardly He kept His resolute demeanor.[4]

Though I sensed the encounter was over, I confess that I did not want to leave! I heard His Spirit say that the entire spiritual audience was waiting for me to leave,[5] but I could not bring myself to turn from Him![6] His Holiness was aligning every fiber of my being![7] I felt perfectly clean! So Yehovah said, "Go."[8] And as soon as He said it, I felt my body turn around and begin to swim away! In my heart I was laughing because I knew my God was driving my body away on my behalf! He knew I couldn't do it, so He kindly did it for me![9]

PRAISE BE TO OUR HOLY GOD, WHO IS BRILLIANTLY COMPASSIONATE![10]

HALLELUYAH!

PRAISE BE TO THE KING OF HEAVENLY HOSTS,[11] WHO RULES WITH KINDNESS AND STRENGTH![12]

HALLELUYAH!

That same night, I was given a dream where I was warned that I would see a long winding staircase that I should not climb.[13] Then I was shown that I would be unfairly apprehended by a principality when I approached a large metal dinosaur.***[14]*** Upon waking, I did not immediately hear in Spirit what the dream

---

[1] 1 Corinthians 2:10; Daniel 2:22

[2] Matthew 9:36; 2 Corinthians 1:3

[3] Luke 15:20; Psalm 86:15; 103:10-13

[4] Revelation 20:11; Jeremiah 4:23-26

[5] Acts 8:29; 10:19; 11:7,12; 13:2-4

[6] John 21:7; Song of Solomon 8:7

[7] 1 John 3:2-3; Colossians 3:4; Hebrews 21:14; Matthew 5:8

[8] Acts 8:26; 9:15; Exodus 4:12

[9] Acts 12:9; Daniel 8:18

[10] 2 Corinthians 1:3; Psalm 86:5,15; Daniel 9:9

[11] Joshua 5:14; Revelation 19:11-14

[12] Colossians 3:15; Psalm 9:8; 66:7; Isaiah 40:10

[13] Matthew 2:12-13; 27:19; Genesis 20:6-7; 31:24; Job 33:15-17; Daniel 2:19

[14] Matthew 1:20; Acts 2:17; Numbers 12:6; I did not understand at the time that I had agreed at the Dead Sea to these terms, but Yehovah knew that for the sake of the reward, I would have still agreed even if I had known the details (Psalm 44:21).

meant.[1] But three days later, I visited the ruins of Beit She'an[2] in Israel, and I saw the staircase winding up the south side of the steep hill.[3] When some friends asked me to climb it with them, I refused. And when they asked me why, I explained the dream in front of forty people, many of whom seemed rather unimpressed or even embarrassed. But some of those listening asked if they should also refrain from climbing the stairs, and I told them that I had seen others going up and down without any problems.

Three days after that, our same group visited the region of Bashan,[4] which is located in the North-Eastern part of the Golan Heights. We ascended Mt. Bental, and as I stood on the rim looking down at an abandoned army tank in the valley, I remembered a curse someone had said over me out of fear that I would fall off a mountain in Israel and break my leg.[5] Instead of rebuking the curse and standing on the promises of freedom in Yeshua, I unwittingly accepted the fear from darkness and backed away from the edge.[6] At once I was seized in the power of a dark spirit that snatched my body by force, dragged me up the slope for about ten feet, and snapped my lower leg in mid-air![7] When the dark spirit let me go, I was still standing; only my right foot was facing completely backward! By the power of Yehovah's Mercy,[8] I grabbed my foot, turned it forward, and fell down sideways on the leg to set it. But my effort failed. So I stood back up in His Strength and tried again.[9] Then my leg was set.

As I lay there, many from the group gathered around me and began arguing with each other. Some were saying, "It is because he climbed the staircase," while others were arguing, "No, he never went up!" But then they all grew silent, and one of them asked me, "Did you see it?" And in my soul I knew exactly what he meant. Yes, I had seen it. When I had been picked up by the dark spirit and dragged

---

[1] Daniel 2:16-19; 4:24

[2] 1 Samuel 31:10-12; 2 Samuel 21:12; Judges 1:27; 1 Kings 4:12

[3] The hill is an ancient tell composed of the ruins of many cities built on top of one another. Canaanites, Egyptians, Greeks, and Romans were among those who lived there and built many temples, so it was not strange to me that Yehovah did not want me to ascend to their sites of worship.

[4] Numbers 21:33; Amos 4:1; Nahum 1:4

[5] Proverbs 18:21; Though I had heard the person say the curse over me, I had told them that I would go to Israel even if that happened. Instead, I should have rebuked that curse in the Name of Yeshua! (Romans 8:1; Matthew 21:21; Psalm 91: 1-16; Deuteronomy 28:6)

[6] Job 1:5 – Job unwittingly opened a door through fear for Satan to curse him.

[7] Luke 9:42; 2 Kings 19:35

[8] Romans 9:16; 1 Peter 2:9-10

[9] Judges 16:18; Proverbs 24:16

up the slope, I saw that I had been pulled toward a large sculpture of a dinosaur made from scrap metal.

Eventually, an ambulance came. They loaded me in the back, and we began the trip toward the city of Tiberius. As we descended the mountain, Yehovah spoke to me and said, "You have heard it said that in the days of old, when a shepherd had a lamb who would stray, he would pick up the lamb, break its leg, and carry it on his shoulders until the lamb was healed. This way, the lamb would learn his voice, understand that the shepherd was its provision, and would never stray again. So I have done for you."[1] And I was deeply moved in spirit and cried grateful tears of joy because He had honored me far more than I could ever deserve.[2]

Now, I had previously broken bones that Yehovah had miraculously healed immediately upon request. But this time I did not ask, because I understood that I had formally agreed to suffer before an audience of what appeared to be the entire spiritual realm. I was overjoyed that He had chosen to free me from soulical stumbling, and I considered the physical suffering almost unnoticeable. Though at the time I assumed that the leg was the suffering, I later learned that it was just the beginning. Both the crippling[3] and the dinosaur[4] were symbolic of much more. I was subsequently attacked unfairly from several directions by the Bulls of Bashan.[5] For three years they pounced on me. I begged Yehovah every day to replace me with Himself, to erase me from existence and fill my body with His Spirit for the sake of everyone else, but each day I woke up again in my body. My soul was in agony, suffocating in darkness.[6] I longed for the smallest drop of His

---

[1] Some argue such methods are not found in the Scriptures and were not used because they were cruel. And yes, technically, it was the enemy who broke my leg. However, the Scriptures are full of examples where Yehovah uses tough discipline (often through the enemy; Job 1:12) to lead people into greater righteousness (Hebrews 12:7). Regardless, I testify that I had never felt so loved as when Yehovah said this to me. I had some large rocks in the soil of my soul that were hard to break, but Yehovah broke them to help me because He loves me (Mark 4:16-17)! But now I know that it is possible to *bypass* discipline if we enter the Kingdom, because the point of discipline is to *guide us into* the Kingdom (Hebrews 12:10)! AND I WOULD ENCOURAGE EVERYONE TO TAKE THIS BETTER PATH! HAHA! HALLELUYAH!

[2] Jude 1:24; 1 Kings 3:13; 2 Samuel 7:18-19

[3] Genesis 32:25,32; 2 Corinthians 12:9

[4] Revelation 12:9; The sculpture of the dinosaur even looks like some sort of red dragon with the mouth of a snake!

[5] Psalm 22:12; Amos 4:1; Ezekiel 39:18

[6] Psalm 6:1-10; Isaiah 38:15

Water.[1] This was actually what Yehovah meant by "learning to hear His Voice."[2] Because through that process, I learned that I had been listening to many voices, all of which wanted to destroy me.[3] And on one particular day, I heard His Whisper that I had strayed from perfect loyalty to Him and that such decisions had provided the footholds[4] used by the enemy against me.[5] When I heard this, I was then filled with the Spirit,[6] and I repented for allowing the concerns of this life to choke me like thorns.[7] I asked Him to take me out of the life into which I had stumbled and to place me into the life that He had intended for me.[8] Within three days, He answered that prayer with such great speed and power that I was shocked almost speechless.[9] And from that day forward, I began to walk in the pure loyalty provided to me through Christ.[10]

By the next year, I was dwelling in the Kingdom of Heaven.[11] I had seen victory over every sickness, over every attack on my soul.[12] My whole being was overflowing with immeasurable faith, joy, hope, purity, love, kindness, and goodness.[13] I was astounded at the abundance of the wonders![14] And I received the understanding that all of this was simply the result of His promises flowing unhindered through me![15] When I had received His Loyalty toward Him, I began to experience His toward me![16] When I ministered to Him, He ministered to me![17] AND MY TESTIMONY TO YOU IS THAT YOU CAN BYPASS "THE CRIPPLING" AND ENTER DIRECTLY INTO HIS KINGDOM THROUGH HIS PROMISES!!!!!!!!!![18]

---

1 Luke 16:24; Isaiah 65:13-14; John 4:10
2 Hebrews 3:15; Matthew 13:15; 19:8; Mark 6:52; 8:17; 10:5; Ephesians 4:18
3 Genesis 3:1; Colossians 2:8,20; 1 John 4:1; 1 Corinthians 2:12
4 Ephesians 4:27; Acts 5:3; 2 Corinthians 2:10-11; 11:3
5 James 4:8; Hebrews 10:22; 1 Peter 3:21; 2 Corinthians 7:1
6 Acts 13:9; 2:4; 4:8,31; 7:55; Micah 3:8
7 Matthew 13:15,20-21; Acts 8:21-23; Mark 6:52; 10:5; Ephesians 4:18; Hebrews 3:8
8 Proverbs 3:5-6; Psalm 37:3-9; 62:8; 115:9-11; 125:1; 146:3-5; Isaiah 12:2; 26:3-4; Jeremiah 17:7-8
9 1 John 5:14; Mark 6:51
10 1 Timothy 1:12; Philippians 4:13
11 Matthew 12:28; 13:44,46 Luke 17:20-21; John 3:3; 18:36; Colossians 1:13
12 Luke 10:19; Psalm 91:13; Ezekiel 2:6; Mark 16:18; Acts 28:5; Romans 16:20
13 See Chapter 34 of this testimony for more on souls conformed to the image of Yeshua (Romans 8:29).
14 Ephesians 1:3; 2:6; Genesis 12:2-3; 1 Chronicles 4:10; Isaiah 61:9; Galatians 3:9
15 Matthew 7:8; 21:22
16 John 15:9; Joshua 1:5
17 James 4:8; Revelation 7:15-17 – *Minister,* from the Greek λατρεύω, pronounced "lah-treh-oo'-oh," meaning *to minister, render homage,* or *to serve.*
18 Matthew 17:20; Mark 9:23; Luke 1:37; 18:27

HALLELUUUUUUUUUUUUYAAAAAAAAAAAAAH!!!!!!

GLORY BE TO OUR FAITHFUL GOD, WHO KEEPS EVERY SINGLE ONE OF HIS PROMISES![1]

HALLELUUUUUUUUUUYAAAAAAAAAAAAAH!!!!!!

PRAISE BE TO OUR WONDROUS KING,[2] WHO HAS PREPARED UNSPEAKABLE JOY AND BLESSING FOR ALL WHO ENTER INTO HIS GRACE!!![3]

HALLELUUUUUUUUUUYAAAAAAAAAAAAAH!!!!!!

HALLELUUUUUUUUUUYAAAAAAAAAAAAAH!!!!!!

HALLELUUUUUUUUUUYAAAAAAAAAAAAAH!!!!!!

AMEN!!!

Almighty Yeshua Yehovah! You conquered the world,[4] and You are what conquers the world![5]

HALLELUYAAAAAH!!!!!!

Thank you for making us aware of the enemy's schemes![6]

HALLELUYAAAAAH!!!!!!

AMEN!!!

Holy children of Yehovah![7] Listen carefully![8]

---

[1] Joshua 23:14; Numbers 23:19; 1 Kings 8:56; Luke 21:33
[2] Revelation 1:5; 17:14; 19:16; Deuteronomy 10:17; 1 Timothy 6:15
[3] 1 Corinthians 2:9; 1 Peter 1:12; Psalm 31:19; Hebrews 11:16
[4] John 12:31; 16:11,33d; Psalm 68:18; Romans 8:37; 1 John 4:4; 5:4
[5] 1 John 5:4-5; 4:4; John 16:33
[6] 2 Corinthians 2:11; Ephesians 6:11
[7] John 12:36; Ephesians 5:8; 1 Thessalonians 5:5
[8] Luke 8:18; 19:26; Deuteronomy 32:46-47; Proverbs 2:2-5; Mark 4:23-24; Acts 17:11; Hebrews 2:1; James 1:22-25; Matthew 13:12; John 15:2

If the heart is attacked with dark affections, but the will is not engaged in unrighteousness, then the gate of heart-toward-will, or considering affection, has a door open for invasion. This contrast of His Loyalty is disloyalty, which is better known as the spirit of lust.[1] It can quickly take a foothold[2] in the heart and push for consideration and reception of all kinds of desires.[3] Foremost among such fiery arrows[4] are "pleasures" of some sort,[5] especially those of sex or wealth.[6] And though the will is not yet engaged in unrighteous behavior, the goal of a lustful spirit is to acquire the cooperation of the will through suggested affections.[7]

Understand that such affections, feelings, and desires are not natural to any of the redeemed![8] They are persuasions brought by destructive spirits![9] They only become residents in a human being if the person accepts them.[10] Because of this, these spirits do their best to persuade their host that such lusts, appetites, affections, feelings, and desires are properties of the human soul.[11] Of course, this is not at all true, which is why Yeshua said, "If your right eye causes you to stumble, tear it out and throw it away. It is better for you to lose one part of your body than for your whole body to be thrown into Hell!"[12] He said this to reveal that it is not the body that causes unclean lusts, appetites, affections, feelings, or desires.[13] Such unclean things come through the heart gates from unclean spirits waging war against the soul.[14] The person does not need to pluck anything out of their own

---

[1] Lust is a form of greed (1 John 2:16); 1 Thessalonians 4:3-5,8; Colossians 3:5; 2 Peter 2:14

[2] Ephesians 4:27; Acts 5:3; 2 Corinthians 2:10-11; 11:3

[3] 2 Peter 2:10; James 1:15; Psalm 7:14; Isaiah 59:4

[4] Ephesians 6:16; 1 Peter 5:8-9

[5] Titus 3:3; Obadiah 1:3; Isaiah 44:20

[6] 1 John 2:16; Ecclesiastes 5:10; Luke 12:15

[7] 2 Peter 2:10; Romans 1:26-27

[8] John 8:44; 1 Peter 1:13-14

[9] 1 Peter 2:11; Galatians 5:17

[10] Genesis 4:7; James 1:15

[11] Genesis 3:11, "And he said, 'Who told you that you were naked? Have you eaten from the tree that I commanded you not to eat from?'" – Once the humans listened to the evil spirit about what to *eat*, they also listened to its lies about what they *were*.

[12] Matthew 5:29

[13] Matthew 15:19, "For out of the heart come διαλογισμοι πονηροι—murder, adultery, sexual immorality, theft, false testimony, slander." – διαλογισμοι πονηροι, meaning "lewd/hurtful discussions/considerations/debates."

[14] John 8:44; 1 Peter 2:11

spirit any more than they need to pluck an eye out of their physical body![1] Instead, they need to obediently rid their soul of the influence of unclean spirits![2]

To overcome lust, the person must first cover the heart by receiving the Love of Yeshua's Sacrifice on the Cross.[3] These Scriptures must be read and reflected upon until His affection is experienced in the heart.[4] Simply speaking, a *statement* of the truth is enough for the mind, but *it is not enough to fill the heart.*[5] The heart *only* communicates in affection and must observe godly affection as a received and experienced affection.[6] Receiving the Cross and picking up one's cross is the only way to cover the heart effectively.[7]

What does it feel like to pick up the cross? It feels like saying, "God's affections and desires matter more than my own."[8]

What does it *feel* like to pick up the cross? It *feels* like saying, "GOD'S AFFECTIONS AND DESIRES MATTER *MORE* THAN MY OWN!"[9]

Don't just listen with your mind! *Listen with your heart!*[10]

Once the heart is covered with the Blood, it is brought back into connection with the righteous will.[11] Then the Scriptures of Christ's Loyalty,[12] especially concerning His death on the Cross,[13] can be applied to the gate of considering affection, and the spirit of lust can be bound, silenced, and cast away.[14]

---

[1] Matthew 5:28-30 – Yeshua is making the obvious point that it is not the body (Genesis 1:31) that causes people to sin but corruption in the soul (Matthew 15:17-19).
[2] Romans 6:13-14; Ephesians 6:12,16
[3] Hebrews 12:2; 1 John 3:16; Romans 5:8; John 10:17
[4] Mark 7:6; Ezekiel 33:31
[5] John 4:24; Colossians 3:16; 1 Samuel 16:7
[6] 1 Peter 1:22; 1 Timothy 1:5
[7] Romans 5:12-19; Matthew 16:24-27
[8] Matthew 10:37-39; Luke 9:23-24
[9] Mark 10:21; John 12:26
[10] Luke 8:18; 19:26; Deuteronomy 32:46-47; Proverbs 2:2-5; Mark 4:23-24; Acts 17:11; Hebrews 2:1; James 1:22-25; Matthew 13:12; John 15:2
[11] James 4:8; Hebrews 10:22; 1 Peter 3:21; 2 Corinthians 7:1
[12] John 5:19; Philippians 2:8
[13] Galatians 6:14; Isaiah 45:24-25; Philippians 3:7-11
[14] Matthew 10:1; 16:19; Mark 1:34; 16:17; James 4:7; Luke 10:17; Acts 16:18; Psalm 31:18

A key response to a temptation of lust is, "No lust is for me or of me;[1] Yehovah has a different path than that for me."[2] Understand that many are deceived by lust because they accept it as their own.[3] But loyalty to Yehovah is what flows from the Holy Spirit in the redeemed.[4] No redeemed person ever has to lust in any way![5] It is a dark spirit, a very deceptive one![6] It presents its own thoughts as if they are yours and then demands that you wrestle with them![7] But they are not your thoughts![8] You don't have to explain them or "deal" with them![9] All those lustful thoughts belong to the attacking spirit of darkness![10] So, do not allow yourself to be enslaved by that deceptive dark spirit![11] Command that dark spirit to be silent and then cast it out[12] for the Glory of Yehovah![13] And enter into the Kingdom of Heaven *this very moment*,[14] where *no one* ever lusts but only lives in perfect loyalty all the time![15]

HALLELUYAH!
YOU ARE CLEAN![16] DON'T LISTEN TO ANY UNCLEAN SPIRIT'S LIES![17] THERE IS NOTHING LUSTFUL ABOUT YOU![18] YOU ARE REDEEMED![19] YOU HAVE A NEW,[20]

---

[1] 1 Thessalonians 4:4-5; 1 Corinthians 6:15
[2] Proverbs 3:5-6; Psalm 37:3-9; 62:8; 115:9-11; 125:1; 146:3-5; Isaiah 12:2; 26:3-4; Jeremiah 17:7-8
[3] 1 John 2:16; Psalm 73:6; 119:36-37; Titus 3:3; 1 Peter 2:11; 2 Peter 2:22
[4] 1 Chronicles 29:18; 2 Thessalonians 2:16-17
[5] Ephesians 4:22; Colossians 3:9; Romans 6:6
[6] Ephesians 2:1-3; 1 John 2:15-17; 1 Corinthians 2:12; Galatians 5:16,24 – Since the Holy Spirit can dwell in flesh without lust, we know that lust is not a property of the body but one of corrupted flesh through a dark spirit.
[7] Genesis 3:11; Matthew 16:22-23; Luke 22:31
[8] 1 Corinthians 2:16; John 15:15; 16:13-15
[9] 1 John 4:1-6; 1 Corinthians 2:12; Ephesians 6:12
[10] Romans 1:28; 8:7; Ephesians 4:18-19
[11] Titus 3:3; 1 Corinthians 6:18
[12] Matthew 10:1,8; 12:28; Luke 19:45; Ezekiel 18:31; 20:7; Isaiah 1:16-17; 55:7; Romans 8:13; Ephesians 4:22-32; Colossians 3:5-9; James 1:21; 1 Peter 2:1
[13] John 15:8; Luke 6:35; Psalm 92:12-15; Isaiah 60:21; Matthew 5:16
[14] Luke 17:21; 1 Corinthians 3:16; Matthew 10:7
[15] Colossians 3:1-2; Romans 8:6-7; 2 Corinthians 5:15; Matthew 6:10,33; 13:11,44; 16:19
[16] John 13:10; Acts 11:9
[17] John 8:44; Romans 1:25; 1 John 1:6; 2:21; Revelation 14:5; 2 Thessalonians 2:9,11; Titus 2:11; Hebrews 6:18; Colossians 3:9; Numbers 23:19; Psalm 38:12
[18] John 15:3; 17:17; Acts 11:9
[19] Galatians 3:13-14; 5:24; 1 Peter 1:18
[20] Ezekiel 36:26; Deuteronomy 30:6; Psalm 51:10; John 3:3-5; 2 Corinthians 5:17

PURE,[1] RIGHTEOUS[2] SPIRIT! DON'T LISTEN TO ANY FOREIGN, DARK, LYING SPIRIT THAT SAYS YOU THINK ABOUT LUSTFUL THINGS OR WANT LUSTFUL THINGS![3] YOU HAVE THE MIND OF CHRIST![4] YOU HAVE THE GRACE OF CHRIST![5] LUST HAS NO PART OF YOU![6] CAST THAT LYING SPIRIT DOWN AND TRAMPLE IT UNDER THE TRUTH OF GOD![7] FOCUS YOUR EYES THROUGH YOUR LOYALTY AND DEVOTION TO YEHOVAH AND BE THE PURE AND LOYAL PERSON HE HAS MADE YOU TO BE![8]

YOU HAVE HOLY THINGS TO THINK ABOUT AND DO![9]

HALLELUYAAAAAAAAAAAAAAAH!!!!!!!

YOU ARE PURE,[10] CLEAN,[11] UPRIGHT,[12] AND RIGHTEOUS!!!!![13]

HALLELUYAAAAAAAAAAAAAAAH!!!!!!!

YOU NEVER EVER HAVE TO LUST AGAIN!!!!!![14]

HALLELUUUUUUUUYAAAAAAAAAAAAAAAH!!!!!!!

If the gate of the will is repentant and the heart is full of love, then the gate of deciding pursuit is steadfast.[15] The result is the expression and revelation of His Humility, and its quality is pure.[16]

"At that time the disciples came to Yeshua, saying, 'Who is the greatest in the Kingdom of Heaven?' And calling to Him a child, he stood him in the midst of them

---

[1] 2 Corinthians 11:2; Titus 1:15; 2 Timothy 2:22
[2] Romans 6:18; Ephesians 4:24; 2 Corinthians 5:21
[3] 2 Corinthians 11:15; Colossians 3:2-3
[4] 1 Corinthians 2:16; John 15:15; 16:13-15
[5] John 1:16-17; Romans 1:5; 5:21; 12:6
[6] 1 John 2:16; Psalm 73:6; 119:36-37; Titus 3:3; 1 Peter 2:11; 2 Peter 2:22
[7] Luke 10:19; Psalm 91:13; Ezekiel 2:6; Mark 16:18; Acts 28:5; Romans 16:20
[8] Matthew 6:22-23; 2 Corinthians 11:3; 1 John 3:3
[9] Philippians 4:8; Ephesians 1:4; Hebrews 12:14; 1 Peter 1:15-16; Revelation 22:11
[10] 2 Corinthians 11:2; Titus 1:15; 2 Timothy 2:22
[11] John 15:3; 17:17; Acts 11:9
[12] Titus 2:12; 2 Corinthians 1:12
[13] 2 Corinthians 5:21; Philippians 3:9
[14] 1 Corinthians 10:13; 2 Timothy 4:18
[15] Ephesians 4:2; 1 Peter 3:8
[16] 1 John 2:10; Romans 14:13

and said, 'I assure you, unless you turn and become like children, you will not enter the Kingdom of Heaven. Therefore, whoever humbles himself like this child is the greatest in the Kingdom of Heaven.'"[1]

Many have heard this word and misunderstood it.[2] Yeshua is not making a point of who is the greatest but rather revealing that no one in the Kingdom harbors any selfish ambition at all.[3] Heavenly humility is obedient,[4] selfless,[5] considers others equally valuable,[6] and describes the love of Heaven's inhabitants as it transfers into action toward each other.[7]

When I first entered Heaven after Yehovah transfigured me,[8] I was met by a large crowd standing on two sides of a cleared path.[9] The very atmosphere was full of revelation,[10] and I immediately perceived everyone's thoughts toward me.[11] Without exception, each of them loved me as dearly as their most beloved friend or son.[12] At that moment, I was suddenly aware that all of them knew everything about me,[13] including my most secret sins![14] However, they loved me! They loved me as He loved me![15] They forgave me[16] and even celebrated me![17] And at that moment, I received great joy because I learned that no one would ever discover anything about me that would cause their love to diminish! I had already been washed clean![18] I was overflowing with gratitude and peace, and I breathed in the camaraderie as I perceived that I also forgave all of them and loved each of them

---

[1] Matthew 18:1-4

[2] Luke 8:18; 19:26; Deuteronomy 32:46-47; Proverbs 2:2-5; Mark 4:23-24; Acts 17:11; Hebrews 2:1; James 1:22-25; Matthew 13:12; John 15:2

[3] Philippians 2:3a; 1 Corinthians 3:3

[4] Philippians 2:8; Proverbs 15:33; Acts 8:33; Hebrews 5:5-7

[5] Philippians 2:7-9; Acts 8:33; Hebrews 5:5-7; 10:7-9

[6] Philippians 2:3b; Luke 14:7-11

[7] 1 Corinthians 13:5; Matthew 6:14; Luke 5:32

[8] 2 Corinthians 12:2; Job 19:26; See the Preface of this testimony.

[9] Revelation 7:9; 21:21b

[10] Ephesians 1:17; Luke 12:12; 21:15; Matthew 16:17; 1 Corinthians 2:10

[11] Luke 11:17; Matthew 9:4; 12:25; John 2:25; Revelation 2:23

[12] John 15:12; 1 Peter 1:22

[13] 1 Corinthians 13:8 – "Knowledge" becomes useless, not because no one knows anything, but because *everyone knows everything*; it is the *measure* of knowledge that becomes useless.

[14] Hebrews 4:13; Luke 12:2

[15] John 15:12; Romans 12:10; 1 Thessalonians 3:12

[16] Matthew 18:35; 7:1-2; Proverbs 21:13; Luke 6:37-38

[17] Luke 15:10,23; Ezekiel 18:23; Philemon 1:15

[18] Hebrews 10:19-22; 9:15; 12:24; Luke 22:20; John 6:54-56

every much as dearly! And I saw the souls of some dear ones I had known before they had passed,[1] and I realized that I loved them more in Heaven than I ever had on earth![2] The sweetness of our relationships had just begun!

HALLELUYAH!

WHAT WONDROUS RELATIONSHIPS AWAIT THE REDEEMED![3]

GLORY TO GOD!!!

Therefore, know that *real humility does not compare itself with anyone but rejoices in mutual love!*[4]

HALLELUYAH!

On the other hand, if the gate of the will is compromised by darkness, but the heart is secure, then the gate of will-toward-heart, or deciding pursuit, is vulnerable. In this case, dark force pushes through the will with an inebriating effect to propose dark affection for acceptance by the heart.[5] The spirit is pride,[6] and it will suggest any lie and twist any truth to gain affection for itself.[7] When confronted, the spirit of pride will offer its own force as proof of justification,[8] sifting any outside advice or perspective through the sieve of self-rule.[9]

BEWARE OF THE SUBTLENESS OF THIS DECIDING SPIRIT![10] It always decides in favor of itself![11] It can latch on to any credit taken by the human soul.[12] There is

---

[1] Revelation 6:9; 2 Corinthians 5:8; Philippians 1:23

[2] 1 Corinthians 13:12; Revelation 22:4; 2 Corinthians 3:18; 1 Peter 1:22

[3] Luke 16:9; 14:14; Matthew 19:21; 25:35-40; 2 Corinthians 9:12-15; 2 Timothy 6:18-19

[4] Philippians 2:3; 2 Corinthians 10:12; Matthew 7:2

[5] Ezekiel 28:15; Jeremiah 48:29; Isaiah 3:16

[6] 1 John 2:16; Psalm 73:6; Proverbs 16:18; 29:23; 1 Peter 2:11; 2 Peter 2:22

[7] Ezekiel 28:17; John 12:43

[8] Matthew 23:5,15; Jude 1:10-13

[9] Ezekiel 28:2; Luke 16:14-15

[10] Matthew 27:42-43,49; Mark 12:7

[11] Matthew 20:20-28; 23:4-8; 3 John 1:9, "... loves to be first ..." – *Loves to be first,* from the Greek φιλοπρωτεύω, pronounced "fih-law-proh-tyoo'-oh" and meaning *loves to be first, loves to be chief,* or *ambitious for preeminence.*

[12] James 4:13-17; 1 Corinthians 5:6

only One from Whom all good gifts come, [1] whether provisions, [2] skills, [3] understandings,[4] or blessings[5] of any kind. If anyone is anything good, it is because they have received it from the One Who is Good.[6] We draw goodness from the Vine.[7] We are nothing in and of ourselves, but we are everything wonderful in Him![8]

HALLELUYAH!

To rid this gate of pride, a person must receive the decision to embrace the truth that pride is not a mere condition of the soul but a spirit.[9] When confronted, the spirit of pride will insist that the soul thinks and feels highly of itself because it is actually superior to other souls.[10] However, the foundation of such a claim is that the soul *chooses* to function in a superior manner.[11] Of course, the truth is that no one can choose *anything* beyond what they have received from God.[12] Those of us who are redeemed know this in spirit.[13] We remember that God raised Nebuchadnezzar to be a great king and then sent him out into the field to eat grass like an animal for seven years until he became humble![14] In this same way, we know that Yehovah can raise anyone up or cut anyone down as He chooses![15] We praise the Name of Yehovah because He has not hidden these things from us![16] And we rejoice that he has not given us a spirit of pride but one of gentleness and humility![17] He is the One Who has given us the Mind of Christ,[18] strengthened us with the Power of the Holy Spirit,[19] and filled us with His Love![20] Were it not for

---

1 James 1:17; John 1:9; 1 John 1:5; Revelation 21:23; 22:5; Isaiah 60:19-18
2 John 1:10; Revelation 4:11
3 Exodus 35:35; 36:1; 1 Kings 7:14
4 1 Chronicles 22:12; Job 32:8
5 Ephesians 1:3; Hebrews 6:7
6 1 Corinthians 4:7; 1 Peter 4:10; James 1:17
7 John 15:1; Zechariah 3:8; Isaiah 4:2
8 John 15:4-5; 5:19; 2 Corinthians 13:8; Philippians 4:13
9 Proverbs 16:18; 18:12; 29:23; Ester 6:6; Isaiah 2:11-12; James 3:14,16
10 2 Corinthians 10:12; Luke 18:11-14
11 Proverbs 26:12; 1 Corinthians 4:7
12 Romans 12:3; 1 Corinthians 4:7; 1 Peter 4:10; James 1:17
13 Deuteronomy 29:29; 1 Corinthians 2:10
14 Daniel 4:31-37; Jeremiah 28:14
15 Luke 14:11; 1 Peter 5:5-6
16 Matthew 11:25; 16:17; John 17:6; Romans 16:26; 1 Corinthians 4:1
17 Matthew 11:29; Romans 8:29
18 1 Corinthians 2:16; John 15:15; 16:13-15
19 Acts 1:8; Micah 3:8; Zechariah 4:6; Luke 10:19; Romans 15:19
20 Ephesians 3:16-19; 1 Peter 1:8

His great Mercy, none of us would have any of these things![1] And the more we have received these, the more we recognize that pride is foreign to us![2] We have not been made in the image of pride but the image of the Humble One, Yeshua HaMashiach, Jesus Christ![3] We do not scoff at the weak but help them and strengthen them![4] The gifts we have we use for His Glory, for such is their purpose![5] Praise be to the King of Kings Who reached down to pick us up and enabled us to behave likewise on behalf of His Name![6]

HALLELUYAH!

When we have recognized pride as a spirit,[7] we can cover the will gate with the Blood of Yeshua's Repentance by obediently engaging in repentance from a focus on worldly behavior to a devoted focus on the perfect behavior of Yeshua.[8]

Now, understand that a devoted attempt to live in perfect righteousness is considered a valid reception of the free gift of Grace.[9] Yehovah does not expect you to part seas or multiply "loaves and fishes" fresh from the starting line![10] However, if you obediently persist in repentance, you will experience such authority through the Name of Jesus Christ[11] (And I testify that I have personally witnessed both the manipulation of water and the multiplication of food through His Authority and for His Glory)! Anyone who perseveres in repentance will receive such blessings and much more[12] because we do not walk by the authority of the Second Jurisdiction but by that of the First![13]

Praise our God, Who gives us such authority to reveal His Goodness![14] Those Who know Him will walk with Him, and those who walk with Him will do what He does![15] Amen!

---

[1] 1 Peter 1:3; Romans 9:23
[2] John 17:14,16; 1 John 4:5-6; 5:19-20
[3] Romans 8:29; Matthew 12:50; 25:40; Colossians 1:15-18; Revelation 1:5-6
[4] Romans 14:1; 15:1; 1 Corinthians 9:22
[5] Isaiah 43:7,21; 48:11; John 15:8; Romans 9:23; Ephesians 1:12
[6] 1 John 2:6; 1:7; Psalm 85:13; Matthew 11:29; John 13:15; 1 Peter 2:21
[7] 1 John 2:16; Psalm 73:6; Proverbs 16:18; 29:23; 1 Peter 2:11; 2 Peter 2:22
[8] Acts 3:19; Revelation 2:5
[9] Hebrews 13:18; Acts 23:1; 1 Peter 3:21
[10] 2 Peter 3:18; Hebrews 6:1; 1 Peter 2:2-3
[11] John 14:12; Acts 5:15; 19:12
[12] John 14:12; Acts 5:15; 19:12
[13] See Chapters 13-16 of this testimony.
[14] 2 Corinthians 4:7; 1 Peter 2:12
[15] John 14:17; 13:15; 1 John 2:6; 1:7; Psalm 85:13; Matthew 11:29; 1 Peter 2:21

HALLELUYAH!

After repentance has been embraced, the gate of deciding pursuit can be covered with the Blood of Yeshua by speaking the Scriptures about His Humility,[1] His commands of humility for us,[2] and other Scriptures about humility found throughout His Word.[3] Then the spirit of pride can be easily cast out.[4]

When attacked by a spirit of pride,[5] a key response is, "I didn't create goodness, Yehovah did;[6] even if I could count the leaves on all the trees, the sand on all the shores, and the hairs on every head, I would not know enough to exalt myself,[7] because God alone is Good!"[8] Remember that the Humility of Christ overflows through your spirit![9] There is no pride that comes from you![10] Pride is a spirit![11] You were not given a spirit of pride[12] but a new spirit that is revealing the Humility of Christ![13] Prideful thoughts come from spirits of darkness![14] And do not be fooled by a dark spirit saying pride is a consequence of knowledge![15] It's a consequence of an attack![16] "Knowledge puffs up"[17] because it gives pride more to work with, but "My children perish for lack of knowledge,"[18] not because they have no knowledge but because they don't value the *right* knowledge![19] The right knowledge is the Word of God, and to "know" it means to abide in it![20] Therefore, abide in the Counsel of Yehovah, and do not be lured into the trap of pride! Reject

---

[1] Philippians 2:5-8; Hebrews 10:7-9; John 15:10

[2] Luke 14:11; Psalm 18:27; Proverbs 15:33; James 4:6

[3] Ephesians 4:2; 1 Peter 3:8

[4] Matthew 10:1; 16:19; Mark 1:34; 16:17; James 4:7; Luke 10:17; Acts 16:18; Psalm 31:18

[5] Ephesians 2:1-3; 1 John 2:15-17; 1 Corinthians 2:12

[6] James 1:17; John 1:9; 1 John 1:5; Revelation 21:23; 22:5; Isaiah 60:19

[7] Psalm 139:17-18; Luke 12:7

[8] Matthew 19:17; 1 Samuel 2:2; Psalm 145:7-9; James 1:17

[9] 2 Corinthians 10:1; Matthew 11:29; James 4:6

[10] 1 John 2:16; Psalm 73:6; Proverbs 16:18; 29:23; 1 Peter 2:11; 2 Peter 2:22

[11] Proverbs 16:18; 18:12; 29:23; Ester 6:6; Isaiah 2:11-12; James 3:14,16

[12] Ezekiel 36:26; Deuteronomy 30:6; Psalm 51:10; John 3:3-5; 2 Corinthians 5:17

[13] Romans 8:29; Matthew 12:50; 25:40; Colossians 1:15-18; Revelation 1:5-6

[14] Proverbs 13:10; 16:18

[15] Proverbs 11:2; 15:33

[16] Proverbs 21:4; 16:18

[17] 1 Corinthians 8:1

[18] Hosea 4:6a; Jeremiah 5:21

[19] Hosea 4:6b-7; 2 Corinthians 4:3-6

[20] James 1:22; 4:17; John 8:31; 13:17; Matthew 7:21-25; 12:50; 28:20; Luke 11:28; 12:47-48; Romans 2:13; 1 John 2:3, 3:7; 3 John 1:11; Revelation 22:7

its lies,[1] bind its pursuits,[2] silence its thoughts and affections,[3] and cast it away.[4] Enter into the Kingdom of Heaven *today,*[5] where *no one* is ever prideful but only lives in perfect humility all the time![6] *Today* is the day of salvation![7]

HALLELUYAH!

When the Light of Yeshua shines with His Truth through the mind toward obedience and with His Power through the will to pursue truth, the convergence gate between the mind and the will resonates with integrity.[8]

About twenty-five years ago, I was visiting a refugee ministry in a certain European town with the plan of leading arriving immigrants to Christ.[9] Late one night, I was led by the Holy Spirit to "go out and wander around the town."[10] I was walking along the town's empty streets when I turned a corner and met twelve Iraqi immigrants. At that moment, the Holy Spirit encouraged me to speak, but I hesitated.[11] Then Yehovah said to me, "You have said to Me that you believe the disciples spoke the languages of the nations at Pentecost,[12] so why do you hesitate to trust Me now?"[13] While the twelve young men were looking at me, I began to speak in a language that I did not know.[14] To my astonishment, they understood what I was saying![15] They were equally astonished when they realized I was speaking their native tongue but did not understand it![16] They did their best by using words from several other languages, hand motions, and sounds to explain to me what I had said. Apparently, I had said something about how they had heard

---

[1] John 8:44; Romans 1:25; 1 John 1:6; 2:21; Revelation 14:5; 2 Thessalonians 2:9,11; Titus 2:11; Hebrews 6:18; Colossians 3:9; Numbers 23:19; Psalm 38:12

[2] Mark 3:27; Matthew 16:19

[3] Mark 1:25,34; Luke 4:41

[4] Matthew 10:1; 16:19; Mark 16:17; James 4:7; Luke 10:17; Acts 16:18; Psalm 31:18

[5] Luke 17:21; 1 Corinthians 3:16; Matthew 10:7

[6] Ephesians 5:5; Philippians 2:3; Colossians 3:12; James 3:13; 1 Peter 5:5; Matthew 6:10; 13:11,44; 16:19

[7] Luke 19:9; Hebrews 3:15

[8] Mark 12:14; 2 Corinthians 1:12; Psalm 25:21; Proverbs 11:3

[9] Acts 1:8; Micah 3:8; Zechariah 4:6; Luke 10:19; Romans 15:19

[10] Acts 8:26,29; Matthew 4:1; Romans 8:14; Galatians 5:18

[11] Ezekiel 37:4; Mark 13:11

[12] Acts 2:6; 1 Corinthians 14:13

[13] Matthew 14:31; James 1:6-8

[14] Acts 2:4; 1 Corinthians 14:14

[15] Acts 2:6,11; 1 Corinthians 14:27

[16] Acts 2:7; 1 Corinthians 14:14

not to cook a young goat in its mother's milk[1] but that they were doing just that when they refused to listen to the Gospel of Christ just because they had been at enmity with Israel.[2] They were so amazed by the Wisdom of God that all twelve of them gave their lives to Yeshua![3]

Such an experience demonstrates that integrity demands that we are spiritually the same in public as in private.[4]

About ten years ago, I had been having many discussions with the redeemed about foreign nations and their spiritual conditions.[5] But one night, when I was sitting alone before Yehovah, He asked me why I did not spend time having such conversations with Him.[6] Even before He was done speaking, I began to be filled with the Holy Spirit.[7] I was suddenly greatly stirred and disturbed at the rebellion within a certain nation.[8] Yehovah's Wrath poured through me,[9] and I spoke, "Let the nation shake at its foundations because of the darkness it has welcomed at the expense of corrupting its own children!"[10] And then I added, "Let its capitol split in half, and let the number of the dead stand as a warning against the entertainment of darkness!"[11]

The next day, that nation experienced a devastating earthquake. Its capitol building split in half, and the casualties numbered near a quarter million.

I did not rejoice.[12] I confess that at the time I was soberly surprised. I mourned for the human beings,[13] but I remained resolute against the spirits of darkness.[14] And though I am certain that Yehovah had planned everything ahead of time,[15] He

---

[1] Deuteronomy 14:21; Exodus 34:26
[2] Genesis 17:18; 1 Chronicles 1:28
[3] 1 Corinthians 14:22; Acts 2:12
[4] Luke 12:3; Matthew 12:36
[5] Titus 1:12; 1 Peter 5:13; Revelation 18:10
[6] Romans 13:1; Psalm 82:1-8
[7] John 2:17; Revelation 18:2
[8] Matthew 18:21; Luke 10:13
[9] Ezekiel 3:14; Nahum 1:14
[10] Matthew 18:7; 2 Peter 2:15-17
[11] Revelation 2:23; Romans 2:5-11; Luke 16:25
[12] Proverbs 17:5b; Obadiah 1:11-13
[13] Romans 12:15b; Hebrews 13:3
[14] Proverbs 23:17-18; Hebrews 1:9
[15] Isaiah 54:16; Daniel 4:35; Proverbs 16:4

taught me that my words had repercussions and that I should be careful with what I said no matter who was listening or where I was.[1]

Therefore, we understand that integrity also demands we are spiritually in private who we are in public.[2]

BEHOLD, THE HOLINESS OF GOD! [3]

HOW LONG, WORLD OF HUMANITY, WILL YOU TEST HIS LOVE?[4]

EVERY DAY HE HOLDS HIS HAND OUT TO YOU,[5] OFFERING YOU ALL HIS WEALTH AND BLESSING![6]

IF ONLY YOU WOULD LET GO OF YOUR IDOLS [7] OF ENTERTAINMENT, [8] REPUTATION,[9] SELFISHNESS,[10] AND GREED![11] DO YOU STILL NOT UNDERSTAND THAT SUCH DECEPTION COMES FROM EVIL SPIRITS?[12] DO YOU NOT LISTEN TO WHAT CHRIST HAS SPOKEN?[13]

IF ONLY YOU WOULD TRADE YOUR WORLDLY RAGS OF DECEIT FOR HIS HEAVENLY RICHES OF TRUTH![14] YOU HAVE BEEN GIVEN THE POWER TO DECIDE![15] WHY NOT DECIDE TO DO THAT?

---

[1] Proverbs 18:21; Matthew 21:21
[2] Matthew 23:27; Isaiah 58:1-10; Acts 23:3
[3] Psalm 89:35; Amos 4:2
[4] Matthew 4:7; Hebrews 3:9; 1 Corinthians 10:9
[5] Revelation 3:20; Luke 12:36
[6] Luke 13:34; Psalm 17:8; 36:7; 57:1; 91:4; Ruth 2:12; Deuteronomy 32:9-12
[7] Revelation 9:20; Romans 1:21-23
[8] 2 Timothy 2:4; 4:3-4; 1 Corinthians 9:25-26; 1 Timothy 6:9-12
[9] John 12:43; Matthew 23:5-7
[10] Ephesians 2:3; 2 Corinthians 12:20; James 3:16
[11] 1 Timothy 6:9; Luke 18:25
[12] Revelation 12:9; 1 Timothy 4:1; Luke 4:41
[13] John 8:43; 6:60; Isaiah 6:9; Jeremiah 6:10; Acts 7:51; Romans 8:7-8
[14] Matthew 13:44-46; Revelation 3:18
[15] Joshua 24:15; Deuteronomy 30:19

REPENT! TODAY IS THE DAY OF SALVATION![1] BE SET FREE FROM EVERY DARKNESS![2] COMMIT YOURSELF TO THE LIGHT,[3] AND HE WILL SHINE ON YOU![4]

HALLELUYAH!

Nevertheless, a human will reap what they sow![5] Whenever there is a complete disconnection between the will and the heart, the will-heart-convergence gate will be vulnerable to a spirit of duplicity.[6] This spirit consists of multiple, simultaneous, and often conflicting *intentions* (as opposed to a spirit of doubt, which causes *wavering* between *decisions*).[7] This is the spirit that causes souls to seem loyal one moment and disloyal the next,[8] honest with one statement and dishonest with one immediately following.[9] It is the driving force behind the person who behaves differently in different environments,[10] who behaves like an angel in fellowship and returns home to act like a devil.[11] If exposed, this spirit will respond by suggesting all sorts of thoughts concerning the cost of wisdom and how it has been obtained through good judgment and hard work.[12] It will feign humility by saying, "I might not always have done right, but I sure know what should be done!"[13] It seeks to judge but not be judged,[14] to lead but not be led,[15] to teach but not be taught,[16] to counsel but not be counseled,[17] to advise but not be advised,[18] to receive honor but not give it,[19] to receive mercy but not give it,[20] to receive

---

[1] 2 Corinthians 6:2; Isaiah 49:8; Hebrews 3:7,13; 4:7
[2] Galatians 5:1; Acts 13:39; Colossians 1:13
[3] Psalm 37:5-6; Matthew 6:33
[4] Ephesians 5:14; Isaiah 60:1; 1 Thessalonians 5:6; 2 Timothy 2:26
[5] Galatians 6:7-9; Job 4:8; Proverbs 11:18; Romans 2:6-10
[6] James 1:8; 1 Kings 18:21: Isaiah 29:13; Luke 20:23
[7] Matthew 14:31; 21:21; Acts 12:11; James 1:6
[8] 2 Kings 18:21; Jeremiah 12:6
[9] Proverbs 26:18-19; 2 Peter 2:13
[10] Jude 1:12; Matthew 23:27
[11] Matthew 6:2,5,16; John 5:44; 7:18; 1 Thessalonians 2:6
[12] John 7:47-48; Daniel 4:30
[13] Luke 6:42; Matthew 23:13
[14] Matthew 21:31-32; 23:13; Luke 11:52
[15] Luke 19:39-40; Acts 4:16-18
[16] Matthew 23:15; Acts 14:2
[17] John 8:13; Romans 2:21
[18] Matthew 23:25; Isaiah 28:7-8
[19] Luke 11:43,46; Matthew 23:6
[20] John 8:2-11; Luke 11:46

forgiveness but not give it,[1] to receive compassion but not give it,[2] and to receive support but not give it.[3] Its lies are myriad because they come in pursuits and affections contrary to one another[4] instead of mismatched statements and philosophies.

When I was a teenager, I also lived in duplicity. With the musical skill Yehovah had given me,[5] I joined a worldly band. During that time, I believed myself to walk in the Light, though I fellowshipped with many who were in darkness.[6] While I knew the truth, I also ate and drank with drunkards and joined with them in mockery of wayward church leaders.[7]

Then one night, when the band was becoming quite popular, I was sitting alone in the master bedroom of our home. As I sat up thinking, and to my sheer amazement, my eyes were opened,[8] and I saw one of the fallen elohim enter the room and stand at the foot of my bed![9] At that time, the Spirit of Wisdom and Revelation fell upon me,[10] and I understood that I had entertained many lies about how I could overcome obstacles in my life by being smarter, tougher, or meaner than whatever confronted me.[11] Yet, as the elohim stood before me, I perceived that I could not best it in any of these ways.[12] It had great authority[13] as some sort of principality,[14] and it clearly sought jurisdiction over me.[15]

Just as I was about to cast out the fallen elohim in the Name of Jesus,[16] my eyes saw something else: I saw the ceiling roll open like a scroll made of clouds,[17] and there above me was Yehovah and two unidentified loyal elohim standing on each

---

[1] Luke 15:1-7; Matthew 18:23-35

[2] Luke 10:30-37; 14:3-6

[3] Matthew 23:23; John 12:17-19

[4] Luke 12:1; 1 Corinthians 5:8

[5] 1 Chronicles 25:7; Exodus 31:3; 1 Corinthians 4:7

[6] 2 Corinthians 6:14; 1 John 1:6; 3:14; 1 Corinthians 10:21; 15:33; James 4:4

[7] Matthew 24:48-49; Ezekiel 12:27; 2 Peter 3:3-5

[8] 2 Kings 6:17; Numbers 22:31

[9] Matthew 4:3; Zechariah 3:1

[10] Ephesians 1:17; Luke 12:12; 21:15; Matthew 16:17; 1 Corinthians 2:10

[11] Matthew 9:4; Ezekiel 38:10; Haggai 2:13-14

[12] Jude 1:9; Zechariah 3:1

[13] Luke 4:6; Ephesians 2:2; John 12:31; 14:30; 16:11; 1 John 5:19; Psalm 82:1-8

[14] Ephesians 6:12; Romans 8:38; Colossians 2:15; 1 Peter 3:22

[15] Luke 22:31; Job 1:8-11; 2:2-6; Zechariah 3:1; 1 Peter 5:8; Revelation 12:10

[16] Matthew 10:8; John 14:14; 15:16; 16:24,26

[17] Revelation 6:14; Isaiah 34:4

side of Him.[1] Yehovah called me by name[2] and said to me, "Up until this time, I have protected you because of the Name of Jesus,[3] but now you need to make a decision."[4]

I was overwhelmed with the weight of the moment. But then the Spirit of Wisdom and Revelation rested on me again,[5] and Yehovah quickly walked me through many thoughts concerning how my destiny could be secure.[6] And so I answered, "Father of my Lord Jesus Christ, I sell my soul to You for inclusion in Your Kingdom.[7] I am no longer my own.[8] Do with me whatever you desire."[9]

Yehovah answered, "Good decision."[10] Then I saw the ceiling roll back to normal.

I knew I had been greatly blessed, and I rejoiced![11] But then I noticed that the disloyal elohim had not left. It continued to stand there like a judge, watching but without emotion.[12] After a couple of minutes, I again became quite serious, wondering if I had missed something. So I lifted my eyes to Heaven,[13] and then the elohim suddenly turned around and simply walked out as if it had somehow been dismissed.[14]

Of course, the delay was because the disloyal elohim was waiting to see if I was going to turn away from integrity again![15] And that was not the last time that particular elohim would be disappointed. Because that elohim continued to periodically check up on me even after I left the band, became a student of the Living Word, and gave up all I had to follow Yeshua![16]

---

[1] Revelation 4:2; Ezekiel 1:16,28; 10:1
[2] 1 Samuel 3:4; Genesis 22:1; Exodus 3:4; Acts 9:4
[3] 1 John 2:12; John 17:12
[4] Galatians 6:7-9; Job 4:8; Proverbs 11:18; Romans 2:6-10
[5] Ephesians 1:17; Luke 12:12; 21:15; Matthew 16:17; 1 Corinthians 2:10
[6] Colossians 1:9; James 1:5
[7] Matthew 13:44-46; Revelation 3:18
[8] 1 Corinthians 6:19-20; 2 Corinthians 5:15: Titus 2:14; Romans 14:7-9
[9] Luke 1:38; John 12:26
[10] 1 Kings 3:11-14; 2 Kings 20:5
[11] Luke 10:20; Revelation 3:5
[12] Zechariah 3:1; 1 Peter 5:8
[13] John 11:41; Psalm 123:1
[14] James 4:7; Matthew 4:3-11; Ephesians 6:11-12; 1 Peter 5:8-9; Revelation 12:11
[15] 1 Peter 5:8; John 8:44; Ephesians 4:27; 6:11; Revelation 12:9; Zechariah 3:1
[16] Luke 4:13; 1 Peter 5:8

Do you see what happened there? Yehovah protected me by leading me into His Light of Integrity![1] He protected me from the principality by releasing the Light, Victory, and Grace that had been freely given to me through Yeshua![2]

HALLELUYAH!

YEHOVAH TRANSFORMS US FROM THE INSIDE OUT![3]

HALLELUYAAAAAAAAAAAH!!!!

HE SPEAKS FORTH FROM SPIRIT INTO SOUL, THEN BODY, THEN CREATION![4]

HALLELUYAAAAAAAAAAAAAAAAAAAH!!!!!!!!!

WHEN OUR EYES ARE FOCUSED ON THE LIGHT, OUR WHOLE BODY IS FILLED WITH LIGHT!!!![5]

HALLELUUUUUUUUUUUUYAAAAAAAAAAAAAH!!!!!!

WE HAVE BEEN GIVEN EVERYTHING WE NEED[6] TO CONQUER AND RULE WITH COMPLETE DOMINION!!!!!!!![7]

HALLELUUUUUUUUUUUUYAAAAAAAAAAAAAH!!!!!!

FOR THE GLORY[8] OF OUR VICTORIOUS[9] AND RIGHTEOUS KING!![10]

HALLELUUUUUUUUUUUUYAAAAAAAAAAAAAH!!!!!!

GREAT IS OUR KING!!!!!![11]

---

[1] Psalm 25:21; Proverbs 11:3

[2] 1 Kings 9:4-5; Romans 8:32-33; Ephesians 1:3; James 4:7

[3] Romans 12:2; Ephesians 4:22-24; Colossians 1:21-22; 3:10; Titus 3:5

[4] 2 Corinthians 3:18; Matthew 17:20

[5] Matthew 6:22-23; Luke 11:34-36

[6] 2 Peter 1:3; Psalm 84:11; Romans 8:32; 1 Corinthians 3:21-23; 1 Timothy 4:8

[7] Romans 8:37; Revelation 5:10; Matthew 18:18

[8] Hebrews 13:21; Ephesians 3:16-19; 2 Thessalonians 2:17

[9] Ephesians 1:21; John 16:33

[10] 1 John 2:1; Zechariah 9:9

[11] Matthew 5:35; Psalm 47:2; 48:2; 95:3; Malachi 1:14; Revelation 15:3

AMEN!!!

I subsequently learned that to overtake this convergence gate with the Light, a person must obediently force the Blood of Yeshua's Repentance through the will gate[1] and embrace the Blood of Yeshua's Affection in the heart gate.[2] Then the Blood of Yeshua's Integrity[3] must be applied to the convergence gate by the person obediently embracing the selfless affection of integrity through that gate.[4]

IN OTHER WORDS, YOU HAVE TO LIVE THE WORD TO LOVE IT[5] AND LOVE THE WORD TO LIVE IT![6]

LIVE IT TO LOVE IT AND LOVE IT TO LIVE IT!

HALLELUUUUUUUUUUUUYAAAAAAAAAAAAAH!!!!!!

DO NOT let any voice of thought or feeling persuade you that you cannot do this! You can do all things through Christ, Who strengthens you![7] Let the weak say, "I am strong in the Lord!"[8] If you perceive that you need more strength, then speak the praises of God because the Joy of the Lord is your strength![9] Praise until joy abounds![10] Lift up the Name of God,[11] and He will lift you up with Himself![12] How do you rise in power? You rise in power by proclaiming the Risen Power![13] Be strong in the Lord![14] Worthy is His Name![15]

---

[1] Acts 8:22; 17:30; Romans 2:4; 2 Timothy 2:25-26; Revelation 2:21

[2] Ephesians 5:2; John 15:12; 2 Corinthians 5:14-15; 1 John 3:16; Revelation 1:5

[3] Hebrews 13:8; Matthew 6:1-4; 23:5,28-30

[4] That is to say, one must persevere in pursuit until one *feels* the affection for integrity because integrity is the unity of holy pursuit and holy affection (2 Timothy 1:7). This is not difficult for us! It is our nature in Christ! HalleluYah! (John 14:12)

[5] John 15:10; 14:21; 1 Corinthians 7:19; 1 John 2:5; 3:21-24; 5:3

[6] Matthew 22:37,40; Psalm 119:97,113,159,163,165

[7] Philippians 4:13; Ephesians 3:16

[8] Joel 3:10 has the often-quoted phrase, but it is in reference to the wicked foolishly challenging Yehovah. Nevertheless, Yehovah certainly makes His children strong, and He does command them to be strong in Him; Isaiah 41:10,29; Exodus 15:2; 1 Corinthians 16:13; Deuteronomy 31:6

[9] Nehemiah 8:10-12; Isaiah 12:2; 61:3; Psalm 71:23

[10] Romans 15:13; Psalm 149:1-9; Isaiah 55:12; Galatians 5:22; 1 Peter 1:8

[11] Psalm 145:1-21; Exodus 15:2

[12] Psalm 30:1; James 4:10

[13] Ephesians 5:14; Isaiah 52:1; 60:1; Romans 6:5; Colossians 3:1

[14] Joshua 1:9; 2 Thessalonians 3:3

[15] Psalm 18:3; 2 Samuel 22:4

YESHUA IS WORTHY TO RECEIVE GLORY AND HONOR AND POWER BECAUSE HE WAS SLAIN![1]

HALLELUYAH!

AND WITH HIS BLOOD, HE PURCHASED PEOPLE FOR YEHOVAH FROM EVERY TRIBE, LANGUAGE, AND NATION![2]

HALLELUYAH!
HE HAS MADE THEM TO BE A KINGDOM AND PRIESTS TO SERVE YEHOVAH, AND THEY WILL REIGN ON THE EARTH![3]

HALLELUYAH!

PRAISE THE NAME OF YEHOVAH, WHO MADE THE HEAVENS, EARTH, SEA, AND ALL THAT IS IN THEM![4]

GLORY TO GOD!

ALL THINGS FIND THEIR BEING AND HOLD TOGETHER IN HIM![5]

HALLELUYAH!

HIS ARM IS NOT TOO SHORT!![6]

GREAT IS OUR GOD!!![7]

HE HEARS ALL THINGS,[8] KNOWS ALL THINGS,[9] AND CAN DO ALL THINGS![10]

HALLELUYAAAAAAAAAAAAH!!!!!!!!!!

---

[1] Revelation 5:12; 7:12; 19:1
[2] Revelation 5:9; Matthew 20:28; 26:28; Acts 20:28; Romans 3:24-26
[3] Revelation 1:6; 5:10; 20:6; 22:5; Exodus 19:6; 1 Peter 2:5-9
[4] Revelation 14:7; Nehemiah 9:6
[5] Revelation 4:11; Colossians 1:17; 1 Samuel 2:8; Isaiah 44:6; John 1:3; 1 Corinthians 8:6
[6] Isaiah 59:1; Numbers 11:23; Jeremiah 32:17
[7] 2 Chronicles 2:5; 1 Chronicles 16:25; Psalm 86:8-9; 135:5; 145:3; Jeremiah 10:6
[8] Psalm 139:4; Matthew 12:36-37; Hebrews 4:13
[9] Romans 8:27; Ecclesiastes 2:19
[10] Luke 1:37; Ephesians 3:20

HE IS POWER![1]

HE IS OUR GOD![2]

HE IS OUR SAVIOR![3]

HALLELUYAAAAAAAAAAAAAAAAH!!!!!!!!

HE IS THE ONE WHO LOVES US![4]

HALLELUYAAAAAAAAAAAAAAAAH!!!!!!!!

HE IS THE ONE WHO PROVIDES FOR US![5]

HALLELUYAAAAAAAAAAAAAAAAH!!!!!!!!

HE IS OUR GREAT REWARD!!![6]

And since He gave up His own flesh on a cross to reveal His Love for us, we know that He will not hold back any good thing but will freely bless us with every blessing![7]

GLORY BE TO GOD!!!

He has made every promise in His Word "Yes" for us![8]

PRAISE BE TO HIS HOLY AND POWERFUL NAME!!![9]

HALLELUYAAAAAAAAAAAAAAAAH!!!!!!!!

HALLELUYAAAAAAAAAAAAAAAAH!!!!!!!!

---

[1] John 13:3; 2 Corinthians 4:7; 2 Chronicles 20:6
[2] Malachi 3:1; John 20:28; Isaiah 9:6; Luke 1:76
[3] Jeremiah 14:8; Jude 1:25
[4] 1 John 4:16; Psalm 36:7-9
[5] Philippians 4:19; Psalm 145:15-16
[6] Genesis 15:1; Ruth 2:12; Psalm 16:5-6; 142:5; Lamentations 3:24
[7] Romans 8:32; Psalm 84:11; 1 Corinthians 2:12; 3:21-23
[8] 2 Corinthians 1:20; Galatians 3:22; Acts 13:32-39
[9] Psalm 96:2; 100:4; 149:3

HALLELUYAAAAAAAAAAAAAAAH!!!!!!!!

SO, DON'T HOLD BACK, MIGHTY WARRIORS OF YESHUA![1] BECAUSE YOU CAN DO ALL THINGS THROUGH HIM![2]

HALLELUYAH!

Now, when we speak of integrity in reference to the soul, we mean the unwavering commitment to be true in deed and affection in all situations![3] That is not to say a person must always behave the same way or have the same affection in every case but rather that the person fully endeavors to be holy, loving, and pure in every situation according to the free gift of Grace received in Yeshua.[4] The person puts on the new self and never takes it off for any reason![5] No matter what the situation is, the person is a devoted servant of Christ![6] There is no dilution, no "vacation" of worldliness, no "cutting loose" from absolute devotion and focus on walking with Yehovah![7]

Are you listening, holy redeemed people of Yeshua?[8]

You are not who you think you are; you are who Yehovah says you are![9] You are not this or that kind of person![10] You are not like this or like that![11] People don't need to understand this or that about you![12] You don't like this or that, and you don't decide who you are, were, or will be![13]

YOU ARE WHO GOD SAYS YOU ARE!!!!!!!!!![14]

---

[1] Romans 8:37; Isaiah 25:8; 1 Corinthians 15:57; 1 John 4:4; 5:4-5; Jude 1:24
[2] Philippians 4:13; Ephesians 3:16
[3] Hebrews 13:8; Psalm 15:1-5; Ephesians 6:6
[4] Ephesians 2:8; 4:24; Titus 2:11
[5] Colossians 3:10; Romans 13:12; Galatians 3:27
[6] 1 Corinthians 7:34; Titus 3:8
[7] 2 Timothy 2:4; 1 Corinthians 9:25-26; 1 Timothy 6:9-12
[8] 1 Peter 1:18; Luke 1:68; Galatians 3:13-14; Revelation 5:9; 14:3
[9] 1 Corinthians 13:12; James 1:23; 2 Corinthians 3:18
[10] James 4:13-17; Psalm 52:1; 1 Corinthians 4:7; 13:12
[11] 2 Corinthians 5:17; John 3:3; Galatians 6:15
[12] John 12:43; Colossians 3:10; 2 Corinthians 3:18
[13] Ephesians 2:10; Jeremiah 10:23; Proverbs 20:24
[14] James 1:23-24; 1 Thessalonians 1:5; Ezekiel 33:31-32; Matthew 7:26-27

SO LAY DOWN INTO DEATH ON THE CROSS[1] THE LIFE OF WHO YOU THINK YOU ARE AND THEN PICK UP THE RESURRECTED LIFE OF WHO YOU REALLY ARE IN YESHUA![2]

HALLELUYAH!

YOU ARE NOT OF THIS WORLD![3]

YOU ARE A HOLY KINGDOM AND PRIESTHOOD![4]

YOU ARE HIS HOLY TEMPLE![5]

YOU CAN DO ALL THINGS THROUGH CHRIST, WHO STRENGTHENS YOU![6]

ALL PROMISES ARE "YES" AND "AMEN" FOR YOU![7]

HALLELUUUUUUYAAAAAAAAAAAAAAH!!!!!!

HALLELUUUUUUYAAAAAAAAAAAAAAH!!!!!!

GLORY TO GOD!!!!!!!![8]

Therefore, understand that part of this consistent pursuit and affection is to speak the Truth of Yeshua's Integrity over the convergence gate,[9] especially reflecting on His steadfast faithfulness in moral obedience and selfless love![10]

YOU ARE THE BODY OF CHRIST ON THE EARTH![11] SO, BE THE TONGUE AND SPEAK HIS WORD![12]

---

1 John 10:17; Matthew 16:24
2 Colossians 3:3; 1 John 3:2; 1 Peter 1:3-5
3 John 17:14,16; 1 John 4:5-6; 5:19-20
4 1 Peter 2:9; Revelation 1:6; 5:10
5 1 Corinthians 3:16; 6:19; 2 Corinthians 6:16; Ephesians 2:21-22; 1 Peter 2:5
6 Philippians 4:13; Ephesians 3:16
7 2 Corinthians 1:20; Galatians 3:22; Acts 13:32-39
8 Revelation 15:4; Luke 1:49; Psalm 99:3
9 Hebrews 13:8; Matthew 5:46-48; 6:1-4,6; 22:16; 23:5,23-28
10 Luke 22:42; John 4:34; 5:30
11 1 Corinthians 12:27; Ephesians 1:22-23
12 1 Peter 4:11; Isaiah 8:20

HALLELUYAH!

After you speak His Word through the mouth of His Temple on the earth,[1] the duplicitous spirit can be easily bound,[2] silenced,[3] and cast into the outer darkness[4] FOR YESHUA'S GLORY![5]

HALLELUYAH!

And know that a key response to a spirit of duplicity is, "I never have to be anything other than what Yehovah has made me to be; if I am going to be anything in Creation, I am going to be what He has made me to be!"[6]

I DO NOT FEAR WHAT OTHERS THINK OF ME[7] BUT ONLY SEEK THE PRAISE OF HIM WHO SENT ME![8]

I NO LONGER LIVE FOR WHAT OTHERS THINK OF ME[9] NOR EVEN FOR WHAT I THINK OF MYSELF[10] BUT ONLY FOR THE GLORY OF THE GOD[11] WHO SAVED ME THROUGH HIS GREAT LOVE![12]
HALLELUYAH!

Remember that you are a new creation![13] You were not made to be duplicitous![14] You have been given a new spirit[15] that overflows with integrity![16] It is the same in the inner rooms as it is on the rooftops![17] You are not duplicitous![18] It is not of

---

[1] Proverbs 18:21; 1 Peter 4:11; Mark 11:23; Isaiah 55:11; 1 Corinthians 6:20; Philippians 2:11
[2] Matthew 18:18; Mark 3:27
[3] Mark 1:25,34; Luke 4:41
[4] Matthew 22:13; Jude 1:6
[5] Romans 11:36; 2 Peter 3:18
[6] Luke 16:15; John 5:44; Romans 8:29-30; Matthew 5:14; 2 Samuel 6:16-22
[7] Proverbs 29:25; John 12:42; Galatians 2:11
[8] John 5:44; 15:8; 1 Peter 4:11
[9] Matthew 10:28; Isaiah 51:12
[10] 1 Corinthians 13:12; Romans 14:22b
[11] John 7:18; 8:49-50; 1 Corinthians 10:31; 1 Thessalonians 2:6; 1 Peter 4:11
[12] Romans 5:8; Isaiah 53:6; 1 Peter 3:18; 1 John 4:9-10
[13] 2 Corinthians 5:17; John 3:3; Galatians 6:15
[14] Philippians 2:2; Romans 15:5-6
[15] Ezekiel 11:19; Psalm 51:10; Acts 8:15; Romans 7:6; 2 Corinthians 3:6
[16] Mark 12:14; Matthew 5:16
[17] Luke 12:3; Matthew 12:36
[18] John 17:21; 2 Corinthians 1:12; Titus 2:7

you![1] It is a dark spirit seeking to confuse and compromise you in all you think or do![2] Bind it, silence it, and cast it away![3] Enter into the Kingdom of Heaven *on this very day*,[4] where *no one* is ever duplicitous but only lives in perfect integrity all the time![5]
HALLELUYAAAAAAAAAAAAAAAAAAH!!!

Praise our REDEEMER,[6] Who removed from us the bonds of lust, pride, and duplicity and INDWELLED[7] us instead with HIS LOYALTY,[8] HUMILITY,[9] AND INTEGRITY![10]

HALLELUYAAAAAAAAAAAAAAAAAAH!!!

WE!!!!! ARE!!!!! FREE!!!!![11]

HALLELUUUUUUUUYAAAAAAAAAAAAAAAAAAAAAAH!!!

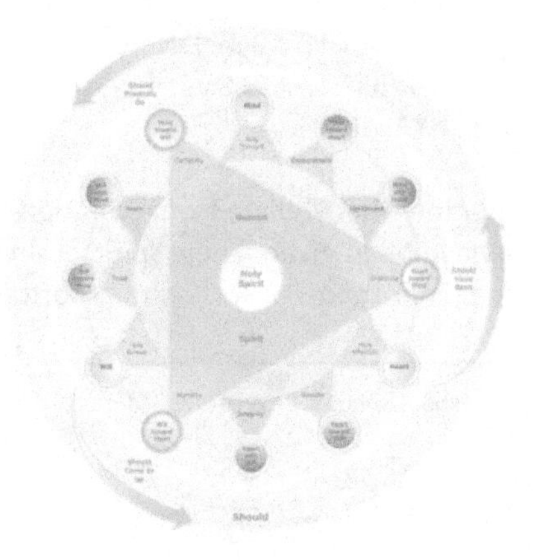

[1] 1 Corinthians 1:10; Acts 4:32; Romans 15:5-6
[2] Genesis 3:1,13; Revelation 12:9; 16:14; 20:2,8; Zechariah 3:1-2
[3] Matthew 10:1; 16:19; Mark 1:34; 16:17; James 4:7; Luke 10:17; Acts 16:18; Psalm 31:18
[4] Luke 17:21; 1 Corinthians 3:16; Matthew 10:7
[5] Matthew 6:10; 13:11,44; 16:19; Titus 2:7 – *Immortality* from the Greek ἀδιαφθορία, meaning *integritous, sound, incorruptible*; Romans 2:7 – *incorruptible* from ἀφθαρσία, meaning *genuine, pure, sincere*; Colossians 3:22 – *singleness/sincerity* from ἁπλότης, meaning *mental honesty, free from pretense and hypocrisy.*
[6] 1 Peter 1:18; Luke 1:68; Galatians 3:13-14; Revelation 5:9; 14:3
[7] 2 Timothy 1:14; John 14:17; Romans 8:11
[8] Philippians 3:3; Romans 14:7-9
[9] 1 Peter 3:8; Philippians 2:8
[10] Hebrews 13:8; Matthew 5:16
[11] Galatians 5:1,13; 2:4; 4:26,31; John 8:32-36; Romans 6:18; 8:2

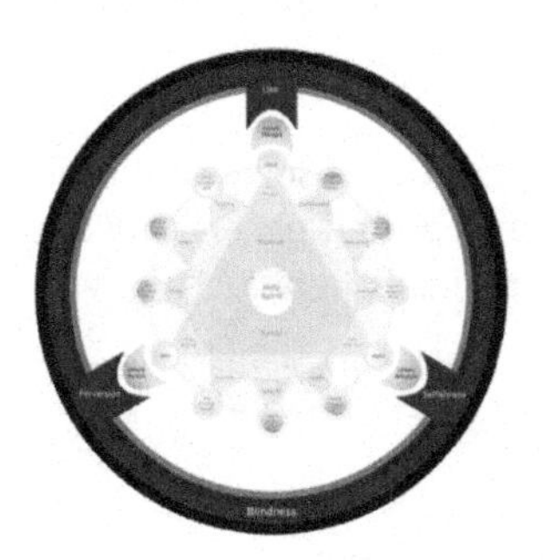

CHAPTER 22

DEFENDING THE TRIAD OF OBSERVATION

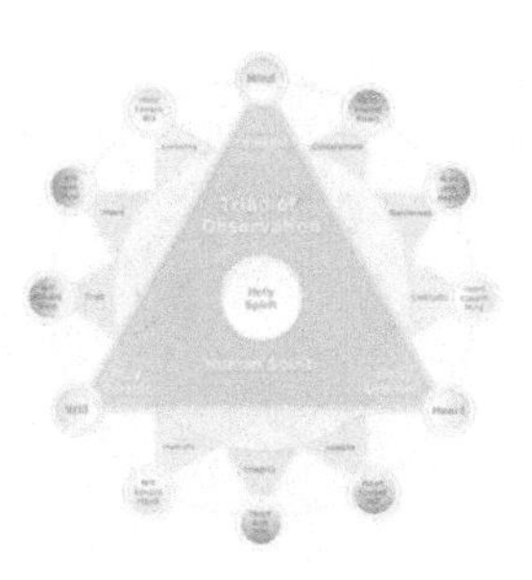

PRAISE THE KING OF KINGS AND LORD OF LORDS![1]

GLORY! HALLELUYAAAAAAAAAAAH!!!!!!!!!!

THE LAND IS OURS![2] GLORY TO OUR MIGHTY GOD,[3] WHO HAS MADE US MORE THAN CONQUERORS![4]

HALLELUYAAAAAAAAAAAAAH!!!! AMEN!!!

Fellow warriors![5] We have only just begun our blessing of revealing His Glory![6] Overtaking the gates is merely the beginning of the spiritual walk! To keep in step with the Spirit,[7] the child of Yehovah must defend the gates![8]

---

[1] Revelation 17:14; 19:6; 1 Timothy 6:15
[2] 2 Chronicles 14:7; Hebrews 3:13-15
[3] Isaiah 9:6; 45:24-25; Psalm 45:3,6; 50:1; Romans 9:5; Titus 2:13
[4] Romans 8:37; Isaiah 25:8; 1 Corinthians 15:57; 1 John 4:4; 5:4-5; Jude 1:24
[5] Philippians 2:25; Philemon 1:2
[6] John 15:8; Luke 6:35; Psalm 92:12-15; Isaiah 60:21; Matthew 5:16
[7] Galatians 5:16-18,25; Romans 8:4-5
[8] Revelation 2:25; 3:11; 1 Chronicles 9:23; Nehemiah 13:22

HALLELUYAH!

As previously addressed, the three primary gates compose the observation[1] triad. The mind,[2] will,[3] and heart[4] are all intimately dependent on the observations of the spirit.[5] This triad forms the foundation of a person's relationship with Yehovah.[6]

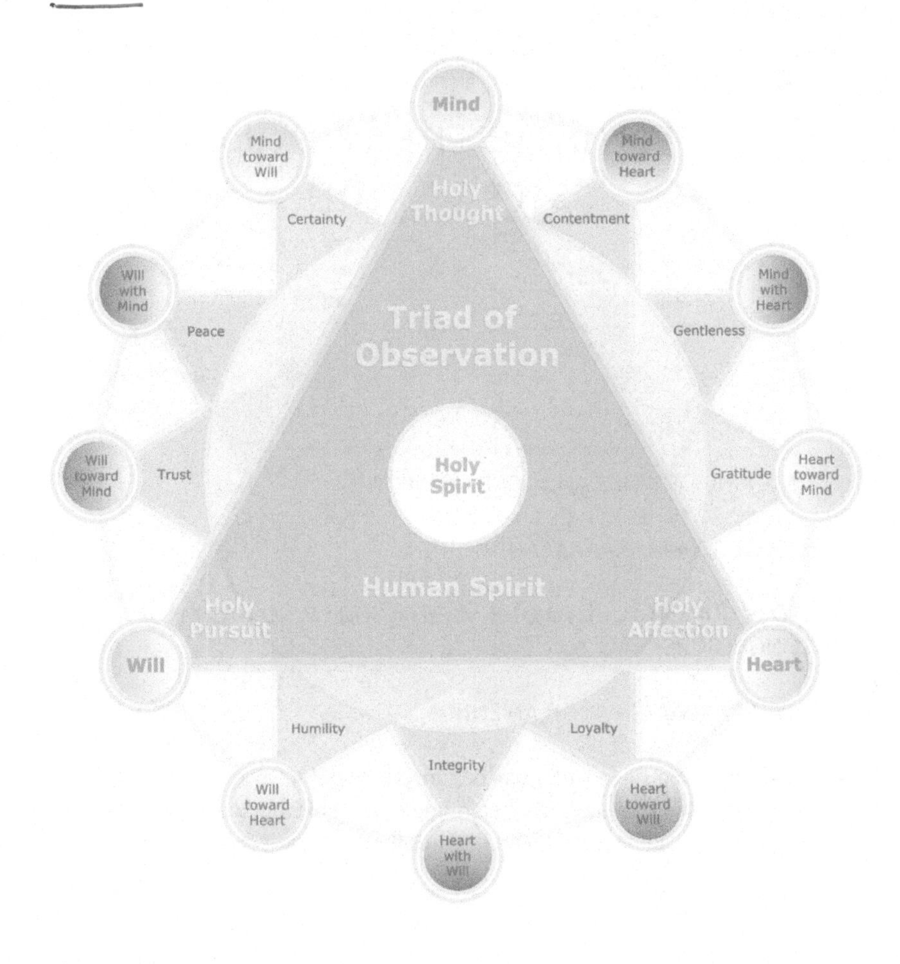

[1] Psalm 14:2 (spirits "look/observe"); Psalm 139:2 (spirits "perceive")
[2] Romans 8:6; Matthew 16:23; Luke 24:38
[3] Ephesians 3:16; Hebrews 11:34; 2 Timothy 4:17
[4] Romans 2:29; Matthew 18:35; Mark 10:5
[5] John 14:7; Colossians 2:2-3; 2 Corinthians 4:6
[6] Luke 10:27; Deuteronomy 30:14

May those who seek Yehovah's Glory[1] be given wisdom and revelation![2] May the Holy Spirit shine forth through your own,[3] and may your soul be full of Light![4] Amen!

The triad functions in observation as a unit.[5] When the Truth shines into the mind, obedience in the will and love in the heart are both increased.[6] Likewise, when the Holy Spirit flows with obedience through the will, the mind and heart benefit.[7] And when love from Yehovah abounds in the heart, a person's whole being is full of Light.[8]

Do you see how important this triad is? It is the foundation of spiritual control over the soul.

Knowing this, the dark kingdom makes every effort to send dark beliefs, pursuits, and affections to distract the person's soul from firmly connecting with the redeemed person's spirit,[9] which is already "seated with Christ in the heavenly realms."[10] By assaulting even one gate, darkness can weaken the others.[11] For example, if impurity is accepted into the convergence between the will and heart, the mind can be plunged into duplicity.[12]

---

[1] John 7:18; 8:49-50; 1 Corinthians 10:31; 1 Thessalonians 2:6; 1 Peter 4:11

[2] Ephesians 1:17; Luke 12:12; 21:15; Matthew 16:17; 1 Corinthians 2:10

[3] Romans 1:9-12; Matthew 5:14; Ephesians 5:8-14; Philippians 2:15

[4] Luke 11:36; Psalm 119:97-105; Proverbs 2:1-11; 2 Timothy 3:15-17

[5] Mark 12:30; Luke 10:27

[6] Romans 12:2; John 8:31-32; 7:17; 1 Peter 1:22; 2 Thessalonians 2:13; Proverbs 2:1-22; Isaiah 2:3, 30:21; Jeremiah 31:33-34

[7] Romans 2:29; Acts 4:32

[8] 1 John 2:10; Matthew 6:22-23; Luke 11:34-36

[9] Galatians 5:7; 2 Corinthians 11:3

[10] Ephesians 2:6

[11] 1 Corinthians 12:26; 2 Corinthians 11:28-29

[12] James 4:8; 2 Timothy 4:3; See Chapter 25 of this testimony for more about how each convergence gate reflects influence toward the main gate across from it, otherwise known as "pouring in through the backdoor."

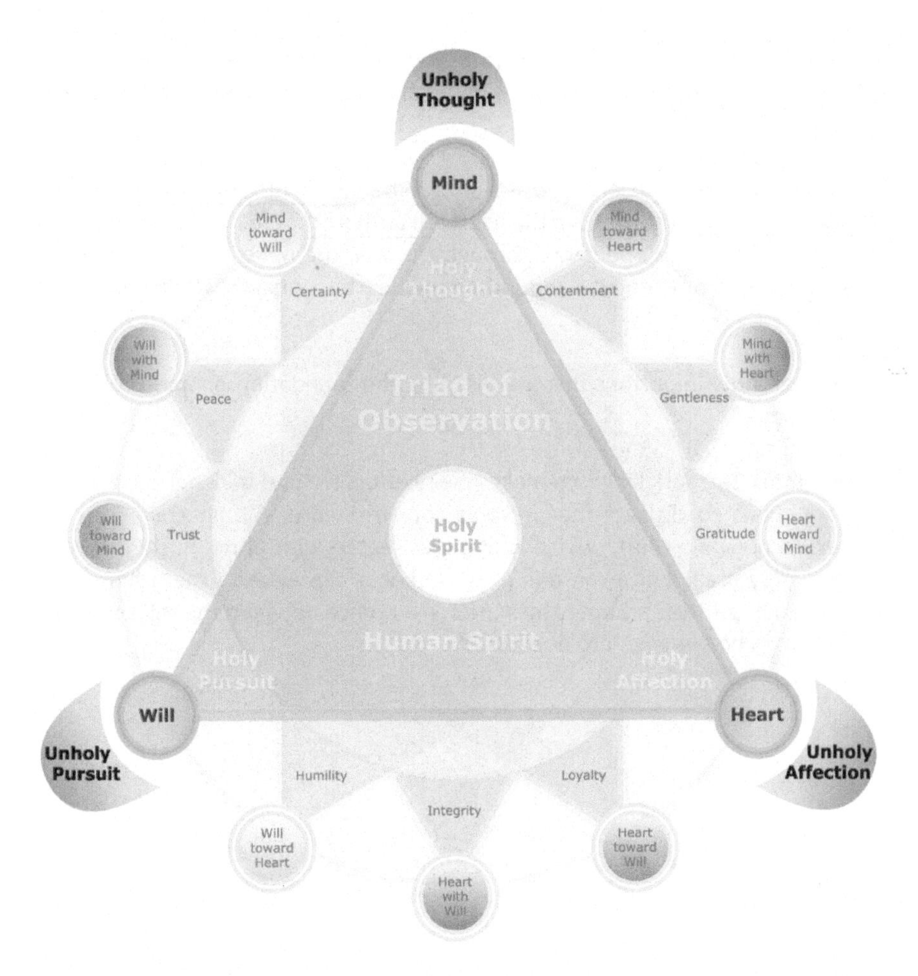

Therefore, it is absolutely vital that the child of Yehovah receives the truth[1] that a redeemed person is not who they think they are but who Yehovah says they are.[2] If the enemy can persuade the person to accept that dark beliefs, pursuits, and affections are the person's own, then the person's soul will remain in turmoil.[3]

Holy children of Yehovah![4] Do you notice we are saying this again?[5]

---

[1] Psalm 119:11; John 4:23

[2] 2 Corinthians 5:17; Colossians 2:10; 1 Corinthians 15:57; 2 Timothy 1:7; Romans 8:9

[3] Galatians 3:1; 2 Corinthians 11:3

[4] Romans 8:14; Galatians 3:26; 1 John 3:1-2; 5:19; Matthew 5:9

[5] Romans 15:15; 2 Peter 1:12

YOU MUST KNOW WHO YOU ARE TO WALK IN VICTORY![1]

Many of the redeemed are wandering around like soldiers with amnesia on a battlefront![2] They don't know what they are fighting for![3] They don't know where to get supplies, ammunition, or support![4] Because of this, they are struck by fiery arrows from both sides![5] The enemy condemns them,[6] and their own forces rebuke them![7]

What we have said before, we will say again:[8]

YOU MUST KNOW WHO GOD IS,[9] AND YOU MUST KNOW WHO YOU ARE![10]

SO LISTEN![11]

Those purchased by the Blood of Yeshua have been purchased,[12] those redeemed have been redeemed,[13] those washed have been washed,[14] those sanctified have been sanctified,[15] and those set free from sin have been set free from sin![16]

DO NOT JUST READ OVER THESE FOUNDATIONAL TRUTHS AND MISTAKE FAMILIARITY AS KNOWLEDGE![17]

---

[1] James 1:22-25; Matthew 7:26-27
[2] Galatians 3:1,3; 2 Corinthians 11:3
[3] Galatians 5:7; 2 Corinthians 11:3
[4] James 4:2; 5:17-18
[5] Ephesians 6:16; Galatians 5:15
[6] Mark 14:64: Romans 2:27
[7] James 4:1-3; Galatians 5:15
[8] 2 Peter 1:12; Romans 15:15; 1 Corinthians 15:1; Jude 1:5
[9] Colossians 2:19; Galatians 1:6-9
[10] Colossians 2:20; Galatians 4:3; John 15:19; 17:14-16; 2 Corinthians 10:3; 1 John 5:19; Romans 7:4-6
[11] Luke 8:18; 19:26; Deuteronomy 32:46-47; Proverbs 2:2-5; Mark 4:23-24; Acts 17:11; Hebrews 2:1; James 1:22-25; Matthew 13:12; John 15:2
[12] 1 Corinthians 6:19-20; 2 Corinthians 5:15: Titus 2:14; Romans 14:7-9
[13] Galatians 3:13-14; 4:5; Titus 2:14; 1 Peter 1:18; Psalm 19:14
[14] 1 Corinthians 6:11; Ezekiel 36:25; John 13:10; Titus 3:5; Hebrews 10:22
[15] 1 Corinthians 1:2; 6:11; John 17:19; Acts 26:18
[16] Acts 13:39; Romans 6:18,22; 8:2; Hebrews 9:15
[17] James 1:22-25; Luke 8:18; 19:26; Deuteronomy 32:46-47; Proverbs 2:2-5; Mark 4:23-24; Acts 17:11; Hebrews 2:1; Matthew 13:12; John 15:2

Ponder them![1] Reflect on them![2] Ask your Father in Heaven for wisdom and revelation to fully absorb them![3] "Bind them to your forehead and your hand"![4]

BE AN EXPERT ABOUT WHO YOU ARE IN CHRIST![5]

HALLELUYAH!

Do this so that you may not be deceived by any contradictory declaration or influence that comes against any of these promises given to you by the God of Truth![6]

Again! Those given the Mind of Christ have been given the Mind of Christ,[7] those given the Grace of Righteousness through Christ have been given the Grace of Righteousness through Christ,[8] and those who have had Yehovah's Love poured into their hearts by the Holy Spirit now have Yehovah's Love in their hearts![9]

KNOW THESE WELL![10]

Know them and do not accept any thought or idea that falls short of the Mind of Christ,[11] do not accept any pursuit in your will that falls short of the Righteousness of Christ,[12] and do not accept any affection in your heart that falls short of His Love for all of us on the Cross![13]

HALLELUYAH!

PRAISE BE TO OUR REDEEMER,[14] WHO HAS TOLD US THE TRUTH![15]

---

[1] Joshua 1:8; Psalm 1:2-3; 19:14; 119:15; Proverbs 2:1-5
[2] 2 Timothy 2:7; 1 Timothy 4:15; Proverbs 24:32
[3] Ephesians 1:17; Luke 12:12; 21:15; Matthew 16:17; 1 Corinthians 2:10
[4] Deuteronomy 6:6-9; 11:18; Exodus 13:9
[5] 2 Timothy 2:3-7; Romans 16:19
[6] 1 John 4:6; John 1:17; 14:6; 16:13
[7] 1 Corinthians 2:16; John 15:15; 16:13-15
[8] Romans 5:17; 6:23; Isaiah 61:10; Philippians 3:9
[9] Romans 5:5; Hebrews 8:10-12; 1 John 4:19
[10] 1 John 3:10; 1 Corinthians 2:16
[11] 1 Corinthians 2:16; John 15:15; 16:13-15
[12] 2 Corinthians 5:21; Philippians 3:9
[13] Romans 5:5; John 3:16; 15:9; 17:23
[14] Galatians 3:13-14; 4:5; Titus 2:14; 1 Peter 1:18
[15] John 1:17; 14:6; 15:1; 18:37; Romans 15:8; Colossians 2:17; 1 John 5:6,20; Revelation 3:7,14; 19:11

HALLELUYAH!

Any belief, pursuit, or affection that falls short of Yeshua is not at all of you![1] It is an attempt by the enemy to suggest darkness for your acceptance with the goal of crippling your soul and providing the dark kingdom influence![2]

The foremost reason there is little observed power in the church today[3] is the complete compromise of the observational triad in those who are redeemed and set free from sin but remain unaware of their freedom![4] Instead of walking in the power of the newness of life,[5] they have been deceived into giving every stray belief, pursuit, and affection equal say to the Word of Yehovah![6]

Know then that the first rule of defense[7] in guarding the observation triad is to observe that Yeshua is exactly and only Who He says He is[8] and that you are exactly and only who He says you are![9]

HALLELUYAAAAAAAAAAAH!!!!!!!!!

DO YOU HEAR THE TRUTH? YOU DON'T HAVE TO ACCEPT ANY BAD THOUGHT, PURSUIT, OR AFFECTION IN ANY PART OF YOU EVER AGAIN![10]

HALLELUYAAAAAAAAAAAH!!!!!!!!!

YOU'RE NOT THE PROBLEM![11]

YOU'RE THE SOLUTION THROUGH JESUS![12]

GLORY BE TO GOD!!!

---

[1] Romans 8:29: Isaiah 54:17

[2] Ephesians 5:1-21; Luke 11:34-36; Matthew 6:22-23

[3] 1 Timothy 1:19; 2 Peter 3:3; 2 Timothy 3:1-9

[4] Galatians 5:1; Romans 6:18,22; 8:2; 2 Corinthians 3:17

[5] Romans 6:4; 7:6; 2 Corinthians 5:17; Galatians 6:15; Ephesians 4:22-24

[6] Matthew 7:26; 1 John 4:1-6; Galatians 1:6; 6:7-10

[7] 2 Peter 1:2-10; John 15:2,6; Titus 3:14

[8] Exodus 3:14; Hebrews 13:8

[9] John 15:5; 2 Peter 3:18; 2 Corinthians 3:18

[10] John 8:32; Galatians 5:1; Galatians 5:25; Romans 8:37

[11] Romans 4:7-8; 5:1; 8:1; Isaiah 54:17; John 3:18; 5:24; Galatians 3:13

[12] Colossians 1:24-26; Romans 15:15-18; Acts 13:47

LOOK WHAT HE'S DONE FOR US![1]

HE'S SAVED US![2] HE'S REDEEMED US![3] HE'S MADE US WHOLE![4]

GLORY BE TO GOD![5]

HE'S LOVED US![6] HE'S COME TO RESCUE[7] AND EMPOWER US![8]

HE'S MADE US INTO NEW BEINGS,[9] HOLY[10] AND PURE![11]

GLORY BE TO GOD![12]

YESHUA MADE US TO BE LIKE HIM![13]

WE'RE NEW! WE'RE HOLY! WE'RE SAVED! WE'RE FREE![14]

WE ARE HIS![15] GLORY TO YEHOVAAAAAAAAAAAAAAAAAH!!!!!!!!

HALLELUYAAAAAAAAAAAAAAAAAAAAAAAAH!!!!!!!!!

SO, let us move FORWARD,[16] CONFIDENT[17] in Him! And let us learn together how to battle as WHO WE ARE and with what we have been given![18] For we fight in the

---

[1] Psalm 46:1-11; Romans 9:23; 1 Corinthians 2:9
[2] 2 Timothy 1:9; Ephesians 2:8; Titus 3:4-5
[3] Galatians 3:13-14; 4:5; Titus 2:14; 1 Peter 1:18
[4] Ephesians 1:3; 2:6; Genesis 12:2-3; 1 Chronicles 4:10; Isaiah 61:9; Galatians 3:9
[5] Luke 2:14; Revelation 14:7; 15:8; 19:1
[6] 1 John 4:19; Ephesians 2:4-5
[7] Colossians 1:13; Isaiah 49:24-25; Matthew 12:29-30; Acts 26:18; Hebrews 2:14
[8] Acts 1:8; Micah 3:8; Zechariah 4:6; Luke 10:19; Romans 15:19
[9] 2 Corinthians 5:17; Galatians 6:15
[10] 2 Peter 2:9; 1 Corinthians 1:2
[11] Philippians 2:15; Matthew 5:14-16; John 5:35; Ephesians 5:8
[12] Romans 3:21-26; Luke 2:14; Revelation 14:7; 15:8; 19:1
[13] Colossians 3:10; Romans 13:12; Galatians 3:27
[14] Acts 13:39; Romans 6:7,22; 8:2; Galatians 5:1
[15] Hebrews 3:6; 1 Corinthians 3:16
[16] Philippians 3:13; Philippians 3:14
[17] Philippians 1:6,14; 1 John 2:28
[18] Romans 8:37; Isaiah 25:8; 1 Corinthians 15:57; 1 John 4:4; 5:4-5; Jude 1:24

TRUTH[1] and by means of the TRUTH![2] We are warriors of the TRUTH[3] because we live in the TRUTH[4] and overcome all darkness with the Light of TRUTH,[5] forever bright and shining with no shifting shadows![6]

GLORY TO YEHOVAAAAAAAAAAAAAAAAAAH!!!!!!!!

HALLELUYAAAAAAAAAAAAAAAAAAAAAAAAAH!!!!!!!!!

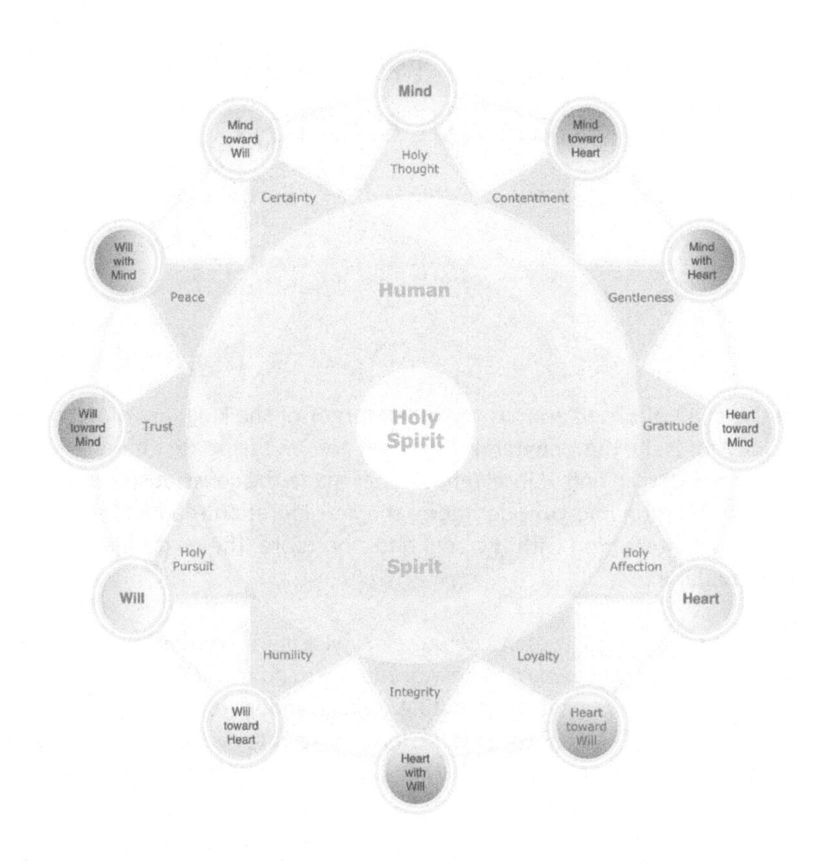

---

[1] Ephesians 6:14; 2 Corinthians 13:8
[2] John 17:17; 2 Timothy 2:25-26
[3] 2 Timothy 2:15; 2 Corinthians 4:2
[4] James 1:18; 2 Thessalonians 2:13
[5] John 8:32,36; Psalm 25:5; 119:45; Proverbs 2:1-7; 4:18; Isaiah 2:3; 61:1; Romans 6:14-18,22; 8:2,15; 2 Corinthians 3:17-18; Galatians 5:13; 2 Timothy 2:25-26
[6] James 1:17; John 1:9; 1 John 1:5; Revelation 21:23; 22:5; Isaiah 60:19

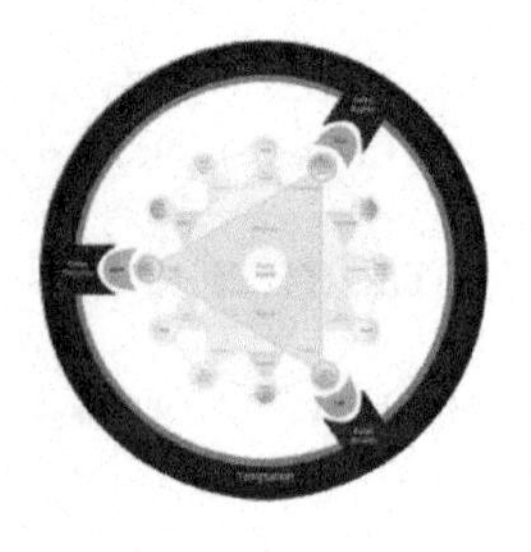

CHAPTER 23

DEFENDING THE TRIAD OF CONSIDERATION

While the triad of observation is the initial target of the kingdom of darkness, it does not represent the only target, nor is it the endgame for the enemy.[1] It is merely a means to an end.[2] Since Yehovah has made the consciousness of spirit to process observation into consideration,[3] the consideration triad is the next layer of the spirit's interaction with the soul and, therefore, the next objective of the kingdom of darkness.[4]

The consideration triad consists of the clockwise gates representing the heart toward the will, the will toward the mind, and the mind toward the heart. Spiritual consideration is the pursuit of gathering understanding for making a decision.[5] When filled with the Light of Yehovah's Glory, these gates become the considering belief of contentment,[6] affection of loyalty,[7] and pursuit of trust.[8] In other words,

---

[1] 2 Corinthians 2:11; 1 Peter 5:8; Ephesians 6:11-12; Revelation 12:9-11; 13:8

[2] 2 Corinthians 11:3; Revelation 12:9; 2 Timothy 4:3-4; 2 Peter 3:17

[3] 1 Samuel 24:15; Psalm 5:1 – Spirits "consider."

[4] Jeremiah 5:1 – "...look around and consider..." First comes observation, then consideration follows; also Lamentations 1:11; 2:20

[5] Jeremiah 5:1 – "consideration to forgive;" 1 Samuel 16:7 – "consideration to reject."

[6] Joshua 7:7; Hebrews 13:5

[7] 1 Chronicles 29:18; Psalm 78:37; 119:80

[8] Exodus 14:31; Psalm 9:10; 13:5; 20:7

when seeking to make a spiritual decision, the redeemed soul will *consider* contentment, loyalty, and trust.[1] Therefore, if a person's spirit strengthens the soul in one of these gates, then the others are strengthened as well.[2] For example, if loyalty is empowered, then certainty and trust will increase.[3]

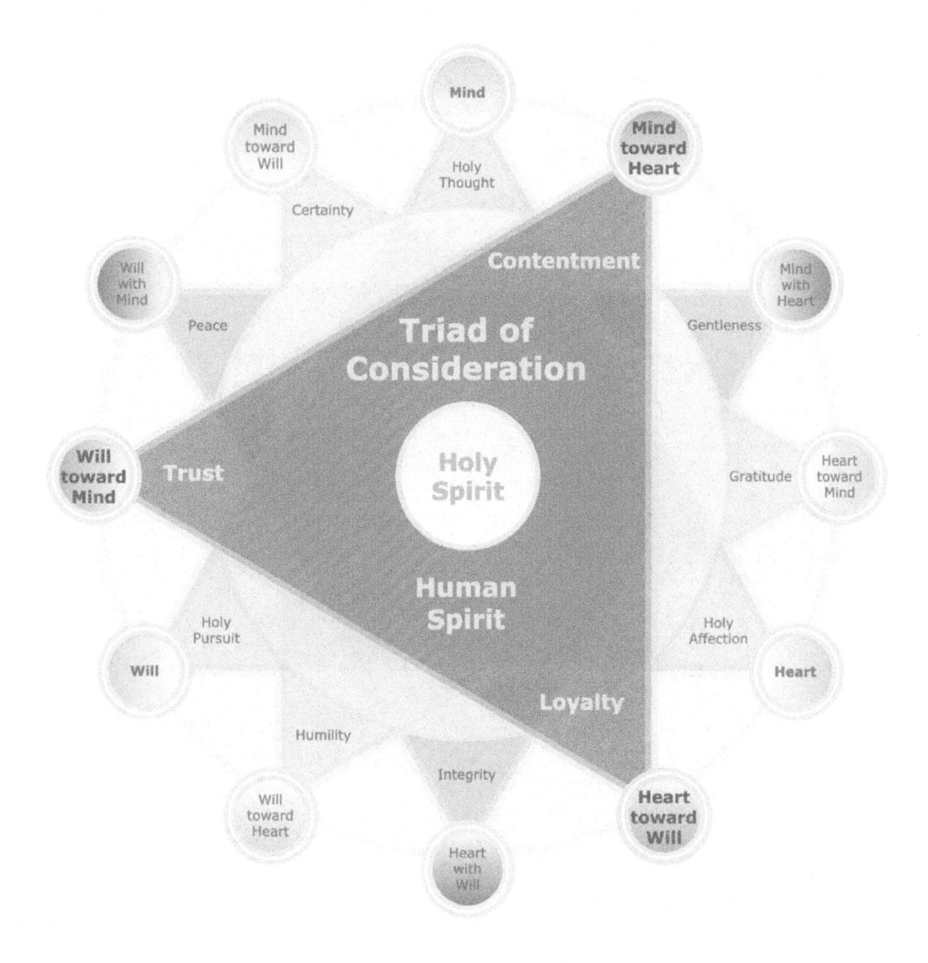

However, when a soul is beset by darkness, these same three gates become vulnerable to dark considering belief, affection, and pursuit.[4] The dark spirits fill

---

[1] Joshua 24:15; 1 Kings 18:21

[2] Matthew 6:33; Psalm 84:12; 1 Timothy 4:8

[3] Joshua 24:15; Hebrews 4:2

[4] Psalm 78:22; 106:24-25

the soul with envy[1], lust,[2] and worry[3] in an effort to misguide decision-making. Therefore, if a dark spirit blocks a soul from contentment, then loyalty and trust will suffer as well, and so on.[4]

When attacking a soul, these dark spirits steadily provide endless considerations[5] to blind the soul from considering the Voice of Yehovah as heard in affection, pursuit, and belief.[6] If any gate in this triad is compromised, the dark spirits will immediately seek to use that gate as backdoor access to reach the other gates

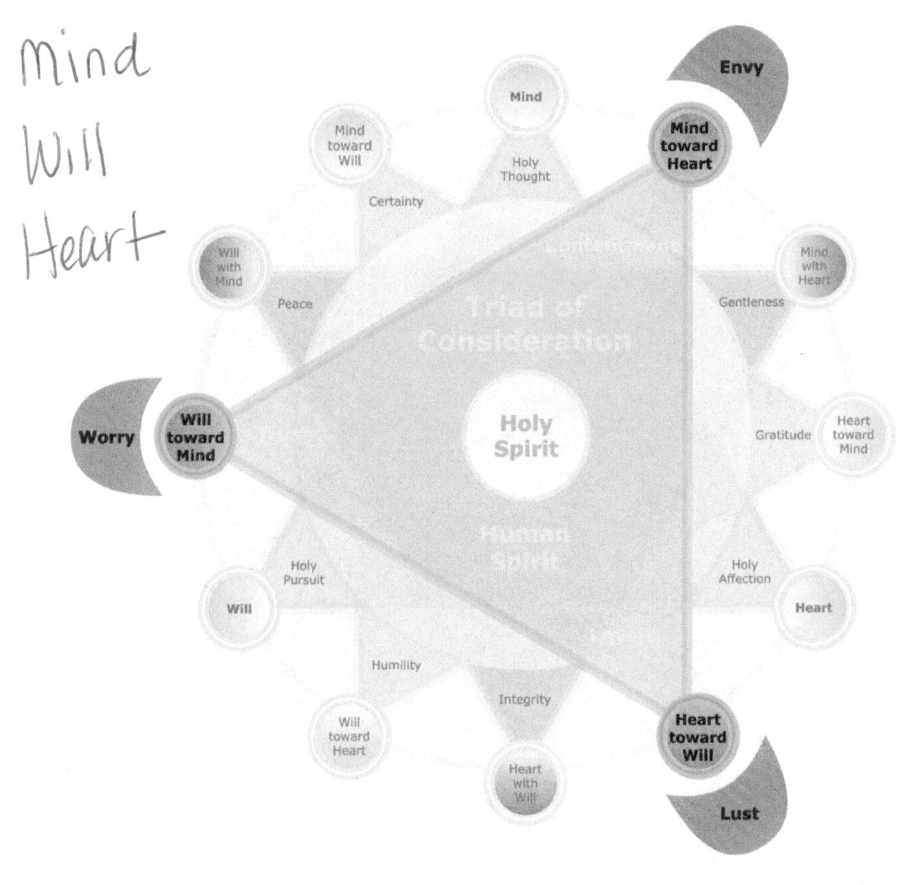

1 Proverbs 3:31; Ecclesiastes 4:4; 1 Samuel 18:8-9; Acts 7:9; 1 John 3:12

2 Ezekiel 16:36-38; Romans 1:27

3 Matthew 6:25-34; Luke 10:41

4 Psalm 106:24-25; Jeremiah 3:19-35

5 Mark 4:19; Matthew 14:28-31

6 John 12:40; 2 Corinthians 4:4; Matthew 4:8-9; Ephesians 2:2; 1 John 2:11; 5:19

with as much distraction and poison as possible.[1] For example, an accepted dark affection will soon be accompanied by a dark belief and a dark pursuit.[2] The evil spirits choose this tactic, not because they like the company of other dark spirits,[3] but because a completely compromised triad offers each of them a more secure foothold.[4]

Understand that a person's overcoming of any triad is a significant accomplishment and greatly fortifies the soul against darkness![5] Such reception of victory[6] glorifies our King and establishes rule on His behalf![7] Amen!

To overtake this triad, a person must first apply the Blood of Yeshua to all the gates in both the observation and consideration triads.[8] This process takes time and commitment, which must be spiritually spurred into momentum for the next step.[9]

Once all the gates have been covered, the soul must be saturated with exposure to upright observations.[10] All subjection to entertainment should consist only of that which is holy and righteous.[11] The soul who wants to live in light but spends time being entertained by darkness[12] is like a person who wants to stay dry but dives into a swimming pool.[13]

---

1 Mathew 12:45; Ephesians 4:27

2 Revelation 16:13 (Let those who have ears to hear, hear what the Spirit is saying through the revelation.)

3 Mathew 7:16; 23:33 – Evil does what it is. While human thieves might be somewhat loyal to each other because they are duplicitous, still having loyalty left over from being made in the image of God, evil spirits became completely evil upon rebellion. They have no residual image of God's Character. They were in the presence of God's Character and *chose* to become the opposite. They are now evil *by definition*, both in essence and behavior (Ezekiel 28:12-19).

4 Ephesians 4:27; Acts 5:3; 2 Corinthians 2:10-11; 11:3

5 Luke 21:19; 1 Corinthians 15:58; Galatians 5:1

6 Romans 8:31-32; 1 John 4:4

7 Matthew 25:21; Luke 22:28-30; Revelation 2:10,26-28; 3:21; 21:7

8 Psalm 103:1; 86:12-13; 111:1; 138:1; Mark 12:30; John 4:24

9 Galatians 6:9; Hebrews 10:36

10 Colossians 3:1-3; 1 Chronicles 22:19; Psalm 119:36-37; Matthew 16:23

11 Philippians 3:19; Job 31:1

12 Matthew 6:21-23; 2 Timothy 2:4; 2 Peter 2:20

13 Romans 8:7; Jeremiah 13:23; Matthew 12:34; 2 Peter 2:14

In this present day, many of the redeemed foolishly hand the reins of their souls to various forms of unrighteous entertainment for hours at a time.[1] Never in the history of humanity has such surrender been so common and so easy.[2] Because of this, so many potentially mighty spiritual warriors have become like King Saul, who was not able to resist antagonizing spirits but craved incessant music as a crutch to drown out the many dark voices plaguing his soul.[3] In the same way, the spirits of many people today have become weak, and their souls have become like untamed horses, running wildly and of no use for war.[4]

Instead of considering matters of the Spirit, these people spend time reflecting on their worldly entertainment, becoming experts in fictional matters and engaging in numerous conversations with one another about which shows or sports they find most entertaining and how they can be improved.[5] They mock previous civilizations such as Sodom and Rome for their unrighteous entertainments and practices while they themselves pay entertainment companies to provide visualization of the very same dark appetites today![6] They saturate themselves with subjects of lust, worry, and envy and then wonder why their souls are lustful, worried, and envious! They plant seeds of darkness and wonder why they harvest its fruit![7]

MAY IT NEVER BE SO![8] DO SOLDIERS DEFENDING LAND IN A WAR LEAVE THE BATTLEFRONT TO GO SEEK ENTERTAINMENT IN THE CITIES OF THE INVADING FORCES?[9]

REPENT![10]

---

[1] 2 Timothy 2:4; Luke 9:59-62; Jude 1:4
[2] 2 Timothy 3:1-7; Hebrews 5:11; Revelation 17:2
[3] 1 Samuel 16:14-23; 19:9-10
[4] Psalm 32:9; Proverbs 26:3; Jeremiah 31:18
[5] 2 Timothy 2:4; 1 Corinthians 9:25-26; 2 Peter 2:20; Luke 9:59-62
[6] Matthew 11:24; Lamentations 4:6
[7] Galatians 6:7-9; Job 4:8; Proverbs 11:18; Romans 2:6-10
[8] Romans 6:2,15; 7:13; 11:1
[9] 2 Timothy 2:4; 1 Corinthians 9:25-26; 1 Timothy 6:9-12
[10] Matthew 3:2; 4:17; 11:20; Revelation 19:8

OR DO YOU INSIST THAT THE SPIRIT OF GOD IS RIDICULOUS FOR DEMANDING ALLEGIANCE TO RIGHTEOUSNESS?[1] WHAT THEN DO YOU WANT FROM GOD?[2] PARTIAL SALVATION?[3]

REPENT![4]

HEAVEN IS NOT FOR THE PARTIALLY SAVED![5] WHATEVER IS NOT SAVED WILL PERISH BY FIRE![6]

YOU SERVE A HOLY GOD[7] WHO HAS HOLY CHILDREN,[8] HOLY SOLDIERS,[9] AND HOLY PRIESTS![10]

WHY IS EVERYONE SO HOLY? BECAUSE HEAVEN IS A HOLY PLACE WHERE NO SIN IS ALLOWED ENTRY![11] THAT'S WHY! AND IF YOU WANT TO LIVE THERE, YOU HAVE TO BE WASHED CLEAN, TOO![12]

REPENT![13] BE FILLED WITH HIS SPIRIT![14] BE PURE[15] AS HE IS PURE,[16] AND ENTER THE KINGDOM OF GOD![17]

HALLELUYAH!

PICK UP YOUR CROSS![18]

---

[1] Matthew 5:6,20; 6:33; 13:49
[2] Mark 10:51; Luke 18:41
[3] Philippians 2:12; 1 Timothy 1:19; Luke 18:25; James 1:8; Colossians 2:9-10
[4] Matthew 3:2; 4:17; 11:20; Revelation 19:8
[5] John 15:6; 1 Corinthians 3:11-15
[6] Mark 9:49; Hebrews 6:8
[7] Revelation 4:8; Isaiah 6:3; Exodus 15:11
[8] 1 Corinthians 7:14; Malachi 2:15; Romans 11:16
[9] Jude 1:3; Philemon 1:2; 2 Timothy 2:3-4; Philippians 2:25
[10] 1 Peter 2:9; Revelation 1:6; 5:10
[11] Revelation 21:27; 22:5; 1 John 1:5; John 12:46
[12] Revelation 22:12-16; 21:27
[13] Matthew 3:2; 4:17; 11:20; Revelation 19:8
[14] Ephesians 5:18; Acts 2:4; 4:8; 13:9,52
[15] Philippians 1:10; 2:15; 1 Timothy 5:22; Titus 1:15; 2:5
[16] 1 John 3:3; Hebrews 7:26
[17] Matthew 7:13; 13:32; Hebrews 4:11
[18] Matthew 16:24; Mark 8:34; Luke 9:23

CRUSH THOSE EVIL INFLUENCES UNDER YOUR FEET![1]

HALLELUUUUUUUYAAAAAAAAAAAAAAH!!!!!!!!!

PRAISE BE TO YESHUA, WHO HAS GIVEN US SURE VICTORY![2]

HALLELUUUUUUUUUUUYAAAAAAAAAAAAAAH!!!!!!!!!!

Now, for that person who picks up their CROSS, [3] DIES to their insatiable appetites,[4] FILLS their soul with upright observations,[5] and DEVOTES their time to the Spirit,[6] that person will see the tree of darkness wither and the tree of life bear fruit![7] The Almighty Resurrection Strength[8] will fill their soul with the Truth,[9] Grace,[10] and Love[11] of Yeshua! The spiritual power of consideration can then be revealed, engaged, and strengthened in the redeemed person through devoted prayer, pouring out the overflow of their heart to Yehovah in sincere transparency.[12] This is not a prayer for self-justification or a promise of intention but rather a request to Yehovah for help in observing and considering life according to the Truth in belief, pursuit, and affection.[13] It is repentance from

---

[1] Luke 10:19; Psalm 91:13; Ezekiel 2:6; Mark 16:18; Acts 28:5; Romans 16:20
[2] 1 Corinthians 15:57; Romans 8:37; 1 John 5:4-5
[3] Matthew 16:24; Mark 8:34; Luke 9:23
[4] Galatians 5:24; 6:14; Romans 6:6; 8:13; 13:14; 1 Peter 2:11
[5] Philippians 4:8; Hebrews 12:2; Colossians 3:2
[6] Matthew 6:33; Colossians 3:17; 4:5
[7] Galatians 6:9; James 5:7; Genesis 2:9 – *Knowledge* comes from the Hebrew word דַּעַת, pronounced "dah'ath" (sounding like the English word *death*) traditionally translated as *knowledge, perception,* or *discernment.* Worth noting is that the core letters דעת were originally written as the symbols for *door, eye,* and *cross.* Interestingly, when the Hebrew letters are read from left to right, they would be pronounced "tawd" or "tohd," which is also the German word for *death* (Tod). The *knowledge* of good and evil led to our *death* and the subsequent death of our Lord on the Cross for our sake (Genesis 2:17; 3:15). PRAISE OUR GOD FOR RESCUING US FROM OUR TRESPASS INTO DEATH (Romans 6:23)! HALLELUYAH! HE OVERCAME DEATH SO THAT WE COULD LIVE (2 Timothy 1:10)! HALLELUYAH! AMEN!
[8] Romans 8:11; John 7:38-39; Ephesians 2:5
[9] John 14:6; Acts 4:12; Hebrews 10:19-22; 1 John 2:23; 2 John 1:9; Revelation 5:8-9
[10] John 1:17; 14:6; Romans 5:21; 6:14; 1 Corinthians 1:4
[11] John 15:9,13; 17:23,26; Ephesians 3:18; Revelation 1:5
[12] 1 Peter 5:7; Psalm 34:15; Philippians 4:6; Luke 12:31-32
[13] Philippians 4:6-8; Colossians 3:2; Matthew 6:33

acquiring and consuming the foul bread of darkness to turn toward a new and permanent diet of His Truth and Righteousness.[1]

HALLELUYAH!

When this exchange has been made, the person will understand the meaning of the promise that whoever loses their life for His sake will find it.[2] They will see torment replaced by peaceful guidance,[3] and they will notice a great increase in their spiritual senses, discernment, and awareness![4]

AMEN!

PRAISE BE TO OUR HOLY GOD, WHO SAVES US *COMPLETELY*![5]

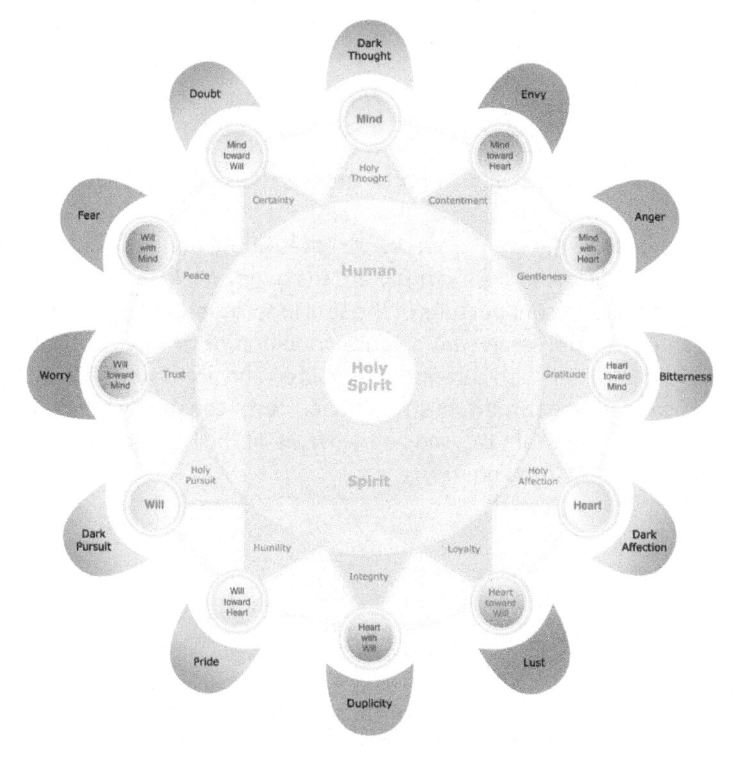

---

[1] John 6:27; Matthew 5:6
[2] Matthew 16:25; Luke 17:33; John 12:25; Revelation 12:11
[3] Romans 8:6; 1 John 4:18
[4] James 3:17; Hebrews 5:14
[5] Ephesians 1:4; Hebrews 12:14; 1 Peter 1:15-16; Revelation 22:11

CHAPTER 24

DEFENDING THE TRIAD OF DECISION

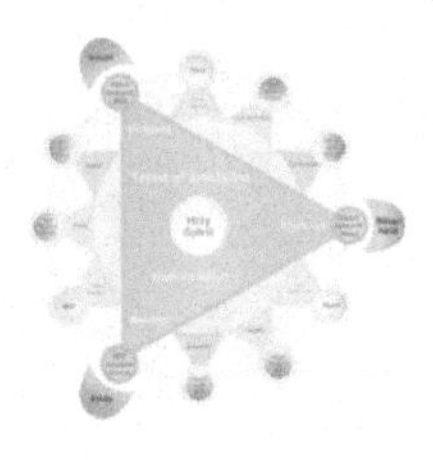

The Triad of Decision[1] is of vital importance. It is the seat of choice in humanity.[2]

This triad consists of the counterclockwise gates of the mind toward the will, the will toward the heart, and the heart toward the mind. While the gates of the Triad of Consideration represent pursuits of the soul in spiritual consideration, the gates in the Triad of Decision represent a soul's condition of spiritual decision.[3] In the Light, these gates shine with certainty,[4] humility,[5] and gratitude.[6] The soul in such a state experiences great spiritual strength and rest,[7] constantly overflowing with praise for God.[8] HalleluYah! Blessed be the Name of the Lord our Savior,[9] the One Who is, and was, and is to come![10]

HALLELUYAH!

---

[1] Exodus 33:5; Judges 11:27; 1 Samuel 24:15 – Spirits "decide."
[2] Deuteronomy 30:19; Joshua 24:15; 1 Peter 4:3
[3] John 14:17; 15:15; Mark 11:24; 2 Corinthians 4:13; Ephesians 3:14-21
[4] Luke 1:4; John 20:31; 2 Peter 1:15-16; Hebrews 11:1
[5] James 4:10; Philippians 2:3-8; Colossians 3:12-13
[6] 1 Thessalonians 5:18; Colossians 2:6-7; Hebrews 12:28
[7] Colossians 2:7; Matthew 11:29
[8] 1 Kings 8:56; Luke 19:37-40
[9] Isaiah 43:11; Luke 1:77-79; 2:11; Malachi 3:1
[10] Revelation 1:8; 22:13; Isaiah 41:4; 44:6; 48:12

COME LORD JESUS[1] AND ESTABLISH YOUR REIGN OVER ALL THINGS FOREVER![2]

AMEN!

Glory be to God!

Now, understand that to darkness these gates represent dark deciding belief, dark deciding pursuit, and dark deciding affection, or the spirits of doubt,[3] pride,[4] and

---

[1] Revelation 22:7,10,12,20

[2] Luke 1:33; Revelation 11:15; 21:27; Hebrews 1:8; Revelation 1:18; 4:9; 11:15

[3] Genesis 3:1; Matthew 4:3,6,9

[4] Proverbs 16:18; 18:12; 29:23; Ester 6:6; Isaiah 2:11-12; James 3:14,16

bitterness.[1] This level of the human spirit's interaction with the soul is where the overall condition of the soul is manifested; it is where control of the soul as a whole is determined and lost or won.[2]

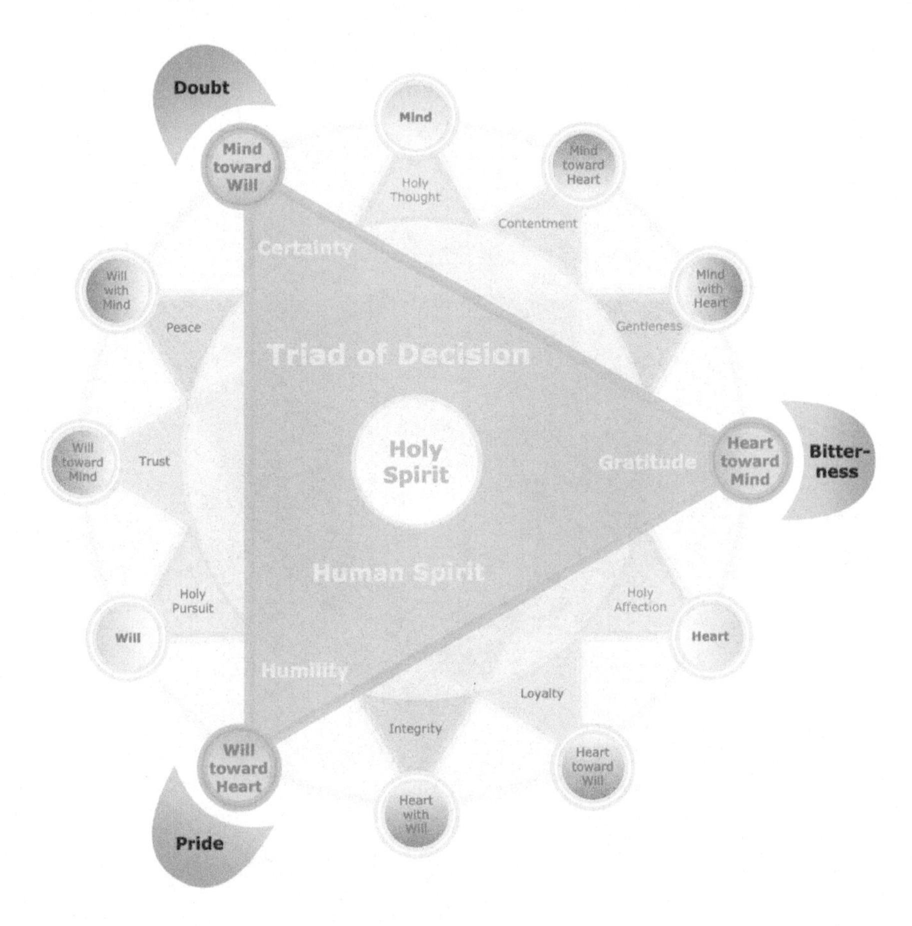

May your spirit be enlightened,[3] may you firmly grasp the reins of your soul,[4] and may you receive established dominion over it in the Name of Yeshua,[5] Who holds

---

[1] 1 Samuel 30:6; Acts 8:23; Romans 3:14; Ephesians 4:31; Hebrews 12:15

[2] Ephesians 4:27; James 1:6

[3] Ephesians 1:18; 2 Corinthians 4:6; Acts 16:14

[4] James 1:26; 3:2-6; Isaiah 44:20; Proverbs 10:19; 11:12; 17:28; Job 10:1

[5] Proverbs 16:32; 25:28; Revelation 3:21

the keys of David! What He opens no one can shut, and what he shuts no one can open![1] Amen! Glory to God!

HalleluYah!

To reign in spirit over the soul, a person must receive the blessing of absolute decision, a function in the spirit.[2] Because of this, the enemy will do their best to hinder the engagement of this spiritual function through misdirection.[3] The dark spirits interacting on this level are vigorous liars, forever babbling, promoting incessant confusion.[4] They will attribute spiritual function to that of the soul and soulical function to that of the spirit.[5] Every aspect of decision will be challenged and accredited to carnality if permitted, for the enemy's tactics on this level involve camouflage, denial, and substitution.[6]

Victory over this triad is not achieved but received.[7] It is not accomplished, worked out, nor computed but discovered, realized, and accepted.[8] It has been made readily available for the redeemed.[9] All that is necessary is its embrace.[10]

Take note that Mount Sinai does not stand in the Promised Land.[11] When Moses, the messenger of the covenant concerning the laws, definitions, and boundaries of the Promised Land, ministered in authority over the Israelites, he was outside of the Promised Land.[12] When he was told to strike the Rock[13] at Horeb to obtain lifesaving water for the Israelites, he was outside of the Promised Land.[14] Nothing done by Moses occurred within the Promised Land.

---

[1] Revelation 3:7; Job 11:10; 12:14; Matthew 16:19

[2] Romans 4:20-21; 2 Timothy 1:12; Hebrews 11:13

[3] Ephesians 4:14; 2 Timothy 2:17-18; 4:3; 2 Peter 2:1-3

[4] Proverbs 26:23-28; 12:5,20

[5] Colossians 2:18; James 3:15; Hebrews 4:12; 2 Corinthians 10:4-5

[6] 2 Corinthians 4:4; 11:14; Matthew 4:8-9; John 12:40; Ephesians 2:2; 1 John 2:11; 5:19

[7] 1 Corinthians 15:57; Romans 8:37; 1 John 5:4-5

[8] 1 Corinthians 4:7; 1 Peter 4:10; James 1:17

[9] 1 John 5:4-5; 3:9; John 16:33; Romans 8:35-37; 1 Corinthians 15:57

[10] Matthew 10:41; Mark 11:24

[11] Exodus 3:1; 19:2; Malachi 4:4; Galatians 4:25

[12] Deuteronomy 3:23-28; Numbers 20:12

[13] 1 Corinthians 10:4; Psalm 106:32-33; Deuteronomy 32:48-52

[14] Exodus 17:5-6; Deuteronomy 8:15; Nehemiah 9:15

However, when the Israelites subsequently grumbled about being thirsty, Yehovah commanded Moses to speak to the Rock again.[1] But out of anger, Moses struck the Rock twice with his staff.[2]

Understand that this action was recorded and addressed for our benefit that we might freely receive the blessing freely given to us.[3]

When Moses struck the Rock a second time, he was forbidden entry into the very Promised Land over which he had been a messenger and authority. This prohibition was a symbolic gesture on behalf of Yehovah demonstrating the transfer of authority from law to promise upon entrance into the Promised Land by Israel, which is a name meaning, "he who wrestles with God."[4] In other words, a person who personally engages God is led to the Promised Land[5] under the authority of the Law,[6] but he enters the land under the authority of Joshua for whom the waters of the Jordan were parted,[7] and whose name means "Yehovah is Salvation."

We are clearly told in the Scriptures that this Rock represented Yeshua[8] and that angels are messengers.[9] Therefore, understand that even the "angel," Moses, who carried the authority of God[10] and guided the Israelites out of Egypt, who led Israel through the waters of baptism,[11] who delivered the Law and provided the very terms and definitions of the Promised Land, was not permitted himself to enter that Promised Land, because "he struck Yeshua" a second time.[12]

---

[1] Numbers 20:7-8; Psalm 105:41

[2] Numbers 20:11-12; 27:14: Deuteronomy 1:37

[3] 1 Corinthians 10:11; Romans 15:4

[4] "Israel" means *to strive/overcome/rule with the Almighty.*

[5] Hebrews 3:11-4:13; Jude 1:5; Revelation 1:6; 5:10

[6] Deuteronomy 3:23-27 – Moses, through whom the Law came, led Israel to the promised land.

[7] Deuteronomy 3:28; Joshua 3:1-17; Hebrews 10:9

[8] 1 Corinthians 10:4; Colossians 2:17; Matthew 26:26-28

[9] Daniel 8:15-16; Luke 1:19; Acts 7:53; מלאך, pronounced "Mah-lahk," the Hebrew word translated "angel," means *messenger, representative*, or *someone dispatched*, like an *ambassador*. The Greek word for *angel,* ἄγγελος, pronounced "ahn-ghel-aws," also means *messenger.*

[10] Numbers 12:1-16; Exodus 34:30

[11] Moses, whose name means "drawn out of the water" (Exodus 2:10), miraculously led the Israelites through the waters of death (1 Corinthians 10:1-2).

[12] Numbers 20:8-12; Deuteronomy 3:23-26

Listen again,[1] holy warriors![2]

Moses was told to strike the rock the first time,[3] but he was told to speak to the rock the second time![4] In the same way, Yeshua was allowed to be struck once,[5] to be placed on a cross once,[6] but anyone who attempts to strike Him again or even dishonor Him again will not be permitted entrance into the Kingdom of Heaven (as long as they continue to do so)![7] Yeshua was crucified once to save us from the dominion of darkness,[8] but now we must humbly ask for entrance into His Kingdom![9] We must speak to the Rock![10] No one who attempts to strike Him again will enter His rest[11] until they stop striking and start asking![12]

Consider the above as you acknowledge that your soul is the land promised to you.[13] Your spirit is the one who has been led out of Egypt by God,[14] who has been rescued from the bondage of sin.[15] Your spirit has been invited into the promised Kingdom of Heaven,[16] a kingdom that does not come at once but is upon you.[17] This kingdom represents the sabbath rest promised to your spirit in Yeshua.[18] He is the Living Water[19] of Eternal Life[20] given to you from the Rock. He saved you from the plagues due to sin[21] by placing His Blood upon you,[22] by leading you through the certain death of the parted waters of baptism,[23] and by inviting you

---

[1] Luke 8:18; 19:26; Deuteronomy 32:46-47; Proverbs 2:2-5; Mark 4:23-24; Acts 17:11; Hebrews 2:1; James 1:22-25; Matthew 13:12; John 15:2

[2] 2 Timothy 2:3; Philippians 2:25; Philemon 1:2

[3] Exodus 17:6; Psalm 78:20

[4] Numbers 20:8; Matthew 21:21

[5] Isaiah 53:5; Zechariah 13:7

[6] 1 John 2:2; 3:5; 4:10,14; Romans 3:25-26; 1 Peter 2:24; 3:18; John 1:29; 4:42

[7] Ephesians 1:21; Revelation 19:15

[8] Hebrews 9:26; Romans 6:4

[9] Romans 10:9; John 16:24; Colossians 1:13

[10] Psalm 95:1; Matthew 21:21

[11] Hebrews 3:19; Jude 1:5

[12] Luke 11:10; Lamentations 3:54-58; Jonah 2:2-8

[13] John 15:8; Hebrews 8:6; 2 Peter 1:4

[14] Ezekiel 11:19; 1 Thessalonians 5:23; 1 Corinthians 14:14-15

[15] Romans 6:6-7,18,22; 8:2; Acts 13:39

[16] Matthew 22:1-14; Revelation 22:17

[17] Luke 17:20-21; Matthew 12:28; John 3:3; 18:36; Colossians 1:13

[18] Hebrews 4:10; 1 Peter 4:1-2

[19] John 7:37-39; 4:10-11; Revelation 7:17; 22:17

[20] John 17:3; 2 Corinthians 4:6; 1 John 5:20

[21] Romans 6:6-7,18,22; 8:2; Acts 13:39

[22] Hebrews 9:12; Acts 20:28; Ephesians 1:7; 1 Peter 1:18-19; Revelation 1:5; 5:9

[23] Romans 6:4; 1 Corinthians 10:2

to establish the land of your soul through conquest according to His Promise.[1] And though the fallen angels who enforced the "law of Egypt"[2] chased your spirit until it reached the promise,[3] they are not allowed to enter that promise.[4] They are not allowed to strike Yeshua again.[5]

Your soul has now become the temple of the Holy Spirit.[6] You are not only a promised land[7] but a promised temple, a promised Jerusalem,[8] and a promised kingdom! He has made you to be a kingdom and priest to serve Yeshua,[9] Who lives in you and reigns in your soul![10]

Therefore, *no angel of any sort is legally allowed to enter your soul as an authority*,[11] nor is any angel or messenger legally permitted to strike Yeshua a second time within you![12] He was struck once at the Cross,[13] but no authority has been given to any angel to strike Him again in any way![14] Any angel or messenger who does so is banished from the Promised Land![15] They are banished from where He dwells![16] They are like Philistines, banished from your soul and destined for death![17] They have no legal authority over you![18]

HALLELUYAH!

---

[1] Romans 8:37; Hebrews 10:36; 2 Peter 1:10-11

[2] Romans 8:2; 6:18; Hebrews 2:14-15

[3] Psalm 82:1-6; Exodus 12:12

[4] Psalm 82:7-8; Deuteronomy 3:27

[5] Deuteronomy 3:26; Revelation 19:15

[6] 1 Corinthians 3:16; 6:19; 2 Corinthians 6:16; Ephesians 2:21-22; 1 Peter 2:5

[7] Hebrews 3:11-4:13; Revelation 1:6; 5:10

[8] Revelation 3:12; Jeremiah 1:18

[9] Revelation 1:6; 5:10; 20:6; 22:5; Exodus 19:6; 1 Peter 2:5-9

[10] Romans 5:17; Colossians 3:15

[11] Matthew 23:8-10; 1 Corinthians 8:6; Ephesians 4:5

[12] 2 Corinthians 10:5; Jeremiah 4:14; Hebrews 4:12; Numbers 14:23; No messenger of any thought contrary to the truth of Scripture is permitted in your soul! HalleluYah!

[13] Isaiah 53:5; Zechariah 13:7

[14] Ephesians 1:21; Philippians 2:9-10; Colossians 2:10; Hebrews 1:4

[15] Numbers 14:23; 33:52; Exodus 23:24; Deuteronomy 7:25-26

[16] Psalm 5:4; 101:7; Habakkuk 1:13; Hebrews 12:14; Revelation 21:25,27; 22:5

[17] Zephaniah 2:5; Ezekiel 25:16

[18] Romans 6:14; 8:2; John 8:36

When you receive this truth, your spirit also receives the authority of this truth.[1] This reception manifests as certainty[2] against the spirit of doubt,[3] gratitude against the spirit of bitterness,[4] and humility against the spirit of pride.[5] It manifests as absolute and undiluted decision in spirit.[6] The reception of this promise is the crossing into this promise.[7] And once you are within the promise, no angel can strike whatever now lives through and because of this promise.[8] No angel has authority to strike the Light Who lives in you![9] Aspects of the soul that have been redeemed by Christ cannot be stricken by any authority again.[10] No striking spirit has any right to any legal authority or consequence of that legality.[11] No spirit can legally enforce any punishment, process, or principle against your soul in the promise.[12] This is why our King rebuked spirits of infirmities and demons;[13] they were not only acting without authority but were not even permitted in the Promised Land![14]

Through His Word, our King has revealed to us His commands concerning these things.[15] Therefore, let us embrace His promises to us and proceed into the Promised Land,[16] leaving the angels of Mount Sinai behind!

HALLELUYAH!

---

[1] Matthew 19:11; 1 Corinthians 4:7

[2] Luke 1:4, "...so that you may know the ασφαλειαν of the things you have been taught." – from ἀσφάλεια, pronounced "ahs-fahl'-ey-ah," meaning *certainty, security, firmness, stability*, or *safety*.

[3] Genesis 3:1,13; Revelation 12:9; 16:14; 20:2,8; Zechariah 3:1-2

[4] 1 Samuel 30:6; Acts 8:23; Romans 3:14; Ephesians 4:31; Hebrews 12:15

[5] Proverbs 16:18; 18:12; 29:23; Ester 6:6; Isaiah 2:11-12; James 3:14,16

[6] 1 Corinthians 15:58; Acts 11:23; Galatians 5:1; 1 Thessalonians 2:2

[7] Luke 8:18; 19:26; Deuteronomy 32:46-47; Proverbs 2:2-5; Mark 4:23-24; Acts 17:11; Hebrews 2:1; James 1:22-25; Matthew 13:12; John 15:2

[8] 2 Peter 1:4; Romans 9:4; 2 Corinthians 1:20; 7:21; Hebrews 9:15

[9] 2 Corinthians 6:14; Romans 8:9; 1 John 2:14; Numbers 14:23

[10] Romans 6:9; Acts 2:24-28; Psalm 16:9-11; Hebrews 7:16,25; Revelation 1:18

[11] Colossians 2:15; Acts 2:32-36; John 12:31; 16:11; Revelation 12:9; 20:2-3,10

[12] 1 Corinthians 8:5-6; Ephesians 4:4-6; No voice, thought, idea, so-called authority, or any spirit of any kind, has any legal right to overrule the commands of the King of kings in or for your soul.

[13] Luke 4:39,41; Matthew 17:18; Mark 9:25

[14] Numbers 33:51-53; Exodus 23:24; Deuteronomy 7:25-26

[15] John 1:14; Ephesians 3:8,18-19; Colossians 2:3

[16] Philippians 3:12,14; 2 Corinthians 4:18

Let us follow "Yehovah is Salvation"*[1]* into the land of "milk and honey,"[2] where He has a temple,[3] where David (meaning "Beloved") has conquered,[4] and where Solomon (meaning "Peace") is reigning on the throne in absolute spiritual authority,[5] wealth, power, and blessing![6]

HALLELUYAH!

Let us cover the gates of decision with the capable Blood of Yeshua, and let us RULE in His Certainty,[7] Humility,[8] and Gratitude[9] over His land for the glory of His Goodness forever and ever![10]

WARRIORS OF GOD,[11] YOUR GOD HAS CONQUERED ALL![12]

GREAT IS OUR KING, WHO HAS RISEN ABOVE EVERY POWER AND DOMINION![13]

HALLELUUUYAAAAAAAAAAAAAAAAH!!!!!!!!!!!!!!

GREAT IS OUR GOD, WHO CREATED ALL THINGS AND HOLDS THEM TOGETHER![14]

HALLELUUUYAAAAAAAAAAAAAAAAH!!!!!!!!!!!!!

GREAT IS OUR ALMIGHTY SAVIOR, WHO WILL SLAY ALL EVIL WITH THE SWORD OF HIS MOUTH!!!!!![15]

HALLELUUUUUUYAAAAAAAAAAAAAAAAAAAAH!!!!!!!!!!!!!

---

[1] That is, "Joshua," who led the Israelites into the Promised Land, and whose name is the same as the Hebrew Name given to our Savior, traditionally translated as "Jesus."
[2] Exodus 3:8,17; 13:5; 33:3; Leviticus 20:24; Numbers 13:27
[3] Exodus 20:24; 2 Samuel 7:13; 1 Kings 8:29; 9:3
[4] 2 Samuel 5:1-10; Isaiah 9:7; 1 Chronicles 12:38
[5] 1 Kings 4:1; 2 Chronicles 9:30
[6] 2 Chronicles 9:1-31; Ecclesiastes 1:12
[7] Luke 1:4; John 20:31; 2 Peter 1:15-16; Hebrews 11:1
[8] James 4:10; Philippians 2:3-8; Colossians 3:12-13
[9] 1 Thessalonians 5:18; Colossians 2:6-7; Hebrews 12:28
[10] Revelation 3:11; 4:10b; Romans 8:37
[11] 2 Timothy 2:3; Philippians 2:25; Philemon 1:2
[12] Psalm 110:1; Colossians 2:15
[13] Ephesians 1:21; Philippians 2:9-10; Colossians 2:10; Hebrews 1:4
[14] Colossians 1:16-17; Psalm 75:3; Acts 17:28
[15] Revelation 19:11-21; 20:7-10; Luke 1:37

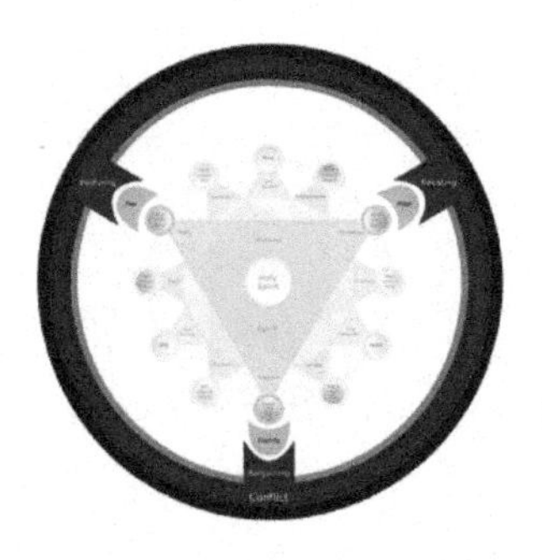

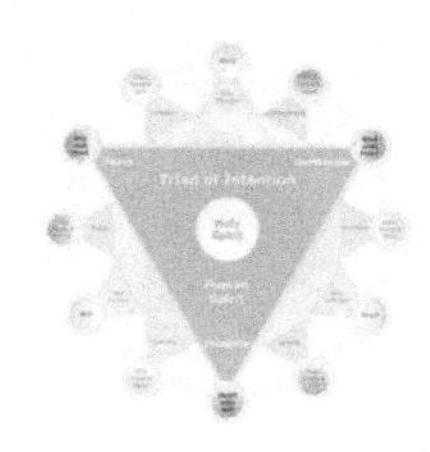

CHAPTER 25

DEFENDING THE TRIAD OF INTENTION

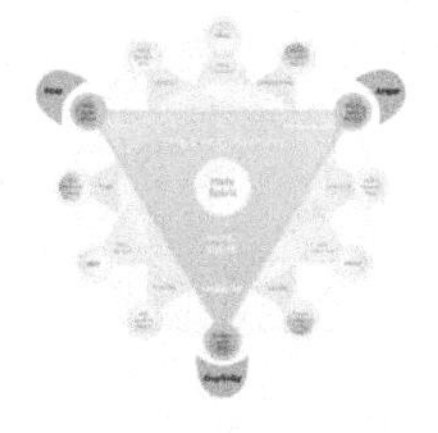

The final layer of the spirit's interaction with the soul occurs at the level of the Triad of Intention.[1]

While the other triads represent functions of one main gate toward another, the gates of this triad represent the connections between any two of the main gates of observation.[2] If the two gates are unified in His Light,[3] then the result is the revelation of His Character.[4] But if the gates are in disagreement through darkness and falsehood, the result contrasts His Character.[5] For just as physical darkness is the absence and "contrast" of physical light, spiritual darkness is the absence and contrast of spiritual Light, which is Goodness.[6]

---

[1] 1 Kings 5:5 – The Scriptural word translated into English as *to intend* or *to purpose* is the Hebrew word אמר, which also means *to speak*. Spirits "intend."

[2] See Chapter 22 of this testimony; Psalm 14:2 (spirits "look/observe"); Psalm 139:2 (spirits "perceive")

[3] John 3:21; 1 John 2:8

[4] Ephesians 5:9; Galatians 5:22-23

[5] John 3:19; Hosea 10:13

[6] Matthew 5:16; John 8:12; 12:46; Acts 26:18; James 1:17

May Yehovah's people be filled with insight![1] May your soul be brought into oneness with Yeshua,[2] and may you overflow with His Peace,[3] Gentleness,[4] and Integrity![5]

Amen!

A unique feature of this triad is that it magnifies ramifications. This is because each gate of this triad represents a relationship between two of the main gates.

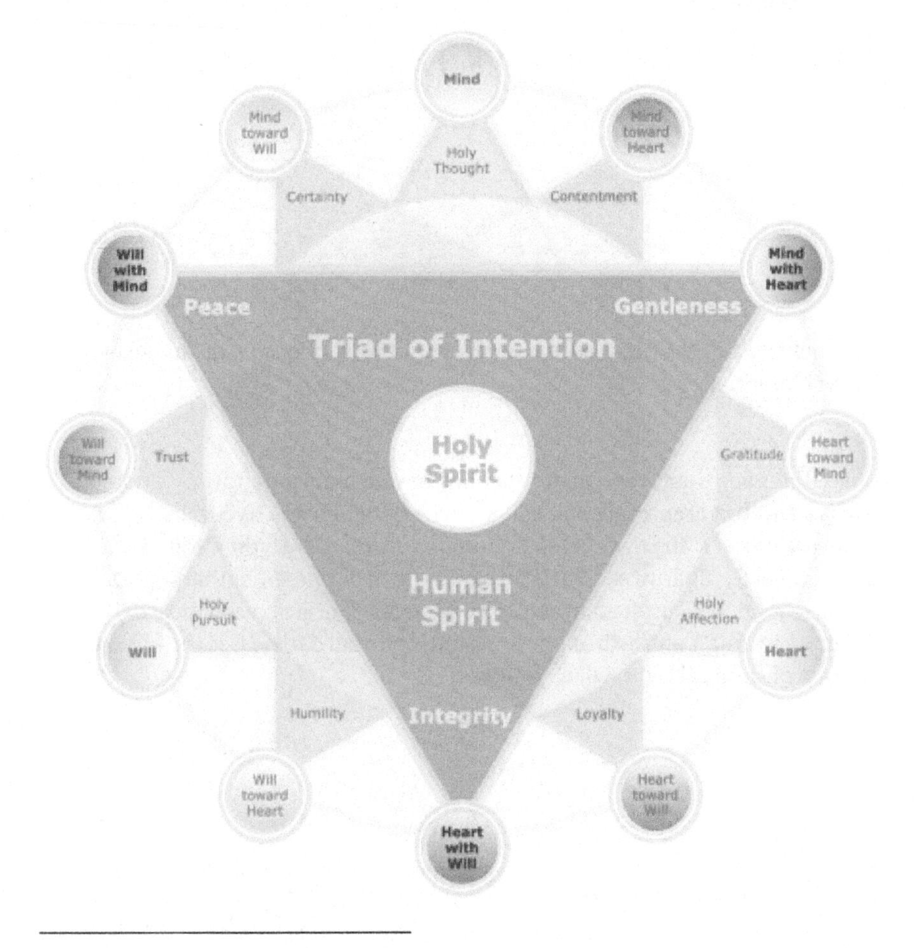

[1] Philippians 1:9; Ephesians 3:4
[2] John 17:11,21-22; 14:20; Romans 15:5-6; 1 Corinthians 1:10-; 12:12-13
[3] John 14:27; 16:33; Romans 5:1-2; Acts 10:36; 1 Corinthians 1:3
[4] Matthew 11:29; 2 Corinthians 10:1
[5] Hebrews 13:8; Matthew 22:16

Anything affecting two of the main gates also has an overflow effect on the third remaining main gate due to its connections with the others.[1] Because of this, each gate of this particular triad represents a functional backdoor to the main gate across from it. And this backdoor effect can work positively or negatively, magnifying the unity or disunity in the soul.[2]

Therefore, if darkness infiltrates the convergence between the will and the heart, duplicity pours into the mind.[3] This influence means that duplicity in the mind cannot be defeated by attempting to renew the mind with statements of Truth, because duplicity's source is not from believing lies in the mind but from accepting

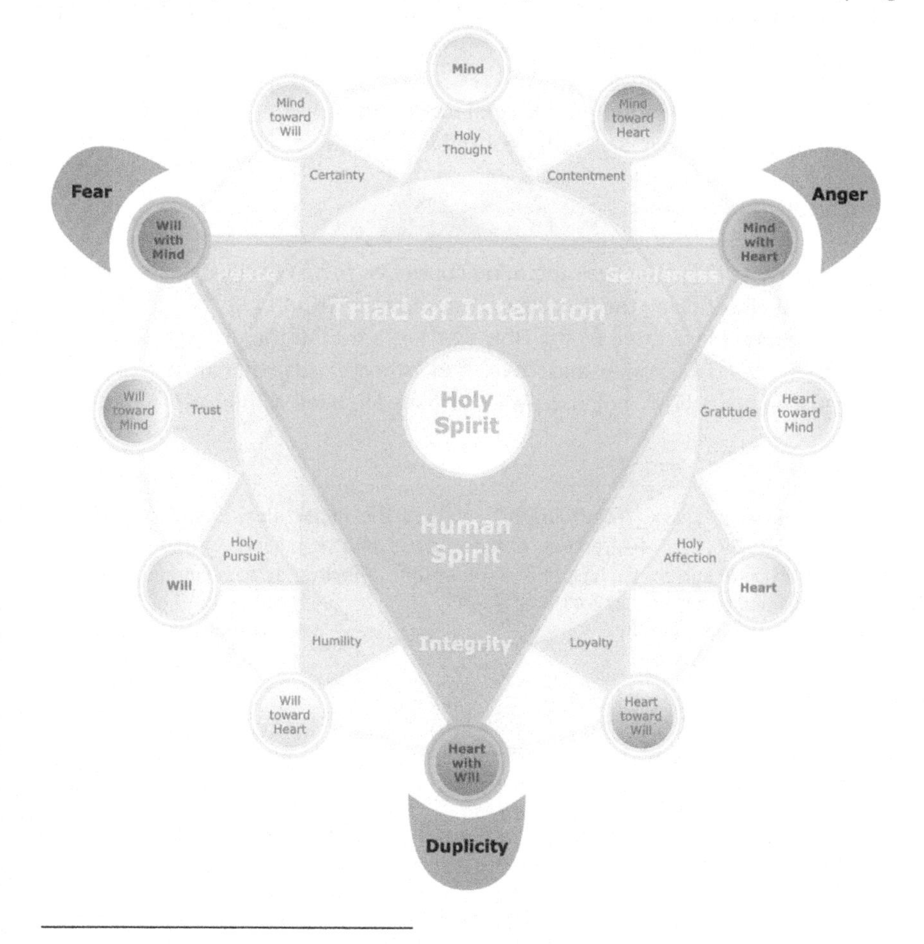

---

[1] 1 Chronicles 28:9; Acts 4:32

[2] Hebrews 12:17; 1 Timothy 6:9; Matthew 6:22-23

[3] Luke 20:20-25; Matthew 23:28; 1 Peter 2:1

darkness in both the will and heart.[1] That is to say, a mind can study without ceasing, but if the soul lacks a righteous and loving life, the mind will not share the strength of Christ.[2] Instead, duplicity is effectively overcome by repentance in the will and love in the heart.[3] Both of these main gates must be covered with the respective Blood of Yeshua.[4] Then the convergence gate between the will and heart must be covered by the Blood of His Integrity,[5] His commands for us regarding integrity,[6] and other Scriptures revealing it.[7] Because of this gate's interaction with the two main gates, this "covering" must include not only the *speaking* of the Scriptures but also the *engagement of their pursuit* through repentance and the *reception of their affection* through reflection and prayer.[8] After all three gates have been overtaken with Light, the spirit of duplicity may be easily bound, silenced, and cast away.[9]

But there's great news! When the connection between the will and the heart is full of Light,[10] the result is integrity poured *into* the mind![11]

HalleluYah!

This pouring effect is one way the mind continues to be renewed even when it is not continually drinking the Word every moment.[12] The integrity flowing from the will and heart is facilitated by the Holy Spirit as a fruit of the unity resulting from sharing in Yeshua's Power and Love.[13] In other words, the mind is not only strengthened by study[14] but also by a righteous life filled with love![15]

---

1 James 4:8; This is why Yeshua sternly rebuked the hypocritical Pharisees (Matthew 23:13,15,23,25,27,29). The affections of their hearts and the pursuits of their wills had to be exposed and stirred to facilitate a repentant affection toward integritous (non-duplicitous) holiness (John 5:42-44).

2 Romans 1:28; John 5:37-47

3 1 Peter 1:22; James 4:8

4 See Chapter 21 of this testimony.

5 Hebrews 13:8; Matthew 22:16; 5:46-48; 6:1-4,6; 23:5,28-30

6 Matthew 6:1,5,16; 22:18

7 Hebrews 4:12-13; Matthew 12:36

8 James 5:16b; Luke 18:1-8

9 Matthew 10:1; 16:19; Mark 1:34; 16:17; James 4:7; Luke 10:17; Acts 16:18; Psalm 31:18

10 Matthew 6:22-23; Luke 11:34-36

11 2 Corinthians 1:12; Revelation 21:23-27

12 2 Corinthians 10:5; Jeremiah 4:14; Hebrews 4:12

13 John 15:2; Hebrews 12:10-11; Philippians 1:9-11

14 Psalm 119:15,23,48,78,97,131,148; James 1:25

15 Mark 5:15; 1 John 3:14,16

HalleluYah!

PRAISE BE TO OUR GOD WHO STRENGTHENS[1] US THROUGH OUR HEARING THE WORD,[2] PURSUING REPENTANCE,[3] AND PRACTICING LOVE![4]

HALLELUYAH!

Now, just as many have been plagued with duplicity, countless children of Yehovah[5] have been attacked by fear.

Let us take a moment for clarification. In English, a physical response to a sudden physical threat is often described as *being scared, afraid, or fearful*. Such perceived threats can often prompt immediate physical reflexes in the body and emotions in the soul before a spirit has time to fully observe, consider, decide, or intend anything.[6] For example, if a person is walking on top of a cliff and momentarily stumbles uncomfortably close to the edge, the resulting rapid heartbeat is *not a spirit of fear* but a physical and soulical reaction to the surprise.[7] However, an uncomfortable foreboding sense that plagues the will's consideration and mind's decision *is most certainly a spirit of fear.*[8]

When darkness breaches the convergence between the will and the mind, it opens the backdoor of the heart to fear.[9] A person receiving fear cannot be rescued by an inward search for peace.[10] Attempts to correct the heart's emotions are futile because the problem is not a weak or wayward heart but an unrepentant will and a mind full of false beliefs.[11] Restoration cannot come by "discovering" peace for the heart but must come through embracing repentance in the will and washing the mind in Truth.[12]

---

[1] Ephesians 3:16; Titus 3:3-8

[2] Luke 24:45; 8:15; 11:28

[3] 1 Timothy 6:11; 2 Timothy 2:22; 1 Peter 3:11

[4] Luke 11:42; Matthew 7:24

[5] Romans 8:14; Galatians 3:26; 1 John 3:1-2; 5:19; Matthew 5:9

[6] Daniel 10:17-19; Ezekiel 1:28

[7] Revelation 1:17a; Daniel 8:18

[8] Deuteronomy 28:66-67

[9] Genesis 3:10; Isaiah 57:11

[10] Numbers 13:27-33; 14:1-4,23-24

[11] Isaiah 59:8; John 20:19

[12] Romans 12:1-2; Daniel 10:19

However, there is good news! While a heart cannot discover peace internally, a fellow soldier can help![1]

HalleluYah!

When a fellow soldier comes with love and the laying on of hands,[2] fear can be cast out through the Power of the Love of Christ![3]

HALLELUYAH!

GLORY TO HIS NAME!

PERFECT LOVE CASTS OUT ALL FEAR![4]

HE LAID DOWN HIS LIFE, AND SO CAN WE![5]

HOLY! HOLY! HOLY[6] IS THE ONE WHO PURCHASED US TO SERVE HIM![7]

HALLELUYAH!

But, even if there are no fellow soldiers around, fear can still be cast out![8]

PRAISE OUR COMPASSIONATE GOD![9]

The soldier can cover the will and the mind with Yeshua's respective Blood,[10] and then the connecting gate must be covered with the Blood of His Peace,[11] His commands for us concerning peace,[12] and other Scriptures revealing it.[13] Once

---

[1] Colossians 3:13; 1 John 4:12
[2] Mark 6:5; Hebrews 6:2
[3] 1 John 4:12,18; Romans 8:15
[4] 1 John 4:18; Romans 8:15
[5] 1 John 3:16; John 15:12-13
[6] Revelation 4:8; Isaiah 6:3; Exodus 15:11
[7] Revelation 5:9-10; Matthew 20:28; 26:28; Acts 20:28; Romans 3:24-26
[8] 2 Peter 1:3; Psalm 84:11; Romans 8:32; 1 Corinthians 3:21-23; 1 Timothy 4:8
[9] Exodus 22:27; 34:6; Psalm 86:15; Joel 2:13; Ephesians 4:32
[10] See Chapter 19 of this testimony.
[11] John 14:27; 16:33; Romans 5:1-2; Acts 10:36; 1 Corinthians 1:3
[12] Luke 10:5; Matthew 10:12-13
[13] Romans 5:1; 8:6; 2 Corinthians 13:11; Ephesians 4:3

these gates are filled with Light, the spirit of fear may be easily bound, silenced, and cast into the darkness of the abyss FOREVER![1]

HALLELUYAH!

But the great news is that when the will and mind are unified in the Light of Yeshua,[2] the result is overflowing peace![3]

OUR GOD PROVIDES![4]

This Peace from the work of the Holy Spirit is the sort that CANNOT fade![5] Even in the midst of pummeling storms, vicious attacks, or significant loss in this world, it will PREVAIL and surpass understanding because it does not come from the heart but is rather poured into it through unity of Yeshua's Truth and Righteousness![6]

HALLELUYAH!

Praise be to our Generous Father,[7] Who withholds from us no good thing,[8] Who gives us Peace overflowing![9]

HALLELUYAH!

And it is important to remember that He gives us good things,[10] because this awareness is an essential blessing for us![11] But the enemy does *not* want us to remember this, because unawareness of it can cause vulnerability to both fear[12] and anger.[13] It is for this reason that darkness attacks the convergence gate between the mind and the heart. Such an assault opens the backdoor of the will to anger.[14]

---

[1] Matthew 10:1; 16:19; Mark 1:34; 16:17; James 4:7; Luke 10:17; Acts 16:18; Psalm 31:18
[2] Matthew 6:22-23; Luke 11:34-36
[3] Romans 8:6; 14:17; Galatians 5:22
[4] 1 Timothy 6:17; Acts 17:25; Psalm 104:28; Matthew 6:32
[5] John 14:27; 16:33; Romans 5:1-2; Acts 10:36; 1 Corinthians 1:3
[6] Philippians 4:6-7; Colossians 3:2; Matthew 6:33
[7] James 1:5; Titus 3:6; 1 Chronicles 29:14
[8] Romans 8:32; Psalm 84:11; 1 Corinthians 2:12; 3:21-23
[9] Romans 15:13; Galatians 5:22; John 4:27
[10] James 1:17; John 1:9; 1 John 1:5; Revelation 21:23; 22:5; Isaiah 60:19
[11] Genesis 3:1; 2 Corinthians 11:14
[12] Luke 12:32; Romans 8:15
[13] 1 John 2:11; Titus 3:3
[14] Psalm 37:8; Proverbs 29:22; James 1:20

Of course, many well-meaning people will often attempt to encourage an angry person to repent from "their temper."[1] But anger cannot be expelled through repentance, because anger does not come from the will but is poured into it through the mind and heart.[2]

Especially unhelpful are the lies propagated by evil in almost every culture, ascribing anger as a "genetic trait" of this or that sort of people from this or that sort of place!

THOSE ARE LIES FROM FALLEN SPIRITS MEANT TO HARM YOU![3]

YOU'RE NOT AN "ANGRY PERSON!"[4]

PEOPLE DON'T "NEED TO WATCH OUT" WHEN YOU GET MAD![5]

YOU'RE THE REDEEMED OF YEHOVAH,[6] FULL OF GENTLENESS,[7] GRACE,[8] AND TRUTH![9]

YOU DON'T *NEED* TO GET MAD![10]

YOU HAVE EVERYTHING YOU COULD EVER WANT, HOPE FOR, OR IMAGINE![11]

HALLELUYAH!

GLORY BE TO THE NAME OF YESHUA, WHO FREED US FROM SELFISH ANGER![12]

HALLELUYAH!

---

[1] 1 Samuel 20:7; Mark 5:2-4
[2] Proverbs 14:29; Ecclesiastes 7:9
[3] 1 Corinthians 10:13; 1 Peter 5:8-9; Luke 22:46
[4] Ephesians 4:32; Mark 11:25-26; Luke 6:37; 11:4; Colossians 3:12-13; Romans 12:20-21; 1 Peter 3:8-9; 1 John 2:12
[5] 2 Timothy 2:24; James 4:2
[6] Galatians 3:13-14; 4:5; Titus 2:14; 1 Peter 1:18
[7] 2 Corinthians 10:1; Philippians 4:5
[8] Ephesians 1:6; John 1:16; Acts 20:32
[9] 1 John 2:20; John 16:13; 1 Corinthians 2:15
[10] Colossians 3:8; Ephesians 4:22; Hebrews 12:1
[11] Ephesians 3:20; Romans 8:32; Psalm 84:11; 1 Corinthians 2:12; 3:21-23
[12] Romans 6:22,14,18; 8:2; John 8:32; 2 Corinthians 3:17; Galatians 5:13

DON'T BUY THE LIE THAT SELFISH ANGER IS A USEFUL THING![1] IT'S NOTHING BUT A STUMBLING BLOCK![2]

YOU WERE MADE TO GLORIFY JESUS CHRIST![3] THAT'S WHAT'S USEFUL! THAT'S WHAT "GET'S THINGS DONE!"[4]

CRUSH THE SELFISH ANGER[5] WITH HOLY GENTLENESS[6] BECAUSE YEHOVAH HAS MADE YOU SO STRONG THAT YOU DON'T EVER NEED TO ENTERTAIN WORLDLY ANGER AGAIN![7]

HALLELUYAH!!!!

HALLELUYAAAAAAAAAAAAAAAH!!!!!!!!!!!

HALLELUUUUUUUUUUUUYAAAAAAAAAAAAAAAH!!!!!!!!!!!

WE WALK IN JOY[8] BECAUSE WE ARE STRONG IN HIM!!!!![9]

BLESS GOD!!!!!

So, expel that fruitless spirit of selfish anger![10] Cover the mind and heart with the respective Blood of Yeshua in Truth[11] and Affection![12] Then cover the gate between them[13] by the Blood of His Gentleness[14] and Peace,[15] His commands for us,[16] and other commands from His Scriptures concerning gentleness and peace.[17]

---

[1] James 1:20; Numbers 20:11-12; 2 Timothy 2:24-25

[2] Ephesians 4:26-27; 2 Corinthians 6:3

[3] Romans 15:6; Romans 15:9-11; Matthew 5:16; 1 Peter 2:12

[4] Ephesians 1:11-12; Isaiah 46:10-11

[5] Romans 16:20; Psalm 91:13; James 1:20

[6] Philippians 4:5; Matthew 11:29; 1 Peter 3:15

[7] Romans 8:37; Isaiah 25:8; 1 Corinthians 15:57; 1 John 4:4; 5:4-5; Jude 1:24

[8] John 15:11; 16:24; 17:13; 1 Peter 1:8; Jude 1:24

[9] 2 Timothy 1:7; Romans 8:15

[10] James 1:20; Numbers 20:11-12; 2 Timothy 2:24-25

[11] Luke 20:21; John 17:17; 14:6

[12] John 15:9-17; 13:34; 17:23,26; Ephesians 3:18; Revelation 1:5

[13] Deuteronomy 6:6-9; Exodus 13:9,16; Numbers 15:38-39; Proverbs 3:3; 6:21; 7:3; Hebrews 2:1

[14] Matthew 11:29; 2 Corinthians 10:1

[15] John 14:27; 16:33; Romans 5:1-2; Acts 10:36; 1 Corinthians 1:3

[16] John 20:19,21,26; Luke 6:27:35

[17] Ephesians 4:2; 2 Corinthians 13:11

After this, the spirit of anger may be bound, silenced, and banished to the outer darkness where that foolish tantrum belongs.[1]

But more good news is that, when the mind and heart are unified in Yeshua's Truth and Love, His Gentleness is poured directly into the will![2] And because this Gentleness is coming from the Holy Spirit acting through the mind and the heart, the will cannot be corrupted even during persecution![3]

BLESS GOD!!!

Even in the face of MARTYRDOM, the will filled with gentleness will be INCORRUPTIBLE because its source is not the will of the soul but the fruit from a persevering life lived in truth and love through the Holy Spirit![4] And this Holy Spirit is the same Spirit that empowered the perfect Soul of Jesus Christ to walk without sin,[5] defeat the Devil,[6] endure the cross,[7] and rise from the dead![8]

HALLELUYAH!

Praise be to the Kings of kings and Lord of lords, our God and Savior, Who has blessed us with every spiritual blessing in Him![9] Through this great Love, we learn that we are one with Him,[10] sharing in His Blessings,[11] His Reign,[12] and His Joy![13]

HALLELUYAH!

ALL PRAISE, GLORY, AND POWER BE TO OUR GOD![14]

---

[1] Acts 1:25; 16:18; Matthew 10:1; 16:19; Mark 1:34; 16:17; James 4:7; Luke 10:17; Psalm 31:18
[2] Matthew 11:29; 2 Corinthians 10:1
[3] Isaiah 53:7; Luke 6:29; Mark 4:17
[4] Revelation 12:11; 2 Corinthians 10:3-5; Ephesians 6:12-18; 1 John 4:4
[5] 2 Corinthians 5:21; Philippians 3:9
[6] Colossians 2:15; Acts 2:32-36; John 12:31; 16:11; Revelation 12:9; 20:2-3,10
[7] Hebrews 12:2; Acts 5:31; Psalms 138:8
[8] John 11:25-26; Romans 8:11
[9] Ephesians 1:3; 2:6; Genesis 12:2-3; 1 Chronicles 4:10; Isaiah 61:9; Galatians 3:9
[10] Galatians 3:28; John 10:16; 11:52; 17:20-21; 1 Corinthians 12:12; Ephesians 2:13-22; 4:4,15-16
[11] Romans 8:17; 1 Timothy 2:10; John 12:26
[12] 2 Timothy 2:12; Romans 5:21; Revelation 2:26-28; 3:21
[13] John 15:10-11; 16:24; 17:13; Romans 15:13; 2 Corinthians 1:24
[14] Revelation 4:11; 5:12-13; 7:12

HE HAS RESCUED US FROM DARKNESS![1]

HE HAS FREELY GIVEN US ALL THINGS THROUGH HIS LOVE![2]

HALLELUYAH!

HE HAS MADE US TO BE PILLARS IN HIS HOLY TEMPLE![3]

CHILDREN IN HIS OWN HOUSE![4]

HALLELUYAH!

WHAT A MIGHTY AND GLORIOUS GOD WE HAVE AS A FRIEND AND FATHER![5]

HALLELUYAAAAAAAAAAH!!!!!!!!!!!!!!

HALLELUYAAAAAAAAAAH!!!!!!!!!!!!!!

HALLELUYAAAAAAAAAAH!!!!!!!!!!!!!!

Glory be to His Holy Name![6]

Now, praise our Holy King, that once all the gates of the Triad of Intention have been sealed, the power of our spirit's governance over the soul will be fully restored![7]

THANKS BE TO YEHOVAH!!!!!!!!!!!!

Therefore, let us understand that each triad of the soul is essential for spiritual dominion.[8] The Triad of Observation permits the spiritual eyes to see.[9] The Triad

---

[1] Colossians 1:13; Isaiah 49:24-25; Matthew 12:29-30; Acts 26:18; Hebrews 2:14

[2] Romans 8:32; Psalm 84:11; 1 Corinthians 2:12; 3:21-23; 2 Peter 1:3

[3] Revelation 3:12; Galatians 2:9; Jeremiah 1:18

[4] Revelation 7:15; Psalm 134:1-2; 1 Corinthians 3:16

[5] Ephesians 5:20; Colossians 1:11-12; Matthew 5:45

[6] Psalm 105:3; Revelation 15:4

[7] Psalm 23:3; Galatians 5:22-23

[8] 1 Thessalonians 5:23; Ephesians 1:18-23; Colossians 1:13

[9] Matthew 13:16; 16:17; Acts 26:18; 2 Corinthians 4:6; Ephesians 1:18

of Consideration provides the spiritual insight to reflect.[1] The Triad of Decision enables spiritual choices to be made.[2] And the Triad of Intention empowers the spirit to grasp the reins of the soul and guide it into His full Character and perfect Power for His Glory![3]

Praise our God for giving wisdom to us![4]

Thank You, Lord.

Thank You, Gracious Father.

Thank You.

Thank You.

Thank You.

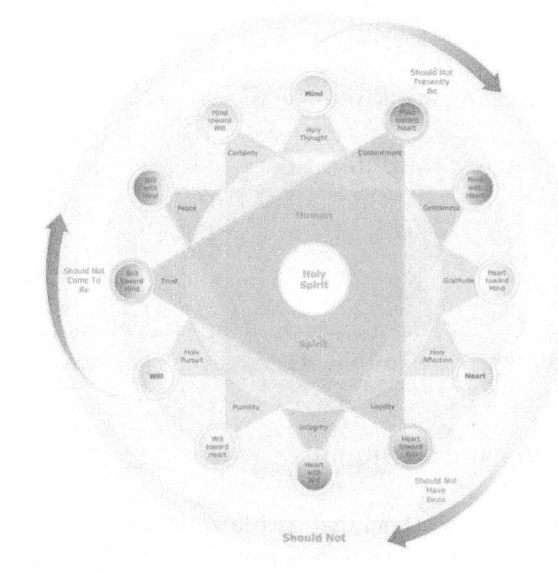

[1] 2 Timothy 2:7; 1 Timothy 4:15; Proverbs 24:32
[2] Deuteronomy 30:19b; Joshua 24:15-22; Psalm 119:173; Luke 10:42; Isaiah 56:4
[3] Matthew 18:18; Revelation 3:7-8; Galatians 5:16
[4] James 1:5; Proverbs 2:6; Ecclesiastes 2:26; Daniel 2:21

CHAPTER 26

THE KEY TO THE CITY

When overtaking and guarding the city of our soul,[1] a child of Yehovah does not always have the convenience of quiet and undisturbed solace.[2] Observations, considerations, decisions, and intentions are often in quick demand, so the person's spirit must have a means to guide the soul in quickly determining what characteristics are simultaneously flowing in or out of multiple gates.[3] To do this, one needs a key to the city,[4] and that key is called "For His Glory."[5]

In recent years many have tried to use many sorts of keys, with the most well-known being "What Would Jesus Do?" However, as useful as this key can prove, it is often not effective enough in more complex situations requiring wisdom. For example, it might not provide ears for quick wisdom regarding whether Yeshua would apologize for a particular sin, because Yeshua never sinned in any way.[6]

However, Yeshua has provided a key that is effective and precise:

---

[1] Matthew 5:14; Ephesians 5:8-14; Philippians 2:15
[2] Mark 1:35; Luke 4:42; John 6:15
[3] 2 Timothy 4:2; John 4:6-10; Acts 16:13,31-33; 20:7,18-21
[4] Matthew 16:19; Isaiah 22:22; Revelation 1:18; 3:7
[5] John 7:18; 8:49-50; 1 Corinthians 10:31; 1 Thessalonians 2:6; 1 Peter 4:11
[6] 1 John 3:5; 1 Peter 2:22; 2 Corinthians 5:21; Hebrews 4:15

"Whoever speaks from themself does so to gain glory for themself, but the person who seeks the glory of the One Who sent them is a person of truth; there is nothing unrighteous in them."[1]

By this we understand that when seeking the glory of the One Who sent us, we are people of truth with nothing false in us. And by "seeking His Glory," we mean that we are seeking to facilitate the revelation of Yehovah's unseen spiritual Characteristics.[2]

To know what glorifies Him, we must know His *decreed* Word, or Logos,[3] and hear His *applied* Word, or Rhema.[4] Therefore, since we have already been given His Holy Spirit with His Living Rhema,[5] let us know His Logos[6] that we may be fully equipped in knowing what glorifies Him.[7]

When we are speaking of His Logos concerning the Key of His Glory, we may refer to those Scriptures that address the twelve gates of the soul as the "Circle of Christ," meaning the "Scriptures testifying to the Character of Yeshua represented in each of the twelve gates."[8]

Though all of the redeemed are children of Yehovah,[9] each of us is unique.[10] Each of us has a special relationship with our Creator.[11] And though He has given His Word to all of us, each of us holds the Sword in our own hand.[12] Therefore, for each seasoned warrior, Yeshua forges our own sword in the fire of battle.[13] It

---

[1] John 7:18; 8:49-50; 1 Corinthians 10:31; 1 Thessalonians 2:6; 1 Peter 4:11

[2] Hebrews 1:3; Ephesians 1:17-21; John 1:4; 17:4-6

[3] Revelation 19:13 – *Word* from the Greek λόγος, pronounced "law'-gaws," and transliterated *Logos*, meaning *word* with an emphasis that it is a *decree, doctrine, mandate,* or *moral precept.*

[4] Matthew 18:16 – *Word* from the Greek ῥῆμα, pronounced "rey'-mah," and transliterated *Rhema,* meaning *word* with an emphasis that it is an *utterance by a living thing, a matter of command, or a matter of narration.*

[5] Matthew 4:4; Luke 7:1; John 6:31-59

[6] John 14:23; 1 John 1:1; 5:7; Revelation 19:13

[7] 2 Corinthians 3:18; 2 Peter 1:3; Psalm 84:11; Romans 8:32; 1 Corinthians 3:21-23

[8] Understand that these Scriptures do not represent methods but reference points in understanding our living relationship with Him (Ephesians 1:17); Revelation 21:12; Isaiah 60:18

[9] Romans 8:14; Galatians 3:26; 1 John 3:1-2; 5:19; Matthew 5:9

[10] 1 Corinthians 12:14-20,27; Romans 12:5; Ephesians 5:30

[11] Revelation 2:17c; Romans 14:4

[12] Ephesians 6:17; Hebrews 4:12

[13] 1Corinthians 12:12; 15:49

becomes an extension of our soul, fitting well and moving deftly with skill and finesse; the Logos becomes Rhema when spoken through us.[1]

Here is an *example* of a Circle of Christ. It is more than able to be wielded for victory in any battle by any of the redeemed:

Mind; Truth-

"'Who has known the mind of the Lord so as to keep pace with Him?' But we have the mind of Christ."[2]

"Love the Lord your God with all your heart and with all your soul and with all your *mind* and with all your will."[3]

Yeshua answered them, "I am the Way and the *Truth* and the Life. No one comes toward the Father except through me."[4]

Mind toward Heart; Contentment -

"I am not saying this because I am facing poverty, because I have learned to exist as content wherever I exist. I have experienced humble living, and I have experienced abundance. All in all I have been intimately acquainted, whether well-fed or hungry, whether living in plenty or in lack. I can do all this through Him who empowers me."[5]

"But godliness with contentment is great gain. Because we carried nothing into the world, and we can carry nothing out of it. But if we have food and clothing, with these we will be content. Those who want to become wealthy fall into temptation and a trap and into many foolish and harmful desires that sink people

---

[1] Luke 6:47-48; Acts 11:14

[2] 1 Corinthians 2:16; See also John 15:15; 16:13-15

[3] Mark 12:30 – *Heart* is from the Greek word καρδία, pronounced "kar-dee-ah," meaning *the seat of affections, appetites, and passions. Mind* is from διάνοια, pronounced "dee-ahn'-oy-ah," meaning *deep thought.* And *strength* is from ἰσχύς, pronounced "ihs-khoos," meaning *forcefulness, ability,* or *might.* While the word does mean *strength,* in this context it is a reference not to a physical strength but to the strength of a soul, that is, a *strength of will.*

[4] John 14:6

[5] Philippians 4:11-13; See also Luke 9:58

into destruction and damnation. The love of money, therefore, is a root of all evil by which some coveters have been led astray from the faith, piercing their souls with all sorts of sorrows. But you, man of God, flee these things and pursue righteousness, godliness, faith, love, endurance, and gentleness."[1]

"But He said to me, 'My grace is sufficient for you, for My power is accomplished in weakness.' Therefore, I will glory in great pleasure about my weaknesses, so that Christ's power may rest on me. That is why I delight in weaknesses, insults, hardships, persecutions, and difficulties for the sake of Christ. Because when I am weak, then I am powerful."[2]

Mind with Heart; Gentleness-

"Take My yoke upon you and learn by practice from Me, because I am gentle and humble in heart, and you will find rest for your souls."[3]

"With all humility and gentleness in patience, bearing with one another in love, endeavor to keep the unity of the Spirit through the bond of peace. There is one body and one Spirit, just as you were called to the one hope of your calling; one Lord, one faith, one baptism; one God and Father of all, who is over all, through all, and in us all."[4]

"But in your hearts venerate the Lord as God. Moreover, be prepared to give an answer to everyone who asks you to give an explanation for the hope within you. Yet do this with gentleness and respect, keeping a good moral conscience, so that slanderers, if they were to bad mouth your good behavior in Christ, may be ashamed of their slander."[5]

Heart toward Mind; Gratitude-

"He told the crowd to sit down on the ground. And having taken the seven loaves and given thanks, He broke them and was giving them to his disciples so that they could continue to distribute them to the people. And they had a few small fish that He blessed and commanded to be distributed as well."[6]

---

[1] 1 Timothy 6:6-11
[2] 2 Corinthians 12:9-10
[3] Matthew 11:29
[4] Ephesians 4:2-6
[5] 1 Peter 3:15-16
[6] Mark 8:6-7

"Rejoice always, cause yourself to continually pray to God, give thanks in all situations; because this is God's will in Christ Jesus for you. Do not suppress the Spirit. Do not dismiss prophecies but discern them all; hold on to what is good, abstain from every appearance of evil."[1]

"Do not be intoxicated with wine, which leads to fallenness. Instead, be well-supplied with the Spirit, speaking among yourselves with psalms, hymns, and spiritual songs. Sing and make music in your heart to the Lord, always giving thanks for everything to God the Father in the Name of our Lord Jesus Christ."[2]

Heart; Love -

"But Yeshua said to him: 'Love the Lord your God with all your *heart* and with all your soul and with all your mind.'"[3]

"To love him with all your heart, with all your understanding, will all your soul, and with all your will, and to love your neighbor as yourself matters more than all burnt offerings and sacrifices."[4]

"Having purified yourselves in obedience of the truth through the Spirit enabling entrance into sincere love for each other, love one another fervently from the heart."[5]

Heart toward Will; Loyalty -

"Therefore, Yeshua answered and said to them, "I assure you, the Son can do nothing at all from Himself; He can do only whatever He sees His Father would be doing. Because, in fact, the very things He would be doing, the Son also does."[6]

"Someone who says, 'I know Him,' but is not keeping His commandments, is a liar, and the truth is not in them. But if someone does keep His Word, the Love of God

---

[1] 1 Thessalonians 5:16-22
[2] Ephesians 5:18-20
[3] Mat 22:37
[4] Mark 12:33
[5] 1 Peter 1:22
[6] John 5:19

is truly consummated in them. This is how we know that we are in Him: someone who says they abide in Him ought themself also to walk just as He walked."[1]

"And He called the crowd to Himself along with His disciples and told them, 'If anyone desires to follow Me, they must utterly deny themself in the same way, pick up their cross, and follow Me continually. Because whoever wants to save their life will lose it, but whoever loses their life for My sake and for the gospel will save it.'"[2]

Heart with Will; Integrity -

"But beware of giving charitable donations before other people in order to be seen by them, because then you will have no reward from your Father Who is in Heaven. Therefore, whenever you donate, do not sound a trumpet before you, like the hypocrites do in the synagogues and in the streets, that they may receive praise from others. I assure you, they have received their reward. But when you make a donation, do not let your left hand know what your right hand is doing, so that your donation may be a secret. And your Father Who sees in secret will reward you."[3]

"So whoever is knowing the right thing to do and is failing to do it, for them it is sin."[4]

"One who is trustworthy with very little is also trustworthy with much, and one who is dishonest with very little is also dishonest with much."[5]

Will toward Heart; Humility -

"Neither be called teachers, because you have one Teacher, the Christ. The greatest among you will be your servant. Whoever honors themself will be humbled, and whoever humbles themself will be honored."[6]

---

[1] 1 John 2:4-6
[2] Mark 8:34-35
[3] Matthew 6:1-4 – If your goal in giving is impure, then impurity will be your reward; but if your goal is pure, you will receive His Purity as it shines through you.
[4] James 4:17
[5] Luke 16:10
[6] Matthew 23:10-12

"Have this mind[1] among yourselves, which is yours in Christ Jesus, Who already being the very image of God, did not consider it robbery to be equal with God, but still emptied Himself of honor, taking the form of a servant born in the likeness of a man. And being found in human condition, He humbled Himself, becoming obedient to the point of death, even death on a cross."[2]

"At that time the disciples came to Yeshua, saying, 'Who is the greatest in the Kingdom of Heaven?' And calling to Him a child, he stood him in the midst of them and said, 'I assure you, unless you turn and become like children, you will not enter the Kingdom of Heaven. Therefore, whoever humbles themself like this child is the greatest in the Kingdom of Heaven.'" [3]

Will; Pursuit -

"Love the Lord your God with all your heart and with all your soul and with all your mind and with all your *will*."[4]

"Actively ask and it will be given to you; actively seek and you will find; actively knock and the door will be opened to you. Because everyone who is asking receives; the one who is seeking finds; and to the one who is knocking, the door will be opened."[5]

"Are you not aware that in a stadium all the runners run, yet only one attains the victor's prize? Desperately run in such a way as to eagerly attain the prize. But all who compete in the competitions train with strict self-discipline. They do this to

---

[1] The Greek word φρονέω, pronounced "froh-neh'-oh," here translated into English as *mind*, emphasizes the meaning *to interest oneself,* or *to set affections on,* which are clearly actions of the will (pursuits). Considering the context of action in this verse, it should rather read, "Have this *pursuit* among yourselves..." Contrast this with the word νοῦς, pronounced "noos" and found in Scriptures like 1 Corinthians 2:16, which is also translated as *mind* and means *mind, intellect,* or *understanding.*

[2] Philippians 2:5-8

[3] Matthew 18:1-4

[4] Mark 12:30 – *Heart* is from the Greek word καρδία, pronounced "kar-dee-ah," meaning *the seat of affections, appetites, and passions. Mind* is from διάνοια, pronounced "dee-ahn'-oy-ah," meaning *deep thought.* And *will* is from ἰσχύς, pronounced "ihs-khoos," meaning *forcefulness, ability,* or *might.* While the word does mean *strength,* in this context it is a reference not to a physical strength but to the strength of a soul, that is, a *strength of will.*

[5] Matthew 7:7-8

attain a crown of leaves that will decay, but we do this to attain a crown that will last forever."[1]

Will toward Mind; Trust -

"Do not let your hearts be troubled. Trust in God, and in Me you are trusting."[2]

So do not worry by saying, 'What will we eat?' or 'What will we drink? 'or 'What will we wear?' Because the worldly run after all these things, and your Heavenly Father knows that you need all of them. But seek first His Kingdom and his Righteousness, and all these things will be added to you as well. So do not worry about tomorrow, because tomorrow will worry about itself. Each day has enough of its own trouble to manage." [3]

"Because you have made 'Yehovah my Refuge, the Most High,' your refuge, no evil will overtake you, nor will an assault come near your dwelling. For He will command his angels over you to guard you in all your ways."[4]

Will with Mind; Peace –

"Peace I leave to you; My Peace I give to you. I do not give to you how the world gives. Do not let your hearts be troubled or afraid."[5]

"Do not be worried about anything at all, but in every situation, by prayer and petition, with thanksgiving, let your requests be made known to God. And the Peace of God, which transcends all understanding, will guard your hearts and minds in Yeshua the Messiah."[6]

"But while they were still talking about these things, Yeshua Himself stood among them and said to them, 'Peace be with you.'"[7]

---

[1] 1 Corinthians 9:24-25
[2] John 14:1
[3] Matthew 6:31-34
[4] Psalm 91:9-11
[5] John 14:27
[6] Philippians 4:6-7
[7] Luke 24:36

Mind toward Will; Certainty -

"We *know* that anyone born of God does not keep sinning; the One who was born of God guards them, and the evil one does not touch them. We *know* that we are children of God, and that the whole world is subjecting itself to evil. We *know* also that the Son of God has come and has given us understanding, so that we may *know* Him Who is True. And we are in Him Who is True, in His Son Jesus Christ, Who is the true God and eternal Life."[1]

"Jesus said to them, 'I am the Way and the Truth and the Life. No one comes near the Father if not through Me. If you really ever knew Me, you will personally know My Father as well. As of now, *you do know Him* and have experienced Him.'"[2]

"Then he said to Thomas, 'Put your finger here and see My hands. Reach out your hand and thrust it into My side. Stop being doubtful but be certain.'"[3]

Again, this Circle of Christ is more than adequate as an effective weapon for any child of Yehovah defending the gates of the soul. However, as a warrior gains experience, the sword will grow and conform into a unique set of blades known only to that person and Yeshua.[4]

HALLELUYAH!

OUR LORD GOD ALMIGHTY REIGNS![5]

JESUS IS MY KINGDOM, AND MY KINGDOM IS JESUS!!![6]

BLESS GOD!

EVERYTHING I NEED IS IN HIM, AND HE IS EVERYTHING I NEED![7]

---

[1] 1 John 5:18-20

[2] John 14:6-7

[3] John 20:27 – *Certain,* from the Greek πιστός, pronounced "pihs-taws'," meaning *believing, trusting,* or *sure.*

[4] Revelation 2:17c; Romans 12:4; 1 Corinthians 14:26

[5] Psalm 99:1; Revelation 1:18; 4:9; 11:15; 19:6; 21:27; Hebrews 1:8

[6] Matthew 4:17; 11:11-12; 12:28; 16:19,28; 25:34; Luke 17:21; 22:29

[7] John 3:15; 5:26; Acts 17:28; 1 Corinthians 1:5,19; 2 Corinthians 5:21; Ephesians 1:11,13; 2:15,22; 3:12; Philippians 3:9; Colossians 1:16-19; 2:6,11; 2 Timothy 1:12; 1 John 1:5; 2:5,27-28; 3:3,15,24; 5:20

HALLELUYAH!

HE IS MY FORTRESS![1]

HALLELUYAH!

HE IS MY PROVISION![2]

HALLELUYAH!

HE IS MY VALUE![3]
HALLELUYAH!

HE IS MY PURPOSE![4]

HALLELUYAH!

HE IS MY LIFE!!!!!!!!!!!!!!!![5]

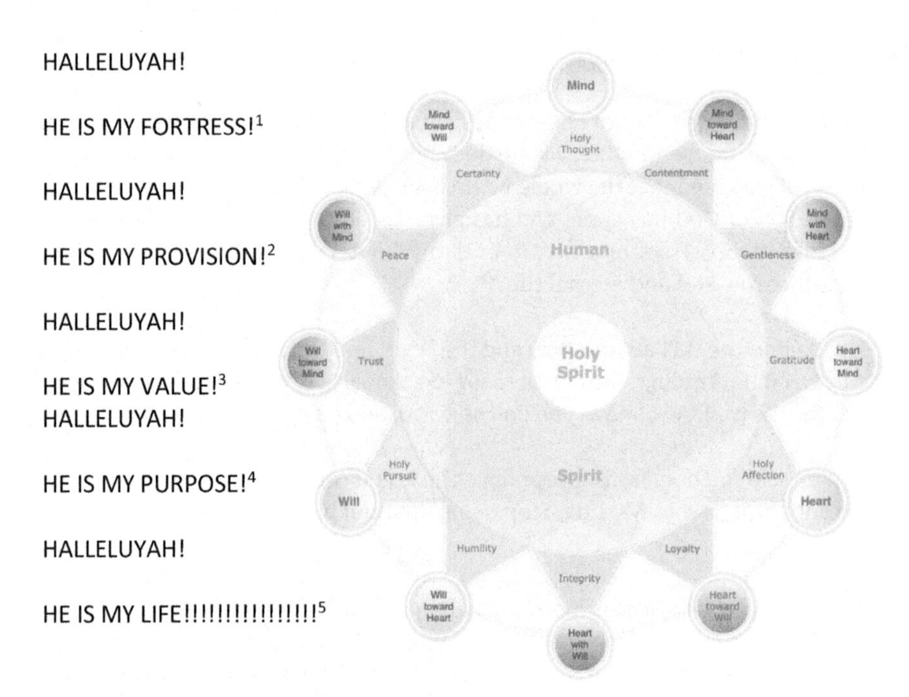

HALLELUUUUUUUUUYAAAAAAAAAAAAAAAAAH!!!!!!!

[1] 2 Samuel 22:2; Psalm 18:2; 31:3; 71:3; 91:2; 144:2
[2] Genesis 22:14; Psalm 22:4-5; Luke 12:32
[3] 1 Corinthians 4:5; 2 Corinthians 10:18; 1 Peter 1:7; 5:4; Romans 2:29; John 5:44
[4] Galatians 2:19; Romans 14:7-8; 1 Corinthians 10:31
[5] Romans 6:23; John 4:14; 6:27; 1 Peter 1:3-4; 1 John 5:11-12

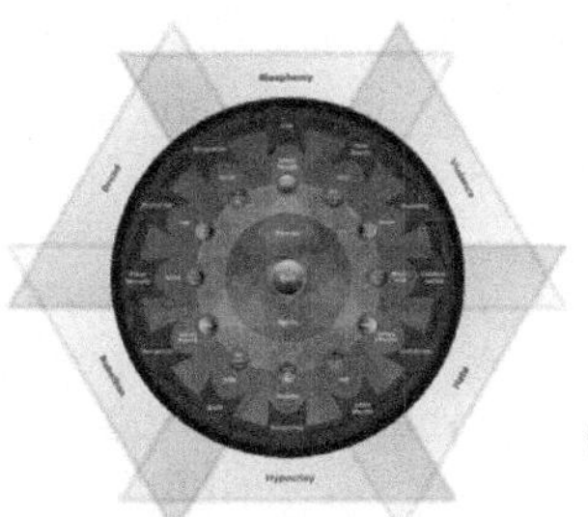

CHAPTER 27

BINDING, SILENCING, AND CASTING OUT DARK SPIRITS

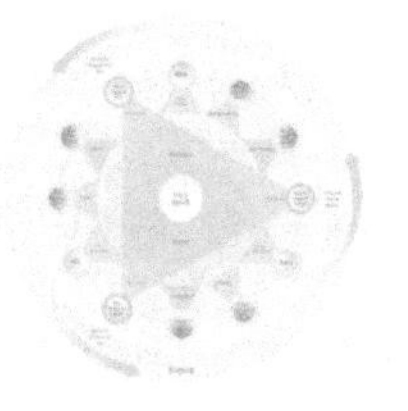

To cast out a dark spirit, a person must first recognize that it *is* a dark spirit.[1]

All dark behaviors are from dark spirits.[2] A good tree grows from a good seed and does not bear bad fruit.[3] Anyone who has been redeemed has been planted as a good seed of Christ.[4] They grow from Christ, and they bear the fruit of His Character.[5] They do not bear bad fruit. Any bad fruit in the soul of the redeemed, in their promised land,[6] is the result of bad seeds planted by the enemy.[7] To be rid of bad fruit, a person must be rid of the bad seeds growing in their land.[8] Their soul must be rid of the dark spirits affecting them.

Or again, demonization is like the experience of a particular homeowner when she heard reports from family members of mysterious damage and thefts in her home. After investigating, she learned that one of her sons had invited a friend to stay in

---

[1] 1 John 4:1; Deuteronomy 13:1-5; 1 Thessalonians 5:21
[2] John 8:43-44; Ephesians 2:2; 6:12
[3] Matthew 7:18; Galatians 5:17; 1 John 3:9-10
[4] Matthew 13:38a; 1 John 3:9
[5] John 15:4-5; Colossians 1:10; Galatians 5:22-23
[6] Hebrews 3:11-4:13; Revelation 1:6; 5:10
[7] Matthew 13:38b-39; 2 Corinthians 11:13-15
[8] Matthew 3:10; Malachi 3:1-3; 4:1; 1 Peter 4:17-18

his room. In tears, the son vouched for his friend, who claimed innocence. But in wisdom, the homeowner sent the friend away, and the damage and thefts immediately ceased.

Understand that you are the homeowner of your soul, and the son represents your personal beliefs and experiences. When you see damage and loss in your peace, righteousness, and joy, know that this is not from you or your efforts.[1] You have been deceived by a destructive and thieving spirit claiming invitation and innocence.[2]

Yeshua does not give as the world gives![3] Freely He has given His blessings to you![4] If they are missing, it is because they are being stolen![5] Stop entertaining that dark spirit,[6] and your soul will overflow with Yeshua's blessings and love for you![7]

HalleluYah!

God does not "partially" save us![8]

He died for us! He died to show that He loves us that much![9]

So be encouraged! Yehovah is not holding victory back from you![10]

To banish a dark spirit, you must fight with the truth of Yehovah's Word in your mind, the pursuit of His Righteousness in your will, and the protective affection of both His Love of Goodness and His Refusal of darkness in your heart.[11]

Just as with anger, there are two different sorts of "hate." In English, they really should be called by two different names. There is the sort of hate that is a combination of hypocrisy and violence.[12] Its root is selfishness, which is the

---

[1] Matthew 13:28; John 10:10
[2] 2 Corinthians 11:3; Revelation 12:9; 2 Timothy 4:3-4; 2 Peter 3:17
[3] John 14:27b; Psalm 27:1; 56:11; 112:7
[4] Matthew 10:8b; Acts 3:6; 1 Chronicles 29:14
[5] John 10:10a; Luke 8:12
[6] Matthew 9:4; Ezekiel 38:10; Haggai 2:13-14
[7] 1 Corinthians 5:7; 10:16-17; 1 Thessalonians 3:12
[8] John 15:6; 1 Corinthians 3:11-15
[9] 1 John 4:9-10; Romans 3:25-26; 1 Peter 2:24; 3:18
[10] 1 Corinthians 15:57; Romans 8:37; 1 John 5:4-5
[11] Hebrews 1:9; Jude 1:23; Revelation 2:6
[12] 2 Samuel 13:4-15; Genesis 37:4-5,8

essence of evil,[1] and it is the opposite of godly love.[2] Then there is the sort of *selfless* hate that abhors evil,[3] that has no tolerance for anything less than moral perfection.[4] It is this sort of selflessness that is willing to risk personal inconvenience and injury to eradicate evil.[5] So, in this testimony, "hate" is a reference to the evil sort, and "refusal" is a description of the holy sort.

Yehovah is a Good Father![6] He's the Best in every way![7] If you ask Him for "bread," He will not give you a "stone."[8] That is, if you ask for nourishment for your faith, He's not going to give you something that will "break the teeth" of your soul! If you find a "stone" when you're looking for "bread," it is because a dark and lying spirit has stolen the bread[9] and left a stone![10]

PRAISE YEHOVAH THAT NO SUCH LYING, THIEVING, DESTROYING SPIRIT WILL ENTER HEAVEN![11]

HALLELUYAH!

PRAISE OUR GOD, WHO IS HOLY,[12] PURE,[13] AND GOOD[14] ALL THE TIME[15] AND IN WHOM THERE IS NO DARKNESS![16]

AMEN!

---

[1] James 3:16; Philippians 2:3; Galatians 5:20

[2] In Greek, *godly love* is ἀγαπάω, pronounced "ah-gah-pah'-oh," meaning *godly or moral love* (John 21:16). Other words referring to sorts of "love" in Greek include φιλέω, pronounced "fih-leh'-oh," meaning *friendly affection or approval* (John 21:17), and ἔρως, pronounced "ehr'-ohs," meaning *erotic love* (Septuagint: Esther 2:17; Proverbs 4:6).

[3] Psalm 97:10; Proverbs 6:16-19

[4] Proverbs 8:13; Amos 5:15

[5] Hebrews 12:2; Judges 6:25-27

[6] Psalm 103:13; Proverbs 3:11-12

[7] James 1:17; Matthew 19:17; 1 Samuel 2:2; Psalm 145:7-9

[8] Matthew 7:9-11; Titus 3:4-7

[9] Matthew 13:19; Mark 4:15; Luke 8:12

[10] Matthew 13:27-28; Romans 16:17

[11] Revelation 22:15; 1 Corinthians 6:9-10; Galatians 5:19-21

[12] Revelation 4:8; Isaiah 6:3; Exodus 15:11

[13] Habakkuk 1:13; Job 15:15; Psalm 5:4-5; 11:4-7; 34:15-16; 1 Peter 1:15-16

[14] Matthew 19:17; 1 Samuel 2:2; Psalm 145:7-9; James 1:17

[15] Hebrews 13:8; Psalm 102:27-28; 103:17; Malachi 3:6; James 1:17

[16] 1 John 1:5; James 1:17; 1 Timothy 6:16; John 1:4; 8:12

So, do not allow the dark spirit to continue to work![1] Bind it from stealing bread and leaving stones! If you do not, it will continue to work while you are confronting it![2] Therefore, bind that dark spirit with the Word of Truth in the Legal Name,[3] Provision of Power,[4] and Ordained Authority of Yeshua![5] Come against it with Yeshua's Strength in your will to stop that spirit's pursuit![6] Come against that darkness with Yeshua's Refusal of darkness and His Love for what is Good in your heart![7]

Understand that you speak with power because you have trusted His Testimony, and all promises are "yes" for those who trust in His Testimony![8]

Bless Yehovah!

Listen to the Holy Word!

"But we hold to the same Spirit of the faith of which it was written, 'I believed; therefore I have spoken!' Since we have that same Spirit of faith, we also believe and therefore speak, knowing that the One Who resurrected the Lord Yeshua will also resurrect us through Yeshua and present us with you!"[9]

HalleluYah!

"But because God is faithful, our word toward you does not become 'Yes' and 'No.' Because the Son of God, Jesus Christ, Who was preached among you by us—delivered through me, Silas, and Timothy—did not become 'Yes' and 'No.' Rather, in Him it has always been 'Yes'! Because no matter how many promises God has made, they are 'Yes' in Him! And through Him the 'Amen' is spoken by us for the glory of God! Now it is God Who establishes us with you in Christ and has anointed us. And He marked His seal of ownership on us, giving the Spirit in our hearts as a security deposit."[10]

---

[1] 1 Corinthians 5:13; Deuteronomy 13:5; Ephesians 5:11
[2] James 4:7; Matthew 4:3-11; Ephesians 6:11-12; 1 Peter 5:8-9; Revelation 12:11
[3] John 16:23; Hebrews 10:19-23; 1 John 5:14-15
[4] Philippians 3:10; Ephesians 1:19; 1 Peter 1:5
[5] Matthew 28:18; John 5:27
[6] 1 Timothy 1:12; 2 Corinthians 3:5-6; Philippians 4:13; 2 Timothy 4:17
[7] Hebrews 1:9; Amos 5:15; Zechariah 8:17; Romans 12:9; Revelation 2:6
[8] 2 Corinthians 1:20; Galatians 3:22; Acts 13:32-39
[9] 2 Corinthians 4:13-14
[10] 2 Corinthians 1:18-22

And,

"I will give you the keys of the Kingdom of Heaven, and whatever you bind on the earth will be bound in Heaven, and whatever you loose on the earth will be loosed in Heaven!"[1]

HALLELUYAAAAAAAAAAAAAAAAH!!!!!!!!!

MIGHTY IS OUR GOD![2]

OUR LORD GOD ALMIGHTY REIGNS![3]

HALLELUYAAAAAAAAAAAAAAAAH!!!!!!!!!

HALLELUYAAAAAAAAAAAAAAAAH!!!!!!!!!

HALLELUYAAAAAAAAAAAAAAAAH!!!!!!!!!

THEREFORE, when you are binding a dark spirit, and it presents a thought or understanding to your mind suggesting that you do not believe or do not have the authority promised to the apostles, respond with these Scriptures and continue to bind the dark spirit!

CRUSH IT![4]

Remember, you are fighting a war in spirit by means of spiritual authority, power, and truth![5] You are overtaking soulical territory from a dark spiritual force, insistence, intelligence, and affection! You are fighting a lie that has its own purpose, personality, and strength![6] But your strength is greater because you have the Strength of Yeshua![7]

HALLELUYAH!

---

[1] Matthew 16:19
[2] Revelation 11:17; 18:8; Luke 22:69; Acts 13:17; 1 Peter 5:6
[3] Psalm 99:1; Revelation 1:18; 4:9; 11:15; 19:6; 21:27; Hebrews 1:8
[4] Luke 10:19; Psalm 91:13; Ezekiel 2:6; Mark 16:18; Acts 28:5; Romans 16:20
[5] Ephesians 6:12; 2 Corinthians 6:7
[6] 1 Kings 22:19-23; Ephesians 2:2; Revelation 12:9
[7] Romans 8:37; Philippians 4:13

And your purpose is greater because you come with the Command of Yehovah to overtake and rule over the soul![1]

HALLELUUUUUYAAAAAAAH!!!!

And your truth is greater because every darkness and lie will pass away,[2]

THE TRUTH HAS ETERNAL LIFE AND REIGNS FOREVER![3]

HALLELUUUUUUUUYAAAAAAAAAAAAAAAAH!!!!!!!!!

PRAISE OUR GLORIOUS GOD!!!!!!!!!![4]

HALLELUUUUUUUUUUUUUYAAAAAAAAAAAAAAAAH!!!!!!!!!

AMEN!!!!!!!!!!

Knowing this, do NOT allow any dark spirit to continue to speak its lies![5] Do NOT accept any thought or understanding that justifies the residence of symptoms of sin or sickness in *any* way, whether by excuses from psychological pondering,[6] medical reasoning,[7] or seemingly common sense.[8] All such justifications are idols of lies that insist against the Truth of God's Word,[9] and the soul that exalts and bows to any such idols will certainly find itself in submission to them.[10] Do not even entertain such thoughts nor give them any place to speak in the court of your soul.[11] Silence that lying, distracting, idolatrous spirit! Bind it and then silence it, just as your King demonstrated by silencing many dark spirits.[12] Silence the dark

---

[1] Numbers 33:52; Romans 6:13; 2 Corinthians 10:4-5

[2] Revelation 21:8,25; 22:5; Proverbs 19:9

[3] Proverbs 12:19; Revelation 21:27; Hebrews 1:8; Revelation 1:18; 4:9; 11:15

[4] Revelation 4:11; 5:12-13; 7:12

[5] Psalm 31:18; Mark 1:25; Luke 4:35

[6] Proverbs 3:5; 9:10; Jeremiah 9:23-24

[7] Mark 5:26; Luke 8:43; Job 13:4; Jeremiah 30:15

[8] Isaiah 53:6 – Obviously, such *common sense* is nothing more than *worldly consensus.*

[9] Isaiah 20:5; John 1:5; Revelation 18:23d, "By your φαρμακεια all the nations were led astray" – φαρμακεια, pronounced "far-mah-kay-ah," meaning *medication, magic, sorcery,* or *witchcraft*.

[10] Romans 6:16; Joshua 24:14; Matthew 6:24a-b; 2 Corinthians 10:5

[11] Matthew 9:4; Ezekiel 38:10; Haggai 2:13-14

[12] Mark 1:25,34; Luke 4:41

spirit by the Legal Name,[1] Provision of Power,[2] and Ordained Authority of Yeshua![3] Come against it with Yeshua's Strength in your will to stop its force![4] Come against it with both Yeshua's Refusal of darkness and His Love for what is Good in your heart![5] Come against it with the Truth, and strike it into silence by the Word of God![6]

Command that dark spirit to be uprooted and cast into the sea![7] Keep fighting until you fully possess victory because full victory has been granted to you![8]

HALLELUYAH!

As in any war, someone is fighting to overtake something, and someone else is fighting to defend and keep it. Regardless of who fights, it is always a fight, and one must fight to take hold of victory.[9] However, the redeemed have been assured that if they continue to fight, they will win![10] For He Who commands the redeemed has already won for Himself and has taken authority over all things![11] And having authority over all things, He has promised the redeemed angelic reinforcements to ensure that victory is received and wielded for His Glory![12]

HALLELUYAH!

So, speak the Scriptures from the Circle of Christ over that gate where the dark spirit seeks to influence![13] Stand with Yeshua's Power in the gate![14] Shine with His Goodness in the gate![15] Speak, stand, and shine for, with, and by Yeshua in that

---

[1] John 16:23; Hebrews 10:19-23; 1 John 5:14-15
[2] Philippians 3:10; Ephesians 1:19; 1 Peter 1:5
[3] Matthew 28:18; John 5:27
[4] 1 Timothy 1:12; 2 Corinthians 3:5-6; Philippians 4:13; 2 Timothy 4:17
[5] Hebrews 1:9; Amos 5:15; Zechariah 8:17; Romans 12:9; Revelation 2:6
[6] 2 Timothy 3:16; Hebrews 4:12; Revelation 19:15,21
[7] Luke 17:6; Mark 11:22-23; Matthew 21:21
[8] Romans 8:37; 1 Corinthians 15:57; 1 John 5:4-5
[9] 1 Timothy 6:12; 1:18; 1 Corinthians 9:25-26; 2 Corinthians 6:7; 10:3-5; Ephesians 6:10-18; 1 Thessalonians 5:8-9; 2 Timothy 4:7
[10] Philippians 3:14; 2 Timothy 4:7-8; Hebrews 12:1; 1 Corinthians 15:57; 1 John 4:4
[11] Ephesians 1:21; Philippians 2:9-10; Colossians 2:10; Hebrews 1:4
[12] Colossians 1:11; 2 Thessalonians 3:3; Ephesians 3:20-21
[13] Isaiah 45:19; Deuteronomy 30:11-14; Ezekiel 37:4
[14] Ephesians 6:13; Colossians 4:12
[15] Matthew 5:16; Luke 1:53; John 6:27; 15:8

gate! He has redeemed,[1] called,[2] and chosen[3] you to be true,[4] powerful,[5] and full of light![6] He has made you His image,[7] vessel,[8] ambassador,[9] soldier,[10] and priest![11] You are His child, a child of Yehovah![12]

BE WHO YOU HAVE BEEN MADE TO BE![13]
BE WHAT HE HAS PLANTED YOU TO BE![14]

FOR HIS GLORY, CAST OUT ALL THAT IS NOT OF YOU![15]
DASH THE ENEMY TO PIECES LIKE POTTERY![16]

RULE OVER YOUR SOUL WITH AN IRON SCEPTER![17]

YOU BEAR THE SIGNET RING OF CHRIST![18]
YOU HAVE ABSOLUTE VICTORY AND DOMINION![19]
YOU ARE AS BOLD AS A LION![20]

HALLELUUUUYAAAAAAAAAAAAAAAAH!!!!!!!!!

HALLELUUUUYAAAAAAAAAAAAAAAAH!!!!!!!!!

HALLELUUUUYAAAAAAAAAAAAAAAAH!!!!!!!!!

---

[1] Ephesians 1:7; Galatians 3:13-14; 4:5; Titus 2:14; 1 Peter 1:18; Revelation 14:3
[2] Matthew 22:14; 7:13-14; 20:16; Luke 13:23-24
[3] John 15:19; Mark 13:20; Luke 18:7; Acts 9:15; 1 Peter 1:2
[4] 1 John 5:20; John 14:6; 17:3; Revelation 3:7,14; 6:10; 15:3; 19:11
[5] Acts 1:8; Micah 3:8; Zechariah 4:6; Luke 10:19; Romans 15:19
[6] 1 Thessalonians 5:5; Ephesians 5:8; Luke 16:8; John 12:36; Acts 26:18
[7] Romans 8:29; Matthew 12:50; 25:40; Colossians 1:15-18; Revelation 1:5-6
[8] 2 Timothy 2:21; Romans 6:13; Acts 9:15
[9] 2 Corinthians 5:20; Ephesians 6:20; John 20:21; Acts 26:17-18
[10] 2 Timothy 2:3; 2 Corinthians 10:3-5; Ephesians 6:11-18; 1 Timothy 1:18
[11] Revelation 1:6; 5:10; 20:6; 22:5; Exodus 19:6; 1 Peter 2:5-9
[12] Romans 8:17; Galatians 3:29; 4:7; Ephesians 3:6; 1 Peter 1:4
[13] Matthew 5:14; Ephesians 5:8-14; Philippians 2:15
[14] Luke 13:6-9; Matthew 12:23; 13:38
[15] Romans 13:12; Ephesians 4:22; Colossians 3:8-9; James 1:21; 1 Peter 2:1
[16] Revelation 2:27; 12:5; 19:15; Psalm 2:9
[17] Revelation 2:27; 12:5; 19:15; Psalm 2:9
[18] Genesis 41:42; John 14:14; 15:16; 16:24,26
[19] Luke 10:19; Psalm 91:13; Ezekiel 2:6; Mark 16:18; Acts 28:5; Romans 16:20
[20] Proverbs 28:1; Exodus 11:8; Psalm 27:1-2; 46:2-3; 112:7; Isaiah 26:3-4

HALLELUUUUYAAAAAAAAAAAAAAAAH!!!!!!!!!

OUR GOD REIGNS,[1] AND WE REIGN FOR HIS GLORY![2]

DARKNESS IS DEFEATED AND DOOMED!!!!![3]

HALLELUUUUUYAAAAAAAAAAAAAAAAAAAAAAAAAAH!!!!!!!!!!

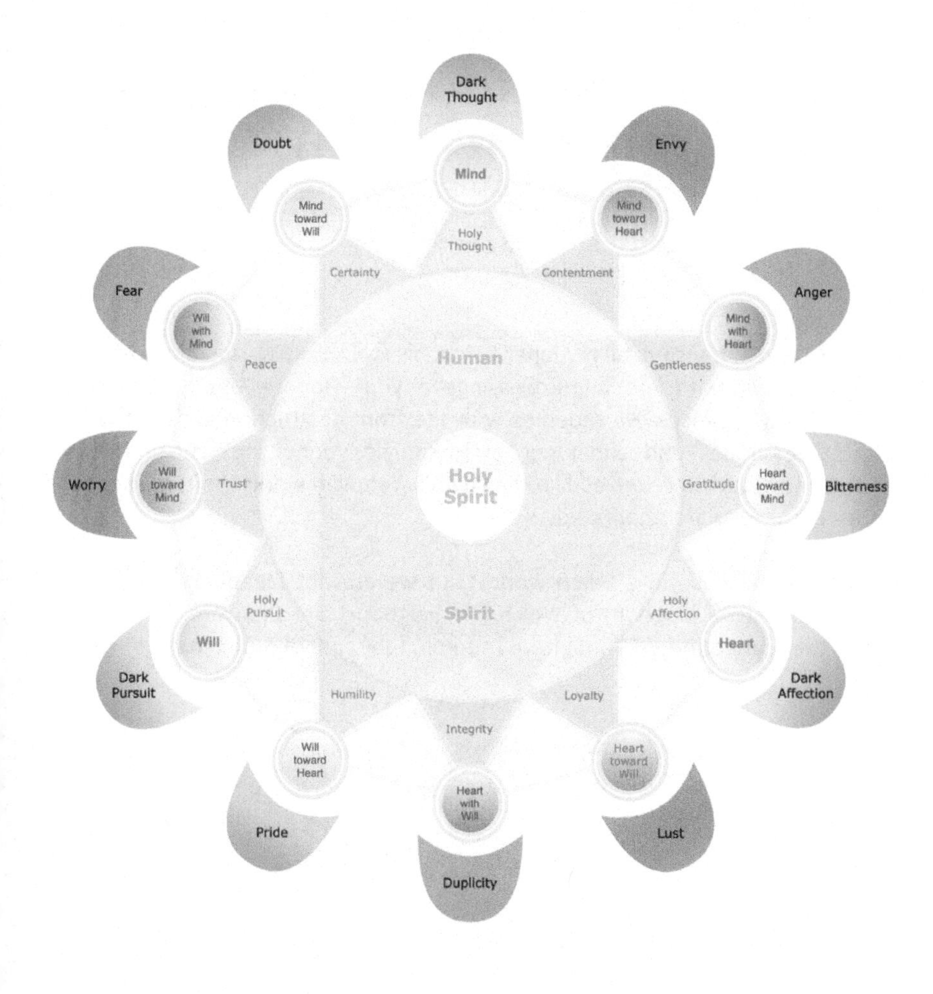

[1] Psalm 99:1; Revelation 1:18; 4:9; 11:15; 19:6; 21:27; Hebrews 1:8
[2] Revelation 1:6; 5:10; 20:6; 22:5; Exodus 19:6; 1 Peter 2:5-9
[3] Revelation 20:14; Luke 10:19; 1 John 2:13; 4:4; 5:4

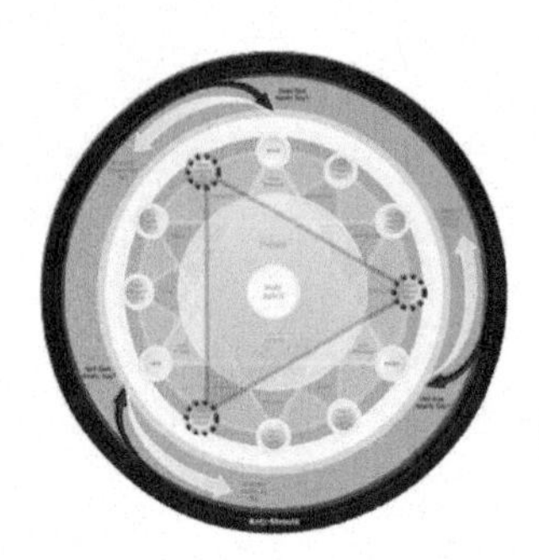

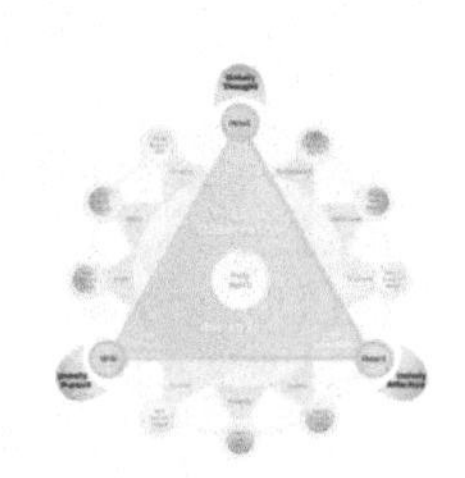

CHAPTER 28

BINDING, SILENCING, AND CASTING OUT INFIRMITY SPIRITS

"Bless Yehovah, my soul; all my inner being, bless His Holy Name. Bless Yehovah, my soul, and do not forget all His blessings for you—He forgives all your sins and heals all your diseases. He redeems your life from destruction and crowns you with loving kindness and tender mercies. He satisfies your desires with good things so that your youth is renewed like the eagle's. Yehovah works righteousness and justice for all who are oppressed."[1]

The truly saved[2] live in a fallen world,[3] but we are not fallen![4] We have been redeemed[5] into a kingdom of which our neighbors are unaware.[6] Though we speak, they cannot hear.[7] Though we triumph, they cannot understand.[8] They are

---

[1] Psalm 103:1-6
[2] Revelation 2:1-3:22; John 15:19
[3] John 12:31; 1 Corinthians 2:12; 7:31; James 4:4
[4] John 17:14,16; 1 John 4:5-6; 5:19-20
[5] 1 Peter 1:18; Luke 1:68; Galatians 3:13-14; Revelation 5:9; 14:3
[6] John 3:8; Luke 17:20
[7] John 8:43; 6:60; Isaiah 6:9; Jeremiah 6:10; Acts 7:51; Romans 8:7-8
[8] John 1:5,10; 3:19; Luke 6:39; Jeremiah 5:31; 2 Peter 2:1

lost.[1] They do not perceive the Light, because the darkness has stolen it from them.[2] The darkness enslaves them[3] and works through them as if unhindered.[4]

Understand that this is a battle for authority.[5] The Covenant of Creation has granted all spirits authority that can be willfully used, neglected, lost, or increased according to how it is used by each spirit.[6] Obviously, any unused authority has no effect.[7] For example, if a person has authority over their own body in Creation, their body will not move for them until it receives their command.[8] But even when enacted, such authority can only have an effect when it is the highest active commanding authority under Yehovah.[9] For example, a thief might physically attempt to steal money from a bank, but he will be unable to succeed if the police physically capture him. Though the thief has authority over his body,[10] the police have been given greater physical authority to capture that body.[11]

The basis of all authority is spiritual, but the parameters of Creation allow it to be used "unspiritually."[12] Consider the dynamics of authority in the example above. The thief tries to steal something he believes he wants from someone else,[13] yet he is not really the one in spiritual authority.[14] His soul has been hijacked by dark spirits that are supplying the affections, thoughts, and pursuits for thievery.[15] At the same time, the police officers might understand they are working as agents of the state but not understand they have been called and empowered by Yehovah's Authority.[16] If the enemy manages to infiltrate the souls of officers or those in leadership within the police or government, they can also misuse the police authority for dark purposes.[17]

---

[1] John 14:17; 1 Corinthians 2:14
[2] 2 Corinthians 4:4; Matthew 4:8-9; John 12:40; Ephesians 2:2; 1 John 2:11; 5:19
[3] Titus 3:3; Obadiah 1:3; Isaiah 44:20
[4] 1 Peter 4:4; Acts 17:30
[5] Job 1:6-12; 2:1-6; Isaiah 14:13
[6] Genesis 1:26,28; 2:16-17; 3:14-19,22-24; Ezekiel 5:17; Deuteronomy 28:1-68
[7] Deuteronomy 1:19-36; James 1:22-25
[8] Proverbs 10:4; 12:27; 19:24
[9] Numbers 14:39-45; John 19:11
[10] Jude 1:8; Deuteronomy 4:31-37
[11] Romans 13:2; John 19:11
[12] John 19:11; 1 Peter 3:22; Colossians 1:16
[13] James 4:1-3; 1 Kings 18:21
[14] Romans 1:24,26,28; Acts 7:42
[15] Acts 26:18; Matthew 12:29-30; Isaiah 49:24-25; 1 John 2:10; 3:8; Ephesians 6:12; 2 Corinthians 4:4
[16] Romans 13:1-4; John 19:11
[17] John 19:11; Luke 3:14

Therefore, understand that all misuse of spiritual authority comes from the enemy.[1] We can see this in the experience of Job, who was a morally upright man.[2] His soul, though mostly righteous, was infiltrated by a dark spirit of fear concerning his children.[3] When he attempted to intercede with sacrifices made to Yehovah, he was unwittingly serving fear with his time and efforts — time and efforts which should have been focused on seeking and serving Yehovah.[4] Because of Job's ignorant acceptance of this idolatry, Satan argued that Job's seeming devotion was nothing more than self-preservation due to darkness.[5] And for the sake of Yehovah's Holy Righteousness[6] and the future blessing of Job's soul,[7] Yehovah temporarily removed His Mercy's protection and authorized Satan to test Job's soul.[8]

Notice that Yehovah had been protecting Job's soul from the rule of darkness[9] even though Job had been allowing darkness into his soul.[10] But as soon as Yehovah removed His hedge, the authority of Satan overruled Job's.[11] Satan was now permitted to use his authority over Creation against Job.[12]

As a spirit, Satan's authority remains active as long as it is not lost or overcome.[13] During Job's lifetime, Satan was like a corrupt general in the early stages of a coup d'état.[14] He still retained his access to Yehovah,[15] and he was able to procure authority to attack Job's body, provisions, and family.[16] Because Satan's authority was given directly by Yehovah,[17] he was able to command Creation in numerous ways, including the use of armies, lightning, and a tornado.[18] When his attempts

---

1 John 3:7; 1 John 3:8-10; Acts 13:10; Matthew 13:38
2 Job 1:1,8; 2:3; 23:11-12; 31:1-40
3 Job 1:5; Ezekiel 14:20
4 Matthew 6:31; 10:37-38
5 Job 1:9-11; 2:4-5; Ezekiel 27:3; 28:6,15; 31:10; Isaiah 14:12-14
6 Job 42:7; Psalm 51:4
7 Job 42:12; James 5:11
8 Job 1:12; 2:6
9 Job 1:10; 2:4
10 Job 1:5; 38:2; 1 Timothy 1:6-8
11 Job 1:12; 2:6
12 Job 1:13-19; 2:7
13 Romans 11:29
14 Job 2:3c; Revelation 12:4
15 Job 1:6; 2:1
16 Job 1:12; 2:6
17 Job 1:11-12; 2:5-6
18 Job 1:13-19; Jeremiah 4:11-12; Ephesians 2:2

failed to further corrupt Job,[1] Satan sought and received authority over Job's body.[2] Job had no form of appeal or recourse aside from prayer[3] because Satan was the primary authority under God.[4]

Today, we are in a different situation.[5] As the Second Man,[6] our Glorious Savior overcame the authority of Satan.[7] And after Yeshua rose into Heaven,[8] its inhabitants refused to allow reentry of the dark spirits[9] who had facilitated the unjust execution of the King of Justice.[10] Therefore, dark spirits no longer have granted permission by Yehovah to enter the soul or body of the redeemed.[11]

What does this mean? It means that those of us granted authority through Yeshua cannot be overruled.[12] If we stand in the Kingdom of Heaven, no one but Yehovah is over us![13] However, the unrighteous are still under the authority of Satan,[14] who continues to retain the greatest authority *under* Heaven.[15] Because of the legal precedent established during the time of Job, weather and flesh remain under Satan's command.[16] He maintains such authority because he does not have human weakness[17] and still has the gifts he was given when standing in the Presence of the Almighty.[18] While the least in the Kingdom of Heaven is greater than Satan,[19] those who have not entered remain under his authority.[20]

---

[1] Job 1:22; 2:3
[2] Job 2:5-7,12
[3] Job 7:7-21; 10:2-22
[4] Job 1:12; 2:6
[5] Romans 8:2,10-11; 6:18,22; John 8:36; Hebrews 2:9,14-15
[6] 1 Corinthians 15:47; Matthew 1:23
[7] Colossians 2:15; Acts 2:32-36; John 12:31; 16:11; Revelation 12:9; 20:2-3,10
[8] Acts 1:9; Luke 24:50-51
[9] Revelation 12:7-10; Luke 10:18
[10] Matthew 27:20; John 8:44
[11] Revelation 12:7-10; 21:25; 22:5
[12] 2 Corinthians 1:20; Galatians 3:22; Acts 13:32-39
[13] 1 Corinthians 8:6; Ephesians 4:5
[14] 2 Corinthians 6:14; 1 John 2:9-11
[15] 2 Corinthians 4:4; Revelation 12:9
[16] Job 1:12; 2:6
[17] Hebrews 2:5-15; Psalm 103:20; Judges 13:20; 1 Chronicles 21:16; Luke 1:19
[18] Romans 11:29; Numbers 23:19; Malachi 3:6
[19] Hebrews 2:7-8; 1 Corinthians 6:3
[20] 2 Corinthians 4:4; Revelation 12:9; Ephesians 2:2

Those of us who have received authority through Jesus remain invincible[1] as long as we remain in His Kingdom.[2] But if we turn from His Light of Righteousness in *any* way,[3] Satan can claim that we have entered his domain.[4] Therefore, understand the difference in our situation from that of Job: Just as Satan could accuse and test Job to validate his claim,[5] he can do the same to any of the redeemed who accept darkness today.[6] The difference is that while Job had no way to contend against the testing,[7] we do![8] When we repent and are washed by Yeshua's Blood, we can come against the enemy and overrule him![9]

HALLELUYAH!!!

So let us be wise and diligent![10] Let us keep watch[11] and prevent access from the enemy![12] Let us put him to shame by our good behavior,[13] standing firmly in the Truth[14] and Power of the Holy Spirit[15] and persevering in doing good![16] Because anyone who occasionally fails to do good is like a person who occasionally worships idols![17] Though they might not do so all the time, they are still an idolater![18] But we are those who repent from wrongdoing[19] and live powerfully through the Grace given us by the precious Blood of Jesus Christ![20] We are those who receive salvation from Him and walk in it with Him![21]

BLESS GOD!!!

---

[1] Romans 8:37; 1 John 4:4; 5:4-5; 1 Corinthians 15:57
[2] John 15:4-7; Acts 11:23; 14:22; Colossians 1:23; 1 John 2:24-28
[3] Romans 8:13; Galatians 6:8
[4] 1 Peter 5:8; Job 1:11; 2:4-5
[5] Revelation 12:10; Job 1:11; 2:4-5; Luke 22:31; Zechariah 3:1
[6] 1 Peter 5:8; Galatians 6:8; Romans 8:13
[7] Job 1:12; 2:6; 7:3
[8] James 4:7; 1 Peter 5:8-9
[9] Revelation 2:5,7,16-17,21-22,26-29; 3:3,5-6,19-22
[10] Romans 16:19; 1 Timothy 4:15
[11] Matthew 24:42; 25:13; Acts 20:28
[12] Acts 20:29-31; 2 Peter 2:1
[13] 1 Peter 2:12; 3:16; Titus 2:8
[14] 2 Peter 1:12; Colossians 2:7; 1 Peter 5:12
[15] Acts 1:8; Romans 15:13; 1 Thessalonians 1:5
[16] Romans 2:7; James 5:11; Hebrews 10:36; 11:27
[17] James 2:9-11; 4:17
[18] 1 John 3:4; Colossians 3:5
[19] Hebrews 6:1; 2 Timothy 2:25-26; Acts 20:21; 26:20
[20] Ephesians 1:7; 1 Peter 1:2
[21] Galatians 5:16; 1 John 1:7; Ephesians 1:13; Philippians 2:12; Hebrews 5:9; 1 Peter 1:9, 2:2

Nevertheless, since we understand that we can still be unjustly accused and attacked,[1] let us continue on and learn the details about the schemes of the enemy and how to resist them![2]

GLORY TO GOD! THANK YOU, YEHOVAH, FOR YOUR WISDOM![3]

HALLELUYAH!

As we have been discussing, there are many sorts of dark spirits.[4] Although Heylel is chief among them,[5] the kingdom of darkness includes a myriad of beings,[6] each specializing in their own vice and purpose.[7] Among them are infirmity spirits,[8] or spirits that seek to steal, destroy, or kill the body.[9] Because sin occurs in the soul, infirmities must seek legal access to the body through the soul.[10] They rely on a soul's granted or implied legal permission to enter and establish their foothold of influence in a body.[11]

The body and soul of the redeemed are a "holy land"[12] and "purchased temple mount"[13] for the Holy Spirit. More specifically, the body is the holy land with its people, warriors, and Levites, the soul is the constructed holy city[14] with its holy temple courts,[15] prophet, priest, and king, and the spirit is the holy temple built in the image of Yehovah[16] where the presence of the Holy Spirit dwells.[17]

Any infirmity seeking to invade the body can only do so if the soul and spirit have a weakness permitting the invasion to go unnoticed,[18] because attacks from

---

[1] Revelation 12:10; 2 Timothy 4:18

[2] James 4:7; Matthew 4:3-11; Ephesians 6:11-12; 1 Peter 5:8-9; Revelation 12:11

[3] Ephesians 1:17; Luke 12:12; 21:15; Matthew 16:17; 1 Corinthians 2:10

[4] Matthew 12:45; Luke 7:21; Acts 23:8; 1 Timothy 4:1; Revelation 16:13

[5] Ephesians 2:2; Revelation 12:7-9

[6] Revelation 12:4; Daniel 8:9-12

[7] Luke 11:26; Revelation 16:14; 1 Kings 22:22

[8] Revelation 12:3-4; 16:13-14; 18:2; 1 Timothy 4:1; 1 John 4:1-3

[9] Luke 13:10-17; Job 2:7

[10] 1 Corinthians 11:31; Psalm 32:3-5; James 5:16

[11] 1 Corinthians 11:29-30; Romans 13:2

[12] Joshua 1:3; Exodus 19:6; Danie 7:27; Romans 14:17

[13] 2 Samuel 24:18-25; 1 Corinthians 6:19; Ephesians 2:19-21

[14] Matthew 5:14; Ephesians 5:8-14; Philippians 2:15

[15] Mark 11:15; Matthew 21:12-16; Luke 19:45; John 2:13-17

[16] Romans 8:29; 1 Corinthians 15:49; 2 Corinthians 3:18

[17] 1 Thessalonians 5:23; 1 Corinthians 3:16

[18] James 1:15; Psalm 7:14; Isaiah 59:4

infirmities on a well-guarded body are unsuccessful.[1] But if accepted dark spirits have infiltrated a soul, that soul's "prophet" (mind),[2] "priesthood" (heart),[3] and "king" (will) [4] can be distracted. [5] Such infiltration provides the enemy "intelligence" (obtained soulical agreement) to wage an attack on the body at an opportune place and time.[6]

Since the enemy has no shortage of infirmity spirits waiting for opportunities to drink from the life given to a person's body,[7] it is useless for a person to focus on recapturing the body if there continue to be problems in the soul[8] — just as it would be foolish for a prophet king to send his army to fight in the outskirts of the land while disloyal generals in his own city work from within to take his life.[9]

Though it is possible for a person to experience victories against infirmities in the body when fighting directly against them or when receiving help from the prayers of redeemed brothers and sisters,[10] such victories tend to be sporadic and often temporary.[11] This is because one or more gates for "dark generals" still remain open in the "city" of the soul.[12] However, if the soul's gates are sealed,[13] and the priesthood of that soul ministers in righteousness and truth, then the security of that soul is established,[14] and its loyal generals and armies are ready to guard and enforce the borders of the body.[15] Therefore, to ensure successful riddance of infirmities from a body, the redeemed must first purify and secure the soul![16]

Consider the following examples:

---

[1] Isaiah 53:5; Proverbs 4:20-22; Jeremiah 30:17; Exodus 15:26
[2] Acts 28:25; Ezra 33:33
[3] Ezra 1:5; 1 Samuel 2:35; Numbers 25:13; Hebrews 7:12; 1 Peter 2:5
[4] Isaiah 32:1; 28:6; 2 Samuel 23:3
[5] 1 Samuel 18:17-25; 2 Samuel 15:1-12
[6] 1 Peter 5:8; Mark 4:15; 2 Corinthians 2:11
[7] Mark 5:9; 1 Peter 5:8
[8] 1 Corinthians 11:30; 2 Chronicles 16:12; Deuteronomy 28:61; Acts 12:23
[9] 2 Samuel 15:1-10; 2 Kings 12:18-21
[10] James 5:16; Colossians 1:9
[11] James 5:14-15; 1 Corinthians 11:30
[12] Matthew 9:2; 1 Corinthians 11:30
[13] 2 Chronicles 8:14b; Nehemiah 3:29; 13:22
[14] 1 Corinthians 11:31; Psalm 32:3-5; James 5:16
[15] Exodus 23:22-28; Isaiah 26:15; 1 Kings 4:21
[16] 2 Peter 1:10-11; 3:17; 1 Peter 1:5; Revelation 3:10-11; Psalm 37:24; 62:2,6; 112:6

One day a certain man learned that some of his financial investments were drained, and he was tempted by a spirit of worry.[1] Using the Scriptures to confront the spirit, he obtained some degree of relief and noticed that the spirit of worry became mostly silent.[2] But when the man sat down to read the Word of Yehovah shortly thereafter, he suddenly began to experience a runny nose. Immediately recognizing this as an attack of darkness to distract him from absorbing the Logos, the man struck back at the infirmity with Scriptures concerning healing. However, after fighting for two hours, though the symptoms did seem to wax and wane occasionally, the man became discouraged because the symptoms still remained and were finally growing worse.

On the same day in another place, a different man experienced the same financial loss, the same spirit of worry, and the same physical attack. However, upon noticing the physical symptoms, this second man immediately returned to finish the battle against the spirit of worry until trust in Yehovah overflowed in truth, power, and thankfulness from his soul.[3] After patiently persevering until he received assurance of the gate's victory, the man then turned to wage a passionate war of truth, power, and absolute refusal against the infirmity spirit.[4] He struck the spirit with the Word of God until the symptoms regressed and strength and comfort filled his body where the weakness and discomfort had formerly attacked.[5]

May your mind be enlightened with His Truth,[6] may your will be empowered with His Power,[7] and may your heart be filled with the healing of His Love, Peace, and Joy![8]

Listen, holy people![9] You can do this![10] You were *made* for this![11] You have victory in your very being![12]

---

[1] Luke 12:22; Philippians 4:6; Hebrews 13:5
[2] James 4:7; Matthew 4:3-11; Ephesians 6:11-12; 1 Peter 5:8-9; Revelation 12:11
[3] Psalm 100:4; 116:17-19; Isaiah 35:10
[4] Galatians 5:1,13; 2:4; 4:26,31; John 8:32-36; Romans 6:18; 8:2
[5] Galatians 6:9; 1 Corinthians 15:58; 2 Thessalonians 3:13; Hebrews 12:3
[6] 2 Peter 1:12; Colossians 2:7; 1 Peter 5:12
[7] Acts 1:8; Micah 3:8; Zechariah 4:6; Luke 10:19; Romans 15:19
[8] Galatians 5:22; Romans 14:17; 15:13
[9] 1 Peter 2:9; Revelation 1:6; 5:10
[10] Philippians 4:13; Ephesians 3:16
[11] Ephesians 1:5,11-12; Romans 8:29-30
[12] 1 Corinthians 15:57; Romans 8:37; 1 John 5:4-5

YOU ARE A WARRIOR![1]

YOUR GOD IS A WARRIOR![2]

YOUR GOD IS VICTORIOUS![3]

SO, YOU ARE VICTORIOUS![4]

HALLELUYAH!

Learning to read was much more difficult than learning this![5] So, "gird up the loins" of your soul, and learn this![6]

HalleluYah!

Remember that when fighting legal claims against your soul, you must vocalize your residency in the First Jurisdiction, the Kingdom of Heaven.[7] Do not attempt to wage war according to the covenant given in the desert,[8] or else you will remain in the spiritual desert![9] The only Person Who was able to do that successfully was Yehovah Himself![10] Fight only by the rules and blessings of the New Covenant[11] given in the Promised Land through Yeshua[12] for the Promised Land of the Kingdom of Heaven![13] Fight by the Word and deeds[14] in spirit and in truth![15] If a person says with their mouth that they believe yet implies with their deeds that they do not, darkness will continue to contend for whatever gates

---

[1] 2 Timothy 2:3; 2 Corinthians 10:3-5; Ephesians 6:11-18; 1 Timothy 1:18

[2] Deuteronomy 20:4; Exodus 14:14; Joshua 10:42

[3] John 12:31; 16:11,33; Psalm 68:18; Romans 8:37; 1 John 4:4; 5:4

[4] Revelation 3:21; Matthew 19:28; Luke 22:30; 1 Corinthians 6:2-3; 2 Timothy 2:12

[5] Matthew 11:30; 2 Corinthians 4:17; Philippians 4:13

[6] 1 Peter 1:13 – *Gird your loins,* from the Greek "ἀναζωσάμενοι τὰς ὀσφύας," meaning *to pull the hanging part of a long robe up between the legs and tuck it into the belt to facilitate unhindered bodily movement (especially running), to prepare for action.*

[7] Luke 4:8; 1 Samuel 7:3; Romans 10:9

[8] Deuteronomy 5:2; Hebrews 7:12

[9] If you try to justify yourself by the Law, then you will be judged by the Law (Galatians 2:16; 3:11; 5:4; 6:13)!

[10] 1 John 3:5; 2 Corinthians 5:21; Hebrews 4:15

[11] Hebrews 8:13; 9:15; 12:24

[12] Luke 22:20; Hebrews 12:24; 13:20

[13] Galatians 2:16,21; Acts 13:39

[14] Colossians 3:17; 2 Thessalonians 2:17; Revelation 2:2,19,23; 3:1-2,8,15; 14:13

[15] John 4:24; 2 Corinthians 3:17; Galatians 4:6

apply.[1] The enemy will do this by insisting that the person's *more recent deeds* represent a *more recent allegiance* to the Second Jurisdiction and, therefore, a change of mind from *anything* the person had previously spoken in favor of the First Jurisdiction.[2]

For example, if the first man in the example above says he has repented of worry, yet he returns every thirty minutes to check his investments online, then darkness will contend for the worry gate based on the man's deeds.[3] If he does not repent in spirit, truth, word, deed, and affection and enter the rest provided by the First Jurisdiction,[4] he will not be able to shut the gate regarding any of these[5] because his actions display agreement with the Second Jurisdiction.[6]

So it is with infirmities. It is difficult to win a case against a legal claim from an enemy if you do not even know which court to fight in![7] If you do not contend the claim, it will often be granted to the enemy by default, especially if the claim is never appealed up to the higher court of the First Jurisdiction.[8] How tragic it is for the redeemed to suffer claims against them waged in a lower court governed by a fallen principality when the redeemed could have appealed out of that court and into the court presided over by their own Father![9] Not only is He sympathetic, but He has already firmly promised to rule in their favor over such matters![10]

Praise be to God that any of the redeemed who appeal to the jurisdiction of the Kingdom of Heaven may claim the full rights ascribed to the members of that kingdom![11] Not only are *all* promises of the First Jurisdiction applied in favor of the redeemed, but *all* promises of the Second Jurisdiction are also judged in favor of the redeemed![12] These benefits are possible because Yeshua, their Benefactor,

---

[1] Isaiah 29:13; Jeremiah 3:10; 5:2; Ezekiel 33:31-33; Matthew 15:7-9

[2] James 2:16-17; 1 Thessalonians 1:3

[3] James 2:24; Revelation 2:2,19,23; 3:1-2,8,15; 14:13

[4] John 4:24: Revelation 3:1-2

[5] James 2:18; Ephesians 2:8-10; 1 Corinthians 15:2

[6] James 2:17,26; Romans 2:25

[7] 1 Corinthians 9:26; Ephesians 4:14; James 1:6

[8] Hosea 4:6; Jeremiah 5:21; 2 Corinthians 4:3-6

[9] Acts 25:8-12; 1 Corinthians 6:1-11

[10] 1 John 2:1; Romans 3:24; 5:1,9; 1 Corinthians 6:11; Galatians 2:16

[11] James 2:12; Galatians 2:16

[12] 2 Corinthians 1:20; Galatians 3:22; Acts 13:32-39

made a full payment against *all* adverse claims, including all curses,[1] processes of death (sicknesses),[2] and death itself![3]

HalleluYah!

Therefore, to completely overcome an infirmity spirit, the redeemed person must first firmly establish their appeal to the First Jurisdiction.[4] Then they must progress through the procedures of casting out *all* dark spirits from the gates of the soul.[5] Even if the infirmity's legal access originally came through a gate that is now closed to darkness, as long as other gates remain open, the infirmity will transfer the claim of rightful dominion to any open gate.[6]

For example, the other night, I put on an oven mitt, reached into the oven, and grabbed the rack to slide out a tray of food that had been cooking on broil. As I began to pull on the rack, the glove split, and my fingers made direct contact with the 500°F metal.[7]

When this sort of thing happens, the Holy Spirit has taught me not even to look at the area of assault since what we perceive in Creation does *not* determine truth or victory.[8] Immediately, I went to war for the "land."[9] Fear was already insisting that my hand was burned. Yet through the Power of the Holy Spirit,[10] I refused to agree with the spirit of fear.[11] But then doubt tried to take its place.[12] If I had assumed that doubt was a product of my own thinking, then I would have been defeated.[13] Instead, I acknowledged that doubt was not of me, and I claimed the full Victory of Christ that every promise of Yehovah is "yes" for me.[14] I reminded

---

[1] Romans 8:1; Galatians 3:13; Revelation 22:3
[2] Psalm 103:3; James 5:15
[3] 2 Timothy 2:11; John 14:19; 1 Thessalonians 4:17; 5:10
[4] Matthew 8:17; Isaiah 53:4-5; 1 Peter 2:24
[5] This is necessary whether the person is aware of the procedures or simply being led unaware through the process by the Holy Spirit (Romans 8:26).
[6] Matthew 8:31-32 – Evil will seek any possible avenue of continued dominion in Creation, even if that foothold is barely viable.
[7] Isaiah 43:2; Acts 28:3
[8] Matthew 14:30; 2 Kings 6:15-17; Numbers 22:22-35
[9] Matthew 14:31; Mark 16:7
[10] Acts 1:8; 10:38; Luke 1:35; Romans 15:13; 1 Thessalonians 1:5
[11] John 20:27; 2 Timothy 1:7
[12] Matthew 14:26,31; James 1:2-3,6
[13] Luke 11:26; James 1:6-7
[14] 2 Corinthians 1:20; Galatians 3:22; Acts 13:32-39

that spirit of Nebuchadnezzar's furnace,[1] and I spoke the truth that Yeshua has given me full authority to overcome all power of the enemy.[2] Nothing will harm me![3] The battle continued on and off for about three hours. Though I periodically bound[4] and commanded the infirmity spirit away,[5] the focus of the battle involved the lies spewing from doubt.[6] Even two hours later, I would feel my fingers begin to blister. But I would shake my hand out, like I was shaking off the enemy, and I would speak the Truth from God.[7] After three hours, I had embraced complete victory, and my fingers were uninjured in *any* way whatsoever.[8]

Last night, a *different* mitt failed me, and I had to fight another battle just like the first![9] But Yeshua's Victory proved perfect again![10]

BECAUSE HE IS FAITHFUL![11]

HALLELUUUUUYAAAAAAAAAH!!!!!

Now listen! THIS IS *VERY* IMPORTANT![12]

Vulnerabilities in the soul are not only caused by "willful sin," or rebellion,[13] but *any* sort of darkness whatsoever![14] While willful sin certainly creates breaches in the soul,[15] many holy people who are suffering from attacks in their bodies have not willfully sinned![16] Instead, their souls have been injured by some sort of dark assault![17] Such assaults include *any* sort of unheavenly experience that falls short

---

[1] Daniel 3:25; Isaiah 43:2

[2] Luke 10:19a; 21:15-19; Psalm 91:13; Ezekiel 2:6; Romans 16:20

[3] Luke 10:19b; 21:18; Psalm 91:13; Ezekiel 2:6; Mark 16:18; Acts 28:5; Romans 16:20

[4] Matthew 16:19; 18:18; John 20:23; 2 Corinthians 2:10

[5] Matthew 10:8; Mark 16:18; Luke 10:9; Acts 4:9-10,30; 5:12-15

[6] Revelation 12:16

[7] Isaiah 43:2; Hebrews 11:34

[8] Luke 8:15; 21:19: Hebrews 6:11; 10:36; Revelation 3:10

[9] My lovely wife just brought home some new mitts! Haha! Proverbs 31:10-31!

[10] Hebrews 6:11; 13:8; Luke 21:19; 10:36; Revelation 3:10

[11] 2 Timothy 2:13; Matthew 24:35; Isaiah 25:1; 1 Thessalonians 5:24

[12] Luke 8:18; 19:26; Deuteronomy 32:46-47; Proverbs 2:2-5; Mark 4:23-24; Acts 17:11; Hebrews 2:1; James 1:22-25; Matthew 13:12; John 15:2

[13] Mark 2:9; Acts 13:10-11; John 9:3

[14] Hebrews 4:15; 5:2; 1 Thessalonians 5:14; Luke 22:32

[15] Luke 5:23; James 5:15; Matthew 13:15

[16] John 9:3; 1 Corinthians 11:30; Genesis 20:17

[17] Luke 13:16; John 8:44; 2 Timothy 2:26

of the Light.[1] For example, if a person is walking along and is bumped on the shoulder by another seemingly careless pedestrian, the person might feel a sense of offense or indignation. To experience such a feeling is not a sin, and it may not have been intended by the pedestrian at all![2] The person's disturbance is not the result of either human's intention or rebellion but an assault from the unseen realm by a spirit of darkness[3] bearing a "feeling" or "awareness" that falls short of the Light.[4] If the person even momentarily accepts the offense as their own and does not subsequently refill that part of their soul with light,[5] the dark spirit can claim any acceptance as implied agreement with the Second Jurisdiction and hold position in that part of the soul to allow entrance of an infirmity.[6] This could result in the person who was unintentionally offended by the pedestrian later experiencing the onset of an illness, pain, or physical discomfort even while remaining repentant from *willful* sin.[7]

However, once all the souls's gates are overflowing with confirming light, righteous pursuit, and affection for goodness, they form a powerful testimony on behalf of the Grace given for the soul's dominion by the Victorious King of Kings.[8] The grip of darkness will fail.[9] Then the redeemed may set out to bind, silence, and cast out the infirmity spirit from the promised land of the body.[10]

Understand that when an infirmity spirit is cornered, it will often protest with both physical symptoms and soulical lies.[11] It can suggest many physical sensations to push back against any attack on its position, claim, or force.[12] As soon as the person binds the infirmity and its symptoms, the dark spirit will typically switch tactics and begin suggesting various thoughts on why the infirmity should be there, why the symptoms are justified, and why they will be "staying for a while"

---

[1] 1 John 1:5; James 1:17; Luke 11:33-36; 2 Corinthians 6:14; 1 Timothy 6:16
[2] Matthew 11:3-6; Mark 1:41a
[3] Ephesians 6:12; Romans 8:38; Colossians 2:15; 1 Peter 3:22
[4] Philippians 4:8; Hebrews 12:2; Colossians 3:2
[5] Matthew 16:21-23; Mark 1:41; Luke 9:54-55
[6] Matthew 6:23-24b; Romans 6:16; Galatians 1:10; James 4:4; 1 John 2:15-16
[7] John 9:3; Luke 13:4-5
[8] 1 John 1:7; Zechariah 13:1; 1 Corinthians 6:11; Ephesians 1:7; Hebrews 9:14
[9] John 1:5,10; 3:19; Luke 6:39; Jeremiah 5:31; 2 Peter 2:1
[10] Acts 1:25; 16:18; Matthew 10:1; 16:19; Mark 1:34; 16:17; James 4:7; Luke 10:17; Psalm 31:18
[11] Luke 9:42; Mark 1:26-27; 9:26-27; Revelation 12:12
[12] Matthew 21:33-40 – The behavior of the wicked in this parable reveals the behavior of wickedness itself; the wicked behave wickedly because of the wicked spirits that drive them (Luke 22:3).

or "forever."[1] It will argue that symptoms are not spirits at all but some sort of inevitable consequences resulting from natural processes.[2] Of course, on one level, that is exactly what the symptoms are; they are "results of natural consequences"![3] They are the Second Jurisdiction's consequences[4] set in motion by the fallen principalities that continue to work within it![5] Anyone who abides in that jurisdiction is subject to its rule, but the children of God[6] are free from that jurisdiction and can even rule over it![7]

Praise the Holy Name of Yeshua HaMashiach for setting us free[8] and anointing[9] us with such Power![10]

BLESS GOD!

Therefore, do not be personally deceived like the world that is perishing in darkness[11] with its plagues of doubt, worry, fear, unrighteousness, pride, duplicity, lust, hate, bitterness, anger, envy, and lies![12] Do not count yourself among the world's servants, students, disciples, or apostles![13] Do not adopt their doctrines, accept their language, defer to their scholastic priests, practice their methods, trust in their pharmakeia,[14] or join their medical assemblies and rituals.[15] Although an emergency room can be a noble "Samaritan,"[16] do not trade your heavenly inheritance for its doctrine, lest you become merely a Samaritan yourself and forget from where your salvation comes![17]

---

1 Luke 14:31-32; Matthew 8:31

2 2 Corinthians 11:14; 1 Timothy 1:10; 4:16; 2 Timothy 4:3; Titus 1:9; 2:1

3 Romans 1:21,25,28; 2 Thessalonians 2:10-12

4 Deuteronomy 27:1-26; Romans 3:19

5 2 Corinthians 4:4; 1 John 5:19; Ephesians 6:12; Colossians 2:20; Galatians 4:3

6 Romans 8:14; Galatians 3:26; 1 John 3:2; 5:19; Matthew 5:9

7 Romans 8:1-2,17; 5:21; 2 Timothy 2:12; Revelation 5:10

8 Galatians 5:1,13; 2:4; 4:26,31; John 8:32-36; Romans 6:18; 8:2

9 2 Corinthians 1:21; 1 John 2:20,27

10 Ephesians 1:19; 3:7,20; Colossians 1:29

11 Luke 13:5; 1 Corinthians 1:18; 2 Corinthians 2:15; 4:3; 2 Thessalonians 2:10

12 1 Corinthians 6:9-10; Romans 1:29; 1 John 2:16

13 1 John 2:15; 3:1,7; 1 Timothy 1:3,10; 2 Timothy 4:3; John 15:19

14 Isaiah 20:5; John 1:5; Revelation 18:23d, "By your φαρμακεια all the nations were led astray" – φαρμακεια, pronounced "far-mah-kay-ah," the etymon of *pharmacy* and meaning *medication, magic, sorcery*, or *witchcraft*.

15 Colossians 2:8; Acts 17:18,32; Romans 1:21-22; 1 Corinthians 1:19-23; 3:18-19

16 Luke 10:33-34; 7:13; Exodus 2:6; Matthew 18:33

17 John 4:22; Psalm 147:19; Romans 3:2

May you understand the words of our King at the well of Jacob:

"'Dear woman,' Yeshua replied, 'believe Me, a time is coming when neither on this mountain nor in Jerusalem will you worship the Father. You all worship what you do not know; we worship what we do know, because salvation is from the Jews. Yet a time is coming and has now come when the true worshipers will worship the Father in the Spirit and in truth, because they are the kind of worshipers the Father seeks. God is a Spirit, and His worshipers must worship in the Spirit and in truth.' The woman said, 'I know that Messiah (the One called Christ) is coming. Whenever He comes, He will explain everything to us.' Yeshua said to her, 'I, the One speaking to you, am He.'"[1]

Are you or ***are you not*** a student of Christ? ***Are you*** or ***are you not*** His disciple? ***Do you*** or ***do you not*** accept His teaching as from Yehovah and True?

If you hear in your inner being that you might not be His disciple or might not accept His teaching, then you are providing residence for a spirit of doubt that demands your submission and service on its behalf![2] That doubt is not a product of your mind but a spirit waging war against the generous gifts of faith, power, and victory served to you on a silver platter through Yeshua's Blood![3] The dark spirit will never be satisfied with enough information, because it is a spirit that is always doubtful of Truth in any circumstance.[4] The dark spirit's very existence depends on its resistance to Truth. It is a shadow. It does not become light; it is cast out by light.[5] Therefore, cast out that dark, arguing, lying, deceitful, impeding, thieving, destroying spirit and become the mighty child of Yehovah you have been called and chosen to be![6]

TRAMPLE IT FOR THE GLORY OF JESUS CHRIST![7]HALLELUYAH!

---

[1] John 4:21-26
[2] John 6:29; 14:11; 20:27; Mark 1:15
[3] Romans 8:32; Psalm 84:11; 1 Corinthians 2:12; 3:21-23
[4] Romans 8:7; Ephesians 2:2
[5] 1 John 1:5; James 1:17; Luke 11:33-36; 2 Corinthians 6:14; 1 Timothy 6:16
[6] Ephesians 5:8-14; 1 Peter 2:9-11; 1 John 1:7
[7] Luke 10:19; Psalm 91:13; Ezekiel 2:6; Mark 16:18; Acts 28:5; Romans 16:20

TRAMPLE those SNAKES and SCORPIONS by means of His promises given you[1] and pick up your smooth stones with confidence![2] Sling them into the forehead of that doubting spirit and remove Goliath's doubting head with his own sword![3]

OUR GOD IS A MIGHTY GOD!!!!!!!!![4]

Now, when you have returned to your senses[5] and have made the unwavering choice to place your confidence in the teachings of the One Who conquered all infirmities, sin, and death,[6] then take up His promises[7] like those extra smooth stones provided to our father, David! He chose *five* stones, knowing that Goliath had *four more giant relatives*![8] Sling your stones of Truth and strike those infirmity giants between the eyes with the confidence of doing the same to any giant that might follow! Strike those infirmity spirits and remove them from the life of the land given to you in the Name of Yeshua Yehovah![9] Then take their armor as spoils of authority for the glory of your Holy God![10] For it is written,

"Or, how can someone go in a strong man's house and carry off his possessions unless they first tie up the strong man? Then they can plunder his house. Whoever is not with Me is against Me, and whoever is not gathering with Me scatters."[11]

Once you have conquered the resistance of an infirmity spirit's lies,[12] then you can go into the body to take authority over it.[13]

Listen again, holy warriors of Yeshua![14]

---

[1] Luke 10:19; Psalm 91:13; Ezekiel 2:6; Mark 16:18; Acts 28:5; Romans 16:20
[2] 1 Samuel 17:40; 1 Corinthians 1:27-29; Jeremiah 23:29
[3] 1 Samuel 17:46,51; 2 Samuel 23:21; Ester 7:10; Psalm 7:15-16
[4] Revelation 1:8; 4:8; Isaiah 5:16; 48:2; 54:5; Jeremiah 51:5
[5] 1 Corinthians 15:34; Joel 1:5; Romans 13:11; Ephesians 5:14
[6] John 6:29; 16:33; 1 John 5:5
[7] 2 Peter 1:4; Romans 9:4; 2 Corinthians 1:20; 7:21; Hebrews 9:15
[8] Saph, or Sippai, (2 Samuel 21:18; 1 Chronicles 20:4) Ishbi-Benob (2 Samuel 21:16), Goliath's brother, Lahmi, (2 Samuel 21:19; 1 Chronicles 20:5), and the giant with six fingers, or "Hexadactylus"(2 Samuel 21:20; 1 Chronicles 20:6).
[9] Numbers 33:52; Romans 6:13; 2 Corinthians 10:4-5
[10] 1 Samuel 17:51d-54; Mark 3:27
[11] Matthew 12:29-30
[12] James 4:7; John 10:10; Hebrews 4:15
[13] Luke 10:19; Psalm 91:13; Ezekiel 2:6; Mark 16:18; Acts 28:5; Romans 16:20
[14] Luke 8:18; 19:26; Deuteronomy 32:46-47; Proverbs 2:2-5; Mark 4:23-24; Acts 17:11; Hebrews 2:1; James 1:22-25; Matthew 13:12; John 15:2

"Because we do not have a High Priest Who is unable to sympathize with our ασθενειαις;[1] but One Who in every respect has been tested as we are, yet took on no sin."[2]

Many English versions simply translate ἀσθένεια[3] as *weakness*, but it is a "weakness" in the sense of an *infirmity or sickness* of the soul or body! Understand that infirmities can be brought to the body as temptations![4] And just as *moral temptations* can masquerade as functions of our own soul, so also *infirmity temptations* can masquerade as functions of our own body![5] In other words, just as you would identify a sudden evil thought as a temptation, understand that a sudden assault by a physical symptom is also a temptation of a different form. Therefore, do not accept either sort of temptation as belonging to the soul or body in any way![6]

And do not be deceived by the many doctrines of your culture that stand against the clear authority given to you by Yehovah.[7] He has given you full command and inheritance over your body for His Glory![8] Go into your body as His disciple with His Truth, Pursuit, and Love and overtake it with His healing![9]

HalleluYah!

For instance, when the second man in the example above fought against the infirmity that was causing his nose to become itchy, inflamed, congested, and runny, he commanded those symptoms to stop. However, his efforts did not stop there. He also used Christ's Power through His will to take control over the tissues and stop each of the symptoms by force.[10] To do this, he first sought awareness of the tissues in the same way that he would have sought awareness of his hand if he intended to move it.[11] He understood that, as a human spirit given dominion

---

1 Pronounced "ahs-then'-ey-ayees"
2 Hebrews 4:15
3 Pronounced "ahs-then'-ey-ah"
4 2 Corinthians 12:7; 2 Chronicles 16:12; Acts 19:12; Job 2:6-7
5 Mark 9:29; Matthew 12:45; James 5:15
6 2 Corinthians 10:4-5; Ephesians 6:12-18; James 5:15
7 Matthew 18:7; John 14:17
8 2 Peter 2:18-20; 3:17; Romans 16-18; 2 Corinthians 11:3,13-15; Hebrews 3:14
9 2 Timothy 2:21; Matthew 10:1
10 Ezekiel 37:1-14; 36:1; Isaiah 42:18; Jeremiah 22:29
11 Ephesians 5:13; Romans 6:13; James 3:2

over his soul,[1] he was able to use his soul to force his body's compliance.[2] Once he felt the body's tissues with authority, he was able to command them to be calm,[3] stop the itchiness, reduce the swelling, and cast away the symptoms of irritation and rhinorrhea (runny nose).[4]
But where did this authority come from? The act of taking authority over tissues in the body is one of cooperation between the Holy Spirit, human spirit, soul, and body.[5] A person's spirit must first learn to recognize and accept the Authority of the Voice of the Holy Spirit.[6] Then the person's soul can learn how to recognize the voice of the human spirit.[7] After this, the body must be trained to listen to the spirit-led soul.[8]

And tissues will listen![9]

Presently, many of the redeemed have been deceived by the voices of infirmity spirits in the body.[10] Not every feeling, sensation, perception, or pain is actually "of" the body.[11] On the contrary, many such voices are not resident in the body at all. The assaults are what they are: assaults.[12] They do not "belong" to the body or the soul in any way. The dedicated disciple will learn to sift through all the "voices" and reject any that are not of the Truth.[13] For there are many voices heard by a spirit, soul, and body,[14] but the spirit of the redeemed person learns to recognize them all when accepting only the Voice of Truth.[15]

---

[1] Genesis 1:28; Romans 8:13; 1 Corinthians 9:27; 2 Corinthians 7:1; Luke 11:36
[2] Ezekiel 37:1-4; Matthew 21:21; Romans 4:19-20
[3] Ezekiel 37:7-14; Luke 8:46
[4] Hebrews 4:12; Matthew 10:8; John 15:8
[5] 1 John 5:8; 1 Thessalonians 5:23; Hebrews 4:12
[6] John 10:3-5; Matthew 11:15; Mark 4:9,23; Luke 8:8; Revelation 2:7,11,17,29; 3:6,13,22
[7] Hebrews 4:11-12; Psalm 42:5; 84:2; 116:7; 119:28; Isaiah 61:10
[8] Luke 4:39,41; Matthew 17:18; Mark 1:25; 9:25
[9] Ezekiel 37:1-4; Matthew 21:21; Romans 4:19-20
[10] Romans 7:11; Isaiah 44:20; Hebrews 3:13; James 1:22
[11] Hosea 5:12-15; Judges 10:10-16; 2 Chronicles 33:12-13; Proverbs 1:27-33
[12] Matthew 13:28; 16:23; 1 Corinthians 5:3-7
[13] Hebrews 5:14; 1 John 4:1
[14] 1 Thessalonians 5:23; Hebrews 4:12
[15] Genesis 4:10; Jeremiah 51:55; Nahum 2:13

Praise Yehovah, Who gives us Truth,[1] Power,[2] and Authority[3] in the Name of Yeshua!

To take authority over the tissues in a body, you must become the reigning voice in the body![4] This conquest is not as mysterious as it may sound to the inexperienced ear.[5] It is no more complex than moving, blinking, or swallowing under normal circumstances. Through faith, you accept the authority to "speak" to the body's tissues.[6] You move them as your own rather than tolerating them as some foreign substance you have been "told" you cannot access. Do not accept any thought, idea, feeling, impression, pursuit, emotion, symptom, pain, ache, or discomfort that resists the healing freely given to you through Jesus Christ![7] He did not die on the Cross to save pieces of you![8] No! Your soul and body have been given over to your authority in Christ![9] There is no part of your body that can escape the full authority of your soul and spirit![10]

Glory be to our God in the flesh, Jesus Christ,[11] Who overcame sickness[12] and healed *everyone who came to Him of all their diseases*![13]

HalleluYah!

Praise our God, Who revealed through Jesus that He *always* wants to heal us![14]

GLORY TO GOD!

HALLELUYAAAAAAAAAAAH!!!!!!!!!!

---

[1] John 1:17; 14:6; 15:1; 18:37; Romans 15:8; Colossians 2:17; 1 John 5:6,20; Revelation 3:7,14; 19:11

[2] 1 Corinthians 1:24; Romans 1:4; Matthew 22:29; Mark 13:26; Colossians 1:16; 2:15; Hebrews 6:5; 1 Peter 3:22

[3] 1 Thessalonians 2:6; Luke 10:19; 2 Corinthians 10:8

[4] Romans 6:12-14; Philippians 1:20; Proverbs 12:18

[5] Acts 17:20; Hosea 8:12; 1 Corinthians 1:18

[6] Ezekiel 37:1-4; Matthew 21:21; Romans 4:19-20

[7] Acts 9:34; Luke 4:40

[8] Revelation 5:9; Matthew 20:28; 26:28; Acts 20:28; Romans 3:24-26

[9] Galatians 5:16-18; Matthew 26:41b

[10] Judges 18:10; James 3:2

[11] John 1:14; Luke 2:11; Philippians 2:6-8; 1 Timothy 3:16; 1 John 4:2-3; 2 John 1:7

[12] John 12:31; 16:11,33; Psalm 68:18; Romans 8:37; 1 John 4:4; 5:4

[13] Matthew 4:23-24; 9:35; Exodus 15:26

[14] Luke 5:12-13; Ezekiel 36:25-27; Hosea 14:4; Matthew 9:29

JESUS IS ABOVE EVERY AUTHORITY!!!!!!!!![1]

HALLELUUUUUUUUUUUUUUYAAAAAAAAAAAAH!!!!!!!!!!

AND HE HAS GIVEN THAT AUTHORITY TO US!!!!![2]

HALLELUUUUUUUUYAAAAAAAAAAAAAAAAAAAAH!!!!!!!!!!

THEREFORE, HOLY PEOPLE[3], PICK UP YOUR SWORDS[4] AND CONQUER!!!!!![5]

Conquer the soul with your spirit through His Love, Power, Truth, and Authority that dwells in you![6] Conquer the body in the same way through the conquered soul that shines brightly in the Hand of our God![7] Take dominion for the Glory of His Name![8] Your soul and body are His![9] They are the "land" entrusted to you through sacred promises from the only truly trustworthy Source in all existence![10] It is Yehovah's Will to form you into the image of Christ![11] It is His Will to make your soul perfect![12] It is His Will to heal your body![13] He is your Healer![14] He is the One Who makes your joy complete![15]

"Wake up, sleeper, rise from the dead, and Christ will shine on you!"[16] Conquer what has been given to you, mighty warrior![17] Conquer in the Name of Yeshua HaMashiach Yehovah, the Alpha and Omega, the Wonderful Counselor, and the Prince of Peace![18]

---

[1] Ephesians 1:21; Philippians 2:9-10; Colossians 2:10; Hebrews 1:4

[2] Luke 10:19; Psalm 91:13; Ezekiel 2:6; Mark 16:18; Acts 28:5; Romans 16:20

[3] 1 Peter 2:9; Revelation 1:6; 5:10

[4] Ephesians 6:17; Hebrews 4:12

[5] Romans 8:37; Isaiah 25:8; 1 Corinthians 15:57; 1 John 4:4; 5:4-5; Jude 1:24

[6] 2 Peter 1:3; Psalm 84:11; Romans 8:32; 1 Corinthians 3:21-23; 1 Timothy 4:8

[7] Numbers 22:31; Romans 8:37; 1 Corinthians 15:45-49

[8] Genesis 28:4; Numbers 33:53; Deuteronomy 1:8,21; 4:1; 6:18; 9:5

[9] Romans 6:13; 1 Peter 2:9

[10] Psalm 62:1-12; 22:4-5; Isaiah 26:4; 50:10

[11] Romans 8:29; Matthew 12:50; 25:40; Colossians 1:15-18; Revelation 1:5-6

[12] Hebrews 10:14; 11:40; 12:23

[13] 1 Peter 2:24; 3:18; 1 John 2:2; 3:5; 4:10,14; Romans 3:25-26; John 1:29; 4:42

[14] Exodus 15:26; Acts 9:34

[15] John 15:11; 16:24; 17:13; 1 Peter 1:8; Jude 1:24

[16] Ephesians 5:14; Isaiah 60:1; 1 Thessalonians 5:6; 2 Timothy 2:26

[17] Romans 8:37; Isaiah 25:8; 1 Corinthians 15:57; 1 John 4:4; 5:4-5; Jude 1:24

[18] Matthew 10:7-8; Isaiah 9:6; Psalm 32:8; Proverbs 8:14

Praise be to the Almighty Conqueror,[1] Who made all things,[2] Who is Supreme in all things,[3] and Who oversees all things for Good![4]

HALLELUYAH!

How blessed we are to be drawn to Him as children of God![5]

PRAISE HIS NAME!

Give Him thanks and glory,[6] for He has done marvelous things![7]

GLORY BE TO GOD!

Let everyone bless His Name,[8] for He is making all things new![9]

HALLELUYAH!

He is removing all death, mourning, crying, and pain, and He is replacing them with life, peace, comfort, and joy![10]

BLESS YEHOVAH!!!!

Praise our God, Who even now grants us entry into the Kingdom of Heaven![11]

HALLELUUUUUUUYAAAAAAAAAAAAAAAAAAAH!!!!!!!!

HALLELUUUUUUUYAAAAAAAAAAAAAAAAAAAH!!!!!!!!

HALLELUUUUUUUYAAAAAAAAAAAAAAAAAAAH!!!!!!!!

---

[1] Romans 8:37; Colossians 2:15
[2] John 1:3,10; Jeremiah 10:11-12; Hebrews 1:2
[3] Colossians 1:18; Psalm 89:27; Isaiah 52:13; Matthew 28:18; John 3:35
[4] Romans 8:28; Matthew 5:45; 19:17
[5] Romans 8:14; Galatians 3:26; 1 John 3:1-2; 5:19; Matthew 5:9
[6] Revelation 4:11; 5:12-13; 7:12
[7] Psalm 72:17-18; 77:14; 86:10; 136:4; Exodus 15:11; Job 9:10; Daniel 4:2-3
[8] Psalm 103:1-22; Deuteronomy 8:10; 1 Chronicles 29:20; Nehemiah 9:5
[9] Revelation 21:5; Isaiah 42:9; 43:19; 2 Corinthians 5:17
[10] Revelation 21:4; Isaiah 25:8; Hosea 13:14; 1 Corinthians 15:54-58
[11] Hebrews 4:3,10; Matthew 11:12; Luke 17:20

HALLELUUUYAAAAAAAAAAAAAAAAAAAAAAAAAAAAAAH!!!!!!!!

HOLY IS HIS NAME!!!

AMEN!

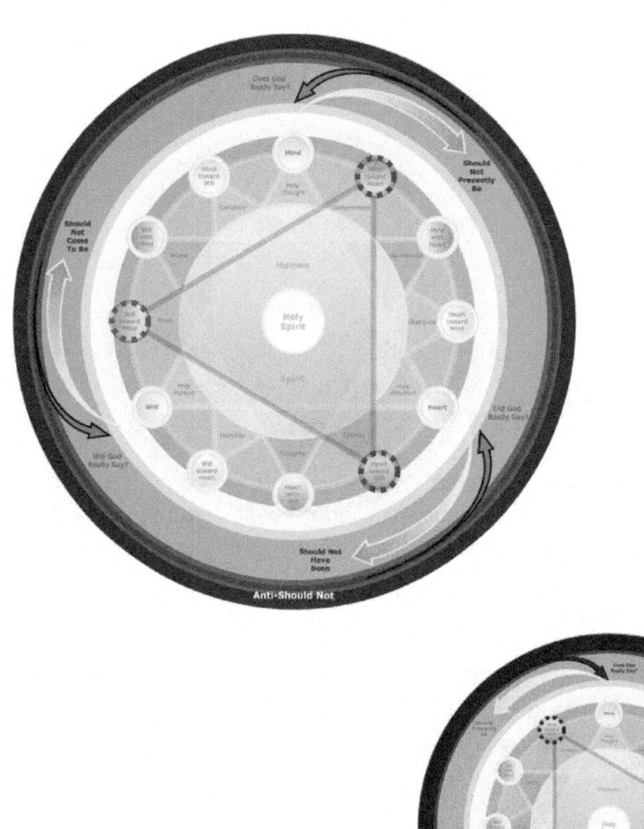

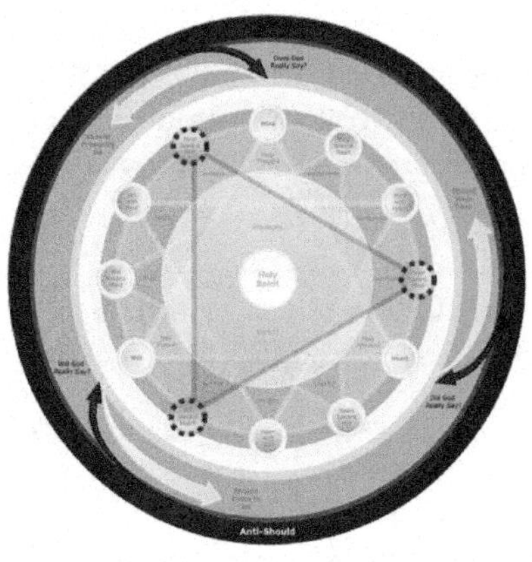

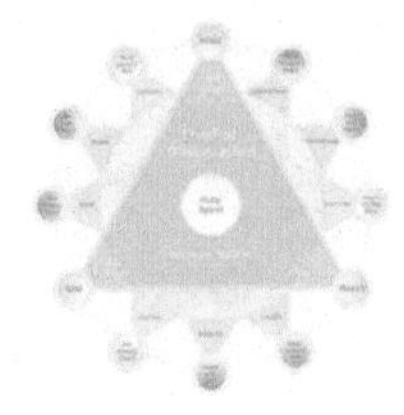

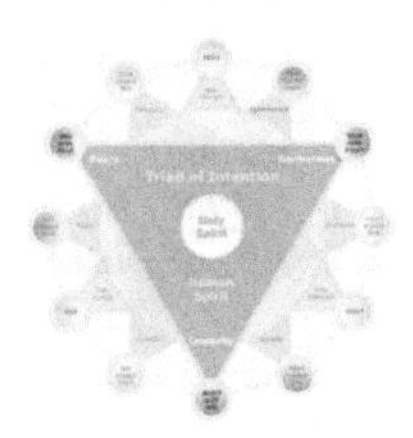

CHAPTER 29

MINISTERING TO THE BODY

Just as the soul requires love and attention to facilitate the healing readily available to it, the body requires love and attention to receive and accept the healing made readily available to it.[1]

"Do you not know? Have you not heard?"[2] Yehovah knitted you together in the womb![3] "No one ever hated their own body,"[4] and Yehovah certainly doesn't hate your body![5] He has even promised to transform it and raise it into Heaven![6]

HalleluYah!

The body is a good thing![7] It is like the Promised Land![8] Wonderful potential has been granted to it, but its development, management, and productivity are dependent on the soul.[9] Crops will not grow for harvest if seeds have not been

---

[1] Ephesians 5:29; Ezekiel 34:27; Matthew 23:37
[2] Isaiah 40:28; Jeremiah 4:22; Mark 8:17-18; Luke 24:25
[3] Psalm 139:13; Job 19:9-12
[4] Ephesians 5:29; Ezekiel 34:27; Matthew 23:37
[5] Proverbs 3:8; Exodus 15:26; Acts 9:34
[6] 1 Corinthians 15:42-49; Luke 20:35-36; 1 Peter 1:4
[7] Genesis 1:27-31; Romans 6:12-13; 12:1; 1 Corinthians 6:15,19-20
[8] Genesis 26:2-5; Hebrews 3:7-4:13
[9] 2 Chronicles 7:14; Luke 13:6-9

planted and the fields have not been irrigated.[1] Sheep will not be available for shearing if they have not been gathered and shepherded.[2] And horses will not be available for riding or war if they haven't been tamed and trained.[3] That is to say, a body that has lived under dark influences has been conditioned to serve the needs of those influences.[4] Like a land mistreated, it often needs tender ministry.[5]

After infirmity spirits have been cast out of a body, it needs to be blessed.[6] While someone could argue that this includes wise choices concerning nutrition, exercise, and rest,[7] far more important are the blessings said over the body in power, love, and truth through the Spirit.[8] Sincere blessings condition the body to receive specific healings and walk in a general acceptance of Heaven's supernatural principles.[9]

For example, a certain man was plagued with breathing problems ever since a time of childhood trauma. For over twenty years, he listened to human experts, practiced their treatments, and consumed their medicines. Still, he continued to suffer between doses and from all sorts of irritants, like mowed grass, strong perfume, and pollen. When he became a true disciple of Christ, he fought a mighty battle, received complete victory,[10] and was fully restored.[11] However, after continuing to minister blessings in Yeshua to his body, he noticed over the progressing years that it had become completely immune even to thick smoke, severe allergens, and toxic fumes! His body had embraced its role according to the Kingdom of Heaven![12]

How did this happen? How did this man's body become "invincible" in Christ?[13] It gained supernatural strength through the Power of Resurrection blessing![14]

BLESS GOD!

---

[1] Galatians 6:7-9; Genesis 26:12
[2] Matthew 12:11; 18:12; Proverbs 27:23
[3] Proverbs 21:31; 1 Chronicles 5:18; 25:7; 2 Chronicles 2:14; 26:11; Hosea 10:11
[4] Romans 1:27; 8:7-8; James 3:6; Jude 1:23
[5] 2 Chronicles 36:21; Leviticus 25:4; Exodus 23:11
[6] Hosea 3:5; Acts 3:19; 1 John 1:9
[7] Proverbs 25:27; Leviticus 11:1-47
[8] Matthew 4:4; Exodus 23:25; 1 Timothy 4:4
[9] Romans 6:13-14; 8:11; Proverbs 12:18; John 5:24
[10] 1 Corinthians 15:57; Romans 8:37; 1 John 5:4-5
[11] 1 Timothy 6:12; 1 Peter 5:10; Galatians 6:1; Acts 9:12
[12] 2 Kings 4:39-41; Luke 10:19; Psalm 91:13; Mark 16:18; Acts 28:5
[13] Luke 10:19; Psalm 91:13; Ezekiel 2:6; Mark 16:18; Acts 28:5; Romans 16:20
[14] John 11:25-26; Hebrews 6:7

Christ filled this man's soul with resurrection POWER![1]

YESSSSSSSSSSSS!!!!!

Praise our Almighty God, Who gives Victory to His children![2]

HALLELUUUUUUUUUYAAAAAAAAAAAAAAAAAH!!!!!!!!

And this is what He has for ALL of us![3]

Our brother believed,[4] put the Word into practice,[5] conquered his soul for the Glory of Yeshua,[6] and proceeded to push that victory throughout his body![7]

He blessed his body as if he were blessing the Promised Land for the service and glory of Yehovah![8]

HALLELUYAH!

You can do this, too! Yehovah does not show favoritism![9] He loves you just as much as He loves this man![10] He loves you just as much as He loves Moses, Elijah, Mary, Peter, and John![11]

HALLELUYAH!

So, stop listening to "every idea under the sun" about how you should live,[12] and start listening carefully to Yehovah's instructions! And then DO WHAT HE SAYS![13]

---

[1] Philippians 3:10; Romans 6:4-11; 8:10-11
[2] 1 Corinthians 15:57; Romans 8:37; 1 John 5:4-5
[3] 2 Timothy 1:9; Ephesians 2:8; Titus 3:4-5
[4] Matthew 8:13; 9:29-30; 15:28; 17:20; Mark 9:23
[5] James 1:22; 4:17; Matthew 7:21-25; 12:50; 28:20; Luke 11:28; 12:47-48; John 13:17; Romans 2:13; 1 John 2:3, 3:7; 3 John 1:11; Revelation 22:7
[6] John 15:8; Luke 6:35; Psalm 92:12-15; Isaiah 60:21; Matthew 5:16
[7] Romans 6:12; 2 Corinthians 10:4; 1 Corinthians 9:26; 1 Timothy 6:12
[8] Deuteronomy 28:1-12; Hebrews 6:7
[9] James 2:1; Acts 10:34-35
[10] 1 John 4:9-10; Romans 2:1; 3:25-26; 1 Peter 2:24; Ephesians 6:9; Acts 10:34
[11] Matthew 11:11; 1 John 2:2; John 15:9
[12] Acts 17:21; 2 Timothy 4:3
[13] John 13:17; James 1:22; 4:17; Matthew 7:21-25; 12:50; 28:20; Luke 11:28; 12:47-48; Romans 2:13; 1 John 2:3, 3:7; 3 John 1:11; Revelation 22:7

GLORY BE TO GOD![1]

THEREFORE, to bless the body, one must speak the full ministry of the soul over it as if speaking the blessings of Scripture over a warhorse or an area of land.[2] Calming assurances and encouragements of His gifts of healing, strength, prosperity, and purpose should be poured out on behalf of the body, showing love, concern, and value for it in His Kingdom.[3]

Your body is not your enemy![4]

Though it might initially seem to resist, perseverance will cause the body to respond favorably, even surpassing expectations.[5] Again, treat it with the patience you would show when attempting to restore some land or train an animal.[6] Continue to show your body the Righteous Love of Yeshua, and in time it will begin to obey on command.[7] You may even command a disk in the spine to move or a knee to stop cracking, and the body will immediately cooperate with awareness and obedience of His authority that has come to live in you.[8]

Once you experience the power of His blessing flowing through your soul for your body,[9] you will also begin to understand how to bless the souls and bodies of others[10] for the Glory of His Love and His Name![11]

HalleluYah!

Praise be to our King,[12] Who *will* find us doing His work when He returns![13]

GLORY TO THE KING OF VICTORY![14]

---

[1] Revelation 4:11; 5:12-13; 7:12
[2] Leviticus 25:21; Deuteronomy 7:13; 28:4,8,11-12; 33:13; Job 1:10; Isaiah 65:16
[3] Ephesians 5:29; Proverbs 12:10a; Isaiah 40:11; Ezekiel 34:14-15
[4] Ephesians 5:29; Ezekiel 34:27; Matthew 23:37
[5] Luke 8:15; Romans 6:22; Colossians 1:6; Hebrews 6:11-12; 10:36; James 1:4
[6] 2 Kings 5:9-14; Luke 13:8
[7] Galatians 6:9; 1 Corinthians 15:58; 2 Thessalonians 3:13; Hebrews 12:3
[8] Ezekiel 37:1-4; Matthew 21:21; Romans 4:19-20
[9] Hebrews 10:36; Luke 8:46
[10] James 5:16; Acts 15:32; Luke 6:28; 22:32
[11] 2 Corinthians 1:3-4; Philippians 2:11; Micah 7:18
[12] John 1:49; 12:13-15; 18:37; 19:19-22; Ezekiel 37:21-25; Revelation 5:5; 22:16
[13] Luke 12:42-43; Revelation 20:6; 22:14
[14] 1 Corinthians 15:57; Romans 8:37; 1 John 5:4-5; Colossians 1:18

HALLELUYAH!

GLORY TO THE KING OF MERCY![1]

HALLELUUUUYAAAAAAH!!!

GLORY TO THE GREAT HEALER![2]

HALLELUUUYAAAAAAAAAAAAAH!!!!

GLORY TO THE RESTORER OF SOULS![3]

HALLELUUUUUYAAAAAAAAAAAAAAAAAAAH!!!!!!!

HALLELUUUUYAAAAAAAAAAAAAAAAAAAAAAAAAH!!!!!!!!!!!!

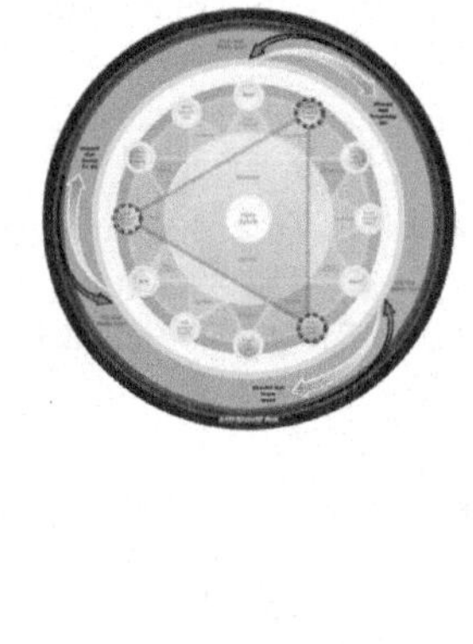

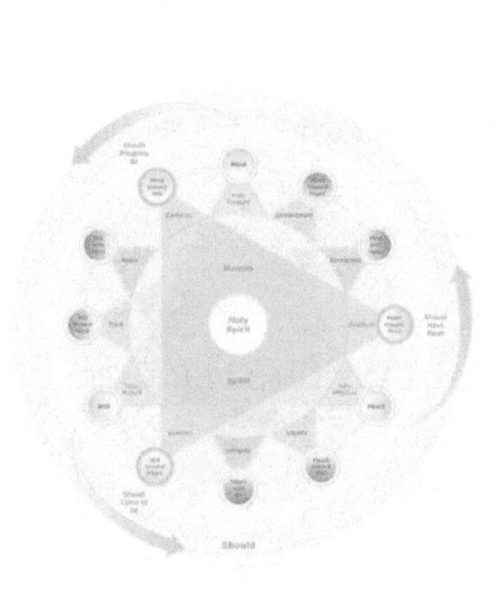

---

[1] Hebrews 4:16; James 3:17; Ephesians 2:4; Romans 15:9

[2] Matthew 12:15; 4:24; 8:16; 12:15; 14:36; Luke 4:40; 5:15; 8:47; Mark 6:56

[3] 1 Peter 5:10; Psalm 23:3

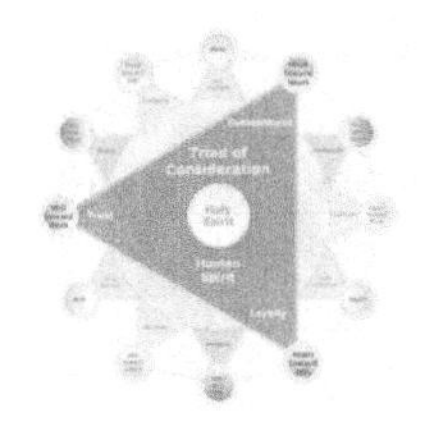

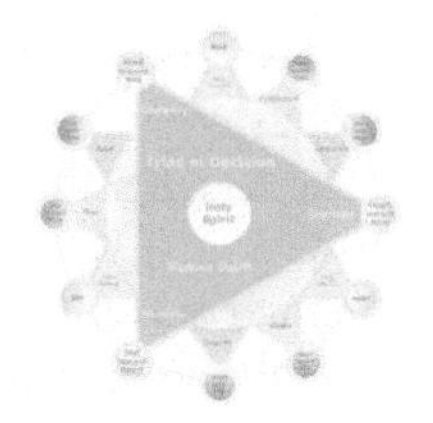

CHAPTER 30

TRAINING STRENGTH IN SPIRIT

HOLY PEOPLE OF GOD!!!![1]

HALLELUUUYAAAAAAAAAAAAAAAH!!!!!!!

YOU ARE MORE THAN CONQUERORS!!!!![2]

HALLELUUUUUYAAAAAAAAAAAAAAAH!!!!!!!

There IS NO ONE stronger than YOU,[3] HOLY PEOPLE, because YOU have the STRENGTH OF CHRIST!!!![4]

YOU ALREADY HAVE IT IN YOU![5]

BLESS YESHUUUAAAAAAAAAAAAAAH!!!!!

HALLELUUUUUUYAAAAAAAAAAAAAAAH!!!!!!!

---

[1] 1 Peter 2:9; Revelation 1:6; 5:10

[2] Romans 8:37; Isaiah 25:8; 1 Corinthians 15:57; 1 John 4:4; 5:4-5; Jude 1:24

[3] Psalm 28:7; 46:1; 2 Timothy 1:7; Joshua 1:9

[4] Philippians 4:13; Ephesians 3:16

[5] Colossians 1:27; Ephesians 3:16; 2 Corinthians 4:16

Because Yehovah's Power is *already* in you,[1] the enemy's assaults are merely *suggestive* in soul and spirit.[2] The enemy will bring dark emotions, thoughts, or desires, with the goal of gaining your acceptance of them as your own.[3] BUT THAT'S NOT WHO YOU ARE![4] You don't have to accept *any* of those dark things![5] On the contrary! You need to shine with who you are![6] You need to stop believing the world's lies about who you are[7] and start acting on who Yehovah says you are![8] By doing this, you flow in the Mighty Power of His Light![9]

HALLELUYAAAAAAAAAAAH!!!!!!!

YOU HAVE BEEN MADE HOLY! SO, BE HOLY![10]
YOU HAVE BEEN GIVEN JOY! SO, BE JOYFUL![11]
YOU HAVE BEEN GIVEN PEACE! SO, BE PEACEFUL![12]

DO NOT let the enemy discourage you from behaving as who you are in spirit![13]

DO NOT let any dark voice convince you that your past troubles with lifting some spiritual weight are any sort of indication that you should not bother practicing, expressing, and living with that particular spiritual characteristic![14]

For example, a certain man experienced a tragic childhood full of abuse that left him heartbroken. After becoming a true disciple of Yeshua, he learned through the Holy Spirit that he was constantly being attacked with illnesses due to an open gate of bitterness.[15] When he confronted the bitter spirit, that spirit began to insist that the man could never be grateful to Yehovah because his childhood would prove too painful to ever result in gratitude. As a result of the attack, the man fell into even deeper heartbreak and threw himself at the Lord's Feet in prayer.

---

[1] 2 Corinthians 4:7; 13:4; Ephesians 1:19-20; 1 Thessalonians 1:5
[2] 1 Corinthians 10:13; 1 Peter 5:8-9; Luke 22:46
[3] 2 Corinthians 11:14-15; 1 Timothy 1:10; 4:16; 2 Timothy 4:3; Titus 1:9; 2:1
[4] Ephesians 5:8,11; 1 Thessalonians 5:4-8; 2 Corinthians 3:18
[5] Romans 6:14,17-18; Galatians 5:1; John 8:32
[6] Matthew 5:14-16; Ephesians 5:8-14; Philippians 2:15
[7] 1 Peter 4:4; Acts 17:30
[8] John 17:14,16; 1 John 4:5-6; 5:19-20
[9] 1 John 1:7; Isaiah 2:5; Psalm 89:15; 97:11; Romans 13:12; Ephesians 5:8
[10] Ephesians 1:4; 2:10; 2 Peter 1:5-10; Titus 2:11-12; 2 Timothy 1:9
[11] John 15:11; 16:24; 17:13; 1 Peter 1:8; Jude 1:24
[12] John 14:27; 16:33; Romans 5:1-2; Acts 10:36; 1 Corinthians 1:3
[13] Ephesians 6:10; 2 Timothy 2:1; 4:17; Colossians 1:11; Philippians 4:13
[14] Exodus 4:10; James 3:2; 1 Peter 5:10
[15] Numbers 5:24; Deuteronomy 29:18

Notice that the man's soul is strong in certainty and humility; the Triad of Decision has not been overcome by darkness.

After spending time in prayer, the man heard encouragement from the Voice of the Holy Spirit as gentle thoughts rising up,[1] suggesting that the man simply begin to spend time thanking Yehovah for things that he was already sincerely grateful for.[2] Invigorated, the man received a plan to thank Yehovah for as many things as possible for at least thirty minutes every morning.[3] As he proceeded to do this, he discovered after several days that He genuinely ALREADY had the gratitude of Christ, and it was flowing powerfully through his heart![4] Over time, he even grew strong enough to know how to be grateful for his childhood as a whole without excusing the dark spirits that had caused people to do him harm![5]

HalleluYah!

Understand that encouraging, expressing, or "growing" spiritual strength to manifest soulical character is very much like physical training.[6] When first seeking to become physically fit, no person enters a gym as a champion or walks onto a track as an Olympian![7] No matter how much potential talent they might possess, they begin at a novice level. What matters for this person is strength in spirit.[8] Either the novice will choose to accept the physical challenges as too demanding and uncomfortable, or they will choose to view them as mere hurdles in their path to victory.[9]

For example, two young men entered a workout gym. Neither having weight trained before, both were thin and immediately experienced unpleasant difficulty when attempting to curl a thirty-pound dumbbell more than a few times. Each of the men heard various thoughts in their souls. The first heard a "voice" discouraging him from continuing by saying that he had always been weak and didn't need to be strong. When he saw an experienced trainer curling a fifty-pound dumbbell, the voice pointed out that the size of the trainer's arm was at least twice that of the young man's own. Then the voice began to distract him with thoughts

---

[1] 2 Thessalonians 2:16-17; Hebrews 6:18
[2] Ephesians 5:20; 1 Thessalonians 5:18; Colossians 3:17
[3] Galatians 6:9; Mark 1:35; Psalm 5:3; 59:16; 88:13
[4] 1 Thessalonians 5:18; Ephesians 5:20; Philippians 4:6; Colossians 3:17
[5] Jude 1:23; Matthew 6:14-15; Romans 5:6-8; Matthew 7:1-29
[6] 1 Timothy 4:8; Daniel 1:5
[7] 1 Corinthians 9:25; 2 Timothy 2:5
[8] Judges 14:6; 1 Samuel 17:34-37,46; Zechariah 4:6
[9] Matthew 21:28-32; Luke 19:12-27

and understandings of how much the young man would have to eat, how often he would have to go to the gym, and how much time he would have to sacrifice from his current schedule to pursue such a goal. However, while the second young man also heard the same voices, he heard another Voice that said physical training takes time and commitment but offers valuable rewards. Choosing to listen to that Voice when seeing the size of the trainer's arm, the second man ignored the voices of discouragement and heard the encouraging Voice suggest that the trainer had also been a beginner at one time. When he asked the trainer how long he'd been lifting, the trainer shared that it had only been a few years, and so the second man decided firmly in his spirit that he would pursue the same goal or even exceed it.

Understand that spiritual training is the same in many ways! One person sees a powerful spiritual warrior and listens to voices that insist the warrior was born that way or had an easy life.[1] In contrast, another person observes the same warrior and chooses to listen to a Voice that says such a blessing is attainable with perseverance.[2]

Be like the SECOND PERSON! BE LIKE JOSHUA AND CELEB![3] BE LIKE MARY[4] INSTEAD OF ZECHARIAH![5]

HALLELUYAH! VICTORY IS OURS![6]

OUR KING HAS OVERCOME FOR US![7]

HALLELUUUUUYAAAAAAAAAAAAAAAAH!

Consider the map of the soul! Note its twelve gates.[8] Are you experiencing weakness at any of them? If you are young in the spiritual fight, then your honest

---

[1] Hebrews 11:23; Acts 7:20

[2] Exodus 2:11; 4:24-26; Numbers 12:3,8; James 5:17

[3] Numbers 13:25-14:38

[4] Luke 1:28-38; Romans 4:20-21

[5] Luke 1:11-20; 2 Kings 7:2; Mark 9:19; 16:14

[6] 1 Corinthians 15:57; Romans 8:37; 1 John 5:4-5

[7] John 16:33; 1 John 2:13-14; 4:4; 5:4

[8] Revelation 21:21," The twelve gates were twelve pearls, each gate made of a single pearl." Consider that pearls in oysters are formed from extensive suffering against irritants. In the same way, our gates are constantly tested and irritated but result in the formation of great spiritual wealth in relationship with Yehovah (Mounted on the gates are the respective

answer is "yes." Acknowledging this, will you now choose to listen to the voices that are attempting to discourage you, or will you listen to the gentle Voice that is encouraging you to take hold of the goal to win every gate of your soul and the dominion over your body as well?[1]

"The one who is faithful in a very little thing is also faithful in much!"[2]

I tell you the truth: if you learn to be faithful with little, you will gain strength to be faithful with much! If you make an effort to be loyal to Yehovah with your time, you will discover that you will receive loyalty in resisting sin.[3] Loyalty is honor.[4] The one who honors Yehovah will be honored by Him.[5] If you make an effort to shift your trust to Yehovah by reading the Word, you will soon discover that you are overflowing with faith to encourage others![6] And if you make an effort to embrace integrity, you will soon experience abundant courage to proclaim the Truth boldly in even the most challenging situations![7]

Listen for the gentle Voice[8] that encourages victory, righteousness, and the pursuit of a faithful life. Begin where you are![9] Remember, our battlefront is the soul.[10] Even if you have been assaulted in your body, the battlefront is the soul.[11] Many warriors have been exhausted from being overstretched by the enemy.[12] The enemy will encourage the believer to spend time focusing on the physical attack and exhaust the believer by engaging in an endless tug-of-war match over physical dominion.[13] This is not how we fight![14] No! We fight where we are, not beyond where we are![15] We fight where we *already* have complete authority![16]

---

colorful stones with the names of the twelve tribes of Israel; Revelation 21:12, Exodus 28:21).

1 Philippians 3:12,14; 2 Corinthians 4:18

2 Luke 16:10

3 Galatians 6:7-9; Job 4:8; Proverbs 11:18; Romans 2:6-10

4 1 Corinthians 6:20; 10:31; Matthew 5:16

5 John 12:26; 14:21-23; 1 Samuel 2:30; Proverbs 27:18

6 2 Corinthians 1:4; 1 Thessalonians 4:18; 5:11; Psalm 66:16

7 Titus 2:7-8; 2 Timothy 4:2

8 1 Kings 19:11-13; Job 4:12-16

9 Zechariah 4:10; Isaiah 43:18-19

10 Matthew 6:33; Luke 12:31; Psalm 34:9; 37:19; 84:11; Isaiah 33:16; John 6:27

11 James 5:15; 1 Corinthians 11:30

12 Mark 5:26; Job 13:4; Jeremiah 30:15

13 Mark 9:18; Matthew 17:19-21

14 2 Corinthians 10:4; Ephesians 6:12

15 2 Peter 1:3; Psalm 84:11; Romans 8:32; 1 Corinthians 3:21-23; 1 Timothy 4:8

16 Ephesians 1:3; Romans 8:37; 2 Corinthians 1:20

We fight for the dominion of the soul right where our spirit is with the full Power of Christ![1] We take hold of every thought![2] We destroy soulical strongholds![3] We overcome darkness with light![4]

"What does this look like?" It looks like believing Yehovah and letting go of every bit of bad news![5] It looks like agreeing with the Word:

"His Divine Power has given us everything we need for life and godliness through our knowing the One Who has called us by His own Glory and Goodness!"[6]

"Therefore, if someone is in Christ, they are a new creation. The old has gone; what has become is completely new!"[7]

"But now that you have been set free from sin but have become slaves of God, the fruit you reap leads to purification, and the result is everlasting life!"[8]

"But the fruit of the Spirit is love, joy, peace, hope, kindness, goodness, faith, gentleness, and purity! Against such things there is no law! Those who belong to Christ Jesus have crucified the flesh with its affections and pursuits! Since we live by the Spirit, let us march in step with the Spirit!"[9]

"Because God has not given us a spirit of fear; but of power, and of love, and of a sound mind!"[10]

"... whatever is true, whatever is honorable, whatever is righteous, whatever is pure, whatever is friendly, whatever is reputable—if anything is virtuous or praiseworthy—think about such things!"[11]

"... to be spiritually minded is life and peace!"[12]

---

[1] Romans 6:13; Ephesians 1:3; 2 Corinthians 10:5
[2] 2 Corinthians 10:5; Jeremiah 4:14; Hebrews 4:12
[3] 2 Corinthians 10:4; Hebrews 11:30
[4] Romans 12:21; Luke 11:35; Romans 13:12; 1 Thessalonians 5:5; 1 Peter 2:9
[5] 1 John 1:5; James 1:17; Luke 11:33-36; 2 Corinthians 6:14; 1 Timothy 6:16
[6] 2 Peter 1:3
[7] 2 Corinthians 5:17
[8] Romans 6:22
[9] Galatians 5:22-25; See Chapter 34 of this testimony for more on this translation.
[10] 2 Timothy 1:7
[11] Philippians 4:8
[12] Romans 8:6

"... for the Joy of Yehovah is your strength!"[1]

Therefore, if you are weak in certainty, focus on filling your mind with truth[2] and being content with the blessings you've been given.[3] If you are struggling with lust, reflect on Yeshua's Sacrifice, which was an act of loyalty toward you,[4] and spend time thanking Him for all He has given you and done for you.[5] If you are wrestling with worry, join in Yeshua's commitment to righteousness[6] and practice receiving His Humility in your weakness.[7] Make an effort to pick up the practice of His Characteristics wherever and however you can today.[8]

"Commit your way to Yehovah. Trust in Him, and He will do this: He will bring forth your righteousness like the light of the dawn, your vindication like the noonday sun!"[9]

CHILDREN OF GOD![10]

HIS YOKE IS EASY! HIS BURDEN IS LIGHT![11]

HE HAS DONE EVERYTHING FOR YOU![12]

THERE IS NO BAD NEWS IN THE GOOD NEWS![13]
HIS STRENGTH IS ALREADY IN YOU![14]

The ONLY things inhibiting your full strength are LIES that you have accepted from the LIAR![15]

---

[1] Nehemiah 8:10
[2] Romans 12:2; Ephesians 4:22-24; Colossians 1:21-22; 3:10; Titus 3:5
[3] Philippians 4:11; 3:8; Matthew 6:31-34; 1 Timothy 6:6-9; Hebrews 10:34; 13:5-6
[4] 1 Thessalonians 5:10; Matthew 20:28; John 10:11,15,17; 15:13; Romans 5:8
[5] Colossians 3:3; 1 John 3:2; 1 Peter 1:3-5
[6] 1 John 2:29; 3:7; Psalm 45:7; 72:1-7; Romans 5:19; Revelation 19:8
[7] Matthew 11:29; Philippians 2:7-8
[8] Romans 8:29; 2 Corinthians 6:2
[9] Psalm 37:5-6
[10] Romans 8:14; Galatians 3:26; 1 John 3:1-2; 5:19; Matthew 5:9
[11] Matthew 11:30; Micah 6:8; Acts 15:10; Galatians 5:1; 1 John 5:3
[12] 2 Peter 1:3; Psalm 84:11; Romans 8:32; 1 Corinthians 3:21-23; 1 Timothy 4:8
[13] James 1:17; Romans 8:28
[14] Ephesians 6:10; 2 Timothy 2:1; 4:17; Colossians 1:11; Philippians 4:3
[15] Galatians 3:1; 2 Corinthians 11:3

REPENT! STOP LISTENING TO THE VOICE OF DISSENSION![1]
STOP LISTENING TO THE WORLD![2]

Are you of the world?

NO! YOU'RE NOT OF THE WORLD![3] YOU ARE A SPIRIT BEING, BORN OF GOD,[4] FILLED WITH HIS SPIRIT! [5]

HALLELUUUUUYAAAAAAAAAAAAH!!!!!!!!!!!

YOU DON'T HAVE TO BELIEVE DISCOURAGEMENT ANYMORE![6]

HALLELUUUUUYAAAAAAAAAAAAH!!!!!!!!!!!

YOU DON'T HAVE TO ACCEPT BAD NEWS ANYMORE!!!!![7]

SIBLINGS IN THE LORD! LISTEN CAREFULLY![8]

In the world, people live under the conditions of the world's principalities.[9] They listen to all sorts of rules, such as, "If I make a lot of money, I can be happy," "If everyone approves of me, I can know I'm valuable," "If I can accomplish this or that goal, I can relax," or "If I can see this or that, I can believe."[10]

NONSENSE! THOSE ARE ALL LIES FROM OPPRESSIVE SPIRITS![11]

THERE ARE NO SUCH "STEPPING STONES" IN THE KINGDOM OF HEAVEN![12]

---

[1] Galatians 5:19-25; Genesis 3:1
[2] 1 John 4:5-6; John 8:23; 15:19; 17:14
[3] John 17:14,16; 1 John 4:5-6; 5:19-20
[4] John 3:7; 1 Peter 1:23; Ephesians 4:22-24; 1 John 2:29; 3:9; 4:7; 5:1,4,18
[5] Ephesians 5:18; Acts 2:4; 4:8; 13:9,52
[6] Deuteronomy 31:8; Colossians 2:2-3
[7] Philippians 4:8; Hebrews 12:2; Colossians 3:2
[8] Luke 8:18; 19:26; Deuteronomy 32:46-47; Proverbs 2:2-5; Mark 4:23-24; Acts 17:11; Hebrews 2:1; James 1:22-25; Matthew 13:12; John 15:2
[9] Ephesians 2:2; 1 Corinthians 3:1
[10] James 4:14; 1 Corinthians 7:31; 2 Corinthians 10:3; 1 John 2:17
[11] Galatians 3:3; 4:7-10; 5:1,4-8; 6:12-14; 1 Timothy 6:9; Matthew 13:22
[12] Galatians 3:14; 1 Corinthians 12:13; Ephesians 1:13-14; Hebrews 12:1

In the Kingdom of Heaven, you ALREADY have happiness, joy, value, rest, and faith![1] You don't have to do ANYTHING to achieve any of these![2] THEY ARE GIFTS TO YOU!

HALLELUUUUUYAAAAAAAAAAAAAAAAAAAAAH!!!!!!!!

ALL YOU HAVE TO DO IS *LET GO* OF THE BAD NEWS AND *ACCEPT* THE GOOD NEWS!

"... testifying to the good news of God's Grace!"[3]

This is God's GRACE! God's GIFT of "*righteous finesse in your soul*" for YOU![4]

Children of Yehovah![5]

He has always been Good![6]

He has always been the Good News![7]

He is immeasurably Marvelous, exceedingly Wonderful![8]

There is no darkness in Him, only Light, even the very "light of humanity!"[9]

---

[1] Ephesians 1:3; 2:6; Genesis 12:2-3; 1 Chronicles 4:10; Isaiah 61:9; Galatians 3:9

[2] Ephesians 2:5,8; Titus 2:11; 3:5

[3] Acts 20:24

[4] See Chapter 19 of this testimony for more discussion about "grace."

[5] Romans 8:14; Galatians 3:26; 1 John 3:1-2; 5:19; Matthew 5:9

[6] Matthew 19:17; 1 Samuel 2:2; Psalm 145:7-9; James 1:17

[7] Hebrews 4:2,6; Mark 1:1; Luke 2:10; 16:16

[8] Revelation 15:3; Psalm 72:17-18; 77:14; 86:10; 136:4; Exodus 15:11; Job 9:10; Daniel 4:2-3

[9] John 1:1-5; 8:12; 9:5; 12:35,46; Ephesians 5:14; 1 John 1:5-7; Revelation 22:16

He is Pure,[1] Trustworthy,[2] Faithful,[3] Joyful,[4] True,[5] Content,[6] Gentle,[7] Kind,[8] Grateful,[9] Loving,[10] Holy,[11] Loyal,[12] "Integritous,"[13] Humble,[14] and Powerful![15]

He is Better than Best![16]

He is more than Lovely![17]

He is more than a Dream come true![18]

He is Hope,[19] Faith,[20] Love,[21] and More![22]

He surpasses everything and anything you could ever even begin to want![23]

HE IS ALWAYS GOOD ALL THE TIME![24]

HALLELUUUUUUUUUUUUYAAAAAAAAAAAAAAH!!!!!!!!!!

---

[1] 1 John 3:3; Hebrews 7:26
[2] 2 Samuel 7:28; Numbers 23:19; Titus 1:2
[3] Deuteronomy 32:4; Psalm 25:10; 33:4; 145:17; Isaiah 55:3; Jeremiah 3:12
[4] Nehemiah 8:10-12; Isaiah 12:2; 61:3; Psalm 71:23
[5] Romans 3:4; Revelation 3:7,14; 1 John 5:20; John 14:6,17; 15:26; 16:13
[6] Philippians 4:11; 3:8; Matthew 6:31-34; 1 Timothy 6:6-9; Hebrews 10:34; 13:5-6
[7] Matthew 11:29; 2 Corinthians 10:1
[8] Romans 2:4; Proverbs 14:31
[9] John 6:11; 11:41; Matthew 26:26-27; Luke 10:21
[10] 1 John 4:8; Exodus 34:6-7; Psalm 86:5,15; 2 Corinthians 13:11; Ephesians 2:4
[11] 1 Peter 1:16; Leviticus 11:44; 19:2; 20:7; Amos 3:3
[12] Luke 22:42; Romans 5:8
[13] An adjectival form of *integrity. Integrity + ous = integritous;* Hebrews 13:8; Psalm 102:27-28; 103:17; Malachi 3:6; James 1:17
[14] Matthew 11:29; Philippians 2:7-8
[15] Revelation 11:17; 18:8; Luke 22:69; Acts 13:17; 1 Peter 5:6
[16] Colossians 1:18; Psalm 89:27; Isaiah 52:13; Matthew 28:18; John 3:35
[17] Psalm 27:4; 63:2-5; Isaiah 4:2; 28:5
[18] Ephesians 3:20; Genesis 15:1
[19] 2 Corinthians 1:10; 2 Timothy 4:17
[20] Galatians 2:16; Romans 3:30; 5:1-2; Philippians 3:9
[21] 1 John 4:8; Exodus 34:6-7; Psalm 86:5,15; 2 Corinthians 13:11; Ephesians 2:4
[22] Matthew 11:27; 1 Corinthians 2:9
[23] 1 Corinthians 2:9; 1 Peter 1:12; Psalm 31:19; Hebrews 11:16
[24] Matthew 19:17; 1 Samuel 2:2; Psalm 145:7-9; James 1:17

He is LIFE[1] and WONDER!!!!![2]

HALLELUYAH!!!

And Life and Wonder are what He has for you; no darkness, no bad news, no disappointment, no discomfort, no "less than," only far better than you can possibly imagine![3]

All curses came through Adam,[4] but all blessings come through Jesus Christ! *Only* blessings![5]

He has all of this on a silver platter, ready for you right now![6]

RIGHT NOW!!![7]

And the only thing hindering you from living fully in the Kingdom of Heaven right now[8] is "accepted" darkness![9]

So don't accept darkness![10]

Don't accept that thought that so-and-so irritated you![11]

Don't accept that feeling of a wary concern![12]

Don't accept that sense of worldliness![13]

Don't accept that distraction of discomfort![14]

---

1 John 1:4; 4:14; 5:21,24; 6:27,33,48,51,63; 8:12; 10:28; 11:25; 14:6; 17:3

2 John 1:5,10; 3:19; 12:36,46; Matthew 4:16

3 Romans 8:28,35-39; Hebrews 12:6-12; James 1:3-4; 2 Thessalonians 1:5-7

4 Romans 5:12-19; 1 Corinthians 15:21

5 Ephesians 1:3; Romans 5:15

6 Matthew 10:8; Ephesians 1:3

7 2 Corinthians 6:2; Isaiah 49:8; Hebrews 3:7,13; 4:7

8 Luke 11:20; 17:20-21

9 1 John 2:11; 2 Corinthians 4:4; Ephesians 6:12; Genesis 3:1

10 Acts 26:18; 1 Peter 2:9,25; 1 John 2:8-9; 1 Thessalonians 5:4-8; Ephesians 5:8

11 1 John 2:11; Titus 3:3; Colossians 3:13

12 2 Timothy 1:7; Romans 8:15

13 2 Peter 2:10; Romans 8:5

14 1 Corinthians 6:7; 1 Peter 2:19-23; 3:9; 1 Thessalonians 5:15

If you are living for Yehovah, don't accept any idea that "things" won't go well![1]

YOU ARE MORE THAN A CONQUEROR![2] THIS DOES NOT CHANGE WHETHER YOU ADMIT IT OR NOT![3] IT'S WHO YOU ARE IN HIM![4]

HALLELUUUUYAAAAAAAAAAAAAAAH!!!!!!!!!!

So, CONQUEROR, don't accept anything that isn't Heavenly![5] Because Yehovah's promises are Heavenly for your soul![6] You can be happy,[7] joyous,[8] fulfilled,[9] valuable,[10] appreciated,[11] trustworthy,[12] pure,[13] humble,[14] wise,[15] loving,[16] peaceful,[17] certain,[18] grateful,[19] content,[20] loyal,[21] kind,[22] understanding,[23] gentle,[24] and integritous,[25] right now!

RIGHT NOW![26]

---

[1] Matthew 8:26; That is not to say that one should expect acts of sin to go well (Hebrews 10:26)! We are speaking of a person who is living for Yehovah (Romans 8:28)!
[2] Romans 8:37; Isaiah 25:8; 1 Corinthians 15:57; 1 John 4:4; 5:4-5; Jude 1:24
[3] James 1:17; John 1:9; 1 John 1:5; Revelation 21:23; 22:5; Isaiah 60:19
[4] Colossians 3:1-3; John 4:14; 6:39-40; 10:28-30; Romans 5:10; 8:34-39
[5] Colossians 3:5-17; Romans 6:6; 8:13; Galatians 5:24; Ephesians 5:3-6
[6] Ephesians 2:6; Luke 12:37; 22:29-30; John 12:26; 14:3; 17:21-26; Revelation 3:21
[7] James 5:13; 2 Corinthians 7:13
[8] John 15:11; 16:24; 17:13; 1 Peter 1:8; Jude 1:24
[9] Philippians 2:13; Ephesians 2:4-5; John 6:65
[10] Matthew 10:31; 12:11-12; Luke 12:24; 1 Corinthians 9:9-10
[11] Romans 2:29; John 5:44; 12:43; 1 Corinthians 4:5; 2 Corinthians 10:18
[12] Luke 19:17; 16:10; Revelation 2:26-29
[13] Philippians 1:10; 1 Timothy 5:22; 1 John 3:3
[14] Ephesians 4:2; 1 Peter 3:8
[15] Ephesians 5:15; James 3:13; 2 Timothy 3:15
[16] Hebrews 13:1; 1 Corinthians 16:14; Ephesians 3:10; Philippians 1:9
[17] 2 Peter 3:14; James 3:17-18; Hebrews 12:14; Jude 1:2
[18] John 17:8,25; 16:27,30
[19] 1 Thessalonians 5:18; Ephesians 5:20; Philippians 4:6; Colossians 3:17
[20] Hebrews 13:5; Philippians 4:11; 1 Timothy 6:8
[21] Philippians 3:3; Matthew 25:21; Titus 2:10; Hebrews 8:10
[22] Ephesians 4:32; Mark 11:25-26; Luke 6:37; 11:4; Colossians 3:12-13; Romans 12:20-21; 1 Peter 3:8-9; 1 John 2:12
[23] Ephesians 1:8; 3:5; Colossians 1:28; 2 Peter 1:5
[24] Titus 3:2; 1 Corinthians 13:4; Colossians 3:12; 2 Timothy 2:24
[25] Titus 2:7; James 5:12; Matthew 5:20
[26] 2 Corinthians 6:2; Isaiah 49:8; Hebrews 3:7,13; 4:7

YOU CAN ENTER HIS REST, RIGHT NOW![1]

HALLELUUUYAAAAAAAAAAAAAAH!!!!!!!

HALLELUUUYAAAAAAAAAAAAAAH!!!!!!!

HALLELUUUYAAAAAAAAAAAAAAH!!!!!!!

HE IS THE ALPHA AND OMEGA, THE BEGINNING AND THE END![2]

HE IS THE GREAT "I AM"![3]

HE IS THE SAME YESTERDAY, TODAY, AND FOREVER![4]

HE IS THE WAY, TRUTH, LIFE,[5] AND OUR VERY GREAT REWARD![6]

HE IS LOVE![7]

HE IS PEACE![8]

HE IS GOOD![9]

HALLELUYAH!

HALLELUYAH!

CONQUERERS[10] CONQUER!!!!!

---

[1] Hebrews 3:11,18; 4:3,5-6,10
[2] Revelation 1:8; 22:13; Isaiah 41:4; 44:6; 48:12
[3] Hebrews 13:8; Psalm 102:27-28; 103:17; Malachi 3:6; James 1:17
[4] Hebrews 13:8; Psalm 102:27-28; 103:17; Malachi 3:6; James 1:17
[5] John 14:6; Acts 4:12; Hebrews 10:19-22; 1 John 2:23; 2 John 1:9; Revelation 5:8-9
[6] Genesis 15:1; Ruth 2:12; Psalm 16:5-6; 142:5; Lamentations 3:24
[7] 1 John 4:8,10,12-13,16,19; Deuteronomy 7:9; 1 Kings 8:23
[8] Isaiah 9:6; Colossians 1:20; Revelation 1:4
[9] Matthew 19:17; 1 Samuel 2:2; Psalm 145:7-9; James 1:17
[10] Romans 8:37; Isaiah 25:8; 1 Corinthians 15:57; 1 John 4:4; 5:4-5; Jude 1:24

CONQUER THE SOUL THROUGH HIS HOLY POWER[1] FOR THE GLORY OF GOD![2]

HALLELUUUUUYAAAAAAAAAAAAAAAAAAAAAAAAAAAH!!!!!!!

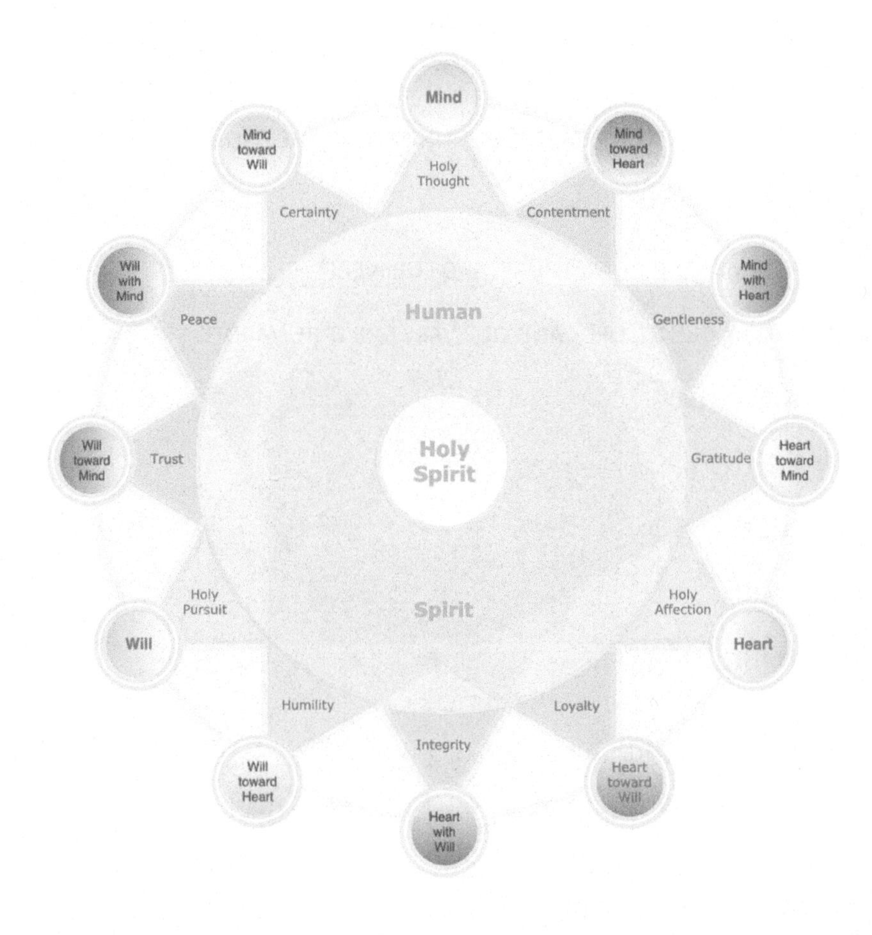

[1] 2 Timothy 1:7; Acts 1:8; 6:8; 9:22; 10:38; 1 Corinthians 2:4

[2] Revelation 4:10-11; Jude 1:25; 2 Peter 1:3

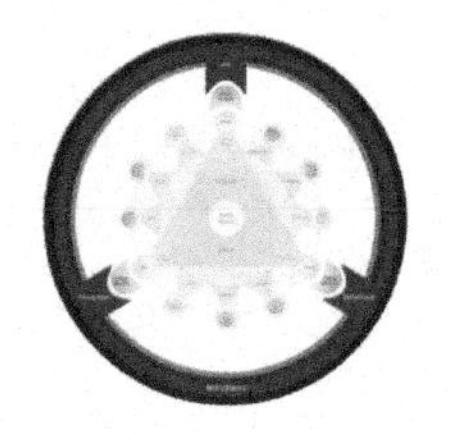

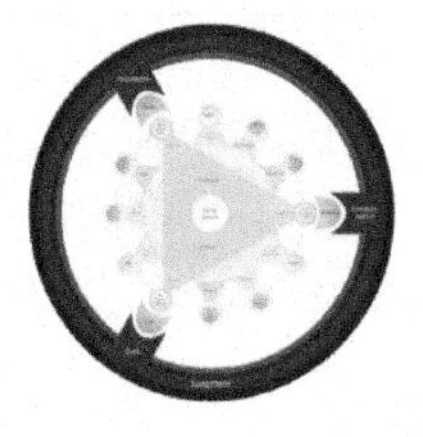

CHAPTER 31

TRIAD ASSAULTS

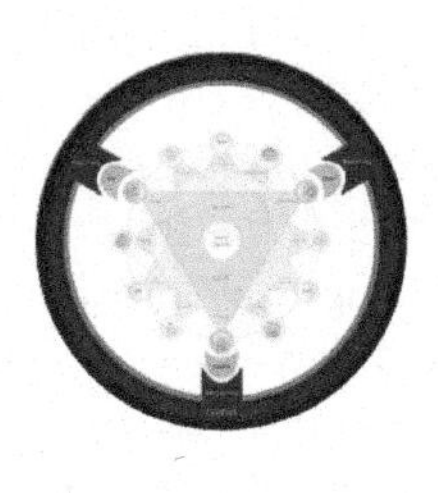

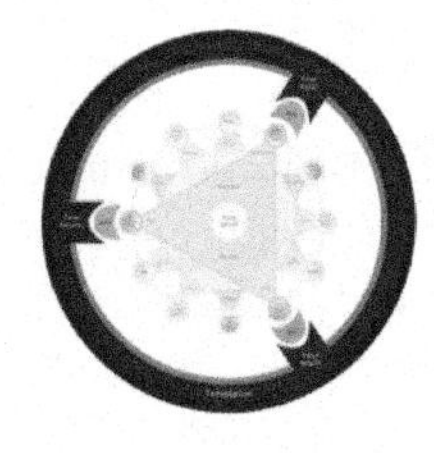

While they might not be able to define them spiritually, even unbelievers can testify to the enemy's main tactics. Every child of Adam has been their victim.[1]

Father in Heaven! In the former days, Your children perished because of a lack of knowledge,[2] but now You have intervened,[3] turned us from willful ignorance,[4] and given us great weapons of Truth![5] HalleluYah! May Your children be blessed, may their souls be full of Light,[6] and may they be victorious over darkness for the Glory of Your Name![7]

HALLELUYAH!!

CHILDREN OF LIGHT![8] LISTEN![9] BE BLESSED!

---

[1] 1 Corinthians 10:13; 1 Peter 5:8-9; Luke 22:46
[2] Hosea 4:6; Jeremiah 5:21; 2 Corinthians 4:3-6
[3] John 1:9,14; Acts 15:14; Romans 1:16
[4] John 1:12-13,16-17; 2 Timothy 3:8
[5] John 8:32,36; Psalm 25:5; 119:45; Proverbs 2:1-7; 4:18; Isaiah 2:3; 61:1; Romans 6:14-18,22; 8:2,15; 2 Corinthians 3:17-18; Galatians 5:13; 2 Timothy 2:25-26
[6] Luke 11:36; Psalm 119:97-105; Proverbs 2:1-11; 2 Timothy 3:15-17
[7] John 15:8; Luke 6:35; Psalm 92:12-15; Isaiah 60:21; Matthew 5:16
[8] Ephesians 5:8; John 12:36; 1 Thessalonians 5:5
[9] Luke 8:18; 19:26; Deuteronomy 32:46-47; Proverbs 2:2-5; Mark 4:23-24; Acts 17:11; Hebrews 2:1; James 1:22-25; Matthew 13:12; John 15:2

ALL dark spirits function through various forms of deception,[1] distraction,[2] and destruction![3] When summarizing the enemy's tactical strategies, it is beneficial to see their correlation[4] with the four levels of spiritual operation in the soul.[5] That is to say, the various methods of attack have specific targets in the soul.[6] Therefore, when made aware of a certain form of attack, the redeemed person can reinforce the targeted areas.[7] By doing so, the redeemed person can successfully resist the attack[8] and even mount a counterattack, absolutely crushing the enemy.[9]

In an attempt to compromise the Triad of Observation, the enemy spirits will primarily focus their efforts on blinding the soul.[10] Their goal is to *separate* the person made in the image of Yehovah *from* Yehovah.[11] By doing this, they can prevent the spirit of the targeted person from perceiving true observations, causing their presentation of His image to become polluted and corrupt.[12] The central weakness at this level is a lack of intimacy with Yehovah, a lack of awareness.[13] Because of this, the enemy presents as many decoys as possible in place of the Truth to overwhelm the person's weak spiritual senses.[14] Such suggestions include thoughts of untruth in the mind, perversions in the will, and selfish and unholy affections in the heart.[15]

Let those who have ears hear what the Holy Spirit is saying to His holy people![16] If someone is attacked with thoughts of lies, perversions, or selfishness, the enemy

---

[1] Genesis 3:1,13; Revelation 12:9; 16:14; 20:2,8; Zechariah 3:1-2

[2] 2 Corinthians 11:3; Jude 1:4; 1 John 4:1; 2 Peter 3:17

[3] John 10:10; Luke 8:12; John 8:44; Acts 13:10; Hebrews 2:14; Revelation 12:9

[4] John 3:20; Ephesians 5:11

[5] 2 Timothy 3:16: Revelation 4:7 – Eagle = observe (see); man = consider (think); lion = decide (judge/rule); ox = intend (do/labor/act). These functions of spirit are discussed more in Chapters 22-25 of this testimony.

[6] James 4:16; Ephesians 6:11; 2 Corinthians 2:11

[7] Revelation 3:2; Hebrews 12:12; Ephesians 3:16; 1 Thessalonians 3:13; Luke 22:32

[8] James 4:7; Matthew 4:3-11; Ephesians 6:11-12; 1 Peter 5:8-9; Revelation 12:11

[9] Luke 10:19; Psalm 91:13; Ezekiel 2:6; Mark 16:18; Acts 28:5; Romans 16:20

[10] 2 Corinthians 4:4; Matthew 4:8-9; John 12:40; Ephesians 2:2; 1 John 2:11; 5:19

[11] 2 Corinthians 3:18; Galatians 5:4

[12] 1 Timothy 6:5; Titus 1:15; 2 Peter 1:4; 2:10

[13] Zechariah 1:3; Jeremiah 31:18-20; Nehemiah 9:28

[14] 2 Corinthians 11:3; Luke 12:1; Galatians 1:6; Hebrews 4:15

[15] Revelation 17:17; John 13:2; Luke 22:3; Acts 5:3

[16] Revelation 2:7; Luke 8:18; 19:26; Deuteronomy 32:46-47; Proverbs 2:2-5; Mark 4:23-24; Acts 17:11; Hebrews 2:1; James 1:22-25; Matthew 13:12; John 15:2

is attempting to use the soul to blind the human spirit's ability to see and observe in the spirit realm.[1]

It is worth noting that it is primarily for this purpose of blinding that the enemy employs various forms of lying in Creation.[2] When the dark spirits do manage to persuade a soul to lie, they are using that soul to accomplish their objective on a much larger scale with the intention of misleading all of the lie's targets via illegal spiritual avenues.[3] In other words, dark spirits know that they are limited in their

---

[1] Luke 16:31; See Chapter 22 in this testimony to defend this triad.

[2] John 8:44; Romans 1:25; 1 John 1:6; 2:21; Revelation 14:5; 2 Thessalonians 2:9,11; Titus 2:11; Hebrews 6:18; Colossians 3:9; Numbers 23:19; Psalm 38:12

[3] Matthew 15:13-14; Revelation 22:15; 2 Peter 2:1,17

permissions to tempt souls.[1] But when these spirits persuade a soul to cooperate with their bidding,[2] the dark spirits can use that soul to bypass legal constraints in the spiritual realm in favor of the more lax permissions of the physical realm.[3] In other words, the lie is their temporary means to circumvent the constraints of the Heavenly Law of Righteousness.[4] Lies are the foundational power of darkness in the world.[5]

However, when the soul is saturated with the Light of Truth[6] through the human spirit[7] and from the Holy Spirit,[8] the three gates of the observational triad are impervious to evil.[9] The mind shines with the Word of Truth,[10] the will erupts with the Power of Representation,[11] and the heart overflows with Selfless Love.[12] The person who freely receives[13] and resonates with the Light of Yeshua[14] cannot be overcome by any darkness![15] They have crossed over from death to life![16] They are dwelling in the Kingdom of Heaven,[17] and nothing can steal, kill, or destroy[18] their faith, hope, and love[19] in their Victorious Savior![20]

HALLELUYAH!!!

KNOW WHO YOU ARE IN OUR SAVIOR![21]

---

[1] Job 1:9-12; 2:4-6; Mark 5:12
[2] Galatians 3:1a-b; 2 Corinthians 11:3
[3] Acts 16:16-18; 1 Samuel 28:8-14; Luke 8:28
[4] 2 Thessalonians 2:9; John 8:44; Mark 13:22; Revelation 13:11-15
[5] 2 Thessalonians 2:10; John 3:19-21; 8:44-47; Romans 2:7-8
[6] John 1:3-4,9; 3:21; 8:12; 9:5; 12:46; Isaiah 42:6-7; Malachi 4:2; Matthew 4:16; Luke 1:78-79; 2:32; Acts 26:23; Ephesians 5:124; 1 John 1:5; Revelation 22:16
[7] Matthew 5:16; Luke 1:53; John 6:27; 15:8
[8] John 1:4; 14:26; Matthew 3:11; Luke 12:12
[9] Luke 11:36; Psalm 119:97-105; Proverbs 2:1-11; 2 Timothy 3:15-17
[10] John 17:17; 2 Timothy 2:15; James 1:18
[11] Romans 8:29; Matthew 12:50; 25:40; Colossians 1:15-18; Revelation 1:5-6
[12] Romans 5:8; Isaiah 53:6; 1 Peter 3:18; 1 John 4:9-10
[13] Matthew 10:8; 1 Corinthians 2:12
[14] Matthew 5:14-16; Ephesians 5:8-14; Philippians 2:15
[15] John 1:5,10; 3:19; Luke 6:39; Jeremiah 5:31; 2 Peter 2:1
[16] John 5:24; Romans 8:16-17; 1 Thessalonians 5:9; 2 Thessalonians 2:13-14
[17] John 3:3; Luke 16:16; 17:21
[18] John 10:10; Luke 8:12; John 8:44; Acts 13:10; Hebrews 2:14; Revelation 12:9
[19] 1 Corinthians 13:13; Galatians 5:22
[20] 1 Corinthians 15:57; Romans 8:37; 1 John 5:4-5
[21] John 8:32; Colossians 3:3

YOU HAVE THE MIND OF CHRIST![1] TO FIGHT LIES, SPEND TIME READING AND LISTENING TO THE WORD![2]

HALLELUYAH!

YOU HAVE THE WILL OF CHRIST! [3] TO FIGHT AGAINST PERVERSION AND REBELLION, SPEND TIME DOING THE WORK OF CHRIST![4]

HALLELUYAH!

YOU HAVE THE HEART OF CHRIST![5] TO FIGHT SELFISHNESS, SPEND TIME PRAISING GOD![6]

HALLELUUUUUUUUUUYAAAAAAAAAAAAAAH!!!!!!!

OUR GOD IS GOOD!!!!!!![7]

Now, when attempting to inhibit the Triad of Consideration, temptation is the enemy's preferred tool.[8] The primary vulnerability targeted by this tactic is a soul's unawareness of sufficiency in Yehovah, a weakness that, when tapped, is called "greed." [9] To accentuate the effect of temptation, the enemy will present countless opportunities, filling the person's mind with a multitude of all sorts of possible scenarios.[10] Loyalty will be minimized by "better offers" of wealth,[11] trust will be challenged with "better insights" of security,[12] and contentment will be mocked by "better rights" of access to various sorts of value and benefits.[13] Imagined sensations of various pleasures will overflow until embraced by the

---

[1] 1 Corinthians 2:16; John 15:15; 16:13-15

[2] 2 Timothy 2:15; Revelation 1:3; Deuteronomy 6:6-9

[3] Philippians 2:13; Ephesians 2:4-5; John 6:65

[4] Matthew 28:19; Acts 1:8; Colossians 1:23

[5] 1 John 4:12; Ephesians 6:6; Philemon 1:20

[6] Hebrews 13:15; Hosea 14:2; Romans 12:1

[7] Matthew 19:17; 1 Samuel 2:2; Psalm 145:7-9; James 1:17

[8] James 1:14; Ephesians 4:22; Hebrews 3:13

[9] Luke 11:39; 12:15; Colossians 3:5; 2 Peter 2:14

[10] 2 Peter 2:10,18; 3:3; Romans 7:8; 8:5-14; Ephesians 2:3; 4:22-24; Galatians 5:24; 2 Timothy 2:22

[11] Genesis 3:5; Jude 1:11; 2 Peter 2:15

[12] Genesis 3:4-5; John 8:44; Acts 13:10; 1 John 3:8

[13] Genesis 3:5; Jude 1:11; 2 Peter 2:15

person,[1] and then they will be followed with innumerable predictions of seemingly avoidable and undesired consequences.[2] This tactic aims to fill the soul with so many considerations that the person either indefinitely continues to hesitate or eventually chooses wrongly simply because of the overwhelming number of possible choices.[3]

Let those who have ears hear what the Holy Spirit is saying to His holy people![4] If someone is tempted with thoughts of worldly rights, wealth, and security, the

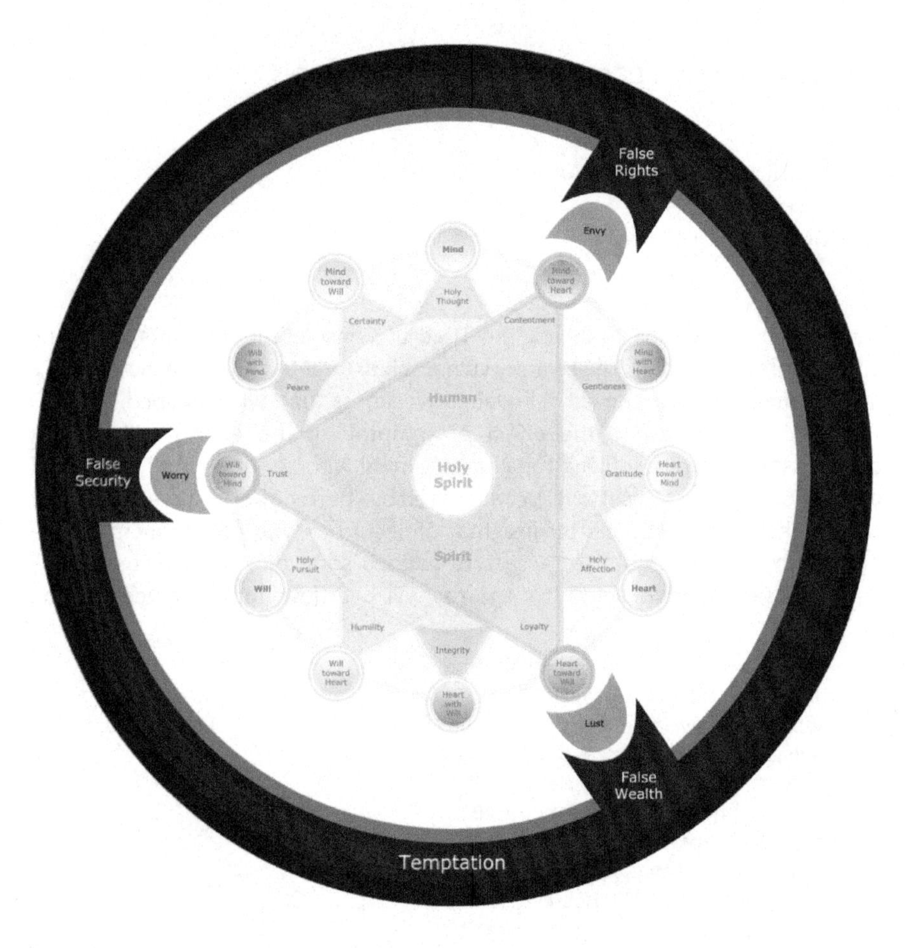

---

[1] James 1:14; Ephesians 4:22; Hebrews 3:13; 1 Thessalonians 3:5
[2] Romans 16:17; Titus 3:9-11; Galatians 5:12; 2 Thessalonians 3:6
[3] Matthew 6:34; Jeremiah 17:7-8
[4] Revelation 2:7,11,17,29; 3:6,13,22

enemy is attempting to manipulate the soul to confuse a person's ability to process spiritual information.[1]

However, a soul filled with the Light of Yeshua is protected from such assaults. For example, a truly content soul cannot be offended,[2] because offense is a reaction against perceived theft or destruction of some sort of spiritual right.[3] That is, if a person measures their value based on how they are respected by others,[4] then they can be offended if anyone disrespects them.[5] But if a person knows the truth about how their true value comes from Yehovah alone,[6] then no disrespectful act from anyone else can offend them.[7] Their value remains steadfast through their contentment in Yeshua.[8]

KNOW WHO YOU ARE IN YESHUA![9]

YOU HAVE ETERNAL WEALTH BEYOND MEASURE! [10] FIGHT VOICES THAT PRIORITIZE TEMPORARY WORLDLY WEALTH BY SPEAKING OF YOUR ABUNDANT AND ETERNAL HOLY WEALTH PROVIDED FREELY TO YOU IN YOUR SAVIOR![11] AND MAKE A POINT TO DO SOMETHING OUT OF LOYALTY TO YEHOVAH![12]

HALLELUYAH!

YOU HAVE ETERNAL SECURITY IN THE KINGDOM OF HEAVEN! [13] FIGHT SUGGESTIONS OF TEMPORARY WORLDLY SECURITY BY SPEAKING OF YOUR

---

[1] James 1:14; Ephesians 4:22; Hebrews 3:13; 1 Thessalonians 3:5; Galatians 6:1
[2] Matthew 5:39-48; Colossians 3:13
[3] Matthew 17:27; Galatians 5:11
[4] John 5:44; 12:43; 2 Corinthians 10:18; Romans 1:32
[5] Matthew 15:12; Proverbs 12:16; 24:19
[6] John 5:41; 7:18; 1 Thessalonians 2:6
[7] Proverbs 19:11; 16:32; 20:3; Matthew 18:21-22; Romans 12:18-21
[8] 1 Corinthians 4:5; 2 Corinthians 10:18; 1 Peter 1:7; 5:4; Romans 2:29; John 5:44
[9] John 8:32; Colossians 3:3
[10] Romans 9:23; Ephesians 1:7; Philippians 4:19
[11] Ephesians 1:3; 2:6; Genesis 12:2-3; 1 Chronicles 4:10; Isaiah 61:9; Galatians 3:9
[12] James 2:26; Do something that shows service to God, like spending some real time reading the word (2 Timothy 2:15), fellowshipping with others (Hebrews 10:25), or making disciples (Matthew 28:19).
[13] Hebrews 6:19; 2 Peter 3:17

ETERNAL HOLY SECURITY IN YOUR SAVIOR![1] AND DO SOMETHING THAT REQUIRES YOU TO TRUST IN GOD'S WORD![2]

HALLELUYAH!

YOU REIGN WITH THE RIGHTS OF SOVEREIGNTY THROUGH CHRIST![3] FIGHT SUGGESTIONS OF THE NEED FOR WORLDLY RIGHTS BY SPEAKING OF YOUR SUPREME HOLY RIGHTS IMPUTED TO YOU THROUGH THE KING OF KINGS AND LORD OF LORDS![4] AND DO SOMETHING THAT DEMONSTRATES CONTENTMENT IN HIM![5]

HALLELUYAH!

YOU ARE WEALTHY, SECURE, AND SOVEREIGN IN THE KINGDOM OF HEAVEN FOR HIS GLORY![6]

HALLELUUUUUUUUUUUUUYAAAAAAAAAAAH!!!!!!

WELCOME TO THE FAMILY OF THE CHILDREN OF THE LIVING GOD![7]

HALLELUUUUUUUUUUUUUYAAAAAAAAAAAH!!!!!!

But the enemy still won't give up, because they are desperate![8] So, to compromise the Triad of Decision, the dark kingdom will plague a soul with judgments.[9] This is an effort to cause the person to *retract* or *reassign* their choice of any righteous

---

[1] John 5:24; Revelation 3:12

[2] James 2:26; Step out on faith in response to His Word, such as sharing your faith with others (Matthew 10:20), giving time, effort, or provision toward making disciples (Matthew 28:19), or helping the needy in His Name (2 Corinthians 9:2).

[3] Luke 10:19; Revelation 2:27; 3:21; 5:10

[4] Matthew 25:45; 1 John 3:12-20; John 15:18-20

[5] James 2:26; Instead of seeking your own attention or appreciation, make an effort to lift others up and encourage them (Romans 15:4-6). Do something that actively blesses someone else in His Name (Matthew 23:11; 1 Peter 4:10), even if it's simply blessing them in prayer (James 5:16)!

[6] Ephesians 1:3; 2:6; Genesis 12:2-3; 1 Chronicles 4:10; Isaiah 61:9; Galatians 3:9

[7] Romans 8:14; Galatians 3:26; 1 John 5:19

[8] Revelation 12:12; Mark 5:12

[9] Revelation 12:10; Romans 8:1

decision already made.[1] Certainty will be challenged by arguments of false claims and accusations.[2]

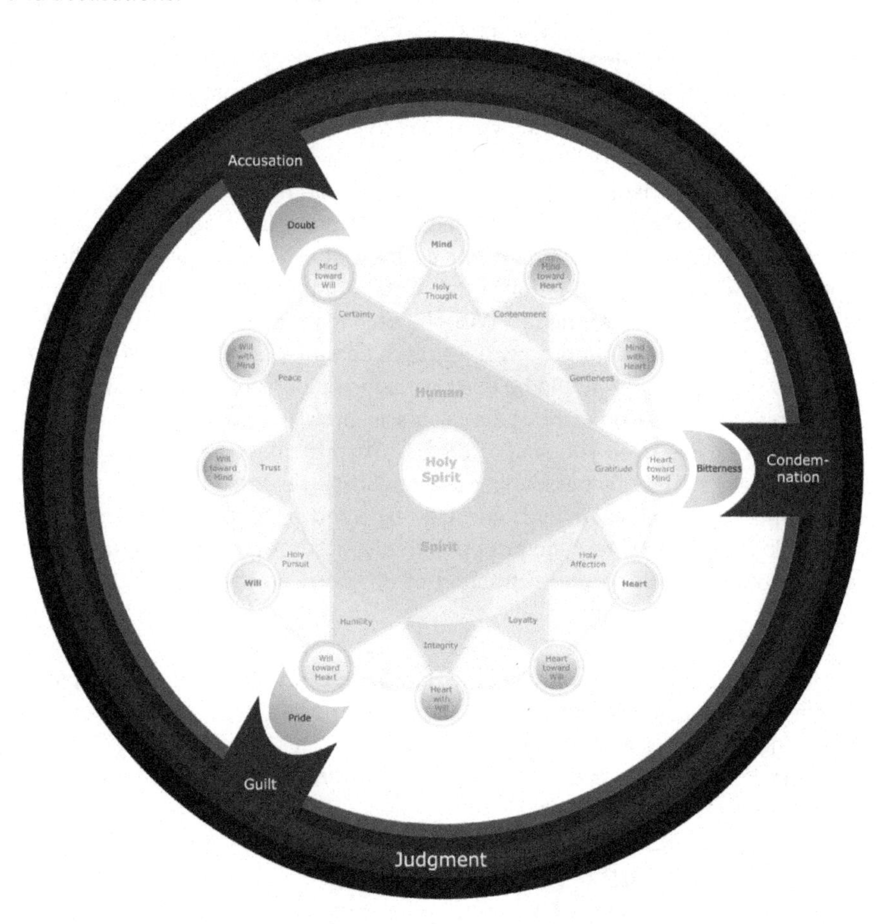

Understand that when an enemy accuses one of the redeemed of a crime or offense, that person has not yet been convicted.[3] However, such an accusation can cause the redeemed to be spiritually placed in a "city of refuge," where their spiritual freedoms are severely restrained.[4] Therefore, the experienced spiritual warrior regularly lifts up the Cross of Yeshua as their standard[5] and requests Him

---

[1] 1 Kings 13:1-32; Numbers 20:12; 1 Samuel 13:13-14; 15:22-24; Acts 23:29

[2] Revelation 12:10; Zechariah 3:1-2; Luke 22:31

[3] Numbers 35:12; Joshua 20:4-5

[4] Numbers 35:25-28; Joshua 20:6

[5] Revelation 12:11; 7:10-14; 15:3

to wash their feet from any crime or offense.[1] By doing this they are willfully entering into court to have their transgressions paid, their innocence restored, and their freedoms and inheritance released from confiscation and returned to them.[2] Upon such restoration, the redeemed may also place that dark spirit into the same restraint and take its freedoms away, for it stood as a false witness, making accusations[3] against one whose penalty had already been paid.[4]

Meanwhile, the enemy will attempt to discredit humility as pride through assignments of false responsibilities and guilt.[5] Upon such assignments, the dark spirits will condemn the redeemed with a variety of false consequences.[6] They will flood the person with accusations of all sorts of unholy or foolish decisions that the person actually never made![7] With the secondary goal of drowning righteous decisions in a sea of unrighteous ones, dark demanders will suggest that many more soulical decisions should be quickly made and pursued.[8] The person may be pressured to decide on various behaviors in an attempt to garner attention, affection, or value from Yehovah or others.[9] Then the dark spirits will compound their strategy's effect by persuading other souls in the person's human audience to hesitate or fail to react in even normally expected or reasonable ways. The dark spirits do this to facilitate pain, disappointment, accusation, and guilt for the sake of promoting indecision and retraction of decisions on the part of the target's soul.[10]

Let those who have ears hear what the Holy Spirit is saying to His holy people![11] If a *redeemed*[12] person is judged with thoughts of accusation, condemnation, or guilt, the enemy is attempting to use that person's soul to *change* spiritual decisions![13] Such judgments are lies![14] Satan comes searching for a speck, even

---

[1] John 13:3-17; Luke 22:26-27; Philippians 2:5-8
[2] Numbers 35:28-34; Galatians 6:1
[3] Deuteronomy 19:16-21
[4] Romans 6:9; John 5:24
[5] 1 John 3:20; Titus 3:11; Luke 19:22
[6] 2 Kings 18:29-32; Psalm 94:21; Proverbs 17:15; James 5:6
[7] Matthew 5:11; Mark 14:56
[8] Proverbs 19:2; 21:5; Isaiah 28:16
[9] Galatians 3:3; Ephesians 2:8-9; 2 Timothy 1:9
[10] Psalm 27:10; 40:4; Romans 3:4
[11] Revelation 2:7,11,17,29; 3:6,13,22
[12] Ephesians 1:7; Galatians 3:13-14; 4:5; Titus 2:14; 1 Peter 1:18; Revelation 14:3
[13] Romans 4:7-8; 5:1; 8:1; John 3:18-19; 5:24; 16:8 – It is the world that He proves to be in the wrong about sin, righteousness, and judgment.
[14] Revelation 12:10; John 8:44

though he has a log in his own eye![1] If any of the redeemed perceive that any voice, whether internal or external,[2] is coming to search for a speck,[3] let the redeemed recognize it is an attack purposed toward changing spiritual decisions![4] Such a voice is not from the Holy Spirit![5] On the contrary, the Holy Spirit comes to His holy children with revelations of approval,[6] innocence,[7] and justification through the Precious Blood of Yeshua![8]

HALLELUYAH!

KNOW WHO YOU ARE IN JESUS![9]

YOU ARE APPROVED BY YEHOVAH![10] FIGHT VOICES OF ACCUSATION BY SPEAKING OF YOUR APPROVAL IN THE LORD![11] AND DO SOMETHING THAT DEMONSTRATES CERTAINTY IN HIS WORD![12]

HALLELUUUYAAAAAAAH!!!

YOU HAVE BEEN PROCLAIMED INNOCENT BY YEHOVAH![13] FIGHT ATTACKS FROM THOUGHTS OF GUILT BY SPEAKING OF THE INNOCENCE GIVEN TO YOU IN YESHUA![14] AND DO SOMETHING TO DEMONSTRATE HIS HUMILITY![15]

HALLELUUUYAAAAAAAH!!!

---

[1] Matthew 7:4; 1 Corinthians 6:3; Revelation 12:10
[2] 2 Corinthians 10:5; Jeremiah 4:14; Hebrews 4:12
[3] Matthew 7:3,5; 2 Chronicles 28:9-10; Psalm 50:16-21; John 8:7-9
[4] 2 Timothy 2:26; Job 1:12; 2:6; Luke 22:31-32; Acts 5:3
[5] John 3:17-18; 8:11; Romans 8:1,31-34
[6] 2 Timothy 2:15; 1 Thessalonians 2:4; Galatians 1:10; 2 Corinthians 10:18
[7] Matthew 10:16; Romans 16:18-19; Philippians 2:15
[8] Titus 3:7; Romans 3:24,28; 5:1-2,15-21; 1 Corinthians 6:11; Galatians 2:16
[9] John 8:32; Colossians 3:3
[10] 1 Thessalonians 2:4; 1 Corinthians 4:5; Matthew 25:21; Romans 2:29
[11] 1 Timothy 1:11-13; 1 Corinthians 7:25
[12] James 2:26; Take action from certainty of the Word. For example, the Word says that you can tell a mountain to move from here to there, and it will obey you (Matthew 17:20). So, speak to some "mountains" in your life! Do something that only makes sense based on the Word!
[13] Matthew 25:31-40; Romans 16:19
[14] Hebrews 10:19-22; 9:15; 12:24; Luke 22:20; John 6:54-56
[15] James 2:26; Find something you can do on behalf of someone else to serve them (1 Peter 4:10). Be a servant for Yeshua (1 Peter 5:2).

YOU HAVE BEEN JUSTIFIED BY YEHOVAH![1] FIGHT ATTACKS FROM FEELINGS OF CONDEMNATION BY SPEAKING AGAINST THEM ABOUT THE JUSTIFICATION YOU HAVE BEEN GIVEN IN YOUR SAVIOR!!![2] AND DEMONSTRATE YOUR GRATITUDE![3]

HALLELUUUUUUUYAAAAAAAAH!!!!!!!!!!!!!

YOU BELONG TO YEHOVAAAAAAAAAAAAAAH!!!!!![4]

HALLELUUUUUUUUUUUUUYAAAAAAAAAAAAAAH!!!!!!!!!!!!!

But after the enemy has failed in their efforts to compromise the Triads of Observation, Consideration, and Decision, the only remaining strategy of darkness is to upset the Triad of Intention through direct conflict composed of resistance, frustration, and destruction.[5] At this level, the enemy is simply engaging in warfare. To attack gentleness, the dark spirits will employ subterfuge by briefly permitting forays of the soul into implied levels of soulical relief.[6] They will lure their opponent with the strategy of giving an appearance of possible soulical confidence or success only to ambush such pursuits with counter attacks of vicious failure.[7] If this strategy fails and the enemy cannot destroy gentleness, they will attempt to make demands or bargain through conditional promises, treaties, or alliances.[8] They will do this by suggesting compromise somewhere between righteousness and unrighteousness, offering conditions for a sort of demilitarized zone in the middle.[9] During these negotiations, the enemy will clandestinely attempt to distance any potentially righteous human relationships from the person, thereby reinforcing dark suggestions that all humanity is unrighteous and integrity is meaningless.[10] However, if the person fails to bargain, the enemy will attempt to paralyze the soul with a spirit of fear through false posturing and

[1] Romans 5:9; 8:30; Titus 3:7; 1 Corinthians 6:11; Galatians 2:16
[2] Romans 3:24; 5:1,9,16; 1 Corinthians 6:11; Titus 3:5-7
[3] James 2:26; Separate out some time just for thanking Yehovah, even if you have to work at it (Ephesians 5:20)! Stretch your soul to do it in obedience to your spirit (James 4:7a)!
[4] Romans 14:8; 2 Corinthians 10:7; 1 John 3:19
[5] John 10:10; Luke 8:12; John 8:44; Acts 13:10; Hebrews 2:14; Revelation 12:9; 1 Peter 5:8
[6] Mark 10:25; 1 Timothy 6:9; Genesis 13:10-13; Numbers 22:17-19
[7] 1 Timothy 6:9; Luke 21:34; Romans 11:9
[8] Ephesians 4:27; Matthew 8:31
[9] Exodus 32:1-35; Matthew 4:9
[10] 2 Timothy 2:16-18; James 5:19; Matthew 15:13; Luke 8:13

discouragement.[1] This tactic consists mostly of "trash-talking," whereby the dark spirits boast of their supposed overwhelming strength and make false predictions of the soul's defeat and woe.[2] Simultaneously, the dark spirits will act in Creation to do everything possible in the person's environment to inhibit, frustrate, or destroy the soul's spiritual intentions.[3] Every traffic light will be red. Every owed bill balance will be unjust. Every social relationship will prove too demanding. To the redeemed, it will seem as if "their life" is against them. [4]

[1] Psalm 143:3-4; 30:11; 38:4; 143:4; Matthew 11:28

[2] 1 Samuel 17:44; 1 Kings 20:10-11; Ezekiel 28:2

[3] Micah 2:1; Psalm 10:2; Daniel 10:4-14

[4] Genesis 42:36; Job 7:7; Isaiah 38:10

Let those who have ears hear what the Holy Spirit is teaching His holy people![1] If someone is attacked with resisting, posturing, or bargaining thoughts or ideas, the enemy is attempting to turn the soul against the human spirit's authority![2] But the person who dwells in the Kingdom of Heaven knows that Yehovah is Welcoming,[3] Genuine,[4] and Resolute!

KNOW YOUR POSITION IN THE KINGDOM OF HEAVEN![5]

YOU ARE WELCOMED BY YEHOVAH![6] FIGHT AGAINST RESISTANCE PERCEIVED IN THE SPIRIT BY SPEAKING THE TRUTH ABOUT YOUR WELCOME RECEPTION IN THE KINGDOM OF HEAVEN![7] AND FIND SOME WAY TO SHOW GENTLENESS ACTIVELY![8]

HALLELUYAH!

YOUR POSITION IS GENUINE![9] WHENEVER EVIL SPIRITS ATTEMPT TO OVER-WHELM YOU BY THEIR POSTURING, FIGHT AGAINST THEM BY SPEAKING THE TRUTH OF HOW YOU ARE FULLY REDEEMED WHILE THEY ARE CONDEMNED![10] AND DO SOMETHING THAT DEMONSTRATES YOUR PEACE IN YESHUA![11]

HALLELUYAH!

YOUR POSITION IS RESOLUTE AND ABSOLUTE![12] WHEN EVIL SPIRITS TRY TO GET YOU TO COMPROMISE IN YOUR SERVICE TO YEHOVAH BY ACCEPTING SOME DEGREE OF SICKNESS, SIN, OR LIMITATION IN MINISTRY, FIGHT AGAINST THEM BY

---

[1] Revelation 2:7,11,17,29; 3:6,13,22
[2] Matthew 4:9; 1 Corinthians 10:20-21; 2 Corinthians 4:4
[3] Ephesians 2:2; John 8:44; 1 Timothy 2:4; 2 Peter 3:9; Titus 2:11
[4] Hebrews 6:18; Isaiah 45:19
[5] John 8:32; Colossians 3:3
[6] 2 Peter 1:11; Mark 9:37; Philippians 2:29
[7] Revelation 3:20; Luke 15:20
[8] James 2:26; Do something in Creation to demonstrate gentleness, even if it simply taking care of plants or animals (Proverbs 12:10)!
[9] 2 Timothy 2:19; Romans 8:29; Philippians 1:6
[10] Acts 13:10; Titus 2:14; 1 Peter 1:18
[11] James 2:26; Do something that actively demonstrates peace. For example, if you are hearing from darkness that your "life is doomed," speak the promises of Yehovah for you and then find someone that you can encourage in their walk. Pour out peace to reveal it (Acts 20:35)! HALLELUYAH!
[12] John 10:28-29; Ephesians 1:11

SPEAKING THE TRUTH ABOUT HOW YOU HAVE BEEN MADE RESOLUTE AND ABSOLUTE IN HIM![1] AND DO SOMETHING THAT OUTWARDLY SHOWS INTEGRITY![2]

HALLELUUUUUUUUUYAAAAAAAAAAH!!!!!!!!!

WHO YOU ARE IS ALREADY PREDESTINED[3] AND ESTABLISHED IN HIM!!!!![4]

THEREFORE, understand who you are in Yeshua and His Kingdom![5] And recognize that when you or others experience one of these four forms of triad attack, all the gates in the matching triad become vulnerable. For example, if a person hears a lie in their mind, they should also be ready to resist perversion in their will and selfishness in their heart, because lies are an attack against the Triad of Observation.[6] An experience of temptation means that the Triad of Consideration is under siege. So, if a worry spirit tempts a person, the soul is also likely experiencing a false sense of rights and a misperception of true wealth.[7] Similarly, if a person is feeling judged, then all the Decision gates are vulnerable. An example would be that an assault of condemnation eventually reduces certainty and humility toward Yehovah.[8] And whenever conflict abounds, the Intention gates are all in need of protection. A breach of darkness in one gate will tend to reduce the brightness of the light shining through the other two gates.[9] This is why selfish anger[10] tends never to be far removed from fear[11] and duplicity.[12]

---

[1] Revelation 2:11; Galatians 5:24; Philippians 1:28

[2] James 2:26; Have you said to Yehovah in private that you want to serve Him, that you desire to do His Will? Good! Then stretch your soul and do something outwardly that is specifically for that purpose! Do something in Creation that proves you are a Child of Yehovah (James 2:18)! Speak to someone about Him (Acts 1:8)! Give in His Name (Matthew 6:3; James 1:27)! Serve in His Name (Galatians 5:13)! DO SOMETHING IN ACTION AND IN TRUTH (1 John 3:18)! HALLELUYAH!

[3] Romans 8:29-30; John 15:16; Ephesians 1:5,11

[4] 2 Peter 1:12; Colossians 2:7; 1 Peter 5:10

[5] John 8:32; Colossians 3:3; Revelation 1:6

[6] Hebrews 3:10; James 4:8

[7] Exodus 17:3; Numbers 14:36; Luke 18:23; Mark 10:25

[8] Psalm 10:6-7; 59:12; Romans 3:14

[9] Matthew 6:23-24b; Romans 6:16; Galatians 1:10; James 4:4; 1 John 2:15-16

[10] 1 Samuel 20:30; Job 5:2; Proverbs 14:29; 25:28

[11] 1 Samuel 15:24; 18:12; Exodus 10:28; 12:31-33

[12] 1 Samuel 28:3,7; Luke 20:19-26; Matthew 23:24-28; 1 Peter 2:1

Brothers and sisters, do not be overwhelmed by the details of spiritual interaction![1] You have already been living through *all* of these complex dynamics![2] And look! You are still alive and even reading this testimony![3]

THANK YOU, YESHUA!!!!!

So, be encouraged![4] Now you can fight with "the light on"![5]

BLESS GOD!!!!!!!!!!!

THE BLINDFOLD IS OFF![6] NOW YOU CAN SKILLFULLY DEFEND YOUR SOUL[7] AND EVEN USE IT TO DASH THE ENEMY TO PIECES FOR YESHUA'S GLORY![8]

HALLELUUUUUUUUUUUUUUYAAAAAAAAAAAAAAH!!!!!!!!!!!

For instance, understanding the Triad Assaults is especially useful when fighting sickness! When suddenly beset by some ailment, the holy warrior can assess any recent exposure they have had with darkness.[9] Again, this may not have been an experience involving willful sin.[10] It could have been a moment of accepting thoughts of "false rights" while driving in traffic.[11] With the Holy Spirit's help, the holy warrior can identify the soulical breach and immediately seal the gate.[12] Being familiar with the triads, the warrior can then strengthen the other triad gates and proceed to go on the offensive, driving the enemy out and taking their authority as plunder![13]

GLORY TO GOD!!!!!!

---

[1] Romans 8:37; Isaiah 25:8; 1 Corinthians 15:57; 1 John 4:4; 5:4-5; Jude 1:24
[2] 1 Corinthians 10:13; 1 Peter 5:8-9; Luke 22:46
[3] 2 Corinthians 6:2; Isaiah 49:8; Hebrews 3:7,13; 4:7
[4] 2 Corinthians 13:11; Romans 15:13; 2 Thessalonians 2:16-17
[5] Ephesians 6:12; Romans 8:38; Colossians 2:15; 1 Peter 3:22
[6] 2 Corinthians 2:11; 1 Peter 5:8; Ephesians 6:11-12; Revelation 12:9-11; 13:8
[7] 2 Corinthians 10:3-5; Matthew 11:12; Revelation 12:11
[8] Revelation 2:27; 12:5; 19:15; Psalm 2:9
[9] See Chapter 28 of this testimony.
[10] John 9:3; Luke 13:4-5
[11] Matthew 7:2; Romans 2:1; 1 Corinthians 11:29
[12] Revelation 3:19-20; Jeremiah 31:18; Job 5:17
[13] 1 Samuel 17:51d-54; Mark 3:27

THE ENEMY WISHES THEY NEVER HUNG OUR SAVIOR ON THAT CROSS![1] WOE TO THEM![2] THEY HANDED THE VICTORY TO US ON A SILVER PLATTER![3]

HALLELUUUUUYAAAAAAAAAAAH!!!!!!!!!

WE ARE THE DISCIPLES OF YESHUA![4]

WE ARE THE REDEEMED OF YEHOVAH![5]

WE ARE THE BODY OF CHRIST,[6] RESURRECTED AND EMPOWERED![7]

HALLELUUUUUYAAAAAAAAAAAH!!!!!!!!!

OUR SAVIOR CONQUERED ALL DARKNESS[8] AND HANDED US HIS AUTHORITY![9]

HALLELUUUUUYAAAAAAAAAAAH!!!!!!!!!

HALLELUUUUYAAAAAAAAAAAAAAAAAAAAAAAAAAAAH!!!!!!!!!

THE KING OF KINGS IS A MIGHTY GOD![10]
GLORY! HALLELUYAH! PRAISE HIM! PRAISE HIM!

HE RULES IN GOODNESS, PEACE, AND JOY![11]
GLORY HALLELUYAH! PRAISE HIM! PRAISE HIM!

HE LAID HIS LIFE DOWN ON A TREE,[12]

---

[1] 1 Corinthians 2:8; John 15:22-25; 16:3; 8:19; 2 Corinthians 3:14
[2] Matthew 18:7; 13:41-42; 2 Peter 2:15-17; Jude 1:11-13; Revelation 19:20; 20:10
[3] Acts 13:27; Genesis 50:20; Colossians 2:15; Hebrews 12:2; Galatians 6:14
[4] John 8:31; 13:35; 15:8; Acts 6:1,2,7
[5] Galatians 3:13-14; 4:5; Titus 2:14; 1 Peter 1:18
[6] 1 Corinthians 12:14-20,27; Romans 12:5; Ephesians 5:30
[7] Romans 6:4; 7:6; 2 Corinthians 5:17; Galatians 6:15; Ephesians 4:22-24
[8] John 12:31; 16:11,33; Psalm 68:18; Romans 8:37; 1 John 4:4; 5:4
[9] Luke 10:19; Psalm 91:13; Ezekiel 2:6; Mark 16:18; Acts 28:5; Romans 16:20
[10] Revelation 17:14; 19:16; Psalm 72:11; Proverbs 8:15-16; 1 Timothy 6:15
[11] Galatians 5:22; Ephesians 5:9; 1 Corinthians 13:4-7
[12] John 10:15,17-18; 15:13; 1 John 3:16

SO WE COULD REIGN ETERNALLY![1]

CREATOR, SAVIOR, LOVE, AND GOD![2]
GLORY! HALLELUYAH! PRAISE HIM! PRAISE HIM!

HALLELUUUUYAAAAAAAAAAAAAAAAAAAAAAAAAAAAH!!!!!!!!!

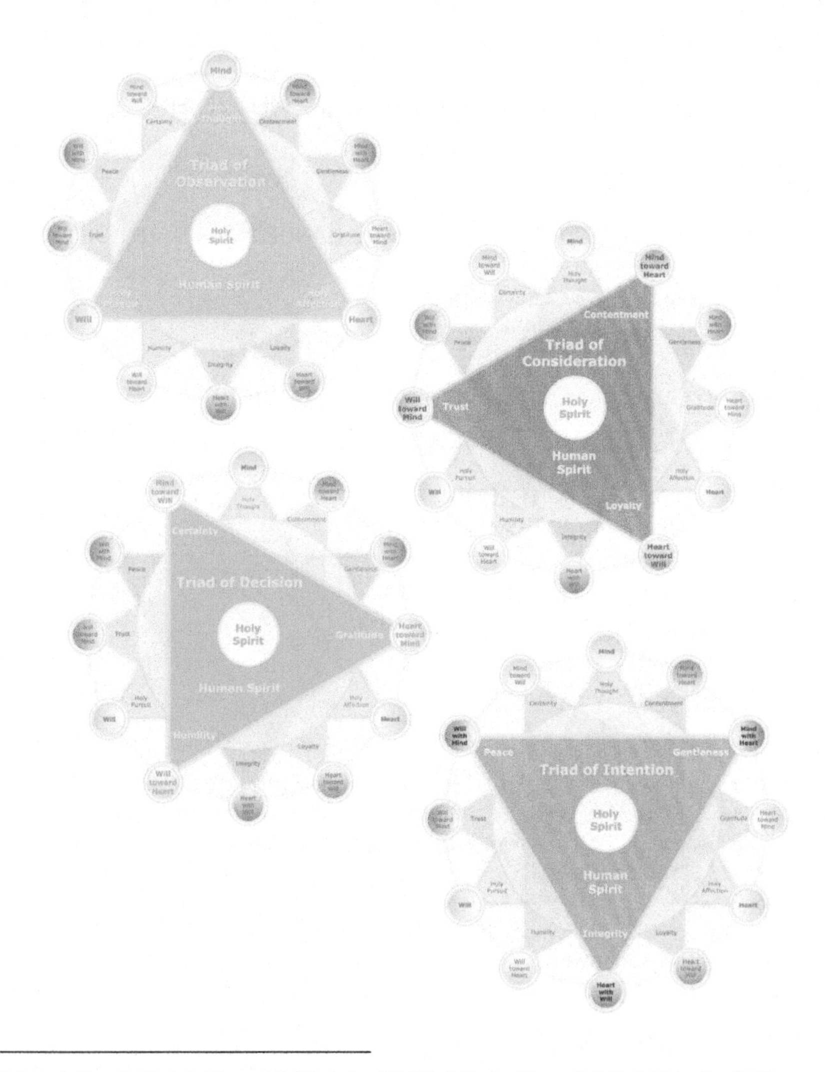

[1] Revelation 3:21; Matthew 19:28; Luke 22:30; 1 Corinthians 6:2-3; 2 Timothy 2:12
[2] Titus 3:4; Psalm 109:26; Hosea 1:7

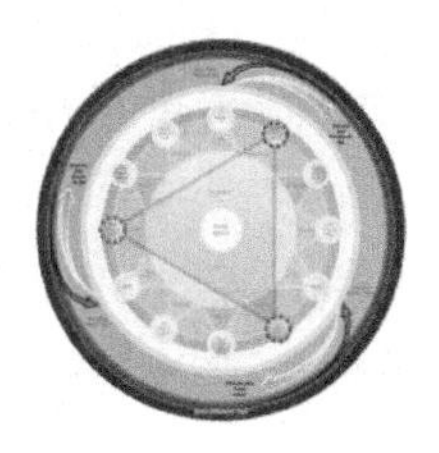

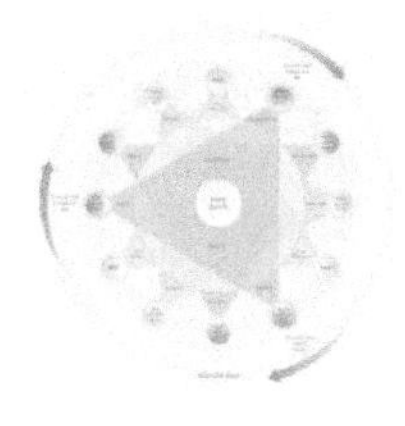

CHAPTER 32

UNDERSTANDING THE CURRENTS OF SHOULD

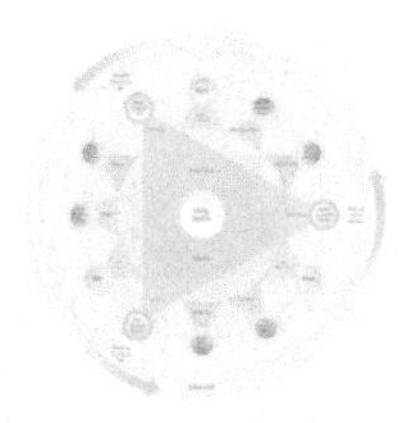

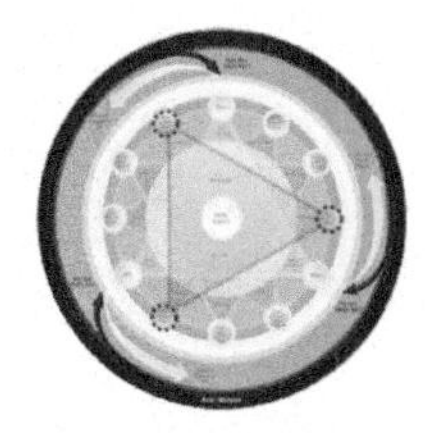

The experienced spiritual warrior is familiar with the "Currents of Should."

In the beginning, Yehovah held all expression of life to a certain standard of His own choosing.[1] He called this "Goodness"[2] and explained that it was a standard of how things should and should not "have been,[3] presently be,[4] and come to be."[5]

May the Holy Spirit grant ears that hear[6] to those who seek understanding,[7] may His wisdom and revelation abound within the redeemed,[8] and may the blindness of darkness be overcome by His Light![9] Amen!

---

[1] Exodus 34:6; Isaiah 6:3; Job 40:8, 11-12

[2] 2 Chronicles 6:41; Psalm 27:13; 31:19; 145:7; 2 Peter 1:3

[3] Genesis 1:4,10,12,18,21,25,31; Leviticus 10:18

[4] Ecclesiastes 12:14; Genesis 2:18; Proverbs 18:5

[5] Exodus 33:19; Genesis 3:5, 22; Micah 2:7; Psalm 23:6; 27:13

[6] Revelation 2:7,11,17,29; 3:6,13,22

[7] Proverbs 4:5-9; Job 12:13; Psalm 111:10: Colossians 2:2

[8] Ephesians 1:17; Luke 12:12; 21:15; Matthew 16:17; 1 Corinthians 2:10

[9] Luke 4:18; John 8:12

Yehovah has made things that were, are, and will be.[1] These facets of being are experienced in the three chief gates of the soul.[2] When addressing these functions in English, we must use awkward language to avoid confusion between present and future conditions.

The mind interacts with what is.[3] Goodness shares with the mind about what "should presently be"[4] and what "should not presently be."[5] When we

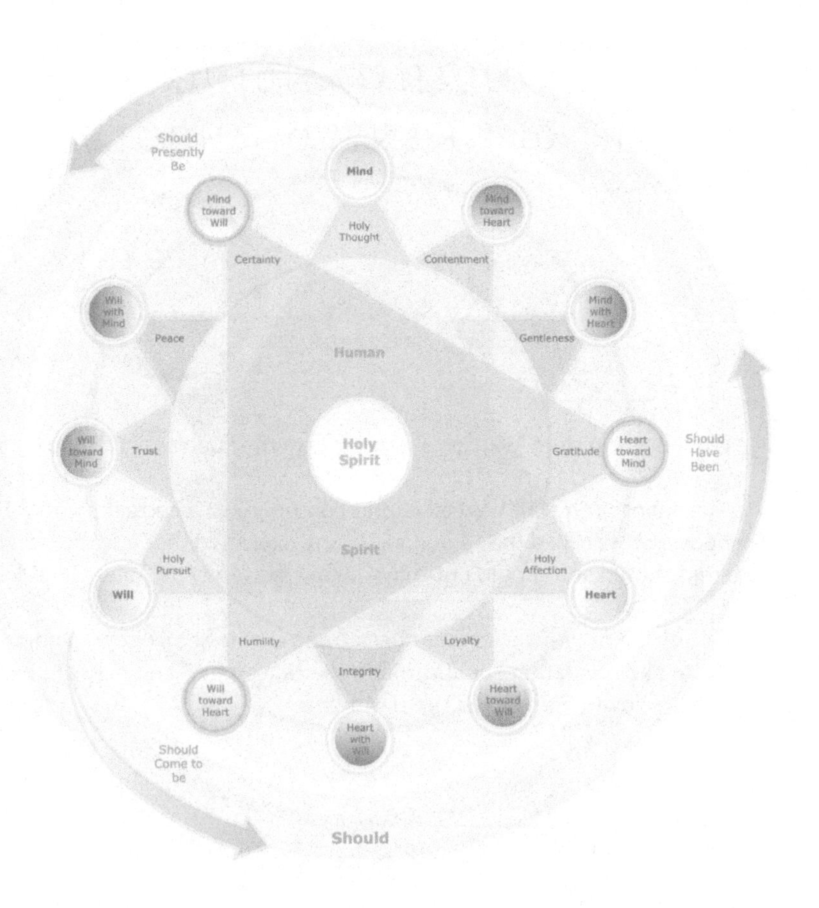

[1] John 1:3; 1 Corinthians 8:6; Acts 17:28; Romans 11:36

[2] See Chapter 22 of this testimony.

[3] Romans 8:6-7; 12:2; 1 Peter 4:7; 5:8; Philippians 2:2

[4] Philippians 2:18; Romans 14:5

[5] James 3:10; 1 Peter 4:15

acknowledge what "should presently be," we experience *certainty.*[1] When we acknowledge what "should not presently be," we encounter *contentment*.[2]

The heart also experiences affections with what "should have been"[3] and what "should not have been."[4] Agreement with what "should have been" results in *gratitude,*[5] while agreement with what "should not have been" manifests in *loyalty*.[6]

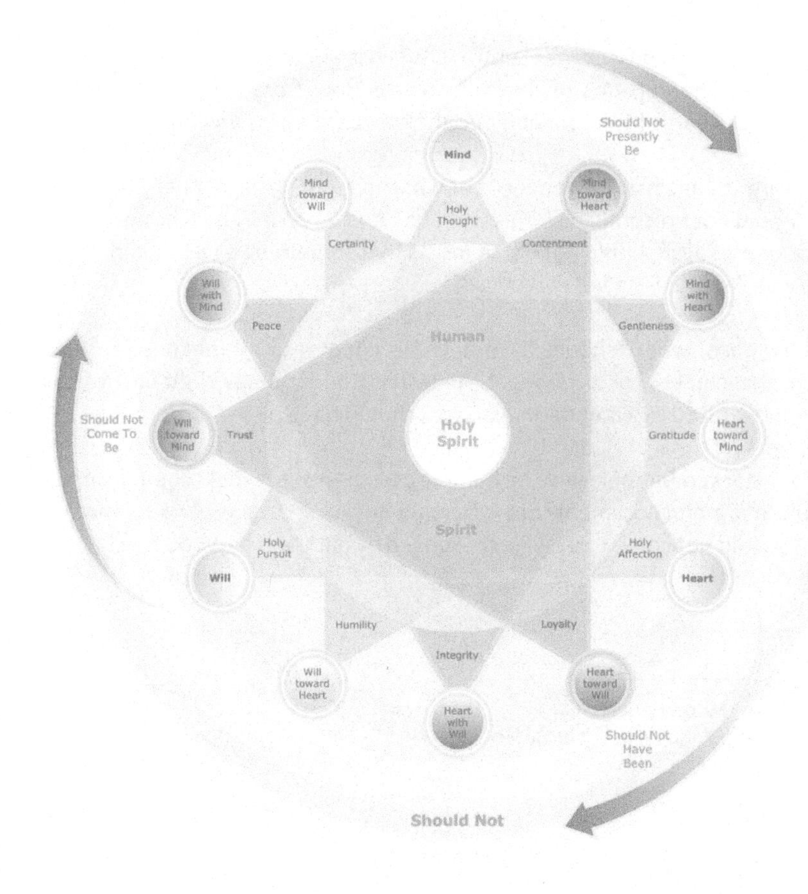

[1] Luke 1:4; 1 John 3:1

[2] Philippians 4:11; 3:8; Matthew 6:31-34; 1 Timothy 6:6-9; Hebrews 10:34; 13:5-6

[3] Matthew 23:23; Isaiah 1:9

[4] Ezekiel 13:19; Isaiah 48:19

[5] 1 Corinthians 1:4; Isaiah 1:9

[6] Joshua 24:14; 119:30; Isaiah 48:19

The will focuses on what will come to be. If we pursue what Goodness insists "should come to be,"[1] then we experience *humility.*[2] And the acceptance of what "should not come to be"[3] is expressed through *trust.*[4]

In the flow of "Goodness," what "should" moves counterclockwise around the map of the soul, while what "should not" moves clockwise.[5] The good currents of light always flow *out* of the spirit and *out* of the mind, will, and heart of the soul. Light shines *outward.*[6]

The fallenness of darkness argues contrarily against Goodness.[7] Therefore, its flow is the reverse. The currents of darkness always flow *from the outside into* the mind, will, and heart of the soul and *into* the spirit. Darkness invades *inward.*[8]

Darkness argues against the goodness of what "should presently be" by insisting that it "should not presently be." This is *doubt.*[9] And when darkness argues against what Goodness says "should not be," it insists that something else "should instead presently be," which is called *envy.*[10]

In the affections, what "should have been" is countered by darkness as "what should not have been," or *bitterness.*[11] And what Goodness says "should not have been" is substituted by what darkness says "should have been," or *lust.*[12]

The will is attacked by replacing the humble acceptance of what "should come to pass" with a *prideful* argument that it "should not come to pass."[13] And the trust of what "should not come to pass" is challenged by darkness as *worry* of what "will come to pass."[14]

---

[1] Matthew 5:4; Hebrews 12:2
[2] Proverbs 15:33; Zephaniah 2:3; Proverbs 22:4
[3] Revelation 2:11; 3:5
[4] Exodus 14:31; Psalm 9:10
[5] Exodus 25:40; Numbers 8:4
[6] Matthew 5:14-16; Ephesians 5:8-14; Philippians 2:15
[7] Galatians 5:17; Romans 8:5-8
[8] 2 Corinthians 7:1; James 4:8; 1 Peter 2:11
[9] Numbers 14:6-11; Matthew 14:23-33
[10] James 3:16; Proverbs 23:17
[11] Exodus 16:3; Numbers 20:3-5
[12] 2 Corinthians 11:3; Revelation 12:9; 2 Timothy 4:3-4; 2 Peter 3:17; Jude 1:4
[13] Genesis 3:4-5; John 8:44; Acts 13:10; 1 John 3:8
[14] Matthew 6:27, 34; 10:19

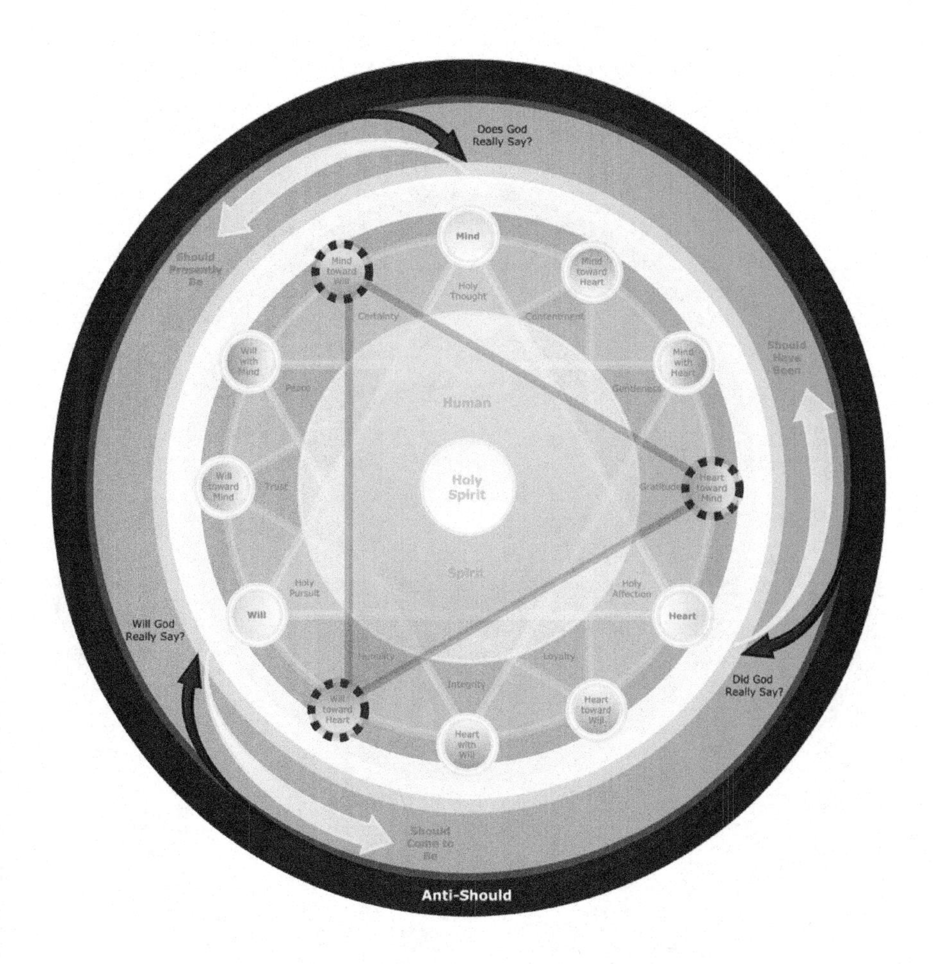

In time, the Eyes of the Spirit[1] will reveal these functions to those who ask, seek, and knock[2] for revelation and wisdom.[3]

---

[1] Isaiah 11:2; Revelation 5:6; See Chapter 34 of this testimony for more on the Eyes and Horns of the Spirit of Yehovah.

[2] Luke 11:9-10; Hebrews 4:16; James 1:5 – If you feel like you have hit a brick wall, that is good! You've found the door! Keep knocking, because the process of knocking prepares you to be able to stand when the door is opened (Luke 18:1-8)! Or, said another way, Yeshua is encouraging you to keep knocking so that you can be transformed and pass *through* the door (Hebrews 10:36)! HalleluYah!

[3] Ephesians 1:17; Luke 12:12; 21:15; Matthew 16:17; 1 Corinthians 2:10

Now, here is a very important function to understand about currents: the currents at a main gate tend to affect both of its neighboring gates. For example, a certain man was battling for many years against worry.[1] Every day he fought from

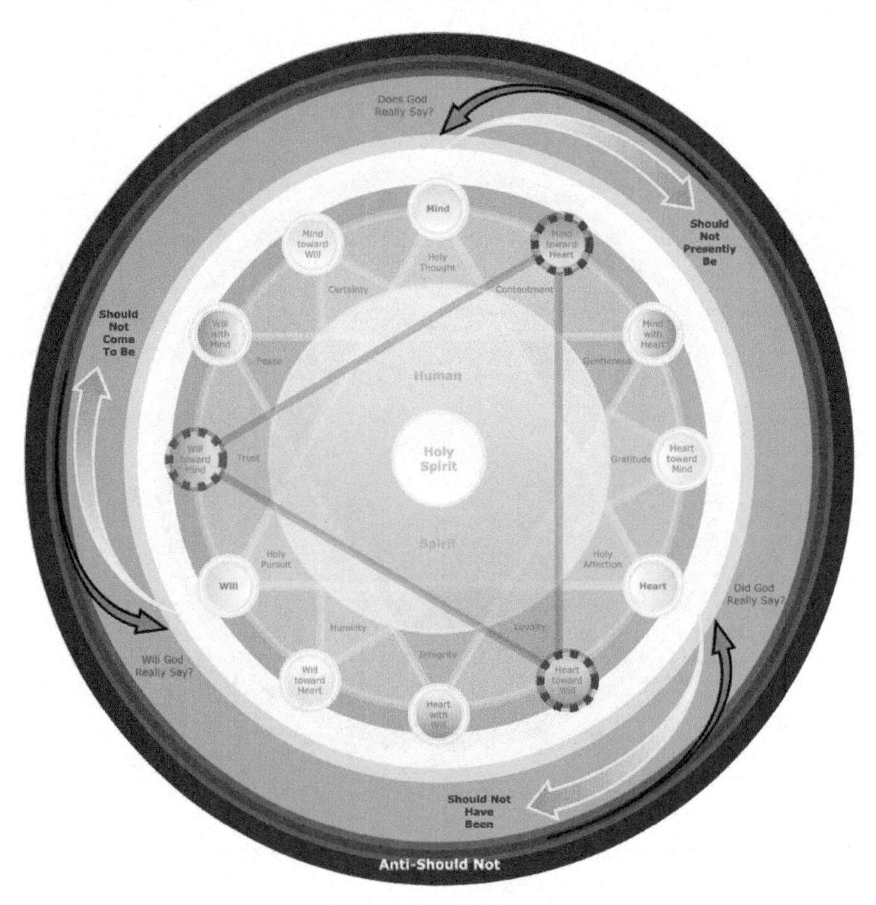

morning till night.[2] Even his dreams were plagued by it.[3] Then one day he heard the Voice of Yehovah say to him,[4] "You worry because you have believed the lie that you are your own keeper."[5] Without hesitation, the man responded, "But

---

[1] Luke 10:41; Mark 4:19; 1 Corinthians 7:32; Philippians 4:6; Matthew 6:25-34

[2] Isaiah 28:19; Hosea 4:5a

[3] Job 4:13-14; Matthew 27:19; Genesis 41:8; Daniel 2:1,3

[4] Hebrews 3:7; 4:7; 3:15; Psalm 95:7

[5] Matthew 4:4; John 6:31-59; 1 Chronicles 29:14

Lord, I know that you are My Provider!"[1] To which the Lord replied, "If you believed that, then worry would have no foothold, but because you have accepted the prideful lie that you have provided for yourself, you have left a door open to worry."[2]

Therefore, if you are experiencing a significant battle at a particular gate, make sure that the opposing current on the other side of the main gate has been addressed.[3] Just as worry can attack someone who's "unhumbly" and maybe even unintentionally taking credit for their own provision,[4] pride can establish residence when someone is trusting their own soul.[5] In the absence of gratitude, lust can find a seat.[6] And where there are assaults of bitterness, loyalty is soon questioned.[7] Doubt often visits when contentment is absent,[8] and envy rears its ugly head whenever certainty cannot seem to be found.[9]

If the dark spirits cannot convince a person of the contrary currents against Yehovah Himself,[10] they will next try to damage the holy relationship by convincing the person of contrary currents concerning other things observed, considered, decided, and intended.[11]

For example, a certain woman is in need of healing. When she begins to seek God for her healing, the enemy suggests contrary thoughts insisting that Yehovah is not presently her Healer.[12] However, the woman decides in her spirit to stand firm on the Scriptures that testify Yehovah is her Healer.[13] In response, the enemy changes tactics, draws her attention to other sick people, and argues that Yehovah is not their Healer.[14] Then the dark spirits draw attention to someone dear who was sick in the past, and they argue that Yehovah was not their Healer back then.[15] If the enemy can gain the woman's acceptance of such arguments, they can turn

---

[1] Philippians 4:19; Luke 12:30-32
[2] Matthew 6:27,33; Genesis 22:14; 1 Chronicles 29:14
[3] 2 Corinthians 2:11; Ephesians 6:11
[4] 1 Corinthians 4:7; 1 Peter 4:10; James 1:17
[5] James 4:16; Psalm 49:13; Proverbs 28:26
[6] 2 Timothy 3:2-5; 1 Thessalonians 4:5; Luke 12:15
[7] Acts 8:23; Exodus 14:12; Hebrews 12:15
[8] Philippians 4:11; 3:8; Matthew 6:31-34; 1 Timothy 6:6-9; Hebrews 10:34; 13:5-6
[9] 1 Timothy 6:4; Romans 2:8; Galatians 5:26; Titus 3:9
[10] Genesis 3:1,13; Revelation 12:9; 16:14; 20:2,8; Zechariah 3:1-2
[11] Genesis 3:4-5; John 8:44; Acts 13:10; 1 John 3:8
[12] Genesis 3:1,13; Revelation 12:9; 16:14; 20:2,8; Zechariah 3:1-2
[13] Psalm 103:2-3; James 5:15; Isaiah 33:24; 53:5
[14] 2 Kings 18:34-35; 17:5-7
[15] 2 Kings 19:12-13; Judges 6:13

the arguments back toward her and try to use sickness in her own past to argue that Yehovah has not been her Healer.[1] All in all, they will do their best to dissuade or distract her from accepting that Yehovah has always been, is, and will always be her Healer. [2] They use such tactics because they know that healing is never a matter of Yehovah's willingness[3] but rather a person's success in drawing near Him in spirit and truth.[4] And they know that when a person fills the cracks in the gates of the soul with the overflowing character of intimate divine relationship, there is no more room for darkness of any kind.[5]

Remember! Yeshua healed EVERY SINGLE PERSON WHO CAME TO HIM![6] EVERY PERSON WHO TOUCHED HIM FOR HEALING WAS HEALED![7]

JESUS CHRIST IS NOT THE PROBLEM![8] HIS WILLINGNESS TO MAKE YOU WHOLE IS NOT THE PROBLEM! [9] HIS ABILITY TO FULFILL HIS PROMISES IS NOT THE PROBLEM![10] THE PROBLEM IS EVIL INTERFERENCE WITH YOUR SOUL'S ABILITY TO DRAW NEAR AND TOUCH JESUS IN SPIRIT![11]

TO DRAW NEAR TO YESHUA IN SPIRIT IS TO DRAW NEAR TO HIM IN ONENESS![12] YOU MUST GUIDE YOUR SOUL INTO ONENESS WITH YESHUA![13] ABANDON THE PRINCIPLES OF DARKNESS[14] AND EMBRACE THE FULNESS OF HIS LIGHT![15] STOP ENTERTAINING LIES[16] AND COMMIT FULLY TO ACCEPTING THE TRUTH FROM CHRIST![17]

HALLELUUUUYAAAAAAAAAAAAH!!!!!!!

---

[1] 2 Kings 18:21; Psalm 28:1; 83:1; Habakkuk 1:13
[2] 2 Kings 18:25; Isaiah 36:10; 37:10
[3] Luke 5:12-13; 2 Chronicles 7:14; Isaiah 19:22; Matthew 13:15
[4] Matthew 12:15; Luke 6:19
[5] Matthew 6:22; Ephesians 5:8; Revelation 7:15-17; 21:3-5
[6] Matthew 4:24; 8:16; 12:15
[7] Matthew 9:21-22; 14:36; Mark 6:56; Luke 8:46
[8] Matthew 5:48; 1 John 3:5; 1 Peter 2:22; 2 Corinthians 5:21
[9] Matthew 8:3; Mark 1:41
[10] Joshua 21:45; Luke 1:37
[11] Galatians 3:1; 2 Corinthians 11:3
[12] John 14:20; 6:56; 15:5-7; Romans 8:1; 16:7; 1 Corinthians 1:30; Galatians 2:20
[13] John 17:11,21-22; Romans 15:5-6; 1 Corinthians 1:10; 2 Corinthians 13:11; Philippians 2:2; Ephesians 4:4
[14] Romans 16:17; 2 John 1:7-10; Ephesians 5:11; Jude 1:19
[15] Ephesians 5:8; John 12:36; 1 Thessalonians 5:5
[16] Matthew 9:4; Ezekiel 38:10; Haggai 2:13-14
[17] Acts 20:32; 1 Kings 18:21; Romans 4:20

PRAISE OUR GOD, WHO HOLDS BACK NO BLESSING FROM US![1]
HALLELUUUUYAAAAAAAAAAAAH!!!!!!!

GLORY TO OUR KING, WHO INVITES EVERYONE TO ENTER HIS KINGDOM OF VICTORY![2]

HALLELUUUUYAAAAAAAAAAAAH!!!!!!!

GLORY TO OUR GOD, WHO POURS OUT HIS BLESSINGS WITHOUT LIMIT ON THOSE WHO DRAW NEAR TO HIM![3]

HALLELUUUUYAAAAAAAAAAAAH!!!!!!!

NOW, you who are still seeking healing, LISTEN![4]

When you are attempting to draw near to Him, you should NOT do so with challenges, complaints, and grumblings! [5] That is how the Roman soldiers "touched" Him, and they were not healed of anything![6] And do not attempt to draw near with apathy, insincerity, or doubts! [7] That is how Yeshua was approached after His transfiguration, and the only reason that boy was healed was for the sake of Yeshua's Name and Testimony![8] No! When you draw near to Him, do not let any stowaways of darkness come with you! Do not bring them to complain, grumble, doubt, or incessantly blabber in double-mindedness! He is not willing to heal THEM![9] It is YOU He wants to heal![10]

HALLELUUUUUYAAAAAAAAAAAAH!!!!!!!

---

[1] Psalm 34:9-10; 84:11-12; Matthew 6:33; Philippians 4:19
[2] 2 Peter 3:9; Matthew 18:14; 1 Timothy 2:4; Romans 2:4
[3] Ephesians 1:3; Hebrews 7:19; 10:22; John 3:34; 4:14
[4] Luke 8:18; 19:26; Deuteronomy 32:46-47; Proverbs 2:2-5; Mark 4:23-24; Acts 17:11; Hebrews 2:1; James 1:22-25; Matthew 13:12; John 15:2
[5] Hebrews 3:11; Numbers 14:27; 17:5,10; John 6:43; Philippians 2:14; 1 Peter 4:9
[6] John 19:2-3; Matthew 26:49
[7] James 1:6-8; Mark 11:22-24; Hebrews 10:32; 11:6; Ephesians 4:14
[8] Mark 9:22-25; James 1:6-7
[9] Matthew 8:28-32; Hebrews 2:16
[10] Exodus 15:26; Matthew 3:15; Romans 11:2a; Mark 6:56

MAY THE HOLY KING BE HONORED IN RIGHTEOUSNESS AND HOLINESS FOREVER!![1]

TO HIM BE THE GLORY!!!!!!!!![2]

THEREFORE, understand that familiarity with the Currents of Should can help immensely with recognizing stowaway darkness![3] Don't allow a single one of those contrary spirits to ever share in your tongue, attitude, or focus, but especially don't allow them to encroach on your time in drawing near to Yeshua![4] May it never be so![5]

GOD DOES NOT HEAL SPIRITS OF DARKNESS![6]

HE GIVES EACH OF HIS CHILDREN A NEW,[7] HOLY,[8] PURE,[9] AND RIGHTEOUS[10] SPIRIT![11]

THAT IS WHO YOU ARE![12] YOU ARE A NEW,[13] HOLY,[14] PURE,[15] AND RIGHTEOUS SPIRIT![16]

DO NOT LET UNCLEAN SPIRITS HAVE A SAY IN YOUR SOUL![17]

REIGN IN YOUR SOUL![18]

---

[1] Revelation 4:11; 5:12-13; 7:12

[2] Revelation 4:11; 5:12-13; 7:12

[3] 2 Corinthians 2:11; 1 Peter 5:8; Ephesians 6:11-12; Revelation 12:9-11

[4] 2 Corinthians 6:14; 1 John 1:6; 3:14; 1 Corinthians 10:21; James 4:4

[5] Luke 20:16; Romans 6:2,15; 7:13; 11:1

[6] Hebrews 2:16; Jude 1:6

[7] Ezekiel 11:19; Psalm 51:10; Acts 8:15; Romans 7:6; 2 Corinthians 3:6

[8] 1 Peter 2:9; Revelation 1:6; 5:10

[9] 1 Timothy 5:22; Titus 1:15

[10] 2 Corinthians 5:21; Philippians 3:9

[11] Ezekiel 36:26; Psalm 51:10; John 3:3-5; 2 Corinthians 3:18; 5:17

[12] 2 Corinthians 5:17; John 3:3; Galatians 6:15

[13] Galatians 6:15; 2 Corinthians 5:17; Ephesians 2:10; 4:24; Colossians 3:10-11

[14] Romans 1:7; Jude 1:3; 2 Peter 3:11; 1 Peter 2:5,9; 1 Thessalonians 3:13

[15] 2 Timothy 2:22; 1 John 3:3; Hebrews 7:26

[16] 2 Corinthians 5:21; Philippians 3:9

[17] Revelation 16:13; 1 John 4:1-3

[18] Romans 6:12; 2 Corinthians 10:4; 1 Corinthians 9:26; 1 Timothy 6:12

REIGN FOR THE GLORY OF JESUS CHRIST![1]

CRUSH THOSE DARK SPIRITS BENEATH YOUR FEET![2]
HALLELUUUUUUYAAAAAAAAAAAAAAAAH!!!!!!!

RECOGNIZE that ALL of the enemy's activities are steeped in rebellion against anything and everything Yehovah was, is, or will be![3] And do not accept discouragement from the enemy that this recognition is difficult![4] You were made to recognize such things![5] It just takes practice![6] Though the understanding of these currents of "should" and "should not" might initially seem elusive, the experienced spiritual victor WILL ABSOLUTELY BECOME skilled in such recognition,[7] able to quickly cut down resistance to Goodness at the root of rebellion![8]

FIGHT FOR YOUR FREEDOM![9]

FIGHT FOR HIS KINGDOM![10]

FIGHT FOR HIS HONOR![11]

HALLELUUUYAAAAAAAAAAAAH!!!!!!!

HALLELUUUYAAAAAAAAAAAAH!!!!!!!

HALLELUUUUUUUUUYAAAAAAAAAAAAAAAAAAAAAAAH!!!!!!!

---

[1] John 15:8; Luke 6:35; Psalm 92:12-15; Isaiah 60:21; Matthew 5:16
[2] Luke 10:19; Psalm 91:13; Ezekiel 2:6; Mark 16:18; Acts 28:5; Romans 16:20
[3] 2 Thessalonians 2:4; Isaiah 14:13; Revelation 13:6
[4] Numbers 32:7; Deuteronomy 1:28
[5] 1 Corinthians 2:16; John 15:15; 16:13-15
[6] Philippians 4:9; 2 Peter 1:10
[7] Hebrews 5:14; Philippians 1:9-10
[8] 1 Thessalonians 5:21-22; Ephesians 4:12-16
[9] Galatians 5:1; 1 Timothy 6:12; 1:18; 1 Corinthians 9:25-26; 2 Corinthians 6:7; 10:3-5; Ephesians 6:10-18; 1 Thessalonians 5:8-9; 2 Timothy 4:7
[10] Matthew 6:33; Luke 12:31; Psalm 34:9; 37:19; 84:11; Isaiah 33:16; John 6:27
[11] 2 Corinthians 8:23; John 15:8

THERE IS NO ONE EQUAL TO OUR GOD!!!![1]

HOLY, HOLY, HOLY IS HE!!!![2]

BUT WE ARE HIS CHILDREN!!!![3]

AND WE FIGHT FOR THE GLORY OF HIS NAME!!!![4]

BECAUSE HE IS GOOD!!!!!!!!!!!!!!!!!!!!!!!!!!!!!!!!!!!![5]

HALLELUUUUUUUYAAAAAAAAAAAAAAAAAAAAAAAAAH!!!!!!!

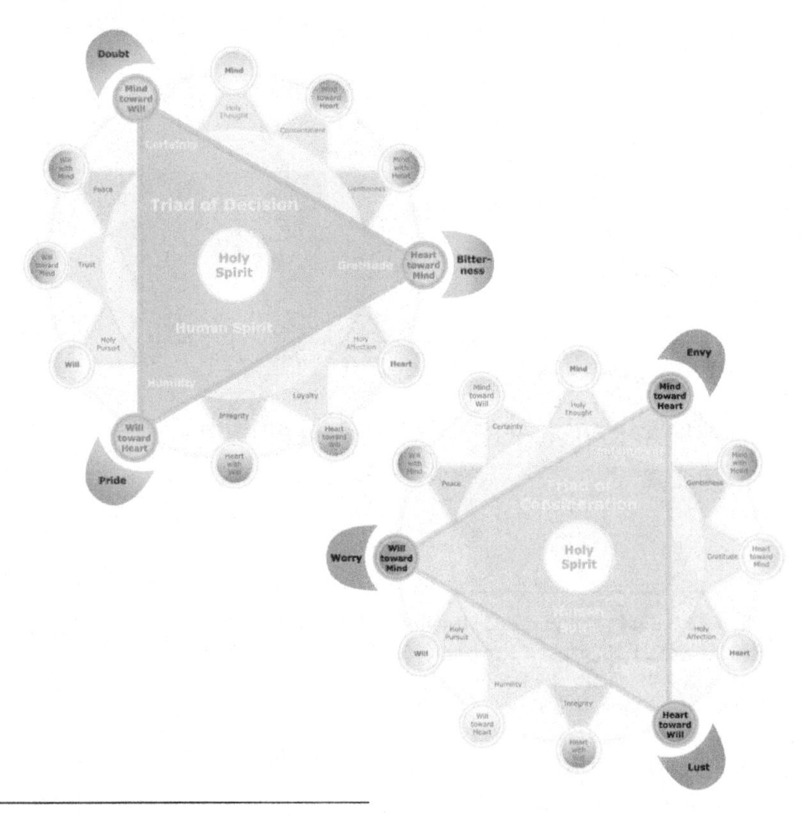

---

[1] Colossians 1:18; Psalm 89:27; Isaiah 52:13; Matthew 28:18; John 3:35
[2] Revelation 3:7; 4:8; Isaiah 6:3
[3] Romans 8:14,16; Hebrews 12:7; 1 John 3:1-2; 5:19
[4] Romans 15:9; John 15:8; 1 Peter 4:14; Revelation 15:4
[5] Matthew 19:17; 1 Samuel 2:2; Psalm 145:7-9; James 1:17

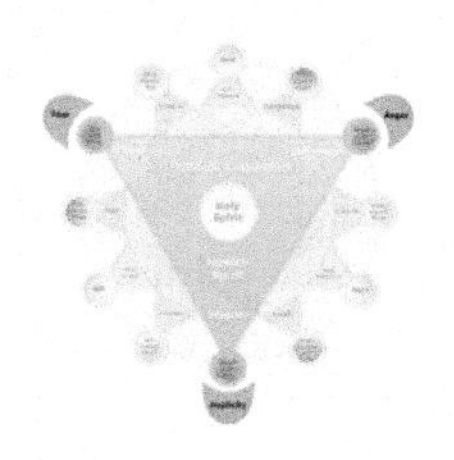

CHAPTER 33

ALTARS IN THE GATES

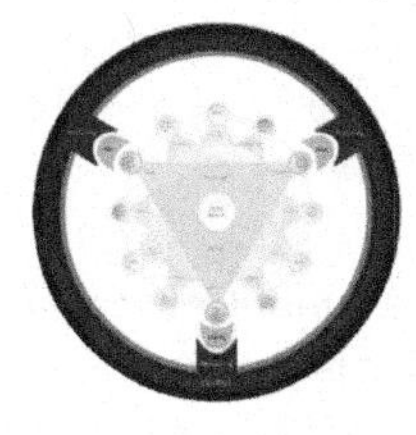

There are many sorts of altars, but the four general groups are altars to the Lord,[1] altars of cut stone,[2] altars in high places,[3] and altars to idolatry.[4]

When a person has a holy encounter with the Lord, they will often take special note of it and refer to the experience as a momentous or "life-directing" event.[5] In soulical terms, this is known as a "memorial" or an "altar to the Lord."[6] It stands as a testimony of Yehovah's faithfulness that cannot be torn down by forces of darkness.[7]

However, after having such an experience, some people will hear encouragement from dark spirits to "alter the altar."[8] That is, they will hear suggestions that they should rewrite the event to better fit certain notions of religious format, cultural

---

[1] Genesis 8:20; Deuteronomy 27:5; Joshua 8:30; 2 Samuel 24:25; Revelation 16:7

[2] Exodus 20:25; Deuteronomy 27:5-6; Joshua 8:31

[3] Hosea 10:8; 2 Kings 23:15; 17:11; Isaiah 16:12

[4] Ezekiel 6:5; 2 Chronicles 33:15; Judges 6:25

[5] Joshua 4:1-9, 20-24 – Yehovah commanded Israel to set up the twelve stones as a remembrance that crossing the Jordan was a "life-directing" event. That is, it represented a point of relationship purposed to affect future behavior (verse 24).

[6] Genesis 8:20; 12:7; Judges 6:24

[7] Proverbs 14:19; Revelation 12:11

[8] 1 Kings 12:28; Exodus 31:1

acceptance, or philosophical rhetoric.[1] Such altars are known as those of "cut stone" and do not meet Yehovah's approval precisely because they are no longer altars of truth to Him but altars of the person's accepted conformity to deceit.[2]

If a person desires a momentous experience or encounter with Yehovah but lacks one, dark spirits will possibly tempt the person to manufacture an experience according to various suggested ideas of how such an experience should appear.[3] Such altars include those testimonies by persons who publicly insist that they heard the Voice of Yehovah tell them this or that when they are inwardly certain that they did not hear Him say anything.[4] Also included would be false claims of experiences with Yehovah, His Voice, or His Wisdom by persons who seek inclusion when attending gatherings, events, classes, or schools.[5] All such altars are really idolatrous tributes to oneself[6] and are known as "altars set in high places."

However, not all altars are built as monuments of genuine or supposed worship. If the enemy has been granted access to a gate for some time, dark spirits will typically attempt to build an altar of their own in the gate. This vulnerability occurs in the person through *willful cooperation* with *unintentional idolatry* and is known as "wounding."[7]

For example, a certain young man began pursuing the Lord. In his zeal, he decided to give away all that he had and become a missionary.[8] He quickly joined a small group with similar goals and left on his first trip full of faith and hope.[9] But during the trip, the enemy viciously turned one of his companions against him, causing the young man to abandon the group in great disappointment.[10] On his journey back to his hometown, dark spirits worked continuously to present many bitter suggestions to him, and the young man accepted a spirit of bitterness.[11] For many years thereafter, the memory of his misadventure was constantly revisited as an

---

1 Jeremiah 8:8; 23:36; Genesis 3:3
2 Jeremiah 23:38-40; Jude 1:8; Zechariah 10:2
3 Colossians 2:18; 1 Kings 22:24; Matthew 23:7
4 Ezekiel 13:6-9; Lamentation 2:14; 2 Peter 2:18
5 1 John 2:4; 2 Peter 2:1; Jeremiah 28:1-17
6 Luke 16:15; John 12:43
7 Lamentations 1:20; Luke 18:10-14; 15:27-30
8 Matthew 19:21; Mark 10:21
9 Luke 8:13; Psalm 106:12-14; Isaiah 58:2-3
10 Acts 15:39; 2 Timothy 4:10
11 1 Samuel 30:6; Acts 8:23; Romans 3:14; Ephesians 4:31; Hebrews 12:15

altar to bitterness.[1] He was *willfully* holding a grudge that was *unintentional* idolatry.[2] Because of this, he remained unable to be grateful in spirit until the Holy Spirit eventually shattered the ignoble altar by filling the young man's heart with His Love.[3] Then the young man was able to clearly understand the events and deceptions that the enemy had brought about on his first mission trip.[4]

Let those with wisdom hear what the Holy Spirit says to the faithful:[5] Dark feelings in the heart are overcome by holy feelings![6] The mind is conquered by holy thoughts,[7] the will is conquered by holy pursuits,[8] and the heart is conquered by holy affections![9] Therefore, choose the appropriate weapon for the applicable battle!

All types of soulical altars are built and stand in a gate. Altars to the Lord shine with His Character in the gate,[10] but any altar that is not of the Lord stands as a wound in the gate.[11] If a gate has a wound, it will not be secured until the unclean altar is destroyed[12] and removed by Yeshua's Blood on that gate.[13] The wound cannot be removed by any means other than His Blood that applies to that gate.[14] His Wounds need to replace the wounds in that gate.[15] This is how any wounds in any gate must be healed.[16]

---

[1] Hebrews 12:15; Deuteronomy 29:18

[2] Colossians 3:5; Ephesians 5:5

[3] Romans 2:4; Luke 15:17-19; 1 Peter 4:8

[4] Romans 12:21; 13:12; Luke 11:35; 1 Thessalonians 5:5; 1 Peter 2:9

[5] Revelation 2:7,11,17,29; 3:6,13,22

[6] 1 John 4:18; John 1:5; Romans 12:21

[7] Romans 12:2; 2 Corinthians 10:5; Jeremiah 4:14; Hebrews 4:12

[8] Matthew 3:8; Acts 26:20

[9] Matthew 5:43-44,46; Mark 12:31; John 13:34-35; 15:17

[10] Exodus 17:15; Genesis 22:14; 33:20

[11] Ezekiel 6:4-6; Revelation 21:21, "The twelve gates were twelve pearls, each gate made of a single pearl." Notice that pearls in oysters are formed from extensive suffering against irritants. Altars built by darkness are irritants that need to be overcome. Even so, victory over such altars results in the formation of holy altars, revealing great spiritual wealth in relationship with Yehovah (Hebrews 5:14).

[12] 2 Chronicles 15:8; 2 Kings 11:18

[13] Philippians 3:8,13b; Ephesians 4:22,31-32; Hebrews 12:1; Luke 9:23

[14] Hebrews 10:3-10,26; Acts 9:34; 1 Peter 2:24

[15] 1 Peter 2:21; 3:18; Hebrews 2:9

[16] 1 Peter 2:24; 1 John 2:2; 3:5; 4:10,14; Romans 3:25-26; John 1:29; Isaiah 53:1-12

Children of the Most Holy God! "Why are you talking among yourselves about having no bread?"[1]

YOU CANNOT SPIRITUALLY HEAL THE SOUL WITH THE SOUL![2]

Understand how the spirit realm works![3] Creation comes from spirit, not spirit from Creation![4] God did not say, "Well, We will see if the land rises up from the water to decide if We can believe it"![5] No! Yehovah decided it, and then He spoke it into completion! In the same way, His children do not rely on what is seen in Creation to decide what to believe in spirit![6] No! The power of the Holy Spirit comes from within![7] We are not changed by Creation; we change Creation![8] We do not serve Creation; Creation serves us![9]

CONSIDER THE GREAT WISDOM OF GOD,[10] WHO MADE IT POSSIBLE FOR US TO DECIDE BEFORE WE SEE![11]

BLESS GOD!

WE HAVE ALREADY RECEIVED EVERY SPIRITUAL BLESSING[12] THROUGH WHAT HE HAS ALREADY DONE FOR US![13] WE ARE" *ALREADY"*![14]

GLORY TO YEHOVAH!

THEREFORE, any gate that is breached in our soul does not need to be "accomplished" in some way[15] but rather needs to be released to express what is *"already"*![16]

---

[1] Matthew 16:8
[2] Galatians 3:3; Hebrews 9:11-15
[3] 1 Corinthians 2:13-14; Ephesians 6:12; Colossians 2:8
[4] Hebrews 11:3; Psalm 33:6; Isaiah 40:26; 2 Peter 3:5
[5] Genesis 1:9; Psalm 95:5; Jonah 1:9
[6] John 20:29; 2 Corinthians 5:7; Hebrews 11:1,27
[7] John 20:22; Acts 2:38; 1 Corinthians 6:19; Luke 17:21
[8] Matthew 17:20; 21:22; Mark 9:23; Luke 1:37; 18:27
[9] Luke 17:6; Mark 11:22-23; Matthew 21:21
[10] Ephesians 3:10; Psalm 104:24; Romans 11:33; 1 Corinthians 1:24
[11] John 20:29; 2 Corinthians 5:7; Hebrews 11:1,27
[12] Ephesians 1:3; 2:6; Genesis 12:2-3; 1 Chronicles 4:10; Isaiah 61:9; Galatians 3:9
[13] Hebrews 7:27; Romans 6:10; Titus 2:14
[14] 2 Peter 1:12; Romans 15:15; 1 Corinthians 15:1; Jude 1:5
[15] Hebrews 4:10; 1 Peter 4:1-2
[16] John 8:12; Ephesians 5:8; 1 Thessalonians 5:5

YESHUA, YOU ARE OUR GATES! BE OUR GATES!!!!![1]

HALLELUYAH!

THE LIGHT IS ALREADY SHINING![2]

WE ARE ALREADY CLEAN BECAUSE OF THE WORD HE HAS SPOKEN TO US![3]

OUR FOREFATHERS HAD TO BUILD ALTARS TO WHAT YEHOVAH HAD SHOWN THEIR SOULS,[4] BUT WE DON'T *NEED* TO BUILD ALTARS![5]

THE ALTARS HAVE ALREADY BEEN BUILT FOR US!!!!![6]

HALLELUUUUYAAAAAAAAAAAAAAAAAH!!!!!!!!!!!!

JESUS DIED FOR US![7] BUT HE LIVED FOR US, TOO![8]

CHILDREN OF GOD! BEHOLD YOUR ALTARS:
HE LIVED IN CERTAINTY FOR US![9]
HE TRUSTED GOD FOR US![10]
HE WALKED IN JOY FOR US![11]
HE WALKED IN TRUTH FOR US![12]
HE LIVED CONTENTLY FOR US![13]
HE LIVED GENTLY FOR US![14]
HE WALKED IN GRATITUDE FOR US![15]
HE WALKED IN LOVE FOR US![16]

---

[1] Ephesians 1:3; Revelation 21:25
[2] 1 John 2:8; 2 Timothy 1:10; John 8:12
[3] John 15:3; 17:17; Acts 11:9
[4] Genesis 8:20; 12:8; 13:18; 35:1; Deuteronomy 27:5; Joshua 8:30; Judges 6:24
[5] Hebrews 10:19-22; 9:15; 12:24; Luke 22:20; John 6:54-56
[6] Hebrews 10:15-18; Jeremiah 31:33-34
[7] Romans 5:8; Isaiah 53:6; 1 Peter 3:18; 1 John 4:9-10
[8] 1 Thessalonians 5:10; Philippians 2:8; Matthew 11:29
[9] John 5:22-27; 13:3; Matthew 11:27; 28:18
[10] Luke 22:42; John 5:19
[11] Hebrews 12:2; Acts 5:31; Psalms 138:8
[12] John 14:6; Acts 4:12; Hebrews 10:19-22; 1 John 2:23; 2 John 1:9; Revelation 5:8-9
[13] Philippians 2:6-8; Matthew 8:20
[14] Matthew 11:29; 2 Corinthians 10:1
[15] John 11:41; Matthew 14:19; 15:36; Luke 24:30
[16] John 13:34; 15:9,12; 1 John 4:10

HE LIVED LOYALLY FOR US![1]
HE LIVED IN INTEGRITY FOR US![2]
HE WALKED HUMBLY FOR US![3]
HE SET HIS EYES ON HEAVENLY THINGS FOR US![4]

HALLELUYAH, HE DID IT *ALL* FOR US![5]

HALLELUYAH, WE DON'T HAVE TO BUILD *ANYTHING* NEW[6] BUT SIMPLY RECEIVE WHAT HE HAS ALREADY DONE FOR US IN OUR SOULS![7]

HALLELUUUUYAAAAAAAAAAAAAAAAH!!!!!!!

DO YOU WANT VICTORY? IT'S IN YESHUA![8]

DO YOU WANT PERFECTION? IT'S IN YESHUA![9]

DO YOU WANT ONENESS WITH YEHOVAH? IT'S IN YESHUA![10]

HALLELUYAH, CHILDREN OF GOD,[11] RELEASE THE POWER OF YOUR ALMIGHTY GOD IN YOUR SOUL AND REIGN![12]

DECIDE AND REIGN![13]

DECIDE AND REIGN![14]

REIGNNNNNNNNNNNNN FOR HIS GLORY!!!!!!!!!![15]

---

[1] John 4:34; 5:19,30; 8:29
[2] Luke 12:3; Matthew 12:36
[3] Matthew 11:29; Philippians 2:7-8
[4] Luke 9:16; Matthew 14:19; Mark 7:34
[5] Romans 8:32; Psalm 84:11; 1 Corinthians 2:12; 3:21-23
[6] 2 Corinthians 5:1; John 14:2-3; Hebrews 11:10
[7] 1 Peter 1:9; 2:25; Matthew 11:29
[8] 1 Corinthians 15:57; Romans 8:37; 1 John 5:4-5
[9] Matthew 5:48; 1 Peter 1:15-16; Colossians 1:28; Hebrews 10:14
[10] John 17:23; Ephesians 1:6-14; Hebrews 11:40
[11] Romans 8:14; Galatians 3:26; 1 John 3:1-2; 5:19; Matthew 5:9
[12] Acts 1:8; 26:18; Mark 9:1; Luke 9:1; Romans 1:16; 1 Corinthians 4:19-20
[13] Romans 5:17; 6:23; Isaiah 61:10; Philippians 3:9
[14] Revelation 1:6; 5:10; 20:6; 22:5; Exodus 19:6; 1 Peter 2:5-9
[15] Colossians 3:5-17; John 15:8

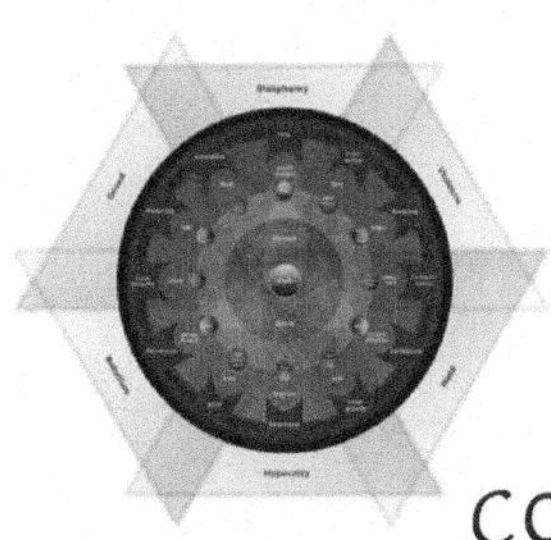

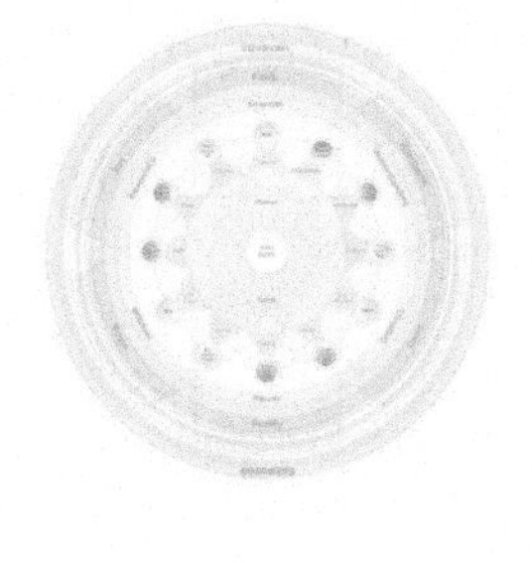

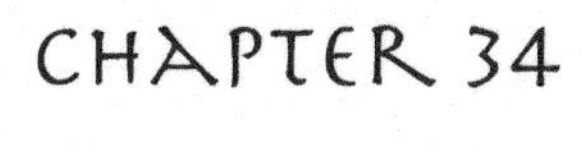

CHAPTER 34

CONQUERED SOULS

The healthy human soul consists of more than the appearance of success.[1] Its conquest is the most arduous of endeavors, and few are those who even find the path to pursue it.[2] Lifetimes are spent pursuing far less valuable goals in a quest for temporal reward,[3] while most who set out to conquer the soul generally do so in anticipation of a reward after resurrection.[4] However, those few who continue forward in sincere righteousness soon discover that the Kingdom of Heaven is not merely a goal for the future but a real place that is extremely difficult yet not impossible to enter in the present.[5]

When a person experiences spiritual dominion over one of the three primary gates,[6] the adjacent gates share in that victory.[7] This unity[8] around the main gate shines forth a facet of the Sevenfold Spirit of Yehovah.[9]

---

[1] 1 Samuel 16:7; John 7:24

[2] Proverbs 16:32; Matthew 7:14; 16:24-25; Proverbs 4:26-27; Isaiah 30:21; 35:8; 57:14

[3] Luke 12:18; 1 Timothy 6:9

[4] John 11:24; 18:36

[5] Matthew 7:13; 13:32; Hebrews 4:11; Mark 12:34; Luke 17:20

[6] See Chapter 22 of this testimony.

[7] Matthew 6:22-23; Luke 11:34-36

[8] Mark 12:29; John 10:30

[9] Revelation 1:4; 3:1; 4:5; 5:6

Now, we know that Yeshua has the Seven Horns and the Seven Eyes which roam throughout the earth and that these represent the Sevenfold Spirit of Yehovah.[1] But these verses do not reveal what facets specifically comprise the "Sevenfold Spirit" of Yehovah.[2]

Yehovah, You have sent Your Sevenfold Spirit[3] into all the earth[4] to testify about You[5] and to guide us into the Truth![6] Gracious[7] and Generous[8] Father, may those who seek Your Kingdom and Your Righteousness[9] receive the revelation![10]

HALLELUYAH!

Warriors of Yehovah![11] The Seven Eyes are the gift of complete spiritual observation given us through the Lamb Who was slain![12] They are the Eyes of the Spirit of Truth,[13] and they perceive the Seven Facets[14] of the Eternal Truth[15] Who was, is, and is to come![16]

GLORY BE TO "HIM WHO IS, AND WHO WAS, AND WHO IS TO COME, AND TO THE SEVENFOLD SPIRIT BEFORE HIS THRONE, AND TO JESUS CHRIST, WHO IS THE FAITHFUL WITNESS, THE FIRSTBORN FROM THE DEAD, AND THE RULER OF THE KINGS OF THE EARTH!"[17]

"The Spirit of Yehovah will rest on Him— the Spirit of Wisdom and Understanding, the Spirit of Counsel and Power, the Spirit of Knowledge and Reverence of

---

[1] Revelation 5:6; 2 Chronicles 16:9a; Zechariah 3:9; 4:10
[2] Revelation 4:5b, "These are the ἑπτὰ πνεύματα of God." – ἑπτὰ πνεύματα, meaning *Sevenfold Spirit* or *Seven Spirits.*
[3] Revelation 1:4; 4:5
[4] Revelation 5:6; 2 Chronicles 16:9; Zechariah 3:9; 4:10
[5] John 15:26; Revelation 19:10
[6] John 14:26; 16:13; 1 Corinthians 2:10-13; Ephesians 4:7-15; 1 John 2:20,27
[7] Psalm 116:5; Exodus 34:6
[8] James 1:5; Titus 3:6; 1 Chronicles 29:14
[9] Matthew 6:33; Luke 12:31; Psalm 34:9; 37:19; 84:11; Isaiah 33:16; John 6:27
[10] Jeremiah 33:3; Deuteronomy 4:29; Psalm 91:15; Isaiah 65:24; Joel 2:32; Luke 11:9-10
[11] Philippians 2:25; 2 Timothy 2:3; Philemon 1:2
[12] John 14:26; Isaiah 11:2-5
[13] John 14:16-17; 15:26; 16:13; Jeremiah 5:3
[14] Revelation 5:6b; 4:5
[15] 1 John 5:11; 2:23; John 14:6; Acts 4:12; Hebrews 10:19-22; 2 John 1:9; Revelation 5:8-9
[16] Revelation 1:8; 22:13; Isaiah 41:4; 44:6; 48:12
[17] Revelation 1:4-5

Yehovah."[1] Notice that the effect of Yehovah's Spirit resting upon Yeshua is divided into four descriptions in this statement, or four areas of awareness in spirit:[2] *one* of "Yehovah,"[3] *one* of "Wisdom and Understanding,"[4] *one* of "Counsel and Power,"[5] and *one* of "Knowledge and Reverence."[6] These groupings are not random but brilliantly organized in His Great Understanding![7]

The world cannot see what the Seven Eyes see.[8] Anyone who is asleep has their eyes shut and cannot see.[9] Blessed are those who wake up, open their eyes, and see![10]

Know then what the Seven Eyes are:[11]

The First Eye is the Spirit of Yehovah. It is singular because It alone sees all things,[12] including the other eyes.[13] It also only belongs to One.[14] Only Yehovah is Good,[15] and only He can perfectly identify *Goodness* and lead us into it.[16] We see Goodness because He gives us an Eye to see it![17] The gift of the Spirit of Yehovah is the gift of His Good Presence and Good Guidance![18] He is the Gift of Goodness![19]

---

[1] Isaiah 11:2

[2] Spirit, from the Hebrew רוּחַ, pronounced "roo-ach," meaning *spirit, breath,* or *wind* (Genesis 1:2 – observation; 2 Chronicles 24:20 – consideration; Luke 3:22 – decision; Genesis 6:3 – intention).

[3] From the Hebrew רוּחַ יְהוָה, pronounced "roo-ach Yehovah," meaning *Spirit of Yehovah* (Genesis 6:3; Numbers 11:25; Judges 14:6; 1 Samuel 10:6).

[4] From the Hebrew חָכְמָה וּבִינָה רוּחַ, pronounced "roo-ach khokh-mah veh-bee-nah," meaning *Spirit of wisdom and wisdom/understanding/discernment.*

[5] From the Hebrew עֵצָה וּגְבוּרָה רוּחַ, pronounced "roo-ach ey-tsah veh-g'boo-rah," meaning *Spirit of purpose/counsel and force/strength/power (to pursue and accomplish).*

[6] From the Hebrew דַּעַת וְיִרְאַת רוּחַ, pronounced "roo-ach da'ath veh-yeer'ath," meaning *Spirit of intimate knowledge and reverence.*

[7] Romans 11:33; Ephesians 3:10; Colossians 2:2-3

[8] John 12:40; 2 Corinthians 4:4; 1 John 2:11

[9] 1 Thessalonians 5:5-8; Isaiah 42:6-7; Acts 26:18

[10] Romans 13:11; Ephesians 5:14; 1 Thessalonians 5:6: Revelation 3:2-3; 16:15; Luke 24:31; John 4:35

[11] Isaiah 11:2; Revelation 5:6

[12] John 5:20; 16:30; Hebrews 4:13; Daniel 2:22; Job 12:22

[13] 1 Corinthians 2:10-11; Daniel 2:22

[14] Ecclesiastes 12:14; John 10:29

[15] Matthew 19:17; 1 Samuel 2:2; Psalm 145:7-9; James 1:17

[16] James 1:17; John 1:9; 1 John 1:5; Revelation 21:23; 22:5; Isaiah 60:19

[17] Psalm 146:8; Proverbs 29:13

[18] Hebrews 13:5; Psalm 37:25,28; Isaiah 41:10; Deuteronomy 31:6

[19] Genesis 15:1; Psalm 16:5-6; 142:5; Lamentations 3:24; Revelation 21:3-4

BLESS OUR GOOD SHEPHERD,[1] WHO GIVES US EVERY GOOD GIFT,[2] INCLUDING EYES TO SEE![3]

The Second Eye is the Spirit of Wisdom. This eye perceives wisdom, which consists of humility[4] and trust[5] in Yehovah. Through these it recognizes godly purpose and affection, thereby enabling us to see ahead.[6] Without wisdom, it is impossible to stay on the narrow way.[7] HALLELUYAH!

The third of the Seven Eyes is the Spirit of Understanding. It perceives understanding, which is the awareness of purpose through contentment[8] and affection through gratitude.[9] Because it recognizes the unity of purpose[10] and affection,[11] it adds strength to wisdom. Since both the Eyes of Understanding and Wisdom see purpose and affection, they are paired together.[12] GLORY TO GOD!

The Fourth Eye is the Spirit of Counsel. This eye, which could also be translated as *the Spirit of Purpose,*[13] consists of certainty and contentment and recognizes what composes true belief![14] Through certainty it perceives godly pursuit,[15] and through contentment it sees holy affection in life.[16] PRAISE BE TO OUR WONDERFUL COUNSELOR![17]

---

[1] Psalm 23:1-6; John 10:11,14

[2] James 1:17; John 1:9; 1 John 1:5; Revelation 21:23; 22:5; Isaiah 60:19

[3] Proverbs 20:12; Exodus 4:11; Psalm 94:9

[4] James 3:13; Proverbs 11:2

[5] Psalm 19:7; 2 Timothy 3:15-17

[6] Proverbs 24:14; 2:1-5; 3:13-18

[7] Matthew 7:12-14; Luke 13:23-30

[8] Jeremiah 9:24; Matthew 6:33

[9] 1 Chronicles 16:34; Psalm 106:1; 107:1,8,15,21,31; 118:1,29

[10] Job 12:13; Proverbs 19:21; Romans 8:28

[11] Psalm 136:5; Proverbs 2:2

[12] Proverbs 3:13,21; 4:5,7; 19:8; 24:3; Ephesians 1:8; Colossians 1:9; James 3:13

[13] From the Hebrew עֵצָה, pronounced "ey-tsah," meaning *counsel, advice, plan, or purpose* (Isaiah 14:26).

[14] Revelation 3:17-19; John 14:7

[15] James 2:22; John 5:19

[16] Hebrews 13:5; Psalm 16:7; 32:8

[17] Isaiah 9:6; Psalm 32:8; Proverbs 8:14

The Spirit of Power is the Fifth Eye. It perceives power in loyalty[1] and humility.[2] Because it sees affection through loyalty[3] and strength in humility,[4] it pours into counsel, and it is paired with the Spirit of Counsel.[5] WE HAVE ONE MASTER AND TEACHER![6] BLESS HIS HOLY NAME!

The Sixth Spiritual Eye is the Spirit of Knowledge, which could also be translated as *the Spirit of Intimacy.*[7] It perceives intimate knowledge in loyalty[8] and gratitude.[9] Through loyalty it recognizes godly pursuit,[10] and through gratitude it discerns holy purpose.[11] PRAISE GOD!

The Seventh Spiritual Eye is the Reverence of Yehovah. This eye perceives trust and certainty.[12] It recognizes the benefit of godly pursuit though trusting Yehovah[13] and holy purpose through certainty in Him.[14] Because it sees the holy unity of pursuit and purpose, it acts as a fountain for affection[15] and is paired with the Spirit of Intimate Knowledge.[16] HALLELUYAH!

Now, we have spoken about how the eyes see, but what happens to the soul and body when these Spiritual Eyes are filled with His Light?[17]

THEY PRODUCE SPIRITUAL FRUIT![18]

---

1 Malachi 3:16; 1 Samuel 2:30; Deuteronomy 11:8; 1 Peter 4:11; Revelation 1:6
2 Proverbs 22:4; James 3:13; 1 Peter 5:6
3 2 Peter 1:17; Romans 12:10
4 Exodus 15:13; 1 Thessalonians 3:13
5 Proverbs 8:14; Job 12:13; Isaiah 59:21
6 Matthew 23:8-12; 17:5; John 13:13-14
7 Genesis 4:1, "And Adam *knew* Eve his wife..." – יָדַע, pronounced "yah-dah" and from the early symbols paring a door with an eye, meaning *knowledge* or *to know someone intimately.*
8 John 8:31-32,38; 5:19; 14:10
9 2 Corinthians 2:14; 1 Timothy 4:3
10 2 Corinthians 5:9-10; 2 Timothy 2:22,25; 1 Timothy 6:11
11 1 Corinthians 15:57; 2 Corinthians 2:14; Colossians 1:12
12 Psalm 9:10; Matthew 19:21
13 Psalm 22:4; 52:8; John 10:27
14 2 Timothy 3:15; 2 Thessalonians 1:11
15 Deuteronomy 12:7-12; Ester 8:17
16 Proverbs 1:7; 2:5; 9:10
17 Matthew 6:22-23; Luke 11:34-36
18 Jeremiah 1:13; 24:3; Amos 7:8; 8:2; Zechariah 4:2; 5:2

"But the fruit of the Spirit is love, joy, peace (an aspect of joy),[1] hope (μακροθυμία – *longanimity, constancy,* or *fortitude,* a description of *hope*),[2] kindness, goodness, faith (πίστις – best translated as *faith, conviction*),[3] gentleness (πρᾳότης – *gentleness, kindness,* an aspect of kindness)[4] and purity (ἐγκράτεια – *self-control, mastering desires and passions,* a description of *holy purity*)."[5]

These *fruits*[6] of the Spirit are *the effects that come from the Spirit;*[7] they are *the results* of the Spirit.[8] They are the Seven *Facets, Results, Powers, or* ***HORNS***[9] of Yehovah's Spirit that blaze forth from His Throne![10] He is their Source, and there is no other![11] They are **LOVE**, **JOY**, **HOPE**, **KINDNESS**, **GOODNESS**, **FAITH**, and **PURITY**!

HALLELUUUUUUUUYAAAAAAAAAAAAAH!!!!!!!!!!!!

OUR GOD IS PERFECT AND HOLY!!!!!!!![12]

HALLELUYAH!

Therefore, understand that each of the Seven Eyes of His Spirit facilitates one of the Seven Horns of His Spirit![13] Each Spiritual Eye of His Observation fills the redeemed with His Light[14] to consider, decide, and intend[15] on behalf of Yehovah[16] and wield a Spiritual Horn of His Power![17]

BLESS OUR HOLY GOD WHO GIVES HIMSELF TO US![18]

---

1 Romans 14:17; 15:13; Isaiah 55:12; Acts 13:52
2 Hebrews 6:12; James 5:10; 2 Peter 3:15
3 Matthew 8:10; Mark 10:52; Romans 3:28
4 2 Corinthians 6:6; Ephesians 2:7; Colossians 3:12; Titus 3:4
5 Galatians 5:22-23
6 *Fruits,* from the Greek καρπός, pronounced "kahr-poss," meaning *fruit, work, act,* or *deed.*
7 Matthew 7:17; John 15:4,8
8 Romans 7:4-6; 8:2; Galatians 2:19-20; 3:13; 5:18; Ephesians 2:15; Colossians 2:14
9 1 Samuel 2:1,10; 2 Samuel 22:3; Daniel 8:7 – Horns represent power.
10 Revelation 1:4; 4:5
11 James 1:17; John 1:9; 15:4-7; 1 John 1:5; Revelation 21:23; 22:5; Isaiah 60:19
12 Matthew 5:48; 1 Peter 1:15-16
13 Matthew 7:17; 13:8,23
14 Matthew 6:22; Matthew 13:15
15 Revelation 2:5; John 15:8
16 John 15:16,19; Matthew 13:20; Luke 18:7; Romans 8:33; Colossians 3:12
17 Luke 10:19; 24:49; Luke 10:19; Psalm 91:13; Ezekiel 2:6; Romans 16:20
18 John 14:16,26; 15:26; 16:7; 20:22; Acts 1:8; 2:38; 8:17; 10:47; 1 Corinthians 6:19

PRAISE HIS HOLY NAME![1]

OUR GOD IS SO WONDERFUL![2]

THE ETERNAL ONE IS SUPREMELY GOOD![3]

GLORY BE TO GOD! WE GET TO CELEBRATE FOREVER!!!!!![4]

HALLELUYAAAAAAAAAAAAAAH!!!!!!!!

HALLELUYAAAAAAAAAAAAAAH!!!!!!!!

HALLELUYAAAAAAAAAAAAAAH!!!!!!!!

THEREFORE, we praise the Glorious Name of Yeshua because, when the mind and its gates toward the will and heart are all filled with truth, ***FAITH*** shines unimpeded through the soul from the spirit![5] This faith is not merely an aspect of the soul but a spiritual facet emanating from shared oneness between the Holy Spirit, human spirit, and human soul![6] It erupts from truth, certainty, and fulfillment and is a quality of Yehovah shared by His children![7] Its presence stretches across the soul to strengthen the connection between the will and the heart![8] Without the Mind of Christ, this faith is impossible,[9] but through a mind steadfast in Yehovah, IT CAN MOVE MOUNTAINS WITH A WORD![10]

BLESS YEHOVAH!

AND, full dominion over the will and its adjacent gates reveals the spiritual facet of ***HOPE***![11] Praise God!

---

[1] Psalm 30:4; 97:12; 103:1; 145:21
[2] Isaiah 9:6; 25:1; Psalm 75:1
[3] Colossians 1:18; Revelation 5:9-13
[4] Revelation 7:9-17; 11:15; 2 John 1:3
[5] Romans 10:17; 1 Thessalonians 2:13; 1 Peter 1:23-25; Luke 8:11
[6] John 14:20; 17:21-23; 1 Thessalonians 5:23
[7] Romans 8:29; 13:14; John 17:16; 1 Corinthians 15:49; 2 Corinthians 3:18; Ephesians 1:4
[8] Acts 15:9; Ephesians 3:17
[9] 1 Corinthians 2:16; John 15:15; 16:13-15
[10] Matthew 17:20; Mark 9:23; Luke 1:37; 18:27
[11] Romans 15:13; 1 Corinthians 13:13

CHILDREN OF GOD![1] LISTEN![2] Because hope is a pursuit and not simply a belief, it is often unappreciated and misunderstood![3] Nevertheless, it is one of the three that REMAIN![4] It is vital to Life, and no life exists apart from it![5] Even Creation itself longs in hope for growth and to be set free from the frustration of having to serve wayward humanity instead of Goodness through the children of God![6] Hope

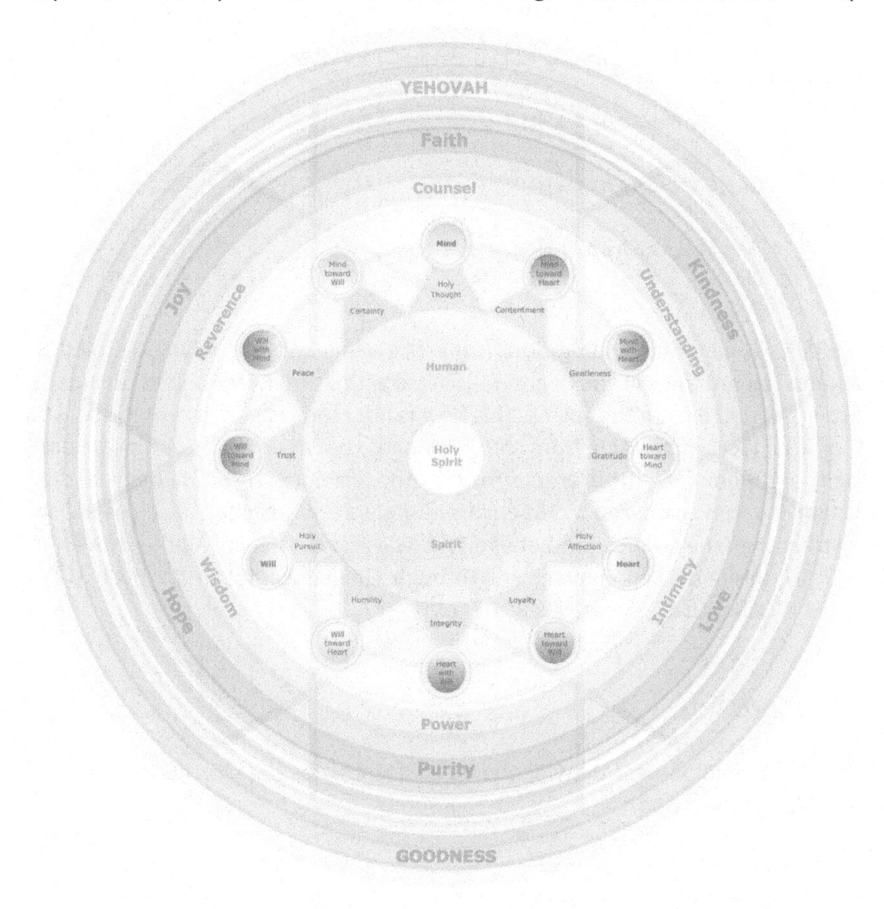

[1] Romans 8:14; Galatians 3:26; 1 John 3:1-2; 5:19; Matthew 5:9

[2] Luke 8:18; 19:26; Deuteronomy 32:46-47; Proverbs 2:2-5; Mark 4:23-24; Acts 17:11; Hebrews 2:1; James 1:22-25; Matthew 13:12; John 15:2

[3] Hebrews 6:18-19; 1 Peter 1:13; 1 John 3:3

[4] 1 Corinthians 13:13; Galatians 5:22

[5] Ephesians 2:12; Proverbs 24:20; 1 Thessalonians 4:13

[6] Romans 8:14,19; Galatians 3:26; 1 John 3:2; 5:19; Matthew 5:9

consists of focused power[1] to serve Goodness,[2] shines through trust and humility,[3] and tramples darkness with light![4] Its effect reaches across the soul as an inner reinforcement for the gate of gentleness![5] IT IS VITAL FOR LIFE!

EQUALLY ESSENTIAL, spiritual dominion accomplished over the heart and its adjacent gates results in ***LOVE***![6] Though faith and hope are indispensable in righteousness, love is the *greatest* indicator of goodness![7] It triumphs against darkness![8] It shines through loyalty, selflessness, and gratitude, and there is no greater reinforcement for peace![9] Love is the very signature of Yehovah Himself![10]

OUR GOD LOVES US!!![11]

HALLELUYAAAAAAAAAAAAAAH!!!!!!!!

BUT THESE THREE FACETS COMBINE INTO THREE MORE! When more than one of the main gates are under holy dominion, each respective convergence gate and its adjacent gates shine forth an additional facet of the Sevenfold Spirit of Yehovah![12]

Therefore, holy unity of the mind and heart reveals not only faith and love but also ***KINDNESS***![13] Consisting of contentment, gentleness, and gratitude, the facet of kindness is paramount to Kingdom living! [14] It is a backdoor for inner reinforcement of the will, pouring in holy serving strength through love and faith![15]

---

[1] Romans 15:13; Isaiah 40:31

[2] Acts 26:7a; Lamentations 3:25; Psalm 52:9; 2 Thessalonians 2:16

[3] 1 Corinthians 13:7; Zephaniah 3:12

[4] Romans 15:13; 5:3-5; Hebrews 6:18-19

[5] 1 Peter 3:4,15; 2 Timothy 2:25-26; Ephesians 4:2; 1 Timothy 3:3; Titus 3:2

[6] Romans 15:30; 2 Corinthians 6:6; Philippians 2:1-2; 2 Timothy 1:7

[7] 1 Corinthians 13:13b; Mark 12:29-31; Colossians 3:14

[8] 1 John 2:10; Colossians 1:13; Romans 12:21

[9] 2 Corinthians 13:11; 2 John 1:3; Colossians 3:14-15

[10] 1 John 4:8,16; Exodus 34:6-7; Psalm 86:5,15; 2 Corinthians 13:11; Ephesians 2:4

[11] Romans 8:39; 5:8; John 3:16; 16:27; 17:26; Ephesians 2:4-7

[12] These gates cannot be won apart from the main gates, because the gates of convergence are dependent on the functions of the main gates. That is to say, a person cannot thrive in the connections between the main gates if the main gates are themselves corrupt.

[13] Colossians 3:12; Galatians 5:22

[14] Romans 11:22; Ephesians 2:7; Colossians 3:12

[15] 2 Corinthians 6:6-7; 2 Samuel 22:51; Romans 2:4

HALLELUYAH!

And when there is unity between a heart and a will ruled in holiness, ***PURITY*** is the result![1] It shines through humility, integrity, and loyalty![2] Of all the facets of Yehovah, it is the most heralded in Heaven[3] because Yehovah is flawlessly pure;[4] He is the holiest of the holy[5] in both Spirit and Soul![6] In the redeemed soul, purity is a vital inner reinforcement of the mind gate[7] and stands as the ultimate armor against lies, dishonesty, and deceit![8]

BLESS GOD!!!!

And, praise our Holy God, when a will and mind are under holy dominion, the resulting shining facet is ***JOY***![9] Trust, peace, and certainty unite to pour inexpressible affection through truth and power into the inner door of the heart![10] This joy is the mood of Heaven[11] and the power of its praise![12]

HALLELUUUUYAAAAAAAAAAH!!!!!!!!

OUR GOD IS A GOD OF JOY!!!!!!!!!![13]

YES!!!!!!!!!

Notice the relationship between the Eyes and the Horns: The paired eyes indicate *fruitful* relationships within the soul! That is to say, wisdom results from understanding,[14] and hope in Yehovah grows from the perception of Yehovah's Kindness![15] Purpose springs from active strength,[16] and faith blooms upon

---

[1] 1 Timothy 4:12; 5:22; 2 Timothy 2:22; James 3:17
[2] Romans 12:1; Hebrews 13:4; Titus 2:5; 2 Timothy 2:22
[3] Revelation 19:8; 20:10; 22:19
[4] 1 Peter 1:19; 2:22; Hebrews 4:15; Isaiah 53:9; 1 John 3:5
[5] Revelation 4:8; Isaiah 6:3; Exodus 15:11
[6] Revelation 5:12-13; 7:12; 19:1
[7] 1 Thessalonians 4:7-8; 2 Timothy 2:21
[8] Ephesians 5:26-27; Colossians 1:22
[9] Philippians 2:2; Acts 2:28; Isaiah 58:13-14
[10] Philemon 1:7; Acts 14:17
[11] Matthew 13:44; Luke 6:23; Hebrews 12:22
[12] Luke 19:37; 10:21; Psalm 28:7; 42:4; 71:23; Isaiah 61:3; Jeremiah 33:9
[13] John 15:11; 16:24; 17:13; 1 Peter 1:8; Jude 1:24
[14] Proverbs 2:6; 10:23; 14:6,33; 19:8; Psalm 119:27
[15] Romans 2:4; Luke 15:17-19; 1 Peter 4:8
[16] Proverbs 8:14; Psalm 92:5

awareness of Yehovah's Integrity and Purity![1] And intimate knowledge erupts when a person serves in reverence of Yehovah,[2] which reveals that love flourishes in response to joy![3]

HALLELUYAH! GLORY TO OUR BRILLIANT FATHER, THE MASTER GARDENER OF THE VINE![4]

BUT THERE IS ONE MORE FACET! The complete unity through the holy dominion of *all* the soulical gates reveals the chief facet of ***GOODNESS***![5] Though all of the spiritual facets have various traits in common, this one *requires* them all and is therefore lifted above all others on the lampstand![6] It is the HALLMARK of Yehovah,[7] the SEAL of His Holiness,[8] the REASON for His Being![9] Yehovah exists because He is GOOD[10] – because Goodness must exist![11] Without Goodness, being is nothing![12]

And this complete revelation of Goodness is the *foremost* purpose of Creation![13] It was for this reason that opposing words, pursuits, and deeds were temporarily permitted to exist![14] Because Goodness could only be revealed by comparison and contrast, Yehovah permitted the Facets of His Spirit to be tested by what was contrary.[15] That is to say, the opposing facets reveal what Goodness is not.[16] They manifest the result of the absence of light, which is darkness, or evil.[17]

---

[1] Psalm 111:7; Romans 15:18-19; Acts 14:27
[2] Proverbs 1:7; 9:10; Job 28:28; Psalm 111:10
[3] John 15:10-11,13; Hebrews 12:2
[4] John 15:1; Isaiah 27:2-3; 60:21; 61:3; Luke 13:6-9
[5] Ephesians 5:9; 2 Thessalonians 1:11
[6] 2 Peter 1:3; Romans 15:14; Revelation 2:5; Exodus 25:31-40
[7] Genesis 1:4,10,12,18,21,25,31
[8] Psalm 143:10; Mark 10:18
[9] Exodus 33:19; 2 Chronicles 6:41
[10] Psalm 145:9; 34:8; 119:68; 1 John 1:5
[11] James 1:17; 1 Chronicles 16:34; Acts 2:24
[12] John 1:3-5; Isaiah 43:10-11
[13] Isaiah 43:7; Ephesians 2:10; Romans 9:23
[14] Romans 9:21-22; Isaiah 54:16
[15] Exodus 9:16; 10:1; 14:17; Proverbs 16:4; Romans 9:22
[16] 1 John 3:10; Revelation 22:11
[17] John 1:5; 1 Thessalonians 5:5; Acts 26:18

When the mind and its adjacent gates are absent of light, they become *antifaith*, which is not only doubt, deceit, and discontentment but moreover ***blasphemy.***[1] The compromise from this spirit of ungodly counsel is so significant that it drives a wedge from inside the soul between the will and the heart.[2] And while unbelief hinders entrance into the Kingdom of Light,[3] blasphemy forbids entrance.[4] However, because of the incredible Mercy of Yehovah, even various forms of blasphemy will be forgiven during this life and on Judgment Day.[5]

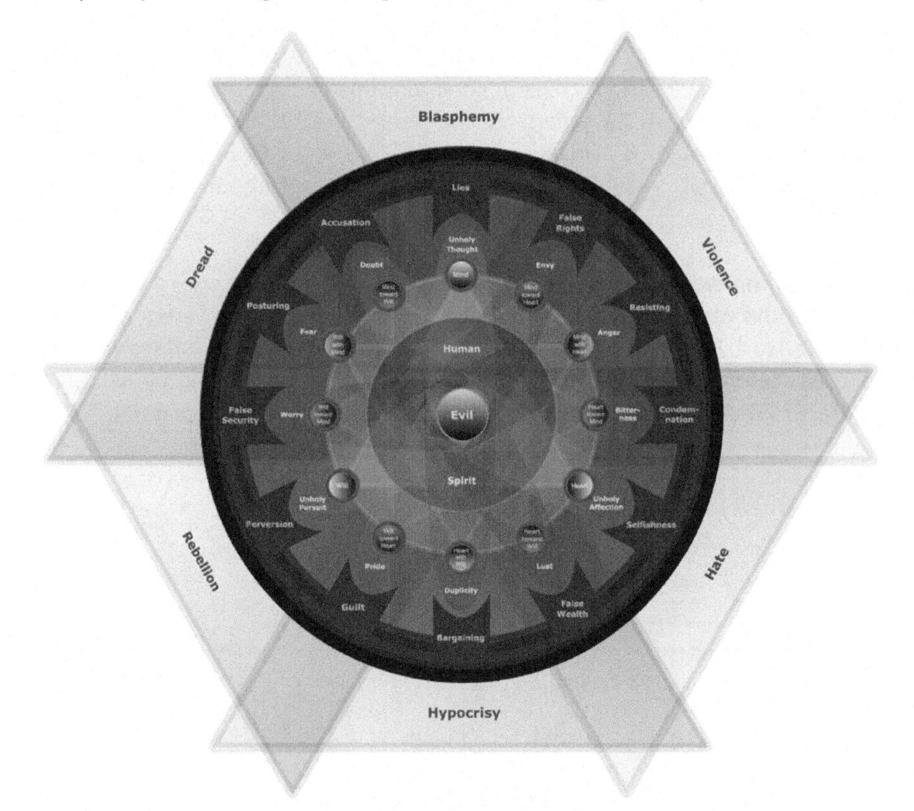

How can we say that blasphemy will be forgiven? How can such darkness enter light? To be sure, no darkness of any kind can enter the Light![6] On the contrary,

---

[1] Matthew 6:23-24b; 12:31; Romans 6:16; Galatians 1:10; James 4:4; 1 John 2:15-16
[2] Jude 1:10; 2 Peter 2:12
[3] Hebrews 3:19; John 3:18,36; 2 Thessalonians 2:12; 1 John 5:10
[4] Matthew 12:31b; Mark 3:29; 1 John 5:16
[5] Matthew 12:31a; Isaiah 1:18; 1 Timothy 1:13-15; 1 John 1:9
[6] 2 Corinthians 6:14; 1 John 1:6; 3:14; 1 Corinthians 10:21; James 4:4

darkness cannot even exist in the Light![1] No shadow can overcome a flashlight; how much more can a lie not overcome the Truth?[2] But Yehovah in His Great Mercy patiently overlooks all sorts of blasphemy[3] in order to continue to pour out His Kindness, Love, Truth, Peace, Power, Purity, and Goodness upon the inhabitants of the earth[4] and even upon those who will stand before Him on Judgment Day.[5] For though blasphemy is the acceptance of antifaith, Yehovah is willing to patiently bring His children into His Light so that their branches of darkness may be pruned off to make room for fruit of the Light.[6] Therefore, He will forgive all sorts of antifaith against Himself,[7] both as the Creator of All and as the Lamp of Heaven.[8] Yet He cannot and will not overlook the blasphemy of His Holy Spirit, because His Holy Spirit is the Voice of Goodness Itself![9] So, He will show mercy to those who show mercy, and He will show kindness to those who show kindness.[10] He will show patience to those who show patience, and He will show love to those who show love.[11] But He will not allow the hatred of goodness to enter into the Kingdom of Goodness, neither now nor on Judgment Day![12] Therefore, understand that any blasphemy can be forgiven if followed by repentance, for we have all refused the Voice of Goodness at one time or another.[13] But continuance in such blasphemy will result in the withdrawal of the Holy Spirit.[14] Yehovah will no longer strive to save such a person,[15] neither in this life nor on Judgment Day,[16] because He agreed in the Covenant of Creation not to force righteousness on anyone.[17] Therefore, Such people stand as memorials to corruption from darkness,[18] as testimonies of why evil should not be permitted in Heaven.[19]

---

[1] James 1:17; John 1:9; 1 John 1:5; Revelation 21:23; 22:5; Isaiah 60:19
[2] John 1:5,10; 3:19; Luke 6:39; Jeremiah 5:31; 2 Peter 2:1
[3] Romans 3:25; Hebrews 10:4; 11:39-40; 1 John 2:2; 4:10; Revelation 13:8
[4] Matthew 5:45; Job 25:3; Psalm 145:9; Acts 14:17
[5] Ephesians 2:4-7; Romans 3:24; 5:10; Titus 3:5
[6] 2 Peter 3:9; Matthew 18:14; 1 Timothy 2:4; Romans 2:4
[7] Matthew 12:31a; Isaiah 1:18; 1 Timothy 1:13-15; Ezekiel 33:11
[8] Matthew 12:32; John 1:3
[9] Matthew 12:31b; Acts 7:51; Hebrews 10:26,29
[10] Matthew 5:7; Romans 9:15
[11] John 16:27; Matthew 6:12; 7:2; Luke 6:31
[12] Psalm 5:4-6; Matthew 25:31-46
[13] Romans 3:23; 1 John 1:10
[14] Genesis 6:3; Matthew 10:14
[15] Mark 6:11; Nehemiah 5:13; Acts 13:50-51; 18:6
[16] Nehemiah 5:13; Romans 1:22-25
[17] Joshua 24:15; Ruth 1:15-16; 1 Kings 18:21; Ezekiel 20:39; John 6:67
[18] Genesis 19:26; Numbers 16:38
[19] Revelation 6:10; 12:10-11; 14:10-11

Additionally, unholy dominion over the heart and its adjacent gates produces *antilove*. Contrary to the Spirit of Intimate Knowledge, this is the spirit of alienation and betrayal.[1] It is selfish ***hate*** that is focused directly contrary to the selfless love of Goodness.[2] In other words, it is not the "hate" of an unpreferred flavor of cheesecake but the hate of godly love that is manifested.[3] And though it might seem as if such a hate should be apparent, it often goes unnoticed, even while weakening the bond between the mind and the will from within.[4] It can be clandestine, not because it is hidden but because its converse, godly love, is often misunderstood.[5]

HOLY WARRIORS![6] LISTEN![7] Many people continue to misunderstand Yehovah's discipline of our ancestors back in the early days of humanity. They read about how our ancestors were sternly rebuked and threatened with real punishment and then wonder if Yehovah ever loved them at all.[8] However, the readers fail to understand that it was precisely *because* of love that Yehovah was so stern![9] Had He not intervened to persuade our ancestors to abstain from accepting evil,[10] they all would have been lost![11] Yet because of His intervention, we are counted as the descendants of the faithful today![12]

HALLELUYAH!
Understand that hate of godly love is not simply a nasty state of affection but rather a replacement of selfless godly love with selfish ungodly love.[13] It is the culmination of greed,[14] selfishness,[15] and bitterness.[16] It is idolatry of the heart,[17]

---

[1] Joshua 22:18; Nehemiah 9:29; Job 19:19; Psalm 41:9; Isaiah 59:13; John 13:18
[2] Galatians 4:16; Micah 3:2; John 3:19
[3] Amos 5:10; John 3:20; 8:44-47
[4] 1 Timothy 4:2; Romans 1:28; Ephesians 4:19
[5] Revelation 3:19; 2:21-22; Romans 9:22
[6] 2 Timothy 2:3; 2 Corinthians 10:3-5; Ephesians 6:11-18; 1 Timothy 1:18
[7] Luke 8:18; 19:26; Deuteronomy 32:46-47; Proverbs 2:2-5; Mark 4:23-24; Acts 17:11; Hebrews 2:1; James 1:22-25; Matthew 13:12; John 15:2
[8] Genesis 18:22-33; Exodus 32:9-10
[9] James 5:20; Exodus 32:22
[10] Genesis 6:5-6; 11:1-9; 2 Peter 2:4-9
[11] Genesis 6:7; Jeremiah 4:22-27; 12:3-4; Hosea 4:3-8; Galatians 3:24; Exodus 32:29-30
[12] Exodus 32:13; 2 Peter 2:4-9; Romans 4:16
[13] Exodus 32:8; Romans 1:23,25
[14] 1 Timothy 6:10; 2 Timothy 4:10; Jude 1:11
[15] James 3:16; Philippians 2:3; Galatians 5:20
[16] Deuteronomy 29:18; Hebrews 12:15
[17] Ezekiel 14:4; 1 Samuel 15:23; Colossians 3:5

adultery,[1] betrayal,[2] and prostitution,[3] the choice of impure for pure,[4] unholy for holy,[5] and wickedness for righteousness.[6] It is the trade of the spiritual for the unspiritual, of inner enlightenment for animal instinct.[7] The unholy heart is desperately wicked,[8] like an open grave, always searching and never satisfied.[9]

Not surprisingly, a will overrun with unholy dominion is what constitutes ***rebellion*** itself. The spirit of rebellion is the contrast of the Spirit of Wisdom.[10] Manifested through the seemingly conflicting priorities of worry, perversion, and pride, rebellion forms the overconfident but desperate villain.[11] It is *antihope* toward Yehovah, the essence of fallenness,[12] self-service,[13] the very pursuit that carries one away from the River of Life.[14] Though it appears to be reserved for the unruly, it is a common trait exhibited through the sons of Adam.[15] Observed in hospital hallways and corporate boardrooms, in higher courts and elementary classrooms, antihope has become the sickness from which few are healed.[16] Its tune is heard in the voices of broadcasters and authors, in professors and psychologists, always offering prognoses while denying prophecies, offering claims of temporal wisdom while denying absolute truth.[17] Like children arguing over territory in a playground sandbox, antihope makes great claims of ownership while denying that any other ownership exists.[18] It pours its conflict into the gate of anger from within the soul.[19]

---

[1] Matthew 15:19; Jeremiah 23:14
[2] Matthew 24:48-49; Ezekiel 12:27; 2 Peter 3:3-5
[3] Ezekiel 16:17; Isaiah 57:7-8
[4] Leviticus 18:26-28; 2 Peter 2:18-19
[5] Isaiah 5:20; Micah 3:2
[6] Romans 1:24; Psalm 35:12; Jeremiah 18:20
[7] 2 Peter 2:12; Jude 1:10
[8] Jeremiah 17:9; Genesis 6:5; 8:21; Job 15:14-16
[9] Romans 3:13; Proverbs 27:20; 30:15; Ecclesiastes 5:10; 6:7; Habakkuk 2:5
[10] Hosea 14:9; 1 Peter 2:8; 2 Thessalonians 2:9-12
[11] John 13:27; Proverbs 1:16
[12] 1 Samuel 15:23; Deuteronomy 9:7; Psalm 107:10-11
[13] James 3:16; Philippians 2:3; Galatians 5:20
[14] Psalm 106:43; Isaiah 65:13; Revelation 22:17
[15] Deuteronomy 31:27; Isaiah 30:1; Ezekiel 2:7
[16] Matthew 13:15; 2 Timothy 2:25-26; Hebrews 6:4-6
[17] Mark 4:12; Genesis 3:4-5; Isaiah 36:18
[18] Revelation 18:7b; Isaiah 47:7-9; Ezekiel 28:2-10; 2 Thessalonians 2:4-8
[19] 2 Chronicles 10:10-11,16; Nehemiah 9:26; Job 34:37

It is resistance for resistance's sake.[1] It is unrest without aspiration,[2] a self-defeating argument.[3]

What's worse is that when more than one of the soulical gates are under unholy dominion, the common convergence gate and its adjacent gates are compromised by the vacuum of darkness.[4] This absence of light results in a manifestation of whatever that particular *anticonvergence* is.

If both the mind and the heart are compromised by darkness, the gates between them are overrun, and the consequence is wicked ***violence***.[5] This spirit is contrary to the Spirit of Understanding.[6] It consists of envy, or discontentment, anger, and bitterness. Violence is more than angry force; it is an attempt toward the acquisition of dark affection regardless of the cost to others.[7] A combination of selfishness and untruth, unholy violence has no real concern for the future but seeks to dominate the past and present.[8] Such brutality is the substance of enraged dark spirits that continue to deceive and destroy even when faced with overwhelming defeat.[9] It pours corruption into the backdoor of the will gate and is the very drunkenness of self-delusion,[10] the intoxication of imagined justification[11] with no regard for reality.[12]

Similarly, a complete dark compromise of both the heart and the will compromises all of the gates in between and results in unbridled ***hypocrisy***.[13] The opposite of the Spirit of Holy Living Purity, hypocrisy spreads like a wasting spiritual disease throughout institutions of learning and cerebral professions,[14] rendering them soulical graveyards filled with spiritual death.[15] Though the penalty for such duplicity hangs in the air like a bird of prey waiting for the inevitable opportunity,[16]

---

[1] Proverbs 17:11; Matthew 15:3,6
[2] Proverbs 25:14; 2 Peter 2:19; Jude 1:12-13
[3] Titus 3:11; Luke 7:30; 19:22; John 3:18; Acts 13:46
[4] Proverbs 25:28; 1 Samuel 25:17
[5] Genesis 6:11; Jeremiah 6:7; Ezekiel 28:16
[6] Proverbs 4:5-17; Ezekiel 22:26; 28:15-17
[7] Proverbs 4:17; Obadiah 1:10-14
[8] Proverbs 13:2; Isaiah 57:20
[9] Jeremiah 6:7; Ezekiel 7:11,23; Micah 3:9-12
[10] Job 12:25; 2 Thessalonians 2:11
[11] Titus 3:9-11; Revelation 18:7
[12] Proverbs 3: 31; 21:7; Psalm 7:16
[13] Matthew 7:5; 23:28; Luke 12:1; 1 Peter 2:1
[14] Luke 12:1,56; Matthew 23:15
[15] Luke 11:44; Matthew 23:27
[16] Luke 12:2-3; Matthew 12:36

this combination of pride, duplicity, and lust, or greed, makes no apology for inconsistency and instead pours itself into the inner door of the mind.[1] It castrates the benefits of intimate knowledge and righteous pursuit, rendering them corrupt, foul, and detestable.[2] It does *not* respond to reason[3] but is only overcome by the unity of repentance and love.[4]

Furthermore, when both the will and the mind are saturated with darkness, all of their joining gates collapse, and the soul is infested with a spirit that is contrary to the Reverence of Yehovah. Known as ***dread,***[5] this spirit is comprised of doubt, fear, and worry. Its heaviness is poured into the backdoor of the heart[6] and *cannot* be overcome by consolation but must be defeated through repentance and truth.[7] The acceptance of dread amounts to a "self-fulfilling prophecy";[8] it is like inviting a panicked bull into an already disorganized dish shop full of delicate china.[9]

The complete collapse of all gates of a soul results in the culmination of darkness known as ***evil.***[10] It is the opposite of Goodness. Having no substance of its own, its essence is mere contrariness.[11] In it no life can be found.[12] It is a vacuum void of Living Truth, Righteous Pursuit, or Selfless Affection.[13] Its sum is zero.[14] It was not, is not, and will not be.[15] It cannot fight the Living Truth, because it has no truth of

---

[1] James 5:12, "...so that you may not fall into ὑπόκρισιν." (See the Byzantine Majority and 1550 Textus Receptus manuscripts) – Pronounced "hoo-pah-krih-seen" and meaning *acting in a staged fashion, feigning a part, deceit, condemnation, dissimulation,* or *hypocrisy.* This word is the source of the English word *hypocrisy.*

[2] Luke 11:37-52; John 9:24-34; Acts 4:17-18; 5:40

[3] Matthew 23:1-36; John 8:43; 9:24-34

[4] Luke 3:7-9; Proverbs 1:23; Revelation 3:19

[5] Deuteronomy 28:66; Job 9:28; Proverbs 10:24

[6] Psalm 53:5; Proverbs 28:1; Job 15:21-26

[7] Isaiah 8:12; Hebrews 3:18; John 8:32

[8] Proverbs 10:24; Jeremiah 1:17b

[9] Isaiah 66:4; Jeremiah 42:16; Proverbs 10:24

[10] Genesis 6:5; Proverbs 13:19; Job 15:15-16; Psalm 55:15

[11] 2 Corinthians 11:3,14; 2:11; Acts 13:10; John 8:44; Genesis 3:1-5; Matthew 4:1-10; Galatians 1:8; Revelation 12:9

[12] John 6:53; Proverbs 11:19; Ezekiel 33:11

[13] Isaiah 26:10; 1 John 3:15; John 6:53

[14] Psalm 34:16; John 6:53; Revelation 14:9-11; Matthew 16:26

[15] Matthew 25:41; Evil itself has never accomplished anything (2 Corinthians 11:14), rather it coopted spirits that had been given authority by Yehovah (Ezekiel 28:15). Therefore, even the dragon once was (Ezekiel 28:14; Revelation 12:9), but because he has been completely co-opted by evil (Ezekiel 28:16-17), he now is defeated (John 1:5; Colossians 2:15), and he will go to his destruction (Revelation 20:10; 21:25-27).

its own.[1] It cannot win against His Power of Righteousness, because it has no other source of power.[2] And it cannot conquer Yehovah's Selfless Affection, because *selfish* affection is by definition as limited in focus as any affection can be.[3] In the final hour, evil will be struck down with the Sword of the Living Word, and then it will be no more.[4] Amen.

BUT KNOW THIS, HOLY WARRIORS![5] WHEN YOU PRACTICE JOY, YOU CONQUER ALL THREE OF ITS GATES! DREAD WILL BE OVERCOME![6]

HALLELUYAH!

WHEN YOU PRACTICE FAITH, YOU DOMINATE ITS GATES! BLASPHEMY WILL BE ERADICATED![7]

BLESS GOD!!!

WHEN YOU PRACTICE KINDNESS, YOU ARE CONQUERING ITS GATES AND EXPELLING VIOLENCE![8]

GLORY TO YEHOVAH!!!!!!!!!

WHEN YOU ACTIVELY PLACE YOUR HOPE IN YESHUA, YOU ARE CONTROLLING THOSE GATES AND TRIUMPHING OVER REBELLION![9]

HALLELUYAAAAAAAAH!!!!!!!!!

WHEN YOU DEVOTE YOURSELF WITH INTEGRITY, YOU CLEAN ITS GATES AND OVERCOME HYPOCRISY![10]
PRAISE HIS HOLY NAME!!!!!!!!!

---

[1] Isaiah 59:4; Ecclesiastes 1:14; 2:11; John 8:44
[2] Isaiah 54:16; Daniel 4:35; Proverbs 16:4
[3] 2 Corinthians 10:12; 2 Timothy 3:2; 2 Peter 2:19
[4] Deuteronomy 28:20; Revelation 19:21; 21:1-8
[5] 2 Timothy 2:3; 2 Corinthians 10:3-5; Ephesians 6:11-18; 1 Timothy 1:18
[6] Nehemiah 8:10; 1 Chronicles 16:27
[7] Matthew 21:21; Romans 1:17
[8] Titus 3:4-5; Ephesians 2:7; Galatians 5:22
[9] Psalm 33:20; 1 Corinthians 1:10
[10] Psalm 25:21; Titus 2:7

AND WHEN YOU SET YOUR HEART TO WALK IN THE LOVE OF CHRIST, YOU WIN LOVE'S GATES AND STAND IN HIS VICTORY OVER HATE AND SELFISHNESS!!!![1]

HALLELUUUUUUUYAAAAAAAAAAAAAAAAAH!!!!!!!!

YESHUA YEHOVAH HAMASHIACH IS THE ALMIGHTY CONQUEROR!!!!!!!!![2]

HALLELUUUUUUUYAAAAAAAAAAAAAAAAAH!!!!!!!!

HE IS WHAT IS GOOD[3] ALL THE TIME!!![4]

HALLELUUUUUUUYAAAAAAAAAAAAAAAAAH!!!!!!!!

AND HE ALONE IS OUR VICTORY!!!!!!!![5]

PRAISE!!! HIS!!!! NAME!!! HOLY!!! HOLY!!! HOLY!!! AMEN!!!

---

[1] 1 Corinthians 13:8; Romans 13:10
[2] John 16:33; Revelation 3:21
[3] Matthew 19:17; 1 Samuel 2:2; Psalm 145:7-9; James 1:17
[4] Hebrews 13:8; Psalm 102:27-28; 103:17; Malachi 3:6; James 1:17
[5] 1 Corinthians 15:57; Romans 8:37; 1 John 5:4-5

CHAPTER 35

YESHUA YEHOVAH IS THE HEALER

GLORY TO YEHOVAH!

YESHUA IS THE SIGN[1] OF THE REVELATION[2] OF THE WILL OF YEHOVAH![3]

BLESSED BE YOUR NAME, YEHOVAH HAMASHIACH![4] AMEN!

WARRIORS OF GOD![5] ALWAYS KNOW THAT YEHOVAH WANTS TO HEAL YOU IN EVERY WAY![6] HALLELUYAH!!!

---

[1] Matthew 12:39; John 8:28

[2] John 1:18; Luke 10:22

[3] Matthew 11:27; Revelation 1:1; John 12:45

[4] Luke 2:11 – *Christ the Lord,* from the Greek Χριστὸς Κύριος, traditionally considered by readers of English to mean *Anointed Lord.* In Daniel 9:25 of the Greek Old Testament, the Hebrew word מָשִׁיחַ, pronounced "mah-shee-ach," meaning *messiah* or *anointed,* is translated into a form of Χριστὸς, pronounced "khris-tahs," also meaning *messiah* or *anointed*. Likewise, the Hebrew Name of God, *Yehovah,* is translated into Greek as both θεός, pronounced "they-os" and meaning *God* or *Supreme* Deity (see how Matthew 4:4 translates Deuteronomy 8:3), and κύριος, pronounced "koo-ree-os," which means *Lord, God, Supreme in Authority* (see how Matthew 4:7 translates Deuteronomy 6:16 and how Romans 15:11 translates Psalm 117:1). Therefore, though traditionally translated into English as *Christ the Lord,* a more Hebrew translation of Χριστὸς Κύριος would be *Yehovah the Messiah*. HALLELUYAH! OUR GOD CAME AND SAVED US! OUR GOD IS ONE! (Deuteronomy 6:4; Mark 12:29, John 10:30)

[5] 2 Timothy 2:3; 2 Corinthians 10:3-5; Ephesians 6:11-18; 1 Timothy 1:18

[6] Mark 1:41; 2 Peter 3:9; John 3:16; Exodus 15:26; Psalms 147:3; Acts 28:27

IT IS EVIL THAT WANTS TO HARM YOU! The kingdom of darkness has the goal of "three for three"; the enemy seeks to kill, steal, and destroy[1] the faith, hope, and love in humanity's relationship with God![2] They do this because humanity is the chosen vessel of Yehovah to reveal His unseen Characteristics of Goodness[3] for all eternity.

The enemy of Good used a tree to pull humanity down from Light into darkness,[4] and the "Enemy of evil"[5] used a tree to lift humanity out of darkness into Light![6]

HALLELUYAH!

Yehovah was and is the Tree of Life![7] He is the Ancient Olive Tree![8] He is the Fruit of Life,[9] the Light of Humanity,[10] the Sound in the Garden,[11] and the Word of God![12] When humans ate from a contrary voice,[13] they bore the fruit of that voice.[14] Their loyalty gates were breached, and greed entered.[15] Their hearts were compromised toward their wills, and the subsequent breach of their will gates was quickly revealed by their fallen deed of darkness.[16] As that deed was performed, humanity became a vessel of darkness,[17] a vessel of contrast[18] rather than comparison for Yehovah's unseen Characteristics.[19] Because they had turned from one purpose to another,[20] humans could not be permitted to eat from the Tree of

---

[1] John 10:10; Luke 8:12; John 8:44; Acts 13:10; Hebrews 2:14; Revelation 12:9
[2] 1 Corinthians 13:13; Galatians 5:22
[3] Romans 1:20; Hebrews 1:3; Colossians 1:15; Romans 8:29
[4] Genesis 2:9,17; 3:1,13
[5] Yehovah is the Enemy of evil (Jude 1:6)!
[6] Galatians 3:13-14; 4:5; Titus 2:14; 1 Peter 1:18
[7] John 6:35,48-58; 11:25; 14:6; 15:1,4-5
[8] Judges 9:8-9; Colossians 1:16; Exodus 25:32; Isaiah 4:2; 11:1; Jeremiah 23:5; 33:15; Zechariah 3:8; Mark 4:30-32
[9] John 14:6; 15:4; Acts 4:12; Hebrews 10:19-22; 1 John 2:23; 2 John 1:9; Revelation 5:8-9
[10] John 1:3-4,9; 8:12; 9:5; 12:46; Isaiah 42:6-7; Malachi 4:2; Matthew 4:16; Luke 1:78-79; 2:32; Acts 26:23; Ephesians 5:124; 1 John 1:5; Revelation 22:16
[11] Genesis 2:16; 3:8-10
[12] John 1:14; Luke 2:11; Philippians 2:6-8; 1 Timothy 3:16; 1 John 4:2-3; 2 John 1:7
[13] Genesis 3:4-6; Psalm 105:28; Ezekiel 2:4-8
[14] Genesis 3:13-24; 2 Corinthians 11:3
[15] Genesis 3:6a; Hosea 6:7; 1 Corinthians 11:3; 1 John 2:16; 1 Timothy 2:14
[16] Genesis 3:6b-7,12; Hosea 6:7
[17] Genesis 3:17; Jeremiah 19:5
[18] Genesis 6:5; Romans 5:12-14; 1 John 2:16; James 4:4
[19] Romans 9:22-24; 2 Timothy 2:21; 1 Corinthians 6:19-20
[20] Genesis 11:4-6; John 3:19

Life.[1] Since their spirits had been corrupted through their souls,[2] restoration would have to come through their spirits overcoming their souls.[3] For this reason, Yehovah had to block access to His Glorified Soul[4] in order not to eclipse intimacy with His Spirit.[5] Human beings needed to hear the gentle whisper of His Spirit[6] and choose life.[7] And with this goal in mind,[8] He later came in an unglorified manner,[9] as a Lamb,[10] to teach everyone how to listen,[11] live,[12] and receive life[13] from their Creator[14] in spirit and in truth.[15]

Now, we do not need to revisit the reasons previously discussed concerning why it was good for Yehovah to allow choice and how He has the ability to redeem even the worst of choices to accomplish Goodness.[16] Rather, we can move forward to acknowledge that the errors made by those choosing against Light were permitted in the great Wisdom of Yehovah,[17] Who knew that unfolding the unseen characteristics of evil was necessary for revealing why Goodness should forever rule over all things for the good of everyone.[18] And because He is able to redeem even the worst and most evil of choices,[19] He took the most evil deed ever committed in all of Creation and turned it into the greatest blessing in all of Creation![20] He did this as a sign of both His Goodness and His Promise to bring perfect Justice,[21] Righteousness,[22] and Joy[23] to Heaven and all of Creation![24] For

---

1 Genesis 3:22; Deuteronomy 18:16-19

2 Genesis 3:6; 2 Corinthians 11:3

3 Romans 8:13; 1 Peter 3:18

4 John 14:19; 16:10,17,19; 17:24

5 John 4:23-24; 14:17; 15:26; 16:13; Acts 28:25; 1 John 5:6

6 1 Kings 19:11-13; Job 4:16; Zechariah 4:6

7 Deuteronomy 30:15,19; Joshua 24:15; Revelation 3:20

8 1 Peter 1:20; Revelation 13:8; Ephesians 1:4

9 Philippians 2:8; Isaiah 50:5-6; Psalm 22:16; Galatians 3:13; Titus 2:14

10 John 1:29; Acts 8:32; Revelation 5:6

11 Luke 10:16; John 18:37

12 John 5:26; 6:57; 11:25-26; 14:26; 17:21; Galatians 2:20

13 Matthew 19:17; John 12:50

14 John 1:3; Romans 11:36; Colossians 1:16

15 John 4:23-24; Ephesians 1:13; 2 Thessalonians 2:13; 1 John 4:6; 5:6

16 See Chapter 6 regarding the purpose of Creation.

17 Romans 11:33; Ephesians 3:10; Colossians 2:2-3

18 Colossians 2:15; Jude 1:7; 2 Peter 2:6-9

19 Romans 8:28,35-39; Hebrews 12:6-12; James 1:3-4; 2 Thessalonians 1:5-7

20 Colossians 2:15; Acts 2:32-36; Galatians 3:14; Ephesians 1:3

21 Matthew 12:20; John 3:14; 8:28; 12:32; Acts 17:31; Revelation 19:11

22 Romans 1:17; 1 John 3:7

23 John 15:11; 16:24; 17:13; 1 Peter 1:8; Jude 1:24

24 Romans 8:20-21; 2 Peter 3:13; Revelation 22:3-5

no greater sin has ever been committed than the brutal beating, mockery, torture, and execution of the only perfectly innocent Man ever to walk the earth![1] Darkness did this as an attempt to rid the world of goodness forever[2] with a plan of eternally enslaving humans as vessels of every sort of darkness, torment, mourning, and pain.[3] But Yehovah, to reveal the blindness of darkness, let the enemy brutally hang Him on a tree.[4] By doing this, He drew the attention of all humanity to Himself.[5] He revealed the hidden Love of God[6] and released humans from all legal binds, setting them free into the perfect freedom of Love, Light, and Joy![7]

LISTEN AGAIN,[8] HOLY REDEEMED CHILDREN OF YEHOVAH![9]

Do you know why the disciples of Yeshua walked in such POWER?[10] They walked in such great power because they knew WHO HE IS[11] and what HE HAS DONE FOR US![12]

They saw Him rebuke the wind and the waves![13] They watched Him walk on water![14] They were there when He rose people from the dead,[15] healed every disease,[16] and threw out dark spirits with a word![17] They marveled as He caused a fish to swim up with money for taxes,[18] turned water into the best wine,[19] and broke a few loaves and fish into feasts for thousands![20] He made fish swim into

---

[1] Acts 3:15; Matthew 27:1-61; John 19:1-42

[2] Daniel 8:10-12; Revelation 12:4,9

[3] John 8:34; 10:10; 1 Peter 5:8

[4] John 10:15,17; 15:13; Isaiah 53:4-10; Daniel 9:26; Zechariah 13:7; Matthew 20:28

[5] John 12:32-33; 1:7; Isaiah 49:6; Romans 5:17-19; 1 Timothy 2:6; 1 John 2:2

[6] 1 John 4:9; John 1:18; 6:46; Romans 5:8

[7] Colossians 2:15; Galatians 5:1

[8] Luke 8:18; 19:26; Deuteronomy 32:46-47; Proverbs 2:2-5; Mark 4:23-24; Acts 17:11; Hebrews 2:1; James 1:22-25; Matthew 13:12; John 15:2

[9] Romans 8:14; Galatians 3:26; 1 John 3:1-2; 5:19; Matthew 5:9

[10] Acts 5:9-10,15; 19:11-12

[11] 1 John 1:2; 2 Peter 1:16; John 20:22; Acts 1:8

[12] 2 Corinthians 5:14; John 21:24; Romans 6:6

[13] Mark 4:39; Nahum 1:4

[14] John 6:19; Job 9:8; Matthew 14:24-25

[15] John 11:43; Luke 7:15; 8:53-55

[16] Luke 4:40; 5:15; Matthew 4:24; 8:16; 12:15; 14:36

[17] Matthew 8:16; Mark 1:25-27; 1:34; 5:8; 9:25

[18] Matthew 17:27; Jonah 2:10

[19] John 2:7-10; 4:46

[20] Matthew 15:32-39; Mark 6:36-44; Luke 9:12-17

nets,[1] restored withered limbs of the crippled,[2] gave sight to the blind,[3] and returned sound minds to those who had been bound by torment![4] He knew their thoughts,[5] their most private moments,[6] and they watched as He knocked down hundreds of trained soldiers with the two words, "I AM!"[7]

EVEN UNTIL THAT TIME, though they knew Who He was, each of the disciples still struggled to embrace the revelation with all their soul.[8] Why? They struggled because they had trouble understanding how a Creator that powerful DID NOT DO MORE![9] They did not understand why He LIMITED Himself, why He didn't simply conquer everything RIGHT THEN![10]

THEY KNEW THE SCRIPTURES, BUT THEY COULD NOT RECEIVE THEM![11]

THEN, even after Yeshua had warned them in great detail about what was about to happen,[12] they watched in astonishment as He ALLOWED Himself to be arrested, insulted, slapped, shoved, beaten, mocked, scourged, stripped, and NAILED TO A CROSS![13]

HOW could such a MIGHTY God allow this HUMILIATION, this ABUSE, this INJUSTICE AT THE VERY HANDS OF THE EVIL POWERS THE DISCIPLES HAD HOPED HE HAD COME TO DEFEAT?[14]

At THAT point, they wondered if they had understood ANYTHING AT ALL![15] BUT, after He rose from the dead, He explained *everything* again![16] And this time, it

---

[1] Luke 5:4-6; John 21:6
[2] Matthew 12:13; Mark 3:5; Luke 6:10
[3] Matthew 9:27-30; 20:34; Mark 8:25; 10:52; Luke 1:6; 7:21
[4] Mark 5:15; Luke 8:2
[5] Luke 11:17; Matthew 9:4; 12:25; John 2:25; Revelation 2:23
[6] John 1:48; 2:25; Psalm 139:1-2; Matthew 9:4; 12:25; Luke 9:47; 11:17
[7] John 18:6, "When Jesus said, 'εγώ εἰμι,' they drew back and fell to the ground." The Greek phrase εγώ εἰμι means *I AM.*
[8] Luke 9:45; 18:34; John 12:16
[9] Acts 1:6; Matthew 16:22; Luke 18:31-34
[10] Isaiah 9:6-7; 2 Samuel 7:16; Psalm 72:8-11; 89:35-37; Jeremiah 33:15-21
[11] Luke 24:45; 2 Corinthians 3:14-18; 4:4-6
[12] Luke 18:31-33; Matthew 12:40; Mark 9:31; 10:34
[13] Matthew 26:47-27:66; Mark 14:53-15:47; Luke 22:47-23:56; John 18:1-19:42
[14] John 12:31; 16:11,33; Psalm 68:18; Romans 8:37; 1 John 4:4; 5:4
[15] Luke 24:11-12; John 20:25
[16] Luke 24:45; Acts 1:3

meant MORE, not because of any new words but because of what He had *DEMONSTRATED*![1]

He explained that He died to show us OUR CREATOR LOVES US, that He will gladly sacrifice HIMSELF for US! [2] HE DEMONSTRATED an extended right hand of FELLOWSHIP,[3] a PROMISE,[4] an INVITATION to TRUST[5] Him even though everything may not immediately make sense to us! And the disciples were finally able to do what they had been unable to do before; they were able to TRUST in Him[6] because He had revealed His LOVE![7]

HALLELUYAH!

THEREFORE, understand that those who walk in POWER know two very fundamental things: Who He is and What He has done![8] If a person knows that Yeshua is the Creator Who came in the flesh, yet they do not understand that He loves them, then they have no power![9] Likewise, if a person knows that Yeshua loves them, yet they fail to understand Who He is, then they have no power![10] A person's received power is DIRECTLY proportional to how much they have encountered both Who He is and how much He loves them! There are no exceptions![11]

Or again, there were many Hebrews in the wilderness who were bitten by snakes.[12] When Yehovah had Moses mount a bronze serpent on a cross, many saw it lifted up.[13] It was a symbol of sin on a cross.[14] It was a symbol that Yehovah knew how to heal them, that Yehovah knew how to defeat the enemy.[15] It was a symbol

---

1 Romans 5:8; Isaiah 53:6; 1 Peter 3:18; 1 John 4:9-10
2 1 John 4:9; John 14:9
3 Galatians 2:9; Matthew 28:20; John 14:18
4 Colossians 1:20; Luke 24:49; Acts 1:4; 13:23,32,34
5 Romans 8:34; John 14:16,26; 15:26; 16:7
6 Acts 2:32; 1:8; 2 Peter 1:16
7 Romans 5:8; Isaiah 53:6; 1 Peter 3:18; 1 John 4:9-10
8 Hebrews 11:6; John 8:24; 2 Timothy 1:9
9 James 1:6-8; 2:19; Mark 11:22-24; Hebrews 10:32; 11:6; Ephesians 4:14
10 Hebrews 8:1; Matthew 7:22-23
11 Hebrews 11:6; Matthew 7:24-27; 1 John 2:3-4
12 Numbers 21:6-7; 1 Corinthians 10:9
13 Numbers 21:8; 2 Kings 18:4
14 Romans 8:3; John 3:14-15
15 Isaiah 45:22; Zechariah 12:10; John 1:29; 1 John 3:8

of Yehovah's Mercy for them.[1] Many people knew about it, but only those who believed and looked upon its message were healed.[2]

LOOK UPON THE CROSS! UNDERSTAND WHAT IT REPRESENTS![3]

Your CREATOR took your IGNORANCE, SIN, GUILT, AND PUNISHMENT UPON HIMSELF![4] Your CREATOR loves you enough to DIE for you![5] He STILL loves you that much![6]

How can you continue to wonder if Yehovah WANTS to heal you? Do you STILL not understand?[7]

HE LOVES YOU! He WANTS good things for you![8] He REJOICES over you with SINGING![9] He SUFFERED and DIED to SHOW you how much HE WANTS GOOD THINGS FOR YOU![10]

If you continue to need healing in your body, then know that indicates you are *still* harboring some sort of darkness in your soul![11] Darkness is the *only* way infirmities can get in![12] But Yehovah is NOT CONDEMNING YOU![13] He's SAVING you from that darkness and ushering you into COMPLETE VICTORY![14] AND HOW IS HE DOING THAT? HE'S DOING IT THROUGH THE CROSS![15] IF YOU ARE NOT HEALED IN EVERY WAY,[16] IT'S BECAUSE YOU HAVE NOT YET DRAWN CLOSE *ENOUGH* TO HIM[17] THROUGH THE CROSS![18]

---

[1] John 12:32; 2 Corinthians 5:21; Matthew 12:7; Luke 1:68-79
[2] John 6:40; Numbers 21:9
[3] John 3:14-15; Colossians 1:20; 2:14-15; Hebrews 12:2; 1 Peter 2:24
[4] John 1:10; Acts 3:15; Hebrews 1:2
[5] Romans 5:8; Isaiah 53:6; 1 Peter 3:18; 1 John 4:9-10
[6] Hebrews 13:8; Psalm 102:27-28; 103:17; Malachi 3:6; James 1:17
[7] Matthew 16:9; 15:16; Mark 7:18; Luke 24:25
[8] Romans 8:28,35-39; Hebrews 12:6-12; James 1:3-4; 2 Thessalonians 1:5-7
[9] Zephaniah 3:17; Luke 15:5-6,32; Deuteronomy 30:9; Jeremiah 32:41
[10] John 15:13; Ephesians 2:4-5; Romans 5:8
[11] 2 Corinthians 6:14; 1 John 1:6; 3:14; 1 Corinthians 10:21; James 4:4
[12] Luke 10:19-20; Though this does not imply that the darkness is always from willful sin (James 5:15b).
[13] John 8:11,15; 3:17; 18:36; Luke 6:37; 12:13-14; Romans 8:1
[14] Romans 8:37; Isaiah 25:8; 1 Corinthians 15:57; 1 John 4:4; 5:4-5; Jude 1:24
[15] 1 Corinthians 1:18,23-24; 2:2; Galatians 6:12-14
[16] Ephesians 1:3; 2:6; Genesis 12:2-3; 1 Chronicles 4:10; Isaiah 61:9; Galatians 3:9
[17] Matthew 14:36; Luke 6:19; Mark 6:56; Hebrews 13:8
[18] Hebrews 10:19-22; 9:15; 12:24; Luke 22:20; John 6:54-56

Someone might say, "I have known of the cross since I was a child, gone to church every week, read my Bible every day, and prayed thousands of hours to be healed!"

GOOD! BUT YOU HAVEN'T DRAWN CLOSE *ENOUGH*![1] YOU HAVEN'T KNOWN HIS LOVE ENOUGH![2] YOU HAVEN'T RECEIVED IT ENOUGH![3] BECAUSE IF YOU HAD, YOU WOULD HAVE DOMINION OVER YOUR SOUL AND BODY![4]

And this is *GOOD NEWS* because it means you have *NOT* done everything, learned everything, or tried everything![5]

JESUS CHRIST NEVER EVER REFUSES TO HEAL ANYONE![6] HE HEALS *EVERYONE* WHO TOUCHES HIM![7]

LOOK AT THE CROSS![8] KNOW WHO DIED ON IT FOR YOU![9] KNOW WHO HE IS TODAY,[10] BECAUSE DRAWING NEAR TO HIM IN THIS WAY HEALS YOU![11]

He LOVES you! He is leading you into brighter and brighter light![12] You can TRUST Him! He WANTS to rescue you MORE than you want to be rescued![13]

And He has done MORE for you than you can POSSIBLY COMPREHEND![14]
Consider WHO He is![15] He is the God Who rotates the ground beneath your feet, Who moves the planets through the heavens like an hour hand, slowly and surely, so that you can have a sense of stability![16] At the same time, He is managing more

---

[1] Matthew 14:36; Luke 6:19; Mark 6:56; Hebrews 13:8
[2] Ephesians 3:18; 1 Corinthians 2:9; John 15:13
[3] 1 Corinthians 4:7; 1 Peter 4:10; James 1:17
[4] Colossians 1:13; John 16:23
[5] James 4:10; Matthew 23:12; Ephesians 4:2
[6] Matthew 15:21-28; 8:5-13
[7] Matthew 14:36; Luke 6:19; Mark 6:56; Hebrews 13:8
[8] Luke 11:34-36; Matthew 6:22-23
[9] 1 Corinthians 2:8; John 1:3,14; 10:30; Malachi 3:1; Luke 1:76-79
[10] Hebrews 13:8; Psalm 102:27-28; 103:17; Malachi 3:6; James 1:17
[11] Matthew 13:15; Acts 3:19; 2 Timothy 2:25-26
[12] James 1:17; John 1:9; 1 John 1:5; Revelation 21:23; 22:5; Isaiah 60:19
[13] 2 Peter 3:9; Matthew 18:14; 1 Timothy 2:4; Romans 2:4; Luke 11:13
[14] 1 Corinthians 2:9; 1 Peter 1:12; Psalm 31:19; Hebrews 11:16
[15] Psalm 46:10; 1 Samuel 2:8; Job 38:4; Psalm 102:25; Proverbs 3:19; 8:29
[16] Genesis 1:1; Job 9:9; 26:7; 38:31; Amos 5:8

chemical reactions per second in your body than the number of all the stars in the universe![1]

He is the God of Time![2] He can wait millennia to respond,[3] or He can think more thoughts between any two words you speak than all the thoughts of humanity since the beginning of Creation![4] He has determined a rate of perception for you, but He can change that if He wills! So, do not doubt Yehovah's sense of timing, because you don't even know what time is![5]

He is the One Who defines all experience![6] He invented the languages of the senses![7] You have perceived many things in Creation through sight, sound, touch, smell, and taste, but such senses do not even begin to compare with His![8] They are superficial![9] They are conversations of perception that were here yesterday and are gone tomorrow![10] So do not explain to Yehovah how you understand things, because you don't even know what perception is![11]

And now you are learning that many thoughts you hear are not even your own![12] Who are YOU, new creature,[13] to even begin to speak to Yehovah as an EQUAL![14] So do not justify yourself to Yehovah,[15] because you don't even know what you are![16] You need to learn from Him who you are![17]

---

[1] Luke 12:7; Psalm 139:17-18
[2] Hebrews 1:2," ...but in these last days He has spoken to us by His Son, Whom He appointed Heir of all things, and through Whom also He made the αιωνας." This plural Greek word means "a perpetuity of time" as opposed to the plural word καιρους, which indicates "occasions of time" (e.g., Revelation 12:14).
[3] 2 Peter 3:8; Psalm 90:4
[4] Psalm 139:17-18; 40:5; 55:8-9
[5] 1 Corinthians 8:2; 1 Peter 1:24-25; James 4:14
[6] Colossians 1:17; 1 Samuel 2:8; Isaiah 44:6; John 1:3; 1 Corinthians 8:6
[7] Proverbs 20:12; Exodus 4:11; Psalm 94:9
[8] Hebrews 4:13; Job 26:6; 38:17
[9] John 7:24; 8:15; James 2:4
[10] 1 Peter 1:24; 2 Kings 19:26; Psalm 90:5; Isaiah 40:6-8; James 4:14; 1 John 2:17
[11] 1 Corinthians 8:2; Job 14:1-2; 1 Peter 1:24-25; James 4:14
[12] Genesis 3:11; John 13:2; Ezra 7:27; Jeremiah 31:33; Revelation 17:17
[13] 2 Corinthians 5:17; John 3:3; Galatians 6:15
[14] Philippians 2:6-8; Isaiah 55:9
[15] Luke 16:15; 10:29; Job 40:8
[16] 1 Corinthians 8:2; Job 14:1-2; 1 Peter 1:24-25; James 4:14
[17] 1 Corinthians 13:12; James 1:23; 2 Corinthians 3:18

THIS GOD, THIS CREATOR, THIS ONE WHO IS UNIMAGINABLY SUPERIOR,[1] IS THE PERSON WHO HUNG ON A CROSS TO SHOW YOU THAT HE LOVES YOU![2]

HALLELUYAH!

AND HE LOVES YOU BEYOND ANY VALUE YOU CAN IMAGINE![3]

HE LOVES ALL OF HIS CHILDREN![4]

AND BECAUSE OF THIS, in the most beautiful and victorious poetic JUSTICE,[5] He has given humanity the good version of EVERY goal that darkness had ever pursued in its quest for independence and greed:[6] Authority for authority,[7] Purpose for purpose,[8] Honor for honor,[9] and Power for power![10] He has shown that the tragedy of darkness is that its proponents COULD have had EVERYTHING they sought if they had MERELY WAITED AND TRUSTED IN HIS GENEROUS AND LOVING GOODNESS![11]

Therefore, since we have been provided such generous victory,[12] let us now endeavor to enter it![13] Let us no longer entertain voices that seek to dissuade us from attaining the blessings that are ours in the Kingdom of Yeshua,[14] for the veil has been torn, giving us open access to full redemption![15] Now having been sanctified,[16] we are free not only to enter but to remain in the overflowing blessings of His Glory![17]

---

[1] Colossians 1:18; Psalm 89:27; Isaiah 52:13; Matthew 28:18; John 3:35
[2] John 1:3,14; 10:30; Malachi 3:1; Luke 1:76-79
[3] John 15:13; 1 Corinthians 2:9
[4] 2 Peter 3:9; Matthew 18:14; 1 Timothy 2:4; Romans 2:4
[5] Luke 18:7; Genesis 50:20; Romans 8:28
[6] Isaiah 14:13-14; Ezekiel 28:2; 29:3; Daniel 4:30; Zephaniah 2:15; Revelation 18:7
[7] Revelation 22:5; 21:4; Isaiah 35:10; 61:3; 1 Corinthians 15:26
[8] Romans 8:29; Matthew 12:50; 25:40; Colossians 1:15-18; Revelation 1:5-6
[9] 1 Samuel 2:30; Revelation 21:26
[10] 2 Corinthians 10:4; 4:7; 13:3-4; Hebrews 11:32-33; 1 Corinthians 2:5
[11] 1 Corinthians 2:8-10; Romans 2:11; Colossians 3:25; Ephesians 6:9; Galatians 2:6
[12] 1 Corinthians 15:57; Romans 8:37; 1 John 5:4-5
[13] Matthew 7:13-14; 13:32; Hebrews 4:11; Mark 12:34; Luke 17:20
[14] John 10:5; Colossians 2:6-10; 2 Timothy 3:5-7; 4:3; 1 John 2:21
[15] 2 Corinthians 3:16; Hebrews 10:19
[16] Hebrews 10:10; John 17:19; Acts 26:18; 1 Corinthians 1:2; 6:11; 7:14
[17] Psalm 23:5; Ephesians 1:3; 2:6

In His Glory, there is no "oh no!"[1] There is only "oh good!"[2] Our gracious Father has not provided us with mixed blessings or diluted healings but perfection and goodness in every way![3] We are not saved only in part.[4] Yeshua did not die to save our hand but not our foot,[5] our spirit[6] but not our soul,[7] or our soul but not our body![8] No! We are freely given every blessing through Him![9]

We are no longer like the citizens of the world who seek healing at a distance and cry out;[10] we are not calling down His Healing to where we are.[11] Instead, we are those who leave "father and mother"[12] and are joined to our Spouse to become one flesh![13] As His bride,[14] we say "yes" to Him for full intimacy with every fiber of our being.[15] We are those who believe His Victory, receive His Invitation of Salvation, and enter into the Kingdom of His Truth, Power, and Love![16] Through His Revelation and Grace,[17] we shed the constraints of darkness from our bodies and souls[18] as we rise into His Righteousness and Life![19] First we see it,[20] then we enter into it![21] For healing rides on revelation,[22] and revelation comes through the grace of righteousness as we abide in His Word![23]

HALLELUYAH! "WAKE UP, SLEEPER, RISE FROM THE DEAD, AND CHRIST WILL SHINE ON YOU!"[24]

---

[1] 2 Timothy 1:7; Romans 8:15
[2] Romans 8:32; Psalm 84:11; 1 Corinthians 2:12; 3:21-23
[3] 2 Corinthians 1:20; Galatians 3:22; Acts 13:32-39
[4] Romans 8:32; Psalm 84:11; 1 Corinthians 2:12; 3:21-23
[5] 1 Corinthians 12:15-18; Matthew 13:15; Revelation 3:18
[6] John 3:5; Romans 8:2; 1 Corinthians 2:12
[7] 1 Peter 1:9; Matthew 10:28; 11:29; 16:26
[8] Matthew 6:22; Matthew 8:16; 10:8; 13:15
[9] Ephesians 1:3; 2:6; Genesis 12:2-3; 1 Chronicles 4:10; Isaiah 61:9; Galatians 3:9
[10] 2 Kings 5:3; Mark 6:33; Isaiah 19:22
[11] 2 Kings 5:11; Luke 7:3; 8:41
[12] Galatians 4:3-5; 6:14
[13] Ephesians 5:31-32; John 17:21-23
[14] John 3:29; Revelation 21:9
[15] Luke 11:10; Revelation 3:20
[16] Revelation 1:6; 5:10; 20:6; 22:5; Exodus 19:6; 1 Peter 2:5-9
[17] John 1:14,17; Ephesians 2:5; Luke 2:32; Romans 16:25
[18] Romans 6:2-14; Colossians 2:20
[19] Romans 6:8-11; 2 Timothy 2:11; John 14:19; 2 Corinthians 13:4; Colossians 3:3
[20] Hebrews 6:18; Philippians 3:14; 1 John 3:3
[21] Matthew 7:13-14; 13:32; Hebrews 4:11; Mark 12:34; Luke 17:20
[22] Mathew 13:15b; Malachi 4:2
[23] John 3:3; 15:5; Romans 6:22; 16:25-27
[24] Ephesians 5:14; Isaiah 60:1; 1 Thessalonians 5:6; 2 Timothy 2:26

Do you want to enter the KINGDOM of the GREAT LORD ALMIGHTY,[1] RULER of Heaven and Earth,[2] CONQUEROR of sickness[3] and death?[4] Then MAKE YOUR WAY TOWARD IT! And you do not have to travel far, because the King has come to knock on your door![5] LOOK! The Kingdom of Heaven has come to YOU! Therefore, OPEN THE DOOR! Stop asking, "Who's there?" and open the door to the Father of your spirit[6] and the Creator of your soul and body![7] The One Who offered HIS OWN FLESH on a cross for you[8] is extending the Right Hand of Fellowship![9] TAKE His Hand! Stop entertaining spirits of doubt and double-mindedness[10] but instead entertain REPENTANCE and BELIEF![11]

NOTHING is impossible for the one who believes![12] NOTHING is impossible for the person who accepts YESHUA at His WORD![13] NOTHING!

Let the weak say, "I AM STRONG!"[14] Let the poor say, "I AM RICH!"[15] Let the sick say, "I AM WELL BECAUSE MY KING HAS GIVEN ALL HEALTH TO ME!"[16]

HALLELUYAH! SPEAK the Word of God![17] SPEAK His Promises![18] Look! He has made you part of His Body![19] Therefore, be His tongue and SPEAK His Words over the earth![20]

---

[1] Revelation 19:6; 21:22; 4:8
[2] Isaiah 66:1; Revelation 11:17; 15:3
[3] Matthew 4:23; 9:35; 10:1
[4] 1 Corinthians 15:54; Revelation 1:18; Romans 6:9; 2 Timothy 1:10; Hebrews 2:14
[5] Revelation 3:20; Luke 12:36
[6] John 3:5; Galatians 4:6
[7] Genesis 2:7; Job 27:3; 33:4; John 20:22: Acts 17:25
[8] John 10:15,17; 15:13; Isaiah 53:4-10; Daniel 9:26; Zechariah 13:7; Matthew 20:28
[9] Galatians 2:9; 1 John 1:3
[10] James 1:6-8; Mark 11:22-24; Hebrews 10:32; 11:6; Ephesians 4:14
[11] Mark 1:15; Matthew 21:31-32; Luke 24:47; Acts 2:36-38; 20:21; 2 Timothy 2:25-26
[12] Matthew 17:20; Mark 9:23; Luke 1:37; 18:27
[13] John 15:7; Psalm 119:11; Proverbs 4:4; Jeremiah 15:16; 1 John 2:27
[14] Joel 3:10 has the often-quoted phrase, but it is in reference to the wicked foolishly challenging Yehovah. Nevertheless, Yehovah certainly makes His children strong, and He does command them to be strong in Him; Isaiah 41:10; Exodus 15:2; 1 Corinthians 16:13; Deuteronomy 31:6
[15] Philippians 4:19; Luke 12:30-32
[16] Romans 8:11; Deuteronomy 7:15; Psalm 103:3; Romans 8:32
[17] 1 Chronicles 16:23-24; Matthew 17:20; Psalm 19:14; Romans 10:9-10
[18] Psalm 89:2; Luke 24:27; Acts 1:8
[19] Romans 12:4-5; 1 Corinthians 12:12-27
[20] 1 Peter 4:11; Acts 1:8; Ezekiel 36:6

SPEAK FOR HIS GLORY!!!!!!![1]

SPEAK, YELL, SHOUT until the earth comes running back like Elijah's servant and says, "There is a tiny cloud forming on the horizon"![2] And when that cloud builds, get ready to sing His praise because you will learn that Yehovah keeps EVERY promise and is PERFECT in His Faithfulness![3]

HALLELUYAH! PRAISE HIM WHO WAS!
HALLELUYAH! PRAISE HIM WHO IS!
HALLELUYAH! PRAISE HIM WHO FOREVER SHALL BE![4]

HALLELUYAAAAAAAAAAAAAAAAAAAH!!!!!!!

GLORY TO HIS NAME!!!!!!!!!!!!!!!!

AMEN!!!

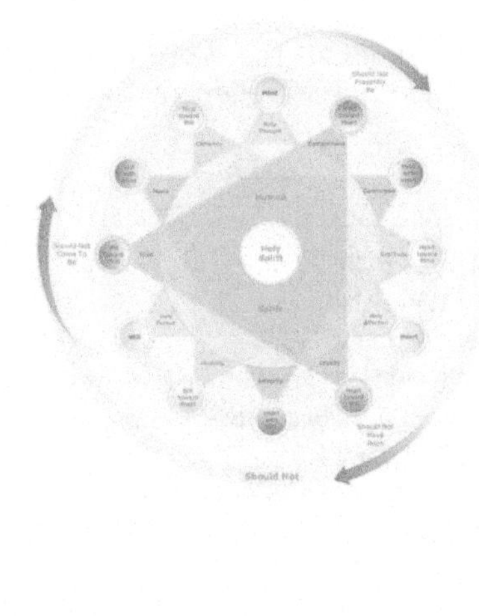

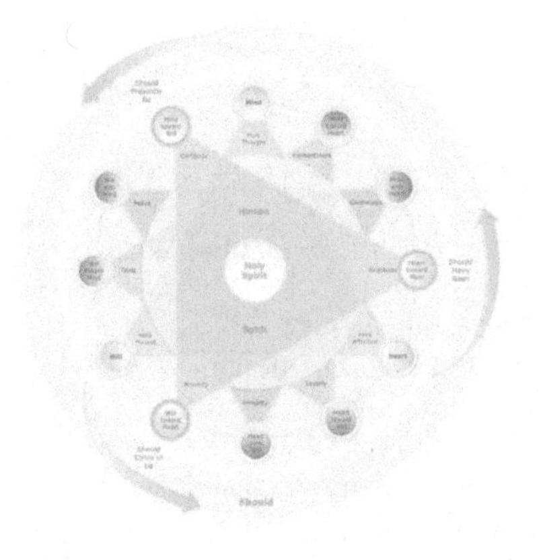

[1] John 15:8; Luke 6:35; Psalm 92:12-15; Isaiah 60:21; Matthew 5:16
[2] 1 Kings 18:44
[3] Joshua 23:14; Ezekiel 12:28; 1 Corinthians 1:9
[4] Revelation 4:8; Isaiah 6:3; Exodus 15:11

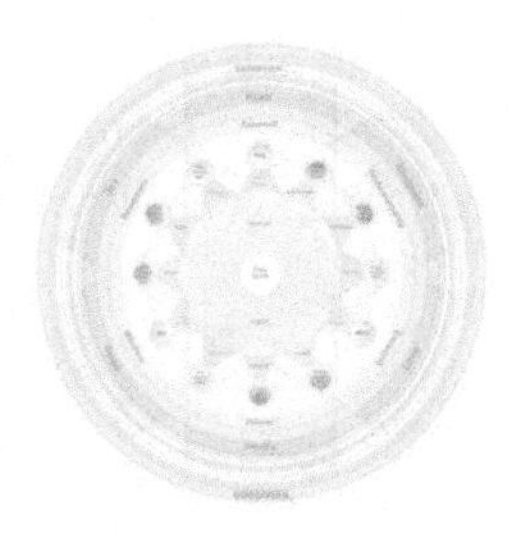

CHAPTER 36

ABIDING AND SHINING

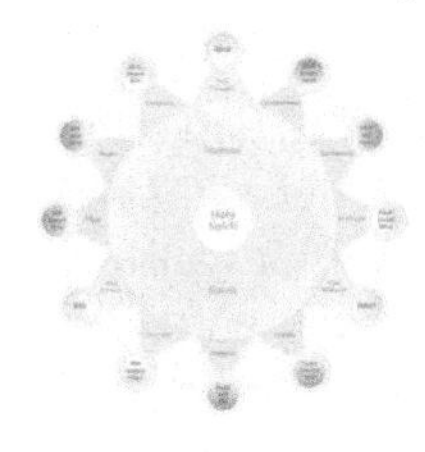

For anything to be, something is.[1] Without something that is, nothing could be.[2] Something has always existed and always will. That Something is Yehovah, Whose very Name means, "He who was, is, and will be."[3]

Creation has not always been,[4] and nothing in Creation always is.[5] Creation is limited, and so is everything within it.[6]

---

[1] Colossians 1:16-17; Isaiah 44:6; Micah 5:2; John 1:1-3

[2] John 1:3,10; Jeremiah 10:11-12; Hebrews 1:2

[3] In Exodus 3:14, God told Moses to say that "אהיה אשר אהיה" or "I AM THAT I AM" sent him. In Hebrew, the sound is "haYah asher haYah." This is why Yehovah calls Himself "יה" or "Yah" fifty times in the Scriptures (e.g., Exodus 15:2). In Exodus 6:2, God told Moses to tell the Israelites, "I am Yehovah, and I will bring you out from under the yoke of the Egyptians." Because Moses knew this when he recorded the Book of the Law, or the Torah (the first five books of the Bible), he used Yehovah as the Name for God as early as Genesis 2:4. "Yehovah" is a combination of the three Hebrew "being" verbs for "He will be," "He is," and "He was." When all three words are said together quickly, they sound like "Yehovah": יהוה "yiheye" (He will be), הוה "hoveh" (He is), and היה "hayah" (He was). yiheye + hoveh + hayah = ye+hov+ah = "Yehovah," "He will be, He is, and He was."

[4] Genesis 1:1; 1 Samuel 2:8; Proverbs 3:19; Isaiah 51:16

[5] Matthew 24:35; Psalm 102:26; Isiah 34:4; 51:6; 54:10; 2 Peter 3:7

[6] 2 Peter 3:7; Revelation 20:11; Psalm 102:25-26

Yehovah made Creation from the seed of His Word, and He grew Creation into a mighty crop.[1] Then He planted His Word in the dust of the earth, and It died;[2] It died as a Seed but sprouted and grew into the Tree of Life[3] and the Lamp of Heaven.[4]

Yeshua was these things, and He became what He was because He is and will always be.[5]

In the same way, we are planted in Him to grow and shine.[6] We die as seeds[7] and are raised as branches in the Vine.[8] We do not remain as seeds but become what we were made to be, lampstands filled and burning with the Holy Oil.[9]

Consider how the oil for the lampstand in the temple was made:[10] To harvest the oil in a reasonable amount of time, the priest first had to shake or beat the olive tree to gather its olives on a tarp placed beneath it.[11] Then the fruit had to be crushed and pressed in order to remove the pits and extract the oil.[12] After this, the oil was regularly added to the lampstand and burned so that light would fill the temple.[13]

In Yeshua, we are such olive trees.[14] He allows us to be shaken with adversity in Creation to gather our fruit that has grown from our relationship with Him.[15] Then He permits spiritual pressure to "remove the pits"[16] from our souls and obtain the oil of His Character from that relationship.[17]

---

[1] Isaiah 45:18; Ezekiel 36:8-12

[2] John 12:23-24; Luke 8:11; John 1:1

[3] Revelation 22:2c (Exodus 15:26 informs us that it is "אני יהוה רפאך" or "I, Yehovah, Who heals you."); Luke 4:40-41

[4] Revelation 4:5; 21:23; Matthew 5:15

[5] John 1:1-3; Hebrews 13:8; Malachi 3:1,6; James 1:17; Psalm 102:25-28

[6] Colossians 2:7; Ephesians 2:21-22; 3:17; Psalm 1:3; 92:13; Isaiah 61:3

[7] Romans 6:3-5,8; 2 Timothy 2:11-12; John 12:24

[8] John 15:5; Romans 12:5; 1 Corinthians 12:12; Acts 4:12

[9] Ephesians 5:8; John 12:36; 1 Thessalonians 5:5

[10] Exodus 39:37; 35:14; 39:37; Numbers 4:9

[11] Isaiah 24:13; Deuteronomy 24:20

[12] Exodus 27:20; Job 24:11

[13] 2 Chronicles 13:11; Exodus 25:31-39; 27:20-21; Leviticus 24:2-4

[14] Psalm 52:8; Romans 11:17-24

[15] Jeremiah 17:10; Psalm 66:10; Isaiah 48:10; Zechariah 13:9

[16] John 15:2; Matthew 13:18-23; Revelation 3:19

[17] Galatians 6:9; John 15:8; James 1:3

And what is this pressing? Is it not the wind and the waves experienced by our brother Peter as he walked toward Yeshua on the water?[1] The winds are those forces that work to drive us toward or push us away from the course that seems best to us, and the waves are those that act on us to lift us up or send us crashing down. And what did Peter experience? He experienced relationship. When he focused on his relationship with the wind and the waves, he experienced the effects of that relationship.[2] But when he turned his attention toward his relationship with His Creator, he experienced the supremacy of that relationship's effects.[3] And look at the oil that came from that pressing; Peter not only learned that the effects from his relationship with Creation could be superseded by embracing his relationship with the Truth in his mind,[4] the Love of His Savior in his heart,[5] and the Grace and Power given him to trust Yeshua in his deeds,[6] but he also learned that His Savior's Trustworthiness, Faithfulness, Patience, Gentleness, and Love were able to save Peter even beyond his own weaknesses.[7] The distractions, denials, hindrances, and attacks throughout the stormy night were the pressure that revealed the Truth, Certainty, Trust, Loyalty, Gentleness, Humility, Gratitude, and Love previously unseen in the relationship with his Creator and Savior.[8] These qualities had always been there, but they were revealed through the struggle.[9]

Therefore, when our brother James exhorts us through the Holy Spirit to consider sufferings as occasions for joy,[10] he is speaking of these eternal benefits that reveal the eternal wealth in our eternal relationship with our eternal Father and Savior.[11]

HALLELUYAH!

---

[1] Matthew 14:24,30; 2 Kings 6:15; Mark 14:66-72; 2 Timothy 4:16-17
[2] Matthew 14:30; 2 Corinthians 4:3-4; Romans 8:5-7
[3] Matthew 14:31; Mark 16:7
[4] Romans 12:2; Ephesians 4:22-24; Colossians 1:21-22; 3:10; Titus 3:5
[5] John 15:9,13; 17:23,26; Ephesians 3:18; Revelation 1:5
[6] Matthew 5:16; James 2:18
[7] Matthew 14:31-2; 8:26; 16:8
[8] Colossians 2:9; 1 John 5:20; 1 Timothy 3:16
[9] Matthew 14:33; 8:27; John 21:5-6
[10] James 1:2
[11] James 1:4,17,25; 4:8; 5:7-8,11

Because these experiences reveal Yehovah's Characteristics as they are pressed out of us,[1] we are also lampstands.[2] The oil of relationship with Him is placed in us and burned to reveal His Characteristics for all to see.[3] Our experiences are put on display in Creation to be observed for everyone's eternal benefit.[4] We do not burn of ourselves, for by ourselves we are nothing.[5] But when our relationship with Yehovah is revealed, we hold the flames of the oil poured into us.[6] We are the expression of His Light, helping everyone to see His unseen Characteristics. We shine with His Truth, Contentment, Gentleness, Gratitude, Love, Loyalty, Integrity, Humility, Righteousness, Trust, Peace, and Certainty.[7]

Knowing this, we should not entertain any suggestions that we cannot fully exhibit all of Yeshua's Light of Righteousness, because it is for this very purpose that He has made us, redeemed us, and prepared us.[8] And we do not allow ourselves to be measured by this world or the darkness that guides it around by bit and bridle,[9] for Yehovah does not measure us or our success in such a way.[10] He is not concerned about our worldly success, popularity, or influence.[11] On the contrary, He has one goal for each of us: to grow us into the perfect representation and revelation of His Soul.[12] If we choose this same goal, we experience it overflowing.[13] Our eyes are opened,[14] our paths are blessed,[15] and our hearts are filled with joy.[16] And even on this earth, as we walk in the Kingdom of Heaven,[17] we hear, "Well done, My faithful olive trees,[18] My precious lampstands,[19] My true children in whom I delight."[20]

---

[1] Romans 5:3-5; Matthew 5:10-12; 2 Corinthians 12:9-10
[2] Romans 5:5; Revelation 2:5; Matthew 5:14-16; Ephesians 5:8-14; Philippians 2:15
[3] Matthew 25:1-13; Hebrews 1:9; Psalm 23:5; 89:20; 133:2; 141:5; Zechariah 4:12
[4] 1 Corinthians 10:11; Romans 15:4
[5] John 15:5; Romans 12:5; 1 Corinthians 12:12; Acts 4:12
[6] John 5:35 Matthew 11:11; 2 Peter 1:19
[7] Galatians 5:22-23; 2 Corinthians 3:18; Proverbs 4:18
[8] 2 Corinthians 4:5-18; Ephesians 5:8; 2 Corinthians 3:18; 1 Peter 2:9
[9] Romans 6:20; 2 Corinthians 4:4; John 12:40; Ephesians 2:2
[10] Luke 16:15; 1 Peter 3:4; 5:5; Isaiah 1:10-20
[11] Mark 8:36; Luke 12:15-21
[12] John 12:26; Romans 8:29
[13] Jeremiah 33:3; Ephesians 1:3-14
[14] 2 Kings 6:17; Acts 26:18; Psalm 119:18; Ephesians 1:18; Revelation 3:18
[15] Proverbs 3:6; 16:9; 25:8-9; 32:8; Isiah 30:21; 48:17; Jeremiah 10:23
[16] John 15:11; 16:24; 17:13; 1 Peter 1:8; Jude 1:24
[17] Luke 17:20-21; Matthew 12:28; John 3:3; 18:36; Colossians 1:13
[18] Romans 11:24; Mark 25:23
[19] Revelation 1:20; Matthew 5:15-16; Philippians 2:15-16
[20] Matthew 25:21; 2 Chronicles 31:20-21; Romans 8:14

YES!!!!!!![1]

ALL GLORY IS YOURS,[2] ALMIGHTY RIGHTEOUS[3] CONQUEROR![4]

WE LAY THE CROWNS YOU HAVE GIVEN US AT YOUR FEET![5]

HOLY, HOLY, HOLY ARE YOU,[6] MIGHTY KING OF KINGS![7]

TO YESHUA HAMASHIACH,[8]

JESUS CHRIST,

THE AUTHOR OF LIFE,[9]

THE LIGHT OF GOODNESS,[10]

THE PRINCE OF PEACE,[11]

AND THE KING OF SOULS,[12]

BE ALL HONOR, GLORY, AND POWER BOTH NOW AND FOREVER AND EVER!!!!!!!!!![13]

LOOK! HE IS COMING WITH THE CLOUDS,[14]

---

[1] 2 Corinthians 1:20; Galatians 3:22; Acts 13:32-39

[2] Revelation 1:6; 4:11; Titus 2:13

[3] 2 Peter 1:1; 1 Corinthians 1:30; Philippians 3:9; Romans 1:17; 3:21-26

[4] John 16:11,33; Colossians 1:15,18; 1 John 4:4; 5:4

[5] Revelation 4:10; 1 Chronicles 29:11-16; 1 Corinthians 15:10

[6] Revelation 4:8; Isaiah 6:3; Exodus 15:11

[7] Revelation 17:14; 19:16; Psalm 72:11; Proverbs 8:15-16; 1 Timothy 6:15

[8] The title "Yeshua HaMashiach" is a transliteration from the Hebrew ישועה המשיח, which is the Name commonly translated into English as "Jesus Christ."

[9] Acts 3:15; John 1:4,10,14; 5:26; 10:28; 11:25-26; 14:6; 17:2; 1 John 5:11-12,20; Romans 8:1-2; 1 Corinthians 15:45; Colossians 3:3-4

[10] John 8:12; Hebrews 9:11

[11] Isaiah 9:6; 53:5; Micah 5:4; John 14:27; Acts 10:36

[12] Ezekiel 18:4; Matthew 10:28; 1 Thessalonians 5:23; Numbers 27:16

[13] Revelation 5:12; 7:12; 19:1

[14] Daniel 7:13; Isaiah 19:1; 30:30; Ezekiel 1:4; Matthew 26:64

AND EVERY EYE WILL SEE HIM,[1]

EVEN THOSE WHO PIERCED HIM![2]

AND ALL THE TRIBES OF THE EARTH WILL MOURN BECAUSE OF HIM![3]

"I AM THE ALEPH AND THE TAV,"[4] SAYS יהוה,[5]
"WHO IS AND WHO WAS AND WHO IS TO COME,
THE ALMIGHTY!"[6]

COME!!!!!!!!!!! LORD!!!!!!!!!! JESUS!!!!!!!!!!!!!![7]

HALLELUYAAAAAAAAAAAAAAAAAAAAAAAH!!!!!!!!!!!!!

HALLELUYAAAAAAAAAAAAAAAAAAAAAAAH!!!!!!!!!!!!!

HALLELUYAAAAAAAAAAAAAAAAAAAAAAAH!!!!!!!!!!!!!

HALLELUYAAAAAAAAAAAAAAAAAAAAAAAH!!!!!!!!!!!!!

HALLELUYAAAAAAAAAAAAAAAAAAAAAAAH!!!!!!!!!!!!!

HALLELUYAAAAAAAAAAAAAAAAAAAAAAAH!!!!!!!!!!!!!

HALLELUYAAAAAAAAAAAAAAAAAAAAAAAH!!!!!!!!!!!!!

AMENNNNNNNNNNNNNNN!!!!!!!!!!!!!!!!!!!!!!!!!!!!![8]

---

[1] Revelation 1:7; Zechariah 12:10

[2] Zechariah 12:10; Psalm 22:16-17

[3] Matthew 24:30; Revelation 1:7

[4] Revelation 1:8; 22:13; Isaiah 41:4; 44:6; 48:12; In the Hebrew alphabet ("aleph-bet"), א "aleph" is the first letter and ת "tav" is the last letter; Yeshua Yehovah is the Beginning and the End! HalleluYah!

[5] יהוה or **יְהֹוָה** is the Holy Name of God in Hebrew that is transliterated into English as "Yehovah."

[6] Revelation 1:8; 22:13; Isaiah 41:4; 44:6; 48:12

[7] Revelation 22:20; 1 Thessalonians 2:19; 3:13

[8] Psalm 41:13; 89:52; 100:1; 106:48; Revelation 22:21

AN ELDER'S CROWN – REVELATION 4:10

Made in the USA
Coppell, TX
17 April 2022